THE GENERAL MANAGER AND STRATEGY FORMULATION:

OBJECTIVES, MISSIONS, STRATEGIES, POLICIES

THE GENERAL MANAGER AND STRATEGY FORMULATION:

OBJECTIVES, MISSIONS, STRATEGIES, POLICIES

John E. Dittrich
Bloomsburg University of Pennsylvania

John Wiley & Sons
New York Chichester Brisbane Toronto Singapore

Library of Congress Cataloging in Publication Data:

Dittrich, John E.
The general manager and strategy formulation: objectives, missions, strategies, policies / John E. Dittrich.
p. cm.—(Wiley series in management, ISSN 0271-6046)
Includes index.
ISBN 0-471-80455-X
1. Industrial management. 2. Strategic planning. I. Title. II. Series.
HD31.D5623 1988 87-29523
658.4'012—dc19 CIP

Printed in the United States of America

10 9 8 7 6 5 4 3 2 1

ACKNOWLEDGMENTS

I would like to express my deep appreciation to following reviewers for their constructive comments during the process of manuscript review: Marc J. Dollinger, University of Kentucky; Kenneth E. Marino, San Diego State University; Robert P. Crowner, Eastern Michigan University; Newman S. Peery, University of the Pacific; Raffaele DeVito, Emporia State University; John R. Schermerhorn, Jr., Southern Illinois University at Carbondale; Arkalgud Ramaprasad, Southern Illinois University at Carbondale; Paul Grambsch, University of Minnesota, Minnesota; Terrell G. Manyak, California State College, San Bernadino; Robert C. Shirley, University of Southern Colorado; Pauline Magee-Egan, St. John's University; James J. Polczynski, University of Wisconsin-Parkside; Dewey E. Johnson, California State University, Fresno; David M. Flynn, Baruch College; Rajendra P. Khandekar, University of Colorado at Denver; Wilma D. Stricklin, Northern Illinois University. In addition, I owe a very special note of thanks to Dr. Jim Lang of the University of Kentucky for the hours we shared discussing the application of the developmental model of instruction to the teaching of business policy. His encouragement and the support of Dr. Bob Zawacki —then Dean of the College of Business at the University of Colorado at Colorado Springs—during the critical periods when the model was tried out in the classroom sustained the work and materially aided its final form.

Over several years, students at the universities of Colorado and Kentucky helped in the process of testing the concepts herein and provided invaluable opinions and information. To all I owe a great debt. To Cheryl Mehalik and her fine staff at John Wiley my thanks for their help in completing the task and seeing it through to production. Finally, I am especially grateful to Rick Leyh of John Wiley for his willingness to undertake the project and to provide the moral and financial support needed to bring about this work in final form.

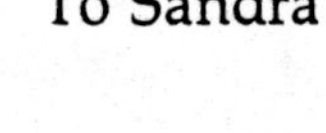

To Sandra

CONTENTS

PART IV Strategy Formulation—Multiple-Business Organizations 635

THE GENERAL MANAGER AND STRATEGY FORMULATION:

OBJECTIVES,
MISSIONS, STRATEGIES,
POLICIES

1

BUSINESS STRATEGY AND POLICY AND OUR APPROACH TO IT

The business policy and strategy course you are now beginning will give you the tools and practice you need to understand what such strategies are and how you may come to apply them. First, we will look at why this course is required by the American Academy of Collegiate Schools of Business (AACSB) of all undergraduate and graduate business students regardless of their chosen major field. Then we will discuss the role of the general manager in strategy formulation, provide you with an overview of the plan of this textbook, and give you an opportunity to review this material through the analysis of a real-life business case.

EVOLUTION OF BUSINESS POLICY AND STRATEGY

The origin of a business policy requirement by AACSB goes back over 20 years. Employers at that time found that graduates of colleges of business were well prepared in the functional areas of business administration (e.g., finance, marketing, accounting, etc.), but that they lacked an understanding of how their own specialty meshed with the specialties of other business graduates. Furthermore, they approached all organizational problems from the perspective of their own specialty rather than focusing on what might be best for the entire organization. The result was a lack of cooperative effort and a less-than-optimum level of performance.

The AACSB took this claim seriously because it, too, felt that business graduates should have gained an understanding of the business organization as a whole. The Assembly commissioned an in-depth study of the curricula of member schools and ultimately concluded that, indeed, graduates did lack the broader perspective of business as a totality. The report found that a great many, if not most, AACSB accredited institutions had curricula lacking a course or courses that addressed the problems of managing an organization as a multifunction entity. As a consequence, AACSB accreditation standards by the early 1970s required that accredited institutions must include a business policy capstone course that would serve to integrate the functional areas of business administration and would provide the overall organizational perspective that employers had found missing among business school graduates.

ROLE OF THE GENERAL MANAGER

For many years, the focus of the business policy course was on the duties and responsibilities of general managers. *General managers* oversee the work of various functional managers and typically have responsibility for profitability of one or more business profit centers. In their work, general managers must integrate the needs, demands, and contributions of each of the business functions within their area of responsibility and work to achieve an optimum level of total organizational profitability.

As we look more closely at the work of general managers, we can see that the field of business policy extends well beyond the day-to-day tasks of the general manager who is busy carrying out the instructions of his superiors. In fact, many general managers are engaged in (1) establishing much longer-range objectives and targets, (2) articulating what they believe to be the mission of the organization, and (3) developing the larger plan to be used to achieve objectives and help in carrying out that mission.

INDEX

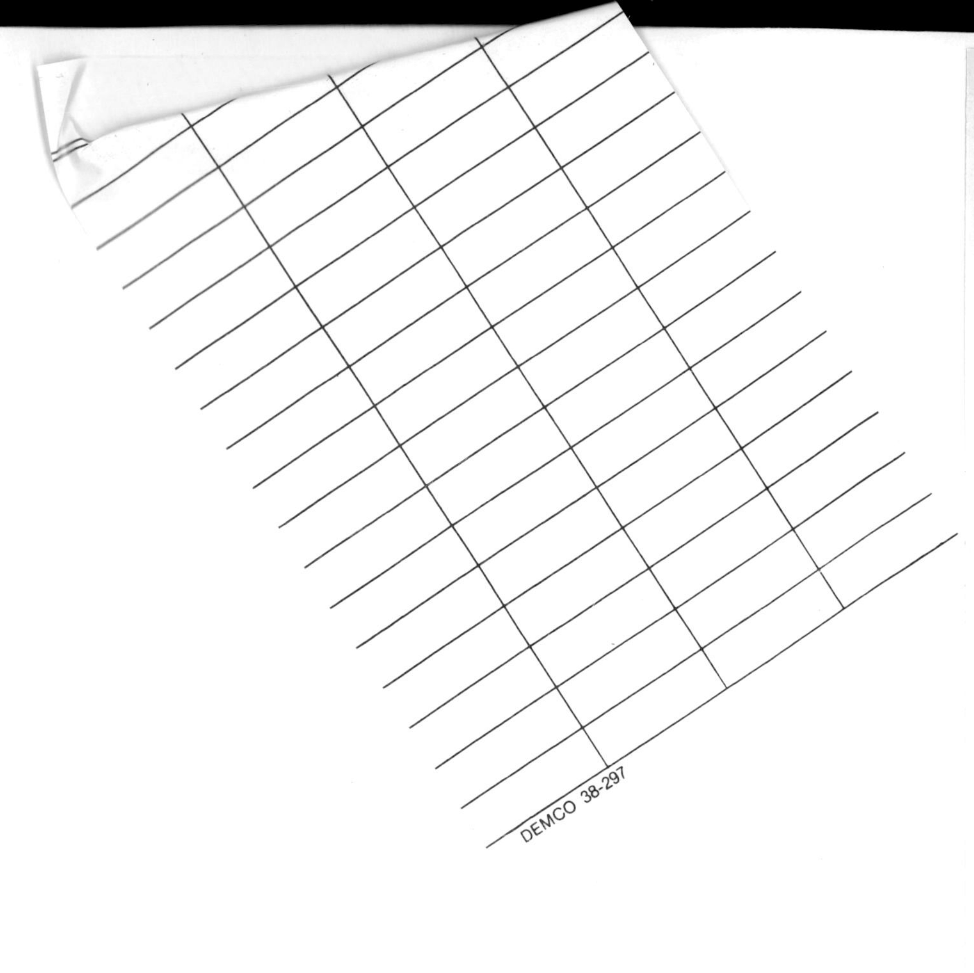
DEMCO 38-297

The activities of the general manager in this part of his or her responsibilities shift from the functions of short-term planning and organizing and the directing and controlling of subordinates (i.e., establishing and executing tactical moves) to those of long-term planning and, to a lesser extent, large-scale conceptual organizing (i.e., developing strategies). Much of this work involves data collection, data analysis, and the exercise of judgment.

The effective use of a hierarchy of integrated plans and objectives is dependent in large part on the competence of managers intellectually capable of spanning the technological, social, competitive, and organizational complexities found in and around the organization. Hodgetts and Wortman contend that managers must overcome their specialties as they move up the hierarchy, "In becoming top level executives, they must put aside much of their previous education and interests and concentrate on being generalists."[1]

The planning activities of general managers are similar in many respects to the functions performed by military commanders in waging war. In military terms, long-range and larger-scale plans used to achieve objectives are called *strategies* and are clearly distinguished from *tactics,* a term that denotes the actual processes for moving military forces. In organizational terminology, the word *strategy* refers to a long-range plan of action designed to achieve long-range objectives or carry out a long-range mission. Some authors in the field consider the term *strategy* to include both the ends to be achieved and the means or plan for achieving the ends.[2] Others distinguish between strategic objectives and strategies for achieving those ends. It seems clear that in either case two components are needed: objectives to be attained and a grand plan (a strategy) to be employed in reaching the objectives.

Some organizations assign long-range or strategic planning to individuals whose entire responsibility is the preparation of plans. Other organizations prepare long-range plans by means of top-level committees of executives and members of the board of directors. Still others make use of consulting firms or research institutes to assist in providing both the data needed and the application of independent judgment. In a great many organizations, however, the responsibility for long-range planning and the establishment of long-term organizational goals is that of the general manager.

DEVELOPMENT OF THE COURSE

By the 1960s, the expansion of the scope of the responsibilities of the general manager and a similar expansion of the field of study was evident as the word *strategy* became more popular in describing the nature of the longer-range management task. The field also began to take a direction toward more rigorous and empirically based

[1] R. M. Hodgetts, and M. S. Wortman, *Administrative Policy,* 2nd Ed. (New York: John Wiley, 1980), pp. 49–50.

[2] Dan E. Schendel and Charles W. Hofer Eds: *Strategic Management: A New View of Business Policy and Planning.* Boston, Little, Brown and Co., 1979, p. 97.

research. Business leaders and recruiters began to request higher levels of skills . . . in analysis, in written and verbal communication, and in the presentation of cogent, sharply focused recommendations for decision making.

The teaching of business policy also followed different modes of thought. For many years, faculty in colleges of business considered the business policy course to be a case course. Because many instructors of business strategy and policy were trained in the use of cases, they naturally preferred that method of instruction. Alternative modes of instruction were not extensively explored or considered. As the course began to take its present form, instructors across the country began to use a wide range of instructional approaches. Cases, of course, were still used extensively, but they were heavily supplemented by readings, text material, business games, and an extensive array of other materials.

The use of cases, although developing analytic and decision-making skills, began to be seen as inadequate in several distinctive ways. First, the exclusive use of cases lacked the structure needed to guide students. In the absence of a framework, or structure, survival, for many, seemed the only goal one might reasonably achieve.

A second problem with the use of cases is the lack of depth of content and the absence of an opportunity for extended practice. New skills are developed through practice. In a wide range of courses in any university, practice is provided to build skills. In contrast, repetitive skill-development exercises are rarely found in the traditional business policy course.

A third problem associated with the use of cases is the lack of feedback. For effective learning, students in all disciplines must have a sense that they have (or have not) adequately grasped the key elements of the material to be learned. Written analysis of cases does offer the opportunity for feedback to students, however the difficulties posed by the mechanics and logistics of feedback by this medium are quite substantial.

DESIGN FOR LEARNING

We believe that the existing methods for teaching this course lack a structure that is designed for effective learning. The sequence of course material in many business policy texts follows a problem-solving framework, but one that would be used by an experienced strategist, or problem solver, rather than by a person who wishes to learn how to master the art of strategy formulation and implementation.

The arrangement of this book is intended to overcome some of these problems. In this text, we will make use of an overall educational design that is intended to achieve three major course objectives. Each objective will be addressed in an order that is dictated by the concept of building toward the development of broad skills to be used in dealing with problems that are, for all practical purposes, unstructured. *The first objective* is to develop in you, the business administration student, the skills and perspectives of the general manager, a person charged with carrying out or *imple-*

menting an organizational strategy by means of business policies and operational decisions.

Effective strategies are best formulated by those familiar with and practiced in the science and art of interfunction integration, namely, those persons well grounded in the perspectives of the general manager. Thus, *the second objective* is to help you to learn and practice the formulation of strategies. This objective, however, is only addressed *after* you have learned and practiced some of the more elemental skills of integrating within and across business functions.

The third objective of this course is to teach you the skills and knowledge you will need to develop and manage strategies for a multibusiness organization. It is an extension of this developmental process and will follow naturally and logically from the attainment of objective number two. Few organizations in our complex economy operate as single businesses. Most have several lines of endeavor, each calling for a strategic plan and for strategic objectives. The typical new-car dealer, for example, offers a line of automobiles to new-car customers. In that business, his or her products compete with other new-car dealers' products by means of product differences, promotion, advertising, price inducements, and sales efforts by the marketing staff. Associated with the new-car business and its strategy are at least two other businesses. Servicing and body work for some dealers has become an important profit center, especially where new car-price competition has been severe. Under these conditions, customers for service work or body repair will be solicited well beyond new-car customers. Advertising will emphasize service to a broad range of customers, and an entire strategy can be found that is independent of the new-car part of the organization. Used-car sales often form an important third business for the new-car-dealer organization. Independent strategies can be seen in the selection of cars for sale, in promotion efforts, and in customers selected as targets.

In effect, top management of the dealer organization is involved in three businesses rather than one. To be sure, new-car customers need a service department and an outlet for their old cars, but the extent of the impact of the new-car business and its customers on the other two businesses can vary considerably from dealer to dealer. In the auto dealer example, top management must examine at least four strategies. The independent strategies of each line of business and then the megastrategy to be used to guide all three businesses toward total organizational objectives.

For you to learn how to formulate multibusiness strategy, two levels or forms of complexity need to be identified and explored. The first is multibusiness *domestic* firms with several distinct lines of business that are either related, as in the new-car dealership, or nonrelated, as in the conglomerate made up of unconnected autonomous divisions. In either instance, this type of multibusiness is located within a single political/economical/social system.

The second type of multibusiness you will need to consider is also one that contains related or nonrelated lines of business but that operates in a *multinational* political/economic context. Oil-based companies such as Mobil or Exxon or communication-based conglomerates such as ITT are examples of this latter form of multibusiness.

Figure 1–1 is a schematic that diagrams the broad learning objectives of the business policy and strategy course we have described. At the beginning of the process, one starts at the lower left of the diagram by studying integration *within* functions, then one examines and develops insights into integration *across* functions as a part of achieving the first objective, learning the skills of the general manager. The learning of single-business strategy formulation is an objective block that occupies the center of this developmental diagram; the development of knowledge and skill in multibusiness strategy formulation is seen at the extreme right. Take a few minutes to look at Figure 1–1 and consider the direction intended by the educational process suggested.

Three elements that are used to help achieve these objectives are depicted by arrows that run from the lower left to the upper, center, and lower right of the diagram. The upper arrow shows the building of *skills.* The lower arrow depicts the acquisition of the new *knowledge* needed to learn and make use of skills. The center, heavier arrow represents the development of *competence*: the acquisition of both knowledge and skills toward the ability to solve complex problems, especially the complex problems of the general manager and strategy formulator.

The developmental approach is used in the learning process to help you build

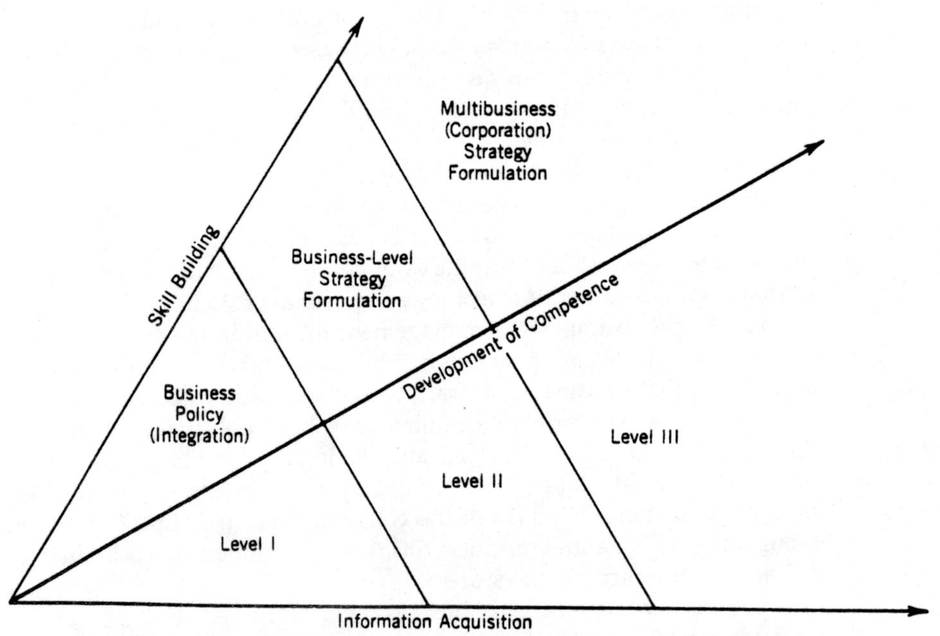

FIGURE 1–1 Course objectives and the developmental process.

abilities from small components of information (much of which you already have) to elemental constructs and from these to go on to larger constructs in developing the macro-organizational concepts needed for you to manage effectively in our complex commercial world. This progressive, developmental approach is also used within each major section of the book.

The text will provide content material that, for most of you, will be new. Exercises will help you learn how to comprehend the full meaning of this new material and will offer the opportunity to test your understanding and to apply your new knowledge, building skills in the process. Despite their many drawbacks, cases offer an excellent opportunity to begin the process of learning analytic skills and of exploring situations that have not been structured by your instructor. This general process is used throughout the book. Each chapter contains content information; exercises for practice, feedback, and skill development; and case material to allow you to practice the application of your new knowledge, to help you learn to deal with increasingly unstructured situations, and to start you in the process of formulating decision alternatives.

APPROACH FOR THIS TEXTBOOK

With this textbook, we plan to help you learn first how to *implement* a given strategy, that is, how to be an effective integrator of functions, a problem solver working to achieve stated objectives. In short, how to acquire the skills of the general manager. From that base, we will begin to address our second objective, the learning and practicing of the strategy-formulation process for single businesses. In this section, you will need to learn the elements of the strategy-formulation process, practice using its elements, and then practice the use of the entire model for single businesses. Here we aim to see you acquire the fundamentals of the skills of the strategy formulator, based on an understanding of the complexities involved in coordinating a multifunction organization toward organizational goals.

From single-business strategy formulation and implementation, we move into the more common multibusiness organization configuration wherein each business has its own strategic goals and its own plans for their accomplishment. It is here that you, as the strategy formulator must not only deal with those tasks, but must also find a rationale for relating these businesses and for knitting the totality into a smoothly functioning, rationally directed entity.

In the next several pages, we will make use of a case that deals with a company called the Holbrook Tire Service to help illustrate some of the points made thus far. You will find some exercise questions at several points along the way. As you read the material, work through the exercises. Write your responses on a sheet of notepaper and bring your notes with you to class to help you in a discussion of the case.

EXERCISE 1–1

Before you begin to read this case, consider the name of the company. In your own mind, is this a single-business enterprise or would it more likely be a multibusiness organization? Make a note, then proceed.

HOLBROOK TIRE SERVICE

"People have accused us of being socialists or Communists. The truth is we just make capitalists out of all employees." Neil Bergh, president of Holbrook Tire Service (HTS), laughed. "Go talk to Ron Turner, one of our assistant managers. He's in my office. He's worked out in the stores and here in central office. He can give you both pictures."

Upon entering the president's office, the casewriter asked Ron about the company.

> *Well, it's fantastic working for a company like Holbrook Tire Service. I don't know many companies where you call the president by his first name. And nobody's better than anybody else. But another guy—someone who sweeps the floors—he's just as important. If he didn't sweep, the ship wouldn't function right, so both the captain and the sweeper are equally important.*
>
> *Everyone can have a piece of the action in this company, too. Do you know about the stock-ownership plan?*

The casewriter assented.

> *Well, as manager of a store, I knew that I would get a paycheck based on my own efforts, but I also knew that my efforts would benefit everyone in the company through dividends and the bonus system. Everyone is part of the larger whole. Now wages aren't so high, but Neil and the other officers, Russ and Bill, they don't have big salaries either. Neil's not out to exploit the company.*

The casewriter watched the animation of the 30-year-old speaker. His enthusiasm about HTS was contagious. He explained that he had worked for HTS for more than 10 years. He had worked in the company's retail branches for 5 or 6 years—2 years as a store manager—and then had come to central office where he had worked in several capacities. For the previous 3 months, since the November 1974 austerity reorganization, Ron had been managing a retail branch again.

As the casewriter listened to Ron, the words of other HTS employees came to mind. Leo James, accountant, talked about the company in terms similar to Ron's.

> *I had completed my sophomore year in college and was looking for summer work. My cousin told me that HTS was demolishing some buildings at the old paint plant.*
>
> *I came out and Bill Lindemann hired me. I knew Bill was an officer, but he came out and worked right along with us. I'd been there a couple of days when someone mentioned that*

This case was prepared by Marilyn L. Taylor and Louis B. Barnes of Harvard University Graduate School of Business.

Tom who also worked with us, was the president's son. Some president's sons would get soft jobs, but Tom worked as hard as anyone else and, as you can imagine, demolition work isn't the easiest work there is, particularly during a hot summer day. I guess I had been there about two weeks when one day Tom referred to another guy as "Dad." That was when I realized that the "Neil" who had been working with the group of us—about six, I think—was Neil Bergh, president of the company. That really impressed me, and when they made me an offer at the end of my senior year I came with them. That was about two years ago.

Will Samuelson, warehouse supervisor, talked about the company.

I was up in Needham earlier this year to see a Firestone warehouse. The thing that struck me was the rigidity. One of the keys to our success in HTS is our flexibility and I like it that way. One of the Firestone employees asked me what I did. I do everything . . . , even drive a truck, I told him. The guy looked at me like I was crazy. At Firestone a guy has a job and that's all he does. A branch manager here at HTS is not a shirt-and-tie guy.

Neil's brother-in-law, Ed Hurley, is treasurer and credit manager for HTS. Ed's wife Sue reminisced about the company. She recalled that when she and Ed first moved to the Charlestown area in the late 1950s, the company was located in a small shop where the company made retreads. In 1974 central headquarters for HTS was a 120,000-square-foot modern facility that housed the warehouse, the retread shop, the support executives and Horns Material Handling–Charlestown. "We have never regretted our decision to come with HTS," said Sue. "Neil is a wonderful man, just like his father. But the amazing thing about the company is that we are all friends."

Lou Fidler is manager of Rally Tire, the HTS subsidiary that sells tires wholesale. Lou talked about the success of HTS:

Hell, it's not tires. It's the management team. With the people we have, we could sell anything.

Still another individual explained the company's record this way:

It's the feeling of invincibility that has led to the HTS success.

EARLY HISTORY OF HOLBROOK TIRE SERVICE (HTS)

Early in 1957 Neil Bergh purchased a small retread shop in his hometown of Charlestown, Massachusetts. The $20,000 capitalization consisted of $5,000 from Neil; $5,000 from the manager of the retread shop; $5,000 from Neil's father, Neil Bergh, Sr., president of Bergh Trucking; and $5,000 from a friend of Neil's who also worked at Bergh Trucking. Although the retread shop had been losing money for several years, Neil felt that by improving the quality of the product and hustling to increase sales, he could turn the company around. The new company was called Holbrook Tire Service, Inc., after the county in which Charlestown, Massachusetts, was located. Neil talked about his father and the decision to get into his own business.

I worked for my dad in the trucking business about twelve years overall. One time when I was seventeen, I was in a truck rodeo. I didn't know until several years later that I had placed third in the rodeo and my dad refused to let me receive the award.

My dad was like that, though. After a couple

of years of college, I started working as a truck driver for Bergh Trucking and eventually became a fleet supervisor. One day I went to my dad and asked for a raise. My dad's reply was, "I believe you are making what a fleet supervisor makes." Psychologically I left Bergh Trucking right then. I began to look around.

Another major trucking company had just purchased an independent trucking concern. After a number of interviews, they asked Neil to come head up the new operation. The salary was a substantial one. Said Neil:

They put me through two days of psychological examinations and after all that made me a handsome offer. I decided that if I was all right to head up a part of their company, I must be all right to run my own. I declined their offer and purchased the retread shop.

Russ Carle, senior vice president for HTS, talked about Bergh Trucking.

Neil and I attended the same Sunday school as youngsters. We were friends even then, although we didn't live in the same neighborhood. I went to work for Bergh Trucking on a part-time basis in my early teens. "Pop" [Neil Bergh, Sr.] had a very profitable business, but he wasn't interested in it getting any bigger. After Neil came back from the marines, he wanted to get out and hustle business.

Neil remained with Bergh Trucking for a number of months and worked nights at the newly purchased retread shop. During the first few months, the operation continued to lose money. The shop manager, fearing he would lose a substantial part of his capital investment, wanted out. "I scraped together four thousand dollars," recalled Neil, "and we gave him the station wagon." The new company became more time consuming. Sherry, Neil's wife, pointed out that he spent more and more time during the day at the shop. Sherry said that Neil's dad was proud of him. She also observed that the father and son were much alike. "But," said Neil, "my father was a truckman, and I am a businessman."

Neil spoke proudly of Bergh Trucking's accomplishments. The company had won a number of awards from the American Trucking Association and numerous safety awards. Neil attributed the excellent safety record to the fact that each driver had his own tractor. Drivers took pride in their tractors and even washed the tractors themselves. At one time, Mack Trucks ran an ad showing two tractors. One tractor was just off the paint line at the factory and the other was a Bergh truck that had a million miles. It was difficult to tell which was which. Neil's father died in 1972. In 1974 the company was run by Jim Bergh, Neil's older brother. Although it had not grown significantly, Bergh Trucking continued to win safety awards and was still very profitable.

EXERCISE 1–2

Stop at this point and see if you can determine six possible profit centers for Holbrook Tire Service. List them on notepaper, then proceed.

In 1958 HTS started in the small retread shop with sales of $200,000 and a profit of $7,000. By 1974 HTS had grown to over $11 million in sales with a $150,000 (estimated) profit after taxes (see 10-Year Summary, Exhibit 1). In 1974 the company had 11 Firestone retail outlets and 4 other subsidiaries (summarized in Exhibit 2.

GROWTH AND DIVERSIFICATION OF HTS

In 1960 HTS opened its first retail branch through which the company sold its recapped tires as well as Firestone and Michelin tires. By 1974 HTS had 10 retail outlets in Massachusetts and 1 in New Hampshire. By the end of 1974 the retail outlets employed 78 people, and sales for the year were nearly $5 million.

Rally Tire was established in 1971. Basically, the purpose of establishing Ralley had been to take advantage of volume-purchase discounts with tire manufacturers. All wholesale tire sales were made through Ralley's four branches. In 1974 sales were nearly $4 million, and at the end of the year, Ralley had 16 employees.

The original retread shop still contributed significantly to HTS sales. In 1974 HTS sold about $1.3 million worth of retread tires, both retail and wholesale. The recap shop was one of the largest on the East Coast. Retreading was done in the shop at the far end of the company's new building. In the old shop, the 8-foot ceiling had made working conditions dirty and hot. By contrast, the 20-foot ceiling and the use of large exhaust fans in the new shop more than met Occupational Safety and Health Administration (OSHA) standards. Ten automated Acutread molds each turned out a quality retread in a 20-minute cycle while the older machines, still used for less popular tire sizes, took an hour to vulcanize the rubber. Very little work, other than truck tires, was done to individual customer specification. The retreads carried the HTS label and were sold through the company's Firestone retail outlets and wholesale through Ralley. Other tire dealers as far away as Ohio had purchased HTS retreads.

Charlestown Safety Equipment, Inc., originally a warehouse distributorship, was purchased in 1973. Holbrook Tire Service converted the company to a wholesale distribution (WD). Eric Mooney, vice president of HTS, talked about his decision to come to HTS and the establishment of Charlestown Safety.

> *I had been an engineer for twenty-five years for a large company. I felt locked in—not able to influence changes. Neil called me one night. . . . My first store was the Boston store. The first year I made forty thousand dollars. By the end of the first year everything was running smoothly and the challenge was gone, so when Neil asked me to open the Burlington branch, I said, "What the heck." In a little more than a year, Neil asked me to come to central office to oversee the warehouse, the recap operation, and Charlestown Safety.*
>
> *I didn't know anything about recapping, but I was a mechanical engineer. . . . After we moved the recap operation into the new factory, I turned my attention to Charlestown Safety Equipment. Holbrook Tire Service had stocked parts and accessories for their own trucks, and they decided that they could purchase wholesale and sell to truck dealers.*
>
> *Tim Joyce was assistant scoutmaster of my scout troop. He ran a wholesale industrial-parts-and-supply house. I didn't feel Charlestown Safety would be a whole lot different. It is multisourcing and multisupplying.*

Under the leadership of Eric Mooney and Tim Joyce, the company made arrangements with a number of quality manufacturers—such as Monroe shock absorbers—to purchase and sell wholesale various car and truck parts and accessories to tire dealers, trucking companies, and car and truck dealers. Ralley and Charles-

EXHIBIT 1
Holbrook Tire Service, Inc. and Subsidiaries 10-Year Summary (1965–74)

	1974	*1973*	*1972*	*1971*
Financial Position at December 31				
Total Assets	$ 9,355,737	$5,334,489	$3,674,220	$2,626,936
Total Liabilities	7,184,552	3,300,554	2,197,590	1,520,383
Stockholders' Equity	2,171,185	2,083,934	1,476,629	1,106,553
Shares of Capital Stock Out*	76,539	76,676	66,214	57,433
Price per Share January 1*	46.58	41.04	32.76	26.61
Price per Share December 31*	43.46	46.58	41.04	32.76
Shareholders	89	82	58	40
Book Value* (1)	28.29	27.10	22.21	17.38
Operating Results for the Year				
Net Sales	11,113,128	8,356,273	6,130,659	5,097,934
Income Before Fed. Inc. Tax	187,367	599,145	494,095	366,709
Net Income	127,463	357,132	271,738	209,043
Dividends	30,406	91,473	69,002	54,449
Per Common Share:*				
Earnings	1.67	4.66	4.10	3.64
Dividends	.40	1.25	1.20	1.00
Other Related Information				
Number of Sales Outlets	19	14	10	10
Number of Employees	217	167	132	132
Dividend as Percentage of Earnings	23.9%	25.6%	25.4%	26.1%

*Adjusted for the five-for-one stock split in May 1969.
(1) Properties are valued at cost and do not reflect appreciated values.

town salespeople did not sell each other's products, but the managers of the two areas encouraged them to talk about the other products.

Small Parts, Inc., came to HTS in an unusual way. Bob Jacob had been known to HTS for several years. He was retired in 1967 when a friend asked him to become a partner in a small company that sold accessories and small parts to tire dealers. By 1972 Small Parts had $250,000 in sales. None of Bob's children were interested in running the business. However, for estate purposes, he wanted to protect the gains he had made, and he realized that the company would fold if he died. Impressed with the HTS record and confident that HTS could provide the necessary managerial talent if something happened to him, Bob sold the company to HTS for stock and a small amount of cash. At 72 he still managed this operation.

Horns Material Handling, Inc.

Horns Material Handling was a result of several brainstorming sessions in 1971–72. Eric Mooney talked about this division of the company.

> *Horns came about because we were looking for diversification. No one had foreseen the gas shortage, but we kicked around the idea*

EXHIBIT 1
Holbrook Tire Services, Inc. and Subsidiaries 10-Year Summary (1965–74) *(Continued)*

1970	*1969*	*1968*	*1967*	*1966*	*1965*
$2,408,405	$2,528,319	$1,985,437	$1,420,730	$ 931,376	$ 571,732
1,471,365	1,706,904	1,271,257	883,025	609,378	369,748
937,040	821,415	714,180	537,705	321,998	201,998
54,651	56,997	57,420	57,515	50,610	45,880
23.13	25.07	22.96	16.11	9.85	8.53
26.61	23.13	25.07	22.96	16.11	9.85
33	37	40	33	26	22
13.98	12.32	10.55	9.35	6.36	4.40
4,424,730	4,232,137	3,554,290	2,787,059	1,799,293	1,273,215
279,114	267,330	228,587	262,854	174,569	55,901
148,445	134,097	118,095	145,108	98,855	36,567
27,238	18,697	40,337	34,508	18,252	5,940
2.72	2.36	2.06	2.52	1.95	.80
.50	.33	.70	.60	.36	.13
9	8	8	7	6	5
132	118	113	90	53	43
18.4%	13.9%	34.2%	23.8%	18.5%	16.2%

that maybe someday people wouldn't ride in vehicles with tires or a tire would be made that wouldn't wear out.

We were having trouble getting service for our own forklift trucks, and so we thought why not go into that. It was wheels, an internal combustion engine and a hydraulic system. Holbrook Tire Service sells tires to industrial customers, so we had some familiarity with the market.

In July 1972 HTS became the distributor for a little-known Japanese manufacturer.

One of the first men Eric hired was Ted O'Malley. Ted had previously been a maintenance supervisor for a well-known forklift distributor. Ted talked about setting up the new company.

Horns was a great opportunity for me to be in on the bottom floor. I had worked for over fifteen years in the forklift truck industry. It is a close-knit industry and everyone knows everyone else. I got some men, some of the best forklift mechanics and salespeople around.

In early 1973 Ted told Eric that a major forklift manufacturer was rumored to be inter-

EXHIBIT 2
Holbrook Tire Service, Inc., Subsidiaries and Divisions

Subsidiary	*Executive in Charge* (Age, Years, w/Co.)*	*Description*	*Personnel*	*Year Established*	*1974 Sales*
HTS–Retail	Russ Carle (45, 11)	Sells tires, accessories, and service through 11 Firestone retail outlets.	11 branches 78 employees	1960	$4,840,484
Ralley Tire	Lou Fidler (27, 4)	Sells tires wholesale to tire dealers in Massachusetts and New Hampshire. Has two outlets—Quincy and Norwood.	4 branches 16 employees	1971	$3,972,192
Horns, Providence	Bob Freeman (52, 1)	Sells and services forklift trucks and accessories.	1 location 22 employees	1974	$336,505
Horns, Charlestown	David Slovakia† (40, 5 months)	Same as Providence.	1 location 13 employees	1972	$669,473
Charlestown Safety Equipment Inc.	Tim Joyce (46, 2)	Distributes truck and auto parts on a WD basis. Installs equipment on and repairs trucks and tractors.	1 location 15 employees	1973	$842,516
Small Parts Inc.	Bob Jacob (72, 2)	Sells small parts (such as valve stems, tools, and equipment) to tire dealers.	1 location 4 employees	1972	$451,958
Retread Shop	Bill Lindemann (45, 9)	Retreads passenger and truck tires on a volume basis. Some individual orders. HTS tires are distributed through HTS Firestone outlets and other dealers.	1 location 20 employees	1958	Included in HTS–Retail

*As of January 1, 1975.
Sales forces for Providence and Charlestown report to David Slovakia.

ested in severing its relationship with their dealer who served the Providence and greater Boston areas. In November Neil, Joe Grossack, Eric Mooney, Ted O'Malley, and a consultant who had been hired to put together the proposal went to company headquarters to make a presentation. The proposal was for HTS to take over the dealership for the greater Boston area.

Several months went by with no decision from the manufacturer. In April 1974 Neil called headquarters. The manufacturer told him HTS could take over the whole distributorship or wait until someone took the Providence area. Shortly after the telephone call, Neil made the decision to take on the whole franchise. The decision essentially meant doubling the *pro forma* estimates.

The HTS dealership for the major manufacturer of forklift trucks officially began on May 1, 1974. During the next three months, Horns Material Handling–Charlestown continued to be developed under the guidance of Eric Mooney and Ted O'Malley. A location in Providence was opened July 1, 1974. This location was about a two-hour drive from Charlestown. Heading up this location was Bob Freeman. Bob had been with another forklift distributor dealer some years before. Later, he set up his own business in which he bought, repaired, and sold used forklifts. Bob was delighted with the opportunity to come with HTS. As he put it, "I wanted to expand my own business, but I didn't have the financial means."

HTS INCENTIVE SYSTEMS

A significant influence on Neil's original purchase of the retread shop was *Incentive Management.*[1] "Before I read Lincoln's book," said Neil, "I could see myself running a sales company. But after I read *Incentive Management,* I knew I had found the key to running a manufacturing concern. The first year we were in operation, we put in a profit-sharing plan. We still have it today."

Each year from 1974 on, 20% of estimated after-tax HTS profit was set aside to be distributed in the profit-sharing program. In 1974, therefore, $30,000 was set aside to be distributed as profit sharing among all employees.

Calculating the profit allocation for nonmanagerial personnel was a three-step process. The first part of the calculation simply divided the total nonmanagerial profit pot by the number of employees. The second part of the calculation took into account the contribution to the total sales and profit picture by unit. The third step, the actual profit distributed to the location, was the average of these two calculations. The manner of determining the amount distributed to the individual employees in the various locations differed by location. Some managers made the allocation entirely on their own. Others asked their assistant and perhaps a senior employee to make the decision. Still others delegated the decision to a committee of employees.

The method used to allocate the managerial pot differed from that used with the nonmanagerial share. Managers were divided into two groups: support people and operating managers. The president, vice presidents, and controller formed the support group. The managers of the retail and wholesale store locations and the heads of the subsidiaries were the operating managers. Each operating manager ranked the support managers and vice versa. The individual profit share was allocated to each person on the basis of an average ranking. If a manager had been with HTS less than a year, the bonus was reduced.

Every employee regardless of length of service with the company, shared in the profit-sharing plan. There were two other incentive systems also in operation in 1974. They were the store manager's share of the store profit and the Individual Bonus for Effort (IBFE) programs. Each of the stores was treated as a profit center. Central office/administrative overhead was allocated on the basis of proportion of total expense incurred by the unit. Wholesale tires from Ralley and retread tires were "sold" to the stores on the basis of established transfer prices. Each manager received an established salary or 40% of the profit from the store, whichever was greater. Since two or three locations had the potential for over a $100,000 profit, a store manager could earn in excess of $40,000. The range of salaries in 1973 was from $14,879 to $42,172, with a median of $23,137.

Store managers did not typically stay in one location. Managers might start in a smaller location and then move to a larger store when the opportunity arose if their experience warranted the move. On the other hand, at times some store managers found their niche and remained with a store indefinitely. In 1974 Dave McCol-

[1] James F. Lincoln, *Incentive Management* (Cleveland, Ohio: Lincoln Electric Co., 1951).

lum, for example, had been manager of the Worcester location since 1966. When HTS purchased the store from the owner, its reputation and sales had been decreasing for several years. Under Dave's management, the reputation of the location was reestablished and sales were steadily increasing.

There may have been some tendency for a store manager to strive for increased current sales and profit at the expense of longer-term customer relationships. However, the philosophy of HTS was that the customer is to be treated with deference. The criteria for the assessment of the operating managers by the support managerial personnel implicitly included adherence to this philosophy.

The IBFE programs were designed for the workers in the retail branches. In working on a car, a retail employee might notice that the car needed some additional parts or service. If the sale to the customer was consummated, the employee received a bonus.

Neil pointed out the delicate balance in setting the amount of the bonus.

> *If you pay too much, the customers will get things they don't need; but if you pay too little, the workers won't go to the extra bother of bringing the need to the attention of the customer or the store manager. We had an incident happen a while ago. Monroe was paying a special bonus of a dollar for a pair of shock absorbers. We passed it along to the managers of the retail outlets. One of the managers told each of his employees that they could have the dollar for each pair they sold. They sold a lot of shock absorbers, but we had some calls from some irate customers who felt they had been oversold.*

EMPLOYEE OWNERSHIP

With three exceptions, all of the HTS stock was owned by the employees of HTS. Almost half the employees owned shares at the end of 1974. Of the three nonemployee owners, two had invested in the company's initial capitalization. The third was an HTS employee who had become a jobber. (A jobber purchases tire casings from service stations and other tire dealers and delivers them to the retread shop for evaluation and purchase.)

Under the employee-ownership plan, any employee who had worked a year or more for the firm could purchase stock. The first purchase had to be in the amount of $500. After the initial purchase of the stock, the employee could purchase any number of shares. On separation from the company, the employee's shares were repurchased as treasury stock at the current price. The current price was established yearly by Smith and Smith, a CPA firm retained by the company since 1958. Dividends had been paid every year since 1965 (see 10-Year Summary, Exhibit 1).

Although employee pilfering was usually a problem in retail operations, at HTS the problem was minimal. Neil Bergh attributed the lack of pilfering to the employee-ownership program.

> *If a guy steals a tire, he knows he is stealing from himself and from the guy who works with him all day. While I was up at Harvard at the Small Company Management Program, I told the professor that some of the people in his class just didn't understand our program. They worried about controlling their companies. I don't control the people in HTS. With employee ownership and a bonus system, you don't have to.*

TOP MANAGEMENT (1974)

Three men headed up HTS. See Exhibit 3 for an organization chart. The president and founder of the company is Neil Bergh. Neil attended the University of Kentucky before joining the ma-

EHXIBIT 3
Holbrook Tire Service, Inc., Organization Chart, January 1, 1975

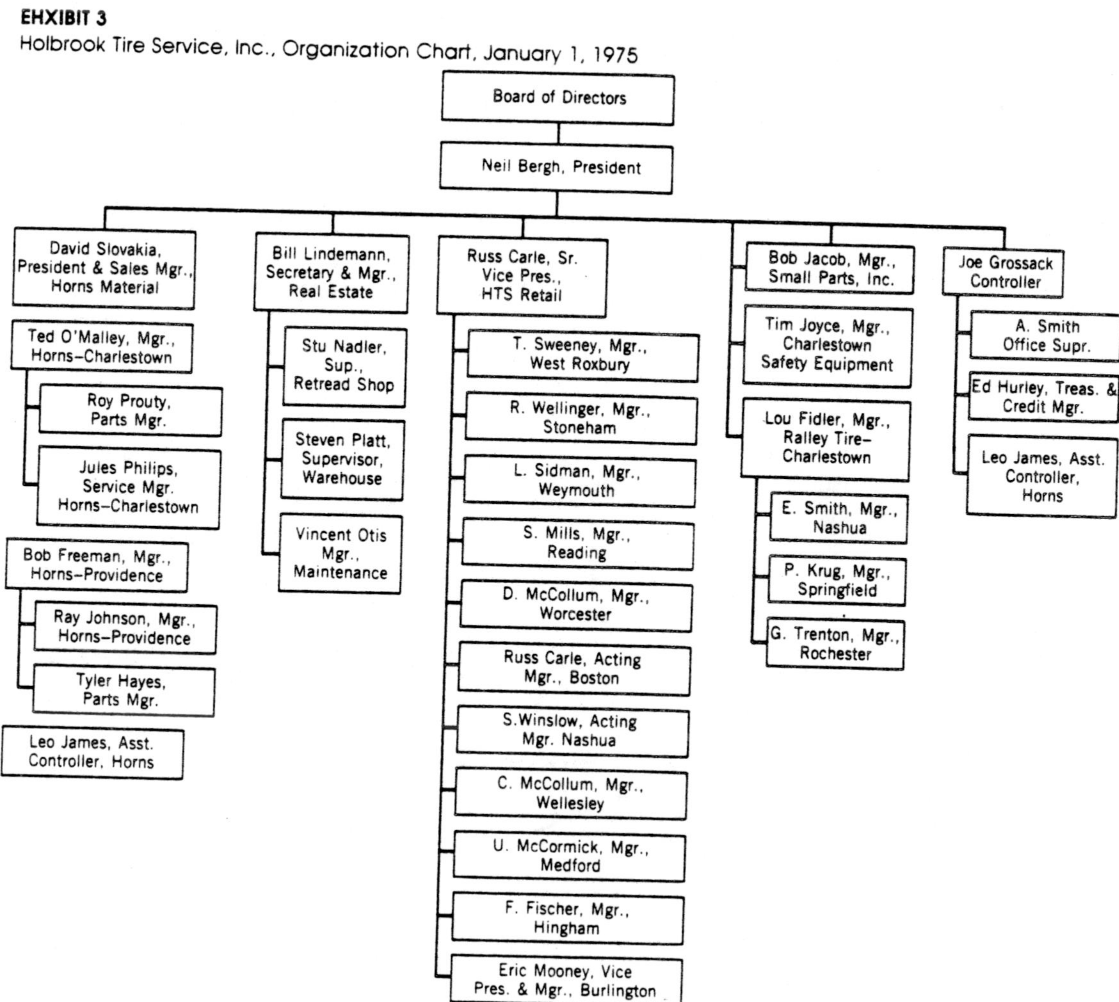

rines during the Korean War. In 1974 Neil was 46.

Russ Carle, senior vice president, was 45. Russ attended the University of Maine and then operated his own business, Carle's Causeway Garage, before coming with HTS in 1963. More than one individual described Russ as a person-oriented man; to those in the company, he was "mother." Russ put it this way:

> *I am a people person. At HTS people are my job and I love it.*

Like Neil and Russ, Bill Lindemann came from a family that had lived in the Charlestown area for several generations. Bill was 45 and had previously worked as an engineer for two larger firms. When he joined HTS in 1965, he was responsible for maintenance, engineering, and construction. Secretary of HTS, Bill talked about the company.

Neil is a leader and I am more of a follower. The balance works well. The informality is great. Phones get used a lot. If we have to write something, we draft it by hand and give it to the girl on the switchboard to type. We don't bother with a bunch of copies like a big company.

In talking about the relationships among Russ, Bill, and himself, Neil Bergh referred to the theory of balance. Neil explained that there are basically three dimensions in all people: the learner, people, and action orientations. Neil felt that he, Russ, and Bill represented a well-balanced combination. In terms of their rankings on each of the three dimensions, Neil saw the following patterns:

Smith Winslow at twenty-eight is a general branch manager. Smith has a bachelor's degree in business administration. He ran his own business for a couple of years and then came with us in 1969. He ran one of the retail stores and then came to central office to work with Russ. In the reorganization last November, Smith went to Nashua, New Hampshire, to head up the branch. He's trying to make that location go and find and develop a manager to replace him.

Joe Grossack has an MBA with a concentration in finance. At thirty-four Joe is our controller. Joe has been responsible for developing the financial controls we need as we get larger. He has developed the computer programs we have as well as cash flow and other financial projections. Joe is another of the younger men we are depending on for the future.

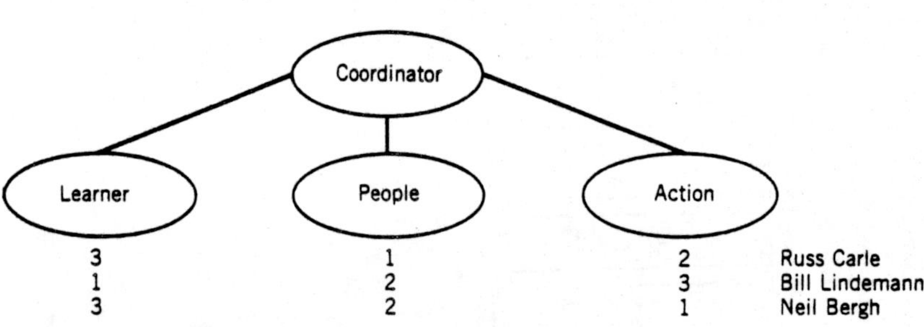

In addition to the senior executives, there were several younger men who were being given substantial responsibility. Neil talked about this aspect of the company.

There's young Lou Fidler. Lou has an economics' degree from BU and is currently enrolled in a master's program. Lou's a born salesman. At twenty-seven he heads up Ralley, which had almost four million dollars in sales in 1974.

None of the children from the families of the three top executives appear to have an active interest in HTS. Neil is not too concerned about the succession issue.

We are developing younger men. We will be around for a good while yet and when we get to be ready for pasture, they will nudge us over.

HORNS MATERIAL HANDLING—THE 1975 DILEMMA

In August 1974 David Slovakia came to HTS. David talked about how this happened.

> *Neil and I were both on the Board of Directors for a local bank in Charlestown. Toward the end of 1973, we began to get friendly and after the April [1974] meeting, we went out for a few drinks. Neil pulled out the ten-year summary and the new future goal for Horns. It was something exciting. His original offer to me was considerably below what I was making at REZ. But Neil said, "Here is an opportunity where you can write your own ticket." I put together some figures. It did look good. . . . [After several talks] . . . , we shook hands . . . Neil really sells people. "We are all equal," I have heard him say. "We are all one big happy family. There are no bosses here." When he says it, he really believes it.*

David began to work for HTS on August 1, 1974; his major responsibility was to develop sales for Horns Material Handling. He described the situation in Horns when he came in.

> *When I first got to Horns, Eric Mooney and Ted O'Malley were involved in everything. Ted assumed that Eric was the guy in charge. Commission policies were different for different people. It was a mess. At the end of the week, I told Neil to find something else for Mooney to do. I was ready to fly by myself. Neil had a talk with him, but it didn't do much good. Finally in November at a Board of Directors meeting, they worked out a reorganization.*

David saw major differences between the forklift truck business and the businesses in which the rest of HTS was involved. He was concerned that others in HTS did not understand the full extent of the diversification that the forklift business represented for HTS. David outlined the differences as follows:

1. *Sales:* Most of HTS is involved in retail sales where people come to the company. There is some wholesale selling to industrial customers, but HTS has not had to do any cold selling for some time. Horns people have to go out on the road to sell. It takes a different breed of cat to do that.
2. *Service:* Service is a big chunk of the money in forklifts. It is a highly skilled endeavor that involves major repairs. The other subsidiaries of HTS never get involved with major repairs such as transmissions. With the move toward electric trucks, the workers have to have more and more of a knowledge of electronics. There is a vast difference between the people in the stores making $2.80 an hour and the mechanics in the highly unionized forklift truck industry making $7.50 an hour; HTS didn't realize that. At the Christmas party, Bill Lindemann said that some of the HTS mechanics would come down and help in Horns during the slack times in the stores. The next day, the Horns mechanics came to me and said, "Is it true that HTS mechanics are going to come to Horns? Does that mean we are going to be replaced?" I tried to make light of it and said Bill must have been kidding when he said that. I went to him and asked if he had said that the HTS mechanics would be coming into Horns. Bill replied, "David, we have got to have some HTS blood in Horns and bringing in HTS mechanics during their slack times is a good way to do it." I went to Neil.
3. *Parts:* Neil thought that some Horns parts could be supplied by Charlestown Safety Equipment. I tried to tell him that wouldn't work. . . . The forklift truck parts are

highly specialized. Nobody comes in off the street and buys forklift truck parts.

The relationship between David and Ted deteriorated as the fall went on. David explained it this way.

I told Neil several times that things just weren't going well between Ted and me [but] Neil strongly suggested that I try to work with Ted. I think that Neil was afraid that if something happened to Ted, the service people would walk out. I doubted that. They had good jobs, good pay. If I had followed my instincts I would have let him go the first month.

The thing with Ted really came to a head at a meeting that was held in Neil's office in early December. Neil asked Ted some questions. I felt he should have had the answers but he didn't.

The day after Christmas 1974, Ted was helping to paint some forklift trucks for one of the largest orders to date. In the hospital later, all he could remember was that he had felt dizzy, perhaps from the paint fumes, although he wasn't sure, and had gone out on the back platform to get some fresh air. The next thing he knew, he was lying on the ground on his side. He could not move.

As of January 16, 1975, Ted could still not move on one side. The doctor's prognosis: "No physiological source." David talked about his relationship with Ted.

Ted understood he was to be general manager of Horns Material Handling. He had been the one to originally tell HTS that a major manufacturer's franchise was available. After I came, Neil kept telling him, "Why don't you work with David?" [Just the fact that] Neil was talking to Ted was implying to Ted that he still had the authority. I finally asked Neil to quit talking to him.

Meanwhile David was becoming very uncomfortable in HTS. He felt that he had always run a tight ship where people weren't left in a state of ambiguity about leadership levels and specific responsibilities. That was one of the ways in which he had managed to turn three plants around for REZ, the large, national company he had worked for before coming to HTS. Although things went well between Neil and David for a time, David felt that the relationship had quickly deteriorated.

Neil and I really stopped talking after I had been there a month or so. I am not saying I am totally innocent. . . . Neil began to interfere more and more then. . . . Neil knew I was drifting away. In the meetings I would say, "Oh, com'on." I wasn't going to be the yes-man in the meetings. Usually, Neil does the talking and people listen. . . . Neil is an interesting man. . . . He never does anything half-assed. Others have tried to compare Neil and me. We compare on ambition. He likes to be number one and so do I. I am not a follower. I have been a leader just like Neil. . . . There are leaders and there are followers . . . each has his part.

Russ Carle was also becoming concerned about how David Slovakia fit into HTS.

David has put a tremendous effort into sales. We have had a lot of pressure from the manufacturer to get sales under way. Now that is moving. The figures aren't out yet, but we think Horns was in the black in December. However, David does not relate to the mechanics. We are convinced that we can do a good job in the forklift service area. We are service oriented in HTS. The forklift maintenance business is no different than the

> *trucking company or any other where people go out on their own. . . .*
>
> *Ted just never understood David. They are two different types of people, and they never developed a respect for each other. They didn't find out what the other was worth. Ted is a people person. He understands people, no question, [but] it was no good between him and David. . . .*
>
> *David has wanted to separate Horns as much as he could. . . . We may have made a mistake in hiring the man and in thinking our philosophy could be implanted. David just isn't buying the way we think. . . . We have learned a great deal over the last couple of months. We need to inbreed our philosophy, not try to breathe it in.*

Over lunch on January 17, Neil talked about his increasing concern about David.

> *David came to us with an impressive record. He was sent to different REZ plants, and he took them to the top [of the company] in a year or two. My assumption was that he got people to pull together. Later, I found out that that wasn't so; rather, he was sent into situations that were racked with union problems and he cleared them out. It takes a different set of skills to be a hatchet man than to grow a business.*
>
> *When David first came with us, it was understood that he was to develop the sales for Horns Charlestown and Providence. Before long, he came to me and said that if he was going to be talking to people in the industrial companies, he would have to have an appropriate title. So we named him vice president, Horns Material Handling, Inc., and Bob Freeman and Ted O'Malley remained managers, Providence and Charlestown, respectively.*

Neil also talked about the expectations of the executive group regarding David and Ted O'Malley.

> *David is a hard driver, but he is not a people man. We thought he and Ted would make a good balance. But that didn't work out. David selected another man as service manager in Charlestown. Ted fell off the dock the day after Christmas—three weeks ago. He is paralyzed on his right side, but the doctors say "Nothing physiologically wrong." So, Ted is either faking it or it is psychosomatic. . . .*
>
> *David has insisted on being completely in charge at Horns. I have allowed that to a certain degree, but maybe I shouldn't have. This morning David came into my office and said, "Well, the worst thing that could have happened has happened; the NLRB [National Labor Relations Board] has called a union election among the service crew." David offered to resign right then. Maybe I should have accepted then and there, but I said, "Let's cool it for a while." I went down and talked with Jules Philips, the service manager, and what has apparently happened is that David has unilaterally changed policies and procedures set by Ted O'Malley and Eric Mooney.*
>
> *I have asked him various times if the guys understood the necessity for the changes, and David has replied, "Of course. I told them."*
>
> *As I see it, we have three alternatives. We can keep David and let the union come in. David is skilled in dealing with a union. We can kick David out, keep the union out, and move someone else in. But then we run the risk of a union in a year or so, anyway, and needing someone like David to deal with them. Or we can move someone, probably Bill or Russ, into my slot here, and I can go down and run Horns myself.*

EXERCISE 1-3

After reading the case, do you wish to change your list from the one you made for Exercise 1-2? Make any changes you wish, then return to page 14 for the profit centers actually used.

EXERCISE 1-4

What sort of person would you want to be manager of the tires and accessories retail sales profit center? List the principal requirements and/or talents that you would like to see in that person. Compare your list with the list found at the end of the chapter.

EXERCISE 1-5

Is the list for this person likely to be different than that for the person charged with responsibility for the retread shop? If not, why not? If so, why?

EXERCISE 1-6

Suppose that an increase in retread tire sales to five or six times the present volume is possible given the demand for tires in the area. What problems might a five- or six-times expansion pose for the other profit centers? List two potential problems for each, and prepare to discuss your list in class.

EXERCISE 1-7

How are the businesses in this company related? Is the relationship horizontal or vertical? Is the relationship based on common materials, technology, or customers? Prepare to discuss this question in class.

EXERCISE 1-8

Give examples of the kind of integration needed by the general manager of Holbrook Tire Service:

- Within functions.

- Between functions.
- Between businesses.

As we conclude Chapter 1, you might wish to reflect on the process we have just completed. Certain new information was provided, and exercise questions helped in the retention of this new information and aided you to understand how it can be applied in a real-life situation. Finally, you had the opportunity to examine an actual business problem by confronting the situation faced by the management of HTS. In the next section of the book, you will encounter the same elements as herein. Although built to present different subject matter, they all are aimed at developing both your knowledge and your skill. As you proceed, you will find yourself reflecting on earlier knowledge and making use of learned skills as you deal with increasingly complex situations. Now, let us begin to explore Part I, a series of chapters designed to help you develop skills in integrating within each of the major business functions.

ANSWER TO SELECTED EXERCISE

Exercise 1-4

The manager of the tires and accessories retail sales profit center should be a customer-oriented marketing person. He or she should be knowledgeable about stock, be capable of providing advice to customers, and be prepared to assist customers in making good choices. The manager should be aware of both the value and cost of advertising and promotion and, in general, of the concept of the combined effect of the characteristics of the Product, its Price (including financing, where needed), Promotion and the importance of merchandising, and the need of an appropriate Place for the customer to reach the buying decision.

PART ONE

INTEGRATION WITHIN EACH MAJOR ORGANIZATIONAL FUNCTION

The generalist must rely on highly educated and advanced specialists for support but must be able to coordinate the work of disparate specialties into a coherent network of directed activity toward desired goals. The generalist, therefore, must first be capable of service as an organizational integrator[1] and serve as a general manager: that is, coordinating the activities of func-

[1] P. R. Lawrence and J. W. Lorsch. *Organization and Environment* (Homewood, Ill.: R. D. Irwin, 1969), p. 244.

tionally separate groups, resolving disputes among functions, acting as a crucial communicator across functional lines, and adjusting functional goal emphasis to achieve an optimum level of organizational goal accomplishment.

In the capacity of general manager, the generalist is primarily concerned with the effective implementation of strategic plans and the achievement of strategic objectives. In doing so, the general manager must be able to understand and make use of integration within business or organizational functions: that is, develop a coordinated *set* of activities in a given functional area of the organization. In marketing, the marketing-mix concept is a mechanism for intrafunction integration. In the production function, the broad operations-management-systems view serves to focus on a *synthesis* within the function rather than concentrating on a more specialized analysis of individualized elements.[2] Similarly, managers in the financial functions make extensive use of highly sophisticated specialists, but they tie the financial elements into a planned financial framework that represents an optimal arrangement of sources and applications of funds in a form of dynamic equilibrium.

The general manager, of course, cannot be expected to have in-depth competence in all of the specialty areas under his or her jurisdiction. Nor can the general manager be expected to be a more expert functional manager than those who are managing the major functions. The general manager is, however, a generalist and can be thought of as an expert in performing the integrative functions: communicating, resolving conflict, coordinating, and developing and assisting in the achievement of integrated objectives. Generalists' perspectives can be gained through academic work such as the deliberately nonspecialized master of business administration (MBA) degree program (or its equivalent at the undergraduate level) or through executive development programs conducted by major universities. (The Advanced Management Program at the Harvard Business School is one. Others are conducted at MIT, Stanford, and at numerous other universities.)

Planned career development for executives has been very helpful in building generalists in many organizations, especially during the period following World War II. The typical program incorporates a lengthy period of initial training for beginners, followed by a planned placement sequence (in a variety of departments or functions) that is designed to build broad exposure and knowledge. On occasion, temporary assignments or job-rotation plans are included to help assure that over a period of years a sufficient supply of well-educated, broadly experienced executives will emerge at the organizational levels where generalist perspectives and skills are required.

Eugene Jennings, in *The Mobile Manager,*[3] observes that these generalist

[2] E. E. Adam, Jr., and R. J. Ebert, *Production and Operations Management,* 2nd Ed., (Englewood Cliffs, N.J.: Prentice-Hall, 1982), p. 678.

[3] New York: McGraw-Hill, 1967.

managers with records of exceptionally fast rates of promotion and with clearly evident success share a common and very highly developed attribute: the ability to *learn*, and learn *quickly*.

Jennings noted that the most far-reaching and significant decisions made by these prominent management superstars were made within the first six months after assuming responsibility for a given position! Generalists—whether trained by means of cross-function training programs, cross-function job assignments, or the sink-or-swim promotion from a single specialized function—must learn the vocabulary, must understand the major techniques available for analysis and decision making, and most important, must learn the critical measures and factors needed for success in each major function. Armed with this knowledge, the generalist can begin to monitor effectively and guide the work of functional managers while beginning the process of assembling the functions into an organizational entity: the integrated business unit. Each of these units represents a coordinated set of business functions designed to achieve strategic objectives.

The general manager of a corrugated box manufacturing plant is an example of such a generalist. His or her market area is defined, in most cases, by transportation costs and the location of competing plants, frequently limited to a 100-mile radius. Within that geographic market, the general manager must oversee the work of a marketing or sales manager, the plant production manager, and a treasurer/controller/office manager. The plant represents an integrated business unit, and the general manager is charged with achieving broad strategic objectives for that unit. Sales growth (in absolute or share-of-market terms), profitability, and return on capital invested are examples of the types of strategic objectives that are commonly found in this industry (and in other industries as well).

In the following two sections, the integrative skills of the generalist will be highlighted and more fully developed. First we will address the generalist's perspective on integration *within* each major function. Following those chapters, the problems of integrating *across* functions will be addressed.

2

ANALYSIS OF ACCOUNTING DATA—THE GENERAL MANAGER'S VIEW

The tools, techniques, and documents used for and by accountants are extremely useful to the general manager. For all organizations, accounting data are needed for financial reporting to owners, to creditors, and to regulatory and taxing agencies. In many organizations, management has extended its requests for information well beyond the data used for financial and tax purposes. In fact, in the accounting profession, managerial accounting has developed into a professional field of its own.

Accounting data are used by the general manager for a wide range of purposes.

Generally, we can relate these very closely to the major managerial functions of planning, decision making, and controlling.

Accounting information provides a fundamental data base for analysis of the past activities of the firm. The financial development of the firm can also be reviewed as a means of understanding and evaluating the effects of the financial policies currently in use. It can be used to provide an in-depth understanding of the cost structure of the business. Accounting information can also be used to assist the general manager in forecasting sales, costs, and capital requirements—all critical elements in effective planning. Forecasting of this type, we must note, requires that one believes that the conditions and patterns of relationships of the past will not be changed significantly during the forecast period. Such an assumption closely parallels the conditions involved in the role of the general manager as an *implementer* of a given strategy.

One example of the use of historical data in forecasting are historical cost records; these can serve as the information base for developing *standard costs* in a cost accounting system. With these standards, managers can plan for specific unit costs and can measure actual unit-cost performance against these standards. Variances from preestablished standards can be identified and flagged for appropriate managerial action. Variances from standard costs might, for example, arise from changes in the price of materials, in the amount of material wasted in the manufacturing process, in labor rates, in productivity of machines and human resources, and in the volume manufactured.

Budgets serve much the same purpose in nonmanufacturing firms or in staff service departments. With budgets, managers review historical data, adjust the data for anticipated conditions, then establish a budget or list of anticipated expenditures for a given time period. As expenditures actually occur, a comparison is made of actual versus budgeted performance, and variances from budget are brought to the attention of management. In both of these examples, accounting data provide the information used in planning and controlling, two key managerial functions.

Conventional financial accounting information helps the general manager in monitoring financial performance and in exerting needed controls in matters related to financial management. In effect, by reading accounting reports, the manager views the same picture as do stockholders, creditors, and regulatory and taxing agencies. Thus, accounting provides valuable data for day-by-day managerial control and somewhat less frequent, but equally meaningful, financial control.

For the general manager, decision making is an integral part of all of his or her management functions. Decisions are made (1) during the planning process, (2) about organizational relationships, (3) about directives to subordinates, and (4) while coordinating and controlling all of the elements of the organization. Management science has emerged in the past 30 years to become an important technological development that aids managers in decision making. Economic orders quantity or economic lot-size decision models have been designed to assist in making decisions for optimum use of facilities or personnel, and waiting-line models have been used to help managers decide when to expand service facilities in the operation of supermarkets and ticket counters. All of these scientific decision-making models employ accounting information as key data in the development, testing, and routine use of the model in the day-to-day conduct of the business. Finally, accounting information can be used to develop and implement the use of sophisticated integrated planning models, models that enable managers to anticipate the effects of altered conditions and resources on the total business.

In short, the data developed by means of accounting techniques represent a key element in enabling the general manager to engage in a wide range of management functions: analyzing, projecting, deciding, and controlling. To the analyst, these data serve to reflect the effects of strategies and to depict areas of strength and weakness.

STATEMENT ANALYSIS

For the general manager, statement analysis is a useful first step in establishing a clear understanding of cost structures, capital funds relationships, and the effects of past strategies. Two statements are the bedrock of business accounting . . . the balance sheet and the income statement.

The balance sheet is, in effect, a financial "snapshot," a picture taken at a moment in time. It portrays the financial health of the organization, but in a static sense. A series of balance sheets provide a dynamic "moving picture" of the organization over several time periods, in the same manner as will a series of photographs. For the moment, let's look at the single "photograph" of the financial makeup of the Cascade Corporation, a company engaged in the manufacture of motor vehicle parts and accessories. In Figure 2–1, five balance sheets are provided. With this much information, we can begin the study of Cascade by examining the most recent "picture" . . . 1986.

To begin our review, let us examine Cascade's debt position. Debt structure provides a good indicator of financial health and also serves to depict the consequences of financial policies. The complete absence of debt, for example, may reflect the policies of a management that is adamant about the issue of owing money to suppliers, banks, or investors. It also may indicate to a diagnostician the possibility of expanding the capital base of the firm by means of credit . . . long and short term.

A highly debt-laden financial structure, on the other hand, raises questions that may be critical. Financial solvency, of course, may be in question. Beyond solvency, though, the diagnostician must examine the coverage of interest payments, the cash flow problems caused by debt-repayment patterns, and the cost of capital for borrowed funds caused by the higher interest rates charged by lenders to more debt-heavy and, consequently, riskier customers.

It is interesting to note that in some industries, a high debt load can be accepted and utilized very effectively. In others, a heavy load of debt is an unsupportable burden. In the case of public utilities, highly predictable demand and regulated prices enable utility companies to utilize long-term debt safely as a major source of capital

	1986	1985	1984	1983	1982
Assets					
Cash	$ 1,506	$ 1,330	$ 939	$ 1,786	$ 1,640
Accounts Receivable	1,757	1,967	1,897	1,597	1,590
Inventories					
Materials	786	861	874	724	512
Goods in Process	2,575	2,112	3,407	2,804	2,246
Finished Goods	4,310	3,524	1,464	1,568	1,555
Total Inventories	7,671	6,497	5,745	5,906	4,313
Prepaid Expenses	68	78	98	104	95
Total Current Assets	11,002	9,872	8,679	8,583	7,638
Land	346	346	346	346	346
Buildings & Equipment	10,337	8,518	7,374	6,171	5,770
Reserve for Depreciation	5,290	5,434	5,066	4,632	4,342
Net Fixed Assets	5,047	3,084	2,308	1,539	1,428
Total Assets	16,049	12,956	10,987	10,122	9,066
Liabilities & Equity					
Accounts Payable	$ 932	$ 786	$ 564	$ 688	$ 241
Notes Payable—Bank	4,564	2,282	978	—	—
Accrued Taxes	1,079	835	773	929	753
Current Liabilities	6,575	3,903	2,315	1,617	994
Common Stock	652	652	652	652	652
Capital Surplus	5,868	5,868	—	—	—
Retained Earnings	2,954	2,533	8,020	7,853	7,420
Total Equity	9,474	9,053	8,672	8,505	8,072
Total Liabilities Owners Equity	$16,049	$12,956	$10,987	$10,122	$9,066

FIGURE 2-1 The Cascade Corporation comparative balance sheets ($1,000's).

for financing the extensive capital equipment needed to generate and transmit power. In other industries, supplier credit is a major source of funding. Suppliers extend credit to firms in order to secure their own sales, and they depend on the *next* level of customer for security. The printing business offers an example. Job printers typically have little capital but often sell large orders of printing work to big customers (book publishers, magazine publishers, sporting-event program producers, etc.). The paper manufacturer willingly extends credit for large shipments of printing paper, not because of the financial security offered by the resources of the printer, but because of the financial strength of the publisher who will pay the bill for printing. The profit made by selling a large order of high-quality printing paper is, of course, an extremely important inducement to the paper company. In effect, the printer can be (and is) seen as a sales agency and converter of paper by paper manufacturers.

In other cases, a firm offers neither the security of its own demand nor the security of large customers and sure orders. In such instances, the account is seen by suppliers as more risky, thus lower levels of debt should be seen.

RATIO ANALYSIS

At the end of 1986, Cascade's total assets reached an all time high of $16,049,000. Liabilities totaled $6,575,000, and owner's equity was $9,474,000. The first ratio to calculate is that of *total debt to total assets*. For Cascade, the ratio is

$$\frac{\$6{,}575{,}000}{\$16{,}049{,}000}$$

or .41. In effect, this ratio says that, for Cascade, each dollar of assets is supported by debts of 41 cents and owner's funds of 59 cents. At the surface, this ratio does not seem particularly alarming. Further investigation, however, should be conducted to see if this ratio is significantly different than ratios for other companies engaged in the same type of business.[1]

Competitors in the motor vehicle parts manufacturing industry, by comparison, had a ratio of .464 in 1986. (See tables in this chapter's Appendix.) The debt structure for Cascade, at .41, is highly comparable, in terms of debt. The low figure for the industry is a ratio of .235. The high figure reaches .662, meaning that 66.2% of total assets were supported by creditors' funds. Cascade, as we can see, has as many owner dollars supporting assets as do the average of its competitors. This, one could conclude, is a competitive debt structure, one that does not overcommit current earnings and that provides for the availability of capital reserve, should additional capital be needed.

A similar ratio that is often used to examine the debt structure of the company is the total debt to owner's equity ratio. (Total debt is sometimes referred to as total liabilities; owner's equity is sometimes called net worth.) Cascade's ratio is

$$\frac{\$6{,}575{,}000}{\$9{,}474{,}000}$$

or .69. Firms engaged in motor vehicle parts and accessories manufacturing in 1986 had a low ratio of .308, a median of .866, and a high ratio of 1.96. Cascade's debt ratio of .69 is below the median of these comparison figures, which is an indicator of better-than-average financial strength in respect to the relationship between owner and creditor funding.

A third diagnostic tool is the relationship between fixed assets and net worth, the extent to which the more permanent assets are supported by permanent ownership funds. In Cascade's case the ratio is

$$\frac{\$5{,}047{,}000}{\$9{,}474{,}000}$$

[1] This ratio can be calculated from the total liabilities to net worth ratio. Let total liabilities/net worth = A. Set net worth = 1. Total assets = total liabilities + net worth = $A + 1$. Then, total liabilities/total assets = $A/(A + 1)$.

or .533. When we compare this ratio with the motor vehicle parts manufacturing industry, we find that the industry's average ratio is .479 for 1986. Generally, It would appear that Cascade's ratio of fixed assets to owner's equity is somewhat above the average of its competitors in this industry.

A fourth major indicator of a healthy financial structure is a comparison by means of the *current ratio:* current assets divided by current liabilities. The current ratio of

$$\frac{\$11{,}002{,}000}{\$6{,}575{,}00}$$

or 1.673 for Cascade compares with a ratio of 2.2 for the motor vehicle parts and equipment manufacturing industry for 1986. Based on these comparisons, Cascade's current financial position is not as secure as it might be. The current ratio of 1.673 is well below the comparable ratio for its comparison group.

When we have gotten this far, we can begin to ask ourselves questions based on more complexity. Here the debt-to-equity ratio is .866 for the industry, but the current ratio is 2.2. We might then begin to conclude that Cascade might be able to make use of additional debt in its financial structure, especially debt of a long-term nature. If, for example, Cascade were to borrow $2,000,000 to be used for a buildup of inventories, accounts receivable, and cash, the current ratio would be

$$\frac{\$13{,}002{,}000}{\$6{,}575{,}000}$$

or 1.978. The total debt-to-equity ratio would rise to

$$\frac{\$8{,}575{,}000}{\$9{,}474{,}000}$$

or .905—still very close to the industry figure of .866.

The *quick ratio* (sometimes referred to as the acid test ratio) is an additional refinement in the diagnostic examination of financial health. The quick ratio is used to determine the coverage of current liabilities by assets that are either cash or equivalents or assets that can be quickly converted to cash. Let's take an abbreviated balance sheet to illustrate the usefulness of the quick ratio.

Cash	$ 6	Current Liabilities	$10
Accounts Receivable	6		
Raw Matl. Inventory	24		
Total Current Assets	36		
Net Fixed Assets	22	Owner's Equity	48
Total Assets	$58	Total Liability & Equity	$58

FIGURE 2–2

With this balance sheet, the current ratio is 36/10, or 3.6 : 1. Of the current assets, however, only cash and accounts receivable are quickly available to pay debts. When we subtract inventory to obtain the quick ratio, we get a ratio of 12/10, or 1.2 : 1. Prepaid expenses are also assets that should be deducted because they, too, are not quickly converted to cash.

EXERCISE 2–1

For the Cascade Corporation, calculate total debt-to-equity ratios for the years 1983 through 1986. (Answers will be found at the end of the chapter.)

EXERCISE 2–2

Calculate fixed assets to net worth for the years 1983 through 1986.

EXERCISE 2–3

Calculate current ratios for the years 1983 through 1986.

EXERCISE 2–4

Calculate quick ratios for the years 1983 through 1986.

ANALYZING THE INCOME STATEMENT

An in-depth analysis of the income statement is made less conclusively than that of the balance sheet because industry comparison data are not available on the detailed composition of the income statement. We can compensate, however, by examining the income statement in terms of the comparisons it provides for itself, as the business progresses from year to year, and by examining the limited data for the industry found in their chapter's Appendix.

In Figure 2–3, all data are expressed in dollar amounts and as a percentage of net sales. With the percentage data, we can look at the information year by year to determine which items of revenue or expense seem to shift in relation to sales.

In Cascade's case, many expenses appear to be well controlled. Little variation is seen in major items of expense from 1982 to 1986, whereas net sales have increased

	1986	%	1985	%	1984	%	1983	%	1982	%
Net Sales	$14,018	100.0	$12,747	100.0	$12,258	100.0	$11,540	100.0	$10,465	100.0
Cost of Sales	11,117	79.3	10,090	79.2	10,139	82.7	9,014	78.1	8,297	79.3
Gross Profit	$ 2,901	20.7	$ 2,675	20.8	$ 2,119	17.3	$ 2,526	21.9	$ 2,168	20.7
Selling Expenses	$ 864	6.2	$ 776	6.1	$ 724	5.9	$ 717	6.2	$ 668	6.4
Commissions	570	4.1	505	4.0	466	3.8	456	3.9	440	4.2
Administrative Expense	619	4.4	665	5.2	626	5.1	603	5.2	580	5.5
Interest Expense	147	1.0	95	.7	59	.5	.4	.4	46	.4
Total Expense	$ 2,200	15.7	$ 2,041	16.0	$ 1,875	15.3	$ 1,825	15.8	$ 1,134	16.6
Net Operations Income	701	5.0	616	4.8	244	2.0	701	6.1	434	4.1
Income Tax	274	1.9	235	1.8	78	.6	274	2.4	147	1.4
Net Profit	$ 427	3.0	381	3.0	166	1.4	427	3.7	287	2.7

FIGURE 2-3 The Cascade Corporation five-year comparative statements of income and expense ($1,000's).

nearly 25% in absolute amount. With the exception of 1984, net profits have held at a figure very close to 3 percent. Cost of sales, with the exception of that same year, has been held at or very near 79%. When we examine the data for the industry, however, we see that Cascade has a much lower-than-average gross margin vis-à-vis the industry (21% vs. 32.8%) vs. and also a much lower percentage of net profit on sales (3.0% vs. 5.4%).

Economies of scale should be reflected in some costs being lower *as a percentage of sales* as volume rises. Costs that tend to be fixed include property taxes, depreciation on plant and equipment, major front office administrative costs, and major portions of utility expenses. If these costs were fixed, then their part of cost of sales *as a percentage of sales* would decline as sales increased, reflecting constant dollar costs for factory overhead expenses. Administrative costs as a percentage of sales would also decline, again reflecting the concept of economies of scale, because the central offices costs would be spread over increased manufacturing and sales activity.

A careful examination of these cost elements over several time periods can provide valuable information as to the extent to which variable costs are held in control as a percentage of sales. It is also possible to assess the extent to which costs that *should* be fixed are managed as fixed, thus permitting the organization to take advantage of increases in scale of operations.

EXERCISE 2-5

List two or three expense categories included in manufacturing costs that should be fixed over a reasonably wide range of sales volume.

EXERCISE 2-6

List two or three expense categories in manufacturing costs that should be variable with respect to sales volume. (Some answers will be found at the end of the chapter.)

EXERCISE 2-7

List two or three types of expenses in the category of selling expenses that should be fixed over a reasonably wide range of sales. (Some answers will be found at the end of the chapter.)

EXERCISE 2-8

List two or three variable cost elements found in the category of selling expenses.

EXERCISE 2–9

List two or three expenses in administrative expense categories that should be fixed over a relatively wide range of sales/manufacturing volume.

EXERCISE 2–10

List two or three variable cost components found in administrative expenses categories.

	1979	*1980*	*1981*	*1982*	*1983*
Net Sales	$332	$350	$405	$448	$422
Cost of Sales	205	219	252	266	248
Total Selling Expense	53	65	80	81	78
Total Administrative Expense	43	44	52	66	62
Net Profit	32	22	21	35	34
Other Income	2	2	3	—	1
Federal Taxes	2	7	6	10	11
Profit After Tax	$ 32	$ 17	$ 18	$ 25	$ 24

FIGURE 2–4 James & Jerrold, Inc.

EXERCISE 2–11

Examine the comparative income statements for James & Jerrold, Inc. What can you say about control of fixed costs from the statement in Figure 2–4?

EXERCISE 2–12

What can you say about the control of variable costs for James & Jerrold, Inc.?

ACTIVITY ANALYSIS

When data from both the income statement and the balance sheet are used, the analyst can assess the effectiveness of the company and its management in several different ways. Profitability is one measure of effectiveness and can be assessed by means of at least three different bases. *profit as a percentage of sales* provides a measure of short-range effectiveness, but it does not reflect the extent to which resources are used. *Profit as a percentage of total assets* provides a measure of the effective use made of the company's fiscal and productive resources. Some of these resources, of course, are provided by suppliers or other creditors. *Profit as a percentage of owner's equity,* therefore, provides an approximation of the return to owners for the funds they have provided and is a measure of the effectiveness of management in utilizing these funds both directly (through the investment in productive assets) and indirectly (by serving as a base from which borrowed funds may be obtained).

For the Cascade Corporation, an abbreviated analysis can be conducted by means of figures seen in Figure 2-5.

In Figure 2-5, we can see several areas of managerial interest and concern. First, in the immediate short range, profits are not being generated from sales activity at the level found among competing firms in the industry and are well below that generated by some competitors. This may be the result of a level of costs higher than is competitively attainable, a product mix that differs significantly from the average for the industry, or the results of systematic pricing and discounting policies that have lowered the net price below that achieved by competing firms.

The low-average level of short-term profit performance is echoed and amplified in longer-term performance measures. Cascade generates less than one-half the profit from the assets employed as do its competitors. This type of performance may be the result of (1) inefficient or inappropriate assets or (2) grossly underutilized assets. Underutilized assets can result from (1) errors made in the decisions to buy plant and equipment that have resulted in excess capacity; (2) from inadequacies in managing not only the existing plant and equipment, but also current assets, which results in

	Cascade Corp.	Motor Vehicle Parts Manufacturing Industry (1986) Low	Average	High
Profit as Percentage of Sales (return on sales)	3.00	1.9	4.4	8.8
Profit as Percentage of Total Assets (return on total assets)	2.66	3.1	7.6	14.2
Profit as Percentage of Owner's Equity (return on net worth)	4.51	7.4	17.5	30.8

FIGURE 2-5 Profitability analysis.

overlarge inventories, excessive accounts receivable, and/or excessive cash balances; and (3) from an ineffective marketing effort that fails to find the volume of sales to justify the financial and physical assets committed for that purpose.

The final measure seen in Figure 2–5 is the profit to owners equity ratio, which again reflects a substantially poorer picture than Cascade's competitors. In this case, because Cascade's debt-to-equity ratio is about the same as that of the average of its competitors, the poor performance is probably the result of inadequacies in asset utilization.

EXERCISE 2–13

From the data provided, in which year did Cascade have the highest profit as a percentage of total assets? How much was it? (Check your answers against those found at the end of the chapter.)

EXERCISE 2–14

What was the best year for profit as a percentage of owners equity? The worst year?

MANAGING CURRENT ASSETS AND CURRENT LIABILITIES

Net working capital represents funds available in current assets that are not committed to the payment of current liabilities. It is easily calculated by deducting current liabilities from current assets. In Cascade's current year, net working capital totals $11,002 - $6,575 or $4,427. One should keep in mind that it is possible to have negative working capital that is, to have current liabilities greater than current assets. In some kinds of business, this condition is relatively common. An example might be a fast foods company. In fast foods, sales are made for cash and inventories are severely limited due to restrictions on storage space and the problems of potential spoilage. Thus, current assets can be relatively limited. Current liabilities, however, are limited only by the patience of suppliers and creditors. If suppliers are willing to grant reasonable commercial terms of sales (net 30 or net 45 days), current liabilities may easily exceed current assets. Net working capital is made up of a fluid balance of funds provided by creditors and converted by the company to inventories and customer's accounts receivable. Although it is fluid, nonetheless, it is an important ingredient in managing a healthy level of sales activity. Net working capital provides an important financial cushion that permits the organization to meet uneven requirements for funds without the necessity of resorting to agencies outside the firm for needed money. Net working capital also serves as a financial buffer in dealing with seasonal or erratic changes in sales revenues. A means of monitoring the level of net working capital is to develop a ratio of *sales to net working capital.* In Cascade's case, net working capital in 1986 is $4,427. Sales for 1986 were $14,018. The ratio is, therefore, $14,018/$4,427, or 3.17. Net working capital sales ratios for 1982 and 1986 are seen in Figure 2–6.

1986	*1982*
3.17	3.23

FIGURE 2–6 Sales-to-net-working-capital ratios, Cascade Corporation.

EXERCISE 2–15

Calculate net working capital for 1983, 1984, and 1985.

EXERCISE 2–16

Calculate sales-to-net-working-capital ratios for the same years.

These data indicate a very slight decline in available net working capital as compared with sales over the past five years. To determine the comparative importance of this information, it is again necessary to examine data from Cascade's industrial competitors. The motor vehicle parts and accessories manufacturing industry had sales-to-net-working-capital ratios in 1986 that ranged from a low of 3.7 through a median of 5.8 to a high of 10.7 sales dollars for each dollar of net working capital. Thus, the values calculated for this ratio for Cascade Corporation seen in Figure 2–6 are of concern, as they might not have seemed initially, and appear to be evidence of inadequacies in the management of assets or less than effective sales management, or both.

Activity ratios can also be calculated for components of current assets. *Inventory turnover* is calculated by dividing *net sales* (for retailers or wholesalers) or *cost of sales* (for manufacturers) by the dollar value of *inventory*. In food retailing, inventory turnover may be as high as 20 to 30 times per year (or even higher) as grocer's shelves offer limited space and as shelf life for many grocery items severely limits the quantities stocked.

Manufacturer's inventories, in contrast to those of retailers, contain raw materials and goods in process, items with values much closer to acquisition cost. Consequently, the use of the cost of goods sold is recommended for calculating turnover because it provides a lower and more conservative measure of activity. Where cost-of-sales are not available, the use of new sales is acceptable so long as the same elements are used in all comparisons. The industry figures in this chapter's Appendix use *sales* for calculating this ratio even though this industry group is involved in manufacturing.

Accounts receivable can also be evaluated by means of an activity ratio. As with inventory, accounts receivable turnover can be calculated by dividing net sales by accounts receivable. Many analysts and managers prefer to calculate accounts receivable activity by means of an *average-collection-period* measure. This measure is derived by calculating one day's sales activity, then dividing that into accounts receivable,

$$\frac{\text{Accounts Receivable}}{\text{Net Sales}/360}$$

The result is the number of days of sales that are contained in accounts receivable or the average time needed to collect an open account. For Cascade, the calculations are

$$\frac{\$1,757,000}{\$14,018,000/360}$$

Simplifying the calculations by inverting the denominator and multiplying, we get

$$\frac{\$1,757,000 \times 360}{\$14,018,000} = 45.1 \text{ days}$$

Accounts payable can be examined in nearly the same fashion. Payables, however, are generated from purchasing activity rather than selling. It is appropriate, therefore, in calculating the *average payment period,* to use cost of sales or cost of goods manufactured as the activity variable. For Cascade, the average payment period for 1986 is

$$\frac{\text{Accounts Payable}}{\text{Cost of Sales}/360} \text{ or } \frac{\$932,000}{\$11,117,000/360}$$

Inverting

$$\frac{\$932,000 \times 360}{\$11,116,000} = 30.18 \text{ days}$$

Cascade, on the average, takes 30.18 days to pay its bills, but 45.1 days to collect from its customers. The extension of trade credit to customers is a time-honored means of enhancing the salability of products and services. In this case, the imbalance between receivables and payables means that sales increases must in very large part be supported by capital derived from sources *other than* supplier credit and may draw upon capital that might otherwise be used to provide machinery, equipment, land, or buildings.

EXERCISE 2–17

Calculate the average collection period for Cascade for 1982 and 1984. (Answers can be found at the end of the chapter.)

EXERCISE 2–18

Calculate the average payment period for accounts payable for the same two years.

Activity ratios related to fixed assets require care in their application because of the uneven rate at which fixed assets are both acquired and used. As economists have long held, all costs in the long run are variable. Similarly, in the long run, a ratio between fixed assets and sales level can be seen to stabilize. If, however, a new facility is constructed and equipped, in its early years the relationship between capital employed and sales volume produced will vary considerably. Suppose, for example, that a small plant is built and equipped for $500,000. The engineer's best estimate of capacity is $500,000 of product per shift, or $1,500,000 at full capacity. If we were unaware of capacity and simply dealt with current volume, the ratio of sales to fixed assets would be 1 : 1 when the plant operated on a one-shift basis, 2 : 1 on a two-shift basis, and 3 : 1 at full capacity. Given numerous plants and a fairly stable level of production, however, dividing sales by net fixed assets can provide a useful indicator of management effectiveness in making use of fixed assets. Fixed-asset-activity ratios for Cascade Corporation for 1982 and 1986 are shown in Figure 2–7.

It is easy to see that a very serious decline has occurred over the five years shown, a factor that should call for a very careful study to determine whether the drop in fixed-asset utilization is the result of excess capacity (a likely cause of part of the decline for Cascade) or whether it is the result of a flagging marketing program. Based on this company's own data, however, it can be said that the company has demonstrated an ability to generate over twice the volume of sales per dollar of fixed assets that it currently is selling. In Cascade's case, sales have increased at an average of 7.02% each year. Capital equipment has increased an average of 13.46% during the same period.

1982	*1986*
2.78	7.33

FIGURE 2–7 Fixed assets to sales, Cascade Corporation.

EXERCISE 2–19

Calculate fixed-asset-activity ratios for 1983, 1984, and 1985. (Answers can be found at the end of this chapter.)

Should further inquiry reveal that present plant and equipment are not fully utilized, then a decision can be made to slow further acquisition of equipment until present equipment is more fully used. Further, the marketing effort should be carefully examined to assure that the company is making best use of capital equipment acquired to support the marketing plan.

The following case is included to illustrate some of the elements discussed and to permit the practice of the analytic skills outlined in earlier parts of this chapter. Once you have completed a careful reading of the case, begin your analysis by responding to the questions you will find in the exercises at its end. Answers to a number of the exercises will also be found at the end of the chapter. Some exercises may be assigned by your instructor for homework.

HERSHEY FOODS CORPORATION

INTRODUCTION

Until 1974 the Hershey Chocolate Company, a division of Hershey Foods Corporation, could validly claim to be second to none in the sales of candy bars. Today, the situation has changed somewhat. Because many candy manufacturers resorted to producing chocolate-coated rather than solid chocolate bars, Hershey has dropped to second place in the industry. But, according to Thomas Null, regional manager of Hershey Chocolate Company in Dallas, Texas, the corporation still leads the market in solid chocolate products, and it is a leading factor in the overall confectionery industry.

Hershey's products can be divided into two major categories: (1) confectionery items such as Hershey Bars, Kisses, and Reese's Peanut Butter Cups and (2) grocery products such as cocoa, syrup, and baking chips. With a dozen manufacturing plants located in Hershey, Pennsylvania; Oakland, California; and Smiths Falls, Ontario, Canada, this largest domestic producer of chocolate and cocoa employs approximately seventy-five hundred people.

This case was prepared by John Reynolds and S. Jauardhavan under the supervision of Professor Sexton Adams, North Texas State University, and Professor Adelaide Griffin, Texas Woman's University. It is intended for class discussion rather than to illustrate either effective or ineffective handling of administrative issues.

Prepared in 1978, this case reflects the facts of that time, not necessarily those of the late 1980s. The issues presented in this case are as significant now as they were at the time of the case. The approaches learned through a careful study of the case, therefore, can be applied in the business world of today and similar business situations well into the future.

Additional manufacturing plants—located in Kentucky and Chicago—produce pasta products for the San Giorgio Macaroni, Inc., subsidiary and coffee-brewing and food-service equipment for the Cory Food Services, Inc., subsidiary respectively. Accounting for only 13% of sales in 1977, these activities comprise the other food products of Hershey Foods Corporation, whereas the Chocolate and Confectionery Division accounts for 87% of sales.

HOW IT ALL BEGAN

After several business reversals, Milton S. Hershey achieved success as the owner of a caramel factory in Lancaster, Pennsylvania, at the age of 40. For several years, he studied the chocolate market until his research convinced him that the nation was ready for a tasty, nutritious, and inexpensive chocolate confection. Thus in 1900 at the age of 43, Milton S. Hershey sold his business for $1 million and returned to his birthplace in Derry Church, Pennsylvania, to start a chocolate factory.

An excellent location surrounded by the rich dairy farms of east-central Pennsylvania was chosen. The Hershey Chocolate Company was situated so as to capitalize on the availability of fresh milk so essential to its two basic produces—milk chocolate and almond chocolate bars. By streamlining production lines and gearing output to large standardized quantities sold at moderate prices, the company achieved immediate success. Production began in 1901, and by 1911 there were reported sales of $5 million.

Though Milton S. Hershey died in 1945, the company still reflects much of his conservative philosophy: at all times, maintain the most modern and efficient equipment capable of producing desired results; provide outstanding benefits to worthy employees; use no artificial substitutes; and employ no advertising. Even though Hershey was opposed to advertising in essence, he broke this policy with his chocolate factory. The largest manufacturing facility of its kind in the world, it provides tours for millions of visitors.

In addition, tourists find in Hershey, Pennsylvania (formerly Derry Church), the storybook town developed from the donations of Milton S. Hershey. It includes the Milton S. Hershey School, which holds 57% of the company's stock.

In 1968 the Hershey Chocolate Company adopted a new name, Hershey Foods Corporation, to reflect its broadened product line with the acquisition of San Giorgio Macaroni, Inc., in 1966 and Cory Food Services, Inc., in 1967. Recently, in 1977, the corporation acquired Y & S Candies, a licorice candy producer, in order to diversify even further.

HUMAN RESOURCES

Bill Dearden, vice chairman and chief executive officer (CEO), had entered the Milton S. Hershey School in 1935 at age 13. The school was designed for orphan boys by the childless founder, Milton S. Hershey.

Dearden moved to this present position of CEO in 1976, replacing Harold Mohler (56), who remains as chairman. At the same time, Richard Zimmerman (43), advanced to the post of chief operating officer. Exhibit 1 shows a partial structure of the corporation.

One of Dearden's main concerns was to restructure Hershey in ways that would enable the company to expand corporate development and increase capital formation.

Dearden obtained a B.S. in economics at Albright College and did graduate work at Harvard Business School. After working at Dun & Bradstreet and serving in the navy, he entered the Hershey School as assistant to the business manager and then became assistant to the chairman of the chocolate company. Between 1961 and 1971, Dearden advanced from marketing manager to divisional vice president to

EXHIBIT 1
Organization Chart, Hershey Foods Corporation

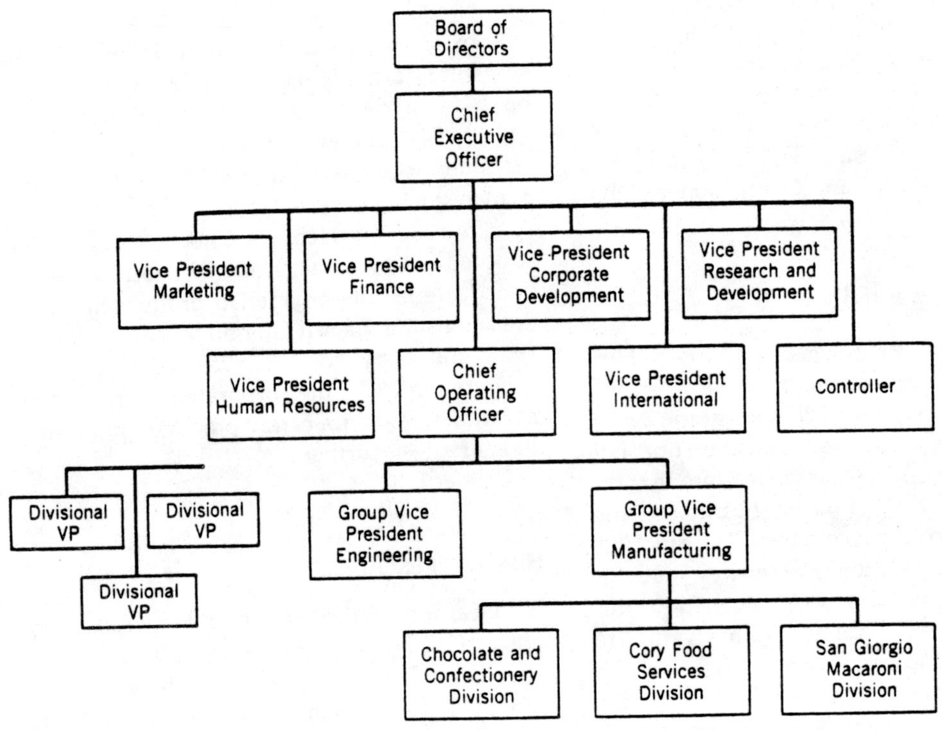

marketing vice president, and finally to his present position as CEO in February 1976.

At this time, the management of Hershey was giving special attention to human resources. It was aware of the continuing need for competent employees in order to meet its strategic objectives. To assist in meeting this need, management initiated a formal program of human resources planning in 1977. Management also launched a longer-range planning program designed to identify the appropriate organizational structure, the skills, and the employee training and development needs required for the next three years. One example is a series of workshops that will train managers in the various financial concepts and techniques needed for more effectiveness in performing their responsibilities.

Critical to the overall planning and development program has been the initiation of the new corporate management succession process. The major thrust of this activity has focused on the identification and development of candidates for key management positions. A top-management committee, chaired by the CEO, has been formed to provide the necessary guidance of this effort.

A savings and stock-investment plan is being set up to facilitate the ownership of Hershey Foods common stock by the corporation's employees. This plan will be available to salaried employees by July 1978.

The company also has a management-incentive plan that provides incentive compensation to eligible employees—both of the company and its subsidiaries—who have substantial managerial responsibilities. The plan currently includes both annual and long-term incentive-compensation programs. The cost of the compensation programs in 1977 was $901,000 and this is expected to double in 1978.

THE CHOCOLATE AND CONFECTIONERY INDUSTRY

Overall, between 1967 and 1977, earnings of the Standard & Poor's composite index of food companies grew at a rate of 7.1% annually. However, producers' sales of chocolate and confectionery products have barely moved above $1.9 billion annually—their 1974 level.[1]

Unit shipments of confectionery products have tended to shift downward throughout the 1970s, although dollar sales are slightly higher. After a high of 3,938 million pounds in 1970, they dropped 17% by 1977. With average value per pound rising to 94 cents in 1977 (from 48.5 in 1970), dollar shipments rose about 60% to $3.1 billion, from $1.9 billion.

In 1977, sales were essentially unchanged from the earlier year level; however, with prices up sharply, unit volume of confectionery products dropped some 5.6 percent to 3,254 million pounds from 3,467 million pounds the previous year. Exhibit 2 illustrates some industrial statistics.

In the industry, about one third of all candy produced is in the bar goods category, roughly the same proportion as 50 years ago. Bar goods generally, are defined as those selling for over 10 cents. Those selling for 5 cents or less are called count goods, whereas those between 5 and 10 cents are termed specialty items. In 1977 the price of candy bars rose to 20 cents while size decreased. Moreover, this appears to be an industry trend, necessary for making only marginal profits for the firm.

HERSHEY'S COMPETITORS

In response to the industry pressures, chocolate and confectionery product manufacturers have resorted to producing more chocolate-coated candies and reducing sizes of bars while increasing prices. Particularly skillful with these tactics is Mars, Inc., currently the nation's number one candy manufacturer and probably the world's leader.

Mars, established in 1964, produces 5 of the top 10 chocolate candy bars (see Exhibit 3).

Through an aggressive sales force of more than seven-hundred persons, Mars captured about 36% of the market in 1977, while Hershey owned 27%.

Emphasizing the aggressiveness of Mars salespeople, an avid Philadelphia confectionery wholesaler said, "You know a Mars salesman is going to come on strong. He's going to know the whole pitch, and he's going to have his arguments ready."[2]

In addition, Mars is split into wholesale and retail units, thus expanding its shelf exposure in retail outlets: Mars has at least 5 or 6 types of candy bars in each store. Five years ago, Hershey had 4 or 5 but has since lost two.

Cultivating a strong loyalty among its personnel, Mars normally pays wages and salaries that are 10% higher than prevailing pay for comparable jobs in a community or in the candy industry.

The remainder of the 5 top candy manufacturers (accounting for about 83% of this market with Hershey and Mars) include Standard Brands, Nestle, and Cadbury with 10%, 5%, and 5% of sales, respectively. All other manufacturers (approximately 39) account for the rest of the market sales.

INDUSTRY FORECAST

The food products industry is expected to enjoy a 10% profit in 1978. However, for the chocolate and confectionery industry, things are not so bright. There is no expected decline in prices of cocoa beans and the 5-cent increase on candy bars does not help matters. However,

EXHIBIT 2
Candy Industry Statistics

					Ingredient Prices ($ per lb)			
Year	*Production (mil. lb)*	*Per Capita Consumption (lb)*	*Mfrs. Sales Value (mil. $)*	*Mfrs. Avg. Price (cents per lb)*	*Refined Cane Sugar*	*Cocoa*	*Corn Syrup*	*Peanuts*
1977	3,254	15.4	3,059	94.0	0.173	1.720	0.082	0.180
1976	3,467	16.7	2,912	84.0	0.192	1.090	0.104	0.190
1975	3,357	16.3	2,830	84.3	R0.314	0.750	0.1525	0.190
1974	3,651	17.8	2,771	75.9	R0.344	0.985	0.1636	0.176
1973	3,807	18.6	2,141	56.2	R0.141	0.647	0.1229	0.157
1972	3,793	18.8	1.977	52.1	0.127	0.321	0.1065	0.144
1971	3,870	19.3	1,974	51.0	0.122	0.268	0.0771	0.134
1970	3,938	19.9	1,909	48.5	0.117	0.342	0.0681	0.128
1969	3,888	19.9	1,848	47.9	0.112	0.458	0.0631	0.123
1968	3,907	20.3	1,756	44.9	0.106	0.344	0.0724	0.119

R = Revised
Source: Adapted from "Confectionery Products," *Standard and Poor's Industry Survey* (August 13, 1978), p.F32.

EXHIBIT 3
Top 10 Candy Bars

Ranking in Sales	*Brand*	*Manufacturer*
1.	Snickers	Mars
2.	Reese Cup	Hershey
3.	M & M's Peanut	Mars
4.	M & M's Plain	Mars
5.	3 Musketeers	Mars
6.	Milky Way	Mars
7.	Hershey Almond	Hershey
8.	Kit Kat	Hershey
9.	Hershey Milk	Hershey
10.	Butterfinger	Standard Brands

Source: Adapted from "Mars," *Business Week* (August 14, 1978), p. 54.

with diversification, the candy manufacturers are expected to receive marginal profits.[3]

RAW MATERIALS

The unique quality and flavor of Hershey's products are the result of skillfully blending several basic foods among which are cocoa beans, milk, sugar, almonds, and peanuts.

Cocoa beans, key to the flavor of chocolate, are grown in the tropics and shipped to Hershey, Oakdale, and Canada for storage until needed. The main storage facility in Hershey has a capacity of more than 90 million pounds—enough for about 5.5 billion Hershey bars.

Fresh whole milk is vital to Hershey. Milk is purchased daily from more than one-thousand farms in the vicinity of Hershey's plants. It is shipped directly to those plants in bulk tankers. The Hershey storage silos have a capacity of more than 300,000 gallons. Everyday, Hershey uses enough milk to supply all the people in a metropolis the size of Salt Lake City.

Sugar is another important raw material. In the East, most of the sugar is obtained through cane refineries in Philadelphia. The Oakdale plant uses both beet and cane sugar processed in California. Almonds are also used. Hershey is the largest user of almonds in America. California grows all the almonds used by Hershey. Peanuts are another important raw material. Many tons of peanuts are used every year for such favorites as Reese's Peanut Butter Cups and Mr. Goodbar. Peanuts come primarily from the southern and southwestern states.

RESEARCH AND DEVELOPMENT

Hershey is continually developing programs to improve the quality of its raw materials. One major program is concerned with cocoa beans. Efforts to improve the growing, harvesting, processing, and shipment of cocoa beans from farm to factory are being pursued.

Research is expanding to provide new products and to improve the quality and safety of existing ones. New and improved chocolate processing techniques are being sought to better control product quality and ingredient usage while conserving energy and maintaining the unique texture and flavor of Hershey's chocolate.

In 1977 several new products were introduced to the marketplace. These included Reese's peanut butter, flavored chips in the Chocolate and Confectionery Division, and both a spaghetti sauce and a twisted noodle product in the Pasta Division.

The Research and Development work that led to new products has provided Hershey with new technologies that will be exploited in the coming years. Work continues on the evaluation of new alternate ingredients, particularly alternate fat ingredients that have the quality and characteristics of cocoa butter. The cocoa butter alternative fat, made available by Procter & Gamble, was studied extensively in 1977; evaluations in manufacturing and acceptance of this alternative fat have been completed with anticipation that final regulatory clearance will be available by mid-1978.

MARKETING AND SALES

Hershey's leadership in the chocolate and confectionery industry is based on three simple criteria: high quality of product, mass distribution, and optimum consumer value consistent with earning a profit in the competitive market place.

The United States is divided into 14 sales regions and 88 districts, each with its own regional manager. The field sales organization totals approximately 300 sales representatives. These sales representatives have separate accounting responsibilities. There are some sales merchandisers who deal mainly with retailers and a few jobbers also. Canada is divided into 5 districts with two brokerages who are independent wholesalers. Altogether, there are about 60 sales representatives in Canada.

Hershey utilizes the brands-manager concept of market management, wherein the brands manager and the new products manager are responsible for development of the total marketing plan for the profitable growth of their assigned brand. They work under the direction of the marketing manager, who along with the managers of marketing research and packing development report to the divisional vice president for marketing. Exhibit 4 depicts a partial marketing and sales structure of Hershey.

Noteworthy in 1977 was Hershey's new thrust into the market for products especially designed for fund-raising projects of the type in which scouting and school groups participate. Five of their bars are now offered in special weights and packaging in this market, and sales in 1977 were more than double those of 1976.

DISTRIBUTION AND ADVERTISING

Hershey's products are distributed in the United States and Puerto Rico through a network of 27 warehouses and by direct shipment to customers from the manufacturing plant.

Location of customers and the quantity ordered determine the method of shipment and warehousing. Hershey's customers include grocery chains, independent grocery wholesalers, candy and tobacco distributors, syndicate stores, drug chains, and vending machine operators. These form the link between Hershey and the consumer. Exhibit 5 typifies the channels of distribution of this company.

For 68 years, Hershey did not advertise in mass consumer media. This attitude was based on the philosophy of the founder, Milton S. Hershey. During the 1960s there arose increased competition in the industry coupled with the fact that young people of that time accepted advertising as an aid to discretionary purchasing.

These environmental changes brought a policy change in 1968 and Hershey's consumer advertising program was inaugurated July 1970. Two months after the inauguration, a national radio and television advertising campaign was begun. Advertising costs were $13.3 million in 1976 compared with $9.4 million in 1975, and they are still growing.

To boost advertising efforts, management announced in December 1977 the appointment

EXHIBIT 4
Organization Chart

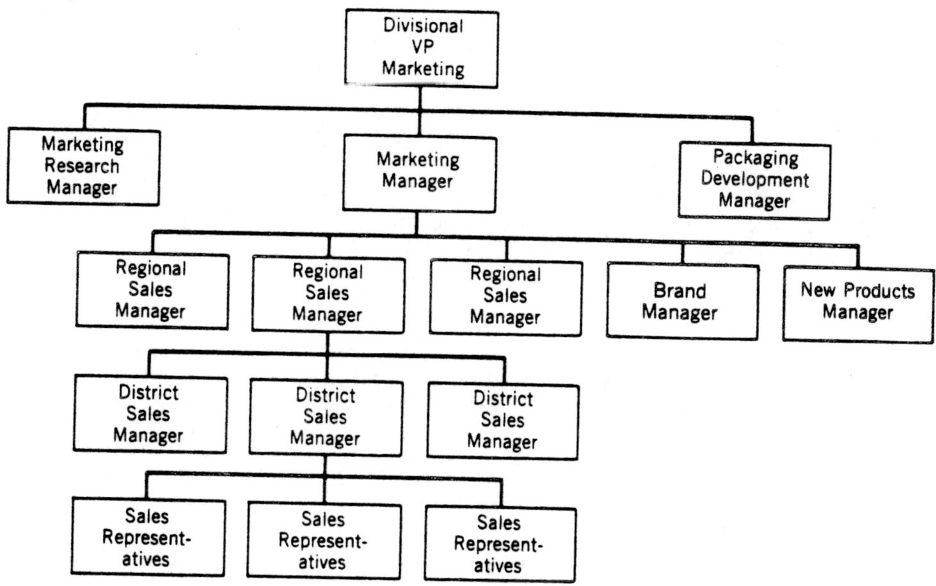

EXHIBIT 5
Channels of Distribution

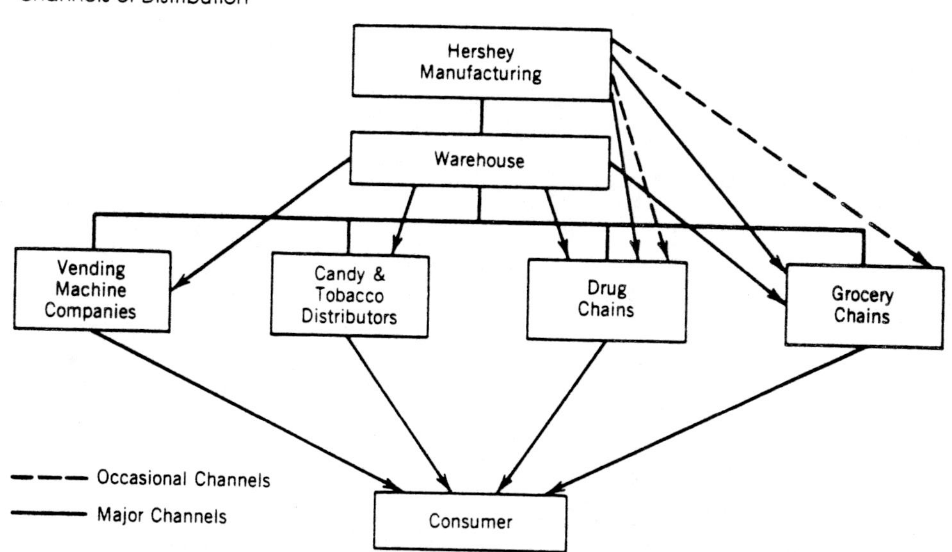

of a second advertising agency besides Doyle Dane Bernbach, Inc., the agency chosen in 1969. Doyle Dane will still continue to handle the major share of the brands, however.

Hershey has always been concerned about the content of its advertising as well as the type of programs it supports. Their ads are constantly reviewed by child psychologists and public affairs specialists to make sure they are not misleading and cannot be misunderstood.

Nearly all Hershey's Chocolate and Confectionery Division products have nutrition information printed on their labels. This practice was begun voluntarily in 1973, and to date they are the only manufacturer in the chocolate and confectionery industry to provide this consumer service.

FINANCE

Sales are the lifeblood of any manufacturing operation and Hershey has experienced considerable increases in sales during these last five years. Exhibit 6 shows the income statement of the corporation from 1973 to 1977. Profits have, however, not shown a good trend. Despite an 11.5 percent increase in sales in 1977, profits have dipped by 7.7 percent.

Income from continuing operations also showed a sharp decrease in 1977. The decrease might be attributed to the rising costs of raw

EXHIBIT 6
Hershey Foods Income Statement 1973–77 ('000)

	1977	*1976*	*1975*	*1974*	*1973*
Net Sales	*$671,227*	*$601,960*	*$566,328*	*$491,995*	*$442,709*
Costs and Expenses					
Costs of goods sold	453,960	383,664	368,992	357,830	314,497
Shipping expenses	28,816	27,650	22,794	21,903	25,322
Selling & Administrative expenses	109,585	93,503	74,768	51,977	62,099
Depreciation	7,995	7,539	7,540	7,912	7,506
Interest (Net)	(509)	357	1,259	2,190	5,632
Income BIT	71,380	89,247	80,975	50,183	27,653
Provision for federal & state income taxes	35,349	45,562	41,682	25,812	13,347
Income from continued operations	36,031	43,685	39,293	24,371	14,306
Gains from discontinued operations	—	1,112	(dr)1,433	2,227	—
Gains on sale of discontinued operations	5,300	—	(dr)4,898	—	—
Net Income	$41,331	$44,797	$32,962	$22,094	$14,306
Retained earnings at Jan. 1	217,775	187,343	163,110	150,715	169,495
Preferred dividends	—	—	240	240	240
Common dividends–cash	15,251	14,365	10,048	9,459	13,007
Other changes	—	—	(2,961)	—	—
Retained earnings at Dec. 31	$243,855	$217,775	$182,823	$16,110	$170,554

materials, especially cocoa, coupled with the inability to raise prices because of competitive retaliations. Net income has also shown a downward trend from $44.8 million in 1976 to $41.3 million in 1977. The costs of goods sold and the shipping and administrative expenses constitute the major increase in expenses.

The balance sheet of Hershey is depicted in Exhibit 7. The current assets show an increase in trend, and the accounts payable on the liability side is triple that of 1976. This is a result of large deliveries of cocoa beans at the end of 1977.

Interest expense declined in 1976 compared with 1975. This reflects improved cash position resulting from increased cash flow from earnings.

EXHIBIT 7

Hershey Foods Balance Sheet (in '000) As of December 31, 1977

Assets	*1977*	*1976*	*1975*	*1974*	*1973*
Cash	$ 7,980	$ 4,828	$ 8,599	$ 8,609	$ 7,326
Short-term securities	109,642	52,647	44,764	14,435	—
Notes & accounts receivable (net)	40,642	44,446	24,711	29,231	27,328
Inventories	61,950	66,304	69,116	71,897	62,452
Prepayments	1,372	1,647	1,284	—	—
Net assets of discontinued operations	—	—	4,013	—	—
Total Current Assets	221,202	169,872	152,487	124,172	97,106
Property, plant, equipment	231,334	214,207	190,274	198,318	193,150
Less: Depreciation reserve	88,164	84,958	76,512	73,326	69,442
Net Property Account	143,170	129,249	113,761	124,992	123,708
Goodwill, etc.	17,777	17,789	17,801	17,813	17,562
Other assets	14,004	14,960	14,339	14,261	13,783
Total	$396,153	$331,870	$298,388	$281,238	$252,159
Liabilities					
Accounts payable	$ 55,650	$ 18,980	$ 23,498	$ 37,176	$ 12,877
Accrued liabilities	14,154	14,578	12,564	7,702	8,128
Income tax payable	13,345	13,751	16,161	12,134	1,597
Loans payable	—	—	271	567	854
Total Current Liabilities	83,149	47,309	52,494	57,579	23,456
Long-term loans	29,440	29,440	29,856	31,730	51,471
Deferred income taxes	23,896	21,593	20,191	18,756	16,455
Preferred stock	—	—	—	1,200	1,200
Common stock	13,730	13,720	13,024	8,863	9,391
Additional paid-in capital	2,083	2,033	—	—	—
Retained earnings	243,855	217,775	182,823	163,110	170,554
Total Stockholders' Equity	259,668	233,528	195,847	173,173	181,145
Less treasury stock	—	—	—	—	20,368
Net stockholders' equity	259,668	233,528	195,847	173,173	160,777
Total	$396,153	$331,870	$298,388	$281,238	$252,159

During 1977, the company reduced inventory quantities (as shown in the balance sheet), primarily cocoa beans. This reduction resulted in a liquidation of LIFO inventory quantities carried at lower costs.

Capital additions in 1977 amounted to $27.5 million. Of this amount, depreciation provided $7.9 million and the company has spent $88 million during the past five years.

Even though management regards the financial potential as challenging and the general improvement of the financial strength in 1977 as significant, Hershey will continue to develop its potentials in order to surpass its present position in the industry. There are many issues to be reflected on by the management of Hershey in order to enhance its financial outlook. Among these issues are:

1 Highly fluctuating commodity prices, especially for cocoa and sugar.
2 Attacks of legislative and interest groups on the nutritional value of candy.
3 Decline in size of the 5–17 age group through the mid-1980s (the biggest per capita consumers of candy).
4 Consumer resistance to higher prices reflected in consumption patterns—from 20.3 pounds in 1968 to 15.4 pounds in 1977.
5 Federal price guidelines.

REFERENCES

1. "Rising Costs Soften the Candy Market," *Business Week* (March 20, 1978), p. 37.
2. "Mars," *Business Week* (August 14,1978), p. 56.
3. *Sami Brand Industry Survey* (December 15, 1978) p. 2.

EXERCISE 2–20

For the Hershey Foods Corporation:

1 Calculate current and quick ratios for 1973 to 1977.
2 Calculate debt-to-equity ratios for 1973 to 1977.
3 Calculate the average collection period for 1973.
4 Calculate the average payment period for 1977.
5 Can you identify any costs that appear to be fixed or nearly fixed? Explain and list, where appropriate.
6 Evaluate the profitability of Hershey, using all three measures suggested.
7 Evaluate the financial structure of Hershey.

QUESTIONS FOR CLASS DISCUSSION

1 As a general manager at Hershey Foods, what issues do you wish to take up with your marketing manager?

2 As general manager at Hershey Foods, what issues do you wish to discuss with your production manager?
3 As general manager at Hershey Foods, what issues do you wish to discuss with your financial manager?
4 In the role of general manager at Hershey Foods, what elements would you like to alter in the situation described in the case? List three to five in prioritized order and be prepared to discuss your list at some length.

Now that you have had some opportunity to consider the types of uses to which accounting data can be put by the general manager, you should be able to address another case in somewhat more detail, with less guidance. The following case (Vermont Tubbs, Inc.) is included to help you to build your analytic skills. The case provides detailed data about a moderate-sized company engaged in the manufacture of showshoes and specialized furniture.

Read the case carefully. Read it first without taking notes. Then re-read the case and make notes on elements worthy of your concern. When you have completed this task, address the general questions found at the end of the case. Prepare your answers in writing, and include notes and arguments on the reasons for your answers. Your instructor may wish you to hand in some answers to some of these questions or may wish you to present your answers and their support in a classroom presentation or discussion.

VERMONT TUBBS, INC.

During the weekend of August 7, 1982, Mr. C. Baird Morgan Jr., (45) President of Vermont Tubbs, Inc., Forestdale, Vermont, was thinking about the upcoming 9 o'clock meeting on Monday morning with his bankers. He was not quite sure how to prepare for it, how he might present his case, and what he should actually say to them. In other words, what strategy should he adopt and in turn what reaction might he expect from them. Sales had fluctuated over the past decade from a high of about $1.2 million in 1979 to a low of nearly $200,000 in the early years of operation. For the fiscal year ending June 30, 1982, the company had a net income of $5,000 on sales of $385,000 (Exhibits 1–4) compared with $30,000 and $338,000 respectively in 1971 (Exhibits 5 and 6).

HISTORY

Mr. Morgan had taken over as the president of Vermont Tubbs, Inc., in 1969. The company, founded in the 1880's had built up a reputation as the manufacturer of high quality snowshoes. During World War II, Tubbs' production of snowshoes reached over 100,000 pairs per year,

This case was prepared by Mrs. Sandra Smith under the direction of Professor W. H. Ellis, McGill University, as a basis for class discussion rather than to illustrate either effective or ineffective handling of an administrative situation.

sold entirely to the U.S. Government for use in Scandinavia, the Alps and the Himalayas. Thereafter the company passed through several owners until it went bankrupt in 1958. Mr. Harold Underwood, a local gasoline station owner, was a creditor and received the business in full settlement of his claim amounting to about $250.

According to Mr. Morgan, Mr. Underwood had run the business successfully with production during the last year of Underwood's ownership reaching approximately 9,000 pairs. This rose to 15,000 in 1970–71 and Mr. Morgan had projected an increase to 20,000 for the year 1971–72.

Mr. Morgan, who had received his MBA from the University of Pennsylvania, Wharton School of Business Administration in 1964, had been looking for a company to buy ("I was single, independent, not afraid of hard work or long hours and did not want to work for someone else"). His search led him to Mr. Underwood* who apparently seemed to prefer to fish and hunt rather than own a small business. The net result was that Mr. Morgan borrowed $10,000 from his father, borrowed $20,000 on a personal note, mortgaged the rest from Harold Underwood and became president of Vermont Tubbs in 1969.

From 1969–1971 Mr. Morgan was able to increase sales through an improved distribution system. In New England he continued to sell directly to retail sporting goods stores and mail-order houses.

The business continued to prosper through 1971–1975. Tubbs purchased a larger plant in Middletown, Vt., in 1971 and then sold it two years later when more suitable facilities were bought in Forestdale. In 1975 there were two plants in operation, one used to manufacture fibreglass canoes and a woodworking shop a quarter of a mile away.

Coincidentally, the financial problems of Vermont Tubbs began in 1975. The office procedures became so involved that Mr. Morgan hired a controller on the advice and recommendation of his banker. This employee, who appeared to have excellent references, embezzled approximately $70,000 from the company in a short period of time. None of this money was recovered and the net result was that by the end of 1976, Vermont Tubbs was virtually bankrupt, and the plant was closed.

At this point, a benefactor appeared on the scene in the person of Mr. Howard Baker. Mr. Baker had been a former New England sales manager for Fuller Brush and currently owned a small woodworking plant outside Boston, Mass. An arrangement was made with the bank whereby he assumed the debts of Vermont Tubbs together with the controlling interest in the company. Having been a salesman all his life, Mr. Baker was accustomed to and enjoyed expense account living. The auditor, in going over the 1977 books, discovered that he had claimed $30,000 in personal expenses, totally unrelated to Vermont Tubbs, and had paid salaries to several of his relatives. He was highly indignant that the books should be questioned and moved the accounting records out of Vermont to an auditor in Connecticut. Mr. Morgan never saw them again until after Mr. Baker's death in May 1981.

FINANCIAL STRUCTURE

Mr. Morgan had originally owned ⅔ of the stock of Vermont Tubbs and his father had held the remaining shares. In 1975 when Mr. Baker came into the company an additional 10,000 shares were issued making a total of 20,000 shares outstanding of which Mr. Baker owned 10,600. The rest were divided between Mr. Morgan and his family.

Mr. Baker had set up a proprietorship called Vermont Tubbs Sales which was a factoring agency for Vermont Tubs and was one way of protecting the accounts receivable from the creditors of Vermont Tubbs. Vermont Tubbs Sales was to receive a 10% commission on the

* Name disguised.

sales revenues of Vermont Tubbs. The intention was also that Mr. Morgan would hold a 50% interest in the sales organization.

ORGANIZATION

Prior to 1975, Mr. Morgan had handled all aspects of Vermont Tubbs' operations. He was familiar with the production techniques and would work along with the superintendents and other plant personnel.

With the entrance of Mr. Baker to the company, Mr. Morgan continued to look after production and quality control. Mr. Baker's duties and responsibilities were mainly finance, office procedures and marketing.

PRODUCTS

Vermont Tubbs . . . manufactures three products: snowshoes, snowshoe furniture and contemporary bentwood furniture. . . .

Snowshoes were made from a light bentwood frame laced with rawhide or neoprene strips. More recently an additional line was added with snowshoes made by using an aluminum frame.

Snowshoes furniture, which consisted of a bentwood frame and snowshoe pattern lacings, had been manufactured by Tubbs many years ago. Some of their pieces had accompanied Admiral Byrd to the South Pole but production had ceased with the concentration on snowshoes during World War II. Tubbs began manufacturing this furniture again in 1973. A natural market was believed to exist and the company hoped to utilize the waste products from the manufacture of snowshoes, in its construction.

The contemporary bentwood furniture production had begun in 1978 and consisted not only of furniture but also gourmet and gift items.

From 1973–1975 Vermont Tubbs manufactured fibreglass canoes. While the design was excellent and the first quality products got excellent acceptance, the quality control problems could not be overcome and more seconds were produced than firsts. Transportation also was a major problem being very expensive because of the bulky nature of the product and many canoes were damaged in transit. This business was sold in 1976 just before the hiring of the infamous controller.

DIVERSIFICATION

In 1971 Mr. Morgan had been receiving on the average of one inquiry per week to sell his business. He had rejected all offers but had considered different possibilities for diversification. He wanted to broaden his product mix so that he had year-round products. Among the possibilities he had considered and to lessen dependence on a product which required snow for continued success were:

1) Bristol Manufacturing. Mr. Morgan had had the opportunity to buy out this company which manufactured Fall Line Wax, considered to be the best wax in the world. Bristol also made Leath-R-Seal which was a leather preservative. In addition Bristol also manufactured paints that could be used for swimming pools and tennis courts. Tubbs advanced $50,000 on a short-term loan basis in June 1971, which held a purchase option for Tubbs. This had to be withdrawn when Tubbs itself subsequently came into financial difficulties.
2) Cross-country skis. Mr. Morgan had considered distributing a Norwegian ski under the Tubbs label. He had finally decided against it as many skiers were moving away from wooden skis to the non-wax fibreglass type. Also, the major manufacturers of downhill equipment, such as Fischer and Rossignal, were also getting into the cross-country marketplace.
3) Canoes. Reference has already been made to the attempts to diversify into this product line.

PRODUCTION

In early 1970's Vermont Tubbs had maintained its share of the snowshoe market. During those early years, production could not keep up with demand.

However, the mid-1970's saw a number of very erratic years in terms of snowfall. If there was snow in the east, there was none in the west or vice versa. Snowshoe production fell to a low during troubled financial times and the unstable snow conditions did not help attempts at rebuilding.

In the late 1970's, efforts were made to spreadout production by making snowshoes year-round, five to six hundred pair per week or fifteen thousand a year. Also during this period the company produced on the average, forty pieces of snowshoe furniture or two thousand pieces a year. The bentwood furniture production had been very erratic, with designers changed frequently and many items manufactured to order.

MARKETING AND DISTRIBUTION

Marketing and distribution have been the major areas of concern for Vermont Tubbs over the past decades. In the early days Mr. Morgan had hired eleven aggressive representatives who handled his snowshoes outside New England across the U.S. including Alaska. In New England he maintained Harold Underwood's network of sporting-goods stores and mail-order houses.

These dealers were a natural outlet for the snowshoe furniture and he continued with them for distribution of this product line. The sales representatives were paid 8% commission on their sales.

Mr. Baker assumed the responsibility for marketing in New England when he took over the company. He did not like to pay salesmen's commissions and announced that he intended to call on the dealers himself. The first year he made several trips; the second year fewer and finally since 1978 had not made any calls. The reduced marketing effort was clearly reflected in the decline in sales.

During the three-year period of 1978–81 with poor snowfall, limited production and sales, Mr. Morgan felt that snowshoe furniture could have been and would now have to be more strongly marketed.

The decision to manufacture upholstered bentwood furniture did present a new set of marketing and distribution problems. The market was now nationwide and not just the States of the snow belt. This furniture could not be marketed through sporting-goods dealers.

The decision was made by both Messrs. Morgan and Baker to market bentwood furniture through a distributor called Raymor-Moreddi (R-M) which was located in New Jersey. R-M represented about forty furniture manufacturers nationwide with showrooms in major U.S. cities. This distributor charged 22% commission on sales plus Vermont Tubbs had to pay a design fee of 3%.

Shortly after this contract was signed Mr. Morgan became disenchanted with R-M. He felt that they were not sufficiently marketing oriented and were simply order takers. At the first furniture show he attended, Vermont Tubbs was pushed off in a corner next to a lot of bric-a-brac from Taiwan.

In 1979 sales of contemporary bentwood furniture reached $200,000, the equivalent of the snowshoe furniture. However, snowshoe furniture was priced to sell with 8% commission whereas bentwood furniture had a 25% commission built into its price. In June 1981, shortly after Mr. Baker's death, Mr. Morgan cancelled the contract with R-M which went bankrupt a year later.

He [then dealt] with a marketing consultant to whom he paid no fee. This consultant was convinced that the way to market bent[wood] furniture was through one or two key accounts in large cities. He was currently trying to sell it in the greater Washington area. The consultant was convinced that he could sell all the bent[wood] furniture that Vermont Tubbs could produce and was willing to take his fees out of future sales.

CATALOGUE SALES

Mr. Baker had decided in 1979 to enter the mail-order business. He was convinced that catalogues were where the money was to be made but Mr. Morgan was vehemently opposed to the idea. He felt that their product line was limited and that their particular market was not geared to mail-order. "Tubbs was definitely not L.L. Bean which sells everything from soup to sleeping bags". However, Mr. Baker persisted and bought mailing lists from different companies, in the anticipation of selling $1,000 per day. In fact, they sold $8,000 worth of goods overall. Mr. Baker spent $50,000 – 60,000 on the catalogue which turned out to be a complete fiasco. . . . In Mr. Morgan's opinion the photography was poor quality and the copy very amateurish. This investment came from Vermont Tubbs Sales and had virtually wiped out all their assets. Mr. Baker had finally realized the folly of the catalogue and had promised to repay Vermont Tubbs Sales. However he died before he could make good on this promise.

COMPETITION AND PRICING

The major competitors of Vermont Tubbs snowshoes came from Canadian manufacturers north of Quebec City. It was believed that these companies had government subsidies and used cheap Indian labour to produce a shoe that retailed for $40.00 in the U.S. Vermont Tubbs had no way of matching this price. Tubbs snowshoes were considered to be of a higher quality than the Canadian products but wholesaled for $40.00. This realization was one of the reasons Mr. Morgan had entered the furniture business.

Vermont Tubbs had very little competition in the snowshoe furniture line and it was not dependent upon snowfall. However, there were many competitors in the bentwood furniture market, and distribution and marketing seemed to be the key to success.

CURRENT (1981) PRODUCTION

In 1979 there wasn't any snow in the east until late in February. Mr. Morgan had wanted to stop production at Christmas time but Mr. Baker had insisted on manufacturing through the winter. Inventory had now been sitting there for two years incurring interest and insurance charges. Mr. Morgan had tried to reduce the inventory but had been unsuccessful. He had even offered L.L. Bean a 40% discount and still could not sell it.

All the staff except two experienced bent[wood] furniture makers had been let go. The payroll was now reduced to $300 per week instead of $3,000. The laid-off workers had been able to find other jobs so that when and if Vermont Tubbs resumed production, the company would have a problem finding skilled workers.

CURRENT (1982) FINANCIAL SITUATION

Mr. Morgan's meeting with his bankers will seemingly decide the fate of his company. Mr. Morgan had no plan presently to suggest to the bank beyond continuing to manufacture snowshoes and bentwood furniture in a very poor economic climate.

The total debt exceeded $350,000 with the current portion nearly $140,000. The statement of income shows $49,000 revenue from Mr. Baker's life insurance. Otherwise the loss in 1981 would have been that much greater (financial statements and sales distribution, Exhibits 1 – 7).

EXHIBIT 1
Vermont Tubbs, Inc. Unaudited Balance Sheet June 30

ASSETS	1981	1982
CURRENT ASSETS:		
Cash	$ 2,588	$ 15,194
Accounts receivable (less allowance for doubtful accounts.)	43,706	41,865
Inventory	230,064	124,209
Prepaid Insurance		4,058
Total Current Assets	$276,359	$185,326
PROPERTY AND EQUIPMENT		
Land	6,000	6,000
Buildings	94,098	94,098
Vehicles and equipment	164,357	166,861
Total Property and Equipment	264,455	266,959
Less accumulated depreciation	141,786	152,366
Net Property and Equipment	$122,669	$114,593
OTHER ASSETS:		
Security deposits	700	700
Energy project	93,178	93,178
Total Other Assets	$ 93,878	$ 93,878
TOTAL ASSETS	$492,906	$393,797
LIABILITIES AND STOCKHOLDERS' EQUITY		
CURRENT LIABILITIES:		
Accounts payable	$ 27,972	$ 3,211
Current portion of long-term debt	190,406	138,286
Taxes payable	50	1,305
Accrued expenses	11,953	1,305
Total Current Liabilities	$230,381	$142,802
LONG-TERM LIABILITIES:		
Long-term debt	228,500	215,923
Other payables	4,000	
Total long-term debt	$232,500	$215,923
Total liabilities		$358,725
STOCKHOLDERS' EQUITY:		
Common stock—20,000 shares authorized, issued and outstanding, net of discount on stock of $98,050	101,950	101,950
Retained earnings	(71,925)	(66,878)
Total Stockholders' Equity	$ 30,025	$ 35,072
TOTAL LIABILITIES AND STOCKHOLDERS' EQUITY	$492,906	$393,797

EXHIBIT 2

Vermont Tubbs, Inc. unaudited statement of income and retained earnings for the year ended June 30

	1981	1982
REVENUES:		
Sales	$511,348	$386,399
Less discounts and allowances	2,240	1,727
Net Revenues	$509,108	$384,672
COST OF SALES:		
Inventory—July 1	368,177	230,064
Purchases and freight	101,196p	61,266
Labor	125,637	62,582
Total Goods Available	595,010	353,912
Less Inventory—June 30	230,064	124,209
Cost of Sales	$364,946	$229,703
GROSS PROFIT FROM OPERATIONS	$144,162	$154,969
GENERAL AND ADMINISTRATIVE EXPENSES (SCHEDULE 1)*	$207,460	$151,638
INCOME FROM OPERATIONS	(63,298)	3,331
OTHER REVENUES:		
Proceeds from officer's life insurance	49,842	
Gain on sale of assets	23,994	1,000
Extraordinary income (fire ins. recovery of $18,025 net or repairs of $17,259		766
Total Other Revenues	$ 73,836	$ 1,766
NET INCOME BEFORE TAXES	$ 10,538	$ 5,097
INCOME TAXES:		
State	50	50
Federal	0	0
Total Income Taxes	$ 50	$ 50
NET INCOME	$ 10,488	$ 5,047
RETAINED EARNINGS—JULY 1	$(82,413)	$(71,925)
RETAINED EARNINGS—JUNE 30	$(71,925)	$(66,878)

In preparing for this meeting Mr. Morgan thought back to offers that he had entertained in the early 1970's. At that time different conglomerates had wanted to buy him out at 18–20 times earnings. He had refused their offers insisting that he would rather have his own small operation than be part of a large company.

Now he wondered if a small manufacturing company would survive the present-day economic climate?

EXHIBIT 3
Vermont Tubbs, Inc. unaudited statement of changes in financial position for the year ended June 30

	1981	1982
SOURCES OF WORKING CAPITAL:		
From Operations:		
Net Income	$ 10,448	$ 5,047
Add back depreciation not requiring an outlay of working capital	21,841	13,561
Deduct gain on sale of property and equipment included in Other Sources below	(23,994)	(1,000)
	$ 8,335	$ 17,608
Other Sources:		
Sale of property and equipment	132,607	2,442
Increase of long-term debt	50,000	5,486
	$182,607	$ 7,928
Total Sources of Working Capital	$190,942	$ 25,536
USES OF WORKING CAPITAL:		
Payments of long-term debt	238,064	(18,063)
Purchases of fixed assets	1,699	(6,927)
Repayment of other payables	16,037	
Cost associated with energy project	93,178	
Total Uses of Working Capital	$348,978	($ 24,990)
INCREASE IN WORKING CAPITAL		$ 546
DECREASE IN WORKING CAPITAL	$158,036	

ANALYSIS OF CHANGES IN WORKING CAPITAL

	1981	1982
CURRENT ASSETS:		
Increase in Cash		12,606
Decrease in Cash	(1,933)	
Decrease in inventory	(138,113)	(105,855)
Increase in prepaid expenses		4,058
Decrease in prepaid expenses	(3,075)	
Increase in accounts receivable	43,707	
Decrease in accounts receivable		(1,842)
	($ 99,414)	($ 91,033)
CURRENT LIABILITIES:		
Decrease in accounts payable	(93,582)	28,761
Increase in current portion of long-term debt	162,087	
Decrease in current portion of long-term debt		52,120
Decrease in accrued expenses	(9,883)	10,698
	58,622	91,579
INCREASE IN WORKING CAPITAL		$ 546
DECREASE IN WORKING CAPITAL	$158,036	

EXHIBIT 4

Vermont Tubbs, Inc. unaudited schedule of general and administrative expenses for the year ended June 30

GENERAL AND ADMINISTRATIVE EXPENSES:	1981	1982
Auto Expense	—	$ 1,595
Commissions	$ 30,266	5,135
Utilities	22,738	20,433
Interest	43,321	41,575
Officers' salaries	29,004	11,685
Depreciation	21,841	13,561
Shop supplies	5,469	3,248
Office expense	4,577	3,982
Insurance	22,366	11,053
Taxes and licenses	7,502	13,475
Travel and entertainment	2,272	1,345
Equipment repairs	1,804	4,846
Telephone	4,324	3,917
Research costs	1,366	1,365
Advertising and promotion	1,168	1,026
Professional fees	4,353	3,715
Bad debt expense	3,000	3,394
Rent	60	-0-
Bookeeping expense	-0-	5,384
Miscellaneous	2,029	904
TOTAL	$207,460	$151,638

EXHIBIT 5

Vermont Tubbs, Inc. comparative balance sheets 6/30/70, 6/30/71

Assets	1970	1971
Current Assets		
Cash	$ 3,945.69	$ 16,058.28
Accounts Receivable (net)	5,270.34	24,576.64
Inventory	55,869.75	64,369.00
Advance to Bristol Chemical	-0-	50,000.00
Other	349.32	69.86
Total Current Assets	$ 65,435.10	$155,073.78
Fixed Assets (net)		
Land	3,000.00	3,000.00
Building & Improvements	50,547.32	49,129.89
Machinery & Equipment	39,553.62	34,303.22
Vehicle	1,833.33	2,907.61
Office Equipment	-0-	187.03
Total Fixed Assets	$ 94,934.27	$ 89,527.75
Other Assets (incl. Goodwill $1,000)	1,211.52	1,159.72
TOTAL ASSETS	$161,580.89	$245,761.25

(continued)

EXHIBIT 5 *(continued)*

Vermont Tubbs, Inc. comparative balance sheets 6/30/70, 6/30/71

Liabilities and Capital	1970	1971
Current Liabilities		
Accounts Payable	$ 6,710.50	$ 13,795.10
Accrued Taxes	2,592.67	2,396.53
Accrued Wages	-0-	1,013.85
Notes Payable: Bank	10,000.00	50,000.00
Notes Payable: H. Underwood (current Portion)	5,572.09	6,430.50
Total Current Liabilities	$ 24,875.26	$ 73,635.98
Long Term Liabilities		
Due Officers & Stockholders	3,395.00	7,394.75
Notes Payable: C. B. Morgan, Sr.	2,000.00	15,000.00
Notes Payable: H. Underwood, Inc.	96,582.77	89,727.37
Total Long Term Liabilities	$101,977.77	$112,122.12
TOTAL LIABILITIES	$126,853.03	$185,758.10
Capital		
Capital Stock	30,000.00	30,000.00
Retained Earnings	4,727.86	30,003.15
Total Capital	$ 34,727.86	$ 60,003.15
TOTAL LIABILITIES & CAPITAL	$161,580.89	$245,761.25

Prepared from the books without audit.

EXHIBIT 6

Vermont Tubbs, Inc. comparative income statement F/Y 1970, 1971

Sales:	1970	1971
Snowshoes	$180,436.22	$283,932.13
Bindings	27,669.44	52,912.75
Repairs	1,734.23	2,276.47
Sawdust & Supplies	-0-	2,304.58
Deduct: returns & allowances	(1,378.49)	(3,481.18)
Net Sales	$208,461.40	$337,944.75
Cost of Sales		
Inventory 7/1/70	37,229.62	55,869.75
Add: Lumber	31,499.40	26,293.02
Rawhide, leather, bindings, neoprene	61,531.24	107,099.72
Operating supplies	10,832.24	14,067.58
Labor	59,691.79	85,767.40
Depreciation	7,728.23	9,321.12
Taxes & Licenses	5,414.83	7,162.57
Heat & Lights	4,464.43	5,196.58
Freight (in)	1,930.26	2,676.03
Other (incl. repairs)	5,354.07	2,435.03
Deduct: Inventory 6/30/71	(55,869.75)	(64,369.00)
Total Cost of Sales	$169,806.36	$251,519.80
Gross Profit	$ 38,655.04	$ 86,424.95

(continued)

EXHIBIT 6 *(continued)*
Vermont Tubbs, Inc. comparative income statement F/Y 1970, 1971

Sales:	1970	1971
General and Administrative		
Salary: Officer	3,600.00	10,000.00
Salary: Office	3,666.50	5,545.22
Commission	6,293.59	9,277.03
Travel Promotion	1,741.46	1,033.25
Telephone	1,009.31	2,320.78
Interest	8,488.07	10,407,67
Advertising	2,397.76	1,821.59
Office Expenses	1,465.73	2,936.00
Repairs	-0-	1,606.62
Legal & Audit	2,551.26	1,687.51
Insurance	3,537.18	5,057.09
Bad Debts	-0-	3,653.60
Other	447.07	2,300.84
Total G&A	$ 35,197.93	$ 57,647.20
Profit on Operations	3,457.11	28,777.75
Other Income (cash discounts)	1,270.75	1,225.40
NET PROFIT	$ 4,727.86	$ 30,003.15

Prepared from the books without audit

EXHIBIT 7
Vermont Tubbs, Inc. comparative data on sales distribution

	1970		1971		1981		1982	
	$	%	$	%	$	%	$	%
Snowshoes	180,436	85.8	283,932	82.8	175,000	34.4	120,000	31.2
Bindings	27,669	13.4	52,912	15.8	50,000	9.8	30,000	7.8
Snowshoe Furniture	—	—	—	—	100,000	19.6	100,000	26.0
General Furniture	—	—	—	—	149,000	29.3	107,000	27.8
Repairs, sawdust and supplies	1,734	0.8	4,581	1.4	35,108	6.9	27,672	7.2
Returns & Allowances $	(1,378)	—	(3,481)	—	(2,240)	—	(1,727)	—
Net Sales	208,461	100	337,944	100	509,108	100	384,672	100
Group Sales	209,839		341,426		511,348		386,399	

Source: Company statistics.

EXERCISE 2–21

Vermont Tubbs, Inc.

- Analyze the debt structure for Vermont Tubbs, noting changes in that structure and possible causes. Note: Industry comparisons should be helpful, even if the time periods are not comparable.
- Analyze the income statements for Vermont Tubbs. Note changes over time. Again, comparisons with industry data can be very helpful.
- Examine the activity of Vermont Tubbs. Use as many activity ratios as you find helpful. Again, comparisons may help.
- What major areas of past performance or present status should Vermont Tubbs's management address? Why? Explain.

ANSWERS TO SELECTED EXERCISES

Exercise 2–1

Total debt-to-equity ratios:

1982	*1983*	*1984*	*1985*	*1986*
.123	.190	.267	.431	.694

Exercise 2–6

Direct Materials
Direct Labor
Shipping Expense
Manufacturing Supplies Expense

Exercise 2–7

Executive Sales Salaries and Benefits Expense
Dues and Membership Expense—Trade Associations
Central Office Sales and Marketing Staff Salaries and Benefits Expense
Directories Expense (e.g., Yellow Pages)
Information or Data Services Expense

Exercise 2–13

.0422, for 1983

Exercise 2–17

1982:	1982: 54.70 days
1984:	59.18 days

Exercise 2–19

1983:	7.50
1984:	5.31
1985:	4.13

APPENDIX

APPENDIX 1

	SIC 3713 Truck & bus bodies (no breakdown) 1986 (169 estab)		SIC 3714 Mot vehicle part, ACC (no breakdown) 1986 (483 estab)		SIC 3715 Truck trailers (no breakdown) 1986 (97 estab)		SIC 3721 Aircraft (no breakdown) 1986 (35 estab)	
	$	%	$	%	$	%	$	%
Cash	66,225	10.1	67,710	8.8	121,837	11.5	651,481	13.1
Accounts receivable	131,139	20.0	171,584	22.3	182,226	17.2	547,045	11.0
Notes receivable	3,278	0.5	6,155	0.8	15,892	1.5	49,731	1.0
Inventory	244,574	37.3	216,981	28.2	358,095	33.8	1,477,022	29.7
Other current	30,818	4.7	32,316	4.2	51,913	4.9	377,959	7.6
Total current	476,035	72.6	494,748	64.3	729,962	68.9	3,103,239	62.4
Fixed assets	101,633	15.5	144,654	18.8	201,296	19.0	805,649	16.2
Other non-current	78,028	11.9	130,035	16.9	128,194	12.1	1,064,252	21.4
Total assets	655,695	100.0	769,437	100.0	1,059,452	100.0	4,973,139	100.0
Accounts payable	102,288	15.6	96,180	12.5	144,085	13.6	482,394	9.7
Bank loans	13,114	2.0	10,003	1.3	24,367	2.3	59,678	1.2
Notes payable	50,489	7.7	36,164	4.7	45,556	4.3	208,872	4.2
Other current	100,977	15.4	103,874	13.5	159,977	15.1	760,890	15.3
Total current	266,868	40.7	246,220	32.0	373,987	35.3	1,511,834	30.4
Other long term	66,225	10.1	134,651	17.5	146,204	13.8	890,192	17.9
Deferred credits	656	0.1	5,386	0.7	2,119	0.2	19,893	0.4
Net worth	321,946	49.1	383,180	49.8	537,142	50.7	2,551,220	51.3
Total liab & net worth	655,695	100.0	769,437	100.0	1,059,452	100.0	4,973,139	100.0
Net sales	1,682,744	100.0	1,347,453	100.0	1,780,760	100.0	350,000	100.0
Gross profit	413,955	24.6	441,965	32.8	388,206	21.8	92,750	26.5
Net profit after tax	38,703	2.3	72,762	5.4	58,765	3.3	(11,200)	(3.2)
Working capital	209,167	—	248,528	—	355,975	—	1,591,405	—

APPENDIX 1 *(continued)*

	SIC 3713 Truck & bus bodies (no breakdown) 1986 (169 estab) $ %			*SIC 3714 Mot vehicle part, ACC (no breakdown) 1986 (483 estab)* $ %			*SIC 3715 Truck trailers (no breakdown) 1986 (97 estab)* $ %			*SIC 3721 Aircraft (no breakdown) 1986 (35 estab)* $ %		
RATIOS	*UQ*	*MED*	*LQ*	*UQ*	*MED*	*LQ*	*UQ*	*MED*	*LQ*	*UQ*	*MED*	*LQ*
Solvency												
Quick ratio (times)	1.2	0.7	0.4	1.8	1.0	0.6	1.3	0.8	0.4	1.6	0.7	0.4
Current ratio (times)	2.9	1.7	1.3	3.8	2.2	1.4	3.0	2.0	1.4	3.6	1.8	1.2
Curr liab to NW (%)	31.9	78.0	159.8	22.4	52.9	125.0	29.9	69.8	132.0	27.8	69.4	110.3
Curr liab to INV (%)	71.9	101.4	144.8	58.5	102.1	171.0	64.3	96.0	158.9	44.7	98.8	274.4
Total liab to NW (%)	41.7	89.2	192.6	30.8	86.6	196.0	43.6	88.4	188.9	49.2	113.8	159.9
Fixed assets to NW (%)	18.9	32.1	58.1	23.8	47.9	82.1	24.9	41.9	82.7	29.9	61.1	86.7
Efficiency												
Coll period (days)	11.9	25.1	37.6	27.0	40.6	54.0	10.7	27.6	46.5	26.8	39.4	52.2
Sales to inv (times)	14.8	9.2	5.5	12.3	6.9	4.6	10.9	7.2	3.9	15.4	6.5	3.8
Assets to sales (%)	22.5	34.1	50.4	34.7	47.7	67.4	28.5	41.7	66.2	35.5	55.8	112.6
Sales to NWC (times)	17.5	9.7	5.6	10.7	5.8'	3.7	13.2	7.5	3.3	21.1	6.8	4.2
Acct pay to sales (%)	3.2	5.0	8.4	3.3	5.5	8.8	3.0	4.3	9.0	3.8	5.8	9.6
Profitability												
Return on sales (%)	4.7	2.2	0.1	8.8	4.4	1.9	6.0	2.6	1.1	4.6	3.0	(7.2)
Return on assets (%)	13.6	7.0	0.5	14.2	7.6	3.1	14.6	7.5	2.3	7.1	5.0	(7.1)
Return on NW (%)	25.5	14.3	2.7	30.8	17.5	7.4	28.7	14.2	5.8	18.8	12.6	(17.1)

APPENDIX 1 (continued)

	SIC 2032 Canned specialties (no breakdown) 1986 (21 estab)		SIC 2033 Can fruits. vegetable (no breakdown) 1986 (110 estab)		SIC 2034 Dried dyhd frts veg (no breakdown) 1986 (27 estab)		SIC 2035 Pikl, sauce, slad dres (no breakdown) 1986 (50 estab)	
	$	%	$	%	$	%	$	%
Cash	70,843	8.4	184,046	5.7	197,124	6.8	81,170	13.8
Accounts receivable	217,589	25.8	497,246	15.4	640,654	22.1	117,050	19.9
Notes receivable	843	0.1	16,144	0.5	11,596	0.4	—	—
Inventory	193,132	22.9	1,252,802	38.8	892,858	30.8	176,457	30.0
Other current	16,867	2.0	90,408	2.8	101,461	3.5	42,350	7.2
Total current	499,275	59.2	2,040,646	63.2	1,843,693	63.6	417,027	70.9
Fixed assets	255,541	30.3	616,714	19.1	518,901	17.9	88,817	15.1
Other non-current	88,554	10.5	571,510	17.7	536,294	18.5	82,347	14.0
Total assets	843,370	100.0	3,228,870	100.0	2,898,889	100.0	588,190	100.0
Accounts payable	99,518	11.8	597,341	18.5	400,047	13.8	77,053	13.1
Bank loans	4,217	0.5	100,095	3.1	95,663	3.3	4,117	0.7
Notes payable	17,711	2.1	193,732	6.0	176,832	6.1	28,233	4.8
Other current	102,048	12.1	387,464	12.0	469,620	16.2	72,347	12.3
Total current	223,493	26.5	1,278,633	39.6	1,142,162	39.4	181,751	30.9
Other long term	181,325	21.5	616,714	19.1	533,396	18.4	82,347	14.0
Deferred credits	843	0.1	12,915	0.4	11,596	0.4	588	0.1
Net worth	437,709	51.9	1,320,608	40.9	1,211,736	41.8	323,505	55.0
Total liab & net worth	843,370	100.0	3,228,870	100.0	2,898,889	100.0	588,190	100.0
Net sales	1,951,423	100.0	5,672,744	100.0	5,704,648	100.0	850,000	100.0
Gross profit	665,435	34.1	1,491,932	26.3	1,688,576	29.6	283,900	33.4
Net profit after tax	95,620	4.9	187,201	3.3	245,300	4.3	54,400	6.4
Working capital	275,782	—	762,013	—	701,531	—	235,276	—

APPENDIX 1 *(continued)*

	SIC 2032 Canned specialties (no breakdown) 1986 (21 estab)			*SIC 2033 Can fruits. vegetable (no breakdown) 1986 (110 estab)*			*SIC 2034 Dried dyhd frts veg (no breakdown) 1986 (27 estab)*			*SIC 2035 Pikl, sauce, slad dres (no breakdown) 1986 (50 estab)*		
	$		%	$		%	$		%	$		%
RATIOS	*UQ*	*MED*	*LQ*	*UQ*	*MED*	*LQ*	*UQ*	*MED*	*LQ*	*UQ*	*MED*	*LQ*
Solvency												
Quick ratio (times)	2.1	1.1	0.9	0.9	0.5	0.3	1.5	0.6	0.3	2.0	1.0	0.6
Current ratio (times)	4.1	2.2	1.4	2.5	1.6	1.2	2.3	1.4	1.1	4.4	2.2	1.4
Curr liab to NW (%)	19.9	41.1	74.3	41.2	88.2	159.5	56.6	86.9	153.1	20.9	52.2	90.2
Curr liab to Inv (%)	44.1	69.3	128.7	58.1	99.4	141.1	65.5	104.0	151.0	36.4	113.7	175.9
Total liab to NW (%)	49.7	70.7	137.1	61.6	36.3	227.7	100.4	139.6	220.4	24.7	77.3	129.7
Fixed assets to NW (%)	39.1	61.8	126.2	30.0	48.5	82.5	25.1	37.7	101.7	22.7	35.4	61.1
Efficiency												
Coll period (days)	24.5	30.1	46.4	17.3	25.9	35.6	17.2	25.5	32.5	16.0	23.5	40.0
Sales to Inv (times)	11.8	9.0	6.5	9.0	5.5	2.5	19.1	6.3	4.7	15.5	10.0	5.3
Sales to Inv (times)	29.8	45.7	62.4	32.4	57.7	80.7	34.2	53.6	68.2	26.2	41.3	68.1
Sales to NWC (times)	8.7	6.2	5.3	19.2	8.7	5.5	24.5	12.1	5.3	13.6	6.8	4.0
Acct pay to sales (%)	2.1	3.4	7.0	3.8	7.4	14.1	2.4	3.8	5.9	1.6	3.5	6.1
Profitability												
Return on sales (%)	5.5	4.9	2.6	5.4	2.0	0.4	10.6	4.1	1.1	6.7	4.0	2.5
Return on assets (%)	10.4	8.1	7.5	10.3	2.9	0.9	8.9	4.9	0.9	13.5	10.4	3.9
Return on NW (%)	34.8	14.4	12.6	22.2	7.8	1.3	19.2	11.9	2.1	25.9	16.6	7.3

APPENDIX 1 *(continued)*

	SIC 2491 Wood preserving (no breakdown) 1986 (71 estab)		*SIC 2499 Wood products, Nec (no breakdown) 1986 (460 estab)*		*SIC 2511 Wood hsehold Furn. (no breakdown) 1986 (413 estab)*		*SIC 2512 Upholst'd hsehold fur (no breakdown) 1986 (350 estab)*	
	$	%	$	%	$	%	$	%
Cash	73,234	8.7	33,221	11.5	30,370	10.7	50,718	11.3
Accounts receivable	145,626	17.3	64,132	22.2	59,321	20.9	107,270	23.9
Notes receivable	2,525	0.3	2,002	0.7	851	0.3	1,795	0.4
Inventory	239,904	28.5	74,532	25.8	80,041	28.2	141.830	31.6
Other current	53,0332	6.3	10,689	3.7	13,056	4.6	22,441	5.0
Total current	514,321	61.1	184,596	63.9	183,640	64.7	324,054	72.2
Fixed assets	180,139	21.4	61,243	21.2	57,334	20.2	79,891	17.8
Other non-current	147,310	17.5	43,043	14.9	42,859	15.1	44,883	10.0
Total assets	841,770	100.0	288,882	100.0	283,833	100.0	448,828	100.0
Accounts payable	69,867	8.3	31,777	11.0	34,344	12.1	65,978	14.7
Bank loans	30,304	3.6	6,067	2.1	3,690	1.3	7,181	1.6
Notes payable	55,557	6.6	11,844	4.1	12,489	4.4	21,095	4.7
Other current	103,538	12.3	35,532	12.3	42,291	14.9	61,041	13.6
Total current	259,265	30.8	85,220	29.5	92,813	32.7	155,294	34.6
Other long term	117,006	13.9	50,265	17.4	45,413	16.0	54,308	12.1
Deferred credits	—	—	867	0.3	568	0.2	898	0.2
Net worth	465,499	55.3	152,530	52.8	145,039	51.1	238,328	53.1
Total liab & net worth	841,770	100.0	288,882	100.0	283,833	100.0	448,828	100.0
Net sales	2,647,093	100.0	625,022	100.0	893,423	100.0	1,280,000	100.0
Gross profit	653,832	24.7	223,133	35.7	286,789	32.1	377,600	29.5
Net profit after tax	127,060	4.8	29,376	4.7	52,712	5.9	57,600	4.5
Working capital	255,056	—	99,376	—	90,827	—	168,760	—

APPENDIX 1 *(continued)*

	SIC 2491 Wood preserving (no breakdown) 1986 (71 estab)			*SIC 2499 Wood products, Nec (no breakdown) 1986 (460 estab)*			*SIC 2511 Wood hsehold Furn. (no breakdown) 1986 (413 estab)*			*SIC 2512 Upholst'd hsehold fur (no breakdown) 1986 (350 estab)*		
	$		%	$		%	$		%	$		%
RATIOS	*UQ*	*MED*	*LQ*	*UQ*	*MED*	*LQ*	*UQ*	*MED*	*LQ*	*UQ*	*MED*	*LQ*
Solvency												
Quick ratio (times)	1.9	0.8	0.5	2.6	1.2	0.7	2.0	1.0	0.5	2.2	1.1	0.5
Current ratio (times)	4.8	2.0	1.3	5.2	2.4	1.5	4.1	2.2	1.3	4.2	2.3	1.5
Curr liab to NW (%)	20.1	54.5	112.4	15.5	39.9	100.8	20.7	48.5	113.3	22.8	52.5	114.1
Curr liab to Inv (%)	52.5	105.6	175.2	42.4	96.5	183.2	55.3	103.0	178.5	57.7	99.8	164.6
Total liab to NW (%)	22.8	60.0	173.9	27.1	71.7	181.7	31.2	75.9	181.4	30.8	74.6	170.4
Fixed assets to NW (%)	22.0	64.9	129.7	22.4	49.0	95.8	27.2	48.4	100.6	15.9	36.1	68.8
Efficiency												
Coll period (days)	15.6	25.5	41.8	20.4	32.8	48.4	18.5	31.0	48.9	12.4	29.0	49.0
Sales to Inv (times)	19.8	8.4	4.5	17.5	9.6	5.5	16.9	9.0	5.9	16.2	10.3	7.0
Assets to sales (%)	34.9	47.3	64.7	28.4	42.1	69.1	25.5	40.2	57.7	20.5	31.6	49.1
Sales to NWC (%)	9.8	7.1	3.6	12.4	6.4	3.6	15.0	7.9	4.6	15.1	8.2	4.6
Acct pay to sales (%)	1.9	3.1	4.6	2.0	3.7	6.6	2.0	3.7	6.7	2.4	4.0	6.5
Profitability												
Return on sales (%)	8.0	3.5	2.1	9.6	3.7	0.7	8.9	4.5	2.2	7.7	3.1	1.1
Return on assets (%)	18.0	7.7	5.1	20.9	7.9	1.2	18.1	9.8	3.8	15.7	7.9	3.4
Return on NW (%)	43.5	27.1	8.1	41.3	16.4	2.5	37.7	17.2	7.2	34.4	16.1	7.1

Source: Industry Norms and Key Business Ratios (Murray Hill, N.J.: Dun & Bradstreet, Inc., 1987). Used by Permission.

3

FINANCIAL MANAGEMENT AND THE GENERAL MANAGER

A systems view of the typical commercial business organization would place the managers of each of the three major business functions—marketing, production, and finance—as interfacing agents for the organization in its relationships with several different external constituencies. In this perspective, the marketing manager is charged with serving as an organizational link to customers and is responsible for maintaining up-to-date information on the competitive dynamics of the marketplace.

The production manager must maintain a close relationship with suppliers of materials and acts in that capacity as an interface agent. The production manager is also concerned with another important ingredient in the conversion process . . . human resources. In that capacity, the production or operations manager must maintain close contact with a variety of labor markets. He or she must act as the intermediary as applicants for employment are screened and selected or as employees return to the population at large through termination, layoff, voluntary separation, or retirement.

In this same perspective, the manager charged with responsibility for financial matters must also serve as a link between the organization and its environment. The financial manager must identify and cultivate numerous potential and actual sources of capital, must know how to husband this critical resource, and must be able to maximize the financial returns for its use. In addition, the financial manager must add technical expertise to decision making by general management in order that the long-run financial investment of stockholders or owners is both secure and adequately rewarded. In performing these functions, the financial manager must have a sound technical knowledge of financial markets, the know-how to use the tools of financial analysis to gauge the relative merits of different investment alternatives, an awareness of the economics of the marketplace of the firm's products, and the ability to plan and manage the flows of funds involved in the operation of the enterprise.

The general manager's responsibility for financial matters is similar to the responsibility for other critical business functions. Of necessity, the general manager must have oversight responsibility and should have an understanding of the relevant critical dimensions in the functional areas, yet he or she need not be as expert, technically, as the functional manager. When faced with capital investment decisions, the general manager should be able to look to financial management both to provide the most suitable tools for analysis and decision making and to perform the analysis and make recommendations based on sound and informed financial management principles. In planning, the general manager should be able to have the informed assistance of a technically proficient financial management staff who can offer advice as it relates to their specialty. The responsibility for the ultimate decision, however, rests with the general manager, and this person should be sufficiently trained in the concepts and skills of financial analysis to have a working comprehension of their use. Thus, our treatment of financial management from the perspective of the general manager will be a somewhat broader and less technical treatment and will concentrate more on the longer-range and integrative problems of financial management rather than on the technical aspects of the function.

FINANCIAL MANAGEMENT AS A FLOW OF FUNDS

An interesting perspective on the management of the financial function in commercial organizations is that of funds as a form of vital liquid stored in cash (its most liquid state); other less fluid, but still current assets; and fixed assets, that is, funds frozen in the form of buildings, equipment, or land. This reservoir of funds has been filled by flows of funds from the original owners; from creditors who have agreed to supply funds in return for "rent" (interest payments) for its use; and from suppliers who have provided the assets for a time, without charging "rent," in return for the firm's willingness to buy their products. This perspective represents a sort of snapshot of the reservoir held in a state of equilibrium, a state captured in the typical balance sheet in a static state (see Figure 3–1).

A more complicated, dynamic view of the system can be had when it is viewed during its normal operating state. In this form, the organization is seen as a vessel that has been provided funds on a more or less permanent basis by stockholders and long-term creditors as well as on a shorter-term basis by customers, suppliers, and employees. The picture is complicated by several different types of major flows of funds into and out of the reservoir and by a certain amount of seepage from the system.

Funds flow into the firm during its normal operation as customers send payments in cash for current or past orders of goods and services. Funds also flow into the firm as goods are shipped by suppliers and as the firm requests and receives borrowed money. Outflows of cash and other funds come about as a consequence of a number of events. First, suppliers of materials expect to be repaid for the "loan" of materials (materials sold and shipped on an open account purchase). Second, creditors expect to be repaid at the end of the term of a money loan. Seepage from the system results from the needs both of permanent suppliers of funds who demand interest payments for the use of funds and of stockholders who, in a similar fashion, expect regular dividends in return for the use of their ownership money. In this dynamic system, profits that are not distributed to shareholders as dividends will cause the reservoir to rise. They represent funds that have flowed in but that have not been drained away. Losses, should these occur, will have the opposite effect, causing the reservoir to fall somewhat. In this latter case, we have drained away more funds

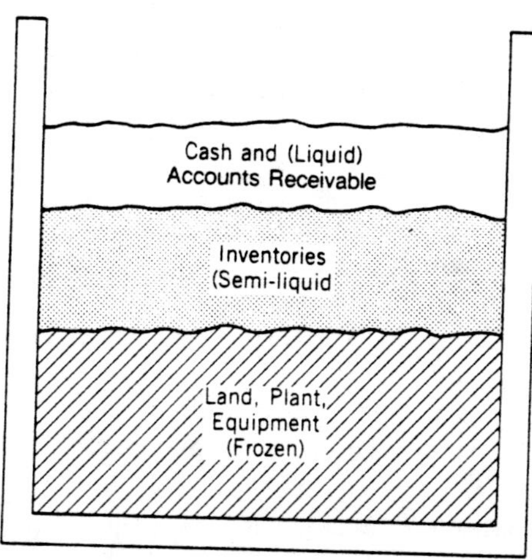

FIGURE 3–1 Static view of the organization as a reservoir of funds.

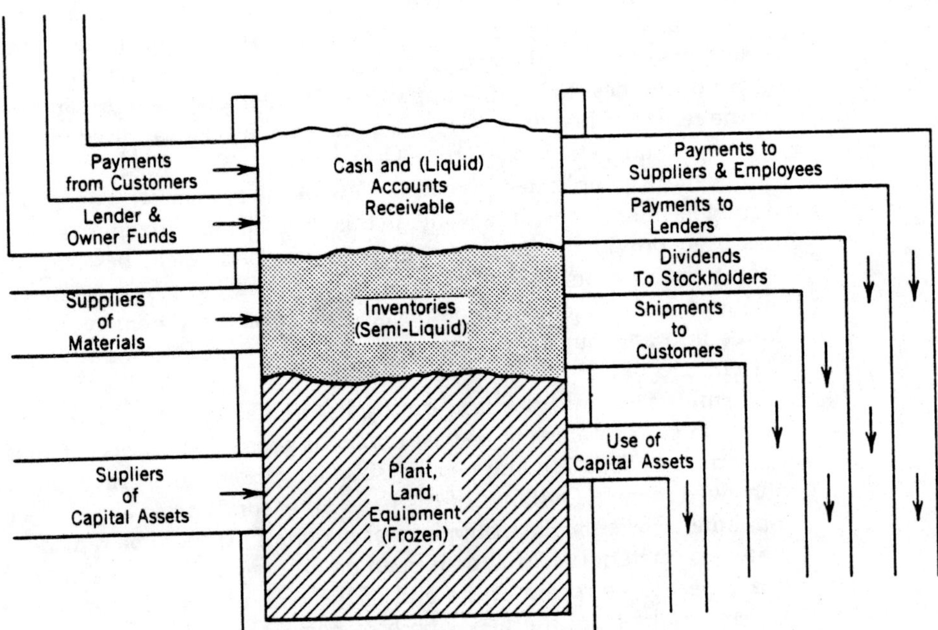

FIGURE 3–2 A dynamic view of the organization as a flow of funds.

in materials and labor than we have regained from customers.[1] Figure 3–2 is a schematic representation of the dynamic model of the organization as a flow of funds.

In the following section we will examine this dynamic system in its parts, looking first at the possible sources of funds, then at the various applications of those funds. In subsequent sections we will discuss the management of this system and, finally, the development of an integrated financial strategy.

SOURCES OF FUNDS

Broadly speaking, sources of funds can be broken into two forms: debt sources and equity, or ownership sources. Each has its own effect on operating costs, on the risk to the organization, on the extent to which it affects the control of the enterprise by management, and on the extent to which it restricts the ability of management to make changes in the future. In the following section, we will first examine some of the more common forms of debt financing and address each of these four major factors. Then we will undertake a brief discussion of equity financing alternatives, again looking at costs, risk, control, and restrictions on future actions.

[1] A detailed development of this concept is contained in Erich A. Helfert, *Techniques of Financial Analysis*, 4th Ed. (Homewood, Ill: R. D. Irwin, 1977), pp. 3–43.

Debt-Financing Alternatives

The most current of debt forms in most organizations is that of current trade obligations: accounts payable. In most instances, these debts are incurred as the result of the purchase of materials and goods for resale and are free of any explicit interest cost. If a cash discount is offered for payment within 10 days, the "cost" of extending the payment period from 10 days to 30 days can be substantial. If the discount for cash were 2%, the 20 days of interest would be the equivalent of a 36% annual rate (using 360 days per year).

EXERCISE 3–1

If the terms of sale are 3% cash discount in 15 days, and net payment in 45 days,

- How would these terms be shown in the abbreviations normally seen on an invoice? (See answer at the end of this chapter.)
- What would the equivalent annual interest cost be for paying the invoice in 45 days?
- What would be the equivalent annual interest cost for paying the invoice in 75 days?
- What does this suggest to you in terms of sources of funds?

An additional source of very short-range debt funding is that of short-term borrowing. Several forms are available:

a Short-term notes, maturing within one year.

b Lines of credit, made available to businesses to accomodate seasonal needs for funds. Typically, as cash is generated at the close of the season, borrowing against lines of credit is reduced.

c Short-term installment credit can also serve to meet short-term borrowing needs. With installment debt, payments against the total are made periodically, and the debt is retired.

Many short-term notes and lines of credit are granted on an unsecured basis. For the financing of the day-to-day operation of a business, these are probably adequate. For more substantial amounts of financing or in situations where the lender perceives a higher degree of risk, the lender may wish to have the loan secured by a lien on a specific article of property. Installment debt is often associated with the purchase of a specific article, which often serves as the security for the loan. Security for short-term working-capital loans can also be provided by accounts receivable. These can serve as collateral for the loan or can be sold at a discount to a factor, who assumes the responsibility for their collection.

The cost of unsecured loans is usually lower than the cost for those that are secured, in part because of the cost of preparing and securing the loan and perhaps, more importantly, because they are often used with firms that represent a greater risk to the lender. The heavy discounting involved in factoring accounts receivable results in a very high cost of borrowing for this method.

Loans from banks may be written in such a way as to deduct the cost of interest for the term of the loan from the principal amount. Thus, a borrower who signs a note for $1,000, on which a nominal 12% annual interest payment will be expected, would receive $880 from the bank but would be expected to repay the face amount of the note at the end of one year. Installment loans also have a substantially higher cost than the nominal rate of interest because the borrower must repay principal over the term of the installment loan.

EXERCISE 3–2

What will be the actual annual interest cost of the loan described above?

EXERCISE 3–3

What will be the interest cost of a $2,000 installment loan written at a nominal interest rate of 15% and payable in 12 equal monthly installments?

EXERCISE 3–4

In accounts receivable you have a total of $87,250 in accounts that a factor will be willing to handle for you. The factor has said that he will discount them to you at 22%.

- What will you receive from the factor when you factor the receivables?
- What will be the annual cost of obtaining these funds, in dollar terms, if you made this same transaction six times each year?
- Is this the equivalent of borrowing? Explain.

The risk to the firm that occurs as a result of short-term borrowing is not inconsiderable. Delinquencies in meeting interest payments, in paying trade creditors, and in meeting repayment schedules to lending institutions can have two fairly dramatic effects in the short run. First, creditors can begin to insist on payment for shipments of materials upon delivery or even with the order. This action can have a nearly catastrophic effect on cash management, especially if the firm has extended credit terms to *its* customers. Funds for as much as 30 or 40 days worth of purchases will be required *in liquid asset form* (i.e., cash) in order to continue to function in a normal operating fashion. The firm that has stretched the goodwill of its trade creditors is unlikely to be able to locate anything like that amount of capital and may be forced to severely curtail operations. Second, creditors can institute foreclosure proceedings, actions that may not only result in high legal fees, but also may restrict the use of key pieces of equipment or other assets. Finally, the institution of collection procedures may be the signal to any and all lenders in the available financial market that the firm is in financial straits and may result in the firm being closed off from nearly all sources of debt financing.

Some of the forms of credit mentioned tend to restrict management actions more than others. Bank loans, for example, often call for compensating balances. These balances restrict the ability of management to draw on those funds and thereby inhibit both the manipulation of liquid assets and add to the real cost of borrowing.

EXERCISE 3-5

Your banker has agreed to a 180-day unsecured loan of $10,000 to help you in your expanding business. He has charged you 13.5% annual interest. In the fine print on the loan document, he has required a minimum balance in your account of 15% of the amount of the loan.

- How much of the $10,000 will you be able to use?
- In annual percentage terms, what is the cost of the capital acquired through this loan?

In addition to minimum balances, lenders have other restrictive practices. A line of credit typically has a provision that the entire line must be cleared at least a stated number of weeks or months each year. Where pledged assets are involved, the secured assets cannot be sold to gain liquidity without repaying the holder of the lien on the property. Borrowers using installment loans must not only pay the interest cost of the loan, but are locked contractually into a rigid repayment schedule. In all of these forms of short-term financing, some flexibility is sacrificed as borrowing occurs.

One factor favoring these short-term types of funding is that of control. In none of the kinds of borrowing mentioned is the control of the company by management diluted by providers of funds. Although the borrower is expected to meet the terms of the loan, the lender has the legal position of creditor to enforce the provisions of the loan and does not normally become involved in the management of the firm.

Long-term debt financing may involve several different types of financing instruments: long-term notes, mortgages, and debentures or bonds. Again, each has different attributes and different levels of cost, risk, and restrictions on management action. Term loans are usually repaid on a quarterly basis and have the interest cost calculated on the basis of the outstanding balance. Payments are high initially but drop as the principal balance declines. Many term loans are based on a variable rate of interest, based on the existing prime rate. Thus, as the prime interest rate moves up or down, so will the interest cost of the variable-rate term loan.

Mortgages are debts that are secured by a specified article of property. In most cases, plant and property usually serve as collateral for long-term business mortgages. If the borrower defaults, the lender has a specific piece of property that serves as security for the specific article of indebtedness and may recover his or her property independent of the other creditors. The traditional mortgage has the interest cost calculated on the basis of the total interest cost prorated over the number of quarters to achieve a constant quarterly payment. In recent years, a variable-rate mortgage has been developed to provide lenders protection against increases in the market interest rate. Quarterly payments will move up or down, given changes in the prevailing market rate of interest.

A bond is a long-term promisory note sold to lenders. A bond is a contract between the borrower and the lender in which the borrower agrees to repay to the lender the face value of the bond at some date in the future. In addition, the borrower agrees to pay the lender an interest payment each year at the coupon rate times the face value of the bond. Usually, these interest payments are paid in quarterly or semiannual installments. The typical bond is unsecured and is called a debenture. Although unsecured, it is a debt instrument and has precedence in liquidation over all owners. Bonds can be repurchased, or called, by the borrower if the terms of the issue include a call provision. When called, the borrower usually has to pay a premium over the face value in order to repurchase the bond from the lender. Some bonds are subordinated to others. This provision means that the subordinated issue will be repaid after the senior issue is paid, but still before stockholders are paid.

EXERCISE 3-6

A bond issue has a $1,000 face value on each certificate and a coupon rate of 9⅜%. Interest payments are to be paid quarterly.

- How much will each payment be?
- The bond issue has a call provision requiring the issuer to pay a call premium equal to one-year's interest. If you held eight certificates, how much would you receive from the issuer if that issue were called?

The market value of bonds is directly related to the market rate of interest for securities of like degree of risk. If, for example, the coupon rate on a given bond is 8% and the market rate is 10%, the present value of the stream of interest payments and the present value of the face amount of the bond to be received in the future would be *less* than other similar securities available to investors. As a result, this 8% bond will sell at a discount, a sum less than its face value. If, on the other hand, the bond we wish to issue has a coupon rate of 12%, the present value of its stream of payments and its redemption at a future time would be greater than that of competing securities, and it would sell at a *premium* over its face amount.

Bonds are attractive to investors because of the fixed stream of relatively high-income payments and the degree of safety provided by the debt instrument. They do not, however, share in exceptional growth, should that occur. For this reason, an attractive feature sometimes included in a bond issue is that of convertibility to common stock. With the convertible bond, the lender has the secured position of the creditor but can take advantage of the growth of the company by converting the bond to a specified number of shares of common stock. The conversion price will normally be set sufficiently high to avoid conversion at its issuance, but low enough so that lenders might find the conversion attractive at some point in the future. Some convertible bonds have a call provision that enables the borrower to force conversion as a means of lowering fixed charges for interest. Yields to investors on convertible bonds are somewhat below conventional bonds, a factor that may make these issues attractive to issuers but somewhat less desirable to prospective lenders. Convertible bonds are subordinated to other issues but precede preferred and common stock in liquidation.

Bondholders may ask that constraints be placed on management in order to enhance the likelihood that their dividends will be paid promptly. One of these types of constraints is an indenture that limits the dividends paid to stockholders or one that requires the firm to maintain a specified current ratio.

EXERCISE 3–7

The following is a list of items taken from the liabilities and owner's equity portion of the balance sheet. Arrange them in order of priority in liquidation. The top of the list should be the item that would be paid first.

Preferred Stock
Taxes Payable
Five-Year Note Payable
Convertible Debentures
Common Stock
Wages Payable

90-day Note Payable
Ordinary Debenture
Accounts Payable
Subordinated Debenture

EQUITY FINANCING

Preferred stock offers another means of providing funds to the organization. For common stockholders, preferred stock and debt offer the advantage of providing funds without in any way relinquishing control. In each of these forms of financing, however, common stockholders must be prepared to agree to the payment of interest to bondholders or other creditors and dividends to preferred shareholders before they may receive dividends on common shares. Preferred stockholders are owners in much the same way as are common stockholders. Consequently, the danger of default does not exist if preferred stock is used instead of debt financing. On the other hand, dividends paid to preferred shareholders are not a tax-deductible expense, therefore may bear a higher net cost of financing.

Several points of distinction between preferred and common stock are worthy of mention. First, preferred stockholders are normally entitled to receive a stated dividend, if a dividend is declared. They are to be paid their dividend before dividends are paid to common stockholders. Second, preferred dividends are usually cumulative . . . if a dividend payment is missed, it must be paid in a future period before current dividends are paid. Third, in some cases, preferred stockholders may *participate* with common shareholders in the proceeds from a particularly profitable year. Finally, preferred stockholders normally do not vote.

EXERCISE 3–8

You are considering the possibility of either issuing a substantial amount of long-term debt financing or the issuance of an equivalent amount of preferred stock. Your investment banker has told you that the cost of issuance of the $20 million will be about 6.5% for the preferred stock and about 5% for bonds. At prevailing market rates, the bond issue could be sold at face value at a coupon rate of 9¾%. The preferred stock issue could be sold at an 8% dividend. Your corporate tax rate is 48%. The underwriter has said that a condition of underwriting the bond issue would be a seat on the board of directors and access to all meetings of the finance committee. Further, an indenture would be required that would restrict any dividends until interest payments had been made on the bond issue. If bonds are used, your commercial banker has said that the resulting debt-to-equity ratio would place you in a very heavily leveraged position and might result in the bank's request for additional security for short-term borrowings, an increased interest rate, or both.

- Which alternative would you choose? Why? Prepare for extended class discussion or as a homework assignment.

In considering the issuance of common stock, two factors must be of principal concern: control of the corporation and return per share. In any common stock issuance, both control and return per share will be diluted unless all of the new issue is purchased by the existing shareholders through the exercise of their preemptive right. To existing shareholders, these factors may represent a considerable "cost" in financing. In situations where a firm is heavily in debt, however, the issuance of ownership shares may be the only practicable means of acquiring funds. Issuing stock will not only gain funds, but also will restore an acceptable ratio of debt to owner's equity and thereby may provide a more acceptable structure for additional debt financing.

The cost of underwriting long-term financing can be high. Schall and Haley report costs as high as 23.7% for issuances of common stock under $500,000. Costs for issuances of preferred stock of issuances of the same size are 14.5%. Bonds at the same issuance size cost 12.3% of the issue amount. When the issuance is very large, of course, the cost of the issue in percentage terms is much lower. For issuances over $100 million, the cost of debt financing is 1.0%, preferred stock 2.4%, and common stock 3.0% of the issue amount.[2]

EXERCISE 3–9

The following balance sheet is that of the Acme Steel Products Corporation before it issues long-term financing.

ASSETS	
Cash	$ 24,000
Other Current Assets	$ 76,000
Fixed Assets (net)	$120,000
LIABILITIES AND OWNER'S EQUITY	
Current Liabilities	$ 40,000
Common Stock	$120,000 (12,000 shares)
Retained Earnings	$ 60,000

[2] L. D. Schall, and C. W. Haley, *Introduction to Financial Management*, 2nd Ed. (New York, McGraw-Hill, 1980), p. 579.

- What will the balance sheet look like with an issuance of $50,000 in common stock, at an issuance price of $12.50 per share, and an issuance cost of $5,000? Calculate the current ratio and the debt-to-equity ratio.
- What will the balance sheet look like with an issuance of $50,000 in bonds at an issuance cost of $3,000? Calculate the current ratio and the debt-to-equity ratio.
- What will the balance sheet look like with an issuance of $50,000 in preferred stock at an issuance cost of $3,500? Calculate the current ratio and the debt-to-equity ratio.
- If the bonds carry a 9.5% coupon rate and the preferred stock an 8.5% dividend, calculate the after-tax earnings per common share on each of the alternatives described above at an Earnings Before Interest and Taxes (EBIT) of $15,000 and a tax rate of 40%.

Financial Leverage

The term *financial leverage* is used to describe an effect that debt can have on stockholder earnings in periods of sales growth and sales decline. Where the rate of return on capital employed is higher than the cost of borrowing, the effect will be to raise the return on shareholder's equity, with no additional investment by shareholders. Similarly, when sales decline, the return to owners will decline dramatically. Let us use an example:

Period 1.

Sales	$1,000
Cost of Sales	$ 950
Profit Before Tax	$ 50
Profit After Tax	$ 25
Total Assets	$ 250
Shareholder's Equity	$ 100

In this situation, return on equity is $25/$100, or 25%.

Return on assets *after* tax is $25/$250, or 10%

Assume that we borrow $100, at a 10% interest rate. In Period 2, the following should have taken place, assuming that the additional sales could be made and that the firm was managed as well as it had been in Period 1:

Period 2.

Sales	$1,400
Cost of Sales	$1,330

Profit Before Tax	\$ 70
Profit After Tax	(\$70 − 10) × .50 = \$30
Total Assets	\$ 350
Shareholder's Equity	\$ 100

Return on equity is now \$30/\$100, or 30%

Return on Assets is now \$30/\$350, or 8.57%

Let us now assume that sales drop back to \$1,000:

Period 3.

Sales	\$1,000
Cost of Sales	950
Profit Before Tax	\$ 50
Profit After Tax	(\$50 − 10) × .50 = \$20
Total Assets	\$ 350
Shareholder's Equity	\$ 100

Return on equity has dropped to \$20/\$100, or 20%

Return on total assets has dropped to \$20/\$350 or 5.71%

It is worth observing that the amount of owner's equity has not changed during these three periods. All earnings were returned to the owners, one must assume. The owners have not invested any more in Period 2 than they had in Period 1, yet the return on their \$100 investment climbed from 25% to 30%, an increase in return on investment of 20%. In Period 3, the decline in sales to the original level now resulted in earnings of \$20 rather than the \$25 earned originally at the same sales volume. While sales and earnings before taxes had declined from Period 2, the cost of interest had stayed at \$10, and earnings were adversely affected, dropping return on equity by 33% from the preceding period, and 20% below the results of Period 1.

EXERCISE 3–10

Use the same sales, cost of sales, assets, and owner's equity figures as above.

- Calculate return on equity for all three periods if the cost of borrowing is 5%.
- Calculate the return on equity for all three periods if the cost of borrowing is 25%.

Cost of Capital

The concept of an average cost of capital is an extremely important element in financial decision making for the general manager and for functional managers. Economic good sense would support the concept held by some that "minimum acceptable rate of return on an investment is equal to the average cost of capital"[3] If returns from a proposed investment do not equal the average cost of capital, then we are required by our fund suppliers to pay them more for funds used than will be returned to the firm in the revenues that would be gained through the investment. The average cost of capital is computed as follows:

AVERAGE COST OF CAPITAL (ACC) =
Proportion of Debt × Cost of Debt +
Proportion of Preferred Stock × Cost of Preferred Stock +
Proportion of Common Stock × Cost of Common Stock

Example:

Debt = 30%, Cost of Debt = 6% (after tax)
Preferred Stock (PS) = 30%, Cost of PS = 8% (after tax)
Common Stock = 40%, Cost of Common Stock = 12%
(historical rate of return, including
dividends and appreciation)

$$\begin{aligned} ACC &= (.30 \times .06) + (.30 \times .08) + (.40 \times .12) \\ &= .09, \text{ or } 9\% \end{aligned}$$

Several points should be made regarding these calculations. First, we must take the tax effects of debt into account in calculating costs. Second, market values of securities should be used as the means for estimating costs, not simply the face value. For preferred stock, the annual dividend divided by the market value of the preferred stock is the appropriate cost. Several methods are suggested for estimating the cost of capital for common stock. One method is to use the historical rate of return to stockholders, a method that would include both dividends paid and the value of stock-price appreciation. An approximation of an acceptable rate of return for common stock can also be obtained by using the rate for debt and adding an amount to compensate for the added risk involved in holding common stock instead of debt. A somewhat more complex means of calculation is to divide the dividend by the current price of common shares, then add an amount to account for the expectations of future

[3] Schall and Haley, *Introduction to Financial Management*, p. 165.

dividends. The amount to be added can be equal to the average growth in earnings per share.

EXERCISE 3–11

The following information is provided on the sources of funding for your company:

OBLIGATION	*COST*	*PROPORTION*
Short-term obligations:	10.0%	25%
10-year note payable	9.0%	5%
20-year bonds	8.5%	25%
Preferred stock	Dividend \$9/share Market price \$87	
Common stock	Dividend \$1/share/qtr. Market price \$95 Price 5 years ago \$44, dividends have been paid each quarter over that period.	

Preferred stock is 15% of total capital; common stock, 30%.

- Calculate the average cost of capital using methods outlined in the text. Explain your reasoning.

Although the cost of capital is extremely valuable in helping to establish a baseline for acceptability of capital expenditure projects, it is most helpful when the projects under consideration involve cost savings or a form of revenue generation that is readily calculated. Some projects, however, are simply *required* for continued operation. Costs and revenues under these circumstances may require somewhat different standards for consideration in the analytic process.

The purchase of a replacement for an irreparably damaged piece of critical equipment may not result in man-hour or materials cost savings. Its purchase, however, may mean survival in the marketplace. A fundamental decision must be made regarding its purchase . . . buy it or go out of that line of business. Some managers might make the decision to remain in that particular business based on strategic interests, without detailed analysis. In other instances, as analysis could be made of flows of funds with the equipment and flows of funds without it, incorporating criterion measures such as the cost of capital in the calculations. In another type of situation, the investment may be needed to aid in the *support* of another segment or product in the organization. In this case, the economic value of that support may be very difficult to estimate, and a decision may be based on the *strategic* value of that support, without an attempt to calculate relative rates of return for the project.

As a practical matter, some managers may ask that investment projects return a somewhat higher rate of return for that investment than the cost of capital. Several reasons exist for this more rigorous standard. First, risk involved in the particular project may be somewhat higher than that for the organization as a whole, either from the uncertainty of savings or revenue generation or because of the length of the project's life. Second, management may believe, understandably, that its role is that of *improving* on the present state of returns rather than simply preserving them. As a consequence, a demand for returns somewhat higher than the average cost of capital is a means of assuring that the organization is something other than a mechanism for converting 11% funds into 11% returns.

ASSET MANAGEMENT

Capital Budgeting

A mechanism that enables managers to allocate capital to projects in ways that maximize the return to the organization is that of capital budgeting. Capital budgeting involves generation of investment proposals, estimating their value to the firm through one of several analytic techniques, and choosing projects based on the criterion measure selected until a minimum acceptance level (sometimes called a "hurdle rate of return") is reached or until the capital budget has been allocated.

Analytic methods used to estimate the relative value of projects to the firm include older methods such as the average rate of return, or the payback period, and more recent, more defensible methods such as the present-value and internal rate of return. Van Horne[4] recommends the use of the discounted cash flow method because it does not assume that savings or revenues generated will be invested at the same rates as those generated by the project, an assumption implicit in the internal-rate-of-return method. In addition, Van Horne suggests that a profitability index be used to arrive at a means of comparing projects using the discounted cash flow method. With this index, the present value of future net cash flows is divided by the initial cash outlay to provide a benefits/costs ratio. This method will provide a ranked list of projects, but it will not aid in decisions that involve mutually exclusive projects. In those cases, the calculation and comparison of present values for each project will suffice. The project with the greater net present value will be the appropriate choice.[5] Mutually exclusive projects can arise as financial and general managers examine alternative proposals for projects designed to accomplish the same objective (lease vs. buy, alternative construction and financing proposals for the same capital need).

[4] J. C. Van Horne, *Financial Management and Policy*, 4th Ed. (Englewood Cliffs, N.J.: Prentice-Hall, 1977).

[5] Van Horne, *Financial Management*, pp. 87–88.

EXERCISE 3–12

The Edwards Corporation is considering three different investment proposals. Each requires a cash outlay of $2,000. Project A has a life of 6 years, B a life of 4 years, and C a life of 5 years. Depreciation is handled on a straight-line basis, and no salvage value is estimated at the end of the life of any of the three projects. The tax rate is estimated at 40%, and the company's expected rate of return is 12%.

NET PRETAX CASH FLOWS (DEPRECIATION AND TAXES NOT INCLUDED):

		Project	
Years	*A*	*B*	*C*
1	600	800	800
2	600	900	800
3	700	900	700
4	700	900	700
5	800		600
6	900		

- Calculate the average rate of return, after depreciation and taxes for each project. (Hint: Average the net after-tax cash flows, then divide by the initial investment.)
- Calculate the payback period for each project. (Again, after depreciation and taxes.)
- Calculate the profitability index for each project. (Here you will need to use a table of present values.)
- If these are three *mutually exclusive* projects, such as three different proposals to do the same thing, which should be chosen? Why?

Asset Structure and Use

In addition to serving in the role of manager responsible for attending to providing funds, the financial manager is responsible for monitoring and managing the effective *use* of the assets provided (as is the general manager). Inadequate assets will cause problems in a variety of ways. If current assets are insufficient for normal operations, the firm may find itself unable to pay current obligations on a timely basis; may find itself out of stock of items, parts, or supplies needed by customers; and may find itself unable to meet competitor's terms of sale in the battle for customers.

When fixed assets are insufficient for effective operation of the business, one may find that plant and equipment operate at or over rated capacity. Costs, as a consequence, tend to elevate as overtime penalties are incurred, as scrap rates increase, and as lowered production from marginally productive equipment and workers becomes more evident.

Assets in excess of needs represent capital that is not being utilized effectively. A principal role in financial management is that of the oversight of the process of effectively using capital. Assets not employed in the generation of revenue will cause the net return to shareholders per dollar invested to be lower than would be the case if all assets were productively utilized. Several factors can contribute to a situation in which assets seem excessive. First, financial conservatism can result in (1) cash balances and inventories maintained at levels in excess of minimum as a means of reducing the risk of stockouts and (2) maintain also an ability to take advantage of purchasing opportunities. An unusually high level of fixed assets may reflect the acquisition (deliberate or inadvertent) of excess capacity or may represent the purchase of assets that might be better called investment properties rather than operating assets.

Several means of assessing the adequacy of current and fixed assets can be used effectively. When possible, a direct comparison of asset structures between and among competitors can provide an excellent perspective on the relative amounts of assets employed. In addition, another useful system can be employed to assess asset adequacy: Activity analysis, which we discussed in Chapter 2, is a means of examining the relationship between assets of various types as well as measures of business activity. Six or seven key ratios should provide sufficient information for effective financial management and control. Activity ratios for the key components of working capital would include

- Number of days disbursements in cash.
- Average collection period for accounts receivable.
- Inventory turnover.
- An overall measure of effectiveness: working capital turnover, or its inverse; working capital as a percentage of sales.

For fixed and total assets, the activity ratios of critical interest would be

- Net fixed assets turnover.
- Total assets turnover.
- Net return after tax on total assets.

These activity ratios can be most helpful in a general evaluation of asset management, but they must be used with some caution. First, although the underutilization of assets can hold down returns to shareholders, any organization that is undergoing expansion will show periods of underutilization as new facilities come on-line. In addition, in rapidly expanding businesses, underutilization of assets may very well mean that the firm is in a sound position to expand its share of market and thereby enhance its market position. Second, overutilization can indeed be costly, as our earlier comments indicate. Until such time as costs, in fact, begin the very sharp climb seen at the extremes of capacity utilization, however, the overall effectiveness of the firm should be at its *maximum* as the plant and equipment approach full capacity. In a stable or slowly growing industry, the truly effective manager of assets, therefore, would want to see asset utilization pushed to just that point where severe cost penalties will begin to be incurred. Where rapid growth is being experienced, the expansion can, and should be, pushed to a point somewhat below that critical cost explosion point to permit time for the construction or acquisition of new facilities.

EXERCISE 3-13

TATANIA PRODUCTS, INC.

	1984	*1985*	*1986*
Cash	$ 24	$ 37	$ 86
Accounts receivable	118	136	160
Inventory	140	149	185
Current Assets	282	322	431
Net Equipment	110	105	188
Net Buildings	260	244	320
Land	80	80	140
Fixed Assets	450	429	648
Total Assets	732	751	1079
Current Liabilities	87	106	219
Long-Term Debt	15	0	150
Owner's Equity	630	645	710
Total Liabilities & Owner's Equity	732	751	1079
Sales	2310	2786	3622
Net Profit	68	101	176

Industry Data (1982/1983)

Days' disbursements of cash	21.3 days
Average collection period	38.5 days
Working capital turnover	12.1 times
Fixed asset turnover	8.6 times
Total asset turnover	4.7 times
After-tax return on total assets	8.3%

- Assess asset utilization in 1984. Prepare for discussion in class or for a homework report.
- Assess asset utilization in 1985. Prepare for discussion in class or for a homework report.
- Discuss changes in asset utilization between 1984 and 1986. Prepare for written assignment or for oral presentation in class.

ALLIED CHEMICAL COMPANY

Allied Chemical is a large, diversified chemical manufacturing firm headquartered in Morristown, New Jersey, with manufacturing and processing plants located worldwide. Allied Chemical operations comprise six business segments.

1) Energy Products and Services—production includes liquefied petroleum gases (LPGs), liquefied natural gases (LNGs), residue gas, crude oil, and ethylene.
2) Inorganic Chemicals—production includes resins; hydrochloric, hydrofluoric, and nitric acids; soda and sodium by-products, and soda ash.
3) Organic Chemicals—production includes resins used in paints, enamels, and other coatings, and textiles.
4) Agricultural Chemicals—includes ammonia-based products used primarily for the manufacture and application of fertilizers.
5) Fibers—production includes nylon, rayon, and other products.
6) Other—production includes coal and coke operations, automotive safety restraints, paving materials, and packaging films.

This case was prepared by Terry Kingston and Billy Sexton under the supervision of Professor Sexton Adams, North Texas State University, and Professor Adelaide Griffin, Texas Woman's University. It is to be used as a basis for class discussion rather than to illustrate either effective or ineffective handling of an administrative situation.

The year 1979 was one of strong contrasts in performance among Allied's business segments. The energy products and services operations, the area of greatest growth in recent years, made a significant gain in sales and earnings. The fibers operations turned in another steady performance. However, these strong performances were offset by lower margins in many of the chemical product lines, substantially higher losses in coal and coke, and a significant loss in agricultural chemicals.

Allied's former chairman and chief executive officer (CEO), John T. Conner, retired under a mandatory retirement program on November 30, 1979. The question of management succession had been under active consideration of the Nominating and Review Committee of the Board of Directors. The committee recommended E. L. Hennessey, Jr., as president and CEO. In a recent discussion, Mr. Hennessey said,

> *The economic environment in 1980 will be a challenging one, with much of American industry caught in a profit squeeze between rising costs and competitive and governmental pressures to keep prices down.*

To deal with the economic uncertainties, Allied has not only moved aggressively to correct loss situations, but has cut costs and trimmed spending plans wherever possible without damaging long-range growth prospects. And Allied continues to believe our growth will pay off in improved earnings for our stockholders over the next few years.

However, Allied, only with other large chemical firms, is having problems in maintaining performance (*Exhibit 1*).

HISTORY

Allied Chemical Corporation was incorporated in New York on December 17, 1920, to consolidate the control of the Barrett Co., Genera; Chemical Co.; National Aniline and Chemical Co.; Semet-Solvay Co.; and the Solvay Process Co. It was called Allied Chemical and Dye Corporation, later changed to Allied Chemical Corporation in 1958. Allied presently operates over two-hundred plants, research laboratories, mines, quarries, and other facilities throughout the United States, Canada, and Europe. Allied operates these in an effort to reduce shipping costs, as most chemicals are shipped in bulk quantities. It also operates research and development laboratories in close proximity to manufacturing facilities.

The corporation is expanding its oil and gas operations and as of December 31, 1979, held leases or other interests in producing oil and gas properties in the: (1) United States, (2) British sector of the North Sea, (3) Canada, (4) Argentina, and (5) Indonesia. They also have interests in or rights to conduct exploratory activities on undeveloped acreage in the: (1) United States, (2) Canada, (3) British and West German sectors of the North Sea, (4) Brazil, (5) Italy, (6) Indonesia, (7) Australia, (8) Tunisia, (9) Bahrain, (10) Jamaica, and (11) onshore and offshore Spain.

ORGANIZATION

With the November 30, 1979, retirement of Chairman and CEO, John T. Conner, and the nomination and election of president and CEO, E. L. Hennessey, Jr., much of the time and energy of the Board of Directors has been diverted away from the task of managing the firm. However, with the nomination and election process completed, the board will be able to direct all attention to managing the company. The company is presently headed by a 15-member Board of Directors that includes 10 external members and 5 internal members. The Board of Directors, as of December 31, 1979, is made up of

EXHIBIT 1
Allied profitability (dollars in millions, except per share amounts)

	1979	*1978*	*1977*	*1976*
Sales and Operating Revenues	$4,332	$3,268	$2,922	$2,630
Net Income	$ 11	$ 120	$ 135	$ 126
Net Income per Share, Common	$ 0.20	$ 4.25	$ 4.93	$ 4.52

Allied Chemical Annual Report, 1980, Allied Chemical Corporation, Morristown, N. J.

Source: Although sales continue to increase, net income continues to decline. Allied along with other large chemical firms is facing hardships, including foreign competition, foreign taxes, governmental regulations, and environmental costs that will only add to the cost-profit squeeze now being felt.

E. L. Hennessey, Jr., Chairman and CEO

John T. Conner, former Chairman and CEO

Joseph B. Collinson, Chairman and CEO, Textron, Inc., diversified manufacturing company

John P. Fishwick, President and CEO, Norfolk and Western Railway

E. Burke Giblin, Chairman of the Executive Committee, Warner-Lambert Company

Robert T. Mulcahy, former President, Allied Chemical Corporation

Robert T. Perkins, retired Chairman of the Executive Committee, Metropolitan Life Insurance Company

Robert R. Shinn, President and CEO, Citibank and Citicorp

Alexander B. Trowbridge, Vice-Chairman, Allied Chemical

Brian D. Forrow, Vice President and General Counsel, Allied Chemical

Roger H. Morley, President, American Express Company

Charles W. Nichols, private investor

John D. Glover, Chairman of the Board, Cambridge Research Institute, Inc., business consultants

Helen S. Meyner, Director, Prudential Insurance Co. of America

Stanley P. Porter, retired partner of Arthur Young & Co

In a recent discussion, President and CEO E. L. Hennessey, Jr., said:

We plan to continue our strategy of redeveloping assets in those businesses we believe have the best future growth potential for Allied Chemical. We will continue to divest ourselves of operations which are marginal in profitability or which for other reasons do not fit into our long-range plans.

Allied Chemical is divided into eight divisions in the six major business segments. Each division is directed by a divisional president who is responsible for the day-to-day operations of his division as well as communicating with the Board of Directors. The current organizational chart is seen in Exhibit 2.

MARKETING

Allied has seen the oil and gas operations grow dramatically in sales and operating income as production continues to grow. The fibers business made significant gains in sales and earnings as 1979 sales were essentially at capacity and work was started to increase capacity at two major production facilities. However, earnings of many of Allied's chemical businesses suffered because of industry overcapacity, which kept process below levels needed to cover rising production and overhead costs. (see Exhibit 3)

CHEMICAL INDUSTRY OUTLOOK

Tightening supply conditions sparked by the Iranian oil curtailment early in the year created unusually strong demand for U.S. manufactured petrochemicals, plastics, fibers, and other products through much of 1979. The demand will lead to increased profits, which should provide enough momentum to allow chemical firms to report a creditable profit performance for 1980. Sales of chemicals and allied products are forecast to rise to $145 billion in 1979, up from $130 billion in 1978, and with estimated sales of $160 billion in 1980 (Exhibit 4).

However, major challenges and opportunities face the chemical industry as it faces a new decade. Mr. Hennessey, CEO of Allied Chemical

EXHIBIT 2
Partial Organizational Chart, Allied Chemical Corporation

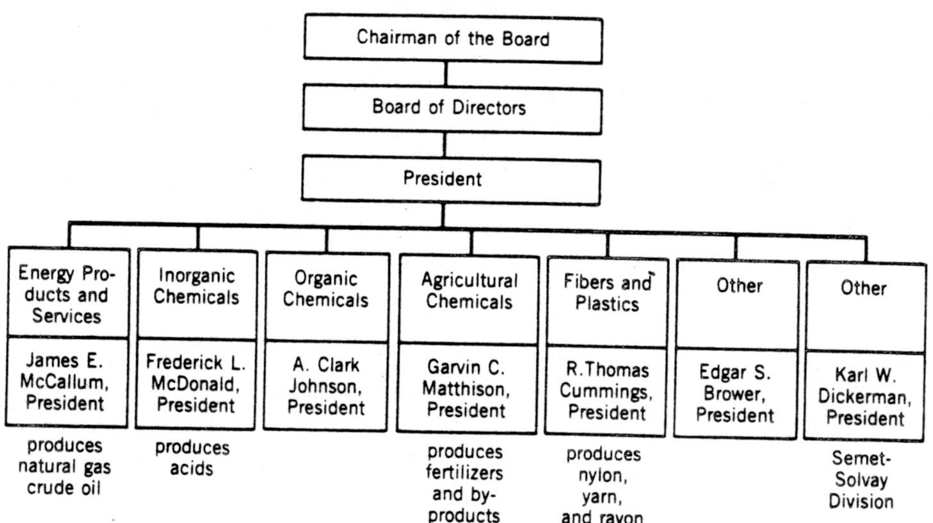

Source: Company records.

EXHIBIT 3
Net sales and income by products group (in millions)

	1979		*1978*		*1977*		*1976*	
	Total sales	*Oper. income*	*Total sales*	*Oper. income*	*Total sales*	*Oper. income*	*Total sales*	*Oper. income*
Energy Products and Services	$1,369	$392	$ 948	$307	$ 676	$193	$ 461	$ 31
Inorganic Chemicals	775	22	657	66	623	80	573	91
Organic Chemicals	725	6	537	15	529	31	573	63
Agricultural Chemicals	155	—	162	(31)	180	—	185	38
Fibers and Plastics	940	120	497	85	441	63	380	60
Other	368	24	467	(41)	474	(37)	458	2
Total	4,332	564	3,268	401	2,923	330	2,630	285

Source: Allied Chemical Corporation Annual Report, 1979.

Corporation, believes the industry has some major concerns, including:

> *One, the tendency for state-controlled nations to subsidize their chemical industries and seek markets for their output at any price; two, the looming development of a petrochemical industry by the Organization of Petroleum Exporting Countries [OPEC] nations in the second half of the decade and the effect this will have on U. S. companies by foreigners through purchases of outstanding stock.*

CHEMICAL INDUSTRY PROFITS

According to John Baker of Dow Chemical:

> *Earnings for most of the large chemical firms should be up about three percent in 1980, and miscellaneous chemicals should have earnings increase above five percent.*

In a recent conversation, Mr. E. L. Hennessey, Jr., of Allied Chemical said:

> *With competition increasing domestically and with more firms trying to capture a larger share of the export market before it shrinks, a moderation or possibly a reversal of recent price increases will be necessary. Prices for all chemicals and related products have risen at a fifteen percent annual rate compared to twenty percent for the previous year. On the other hand, manufacturers are faced with an unrelenting climb in raw material costs, energy and labor costs which should cause profits to decline for the industry. For 1979, the return on sales for the chemical industry was 6.8 percent and should be about 6.3 percent in 1980, and slower price increases should be seen as demand will remain soft through 1980.*

EXHIBIT 4
Chemical industry sales (billions of dollars)

Year	*Industry sales*	*Allied chemical sales*	*Allied's percent of industry sales*
1969	$ 48.3	$1.316	2.73%
1970	49.3	1.248	2.53
1971	51.9	1.325	2.55
1972	57.4	1.501	2.61
1973	65.0	1.664	2.56
1974	83.7	2.215	2.65
1975	89.7	2.333	2.60
1976	104.0	2.629	2.53
1977	118.1	2.922	2.48
1978	130.0	3.268	2.51
1979	145.0	4.332	2.99
1980 (est.)	160.0	5.400	3.40

Source: "Chemicals, Current Analysis," *Standard & Poor's Survey*, July 3, 1980.

CHEMICAL INDUSTRY PRODUCTION

An early projection of 1980 domestic production of chemicals and related products (on a dollar-value basis) calls for stable growth of about 12% compared to the 1973–78 average of 15%. The area most likely to show gains is industrial chemicals, aided by strong demand from foreign countries arising from lower costs for U.S. manufacturers. Other sectors that should do better than average are cosmetics, pharmaceuticals, and industrial inorganic chemicals. With moderate growth in demand, excess capacities should be gradually absorbed and allow for near-optimum operating rates for producers.

RESEARCH AND DEVELOPMENT

In the 1960s, U.S. industry spent close to 3% of sales for research and development, but spent only 1.87% in 1978. A substantial portion of the decline in recent years may be attributable to the 1974 tax code revision, which redefined research and development outlays. Generally, research and development costs are now limited to those expenses that involve the technological aspects of product and process development and that extend knowledge of physical sciences useful in commercial production. Specifically excluded are costs pertaining to routine product improvement, market research, test marketing, seasonal style changes, quality control, and engineering follow-through in production. Also excluded are legal costs related to patents and costs associated with their sale or development outlays (Exhibit 5).

FINANCIAL

According to *Chemical Week* magazine, earnings of the six leading chemical companies are expected to have flat-to-moderate growth in 1980, after an 11% increase in 1979, and an 18% increase in 1978. The chemical industry enjoyed strong market conditions in 1979, but these conditions are expected to weaken in 1980 as the company slumps. In recent years, excess

EXHIBIT 5
Research and development outlays (as a percentage of total sales)

	1979	*1978*
Office Equipment	5.70	5.65
Health Care	4.25	4.30
Leisure Time	4.20	4.50
Aerospace	2.75	2.70
Automobile	2.60	2.50
Electronics	2.55	2.45
Chemicals	2.45	2.55
Machinery	1.90	2.05
Rubber Fabricating	1.65	1.70
Home Furnishings	1.60	1.70
Allied Chemical Corp.	1.87	1.77
Composite Average (all industries)	1.83	1.87

Source: "R & D Costs," *Standard and Poor's Industry Surveys*, September 6, 1980.

capacity hampered the implementation of adequate price relief and squeezed profit margins. The tight supply conditions that prevailed in 1979 created a seller's market and enabled producers to institute long-awaited price increases.

Capital spending is expected to increase 13% in 1980, which will only keep up with inflation. Expenditures for investments in new plant and equipment is expected to remain under 10% for the third year in succession. A review of industry capital spending as a percentage of sales is presented in Exhibit 6.

In mid-1979, the Treasury Department announced that chemical companies would be allowed to reduce to seven-and-one-half years (from nine years) the shortest period over which chemical companies can depreciate their equipment. The new rules should encourage greater spending for new plant expansion.

Industry profitability, measured as a return on stockholder's equity, remained strong at approximately 13%. The dividend pay-out ratio is expected to rise in the next few years, owing to an endless quest for growth capital.

EXHIBIT 6
Capital spending as a percentge of sales

Year	*Percent*
1969	10.9
1970	11.6
1971	10.6
1972	8.9
1973	9.9
1974	11.9
1975	12.8
1976	12.7
1977	11.6
1978	9.8
1979	9.8
1980 (Projected)	13.0

Source: "Chemicals, Current Analysis," *Standard and Poor's Industry Surveys*, September 6, 1980.

An additional capital expense for the chemical industry will be in the area of environmental protection. Stricter laws and regulations passed in recent years will continue to drive experimental costs upward at an increasing rate. This is evidenced in environmental spending at Allied Chemical (Exhibit 7).

EXHIBIT 7
Allied chemical environmental costs (in millions)

Year	*Expense*	*Percentage of Sales*
1975	27	1.15%
1976	29	1.10
1977	35	1.20
1978	72	2.20
1979	101	3.10

Source: Allied Chemical Corporation Annual Report, 1980.

ENVIRONMENTAL POLLUTION AND OTHER LEGAL DIFFICULTIES

Kepone

Kepone is a chlorinated organic compound similar to DDT. Allied Chemical produced the pesticide from 1966 to 1973 at its Hopewell, Virginia, chemical plant. In 1973, Virgil Hundtofte and William Moore, former employees of Allied, formed Life Science Products Company. This company had a total-process contract with Allied to produce Kepone solely for Allied until it was closed on July 24, 1975, by the Virginia Department of Health. Seventy of the plants 150 employees showed symptoms of Kepone poisoning, which included tremors, slurring of speech, chest and joint pains. Disposal of Kepone by Allied and by Life Science Products Company contaminated a large portion of the James River. According to the U.S. Attorney's Office at Richmond, Allied and Life Science actually dumped Kepone into the river. In December 1975, the river was closed to fishing because of the poison being traced to fish caught from the James.

On October 6, 1976, Federal Judge Robert R. Merhige, Jr., fined Allied Chemical Corporation $13,375,000 for its part in polluting the James River with Kepone. Merhige was quoted as saying, "I hope that the size of the fine will deter employees of other companies from polluting the environment." Besides the employees of Life Science suffering from various nerve disorders, the fishermen on the James lost their means to a livelihood by authorities banning the sale of fish caught from the James. Claims of the employees and the fishermen totaled around $200 million in civil suits against Allied. Life Science Products was imposed a fine of $3.8 million. William Moore and Virgil Hundtofte were fined $25,000 each. After the pronounced sentence, Allied's John T. Conner (who was chairman at the time) stated, "We are pleased that the court has found Allied Chemical not guilty of charges of aiding and abetting Life Science Products Company and conspiring with it to break the law." However, Allied pleaded *nolo contendere* to 940 counts of pumping chemicals into the river. Of the 940 counts, 144 were dismissed against Allied. Connor pointed out that only 312 of the counts involved Kepone and 628 covered two low-toxic biodegradable chemicals, TAIC and THEIC.

Allied is not only being held responsible for polluting the James River with toxic chemicals, but it is being held responsible for dredging of about 100 miles of the James. Approximately 100 miles of the James was closed to commercial fishing by state health authorities. The estimated cost to Allied of dredging the James has been around half a billion dollars. Problems exist after dredging the James such as what to do with the soil contaminated with Kepone.

Allied has run into problems with the disposal of the contaminated soil. Allied was planning to dispose around 100,000 pounds of soil and equipment contaminated with Kepone by burying it in a 16-story-deep missile silo in Idaho. However, the state of Idaho rejected the idea of burying the soil in the abandoned silo near Boise. Burning the Kepone stored in barrels turned out to be a nonworkable solution because of the dangerous gases that would be released into the atmosphere. One of the gases released by burning Kepone is a deadly type of gas similar to arsenic fumes. The negative results of the burning have put a damper on Allied's plan of using a mobile incinerator to dispose of contaminated materials in Hopewell. Further plans for continued action in disposing of the Kepone contaminated soil by Allied include finding locations where the material can be safely buried and disposing of the liquid material by chemical-type reactions that will leave a safe residue.

Allied set up an original fund of $8 million to help solve the problems caused by its Hopewell Kepone-making operations. The Virginia Environmental Endowment of $8 million, according to Allied, is to "alleviate the effects of Kepone on the environment and on those whose livelihoods have been impaired by it." The endowment is a separate independent organization whose Board of Directors is appointed by Judge Robert R. Merhige, Jr. The endowment board will, according to Allied, "fund scientific research projects to implement remedial efforts and other scientific programs and measures (including financial and economic assistance in the form of loans or such) as the Board of Directors in its sole discretion shall deem appropriate." Allied concedes that the net financial drain to the corporation will probably be around $4 million rather than $8 million because the endowment is considered a charitable contribution. Judge Merhige points out, however, that the endowment does not affect civil suits against Allied by former plant workers claiming injury from unsafe plant conditions at Hopewell or civil suits against Allied by James River watermen for loss of income owing to the closing of the river to all commercial fishing. Allied hopes that by creating the endowment, it can express its sincerity in alleviating problems caused by the Kepone pollution.

Before leaving the Kepone-related circumstances, it should be pointed out that in the court proceeding, Allied Chemical's experts stated that Environmental Protection Agency (EPA) levels for action of Kepone pollution could quadruple without changing the safety factor recommended by EPA's own experts. Allied Chemical's experts also suggested that raising the action level for fish from 0.1 parts per million to at least 0.4 parts per million would be more realistic and consistent with data and would alleviate some of the economic hardship caused by "unnecessarily severe levels." Allied Chemical's experts also claimed that the action level for Kepone had been set at one far more severe than other chemicals that were of far greater potential danger to the environment.

Armco Suit

Allied supplies blast furnace coke and coke-oven gas to Armco's steel-production plant at Ashland, Kentucky. Armco filed a suit against Allied for $32 million for Allied's failure to deliver coke and coke-oven gas as specified in a contract with Armco's plant. The suit also asked for $185 million for damages that would occur through 1982. Allied denied breach of contract because of certain contingencies within the contract. These contingencies relieve performance by either party because of equipment failures, labor problems, and failure of supply materials. Allied also claimed that Armco caused operational problems at Allied's Ashland plant by supplying coal of inferior quality. All of Allied's output goes to Armco; likewise, Armco furnishes all of the coal used by Allied. Coke battery damage and excessive demurrage was claimed against Armco by Allied as a result of the inferior coal. After court proceedings lasting most of 1979, Allied was found guilty of charges leveled by Armco. Allied was held responsible to Armco for an initial $34 million, but not long-term damages amounting to $185 million from 1978 through 1980. Allied appealed the verdict; however, the appeal was not successful as other court proceedings arrived at the same verdict. Allied paid the fine and suspended coke business transactions involved with Amco.

ALLIED OPERATIONAL STRATEGIES

Plant Modifications

Semet-Solvay is a division of Allied that manages the company's coal and coke operation. In 1977, Allied spent $45 million to rehabilitate a foundry coke plant in Detroit, Michigan. The division's president said, "Rehabilitation of our foundry coke battery in Detroit will serve not only to increase the facility's capacity, but also should serve to end concerns among area residents that the plant is a source of environmental contamination." The project brought the screening capacity to 700,000 tons annually. Not only did this action by Allied improve environmental conditions, it includes improvements in coal preheating, coal preparation and by-product recovery from operations. Allied is the largest producer of coke in the United States. Operations by Allied's management to revitalize older plants in terms of environmental safety and energy savings is an attempted strategy to meet environmental expectations along with decreasing long-run cost of operations.

Energy Endeavors

Allied's first phase of oil and gas exploration development in the North Sea was Piper Field during 1976. Allied owned 20% interest. This 20% cost to Allied was $250 million. John T. Conner, Allied Chemical's former chairman said, "Allied's commitment to participate heavily in the development of oil and gas in the North Sea was made over five years ago and has had a high priority among its capital spending programs and strategy-planning efforts." Allied also owns 20% interest in the Claymore Field in the North Sea. In late 1980, production of 250,000 barrels per day from the Piper Field and 170,000 barrels of oil from the Claymore Field will reach peak levels for both fields. Mr. Connor stated, "When the two fields reach peak production levels, Allied Chemical will experience substantially increased cash flows. In addition, the flow of crude will provide a raw material back-up for Allied's expanding petrochemicals-based operations." The United Kingdom's energy corporation, British National Oil Corporation, has the option to buy up to 51% of the crude oil and natural gas derived from the Piper and Claymore fields. Conner points out that this arrangement protects the legitimate interest of the United Kingdom. Allied's participation in the North Sea represents the company's largest single endeavor among its oil and gas operations.

Although the North Sea ventures are the largest for Allied in oil and gas, other ventures such as the Salou Field in the Mediterranean Sea off the coast of Tarragona, Spain, hold significant promise of 15 million barrels. Allied's Union Texas/Espana division is involved not only in the Salou Fields off Spain, but also in areas around the Bay of Biscay north of Spain. In Indonesia, Allied Chemical and its partners have natural gas production wells in the Bodak Field in east Kalimantan (Borneo). Allied's position and strategy involving energy can best be summarized by Mr. Conner's statement, "Clearly, the cash flows derived from the company's participation in these ventures will be most impressive. Moreover, they serve to vindicate a long-term business strategy of our corporation."

Research and Development in Solar Energy

Allied's shift in strategy to all energy fields can be expressed by research and development into the area of solar energy. Allied's research and development division invented a photochemical diode device that simplifies the conversion of sunlight energy into chemical energy. This discovery has been a leading force in the solar energy development and utilization field. The process uses small wafers that create specific chemical reactions when suspended in a chemical liquid and exposed to sunlight. Allied's Materials Research Center actively pursued practical goals of development for the diode structures. These actions by the Materials Research Center developed into high efficiencies for light-energy conversion for the solar energy field along with long-term stabilities and low-cost manufacturers' units for the solar energy conversion industry. Likewise, Allied benefits from the low cost of manufacture and long-term stability of sales of diodes, as many energy experts look to energy from solar conversion for future needs.

Divestments

As shown previously, Allied Chemical's long-term strategies involve concentrating on improving and expanding the energy aspects of the business. For the last five years, Allied's strategy has been to divest itself of the unprofitable aspects of the business. For example, in 1977, Allied Chemical sold its organic pigments to Harmon Colors Corporation. The sale included all manufacturing facilities, laboratories, and sales offices, which were staffed by approximately 325 employees. By this type of divesture, Allied completely disengaged itself from the organic pigments business, which had turned out to be unprofitable for the past three years. Allied's divestment of unprofitable business segments from 1977 to the present along with its energy expansion reversed a declining shift in earnings per share to an increasing value for earnings per share.

As stated previously, Allied divestment itself from unprofitable business aspects from 1977 to present. By divestment and expansion of their participation in oil and gas, Allied's profits from continuing operations more than tripled in 1980 from 1979. Other chemical firms showed a significant drop in earnings (Exhibit 8).

The $123.7-million loss of Allied in the third quarter of 1979 was a net loss after nonrecurring, after-tax charges of $163.2 million to cover losses connected with the divestiture of several operations and other one-time costs.

All four companies had small sales increases for the third quarter, with Allied having the largest, 6% from $1.25 billion to $1.32 billion. Celanese's sales rose 1% from $778 million to $785 million, and Dow's sales increased 4% from $2.43 billion to $2.52 billion. Rohn & Haas's sales were up 3%, from $391.9 million to $403.8 million. Exhibit 9 shows that except for Allied, the net income of all three chemical companies first nine months of 1980, as compared to 1979, had a negative change.

Rohm & Haas Chairman, Vincent L. Gregory, Jr., attributed the company's nine-month drop in earnings to a drop in volume of shipments. G. J. Williams, Dow's financial vice-president, said, "The third quarter was a definite turnaround in the U.S. in virtually all parts of the economy." However, Williams said that business activity outside the United States, particularly key European markets, had slowed drastically, therefore, causing Rohm & Haas and Dow to reduce operations in order to reduce inventory. All companies emphasized a drastic decline in demand for chemicals with an improvement in fibers demand. As an example of industry conditions, Celanese fiber profits were up 36%. However, profits from the chemicals business were down 62% with profits from plastics and specialties off 70%. Edward L. Hennessy, Jr., Allied's current president and CEO; attributed Allied's higher earnings to sales in fibers and the oil and gas industry. Hennessey expressed his opinion that problems faced in the chemical industry because of poor economic conditions demonstrate the need for large corporations such as Allied to diversify and not depend on one specific industry for survival. Hennessey said that the reason for chemical and plastic sales decline was due to poor economic conditions worldwide and especially the auto

EXHIBIT 8
Third Quarter Net Income

	1980		*1979*		
	In Millions	*Per Share*	*In Millions*	*Per Share*	*% Change*
Allied	$ 66.2	$1.80	($123.7)	($4.35)	
Celanese	$ 21.0	$1.43	$ 37.0	$2.47	−43%
Dow	$160.5	$0.88	$198.4	$1.09	−19%
Rohm & Haas	$ 22.6	$1.75	$ 29.2	$2.26	−14%

Source: Wall Street Journal, October 17, 1980.

EXHIBIT 9
Nine months net income

	1980		*1979*		
	In Millions	*Per Share*	*In Millions*	*Per Share*	*% Change*
Allied	$207.5	$5.88	($ 56.6)	($2.00)	
Celanese	$ 82.0	$5.51	$114.0	$7.67	−28.0%
Dow	$562.2	$3.09	$589.6	$3.25	− 5.0%
Rohm & Haas	$ 76.7	$5.95	$ 84.6	$6.56	− 9.3%

Source: Wall Street Journal, October 17, 1980.

industry recession from 1979 to the present. Hennessey stated that the most important aspect of the third-quarter results for Allied is that 90% of Allied's profit from operations came from its oil and gas enterprises. He also pointed out the direct link of profitability to oil and gas operations through Allied's third-quarter reports. Allied's oil and gas endeavors accounted for 32% of sales whereas chemicals accounted for 24%. However, 90% of Allied's third-quarter-operation profits was from oil and gas.

Future Operations

Allied Chemical has been in a state of transformation for the past five years. This transformation has involved divestiture of certain operations and a strategy of concentrating in areas of oil and gas. As can be seen readily for the third quarter of 1980, Allied's financial strength is improving on the background of its oil and gas operations. The move five years ago to divest of unprofitable business and acquire business strength in oil and gas is turning out to be the successful corporate strategy for Allied. Likewise, W. R. Grace is a chemical company that reported a third-quarter 1980 net income of $68 million. This was up from $44.5 million during three quarters of 1979. John Spelling, Grace's chief financial officer, explained that Grace's oil and gas operations and its oilfield service business helped push the natural resources segment earnings up to 15% in the quarter from the same time in 1979. As a result of the auto industry in the United States from 1979 to the present drastically declining in production, the demand for chemicals and plastics has been drastically reduced. Likewise, because of a slowdown in the economy of the United States along with a slowdown of key European markets, the chemical industries demand has become a great deal less.

Chemical companies have also faced costly capital expenditures to upgrade plants to meet EPA requirements. For example, Allied is bearing the cost of clean-up and lawsuits stemming from Kepone pollution, but also the negative feelings toward Allied. Chemical companies face difficult times with capital-intensive plants producing below capacity because of falling demand for chemicals. Existence of slowing-down economies in the United States and foreign vital markets does not show a promising increase in demand for chemicals. However, the oil and gas industry will continue to be of prime importance with the energy crisis that faces the world.

EXHIBIT 10
Selected financial data

	1979	*1978*	*1977*	*1976*	*1975*	*1974*
Plant Asset Additions (millions)	$ 475	$ 502	$ 465	$ 352	$ 314	$ 306
Net Sales (millions)	4,330	3,270	2,920	2,630	2,330	2,220
Net Income (millions)	11	120	135	117	116	144
Cash Dividend Per Share	2.00	1.85	1.80	1.80	1.80	1.53
Rate of Return on Revenue	.25%	3.7%	4.6%	4.4%	5.0%	6.5%
Rate of Return on Stockholders' Equity	.86%	9.7%	11.8%	11.2%	11.6%	15.8%
Rate of Return on Total Capital	.64%	7.2%	8.4%	8.0%	8.6%	10.8%

Source: Allied's 1979 Annual Financial Statement.

EXHIBIT 11
Allied's geographical operations (in millions)

	Year	*United States*	*Canada and Europe*	*Other*	*Total*
Net Sales	1979	$3,306	$712	$314	$4,332
	1978	2,606	500	162	3,268
	1977	2,530	351	42	2,923
Net Income	1979	(100)	75	36	11
	1978	7	76	37	120
	1977	54	59	22	135
Assets	1979	3,062	825	322	4,209
	1978	2,544	629	164	3,337
	1977	2,430	544	96	3,070

Source: Allied's 1979 Annual Financial Statement.

EXHIBIT 12
Consolidated earning statement (year ending December 31)

	Sales and Operating Revenue	Operating Income	Depreciation Amortization and Depletion	Income Taxes	Fixed Charges	Times Interest Earned	Net Income	Earnings Per Share	Dividends Per Share
1970	1,249[a]	191	120	14	28	2.36	43	1.56	1.00
1971	1,326	207	119	19	29	2.59	52	1.88	1.10
1972	1,500	231	117	31	30	3.06	65	2.38	1.20
1973	1,665	271	109	54	29	4.30	95	2.29	1.29
1974	2,216	363	115	82	28	6.32	144	3.26	1.53
1975	2,333	352	129	73	40	3.88	116	5.17	1.80
1976	2,630	368	136	63	45	3.80	126	4.52	1.80
1977	2,923	446	164	104	55	3.50	135	4.93	1.80
1978	3,268	534	203	148	69	2.75	120	4.25	1.85
1979	4,332	921	225	385	102	2.73	11	0.20	2.00

Source: Allied's 1979 Annual Financial Statement.
Note: [a]Millions $, except Times Interest Earned and Earnings Per Share.

EXHIBIT 13
Allied's financial and operating data

	1979	1978	1977	1976	1975	1974	1973	1972
Current Assets/Current Liabilities	1.21	1.43	1.69	1.96	2.14	1.93	2.43	2.81
% Cash and Securities to Current Assets	7.79	7.22	5.22	7.53	12.24	11.34	19.67	17.33
% Inventory to Current Assets	37.28	36.02	39.53	44.83	43.28	44.86	35.52	34.23
Capitalization								
% Long Term Debt	43.67	36.81	33.63	32.26	32.66	26.78	29.09	32.25
% Common Stock and Equity	56.33	63.19	66.37	67.74	67.34	73.22	70.91	62.75
Sales/Inventory	7.19	9.79	9.03	7.89	7.68	7.70	7.34	7.31
Sales/Receivables	5.73	6.56	6.71	7.74	7.86	8.21	6.06	5.32
% Net Income to Total Assets	0.26	3.72	4.71	4.64	4.97	6.97	4.83	3.62

EXHIBIT 14
Allied chemical comparative consolidated balance sheet, as of December 31 (in thousands of dollars)

Balance Sheets	*1978*	*1977*	*1976*	*1975*	*1974*	*1973*	*1972*
Accounts and notes receivable, net	498,209	435,759	339,838	296,991	269,838	274,537	281,990
Inventories	333,701	323,615	333,247	303,941	287,919	226,855	205,194
Other current assets	27,678	16,589	14,321	15,376	11,298	11,654	8,457
Total Current assets	926,494	818,683	743,369	702,287	641,843	638,683	599,531
Marketable securities, cost	3,096	3,396	3,538	3,640	3,728	3,861	3,956
Investments and advances, cost	165,316	134,649	128,612	133,263	113,284	88,881	80,511
Property, plant, and equipment cost	3,739,889	3,450,819	3,129,926	2,901,046	2,703,504	2,500,660	2,381,383
Less: Res. for depreciation, etc.	1,698,480	1,641,446	1,587,589	1,534,056	1,494,220	1,455,727	1,391,037
Net property amount	2,041,409	1,809,369	1,542,337	1,366,990	1,209,284	1,044,933	990,346
Goodwill, patents, licenses & def. chgs.	91,634	106,065	109,703	122,026	91,903	85,034	84,053
Total	3,227,949	2,872,162	2,527,559	2,328,206	2,060,044	1,861,392	1,758,397
Liabilities							
Accounts payable and accrued liabilities	438,770	388,643	313,214	266,919	254,143	218,589	182,365
Notes and loans payable	47,995	33,176	32,272	25,047	12,411	16,087	8,965
Taxes accrued	144,738	52,963	22,051	24,190	53,148	28,067	22,410
Interest accrued	15,328	10,662	11,309	10,814	7,818	—	—
Long-term debt due in one year	—	—	—	—	4,726	—	—
Total current liabilities	646,831	485,444	378,846	326,970	332,246	262,743	213,740

Long-term debt	741,008	606,612	527,613	503,523	354,071	354,228	383,856
Res. for pensions and contingencies	67,549	70,292	71,109	48,787	61,887	74,086	84,900
Deferred income	46,386	37,369	37,721	26,994	27,894	18,985	19,086
Deferred income tax	247,852	252,197	200,596	170,365	130,544	106,914	91,170
Capital lease obligations	205,999	222,939	203,672	213,366	184,977	180,860	139,178
Common stock (par $9)	375,464	365,932	364,305	364,305	364,305	364,305	364,305
Retained earnings	910,450	846,804	763,508	696,692	631,159	530,117	475,852
Total stockholders' equity	1,285,914	1,212,736	1,127,813	1,060,997	995,464	894,422	840,157
Less: Treasury stock	13,590	15,427	19,813	22,796	27,039	30,846	33,690
Net stockholders' equity	1,272,324	1,197,309	1,108,000	1,038,201	968,425	863,576	806,467
Total	3,227,949	2,872,162	2,527,550	2,328,206	2,060,044	1,861,392	1,758,397
Net Current assets	279,663	333,239	364,523	386,131	309,599	375,940	385,791
Property Account—Analysis							
Additions at cost	502,040	464,638	351,613	313,319	302,217	193,812	147,462
Retirements or sales	212,966	143,749	122,733	116,099	101,116	74,535	113,512
Other additions	—	—	—	322	6,641	—	—
Depreciation, Depl., and Res.—Analysis							
Additions chgd. to income	202,975	164,307	145,049	136,899	123,276	116,469	123,993
Retire renewals changed to res.	145,941	110,430	91,516	97,013	84,783	51,779	76,411
Other deductions	—	—	—	—	1,685	—	—
Other deductions	—	—	—	—	—	16,666	16,947

EXERCISE 3–14

Refer to the concepts found in Chapter 2. Assess and develop a critique of the capitalization of Allied Chemical (sources of funds). Note changes over the past three years, if any. Prepare for class presentation or as a written assignment.

EXERCISE 3–15

Refer to the concepts found in Chapter 2 and develop an analysis of the structure and utilization of the assets of Allied Chemical. Note changes over the past three years, if any. Prepare for class presentation or as a written assignment.

MEETING ANTICIPATED NEEDS WITH APPROPRIATE SOURCES OF FUNDS

The matching principle is a key principle in traditional financial management. It is stated as: "Finance short-term needs with short-term sources, and finance long-term needs with long-term sources."[6] The practical explanation underlying this principle is that if the firm were to finance long-term needs with short-term sources of funds, it would find it necessary to reborrow several times over during the life of the asset in order to sustain the acquisition. In doing so, the firm faces the expense of additional one-time borrowing costs and the risk of high rates that may be charged to borrowers at some future time.

Given the cycles in needs for current assets, the use of longer-term sources of funds such as bonds or stock issues to finance cyclical needs for working capital might mean a surplus of current or liquid assets during slack periods. Because the need for current assets will increase in the next peak period, these funds can only be used inefficiently for relatively low-yielding, readily marketable securities.

There are exceptions to the matching principle, just as there are exceptions to most other principles. As we mentioned in Chapter 2, some companies' balance sheets display a position of *negative* working capital. In this situation, short-term creditors, for a variety of reasons, extend credit beyond the value of current assets. In effect, short-term sources thereby provide funds for the financing of long-term assets. In a positive way, *suppliers* might permit this situation to exist if the payment record of the firm has been good, the profit margin attractive, and the growth pattern strong. They become, one might say, participants in the growth of the firm's future.

Commercial creditors might also be found to be the principal suppliers of short-term credit where a negative working-capital situation exists. The rates of return on most commercial debt, however, are probably not sufficient for this category of creditor to undertake extensions of credit with profit as a principal motive. The commercial lender might extend the credit, however, when the additional debt is seen

[6] Schall and Haley, *Introduction to Financial Management*, p. 559.

as the only practicable means of preventing financial collapse for a troubled borrower.

A second situation in which an explicit match between current sources of funds and current assets is not appropriate is in providing for long-term, or permanent, current assets. This may sound like a contradiction in terms, but let us reflect on the fact that the vast majority of companies operate with a positive level of working capital. If, for example, the "standard" 2:1 current ratio were in fact the current ratio in a company, then fully *half* of the firm's current assets are net working capital. If the firm, as a matter of financial policy and practice, maintains a 2:1 current ratio, then a *permanent feature* of the company's balance sheet will be an amount of net working capital equal to one-half of the current assets. In some respects, this permanent working capital is much like a minimum balance in a bank account. The dollars flow in and flow out, but a minimum balance is always found in the account. The depositor has at least that amount *permanently invested* in the bank account. The financial manager must consider the need for permanent working capital as much a part of the permanent asset structure as other assets used for long-term growth and development. Financing this permanent need can and should be undertaken with long-term sources of funds.

INTEGRATING FINANCIAL ELEMENTS INTO A FINANCIAL STRATEGY

The assembly of financial elements into a coherent financial strategy that is supportive of the primary mission and objectives of the firm involves a series of analytic steps, then the development of a coordinated plan for financial development. The process is one of a contingency approach to strategy formulation. The major contingencies are: the chosen industry, its technology, the stage of development of chosen product/service offerings, the current and prospective status of financial markets, and the stature or reputation of the firm in the immediate and larger financial community. The role of the financial and general managers in this process is that of analysts and diagnosticians first and then that of strategy formulators and decision makers as the strategy takes shape and is implemented.

ROLE OF CHOSEN INDUSTRY AND TECHNOLOGY

The industry and customers chosen by strategy formulators for directing the products and attentions of the firm form a first set of contingencies within which managers must work in the development of financial strategies. If, for example, the industry chosen is that of agricultural implement manufacture, then the seasonal nature of agriculture and the cash flow patterns of firms involved in this business will, in turn, prescribe funding patterns for the supplying firm. Seasonal patterns in sales, even where demand is derived from that of the business of one's customers, will require one of two responses. In the first, the firm must have an ability to *adjust production levels* significantly in response to the cycle, expanding and contracting the scale of operations and using layoff and recall procedures to provide only the manpower needed for the existing level of sales. The second response calls for substantial financial resources to provide support to a production pattern that is *kept at a relatively constant level* while sales revenues rise and fall. With this approach, employment and the scale of operations is held relatively level, and inventories are used as a buffer.

In another industry, ethical drug manufacture, the competition for market share within the industry has resulted in all manufacturers engaging in extensive research. In some cases, the research program must extend over 8 or 10 years or more before the product can be produced for general consumption. This lengthy development period, characteristic of this industry, again calls for significantly higher levels of current assets than might be the case where organizational research and development activities (and costs) are much lower. Cash is needed to fund research activities, to pay for development costs, and to provide for exploratory marketing ventures. Reserves of cash are also needed to fund the extensive promotional efforts used to obtain rapid acceptance of new products and to distribute them to mass markets.

In addition to the need for current assets, advances in technology in the drug industry have called for frequent expenditures for state-of-the-art production equipment. Although not regarded as a capital-intensive industry, the ethical drug industry has had to provide funds for the newer processes used in producing the latest drug products. Because the technology advances quite rapidly in this industry, both the timing of technological change and the impact on capital needs are difficult to forecast. Again, the acquisition of advanced equipment on relatively short notice requires cash reserves and an ability to negotiate effectively to acquire the productive equipment on a timely and cost-effective basis.

In a capital-intensive industry, where the rate of technological change is slow, the need for financial resources has a substantially different character. Equipment needs can be anticipated with more certainty, and the change in technology in most cases is evolutionary. The acquisition cycle for massive investments in productive assets is quite long, and much longer time horizons are required, consequently, for acquiring the equipment and for planning and securing the financial resources needed for its acquisition.

IMPACT ON FINANCIAL MANAGEMENT

In the two industries mentioned above, there is a significantly different set of tasks for financial managers. In situations where extensive research is a means of competition, as in the ethical drug industry, the financial manager must maintain and manage a significantly larger working capital than is the case in a more capital-intensive industry. The financial manager must obtain a significant "permanent" working capital and must maintain funding sources to provide for the cash needed for research, development, early marketing, and the purchase of advanced equipment. In a seasonal or more volatile business, the financial manager has a similar task: very active involvement in managing working capital. In addition, the financial manager must arrange for seasonal-funds requirements through suppliers or lines of credit with lending institutions. The focus is providing for current assets . . . building from a base of "permanent" current assets derived from long-term sources, but then seeking a range of short-term sources of funds and managing working capital to maximize its effective use in the day-by-day operation of the business.

In the capital-intensive industry, the focus shifts to fixed assets. The matching principle, mentioned earlier, calls for funding for fixed assets with long-term sources of funds. These sources (long-term debt and equity issues) carry an obligation of financial return in the form of dividends or interest payments. As a consequence, operating leverage in this type of business is high, and great effort is expended to hold operating volume at high and fairly constant levels. Order backlogs are maintained to assure economic lot sizes, and the business is run as much as possible in a "steady state." Although replacements for existing capital assets can and are obtained in relatively small increments, expansion or new installations in capital-intensive industries may involve expenditures of hundreds of millions of dollars. In addition, the economics of funds acquisition suggest that when seeking long-term funding, the cost of acquiring an issue is significantly related to its size. Here, it would seem, the financial manager must be involved in developing and maintaining relationships with those persons and entities that aid in providing long-term funds. The manager must actively cultivate the favor and interest of stockholders, investment bankers, financial analysts (whose opinions shape the views of investors), and major lenders such as large banks, insurance companies, and pension funds. If this groundwork is properly laid, when the need for funds becomes apparent and the timetable for funding approaches, these individuals and agencies will provide an optimal environment for fund raising.

The form or type of fund that will be used depends on the relative cost of each type of capital. In situations in which borrowing has been extensive and in which financial leverage is high, stock issuance is likely to have the lower cost of capital. In addition, where income streams are less certain, extensive use of debt sources will be seen as risky, and the cost of capital will rise. As a consequence, among capital-intensive industries, some can carry a higher debt load than others (e.g., utilities) because of the higher degree of certainty in income streams over the life of the assets and the life of the debt instrument. Others, (e.g., the steel or auto industries) have a much lower level of assurance of a stream of earnings and, consequently, must be funded by a higher proportion of equity. In this kind of industry, however, many stockholders often expect—and receive—dividends on a regular basis. Their stock is purchased with long-term income in mind, not for short-term gain. Although not legally compelling, as is the case with interest payments, the expectations of these income-seeking shareholders for regular dividends are just as persuasive to the financial manager. Keeping a sound dividend-payment record is an extremely important element in maintaining a receptive environment for offerings in future years.

Funding for industries that have a greater degree of either uncertainty or volatility involves a significantly lower level of long-term debt and a much higher reliance on equity in the permanent capital structure. Here, stockholders may have different financial objectives and may be willing to forego regular dividend payments in order to attain growth in the value of their holdings. In this kind of situation, any and all matters that have an effect on the stock price of the firm's stock may be the object of attention of the financial manager. As shareholders see the price of the company's stock rise, their own holdings rise in value . . . even if they do not sell the holdings to realize the gain. Similarly, "paper" losses are seen when stock prices fall. New-product announcements, news of sales and/or profit improvement, expansion plans, or optimistic outlooks for the industry can all buoy the price of the company's stock and keep shareholders interested and happy with the prospects for their company.

EXERCISE 3–16

Refer to the industry financial data mentioned in Chapter 2 and locate industries that represent

- An industry with a turbulent technological environment, characterized by extensive research and development.
- An industry that is capital intensive with stable demand.
- An industry that is capital intensive with a relatively volatile demand pattern.

1 Select ratios that will help you to understand the assets structure and the makeup of long-term obligations (including owner's equity) for each of these industries.
2 As needed, calculate from the published ratios the information needed to describe the relative importance of working capital and fixed assets.
3 As needed, calculate from the published ratios the information needed to determine the relative importance of debt or equity in the structure of long-term obligations of the firm.

STAGE OF DEVELOPMENT OF PRODUCTS

Although the industry in general may have certain characteristics that can guide the formulation of financial strategy in arranging the sources and applications of funds, the stage of development of the product or service will also have a significant bearing on financial strategy. The choice of a product or service that is mature will probably place the firm in a subset of an industrial environment that is relatively stable. On the other hand, even in an industry that is relatively mature, some products are rapidly developing, and may present managers with a subenvironment that is turbulent and frought with uncertainty. The financial manager should, it would seem, develop an understanding of the state of product and process technologies that will be encountered in the subset of the industry chosen rather than making use of more global and possibly misleading industry statistics.

In general, as the manager encounters a higher degree of uncertainty and volatility, prudence (and the experience of others in similar situations) would suggest a greater reliance on low fixed-charge sources of funds and the expenditure of a greater portion of time on the management of working capital. As stability in product design and product acceptance becomes more evident, the financial manager can begin to make use of the advantages of financial leverage through a more extensive use of debt funding and spend more time on the development and cultivation of sources of long-term financing.

CHOSEN TECHNOLOGY

As a particular company chooses to enter an industry and to select a product to address some market, it incorporates as a part of its overall strategy some choice of technology. As one example, chairs can be made by hand, in a household shop, or in a large factory by automated or semiautomated production processes. Automobiles can be built in multibillion dollar factories or by hand in small shops. Even where the investment amounts may be similar, the types of processes may have significantly different financial effects. In the paper industry, the manufacture of specialty papers is done through batch processes and by means of multiples of smaller-capacity machines. The total investment in this configuration of equipment may be as high (or higher) than an equivalent tonnage single-purpose mill. Despite the higher labor cost involved in operating multiple units, the financial impact of smaller orders of higher-priced products and the flexibility offered by multiple units may mean lower inventories during slack periods, lower risk of loss of orders when a breakdown occurs, and a more stable financial situation as orders are filled for a broader base of customers.

Where the choice of technology is highly capital intensive, long-term sources of funds are of principal concern. In the financial situation in which stability of earnings is expected, the debt component in the capital structure is emphasized. Where the situation is more volatile, a lower level of debt and a greater reliance on equity funding is required.

Where the technology chosen is *labor* intensive, attention to working capital is a critical ingredient in effective financial management. Although long-term sources are needed to provide the base of fixed assets and permanent working capital, suppliers and short-term creditors are the principal sources of funds for day-by-day operations.

STAGE OF THE FINANCIAL MARKET

The elements discussed in the preceding paragraphs are extremely important contingencies in describing a desired financial structure for a company in a given product and industry situation. We must remind ourselves that they prescribe a nominal, or desired, configuration. Once this desired structure is planned, the financial manager must begin the process of working toward that desired structure through a very real financial marketplace that is affected by such diverse factors as concerns about government military and economic policies, foreign-trade balances, national inflation, economic health of the country and various industries, and even the latest health problems of national figures! In addition, the Federal Reserve Board's actions in establishing the discount rate for member-bank borrowing and its purchase or sale of government securities directly affect interest rates to all borrowers.

In addition to these external factors, the financial manager must also deal with the perception of his firm's desirability to the investment community. The securities of larger firms and municipalities are rated by rating bureaus such as Moody's that serve as a notice to potential investors of the relative risk of these securities. Lower ratings indicate a higher degree of risk and the need for a higher return to bond purchasers.

Stocks that are traded on the organized stock exchanges are often evaluated in a similar manner in terms of their price-to-earnings ratio. High ratios are said to reflect an optimistic view of that company's stock by the market in general. Stocks with price-earnings multiples in the 50s and 60s and higher can be found where industries are believed to be positioned for very rapid growth. Investors hope to buy stock at the early stages of that growth and seem unconcerned about low earnings, or even no earnings at all!

A similar, but less formal system for evaluating the riskiness of securities is conducted by investment bankers, brokerage analysts, and individual investors as they examine the prospects for a particular firm. Several factors are considered in their deliberations: the past and anticipated future growth of the industry, the nature of the company's products in that industry, the competitive and financial record of the company in recent months and years, and the perceived ability of the company's management to direct the affairs of the company.

EXERCISE 3–17

Thomas Jenkins, a college classmate, has said that he is interested in establishing a small clothing store for men and boys in Mullins, Nebraska, a city of 45,000 persons. Tom's research has indicated that competition for men's and boy's clothing in the town is moderate and that principal competition would probably come from a major discount store located in Hastings, some 25 miles to the north. Tom is a native of Mullins and is well thought of by members of the business community, several of whom have urged him to open his own store. During his undergraduate college years, Tom worked in the Men's Wear Department of the May D & F store in Colorado Springs, where he advanced to the position of department manager and assistant buyer.

Tom has asked you to help him in the financial planning for his new store. He has been able to accumulate a total of $120,000 in start-up capital from a trust fund, savings, an inheritance, and from several relatives. He is interested in establishing his business on a sound financial footing and does not want to lose the equity capital he has so carefully acquired.

From the information provided above and your research resources, develop a set of *nominal* balance sheets for

- the end of the first six months of operation.
- the end of the first year of operation.
- the end of the first two years of operation.

Note: In developing the nominal balance sheets, use the owner's equity fròm the original capitalization.

EXERCISE 3–18

Use the following assumptions to aid in converting the nominal balance sheets above to a more realistic representation of capital structure that could be used for practical financial strategy formulation.

- The first year's profit will be 10% below the profit shown for the lower quartile firms in the comparative accounting data in Chapter 2.
- The second year's profit performance will be at the median level shown in the data in Chapter 2.
- Years three through five will be at the upper quartile level shown in the data in Chapter 2.
- No dividends will be paid during the first year of operations, but dividends of 20% of profit after tax will be paid each year thereafter.

Next, prepare balance sheets for each period referred to above (Exercise 3–18), adjusting for increases in owner's equity through retained earnings.

EXERCISE 3–19

Describe the sources from which you will seek the funds needed to meet the needs for each period, and your rationale.

ANSWER TO EXERCISE 3–1 3/15/n45

4

MARKETING AND THE GENERAL MANAGER

For the general manager, the work of the marketing staff is a crucial element in helping to analyze past strategies and to develop strategies for use in the future. Peter Drucker has been quoted as saying that because of its unique position in the managerial decision processes, marketing "cannot be considered a separate function (i.e., a separate skill or work) within the business, on a par with others such as manufacturing or personnel. Marketing requires separate work and a distinct group of activities. But it is, first, a central dimension of the entire business. It is the whole business seen from the point of view of its final result, that is, from the customer's point of view."[1]

In spite of its central role in the strategy-formulation process, marketing need not

[1] Peter F. Drucker, *Management: Tasks, Responsibilities, Practices* (New York: Harper & Row, 1974), p. 63.

and should not be managed by both a marketing manager and the general manager. The effective implementation of marketing plans for the accomplishment of organizational objectives is a task requiring the efforts of persons trained and experienced in the techniques and terminology of the field, a background that some general managers may not have. In addition, balancing the attention needed for all functions and for their integration means that the general manager must remove himself or herself from the day-by-day marketing management, but must retain the links that make possible the observation, coordination, and guidance of the marketing effort in its relationships with other functions in the organization.

General management control points will be based on longer-term objectives and more broadly based targets. Contact with the marketing organization will be less frequent than that of the marketing manager, and much of the emphasis will be placed on plans, goals, and results versus the specific tactics used to achieve the goals or the selection and supervision of persons assigned to perform various tasks. From the general manager's perspective, marketing should be governed through a broad practical understanding of several key elements in the marketing effort and on the ability of the manager to appraise the effectiveness of the unit engaged in marketing for the firm. In the following sections, three topics are developed that comprise key *knowledge elements* needed by general managers: (1) the concept of *markets and targets*, (2) an understanding of the *marketing mix*, and (3) an understanding of the concept of *marketing strategy*. Skills in several areas also discussed: (4) skills needed to aid in the development of new strategies, (5) skills needed to aid in *managing* an integrated marketing strategy, and (6) skill in the application of marketing evaluation tools.

As in previous chapters, exercises will be provided to help in assuring that concepts and skills have been successfully retained.

TARGET MARKETS

We begin this discussion with Phillip Kotler's description of a market, "The set of all individuals or organizations who are actual or potential buyers of a product or service."[2]

In this definition, the observation that both existing or *actual* buyers and *potential* buyers are in the market is of considerable importance in identifying areas of opportunity for the expansion of sales. As one example, Arm & Hammer Baking Soda, sold to a long-standing market consisting of commercial and home bakers, had achieved a fairly saturated state. By developing alternative uses for baking soda (e.g., as a water softener for bathing, as a deodorant for refrigerators and drains) the number of potential buyers for baking soda was increased several fold.

Several ways of categorizing or breaking down markets have been suggested.

[2] Phillip, Kotler, *Marketing Management*, 4th Ed. (New York: Prentice Hall, 1980), pp. 129–30

Kotler suggests four fundamental forms based on buyer motives: consumer markets (persons buying for personal use), producer markets (manufacturers buying materials or components for their own products), reseller markets (buying for the purpose of reselling), and government markets (buying for use in government activities.[3] Cravens and others have categorized markets more tightly by considering classes or groups of product markets and matching product-benefits categories with those groups of buyers with both the willingness and the ability to buy.[4] Thus, products that serve as substitutes for each other and both the actual and potential buyers of those products constitute a product market. A *generic* product market is made up of all products and services that can satisfy a particular need. A *specific* product market is somewhat narrower, it includes *all brands* of a particular product category, even those in quite different price ranges. A *brand* product market is made up of those particular brands that are directly competitive.

From the following list, identify products, services, or brands to answer the three questions in Exercises 4–1, 4–2, and 4–3.

Chevrolet Trucks.
Raleigh Bicycles.
Ford Station Wagons.
Chevrolet Corvettes.
Chevrolet Sedans.
Cadillac Coupes.
Buick Rivera Coupes.
Dodge Aries K Sedan.
Chrysler LeBaron Coupes.
Lincoln Continental Coupes.
Roller Skates.
Hertz Rent-a-Car.
Fuji Bicycles.
Huffy Bicycles.
Winnebago Chief Camper.
Ferrari Sports Coupe.

EXERCISE 4–1

Which of the items listed belong in a generic product market? (See one such generic market in the answers at the end of the chapter)

[3] Kotler, *Marketing Management*, pp. 130–31.

[4] David M. Cravens, *Strategic Marketing* (Homewood, Ill.: R. D. Irwin, 1982), p. 128

EXERCISE 4–2

Which of the items listed belong in a specific product market?

EXERCISE 4–3

Are there any brand product markets in this list? Any partial brand product markets? If yes, please identify them.

Think back on the definitions of consumer, producer, reseller, and government markets, take one of the products listed and describe a potential buyer in each market. Then use the *Chevrolet Truck* as the product and list buyers in the categories shown in Exercises 4–4 through 4–7. Note: Some answers will be found at the end of the chapter.

EXERCISE 4–4

Buyer in a consumer market.

EXERCISE 4–5

Buyer in a producer market.

EXERCISE 4–6

Buyer in a reseller market.

EXERCISE 4–7

Buyer in a government market.

A structured approach to developing a product market is suggested by Cravens, Hills, and Woodruff. In the structured development, the manager should develop a market profile, an industry profile, and an aggregate demand forecast first for the generic market, then for the specific product, and finally for the brand-level product market. For the brand-level product market, a market target profile, a key competitor profile, and a brand-positioning strategy are needed.[5]

Kotler suggests another process for breaking down a total market into a portion that can be served effectively. The first step is to segment the market into subsets of customers, each with a distinct set of needs. Segments can vary according to size, resources, locations, product needs, attitudes, and purchasing practices.

Kotler suggests that the hierarchy of variables used by consumers in making buying decisions be used to aid in segmenting a market. Buyers deciding first on a brand, then on a type of product, would call for a brand-form (meaning forms of the product) hierarchy. Product size or other customer or product characteristics might also determine the type of partitioning used in a specific segmentation process. New markets can, of course, also be segmented on the basis of geography, on demographic characteristics of customers, or on personality or life-style. Table 4-1 is a brief list of segmentation variables and their respective breakdowns.

Industrial customers can be segmented on the basis of their size, usage rates, end-use products, and geographic locations.

EXERCISE 4-8

Think of your most recent major purchase as a consumer. Identify, if you can, the sequence of elements that you used in making your final decision. Use brand, form or shape, size or capacity, and your personal product needs as variables in answering this question. Think which variable came first, then next, and so forth. Be prepared to discuss your list in class.

The use of segmentation allows marketers to do a better job of analyzing market opportunities and to adjust their marketing efforts to meet the particular requirements of that segment. According to Kotler, given clearly identified segments, a marketing strategy might follow one of three broad patterns: (1) an undifferentiated approach in which a single appeal (marketing mix) is made to the broadest part of the market; (2) concentrated marketing, in which we zero in on a narrow segment, with an appeal (mix) developed especially for this specific group of customers; or (3) multiple but different appeals (mixes) designed for different segments of the market. The choice of one of these three types of targeting is dependent on company resources, product characteristics, the variety of needs of prospective customers, and the position of one's competitors.

The brief case, Symmetry in Gold, Inc., can serve to help you deal with the concepts of market segmentation and targeting. As you read through the case, refer to Table 4-1 from time to time to keep segmentation variables in mind. When you have completed studying the case carefully, proceed to respond to the exercise questions that follow the case.

[5] David W. Cravens, G. E. Hills, and R. B. Woodruff, *Marketing Decision Making: Concepts and Strategy*, Rev. Ed., (Homewood, Ill.: R. D. Irwin, 1980), p. 120

TABLE 4-1
Major segmentation variables for consumer markets

Variable	*Typical Breakdowns*
Geographic	
Region	Pacific, Mountain, West North Central, West South Central, East North Central, East South Central, South Atlantic, Middle Atlantic, New England
County size	A, B, C, D
City or MSA size[a]	Under 5,000; 5,000–20,000; 20,000–50,000; 50,000–100,000; 100,000–250,000; 250,000–500,000; 500,000–1,000,000; 1,000,000–4,000,000; 4,000,000 or over
Density	Urban, suburban, rural
Climate	Northern, southern
Demographic	
Age	Under 6, 6–11, 12–19, 20–34, 35–49, 50–64, 65+
Sex	Male, female
Family size	1–2, 3–4, 5+
Family life cycle	Young, single; young, married, no children; young, married, youngest child under 6; young, married, youngest child 6 or over; older, married, with children; older, married, no children under 18; older, single; other
Income	Under $2,500; $2,500–$5,000; $5,000–$7,500; $7,500–$10,000; $10,000–$15,000; $15,000–$20,000; $20,000–$30,000; $30,000–$50,000; $50,000 and over
Occupation	Professional and technical; managers, officials, and proprietors; clerical sales; craftsmen, foremen; operatives; farmers; retired; students; housewives; unemployed
Education	Grade school or less; some high school; high school graduate; some college; college graduate
Religion	Catholic, Protestant, Jewish, other
Race	White, black, oriental, Hispanic
Nationality	American, British, French, German, Scandinavian, Italian, Latin American, Middle Eastern, Japanese
Psychographic	
Social class	Lower lowers, upper lowers, lower middles, upper middles, lower uppers, upper uppers
Life style	Belongers, achievers, integrateds
Personality	Compulsive, gregarious, authoritarian, ambitious
Behavioristic	
Purchase occasion	Regular occasion, special occasion
Benefits sought	Quality, service, economy

TABLE 4-1 *(continued)*
Major segmentation variables for consumer markets

Variable	*Typical Breakdowns*
User status	Nonuser, ex-user, potential user, first-time user, regular user
Usage rate	Light user, medium user, heavy user
Loyalty status	None, medium, strong, absolute
Readiness stage	Unaware, aware, informed, interested, desirous, intending to buy
Attitude toward product	Enthusiastic, positive, indifferent, negative, hostile

[a]MSA: Metropolitan statistical area.
Source: Phillip Kotler, *Principles of Marketing* 3rd Ed. (Englewood Cliffs, N.J.: Prentice-Hall, 1986) p. 265.

SYMMETRY IN GOLD, INC.

Symmetry in Gold (SIG), a small manufacturing jewelry firm, is located in attractive showroom/shop facilities on the third floor of a multistory bank building located in a large shopping center mall. Symmetry in Gold employs five people and is engaged in jewelry repair and sizing work (for large retailers such as Zales, O.G. Wilson, J.C. Penney) and in the manufacture of two types of designer jewelry. The SIG line is jewelry designed by SIG goldsmiths, manufactured by a New York casting firm, then sold by SIG to jewelry retailers in the metropolitan area around their location. The second type is custom-designed jewelry made to customer specification. The manufacture of this type of product requires a number of consultations between designer/manufacturer and client, a process usually done at the SIG location.

The manufacturing cycle on these lines of business vary considerably. Ring sizing and other simple repair jobs are normally returned to the retailer the following day. The SIG line items are sold out of inventory or manufactured on contract within a three-to-four-week period. Custom work can take as long as six weeks to go from concept sketches to drawn design, to sculpted wax representation, to completion of the finished piece.

The metropolitan area currently served by SIG contains over 200,000 people and contains a relatively heavy proportion of white-collar professional employees and retired persons. A major city containing over 2 million persons is located 65 miles away. The next nearest major population center is over 350 miles from SIG's present location. Four competitors are found in SIG's home city, and many more than that in the larger city nearby.

EXERCISE 4–9

What kinds of markets is SIG currently serving with its present products and services?

EXERCISE 4–10

Describe how you would segment the market for SIG's custom jewelry. Use Table 4–1 to help in your analysis. Prepare your list to hand in to your instructor or for discussion in class.

EXERCISE 4–11

Can you select a target segment or segments? Describe your rationale for segmentation, and be prepared to discuss it in class.

THE MARKETING MIX

The marketing mix is a major integrative marketing concept developed many years ago. The major elements comprising the mix are the *product,* its *price* (and terms of sale), the *distribution* needed to deliver the product to the customer at the appropriate time (place), and the *promotion* used to convince purchasers to buy. Many marketing texts refer to the four elements of the mix as the four P's (Product, Price, Place, and Promotion).

The importance of the marketing mix to marketing and general managers is its integrative character and the sense of collective integrity that it can have when properly applied. The concept of the marketing mix extends well beyond the simple enumeration of elements—as a sort of abbreviated checklist—to the notion that the customer buys a *complementary set* of marketing factors. Purchases can and will be affected by the extent to which a marketing mix fits together in meeting customer needs.

Convenience goods, for example, must be placed (distributed) into locations that are, in fact, convenient to customers. They must have been promoted (via all forms of promotion) to such an extent that brand identification and product qualities are either known or well established *before* the need or desire for the product comes to the attention of the customer. In the mix for convenience goods, price is of somewhat lower importance to the consumer, but it is important to the retailer, who stocks convenience goods under a discount-pricing system in order to generate sales and to profit from those sales. Doublemint Chewing Gum can serve as an example. We see this product in a wide range of outlets. Vending machines, drugstores, supermarkets, filling stations, restaurants, and other retail outlets sell chewing gum. We are aware of the product because of extensive television advertising—most of us can repeat the opening line or two of the TV commercial's jingle! We buy the product, in most cases, on impulse, from the outlet we are closest to, at the time the impulse arises.

For chewing gum, the marketing mix described above works very well. For other products, a quite different mix of marketing elements is seen. Home computers, ranging in price for $400 to $5,000 or more are sold through a highly selective distribution system. Part of the promotion effort for these products involves the advertising of technical product features to lay customers. A significant element in selling home computers, however, can be the personal selling done by an expert salesperson in the computer retail store. Differences in product features are a key element in the mix. Some home computers have color display, which sets them apart from others. Internal memory capacity, modular additive features, display screen size, and numerous other technical properties serve to distinguish one manufacturer's product from another, even though they serve the same general purposes. Price, within the range of prices mentioned earlier, is a most significant factor to prospective purchasers and may tip the scales in favor of one brand over another, despite differences in technical features. For many customers of home computers, once the critical product features are known, the product's distinctive features of most importance to that particular customer identified, and the price issue resolved, then the *place* where the equipment is purchased is less important. Some customers buy through mail order, others are willing to wait several weeks to get delivery of a unit whose features (and price) best match their needs.

Although the marketing mix for numerous types of goods could be used for illustrations, the two examples cited should help to illustrate the point that the mix for a product is a *combination* of factors that *taken together* serves to induce the person to purchase. The type of good and the buying behavior of prospective purchasers are important elements in shaping the appropriate marketing mix.

Timex developed an entirely new mix for marketing its products and was able to succeed by producing a low-priced, low-cost product that was made attractive to retailers because of its profit margin. Timex obviated the need for a jeweler-service facility by providing a central mail-in service center. The Timex watch could not, however, have been sold through the discount, drug, and grocer outlets had not the product been reliable and customers been made aware of this reliability through television advertising that demonstrated this critical piece of product information.

In the following sections, we will discuss the elements of the marketing mix in more detail and then explore the mix in an application through a case.

Products/Services

For general managers, the term *Product* should, in the marketing sense, include physical objects, places, personalities, organizations, services, and concepts being offered for sale.

A three-level notion of the product includes the *core* benefit, or service, provided by the product and the *formal* product, which includes styling, features, brand name, packaging, and quality. The third level incorporates the *core* and *formal* levels, but adds augmentation in the form of installation, service, warranties, and delivery.[6]

EXERCISE 4–12

Seiko timepieces have gained a well-earned position in the consumer market in the United States and elsewhere throughout the world.

Select, as one example, the most frequently purchased Seiko model at a large timepiece retailer in your own area. Ask to see the timepiece and have its features explained to you. Then, prepare to describe the *product* in marketing terms, making use of the three levels of product described. Prepare your description for class discussion or to be handed in as a homework assignment.

An understanding of the mix of products offered by the company is also an important part of marketing for general managers. A company may have a single line of product. The McIllheny Company concentrates its efforts on a single product, its widely known Tabasco Pepper Sauce. Bic Pen manufacturers and markets three lines, ballpoint pens, disposable butane lighters, and disposable razors. General Electric Corporation sells lines of light bulbs, toasters, radios, ranges, television sets, jet engines, electric generators, industrial motors, and many other types of products. Within each line are the various models, sizes, colors, or product characteristics deemed necessary and desired by customers.

A key responsibility of top management is an analysis and evaluation of the contribution to fixed costs and profits by each product and product line. This analysis is needed not only for current managerial control, but also for product and profit planning as products move along the product life-cycle from development through growth and maturity to decline.

EXERCISE 4–13

	Now (1986)	*1987 (Yr. 1)*	*1988 (Yr. 2)*	*1989 (Yr. 3)*	*1990 (Yr. 4)*	*1991 (Yr. 5)*
Product A	10	20	36	49	72	71
Product B	60	63	68	70	70	64
Product C	(8)	(10)	(20)	0	14	27
Product D	76	69	56	26	5	0
Product E	12	23	29	43	60	89
	150	165	169	188	221	251

[6] Kotler, *Marketing Management*, p. 352.

Your goal, as manager, is to increase total profits by 12% each year (compounding the increase each year). Prepare a graph to depict the profit contribution of each product to the total for each year and to show the total profit expected each year given the goal stated above. A format such as that in Figure 4–1 may be helpful.

EXERCISE 4–14

What, if any, will be the profit gap in the years you have analyzed?

Pricing

To the general manager, pricing forms a second important part of the marketing mix for products and product lines. Generally, pricing decisions are keyed to gains in profit position or to gain in volume. Beyond these two important objectives, pricing decisions may involve improving one's position in the competitive arena. In addition, pricing decisions may be directed toward improving or enhancing consumer impressions of the product or the company.

Pricing decisions based on costs require that both the marketing and general managers consider the relative importance of fixed and variable costs for the firm and its competitors as well as the liklihood that economies of scale are technologically available.

The profits of companies that have a very high-fixed cost component are most sensitive to changes in volume. Airlines, steel mills, hospitals, and public utility companies are examples of organizations that have cost structures containing a very high proportion of fixed costs. In these kinds of companies, pricing decisions are aimed at maximizing long-term profit through high levels of output, making best use of all available capacity.

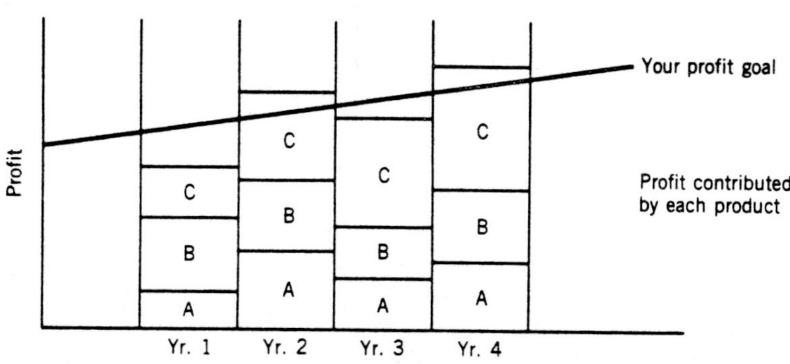

FIGURE 4–1

PRICING

Contribution Pricing is a way of considering prices on products to maintain volume and to obtain a high level of coverage of fixed cost and desired profit. Contribution, in this system of pricing, is the net of selling price less the out-of-pocket variable costs associated with the sale of that product. As an example, let us assume the Crawder Manufacturing, a small steel refining company, has a fixed cost component of $5.2 million per year and a maximum three-shift capacity of 15,000 tons per year. Variable costs are 35% of the present average selling price of $800.00 per ton and present volume is 9,000 tons per year.

Full costing at 9,000 tons per year in volume would mean

- $5.2 million per year fixed cost. Fixed cost per ton at 9,000 tons = $577.77 per ton.
- $800 per ton selling price × .35 = $280.00 per ton in variable cost.
- Total cost per ton = $857.77
- Revenue per ton = $800.00
- Loss per ton = $57.77

Pricing to cover full cost (at present volume) would involve a price increase of $57.77 per ton. If demand for this type (or your brand) of steel is relatively price inelastic, customers should be willing to pay the additional price in order to get the steel. On the other hand, if the demand for your type of steel tends to be price sensitive, then you may find your sales volume to be substantially lower at $857.77 per ton than at $800.00. Conversely, *lowering* the price in a price-elastic demand situation can result in increases in demand sufficient to more than offset the lower level of contribution per ton resulting from the lower price.

EXERCISE 4–15

Your marketing research department indicates that you can sell an additional 4,000 tons of steel per year, but you must sell the new tonnage at an average price of $780.00 per ton. Your marketing manager says that if you sell to one customer at $780.00, you are obligated to sell to all of your customers at that average price. What will be your decision? Explain, using the cost information cited above.

EXERCISE 4–16

At the new volume (13,000 tons of steel per year) what price, on the average, will you need to charge to obtain a 10% profit (before tax) as a percentage of sales?

EXERCISE 4–17

Why might you, as general manager, wish to take the new tonnage, even if it offered no significant profit opportunity at this time? Prepare your answer(s) for handing in or for class discussion.

EXERCISE 4–18

Your market research department has provided you with the following information based on economic estimates of demand for your products:

Price per Ton	*Estimated Volume*
$725	35,800 tons/yr
750	24,200
775	14,500
800	9,000
825	6,800
850	5,200

Plot the demand function on graph paper.

EXERCISE 4–19

Given the cost structure developed for Exercise 4–15 and the demand function graphed, determine the price and volume that you believe will maximize profit.

EXERCISE 4–20

At what price can you maximize market share without draining profits from other products?

Skimming The term *skimming* is used to describe a strategy for setting a high price for new products. It is aimed at taking advantage of the novelty value of new products and the lack of competing or substitute products. It is typically intended as a strategy to be used until competing firms enter the market and until the novelty value has declined. Patent protection provides another shelter because competitors must find ways to circumvent the protected characteristics of the product, thus giving the skimmer valuable time in which to capture the less price-sensitive portion of the market. The Pulsar digital wrist-timepiece was initially priced at $350 and $500 (stainless steel and gold cases, respectively). Within two years, competitors had *functionally* identical models at prices below $20, but Pulsar had sold many $350 or $500 timepieces to the curious, status seekers, or well-to-do customers pleased with the novelty of this new look in timekeeping. The Polaroid Company has consistently skimmed the markets for its products by introducing innovations at its highest-quality levels. Publishers of popular books accomplish the same objective by publishing hardcover editions long before less expensive, mass-marketed paperback editions. Again, these products have a period of protection, provided by patent or copyright, and can use skimming during that sheltered period. An unpatented technological innovation in manufacture or design can serve to provide the period of shelter so long as the processes for manufacture are kept secret (a practice found in some industries) or by making products in such a way as to make copying difficult.

Penetration Pricing If skimming is not used because of a lack of patent protection or a fast-response cycle by competitors, *penetration* pricing is used as a means of introducing new products. This strategy is particularly helpful in entering a mature market occupied by established brands; it involves entering the market with low initial prices as a means of capturing a significant share of the market.

EXERCISE 4–21

You are considering the introduction of a new type of electrical switch for 110-volt household use. Your invention is patented and involves a heat-sensitive panel that will trip the switch by means of the warmth of one's fingers in touching the switch panel.

Present arguments in favor of using (1) penetration pricing or (2) skimming.

Competition-Based Pricing Competition-based pricing presents a wide range of decisions for the general manager. At one extreme, when prices are based on an established price list in a highly competitive market with a specific price for a particular product, management has little incentive to price at any level other than that of the going rate. At the other extreme, where competitive bids are involved, pricing decisions can make or break a firm. A necessary (but not sufficient) element in competitive bidding is a competent cost-estimating staff, one that provides management with accurate estimates of direct and indirect costs. In addition to costs, management's volume and profitability objectives and their assessment of competitors' strengths and weaknesses will all be considered in developing the final price. Tactically, some managers prefer to bid low to gain the volume of business, and they hope to improve estimated profit by operational economies or by alterations of the contract after its acceptance by the buyer. Although price is a critical ingredient in competitive bidding, the quality or reputation of one's products or services will have an important bearing on the acceptability of one's bid and may tip the scale in favor of a particular bidder despite a price difference favoring another competitor.

Distribution of Products

Distribution, or place, the third of the four P's in the marketing mix, involves managing the channels of distribution as a means of assuring that one's products reach customers at the time needed to most effectively complete the sale.

The structure of one's channels of distribution can vary from a zero-level distribution system wherein products are shipped directly from manufacturer to retail customers to multilevel structures involving agents, brokers, wholesalers, and retailers. A zero-level system provides the highest degree of control over the marketing effort, but it requires a high commitment of financial resources for advertising and promotion expenses, funds for inventories, and capital to finance accounts receivable. As the number of levels increases, the requirement for resources diminishes, but control over marketing does as well. For the general manager, the trade-off between financial resources available and the degree of control desired poses an interesting set of choices. Jain[7] describes a four-cell matrix (see Figure 4–2) in which these two variables are matched to frame or constrain management choices.

		Control desired	
		Yes	No
Adequate financial resources	Yes	A	B
	No	C	D

FIGURE 4–2

Cells A and D provide easy choices. Cell A calls for a limited number of levels in the distribution, as the degree of control needed and the resources that are available match well and permit this type of distribution. Cell D, on the other hand, calls for a

[7] Subhash Jain, *Marketing Planning and Strategy* (Cincinnati; Ohio: South-Western Publishing, 1981), p. 336.

larger number of levels. Here, the low level of control needed and the lack of funds match well.

Cells B and C, however, present difficult choices. In the case of cell B, as capital is not a limiting factor, the selection of channel structure becomes less related to capital than to its most effective use and to other important marketing considerations. *Any* of the four levels of distribution could be used. With cell C, capital *is* a limiting factor and the firm may be required to use a less direct system than desired, simply for lack of funds.

Beyond the constraints imposed by financial resources, marketing control can be exercised by *exclusive distribution*. Exclusive distribution by a retailer, for example, means that the retailer is the only outlet for that particular brand in a given area. Exclusive distribution has great benefits to the retailer who gains by the attractiveness of brands or products that are well known and advertised and by close contact with manufacturers for sales support, cooperative advertising, and merchandising assistance. To the manufacturer, exclusive distribution provides greater control over marketing and more support and attention given to products by the exclusive retailer.

Another strategy is that of *intensive distribution,* that is, making your product available for sale at any and all possible outlets. Cigarettes, chewing gum, and ballpoint pens are examples of products sold in a wide range of outlets. Typically, these products are high-volume, low-priced items that require frequent servicing from suppliers to avoid excessive retailer inventories. The result is a multichannel, low-control distribution structure that although leading to increased sales, can have detrimental effect if the products require service or if price competition among outlets becomes severe. Electric hair dryers, for example, have been sold through an intensive distribution to a large number of types of retail outlets. The system of distribution originally included barbershops and hairstyling salons. Over the years, competition from drugstores and discount outlets has lowered profit margins to the point where few barbers or shop operators care to carry the item in stock.

An intermediate position, in *selective distribution,* uses a limited number of retailers to carry one's products. This distribution system is employed by the automobile and home appliance businesses, where customers shop for features, prices, and service. It is especially helpful where brand and product identification has been established and where postpurchase servicing of products may be needed.

EXERCISE 4–22

Consider the *classification* of types of stores and goods as well as the *behavior of customers* in Figure 4–3. Then identify the type of distribution you would most likely use and give an example of a product that fits the general description shown in column 2.

Classification	*Behavior of Customers*	*Distribution*	*Products*
Specialty store/ specialty good	Consumer has both a preference for a particular store and for a specific brand.	________	________
Shopping store/ shopping good	Consumer makes comparisons among both retail-controlled factors and factors associated with the product (brand).	________	________
Convenience store/ Convenience good	Consumer prefers to buy the most readily available brand of product at the most accessible store.	________	________
Shopping store/ specialty good	Consumer has a strong preference as to product brand but shops a number of stores to secure the best retail service and/or price for this brand.	________	________

Source: Adapted from L. P. Bucklin, "Retail Strategy and the Classification of Consumer Goods," *Journal of Marketing* (January 1963), pp. 50–55.

FIGURE 4–3

Promotion

Promotion, the fourth of the four P's in the marketing mix, is a term that includes all forms of communications serving to persuade or induce customers to purchase products or services. Generally, we can categorize promotion activities into four forms: advertising, personal selling, sales promotion, and publicity. General managers establish budgetary limits for promotion activities, a key step in framing the promotional effort of the marketing department. Several methods for setting these limits have been suggested. An economist's approach is one wherein expenditures are made until marginal revenues equal marginal costs. Less theoretical and more applicable methods include *spending what you can afford, spending a percentage of sales,* obtaining a *return on investment,* or *spending a proportion of that paid by competitors.*[8]

The general manager also has an important role in overseeing the development of a *mix* of promotional tools to obtain maximum impact. Cravens suggests that guidelines for developing a promotional strategy should involve a review of (1) the target market, including customer characteristics, needs, and buying processes; (2) the

[8] Jain, *Marketing Planning and Strategy,* pp. 365–67.

previously developed product strategy, including product-line choices, branding decisions, and relevant information to be communicated to customers; (3) distribution decisions, including choice of channels, information needs of intermediaries, and communication functions to be performed by intermediaries; and (4) pricing decisions, including the importance of price in the overall strategy, relative price of products versus those of competitors, and price information to be communicated to customers and intermediaries.[9]

In the development of this promotional strategy, the objectives of the campaign should be clearly delineated. Objectives may be to *inform* prospective customers of product uses (e.g., the message delivered by baking soda ads that stress the product's deodorant properties), to *educate* customers about product features or functions, to *assist* (or force!) *comparisons* with competing products, to *stimulate needs* and to *close sales,* that is, to directly affect the decision to buy. Some forms of promotional work are effective in reaching only some of these objectives. Direct selling, for example, can be a most effective means of closing sales, comparing products, and educating customers, but it may be less effective in a broad-scope product-information or need-stimulation program than might a well-executed publicity or advertising campaign.

The proportion of each element in the mix varies with the type of good and with the intended purpose of the campaign. Figure 4–4 shows that advertising has a much lower use with industrial products than with consumer goods, a pattern almost exactly the opposite of that shown for personal selling.

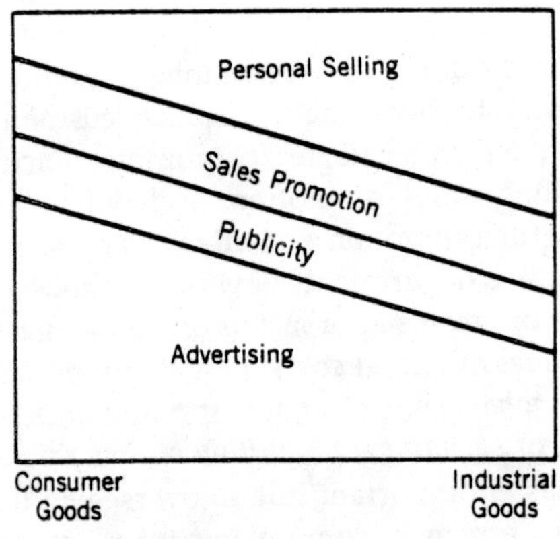

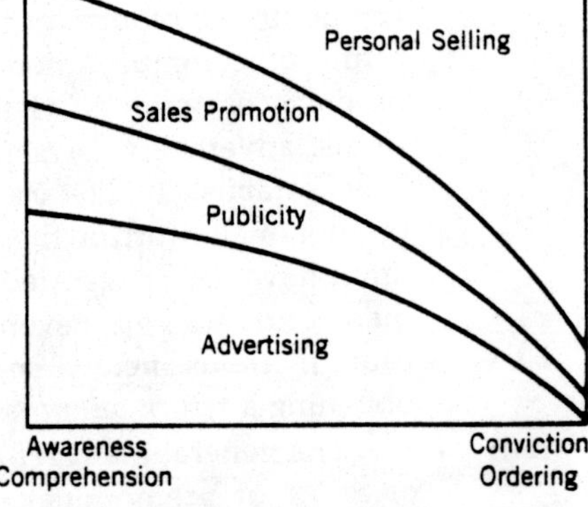

FIGURE 4–4 Communications mix as a function of type of market and buyer readiness stage. *Source:* Kotler, *Marketing Management*, p. 491.

[9] Cravens, *Strategic Marketing*, p. 322

From these two diagrams, it is obvious that the general manager's control actions must be directed toward assuring that the mix of promotional efforts fits the type of product and the promotion objectives and that it be designed to concentrate on those elements deemed most significant.

EXERCISE 4–23

Your company manufactures and sells an extensive line of V-belts (a rubber belt used for connecting motors to fans, pumps, compressors, or other devices) to industrial customers. The market for your line includes a large number of aggressive and large competitors. Product differences are technical in nature and are not immediately apparent to a lay person.

As general manager, what mix of promotional effort would you expect your manager of marketing to suggest?

EXERCISE 4–24

How would you attempt to concentrate your own efforts on those parts of the promotional mix that seem most important to you?

EXERCISE 4–25

As product manager for a new breakfast cereal made of a highly nutritious mixture of sunflower, safflower, and rye grass seeds, what type of promotional mix do you hope to develop with your marketing manager?

EXERCISE 4–26

How would you concentrate your own efforts on those parts of the promotional mix that seem most important to you?

In overseeing the advertising component in promotion, important managerial decisions are made in several areas. The *message* to be delivered is directly related to the objective of the promotional effort. As such, a message to make the public *aware* of a product is quite different than a message designed to achieve conviction, or to close the sale. Messages are evaluated on the basis of desirability, exclusiveness, and believability. A deficiency in any one of these three elements is thought to reduce the impact of the other two in a multiplicative relationship.[10] In effect, if the message is not believed, its value is zero. If the features are not seen as exclusive, the message value is zero, and if the product is not conveyed as being desirable, the value of the message is again zero.

For effective delivery, the selected message needs to be executed properly in a medium that offers the proper contact with the target market and at the right frequency. Exposure can be concentrated, continuous, or intermittant. Frequency can range throughout the day or week, and it can be timed to address the listening, viewing, or reading habits of prospective customers.

As can be seen in Figure 4–4, personal selling, the second of the four major components of promotion, has a wide range in importance, depending on the type of good and the promotional objective. Beyond these general guidelines, the size of the personal selling component in promotion will also depend heavily on the number and location of buyers, their need for information, and the size of the purchase.[11]

Sales promotion activities form a third component in the promotion mix. Most of us have encountered a person offering sample edibles in supermarkets as a promotional device to increase awareness of products or product qualities. In addition to this type of sales promotion, bonuses, free vacations to salespersons, special discounts to retailers, cooperative advertising programs, and discount coupons all serve to promote the sale of specified products. The use of these promotional scheme is widespread.

In industrial markets, promotional efforts include the use of small business-oriented gift articles (e.g., measuring tapes, pocket calculators, rulers, calendars, conversion tables) or user guides that serve to aid the buyer while promoting the company's product line.

Publicity, the fourth part of a total promotion campaign, is the communication of product- or company-related information in *editorial* space as opposed to paid-for commercial advertising. The real estate and foods industries in many communities have developed enough interest and information that sections devoted to these industries appear weekly in major local newspapers. News items about new products, personnel changes, and tips and articles of interest to consumers are packaged by an editorial staff and are combined with extensive commercial advertising (by the same industry) that is presented as a supplement to, or part of, the Sunday paper. Publicity has the effect of providing substantial support for other marketing efforts by *providing credibility* in the minds of consumers and by stimulating salespersons and intermediaries in carrying out their functions.

The concept of the marketing mix offers marketing managers and general managers a great deal of flexibility and challenge in designing appeals that will have maximum effect. A carefully constructed mix provides mutual support for each of its

[10] Kotler, *Marketing Management*, p. 505.

[11] Cravens, *Strategic Marketing*, p. 342.

elements and can serve to ease the entry of new products, sustain its long-term growth, and assist in the development of new markets for established products. In the Selden Sausage Company Case, you should carefully consider the material we have covered so far. You may wish to review the highlights of this chapter before reading the case. Then, carefully read the case and take notes if you find that helpful. When you have gone through the case, then respond to the questions contained in Exercises 4–27 to 4–31.

SELDEN SAUSAGE COMPANY

Selden Sausage Company, a well-established organization, produced sausage in one location and marketed it in five contiguous states. This regional firm produced only sausage but had sales of over $6 million the past year. Throughout its market area Selden had many competitors, including four national brands of well-known producers. The market of another regional firm overlapped into two of the states that Selden served. Local producers with strictly local markets existed in four sizable cities. Several major supermarket chains also had house brands of sausage. In addition, in many rural areas small custom-meat processors, sometimes known as "locker plants," manufactured small quantities of sausage from less desirable cuts of pork, often including trimmings. Sales at one of these plants might be as low as twenty pounds a week. Their price and quality combinations had wide variability. Selden's price for its products was about 15 per cent above the average price in its market area. The company had a modest reputation for better than acceptable quality. It was not, however, considered the most choice brand available.

Because of the fact that food prices, both raw and processed, had been undergoing a rapid rate of inflation over the past eighteen months, Selden Sausage Company was faced with some managerial decisions. Selden had two products, a one-pound roll of sausage that the user sliced to the thickness of her preference and a one-pound package of formed sausage links in thin casings. The latter accounted for about 47 per cent of sales. At present Selden felt no concern for its relatively cheaper rolled sausage product but was worried about the future of its link sausage. This product was priced about 40 per cent higher than the rolled sausage, partly because of labor and partly because the ground mixture was slightly leaner. This price ratio had been traditional with the company and was not based on any current cost accounting.

For the first six months of the price spiral, Selden had cushioned the impact of its increasing costs on the consumer by absorbing the increases, i.e., letting its margin decline on the link sausage. For the past twelve months, however, it had found it necessary to raise the price of this product on five occasions. The food price situation seemed to indicate that consumers should be retrenching on luxuries and, economically speaking, most middle- and lower-class consumers should probably perceive breakfast sausage as a luxury.

Puzzlingly enough, government data indi-

This case is from T. V. Greer, *Cases in Marketing*, 2nd Ed. (New York, Macmillan, 1979), pp. 28–30.

cated that consumption of cured meat products such as sausage, bacon, and ham had increased rather than decreased during the price spiral. This fact was particularly difficult to understand in light of the fact that beef consumption had decreased sufficiently to temporarily stabilize the prices of beef. Was the housewife thinking of the morale generated per dollar spent? She could serve a very popular breakfast with two or three one-ounce sausages per person plus a bulky starch such as waffles, pancakes, or hash brown potatoes. The American top choice for dinner, steak, would require about one-third to two-thirds pounds of steak per adult, at a price per pound at least equal to that of sausage, and perhaps much higher, depending on cut. Yet in each case the family reaction would be that one of the meals of the day had been a particular favorite.

Despite the fact that the expected impact of the price spiral had not yet occurred, Selden felt it was only a matter of time. The situation remained quite fluid, and managers in the company felt it was time to consider various options for future strategy.

The first possible strategy and one that seemed highly desirable to many of the executives was to modify the present equipment, which then produced fourteen to sixteen sausages per pound to produce an *exact* number per pound. (The consumer was not given short weight but was given a variable number of units in the package.) All the executives believed that with the present price situation the housewife would be much more sensitive to precise portioning. Unpredictability as to the unit count in a pound package was seen as a potential alienator of the customer. Four competitors had offered the feature of exact count for several years, but Selden had felt no competitive impact from the factor thus far.

Some of the Selden executives felt that it was not adequate simply to improve the portionability of the sixteen-ounce link package. They were concerned that either through magazine articles, public service information, or their own observation and reasoning, housewives would realize that as a substantial protein source, sausage was not much of a bargain. For example, a ham, if bought whole and kept in the refrigerator for slicing, would give a much more favorable ratio of ounces of cooked protein per dollar. Loss of weight by loss of fat during the cooking of sausage was substantial, resulting in a relatively high cost per ounce of cooked meat. Since luxuries are more often bought in small quantities, it was proposed that Selden convert to either a package containing twelve sausages or one containing eight sausages.

A minority of those involved in the discussion believed that decreasing the package size would decrease total dollar sales immediately and would be a bad move. These people believed that appropriate advertising could counteract any tendency by the consumer to discount breakfast sausage as a reasonably priced source of protein. Since many consumers do not read newspaper articles and magazines that contain information on cost per ounce of cooked protein, these executives believed that they could successfully promote sausage even in small servings as a significant share of daily protein intake. These managers stated that it would be a grave error to accept the assumption that breakfast sausage was a luxury until and unless such a stance was forced on the company by actual consumer purchasing patterns.

Another strategy that was feasible but generally regarded as risky was to change the formulation of the sausage to increase the cheaper ingredients. Since Selden's sausage had always been rather lean, fat content could legally be increased in its brand resulting in a lighter weight portion after cooking. The executives wondered if the housewife would notice this result, provided they were careful to preserve flavor. If she did, they feared she would react angrily and begin brand hopping.

EXERCISE 4–27

Identify the target market that Selden has been addressing with its marketing effort.

EXERCISE 4–28

Identify the four major elements in the existing marketing mix for Selden's sausage product(s).

EXERCISE 4–29

Consider the marketing mix that is now addressing and being accepted by Selden's target market. Explain the fact that Selden's roll sausage is priced 40% below its link sausage and that all of Selden's sausage costs are 15% higher than competing brands.

EXERCISE 4–30

Given this analysis, and the other data in the case, what elements do you think can be changed effectively in the marketing mix for Selden?

- Product? No ____ Yes ____. If yes, changes include ____________________ (explain in detail).
- Price? No ____ Yes ____. If yes, changes include ____________________ (explain in detail).
- Distribution? No ____ Yes ____. If yes, changes include ________________ (explain in detail).
- Promotion? No ____ Yes ____. If yes, changes include ________________ (explain in detail).

EXERCISE 4–31

Does your new mix have balance and coherence? Does it fit the target market?

1 Does the product have appeal to the target customer?
2 Is the price acceptable to the target customer?
3 Will distribution reach the target customer in a timely and sufficient fashion?

4 Is the promotional message likely to be persuasive to the target? Is it directed toward acceptable objective?

5 Is the promotional mix suitable for the product? The objectives? The target customers?

Be prepared to critique your selection in class.

TARGET-MARKET STRATEGIES

The elements of the marketing mix discussed in this chapter should fit together, in the sense that they should logically support each other in successfully addressing the product/service needs of the customers selected as targets. Thus, a large number of potential customers identified as having needs for inexpensive foods offered throughout the day can effectively be addressed by companies serving a limited, but highly controlled, menu through a very large number of outlets convenient to mobile customers. Rigid control over location and control of management practices are imperative to meet customer needs for satisfactory prices, maintain control over costs, and return profit to the corporation. To reach a broad audience, promotion requires frequent and heavy advertising in mass media. We are, of course, describing the mix for marketing fast foods such as that of Colonel Sander's Kentucky Fried Chicken, McDonald's, Burger King, or Long John Silver's Sea Food chains.

At another extreme is the marketing or specialized well-drilling equipment; price may be a much less significant element in this mix than the technical characteristics of the product. Distribution may involve zero- or one-level channels, and promotion will be heavily oriented toward technical advertising and personal selling. Each *set* of marketing-mix elements is designed to help in the implementation of a target market strategy.

Generally speaking, target-market strategies fall into one of three different forms. The *mass-market* strategy is one in which *all* potential customers are felt to be sufficiently similar in their needs and buying characteristics for this type of product to warrant their inclusion in the target. A *single-niche* strategy involves the identification of a specific subgroup of customers from two or more identifiable subgroups within the total market. Each niche should be selected for its members' similarity in needs and buying characteristics. Companies can and do address *multiple niches*, that is, the use of separate products and mixes to address each target. Brewing companies have long maintained multiple-niche strategies wherein a mass-produced and mass-distributed product is mass marketed by using broad promotional appeals concurrently with the promotion and sale of a higher-priced product that is limited in distribution, sold through more selective outlets, and whose advertising is directed toward a narrower market of beer connoisseurs.

Implementing the Target-Market and Competitive Marketing Strategy

Establishing Marketing Policies From the foregoing, it is apparent that the choice of strategies can call for radically different plans of implementation. Distribution policies, for example, will be much different for mass-marketed products that are sold through thousands of different kinds of retail outlets as compared to products or services sold under a strategy in which products may be distributed on a highly personalized basis. At one extreme, we find cigarettes and candy sold in machines by vendors, supermarkets, filling stations, and a myriad of other outlets. At the other extreme, antique or custom-built automobiles are sold through want ads in auto magazines and the product is often personally delivered by the seller to the buyer at any location in the United States.

Policies can be considered operational guidelines that are developed by the general manager and his/her functional managers to aid in carrying out a given strategy. In the case of distribution of products, a managed vertical distribution involves the institution of policies that first *establish* the distribution system and later *manage* the system (e.g., "As of 19 [date], it is the policy of the ABC company to discontinue the use of commercial wholesalers and agents and to commence the warehousing and distribution of ABC's product line to its identified retailers"). An example of a distribution management policy is: "Warehouse managers are expected to ship orders based on the following priority codes,

AA Ship Air Express
A Ship Trailways Express
B Ship First Class Mail
C Ship UPS
D Ship Common Carrier

and "all delivery codes are to be initialed by the sales manager for the district in which the account is located."

Standing instructions of this type form the framework for day-to-day operations in businesses throughout the country and, for that matter, the world. The instructions must be clear to those whose responsibilities include the implementation of the policy. The instructions should be explainable to others and should make good business sense in terms of helping management and staff to carry out the needed business functions.

For another example, let us suppose that we have chosen as a marketing strategy a multiple-niche approach that involves a high-quality, low-volume but high-priced product and a high-volume lower-priced product as items selected for each of two niches. If your organizational resources are currently fully utilized, a reasonable policy on new-product development might be: "New product-development efforts must be directed toward the timely *replacement* of existing products within existing target markets as technological and market changes result in their increasing obsolescence."

If, on the other hand, one had resources available, a policy statement on new-product development might be similar to the one above, but one might add "and to potential profitable (over 10% profit on sales) products that can be marketed to a clearly identifiable market segment through concentrated marketing techniques."

Policy statements and guidelines can help to guide persons in making decisions on price. In some companies, price decisions are clearly the realm of specified persons. "No alteration to the existing price schedule is permitted without the express written permission of the Director of Marketing." Another form of pricing policy is contained in instructions to persons involved in competitive bidding: "In pricing construction work, it is our practice to price overhead at 75% of estimated direct labor. Total cost obtained is then multiplied by 1.48 to obtain quotation price." And, "All prices must be based on published list prices as of April 30, 19XX. Retailer and wholesaler discounts are at 30% and 50% of list, respectively." Policy guidelines on pricing that are not of the formula type are also found: "I tend to bid below total cost, particularly against *(name of a competitor)*, and I often get the job. I can often beat my cost estimates, but when I can't, I'm usually able to reopen the contract when the customer wants changes made. I get the business, I usually make a profit, and I keep *(name of the competitor)* from getting the job."

EXERCISE 4–32

Draft policy statements for each element of the marketing mix (price, promotion, distribution, and product) for a company engaged in selling distinctively styled ladies leather goods. (Use the Aigner line of leather shoes, handbags, coats, etc., as an example.)

Hint: Consider first the target market, next a generic competitive strategy, and then prepare your draft statements. Compare your replies with statements found at the end of the chapter.

EXERCISE 4–33

Draft policy statements for each of the four parts of the marketing mix for a company engaged in selling high-priced, high-quality electronic laboratory equipment to research and development centers in government and industry. Prices range from \$5,500 to \$10,500 and from \$180,000 to \$275,000 for the two product types now being carried.

Evaluating and Auditing Marketing

Assuring That Strategies and Policies Are Working Philip Kotler has developed a Marketing Effectiveness Rating Sheet that can serve several useful functions for the general manager. First, it provides a means of assessing past and present marketing in the organization. As Kotler notes, the superior range of scores on this scale is attained by only a few marketing superstar companies (Procter & Gamble, Avon Products, IBM, etc.). A second use for the rating sheet is as a checklist for establishing marketing-management objectives and for assuring that a *broad* range of marketing concerns are managed and monitored. Third, the rating instrument can help in evaluating the *change* that occurs as marketing and general managers' strategies and policies become operational. In effect, the general manager can extend his or her measurement beyond sales growth, profitability, and market share—each very important *WHAT* objectives—to a long list of *HOW WELL* objectives. Figure 4–5 offers a reproduction of the Marketing Effectiveness Rating Sheet.

A more detailed analysis of areas of deficiency uncovered as the result of the effectiveness rating can be undertaken by means of a detailed marketing audit. Audits, in the form suggested by Miller, should cover a review of (1) the marketing concept, including identification of customers, marketing strategies and their link to organizational objectives; (2) the marketing mix: product, price, place, and promotion; and (3) an analysis of the present situation . . . strengths, weaknesses, problems, and opportunities. Figure 4–6 is the abbreviated skeleton outline for such an audit.[12]

Generally, the audit should be used by the marketing manager on a comprehensive and systematic basis. Periodic audits should be conducted regularly rather than undertaken on a crisis basis. Where possible, the audit should be conducted by persons independent of the marketing group. Outside consultants and the experienced headquarters staff auditors are most likely to provide a truly independent assessment of the marketing program.[13]

The Winkleman Manufacturing Company Case, offers an opportunity to view a company's marketing situation from the perspective of the general manager. Reflect on the material in this chapter (perhaps using one of the audit frameworks as an overview), then read through the case carefully at least twice. When you have finished, please respond to the questions found in the exercises at the end of the case.

[12] John A. Miller, Valparaiso University. More detailed outlines can be found in Kotler, *Marketing Management*, pp. 653–55; and Cravens, *Strategic Marketing*, pp. 415–17.

[13] Kotler, *Marketing Management*, p. 650.

CUSTOMER PHILOSOPHY

A. Does management recognize the importance of designing the company to serve the needs and wants of chosen markets?

Score

0 ☐ Management primarily thinks in terms of selling current and new products to whoever will buy them.

1 ☐ Management thinks in terms of serving a wide range of markets and needs with equal effectiveness.

2 ☐ Management thinks in terms of serving the needs and wants of well-defined markets chosen for their long-run growth and profit potential for the company.

B. Does management develop different offerings and marketing plans for different segments of the market?

0 ☐ No.

1 ☐ Somewhat.

2 ☐ To a good extent.

C. Does management take a whole marketing system view (suppliers, channels, competitors, customers, environment) in planning its business?

0 ☐ No. Management concentrates on selling and servicing its immediate customers.

1 ☐ Somewhat. Management takes a long view of its channels although the bulk of its effort goes to selling and servicing the immediate customers.

2 ☐ Yes. Management takes a whole marketing systems view recognizing the threats and opportunities created for the company by changes in any part of the system.

INTEGRATED MARKETING ORGANIZATION

D. Is there high-level marketing integration and control of the major marketing functions?

0 ☐ No. Sales and other marketing functions are not integrated at the top and there is some unproductive conflict.

1 ☐ Somewhat. There is formal integration and control of the major marketing functions but less than satisfactory coordination and cooperation.

2 ☐ Yes. The major marketing functions are effectively integrated.

E. Does marketing management work well with management in research, manufacturing, purchasing, physical distribution, and finance?

0 ☐ No. There are complaints that marketing is unreasonable in the demands and costs it places on other departments.

1 ☐ Somewhat. The relations are amicable although each department pretty much acts to serve its own power interests.

2 ☐ Yes. The departments cooperate effectively and resolve issues in the best interest of the company as a whole.

FIGURE 4–5 Marketing Effectiveness Rating Instrument.

F. How well organized is the new product development process?

0 ☐ The system is ill defined and poorly handled.
1 ☐ The system formally exists but lacks sophistication.
2 ☐ The system is well structured and professionally staffed.

ADEQUATE MARKETING INFORMATION

G. When were the latest marketing research studies of customers, buying influences, channels, and competitors conducted?

0 ☐ Several years ago.
1 ☐ A few years ago.
2 ☐ Recently.

H. How well does management know the sales potential and profitability of different market segments, customers, territories, products, channels, and order sizes?

0 ☐ Not at all.
1 ☐ Somewhat.
2 ☐ Very well.

I. What effort is expended to measure the cost effectiveness of different marketing expenditures?

0 ☐ Little or no effort.
1 ☐ Some effort.
2 ☐ Substantial effort.

STRATEGIC ORIENTATION

J. What is the extent of formal marketing planning?

0 ☐ Management does little or no formal marketing planning.
1 ☐ Management develops an annual marketing plan.
2 ☐ Management develops a detailed annual marketing plan and a careful long-range plan that is updated annually.

K. What is the quality of the current marketing strategy?

0 ☐ The current strategy is not clear.
1 ☐ The current strategy is clear and represents a continuation of traditional strategy.
2 ☐ The current strategy is clear, innovative, data based, and well reasoned.

FIGURE 4–5 Marketing Effectiveness Rating Instrument. ***(continued)***

L. What is the extent of contingency thinking and planning?

0 ☐ Management does little or no contingency thinking.

1 ☐ Management does some contingency thinking although little formal contingency planning.

2 ☐ Management formally identifies the most important contingencies and develops contingency plans.

OPERATIONAL EFFICIENCY

M. How well is the marketing thinking at the top communicated and implemented down the line?

0 ☐ Poorly.

1 ☐ Fairly.

2 ☐ Successfully.

N. Is management doing an effective job with the marketing resources?

0 ☐ No. The marketing resources are inadequate for the job to be done.

1 ☐ Somewhat. The marketing resources are adequate, but they are not employed optimally.

2 ☐ Yes. The marketing resources are adequate and are deployed efficiently.

O. Does management show a good capacity to react quickly and effectively to on-the-spot developments?

0 ☐ No. Sales and market information is not very current and management reaction time is slow.

1 ☐ Somewhat. Management receives fairly up-to-date sales and market information; management reaction time varies.

2 ☐ Yes. Management has installed systems yielding highly current information and fast reaction time.

TOTAL SCORE

The instrument is used in the following way. The appropriate answer is checked for each question. The scores are added—the total will be somewhere between 0 and 30. The following scale shows the level of marketing effectiveness.

0–5 = None	16–20 = Good
6–10 = Poor	21–25 = Very good
11–15 = Fair	26–30 = Superior

FIGURE 4–5 Marketing Effectiveness Rating Instrument. *(continued)*

Source: Philip Kotler, "From Sales Obsession to Marketing Effectiveness," *Harvard Business Review*, November–December 1977, pp. 67–75.

I. THE MARKETING CONCEPT
   A. Satisfying Consumer Needs
      Current customers identified?
      Target customers identified?
      What *needs* do we satisfy?

   B. Coordinated Effort
      Are marketing and other business activities coordinated?
      Is there a written marketing plan?

   C. Achieving Organizational Objectives
      What are the firm's objectives? Dollars? Percentages? Numbers?
      Share? Profit? Growth? Sales? Other?

II. THE MARKETING MIX
   A. Product/Service
      Current line evaluation?
      New product/service development?
      Competition? Primary Companies . . . products . . . , etc.

   B. Price
      Objectives? Strategies?
      Penetration? Skimming?
      Discounts?
      Competitive levels?

   C. Place
      Firm's location (also that of competition, target markets)?
      Access
      Channels Suppliers
      Delivery of product/service . . . hours of operation . . . parking . . . etc.

   D. Promotion
      Personal Selling—people, training, compensation . . . ?
      Advertising—amounts, media, appeals, messages, etc.
      Sales Promotion—displays, coupons, sampling, premiums, etc.
      Publicity—used?

III. Strengths/Weaknesses Problems/Opportunities

FIGURE 4-6 Skeleton for a simple preliminary marketing audit.

Source. John A. Miller; Valporalso University used by permission.

WINKLEMAN MANUFACTURING COMPANY

In a recent staff meeting, John Winkleman, president of Winkleman Manufacturing Company, addressed his managers with this problem:

> *Intense competitive pressure is beginning to erode our market share in handhelds. I have documented eleven large orders that have been lost to Backman and Wiston within the past three months. On an annual basis, this amounts to nearly 10,000 units and $1.5 million in lost opportunities. Within the last eighteen months at least sixteen serious competitors have entered the market. Two-thirds of these DMMs have continuity indicators. The trend is the same for European and Japanese markets as well. Our sales of handheld DMMs in FY '81 is forecast to grow only 1.7%. According to Dataquest projections, the handheld DMM market will grow 20.9% for the next five years. I think that figure is conservative. Our competitors are gaining attention and sales with added features, particularly at the present time with continuity indicators. Since a new Winkleman general-purpose, low-cost handheld is two years from introduction, it is important that something be done to retain the profitable position of market leader in our traditional direct and distributor channels. Next meeting I want some ideas.*

The Winkleman Manufacturing Company is a major electronics manufacturer in the northwest, producing many varied products. The three products that most concern Mr. Winkleman are the Series A handheld digital multimeters (DMMs). As an innovator in the field of handheld DMMs, Mr. Winkleman saw his business flourish over the last two years. But now, with his three most successful products in late stages of maturity and a recession in full swing, times are not looking as rosy.

The three multimeters of concern are model numbers 1010, 1020, and 1030. These three models form a complementary family line. The 1010 is a low-cost unit containing all standard measurement functions and having a basic measurement accuracy of .5%. The 1020 offers identical measurement functions but has an improved basic measurement accuracy: .1%. The top of the line is the 1030. In addition to a basic accuracy of .1%, the 1030 offers several additional features, one being an audible continuity indicator. (See Exhibit 1 for sales and projected sales of these three models.)

At the next staff meeting, one of the newer management team members, Dave Haug, presented his ideas for tackling the lost market problem:

> *What we need is a facelift of our existing product line to hold us over the next two years. Changes in color, a new decal, some minor case modifications, and, most important, an audible continuity indicator in the 1010 and 1020, should give us two more years of product life to tide us over. We can call this Series B to retain continuity in switching from the old to the new. As my analysis indicates, Winkleman's decline in 1010/1020 sales could be reversed, and show a modest increase in market share over the next two years with the inclusion of the Series B features [see Exhibit 2]. Discussions with*

This case was prepared by Jim Dooley, under the supervision of Dr. William L. Weis, as the basis for class discussion rather than to illustrate either the effective or ineffective handling of an administrative situation.

EXHIBIT 1
Selected sales and projections

	FY '80 actual	*FY '81 forecast*	*Percentage*
1020	67,534	61,800	−8.4
1010	37,455	35,500	−5.5
1030	25,602	35,500	+39.0
TOTAL	130,591	132,800	+1.7

large-order customers indicate that Winkleman could have won 40–60% of the lost large orders that were mentioned at our last meeting, if our entire handheld family featured audible continuity. As you well know, the popularity of continuity indication has been confirmed in several other studies conducted over the past two years.

An estimate of sales of Series B has been generated from inputs from field sales, distribution managers, and discussions with customers. Conservative estimates indicate that sales of Series B will increase 6.9% above current Series A levels, with a marginal revenue increase of $1.5M at U.S. list, and assuming the same list prices as the current Series A models. During this current period of tight economic conditions, the market is becoming increasingly price sensitive. I am aware that our normal policy dictates multiplying the factory cost by three for pricing purposes and that the added factory cost of an audible continuity indicator is $5.00; but for income purposes, we should not tack this on to the current prices. My analysis indicates that an increase of $5.00 would reduce incremental sales by 20%, and an increase of $10.00 would reduce incremental sales by 80%.

Also, remember that we must pay for some non-recurring engineering costs (NRE) [see Exhibit 3]. These must come out of our contribution margin—which, at Winkleman, is calculated by taking the total dollar sales less the 28% discount to distributors less factory cost for those units. I believe that

EXHIBIT 2
Series A and B—projected comparisons

Model	*Unit price*	*Series A FY '81*	*Series B FY '81*	*Change*	*Total $ change*
1020	179	61,800	66,000	4,200 + 6.8%	11.81M (+.75M)
1010	139	35,500	40,000	4,500 +12.6%	5.56M (+.63M)
1030	219	35,500	36,000	500 +1.4%	7.88M (+.11M)
TOTAL		132,800	142,000	9,200 6.9%	25.25M (+1.49M)

EXHIBIT 3
Engineeriing costs and schedule

The objectives for Series B, Models 1010, 1020, and 1030, are:
- All case parts molded in medium gray
- New decal for all units
- Pulse-stretched beeper for 1010 and 1020
- Rubber foot on battery door
- Positionable bail
- Manuals updated as necessary

For these objectives, NRE costs will be:

Manual (updated schematics for 1010, 1020, along with instructions for operation of beeper; model number and front panel changes for all units)	$ 3,500
Battery door mold (add three units)	12,000
Battery door foot die	3,000
Decal	1,900
Bail improvement	8,600
Photo lab	250
PCB fab (prototypes)	500
Engineering labor (25 man-weeks)	81,000
Hard model run	6,000
TOTAL	$96,750

increasing these prices will reduce our margins significantly, hindering our ability to cover the NRE, let alone make a profit. Therefore, I propose we go ahead with Series B and hold the line on prices.

Dennis Cambelot, a longtime Winkleman employee, spoke up with a comment on Dave's proposal:

Dave, I think this Series B idea shows a lot of potential, but price-wise you are way out of line. We have always added the standard markup to our products. We make quality products and people are willing to pay for quality. The only thing your fancy MBA degree taught you was to be impractical. If you had gotten your experience in the trenches like me, your pricing theories would not be so conservative, and this company could make more money.

At the close of the meeting, Mr. Winkleman asked that each manager consider the Series B proposal. He directed that this consideration include: (1) whether or not to adopt the B series; (2) if yes, at what price level; (3) alternative suggestions.

EXERCISE 4-34

Refer to Figure 4-6. Prepare a simple preliminary marketing audit on Winkleman Manufacturing, cover Section I of Figure 4-6, The Marketing Concept.

EXERCISE 4-35

Refer to Figure 4-6. Prepare a simple preliminary marketing audit on Winkleman Manufacturing, cover Sections IIA, and IIB only.

EXERCISE 4-36

Refer to Figure 4-6. Prepare a simple preliminary marketing audit on Winkleman Manufacturing, cover Sections IIC and IID only.

EXERCISE 4-37

Refer to Figure 4-6. Prepare a simple preliminary marketing audit on Winkleman Manufacturing, cover Section III only.

Prepare these audits in written form for presentation in class or as a written assignment. Length should be two-typed pages or less.

ANSWERS TO SELECTED EXERCISES

Exercise 4-1

One generic market might be *powered* (or self-propelled) *transportation vehicles.* From the list, all of the products named except bicycles and roller skates would be a part of that generic market, including the rental car, because that does serve the same purpose.

Exercise 4-32

The following brief statement provides an example of the type of policy statement that might specify the principal elements in the marketing mix for the Aigner line of ladies leather goods. "The Aigner line of high-fashion leatherwear is designed for special appeal to professional women, homemakers in the managerial and professional wage-earner class, and single women with sufficient means to dress well—all ranging from ages 25 to 50. The products are characterized by a distinctive color that permits wear with a wide range of ensembles, and they have a distinctive, artistically designed buckle or clasp that carries the Aigner logo. Prices fall below designer lines but are well above conventional ready-to-wear items. The Aigner line is found in selected higher priced department stores and ladies ready-to-wear retailers. Although the products' distinctive color and logo offer a promotional medium when worn by customers, Aigner also advertises, selectively, in high-quality ladies magazines."

Do you believe that you could write a similar statement for another product? Try to do so for a product of your choice and bring it to class for discussion.

5

PRODUCTION/ OPERATIONS AND THE GENERAL MANAGER

THE CONVERSION FUNCTION

Businesses are organizations that have been established to perform some purpose. A manufacturing firm, for example, performs a transformation function, one in which it converts (transforms) materials into salable products by means of the application of available technologies and human resources. A small company that manufactures window units for homes obtains the wood or aluminum materials used in building window frames, the metal parts used for latches and glides, and the glass used for the windowpanes. These materials are converted into salable units—by mill workers, using shapers, joiners, saws, and sanding machines—into complete window units that can be installed in new or existing homes. The materials gain value in this process because they become more useful to potential customers than they would be as raw materials. The cost of this conversion can be identified as (1) the cost of added labor and supplies and (2) the allocated cost of the technologies and management needed to perform the transformation.

The equipment needed to aid in the transformation is "used up" to some extent in the process. As the equipment is used, we can attribute some of that usage to each unit of output and thereby consider that cost to be a part of the cost of transforming each unit. In a similar way, we can assign part of the cost of the building that is used to house the transformation equipment and workers. Indeed, we can allocate the costs that apply to all parts of the organization involved in transformation of materials into salable products. Thus, the cost of executive salaries, taxes on the building, insurance premiums, building security, and a host of other overhead expenses can be attributed to products produced by the conversion process.

It is important to remember that the economy in the United States today is made up largely of *services* rather than products. We find services in an enormously broad range of application areas. Dog walkers, housecleaning firms, employment agencies, accountants, attorneys, physicians, home decorating firms, engineers, architects, baby-sitters, bodyguards, chauffeurs, and management consultants all offer services to a service-oriented public.

The conversion function also applies to service businesses. A customer who comes to a service station for a lubrication and oil change, for example, will receive some products (oil, grease, filters, etc.) and will also receive services in the form of the help of the staff in actually lubricating the vehicle and changing the oil. The conversion in this type of business involves changing a vehicle from one that needs lubrication service to one that is lubricated. In recent years, gasoline stations have initiated self-service pumps for those customers who simply want to buy the product or products and don't wish to pay for the services offered with the sale of gasoline (pumping the gas, checking oil, battery, tire pressure, etc.). In addition, convenience stores have long sold gasoline and oil to customers who want those products but who have little or no need for the other services.

EXERCISE 5–1

List two types of manufacturing business and describe:

- The materials used in the conversion.
- The general technology and equipment used in the conversion.
- The products sold to the public.

EXERCISE 5–2

List two types of commercial service businesses (other than those listed above) and describe:

- The state of the customer prior to the service conversion.
- The general technology and the equipment used in the conversion.
- The end state of the customer, that is, the service sold to the public.

Scope of Conversion

A number of years ago, it was quite common to encounter textbooks on "production" that described manufacturing operations and facilities, but little else. These textbooks focused on all the activities within the walls of a factory, rarely on the functions performed prior to the time the material or parts arrived at the factory or on products after they left the premises. The focus was on efficiency, developing methods and processes that could convert materials into products in the factory at the lowest possible cost. Decisions related to the costs of components were dealt with by cost-driven make-or-buy decision rules. Similarly, questions on transportation and/or distribution were viewed by production managers primarily from a cost-efficiency perspective. For example, "Can our own trucks deliver the product to our customers at a lower cost than a contract carrier?" Such a question describes the concern of the manager who is focusing on cost efficiency.

In the 1960s and 1970s, the scope of concern began to expand. In order to maintain not only a maximum efficiency in cost terms, but an effectiveness in meeting customer needs, managers charged with responsibility for the conversion process began to broaden the area of their interests. They began to see that accepting a somewhat lower level of efficiency in one element might result in maximizing the effectiveness of the *entire* conversion process. Thus, the scope of the manager of operations has broadened significantly, as has the perspective of the general manager, who must also view the transformation process in its entirety rather than confine his or her concern only to the segment currently occupied by the firm.

In the years when transportation costs per ton of coal were relatively low and the cost of electric transmission high, power plants were located close to the point of the use of power. Later, when transportation costs rose and when the technology of generation and transmission had improved, power plants began to be located close to or, in some instances, *in* the coal mine itself. If one were to concentrate on only one element in the total process of converting coal to electrical energy *delivered to the customer,* the older method might have been more efficient. When the entire conversion is considered, a more effective, and more efficient total operation can be both envisioned and implemented. In this instance, a larger single generating station may have superior operating efficiencies over several smaller units. Coal could be handled by automated equipment and would not have to be loaded and unloaded from the relatively small units represented by railroad hopper cars. Customers too small to afford their own generating units could be supplied by power from the main power network originating at, or close to, the coalfields. These individual operating efficiencies could offset the cost of longer distance transmission of electrical energy and result in a more efficient and more effective conversion process.

The change in the scope of the business outlined here has significance well beyond the concerns of the operator of the generating plant. It involves a significant shift in capital assets and in the ownership of those assets. It should be apparent that the shift in form of operations involves a much wider range of business functions than just production or, for that matter, just operations. Marketing is needed to sell power, capital is needed to finance the large-scale generation facility and the transmission lines needed to carry power to users. The general manager's oversight of the production/operations function, therefore, must be sustained not only for purposes of supervision, but also to recognize the *organizational* impact of decisions reached in the pursuit of production/operations management objectives.

The enlarged scope, as illustrated earlier, also extends to the customer as well as to the origin of materials, and it represents a perspective of overall effectiveness in providing products and services to customers in one's markets.

EXERCISE 5–3

The General Electric Company built a large appliance-manufacturing facility in Louisville, Kentucky, in the 1960s. Appliance Park was designed to produce a number of small appliances for sale to customers in the eastern and central United States. Louisville, a city of nearly 1 million persons, is located on the Ohio River, approximately 500 miles downstream from Pittsburgh, Pennsylvania, a major steel-manufacturing center. It has a largely nonunion labor market and is a major railroad center, with rail lines extending north to Chicago, south to New Orleans, east to Philadelphia and New York, and west to St. Louis and Kansas City.

- From an *operations*-management point of view, what major cost and effectiveness elements were being addressed by the choice of Louisville as a site for a manufacturing plant costing hundreds of millions of dollars? (Some answers can be found at the end of the chapter.)
- If the plant had been located in an area of the lowest labor cost (e.g., Mississippi or Louisiana), what would have been the consequences for the rest of the cost-effectiveness picture?

Today, the term *operations management* has replaced the term *production management* for a number of very good reasons. First, the term *production* tended to have a factory connotation, which was ill suited to the expanded scope of the concern of those who were interested in the total conversion process. Second, *operations management* suggests that managers are concerned with effectiveness as well as with efficiencies. Maximizing the utilization of resources, maintaining sources of supply, and satisfying needs of customers are legitimate concerns of operations managers. Third, the expanded scope of the term permits us to think of ways of addressing the pursuit of both efficiencies and effectiveness in service industries, areas that had been inadequately treated in earlier thinking. Now we see applications of operations-management thinking to the computer room, where payroll checks, sales reports, invoices, and job cost data are calculated and prepared for distribution. It is interesting to note that this part of a data processing department is referred to as computer *operations*. The relative merits of mailing hard-copy reports to "customers" versus establishing a remote terminal for transmission by wire or satellite are among the types of concerns of today's computer operations specialists. They have moved beyond being concerned solely about the monthly cost of equipment and manpower or hardware utilization to questions about the wisdom of performing the operation at all!

MAJOR ELEMENTS IN CONVERSION

Technology

In very broad terms, technology can be partitioned in at least two different ways. First, some technologies are mature and very stable, whereas others are evolving and are seen to change rapidly and frequently. The technology of the paper industry has remained virtually intact for nearly 200 years, dating from the invention of the Fourdrinier paper machine. Improvements in that technology have been made, but they have been incremental in nature: changes in the type and speed of power sources, improvements in materials used in the processes, and increased efficiencies in heat exchange, and so on. The process itself is fundamentally the same. In a more dynamic technological environment, change in production technology is rapid and telling in its impact on production. In the high-technology semiconductor field, developments in production technology made possible the dramatic decline in price of pocket calculators; the use of microcircuits in appliances, automobiles, digital clocks and watches; and extraordinary advances in computer technology, advances that permitted an extension of computer usage to the household and enabled a quantum expansion of computer power in larger installations.

In some instances, changes in technology take place in relatively small increments. In others, change is a more convulsive process and may have a greater impact on those individuals closely associated with the technology. In the steel industry, the open-hearth furnace was the accepted standard technology for 50 or more years. In the late 1950s, the basic oxygen furnace was adopted, a process change that caused the shutdown of hundreds of furnaces across the country. The effect was so dramatic that some newly built open-hearth furnaces were never used; they were simply scrapped. The new technology could produce steel at roughly twice the rate of the older process, tapping heats of several hundred tons of steel in 3 to 3½ hours as compared to a processing time of 7 to 9 hours for the older process. The new technology required vast quantities of gaseous oxygen, a costly addition to the process, but the additional cost was more than offset by the increased production rates.

A second system for partitioning technology has to do with production in a continuous stream or in lots through intermittent or batch-type processes. Each process carries with it a number of associated attributes, issues, and conditions. In the lowest-volume, one-of-a-kind production, the opportunity for individual variation in design is ideal. The technology used here is typically that of a model, or prototype, shop, one in which general-purpose production equipment and artisan's or artist's tools are the means of constructing the product. Examples of this type of production include custom-furniture manufacture, tool-and-die-shop manufacture of metal artifacts, the construction of prototypes for contract bidding and production planning, and the building of models for display or hobby purposes.

At the next higher level of volume, we find the manufacture, or processing, of small batches of similar or identical products. The same tools and equipment used for one-of-a-kind production are frequently employed, but they are adapted to reduce the need for repeated set-up by the use of jigs or fixtures. Also, additional space is provided to permit the accumulation of small quantities of in-process inventories. A worker, therefore, can set up a machine to produce 20 items of a particular product and can provide special stops or guides to aid in the production process at that station. As each of the 20 items are completed, they are set aside to accumulate prior to being moved to the next station, thus permitting a batching for processing at subsequent production stations. The guides, stops, and other specialized equipment used to aid in the batch processing can be constructed so that they can be kept in a toolroom for use on subsequent batches, thereby preserving the technological improvement.

Employees involved in one-of-a-kind and batch production are, of necessity, versatile in their skills. They must understand the sequence of steps needed; be able to set up, adjust, and operate their equipment; and know how to construct and employ the fixtures needed as production aids. The acquisition of the multiple skills required for this type of production is often developed by means of a lengthy apprenticeship process. Typically, these are highly paid employees who are capable of great flexibility, and precise, artful, and highly skillful production.

As batches become larger and larger, the conversion process approaches a continuous flow of products through the facility. In some kinds of production processes, it is possible to batch orders together in such a way as to (a) enlarge each batch to an economically justifiable size and (b) to group and schedule orders through the conversion process in ways that minimize the frequency and time delay caused by equipment changes. In the steel industry, for example, orders for similarly shaped bars are grouped together and rolled as a set of orders. The roll sets are shaped to permit successive reductions in bar size and, as orders for a large size are filled, the operators adjust to the next size in the order sequence but stay within a shape category. This size adjustment takes a relatively short time. When the orders for the entire category are filled for that time period, the mill is shut down for a roll change, and a set of rolls for the next category of production are then set into place. In effect, we have a series of large batches being produced, each scheduled to minimize order-change delay. As order-size increases and product change downtime decreases, we approach a continuous process. Today, however, the technology for achieving these economies of scheduling is well established and built into the capital equipment itself. The jigs and fixtures used to achieve production efficiencies on general-purpose equipment have now become highly sophisticated specialized machines designed to produce batches of products, and to do so with minimum delay between batches. The range of items produced on the newer machines is narrower. But operating speeds are higher, and the skills required for their operation have also become more restricted by the limited purposes to which the equipment can be put and by the limited range of human needs called for by the process. Employees who were formerly responsible for planning production and for the setup and adjustment of the equipment are now responsible for *tending* the machine . . . feeding materials in, removing finished products, and monitoring the work of the machine to minimize waste.

At the extreme of continuous production, we find process industries, where closed manufacturing technologies continually generate output—24 hours per day, 7 days per week. Shutdowns do occur, but they have a profound effect on production and every effort is expended to delay their occurrence and to aid in returning the unit to operating status. Several examples in manufacturing come to mind. In the manufacture of fluorescent tubes for illumination, the furnaces needed to melt glass to the proper chemical composition and plasticity are very large, as are the quantities of material kept at operating condition. A shutdown of one of these furnaces could mean a loss of costly material (or the costly recycling of that material) and the loss of production owing to the time required to close down the furnace, cool it to a temperature where it can be repaired or rebuilt, reheat it to operating temperatures, refill it with materials, and return it to operating status. As a consequence, a plant that manufactures these products will attempt to keep the furnace at operating temperatures as much as possible. In addition, the process works best when glass can be drawn smoothly from the furnace in a continuous flow. New materials can be added as needed, operating temperature and consistency maintained, and maximum efficiencies achieved. Scheduling such a plant to reach maximum efficiency means attempting to run around the clock, maintaining the continuous flow, and working to achieve enough orders for production to minimize the costs of a hot but unused furnace.

A second example is found in the steel industry. The blast furnace is a device that converts iron ore, limestone, and coke (coal that has been refined) into molten iron. It functions by suspending a column of materials on a very hot continuous blast of air. Materials are added in layers at the top, and the mixture gradually settles as the chemical processes occur and as molten iron drips out of the mass to the bottom of the furnace. If the air were to be cut off, the mixture could collapse and cause great damage. For effective operation, the blast furnace operates 24 hours per day, 7 days per week, until its liner of ceramic material is eroded to the point where it must be replaced, roughly 6 to 8 years. Molten iron is tapped off periodically and sent to subsequent steel-making operations. When demand is low for iron, the molten iron is cast into bars and stored in bar form for periods of heavier production. The furnace continues on, as it must, even when demand is low.

In both of the cases cited, we see evidence of the inflexibility of continuous production. In the case of glass, the nature of the process requires continuous production scheduling, with all the attendant problems of manning and staffing a round-the-clock plant as well as the cost of maintaining very high temperatures in a large mass of material when order volume is insufficient to maintain 24-hour-per-day production. In the blast furnace case, there is little control over the volume of material produced, and schedulers must accommodate demand by accumulating inventory in slack periods in anticipation of its use in later, more prosperous times. In addition, the furnace must be manned 24 hours per day, 7 days per week, for years and years of operations. The rebuilding of one of these massive production units is a sizable task, as is the difficult task of relighting the furnace and gradually rebuilding the mass of materials to reach operating status.

Thus far, we have looked at the manufacture of products in our examination of technology. Many, if not most of the same observations apply to various kinds of services. Let us first look at services performed on an individualized basis. An example might be hairstyling for both men and women. The opportunity for individual variation is quite high, the tools are relatively simple, and those performing the service are highly skilled. In clinical psychology, individualized therapy can be tailored to the unique problems faced by the client. In addition, the therapist can readily adjust the rate of progress in therapy to the extent to which the client seems to be making improvement. Similarly, in education, a tutor works on an individualized basis with a single student. The student's individual needs and problems govern topics addressed and the rate of progress when a tutorial system is used.

In a number of service areas, the equivalent of batch processing is a common technology employed to gain economies of scale in dealing with like problems. Weight-loss clinics often have fairly large classes of persons needing assistance in dietary control. Group-oriented approaches to deal with psychological problems are not uncommon, and educators have used batch approaches since time immemorial. Several conditions are needed before batch approaches can be employed. First, the problems needing attention must be very similar. In clinical psychology, persons suffering from similar phobias are often coached and trained to deal with the disorder in groups. They not only face the same kind of problem, but find that the encouragement gained from the group and the examples seen in other group members are materially helpful in making progress in their own case. Second, the service needed must be appropriate to a group or batch approach. Education, for example, can be delivered to a group, as can counseling on drug or alcohol abuse. Surgery, on the other hand, does not lend itself to group delivery!

An interesting solution to the problem of providing individualized services to large numbers of clients is found in the induction process for military service. Inductees must be processed through a series of services in the course of becoming members of the military. Typically, they are sent through an induction center in batches. The center is arranged to provide categories of individualized attention to large batches of recruits. Numbers of clerks will take the same kind of information from a large number of inductees at the same time. Similarly, a group of physicians will conduct physical examinations on groups of inductees, and groups of medical technicians will administer innoculations to groups of inductees. The induction center is arranged to provide these services efficiently, and it uses batch approaches to achieve the needed level of productivity.

Techniques for batch approaches to services often differ from those used for individualized attention. Specialists highly trained in group psychotherapy are employed to make maximum use of the group and its effects on individuals. Educators develop highly refined pedagogic approaches that maximize the learning potential in a conventional classroom setting. The highly controlled tutorial approach, with an individualized dialogue between tutor and pupil, is replaced here by generalized directions to students who use common, but highly refined workbooks and exercises to achieve educational ends. The teacher serves as a guide and as a resource to deal with questions rather than as the immediate source of new knowledge.

Continuous service activities are somewhat less commonly found. In transportation, batch transportation is normal, but escalators and motorized walkways provide a continuous flow of persons through facilities such as airports and some entertainment centers. Pipelines provide a continuous flow of products to customers, as do power-transmission lines and microwave communications networks. These forms of continuous services are, for the most part, technologically driven. They exist because of a technology that permits their existence, and they do not simply represent a multiplicative use of existing small-batch processes.

In many areas of our society, services are available on a continuous, or round-the-clock, basis, but they are used only as needed. Police, fire, and medical services have this characteristic, as do towing services, automated banking, and 24-hour-per-day centralized claim handling by insurance companies. This type of service, although continually available, is largely an extension of an existing technology or an organizational means to make a small batch service available as needed.

EXERCISE 5–4

Identify, if you can, two products (other than those described above) produced on a one-of-a-kind basis. Describe, as well as you can, the tools that are used and the type of training required for the person who makes each product.

EXERCISE 5–5

Identify two services (other than those described above) provided on a batch basis. Describe the degree of specialization required to perform these services and any specialized equipment required. (Some answers can be found at the end of the chapter).

EXERCISE 5-6

Identify any type of service that you can think of (other than those mentioned above) that is provided on a continuous basis. Describe the technology that is required to provide that service and the degree of specialization required for its operation.

Human Resources

A second element in the mix of factors to be addressed in production or operations management is that of the human factors involved in the process. Since the time of the Industrial Revolution, as automated processes expanded, jobs became less and less complex. Our product economy was built on processes that made products of increasing sophistication and complexity by a technology similarly complex, but the processes were operated by employees whose education and skill levels were relatively quite low. Our present economy is now in a state of evolution in services similar to that which took place in the product economy shortly after the time of the Industrial Revolution. Our services have been produced, in large part, by highly trained and well-paid *generalists* in their professions. Physicians, for example, perform a wide number of tasks that are incidental to the performance of their function, in much the same fashion as artisans of the late-eighteenth century performed many tasks in the construction of their product line. As specialization in the manufacture of products was achieved, persons responsible for small segments of manufacture were employed, and the need for the craft generalist declined. In our service economy future, we will see a continuation of specialization in functions as service professionals find means of more efficiently providing their abilities to clients. In the dental-care profession, we have seen many functions formerly performed by dentists now under the highly professional (but more narrowly defined) care of dental assistants. The use of paraprofessionals in a number of fields is evidence of the advancement of this gradual revolution in services delivery.

In general, it is probably reasonable to consider the demands on the human resources employed to be inversely related to the degree of technological complexity used. That is, as the state of the technology required is at the level of a craftsperson who uses relatively simple tools, the production of either products or services requires the talents of highly trained generalists. These individuals must have an expertise that is broad enough to enable them to carry out the full range of tasks required and to supervise the persons engaged in supporting activities. In the manufacture of products, these kinds of persons might be machinists, cabinetmakers, goldsmiths, or weavers. In the services, highly skilled generalists might include physicians, physical therapists, teachers, clinical psychologists, publicists, business agents, or athletic coaches.

At the other extreme of technological advancement, the process type of transformation process, the skills required of human resources are highly specialized but narrow in scope. In manufacturing, automation has sometimes resulted in the development of jobs so narrow that they require only one or two movements and a range of little more than arm's length physical activity. Training time for jobs of this type is often only a few minutes. Operating a machine of advanced type may mean simply feeding raw material into the equipment and monitoring the machine to shut down in the event of trouble. These ultraspecialized and minimum-function jobs offer the natural opportunity for advanced automation and roboticized technologies, and they are targeted by engineers and production technologists for that purpose. For more advanced equipment, one set of specialists are employed to adjust the machine; a second type of specialist sets the machine to new specifications as orders change. In both cases, the specialists are very narrow.

In the services, the same form of specialization is found. In medicine, specialized professionals perform many medical functions once performed by the physician. Laboratory analysis of body fluids is performed by a team of lab specialists and x-rays are taken by radiological technologists. Casts are constructed and applied by orthopedic assistants, and social workers provide counseling to patients and families upset over the complications of illness. In law, attorneys not only specialize to perform a limited list of functions, but they make use of paralegal assistants and junior attorneys to perform law research, file documents and handle the administrative work related to their cases.

As this process becomes more and more advanced, the technology associated with the work of specialists becomes more highly developed and may eventually exceed the ready knowledge and use of the general practitioner. The administrative secretary who has learned to become an expert in the use of a dedicated word processor has access to equipment and a technology that may not be understood well by the manager of the department. The laboratory technician who operates an automated blood-analysis machine may similarly be in control of equipment that is not readily usable by a physician or even a pathologist (the type of physician usually in charge of laboratory activities). In these examples from service industries, we should note that the training and education for these specialists is considerably more time consuming than was described for specialized skills in manufacturing. Indeed, in many of the areas in medicine, certification in the specialty is required prior to practice, and incumbents have been required to undergo several years of training to achieve certification.

In the performance of general accounting practice, various specialists in accountancy address client problems at different times. A managerial accountant may be involved in the construction of a standard cost system for use in manufacturing cost control. Once a year, or more, auditors will examine not only the books of account, but physical assets, employee records, and historical records as a part of the process of assuring that the company's financial position is properly stated. Tax specialists assist in advising clients on tax matters and in the preparation of state and federal returns. Although the general practitioner can offer services in each of these areas, the extent of specialization in each gives the larger service firm a distinct competitive edge in meeting client needs for the broad array of service needs. In a similar fashion, the large university offers both specialized depth and a diversity of offerings to students. As with accounting firms, the larger institution's ability to offer these services is competitively advantageous. Indeed, in service industries, the principle advantage of larger scale is the opportunity for enhancing competitive strength through specialization rather than by means of the economic advantage of size, as might be the case in manufacturing.

In both product and service sectors, we find a general trend of automating to reduce or eliminate the cost and potential error of human factors. Robotics in manufacturing involves the widespread use of complex automated devices to aid in manufacturing processes. In service fields, computerized diagnostic equipment and the on-line availability of data banks has reduced the need for lower level technicians and library researchers. In law, the computer has revolutionized case research, as it has revolutionized research in academic reference libraries throughout the country. In human terms, this inevitably means the continuing loss of narrow-skill occupations and the development of a more limited number of new, more complex, but still narrow specialties. Although robotics has removed people from the assembly line for autos, it has not removed them from the *robotics* construction and repair business! In many service areas, service generalists have found themselves functioning as managers of client services rather than serving as the person providing the service itself. This trend is likely to continue as service functions become more specialized.

EXERCISE 5–7

Assume, for the moment, that you are the operations manager for a moderately large medical laboratory. Your laboratory has enjoyed considerable success and you anticipate that it will more than quadruple in size over the next five-year planning period. Anticipate the effects of this growth on your needs for equipment, facilities, and manpower for the coming 5-year period. Prepare for a detailed discussion in class or for a homework problem to be turned in to your instructor.

EXERCISE 5–8

As the manufacturing manager of a firm that builds ceiling light fixtures for sale to the home renovation industry, you have found that orders have become decidedly smaller over recent years. Retailers and individual customers have seemed to prefer a wide range of highly individualized designs, and they are apparently willing to pay for the cost of manufacture. Your present equipment is moderately automated and your work force semiskilled. Most employees have only the skills they have developed with your firm and are not members of any recognized craft or trade.

- What would be some of the factors you would consider in your equipment replacement plans for the coming years? What kind of equipment would you plan to buy? Why?

- What problems might you anticipate with human resources in the coming years? What will you plan to do about them? Why?

Materials

In the operations-management sense, materials represent the object of the transformation process. In the case of the manufacturer of windows, wood, aluminum, and glass are transformed into salable products. In the service organization, the object of the transformation process may be a person (as in the case of medicine or hairstyling) or some other object needing service attention (one's poodle in need of trimming, perhaps). In either case, some of the same considerations apply. In manufacturing, the materials to be transformed must be specified by type, size, chemical composition, or color in order to produce items meeting customer needs at reasonable costs. Materials can be acquired in raw, or unmanufactured, form, or in semifinished or completely finished states. Some operations make use of entirely finished materials (components or even subassemblies) and concentrate on the assembly and packaging of the finished product. Other organizations make use of the most fundamental form of raw material and transform the raw ingredients into products through a series of transformation steps. The blast furnace is an example of that form of transformation, converting ore, limestone, and coke into iron. In any case, the specification of materials is a significant step. When the technology is relatively simple, the choice of material makes only a modest difference to the craftsperson. A custom-furniture manufacturer cares little whether the customer chooses oak, cherry, or chestnut wood as the material to be used in a desk, so long as the customer pays for any cost differentials involved. In some instances, the craftsperson may find that the customer's choice of a more exotic wood offers a challenge and thereby makes the job somewhat more interesting. The materials chosen have an effect on some of the tools chosen and the techniques employed, but the impact on the process is relatively modest in this form of technology.

When batch processing is undertaken, however, the choice of materials becomes much more important. Batching is predicated on like qualities, and one like quality is choice of materials. In furniture manufacture, mixing maple and oak in the use of materials might result in furniture being constructed of dissimilar materials, a factor that might not be of significance in manufacture, but one that would not be attractive in marketing finished products. Even mixing pieces in a production process can cause problems. In our example of oak and maple furniture, we might be able to see that the pieces were matched successfully to achieve all-maple and all-oak assemblies, but we would still encounter difficulties when we attempted to use oak stain on maple finishes, or vice versa.

The quality level of materials to be transformed also can be the source of problems. If we are planning the manufacture of a batch of products and have purchased materials in anticipation of finishing a given number, any losses that might result from poor quality in materials affect not only the material itself, but all of the other elements that are involved in producing that particular product. Although replacement materials can be acquired, the remainder of the product must be delayed, and it may be lost or damaged while waiting for the missing components to be prepared. Thus, the operations manager must specify quality as well as quantity and must attend to the downstream problems that arise when material quality is inadequate. In some industries, these downstream problems are so difficult to handle that inspectors are permanently assigned to vendor's plants to assure that quality requirements are dealt with quite early in the process. Similarly, in those same industries, repeated inspections of raw materials and goods in process are undertaken to stop problems at the earliest possible stage of production. In many industries where these types of quality problems exist, the identification of a very limited list of highly trusted vendors is extremely important.

In service industries, batching of the "materials" is also extremely important. If the service to be provided is highly individualized and if the provider is a generalist, then the practitioner simply inquires as to need or diagnoses need, and then proceeds with service provision. In a group-service technology, however, considerable care is needed to accurately categorize the individuals or objects needing services. In education, placement in programs follows a careful program of detailed evaluation to assure that the student is affiliated with a class that closely approximates his or her stage of educational development.

In a highly bureaucratized service facility, the appropriate screening of persons needing services helps to assure service specialists appropriate to specific needs work on the particular type of required service and that clients do not spend time needlessly waiting, only to be told that that window doesn't handle the particular service need they want. Signs, lines on the floor, floorwalkers, and service assistants at entrances all aid in the process of categorizing clients into appropriate need categories.

INTEGRATING THE MAJOR ELEMENTS

From the foregoing, it should be apparent that for each category of production, an appropriate, or congruent, mix of machinery, materials, and human resources is required to convert materials into products. Each constitutes a set that serves to accommodate the need for efficiencies and for effectiveness given the needs of customers. The manager of operations and, in a somewhat less tightly focused way, the general manager must think in terms of these congruent sets in planning, organizing and executing strategies in operations. Each carries with it a different set of needs for materials, capital, equipment, and human resources. Markets differ, as do the marketing plans and activities needed to serve customers in each. Figure 5–1 is a simple graphic that represents a range of elements given a range of order patterns.

Integration of Operations-Management Elements

PERSONNEL	Skill Level	High	Semiskilled	Low/ Semiskilled	High/ Narrow
	Training Time	Long	Moderate	Short	Moderate/ Long
MATERIALS	Type	Variable by Order	Variable by Batch	Little Variability	
	Quality Control	By Craftsperson	By Purchasing Standards	By Purchasing Standards and Preproduction Tests	
TECHNOLOGY	Tools	Simple	Modified Simple	Complex	
		One-of-a Kind	Batch	Continuous	

ORDER PATTERN

FIGURE 5-1

The schematic shown in Figure 5-1 should not be interpreted to mean that the categories of order patterns, human resources, materials, or technologies shown are always clearly delineated or sharply defined. Instead, as we have described earlier, the order patterns and technologies tend to gradually shift from very limited quantities to small batches, to larger batches, and, ultimately, to nearly continuous operations. Equipment becomes automated on a progressive basis, in most cases, and intermediate stages of technological development can be relatively easily identified.

EXERCISE 5-9

Use Figure 5-1 to assist you in describing, in as specific terms as you can, the personnel skill level, training time, quality-control needs for materials, and technologies needed for these products:

- Kentucky Fried Chicken.
- A man's three-piece suit.
- An oil portrait of a relative.

Although the transition from one stage to another can take place gradually, one factor should be made clear. The equipment and work force used for one-of-a-kind manufacture is not suitable for continuous production, nor is the reverse true. Indeed, as the change progresses toward batches of articles, the usefulness of the general-purpose equipment rapidly declines, as does the wisdom of employing the expensive skills of the craft generalist. Each broad category of operations has its own unique problems, its own forms of quality standards and quality control, and its own performance standards.

On occasion, operations managers may be asked to produce products that have distinctly different order patterns. Each order pattern carries with it an associated technology, set of material requirements, and personnel needs. Handling one or the other order pattern is easy enough, but many problems arise when more than one order pattern is placed into production in the same facility. Equipment requirements are different, as are needs for employees, training time, and the need for close control on quality of materials.

Unless all members of management are extremely careful, the standards from one part of the operation will migrate, inappropriately, to the other. If standards for a one-of-a-kind operation are used in large-scale production, it is likely that overqualified persons will be employed to run mass-production equipment or that materials quality control will be left to unqualified operators, thus causing delays in production. In addition, it is possible that quality standards will be somewhat higher than the generally accepted commercial standards for mass production.

It is interesting to note that some companies faced with requests for a mixture of order-pattern types have physically separated the different patterns in order to avoid the problem of inappropriate transfer. Firearms manufacturers have a custom shop that handles requests for custom-finished or specially engraved firearms for gifts, collectors, or presentations. They manufacture the regular line of products in classic large-batch fashion in an automated factory, but they handle the custom work in a small bench-type shop and use highly skilled craftspersons to undertake this one-of-a-kind manufacture. It should be pointed out that *functionally* the products produced in the custom shop are identical with those made on the production line. They differ in the need for highly specialized and individualized attention and in the frequency and size of their orders.

SOUTHERN METAL TRIM, INC.

Two small manufacturing plants in rural Alabama provide the output for a company which has the nation's third largest market share in the metal nameplate and decorative trim industry. A very large percentage of the households in the nation own products that Southern Metal Trim, Inc. has helped to produce.

Southern's product line includes a broad array of metal products, ranging from dataplates for automobiles and appliances to very artistic simulated wood grain designs for the control panels of major home appliances and the interiors of automobiles. Many of the control panels for kitchen ranges, washing machines, dryers, small appliances, television sets, and stereo components are manufactured by Southern. The company's customers include a veritable who's who in manufacturing. A few of them are: General Motors, Chrysler Corporation, Zenith, RCA, Quasar, Motorola, Sharp, General Electric, Sylvania, Magnavox, Texas Instruments, White Consolidated, Sears, J.C. Penney, Montgomery Ward, Coldspot, Amana, Electrovoice, Soundesign, Pioneer, and Bose.

Sales during the past 20 years have increased from less than $400,000 to an expected $8.1 million in 1979. The story of this sales growth is one of struggle, disappointment, determination, and triumph.

HISTORY OF THE COMPANY

Jim Evans received an engineering degree from the University of Michigan in the 1930's. With jobs being scarce during those depression days, he took employment as a wet sander with General Motors. His job was to apply emery cloth to wet automobile bodies, a process which prepared them for painting. He advanced to the position of Industrial Engineer by the late 1930's. He was called into military service about two months before the Pearl Harbor attack, and served with the infantry in the European Theatre during World War II.

Having become somewhat disconcerted with the ways of big business and big labor, Mr. Evans decided not to return to his former job with General Motors when he was discharged from the Army in 1946. He chose instead to join his brother, Gerald, in the small firm Gerald had founded in 1932, The Chicago Metal Etching Company. The firm supplied etched metal nameplates made of brass, stainless steel, and zinc to the automative industry. Gerald retired from the business within a year after Jim joined the company. Jim soon joined forces with another partner, Tom Secrest, who also had an industrial engineering background. Beginning with the etching of metal nameplates and dataplates, the two men saw their business grow slowly from 1946 through the early and mid-1950's.

The hourly employees of the company elected the United Auto Worker's Union to represent them in 1955. This soon resulted in a wage and benefit structure competitive with that of the Automotive Industry. It was very difficult for the small company to sustain such expenses and still remain competitive in its pricing. The recession that struck during 1957 compounded this problem as sales slipped while costs increased.

Mr. Evans knew some fellow businessmen in the Chicago area who had recently moved to the southern states. Labor and other costs were not as high in the South, and the recession was not impacting quite as severely there. Mr. Evans

This case was prepared by Dr. Charles W. Boyd of Wingate College as a basis for class discussion rather than to illustrate either effective or ineffective handling of an administrative situation. The name of the firm and the names of all individuals are disguised. Distributed by the Intercollegiate Case Clearing House, Soldiers Field, Boston, Massachusetts, 02163.

traveled through the southeastern part of the country for two months, talking to some of these men and investigating the feasibility of several locations for the company. He became especially interested in the Montgomery, Alabama area. The chief executive of one firm he visited suggested that he also investigate some of the smaller towns in the vicinity of Montgomery. Such a location could offer lower labor costs and taxes plus a supply of labor among those who might prefer not to drive 30 to 40 miles roundtrip to work in Montgomery. The executive suggested the city of Prattville, which was located approximately 15 miles northwest of Montgomery and had a population of about 20,000. Mr. Evans had to return to Chicago before he was able to visit Prattville, but a telephone conversation with a member of that city's Chamber of Commerce convinced him that there was interest in the company locating there. Mr. Evans returned to Alabama and visited Prattville two weeks later. After doing so, he and Tom Secrest decided to move the company there.

The move was completed in 1958 and the company was renamed Southern Metal Trim, Incorporated. A plant with 10,000 square feet of floor space was built to house the operation. This was expanded over the years to 50,000 square feet. The newly relocated operation began with nine employees. There were many production mistakes during the first year of operation, but then the firm began to grow and prosper. Not until 1962 did the organization's earning reach the level they had been during the late 1940's and early 1950's. Although wages began to rise to the former Chicago level, profitability also increased. Both Mr. Evans and Mr. Secrest agree that the reason for this was the greater productivity of the workers in the new location.

A second plant with 25,000 square feet of floor space was opened in 1971. This plant was located in a lovely wooded section by a lake near Tallassee, Alabama, which is approximately 40 miles from the first plant, lying to the northeast of Montgomery. It was first managed by Dan Wellman, a man who had worked with General Foods Corporation for many years. Mr. Wellman was willing to open the additional plant in 1971 and spend a few more active working years, but he had made it clear to Mr. Evans that he wanted to slow his working pace down later on. Consequently, Mr. Evans' son, Jerry, was appointed to the position of Vice President and Manager of the Tallassee Plant in October, 1978. Jerry has a business degree from a larger state university in the south, and had worked several years for a company in Atlanta before joining Southern Metal Trim as Assistant Plant Manager under Mr. Wellman in 1971. Today, Mr. Wellman works three days per week in the Prattville plant, primarily in the area of quality control.

A newly constructed Prattville plant was opened in 1973. The plant has 50,000 square feet of production area and 3,500 square feet of administrative offices. It is located in an attractive wooded area just outside of Prattville, about three miles from the former plant. The primary reason for the move was to obtain a facility with a better floor layout for Southern's production process, and with better ventilation for workers in the oven curing operation, where considerable heat is generated. The former Prattville plant is leased to another manufacturing company.

Since Southern sells its output to consumer product firms, its fortunes are inextricably entwined with those of its customers. Never was this fact of business life more apparent than in 1974. The recession of that year hit many of Southern's customers very hard. Thirty-five percent of Southern's volume at that time was in the television industry, and when sales in that industry slumped, the effect on Southern was devastating. For the first time in the company's history, it was necessary to lay off employees.

The Prattville plant released 60 of its employees and converted temporarily to a four-day workweek, while the smaller plant in Tallassee actually ceased operations altogether for a two-month period. Both plants moved back into full operation during the economic recovery of 1975 and 1976. A valuable but painful lesson had been learned. Never again would Southern permit itself to become overly concentrated in one industry. Diversification would become an important word in the vocabulary of Southern's management.

In 1979, Southern employed 160 people in the Prattville plant and 80 in the Tallassee plant. The long-term pattern of sales growth is indicated by the following selected figures.

Year	*Net Sales*
1962	$ 467,000
1967	1,521,000
1972	3,005,000
1977	5,464,000
1979 (estimated)	8,100,000

KEY PERSONNEL

In 1978, Mr. Evans and Mr. Secrest decided it would be wise to scale back their own day-to-day involvement in company affairs and place younger men in some key positions. Up to this time, Jim Evans had been President, giving his primary attention to production, while Tom Secrest had been Secretary, Treasurer, and Sales Manager. As mentioned earlier, Jerry Evans was appointed as Vice President and Manager of Tallassee plant in October, 1978. Harold Jensen, age 47, was appointed President of the company during that same month. Mr. Jensen was brought into the firm in 1963 to manage the Decorating Section. He already had several years of experience in the decorative metal trim industry. He was acquired to help Southern move into more sophisticated decorative metal technologies and broaden its sales from the automotive industry into consumer product industries.

Mark Williams was appointed as General Sales Manager in January, 1979. He began work in the company as an hourly employee in the Camera Department. In 1977, he was promoted to the position of Assistant Sales Manager, reporting to Tom Secrest. There are now 21 manufacturer's representatives located throughout the eastern half of the United States, working on a commission basis, that report to Mr. Williams.

Jim Evans currently functions as Chairman of the Board, and Tom Secrest is Vice Chairman of the Board, Secretary and Treasurer. Both men feel that the recent appointments of Harold Jensen, Mark Williams, and Jerry Evans to key positions of responsibility will help to provide management continuity for the company. Their plan is to slowly yield increasing authority to these younger men as they grow and mature in their positions.

SALES

The primary sales territory for Southern is all of the United States east of the Mississippi River. In addition, the company has some accounts in Iowa and Texas. Southern's two principal competitors are also located in the eastern half of the country, where the bulk of the country's manufacturing takes place. There are several smaller competitors on the West Coast who service markets in that region.

Southern's sales are to original equipment manufacturers (O.E.M.). The 21 manufacturer's representatives that report to Mark Williams either call on purchasing agents or respond to their requests. The manufacturer's representatives make no price quotations. If a purchasing agent is interested in a new job, he sends a price quotation form (called a quote-in) to Mr. Williams at the Prattville plant. Most of the time, copies of the quote-in are also sent to Southern's competitors. Southern and its competition bid on the job without seeing each other's price quotation. The customer then reviews the bids and decides which company will be awarded the order.

When a quote-in is received at the Prattville plant, the price quotation is made by Mark Williams or other personnel in the Inside Customer Sales and Service Group based on quantifiable factors such as the cost of materials and expected labor time. A final factor in the quote is a markup based on expected problems in the production process. For example, a higher percentage markup would be quoted if history had taught Southern that a substantial amount of rework was usually necessary to meet quality standards for a certain type of job. If a particular customer has in the past been more exacting regarding quality standards, this would also cause the markup quoted to be somewhat higher. The markup is an attempt to insure that Southern can satisfy the customer's standards while still securing a reasonable profit from the job.

There is a wide degree of variance in the skill, and thus the cost, involved in producing Southern's myriad products. For example, a simple dataplate for an automobile transmission requires much less art and design work than a wood grain panel for the interior of the automobile. There is a corresponding difference in the profitability of various jobs. The most profitable ones are those with a high markup or relatively long production run combined with a lower markup. The least profitable jobs are those with short runs and low markups. It is very important to keep a good mix of these different types of jobs moving through both plants at any given time. This provides a smoother production flow and a more cost-efficient utilization of machinery and manpower, resulting in a more profitable operation. Consequently, the success of the sales personnel in obtaining this ideal mix bears heavily on the efficiency of short-term production scheduling in the two plants.

THE PRODUCTION PROCESS

The production lines in Southern's two plants are among the finest in the industry. In the Prattville Plant, the manufacturing process begins when an order is sent from the Sales Department to the Art Department. The personnel here often work with a prototype supplied by the customer. They draw the product into its final form, working when necessary with the adjacent Camera Department which may provide them with blowups or other alterations of the prototype. When the art work is completed, the Camera Department prepares either a photographic or silk screen replica of the product.

The Lithography Department takes the work provided by the Camera Department and imprints it on the appropriate type of metal. This process begins with the cutting of the metal (brass, aluminum, or steel) from flat sheets, or more often, rolled coils. A machine automatically feeds the metal and cuts the sheets to a preset size determined by the size of the product being run. There may be five front panels for an electric range printed on one sheet, or 50 or 60 small dataplates for automobile transmissions could be printed on one sheet.

After cutting the sheets to the appropriate size, the image of the product is imprinted on the sheets either by offset presses or silk screening, depending on the nature of the product. This is a very critical phase of the job from the standpoint of quality, for if there are errors here, no subsequent operation can correct them. Colors must be matched precisely. Reproduction of an unusual wood grain pattern for the interior trim of an automobile or the front panel of a television set is often a very tedious and painstaking operation. Samples of such products must be run and rigidly inspected to insure that they match the customer's specifications exactly. If a product requires three different colors, it must be run through the offset press or silk screening process three times, since only one color can be imprinted per run with the company's present equipment. Products requiring these repeated runs are carefully inspected during and following each run, so that a defective product does not continue to be sent through successive operations before a problem is detected.

After the sheets pass through each offset or silk screening process, they are placed in racks which are carried through 50-feet long natural gas-fired curing ovens. There are three of these ovens in the Prattville plant and one of them in the Tallassee plant. Each plant also has one machine that employs an ultra-violet process which cures the ink on the sheets very quickly without the use of heat.

Some customers specify an etching process for their product. This involves imbedding the printed characters into the metal rather than simply printing them on the surface of the metal. This process is typically used for nameplates and dataplates that will be subjected to weather. These are called "20-year nameplates" because of their durability. A separate Paint and Etching Department consisting of 12 personnel does this type of work at the Prattville plant. No metal etching is done at the Tallassee plant. This department is separated from the Lithography Department because the production process is different. The use of acids is involved, and although silk screening is done, a different type of ink is used in the process. As a result, the Paint and Etching Department has its own silk screen equipment. A relatively small percentage of Southern's current order mix requires the etching process, since the company has moved more in the direction of decorative metal trim work in recent years. The etching process costs the customer 25 percent more than a non-etched job for the same product.

When the product is in final form on the sheets, a clear plastic coating material is placed over each sheet to protect it from scratches as it proceeds through the production process. The sheets then go to the Punch Press and Shearing Department. Here the individual products are first cut (sheared) from the sheets. Then punch presses or kick presses stamp the required holes in the individual products. If required, other presses put a bend or curvature in the item. This department also has two gem-cutting machines which employ a diamond tool to cut an attractive serrated pattern into the border of a product or the border of an opening in the product. The gem-cutting operation is not performed at the Tallassee plant.

The Prattville plant employs approximately 45 females and a male supervisor in the Punch Press and Shearing Department. The Tallassee plant utilizes approximately 30 females in this operation. The machinery is general purpose, capable of being tooled and adjusted to the specifications of any job. This means that a number of different jobs can be flowing through this department simultaneously. Part of the production scheduling problem involves keeping this department operating at a high utilization rate by keeping it supplied with jobs flowing from the Art, Lithography, and Paint and Etching Departments.

The final step in the production process is the Packing and Shipping Department. The Prattville Plant employs 22 females, one male, and a female supervisor in this department. The Tallassee plant utilizes approximately 15 females with a female supervisor in its similar operation. The employees in this department peel off the protective coating material, inspect each finished product, and wrap and pack the products for shipment to the customer. Some products also require the application of a pre-cut adhesive material on the back, which the customer removes in order to place the part on his product. Southern buys this adhesive from an outside supplier.

Both plants also maintain small Tool Rooms with the capability of repairing damaged tools used in the punching operation. A tool is the form for a product which is used in the punching operation. The capability to repair tools is important because a damaged tool on a punch press halts an operation, and without repair capability, the tool would have to be returned to the customer who built it. This would slow the job tremendously.

The tools are expensive items for the customer to build. Preparing a punch press tool for a relatively simple television control knob panel may cost as much as $7,000, which Southern charges back to the customer. Southern and its competitors store these tools for repeat use. If the customer awards a later contract to another company, it is common practice for the company losing the contract to ship the tool for the job to the competitor gaining the contract.

In 1975, the two Southern plants began a 10-hour day, 4-day per week operation in their Act, Camera, and Lithography Departments. The other departments have continued to work an 8-hour day five days per week. The reason for the 4-day workweek is that the natural gas used in firing the three curing ovens became scarce and more expensive during the mid-1970's. The greatest amount of gas is consumed in firing the ovens up to operating temperature in the morning. Management decided to save energy and costs by firing the ovens four rather than five days per week. This decision required the Art and Camera Departments to work the same schedule, since the Lithography Department can do nothing until it receives the product from those two departments. Work can be stored for operations following Lithography, so it is not imperative that they work the same schedule.

QUALITY CONTROL

No Quality Control Department exists within Southern Metal Trim, Inc. Each production worker is responsible for high quality work, and supervisors check the quality of each job before it leaves her or his department for the next stage of production. The Lithography Department inspects work in process and utilizes inspectors to examine the sheets again after the silk screening or offset process is completed. Each error found is marked with red ink so that no subsequent operations are performed on them. Only the unmarked products on a sheet receive further processing. Sometimes an additional 10 percent above the ordered quantity is run in this department to allow a safety margin for quality defects in order to prevent the second run of a job. The greatest single point of inspection is in the Packing and Shipping Department. There is virtually 100 percent inspection there, since each individual product must be handled by the women in this department as they prepare it for shipment.

The rejection rate on shipments to Southern's customers has always been less than three percent until the past couple of years, during which it has crept up to and slightly beyond that figure. The in-house rejection rate is much higher at present. Management has become very concerned about this, and is attempting to combat the trend. Roving inspectors were used for a time in the Tallassee plant, but this created some discontent among the workers and the procedure was abandoned. Quality errors in that plant are presently reported to Jerry Evans, who makes the decision concerning corrective action. He is quite concerned that so many jobs flow through the entire production process with errors that are not discovered until the products reach the Packing and Shipping Department.

Southern's management feels that a good quality control system is difficult in this type of business for two reasons. First, it is difficult to develop quality standards because each job is unique and the jobs are constantly changing. It does not appear to be economically feasible to create a set of standards for such short-run jobs. Secondly, the products' quality is primarily judged on esthetic basis. As a result, one person might be able to detect a flaw in a product that appeared passable to another person. Despite these difficulties, management is attempting to deal with the problem by instituting a program called Quality Circles.

The Quality Circles program was developed in Japan in 1962 as a product of Japanese effort toward improving the general quality level of their products following World War II. Basically, the program involves weekly meetings of production workers in groups of 8–15. They discuss problems related to their work, then think about these problems for a week or two. At a subsequent meeting, they list possible solutions to the problems, discuss them, and select a solution for implementation. The program was started only a month ago in the Prattville plant. Dan Wellman is in charge of the effort, being assisted by a young executive. Their approach is to keep group discussion narrowed to problems focused on the man-machine relationship in the production process. Jerry Evans is waiting to see what type of results the program achieves before implementing it in the Tallassee plant.

MANAGEMENT'S PHILOSOPHY

Southern's top management takes the view that if the employees are given a pleasant environment in which to work and a stake in the fortunes of the organization, they will be committed to producing a quality product. This philosophy is manifested in a number of policies not found in many manufacturing operations of this size.

There are no time clocks. Nor are there written rules concerning behavior on the job. It is assumed that employees know when to come and go from work and how to conduct themselves while on the job. Wages for the production employees are on a straight day rate, slightly above the average for the area. All workers in a particular type of job, such as punch press operators, are paid at the same hourly rate. The higher skilled within such a group are recognized by being given the more challenging jobs.

The supervisors of each department are given a high degree of autonomy. They are responsible for the hiring and dismissal of their employees, and, as mentioned earlier, they are responsible for the quality of the products that leave their departments. They are permitted to use their own discretion in purchasing departmental supplies such as inks, paints, coating materials, tool steel, and nuts and bolts. They are not required to submit purchase orders to any higher level of management for these items.

Jim Evans and Tom Secrest have instituted a profit-sharing plan which they believe will create a greater commitment to excellence on the part of the employees. At the end of the fiscal year, the Board of Directors reviews the company's profits before taxes and typically distributes 25–30 percent of these to the employees in proportion to their earnings level. These monies are distributed in two ways: 50 percent as a cash bonus, and 50 percent deposited in a trust fund. After five years, the employee has a 50 percent vested interest in his portion of the trust fund. The amount of his vesting is graduated over the next five years in a manner such that he has a full vested interest after 10 years. In addition, all quarterly profits in excess of 12 percent of sales are distributed evenly among all employees. Once each year, shares of the company's stock are offered to the employees at recent book value in an amount equal to their annual cash bonus distribution. Additionally, the company will match the amount the employee pays for the stock. For example, if the cash portion of an employee's annual bonus was $100, he or she could keep that amount of cash or purchase up to $200 of stock by paying back the $100 plus the tax involved in the sale of $200 of stock.

At present, Jim Evans and Tom Secrest each own approximately 40 percent of the company's stock and other employees own the remaining 20 percent. Those in supervisory and higher positions have participated most in the stock plan since its inception in 1966. It is hoped that more of the hourly employees will choose to do so in the future. The stock has appreciated well in recent years, making the plan a good investment for the participants.

Profits during the last two quarters of Southern's fiscal 1979 (ending July 31, 1979) were not sufficient to pay out any quarterly bonuses. There is some concern among the management that this may be causing a decrease in morale among some of the hourly employees. Managers are attempting to help these employees see the connection between high quality production and the company's profitability.

Mr. Evans and Mr. Secrest believe strongly in their philosophy. They feel that the picturesque plant locations, relative freedom and autonomy given the employees, and the profit-sharing programs have helped to create a happy and productive work force with a very low turnover rate. Many employees have been with the company in excess of 15 years, and a few have risen from hourly to managerial positions.

FINANCES

Recent financial statements for Southern are presented in Tables 1 and 2. Mr. Evans and Mr. Secrest have attempted to finance as much of the company's operations as possible from earnings and the sale of stock to employees. Long-term borrowing is held to a minimum. The two men intend to continue this general approach to financing in the future.

Inventories are stated at the lower of cost or market. Cost of materials and supplies is determined by actual invoice cost by the first-in, first-out method, and the cost of labor and overhead is based on average cost. Market is based on replacement cost not to exceed net realizable value for raw materials and manufacturing supplies. For work in process and finished goods, market is based on net realizable value less a normal profit margin.

Property, plant and equipment are stated on the basis of cost. Depreciation is computed by accelerated methods based on useful lives of the assets as follows: building and related improvements, 10 to 25 years; improvements to leased property, 15 years; machinery and equipment, 8 and 10 years; and furniture and fixtures, 5 and 10 years.

As mentioned earlier, the department supervisors purchase a variety of supplies for their departments. The aluminum raw stock is purchased by Jim Evans, primarily from Austria. The lower price of the Austrian aluminum is felt to offset the three-month delivery time. Harold Jensen purchases the brass and steel raw stock from domestic markets. The adhesives are purchased by the production planner. Since the supervisors do not submit purchase orders for the supplies they buy, Mr. Secrest must estimate the amount of those purchases when developing monthly cash flow statements. He is usually able to estimate these expenditures within five percent of the actual amounts.

TABLE 1
Consolidated balance sheets for years ended July 31

	1974	*1975*	*1976*	*1977*	*1978*
ASSETS					
Current Assets:					
Cash	7,692	33,604	125,138	185,024	425,099
Accounts Receivable	422,863	474,425	614,602	757,731	1,037,844
Refundable Fed. Income Tax	57,340	—	—	—	—
Investment in short-term commercial note	—	—	—	—	200,000
Inventories:					
Raw Materials	555,437	590,833	388,855	883,020	625,506
Work in Process	128,908	97,371	186,954	172,066	373,369
Finished goods	67,026	77,044	82,224	95,536	89,444
Manufacturing supplies	33,810	19,416	32,946	49,263	57,025
Prepaid Expenses	27,507	10,445	13,063	29,844	29,705
Dies to be charged to customers	2,830	9,515	31,730	31,069	45,910
Total Current Assets	1,303,413	1,312,653	1,475,512	2,203,553	2,883,902
Other Assets	208,169	227,544	253,199	276,181	300,411
Fixed Assets	572,528	509,241	537,588	545,031	562,171
TOTAL ASSETS	2,084,110	2,049,438	2,266,299	3,024,765	3,746,484
LIABILITIES AND STOCKHOLDERS' EQUITY					
Current Liabilities:					
Current Maturities of Long-Term Debt	—	120,286	121,056	231,885	252,775
Notes Payable	454,570	25,000	—	45,000	45,000
Accounts Payable	217,960	119,187	281,014	227,350	531,453
Accrued and sundry liabilities	116,724	89,599	291,162	427,289	524,701
Federal and State income taxes payable	4,109	7,298	173,426	45,797	131,368
Dividend payable	8,570	6,168	36,940	41,320	54,848
Total Current Liabilities	801,933	367,538	903,598	1,018,641	1,540,145
Long-Term Debt	295,852	710,566	208,179	596,294	403,519
TOTAL LIABILITIES	1,097,785	1,078,104	1,111,777	1,614,935	1,943,664
Stockholders' Equity—Capital Stock:					
Common Stock, par value $1 a share	27,333	27,333	27,333	28,637	30,285
Capital in Excess of Par Value	123,019	123,019	123,019	182,846	271,163
Retained Earnings	870,718	904,557	1,089,477	1,288,623	1,594,323
Total Capital Stock	1,021,070	1,054,909	1,239,829	1,500,106	1,895,771
Less: Common stock in treasury	34,745	83,575	85,307	90,276	92,951
TOTAL STOCKHOLDERS' EQUITY	986,325	971,334	1,154,522	1,409,830	1,802,820
TOTAL LIABILITIES AND STOCKHOLDERS' EQUITY	2,084,110	2,049,438	2,266,299	3,024,765	3,746,484

TABLE 2
Statements of income and retained earnings for years ended July 31

	1974	1975	1976	1977	1978
Sales	3,945,771	3,214,991	5,140,569	5,656,028	7,856,085
Less: Sales Returns and Allowances and Sales Discounts	144,697	150,376	179,710	191,703	238,218
Net Sales	3,801,074	3,064,615	4,960,859	5,464,325	7,617,867
Cost of goods sold	3,046,935	2,453,465	3,859,170	4,268,665	5,980,155
Gross profit on sales	754,139	611,150	1,101,689	1,195,660	1,637,712
Selling, general, and administrative expenses	584,781	507,262	672,568	725,868	873,915
	169,358	103,888	429,121	469,792	763,797
Other Charges:					
Interest—net	40,267	67,952	40,482	41,176	75,249
Loss (gain) on disposals of fixed assets	36,992	(23,071)	(22,221)	(22,850)	—
Income before income taxes	92,099	59,007	410,860	451,466	688,548
Provision for federal and state income taxes	40,000	19,000	189,000	211,000	328,000
Net Income	52,099	40,007	221,860	240,466	360,548
Retained earnings as of July 31 of previous year	827,189	870,718	904,557	1,089,477	1,288,623
	879,288	910,725	1,126,417	1,329,943	1,649,171
Cash dividend declared	8,570	6,168	36,940	41,320	54,848
Retained earnings as of July 31 of current year	870,718	904,557	1,089,477	1,288,623	1,594,323

FUTURE PLANS

Southern's top management has some ambitious plans for the future. Sales for the next five years are projected as follows:

Year	Annual sales (in millions)
1979	$ 8.1
1980	9.5
1981	11.2
1982	13.2
1983	15.5

Several actions are being considered to achieve the above sales growth.

To begin with, increased production of sophisticated decorative trim in the Prattville plant is to be provided by the addition of new high-speed lithographing equipment, a multi-color silk screen printing line, and the total replacement of curing ovens by additional ultra-violet curing of all coatings and inks. The purchase of a new mechanical slitter to cope with additional decorating capacity is also planned. Additional equipment expenditures of $75,000 by 1981 are also planned for the Tallassee plant. The major items required there are six punch presses, an electronic shear, and one additional ultra-violet curing unit.

Southern plans to develop additional production capacity by acquiring a third plant in an as yet unselected small community within a 100-mile radius of Prattville by late 1980 or early 1981. The new facility will be leased until the operation is well established, at which time a new facility will be built similar in layout to the Prattville plant. This third plant will specialize in producing low volume orders, prototype orders, and specialty items requiring a short delivery cycle. Top management sees an established need for this service if a competitive advantage in delivery can be achieved. This plant will also diversify into the production of plastic decorative parts. Estimated cost for machinery and equipment for this new plant is $100,000. An additional $75,000 of operating capital is expected to be needed.

A major project now underway is the development of a new decorative trim operation in Ireland to compete for business in the European Common Market. The market for Southern's products in Europe is currently being studied. Tentative plans call for $475,000 of new and $75,000 of used machinery and equipment. Thirty-five percent of the new machinery could be financed by a grant from the International Development Agency. The balance of the financing will be arranged by Southern. Two outside groups have indicated an interest in investing $70,000 each. In addition, it is expected that $250,000 of operating capital would need to be financed in Ireland. If the market looks good, a site for the plant will be considered. It has not yet been decided which method should be used to acquire a plant: lease, lease with an option to buy, or purchase.

The company is attempting to improve all its accounting systems by the recent acquisition of a small computer system. A new inventory control system became operative in June, 1979. It is expected to reduce aluminum inventory by $250,000 and to improve control over the adhesives inventory. The system will also provide an order entry and tracking system for both the Prattville and Tallassee plants. An open item accounts receivable program will be used in an attempt to improve cash flow. The cost of the new system is estimated at $100,000. Complete transformation to this new system is scheduled for December 31, 1979.

Harold Jensen, the President of Southern Decorative Trim, indicates that the company's basic goal is to perpetuate its past philosophy of earning a good return on sales while providing a pleasant place for people to work. He proposes that this be done by maintaining the firm's past record of steady, controlled growth.

EXERCISE 5–10

- Refer back to Figure 5–1. What is the most predominant order pattern for Southern Metal Trim's Art and Camera departments?
- Describe the types of materials, machinery, and human resources associated with this order pattern.
- Is the order pattern different for Southern's Lithography Department? Why? Why Not?

- Describe the predominant order pattern and types of associated major elements that would be most desirable for Southern's Punch Press and Shearing Department. Does your description of the elements match the description in the case?
- With the additional equipment Southern has planned, should they plan to adjust other elements of their production process for a better balance to improve profitability?
- What changes can Southern plan to make in the major elements for their third production plant proposed for 1980–81?

Services

The same type of thinking we applied to a variety of order patterns for products can be applied, with some modification, to the operations of a service firm. Services can be categorized in terms of their amenability to batching or to mass servicing. Surgery or other services performed on the human body have not as yet been found to be amenable to mass performance. Others, such as psychological counseling and education that function, at least in part, through the mind, may not only be suitable for group approaches, but, in fact, may be performed more effectively in a group setting. Figure 5–2 presents a way of examining the class of service delivery, the categories of equipment or technology used, the degree of refinement in problem identification required, and the type of service provider required.

Integration of Operations-Management Elements for Services

		Individual	Group	Mass
PERSONNEL	Qualifications	Broad Qualifications	Narrower Qualifications	Narrow Qualifications
	Education	Highly Advanced	Highly Advanced	Advanced (Technologist)
CLIENTS	Need for Preservice Classification	Low	Moderately High	High
TECHNOLOGY		General and Wide in Scope	Specialized and Moderately Wide in Scope	Specialized and Narrow in Scope

SERVICE DELIVERY TYPE

FIGURE 5–2

The approach to services is similar to that used with products, but with some exceptions. First, the ability to perform services on something other than in individualized basis is, to some extent, determined to a high degree by the existence of a technology for doing so. Second, each level of technology has its own type of specialist. The generalist in service fields is, to a large degree, a specialist in diagnostics and case management. The specialist in group approaches must know the technology of group services and be skilled in their application. In the mass-performance service categories (either large batch or continuous), persons responsible for the advanced technology used for these tasks need specialized training and in many cases may be licensed or certified to perform these unique services. Their training, however, is narrower than that of the generalist and frequently can be accomplished in a shorter period of time.

THE COMP-CARE CENTER

The Bluegrass Region Comprehensive Mental Health–Mental Retardation Care Center (called the Comp-Care Center by its staffers) provided extensive outpatient educational and psychiatric care to a large metropolitan city and county in central Kentucky. The staff of the Comp-Care Center were distributed in a number of outreach centers located in strategic sites throughout the county and city. Each outreach center had a team of psychological counselors, registered nurses, educational specialists, and social workers assigned to work with any and all of the educational, social, and psychological problems encountered by clients in the outreach area. In addition to the team located in the outreach centers, specialists in alcohol abuse, drug abuse, geriatric care, and suicide prevention were available to any of the outreach centers by telephone request. Clients could also be referred directly to these central staff specialists.

Discussions with employees of the Comp-Care Center revealed that many of the problems they encountered were multifaceted. As one example, they described the problems encountered by a family with a member who was mentally ill. It was not uncommon for Comp-Care Center counselors to find that not only was the client mentally ill, but that other members of the family were also ill or were contributive to the client's illness. In some cases, physical health issues involved not only the client, but also the client's family. In these cases, medical help would be needed for the client and often for the members of the family. Educational work was needed to assist family members to understand better the extent to which their actions were a contributing factor in the continuing illness.

In instances of severe emotional or mental distress or illness, clients were referred to custodial care in institutions. In the case of attempted suicides, a hot line was established both to help in counseling and in attempting to get the person to undertake some alternative action rather than his or her own destruction. The suicide crisis specialist had a beeper so that he or she could be called at any hour of the night or day, 7 days per week, to aid persons attempting or in the process of thinking of committing suicide. The drug abuse specialist was called on to act as an expert witness in legal actions and to identify the possible agents that might have produced a given type of observed disorder. In addition, this specialist provided educational programs for educators and law enforcement authorities on current drug abuse patterns.

Social welfare workers aided clients and client's families in seeking assistance for medical care, housing, food, and education. They acted as referral agents to public welfare agencies, and they provided guidance and counseling for persons in need of help. Psychological counselors performed a number of functions in the outreach centers. Directly, they served clients in need of help through individual therapy sessions. Indirectly, they worked with client's families, in a family counseling context, to build a structure of support for the client in the home. In instances of marital problems, they served as marital counselors and worked with both partners in an attempt to resolve problems at minimum economic and psychological cost.

A key position in the Comp-Care Center was that of receptionist. When questioned about the critical nature of this job, Comp-Care Center workers explained, "The receptionist is the first person seen by people who become our clients. The receptionist can turn clients away, by either actions or demeanor, or can reassure and encourage clients to seek help." In addition, they said,

> *The receptionist is in the best position to begin the process of referring the client to the person who can best provide the help that is needed. Frequently, clients aren't aware that they have a problem or what sort of person may be of most help. The receptionist, as that first contact, can often ask the questions that begin to identify the type of problem that may be causing trouble and to make those early referrals to persons in the outreach center and through them to others in the Comp-Care Center system. Frequently, we employ an experienced staffer in this job because of the range of clients they have already seen and the skill they have demonstrated in understanding how to reach clients to help them in subsequent therapy or counseling.*

EXERCISE 5–11

Use Figure 5–2 to help you analyze the Comp-Care Center case.

- Place the family counselor in the matrix. Explain the reasoning used in your analysis.
- Place the suicide crisis interventionist in the matrix. Explain your reasoning.
- Place the receptionist in the matrix. Explain.
- Comment, if you can, on how this arrangement of specialized service professionals is organized to meet the needs of the community.

MANAGING AN EXISTING CONVERSION OPERATION

The management of an existing conversion involves the employment of a careful balancing of materials, human resources, and technologies to achieve desired customer needs. Before this balancing can be undertaken, it is necessary to understand the type of order pattern and to have some knowledge of the technology to be employed.

If the order pattern is that of batch production for customers who, for example, order in quantities of one hundred to five hundred items, we must first assess the extent to which the equipment and our technological approach are compatible with orders of this size. If we have nothing but general-purpose, multiuse equipment, our technology is better suited to smaller orders of specialized types of items. As it now is, our equipment will cause us to incur production-time penalties brought about by excessive setup time for a 100-to-500-item order or by blockades caused by material-in-process stored on the shop floor. If, on the other hand, our equipment is rather more automated, we may have difficulty in adjusting to the individual needs of customers who order in such small lots. One of two actions should be undertaken in either case. We can work toward acquiring equipment that is better suited to our order patterns or, should that not be possible at this time, we can seek to adjust the order pattern to our equipment and its availability, making best use of the advantages inherent in the equipment type now owned.

Given a reasonably close match between the typical order pattern and the capabilities of the existing equipment, we then need to address the two other major elements, human resources and materials. In the case of human resources, we need to examine and evaluate both the depth of available labor sources and the quality of human resources required for the technology to be employed. In the case of a batch operation, operators should be trained broadly enough to be able to make the adaptive shifts needed to move products through one piece of equipment to another, through that one to another, and so on, until manufacture is complete. Similar adaptive skill is required to shift rapidly from one type of product to another, locating the necessary jigs and fixtures, and, where needed, constructing other aids to help in the efficient manufacture of desired products.

The effective operations manager will assess the needed depth and breadth of these human resources, and will begin a process of human resource planning and development to help in assuring a ready supply of adequately trained operators. Where labor markets do not have the needed depth, operatives may be developed from scratch, and elaborate on-the-job training programs can be used to train people for both their current job and other positions immediately adjacent in the workplace. A backup matrix is a simple grid that lists jobs on one axis and individuals on the other. The backup matrix helps the operations manager to determine on short notice who might be qualified to replace a missing worker. The backup matrix also can serve as a development plan for both the supervisor and employees to guide the course of their career growth and to channel that growth in ways that are helpful in meeting work force needs in the future.

Employees	Tasks					
	Cashier	*Payroll*	*Receiving*	*Reception*	*Invoicing*	*Order Entry*
J. Jones	FQ				FQ	
A. McCarthy				FQ		
R. Holmes		Q			FQ	FQ
P. Munn				FQ		FQ
R. Potts		FQ				
L. Ross		FQ				
M. Quinn			FQ		Q	
F. Gault			FQ			
B. Boros			FQ			

FQ = Fully Qualified; Q = Qualified.

FIGURE 5-3 Sample backup matrix.

The third element of major concern to the operations manager is the identification and acquisition of a ready supply of materials of the correct type at a competitive cost. As mentioned earlier, materials can include goods ranging from freshly mined ores in their rawest form to highly advanced, complex, and costly components built under subcontracts from specialty suppliers. The operations manager must make some critical decisions about quality of materials because each added degree of quality assurance has an economic value. For some customers, the additional quality offered by a particular supplier may have little or no commercial value. As one example, a homeowner purchasing 8-foot wooden fenceposts would have little interest in solid mahogany posts if they were to cost twice the price of conventional pine or cedar. The customer may recognize the quality difference but not be interested in paying the cost differential for that particular product's more costly features.

Once a quality level is established that is commercially recoverable through customer interests, the operations manager must identify sources and seek to obtain a steady supply. Sound procurement practices would suggest that more than one supplier should be sought in order to avoid shortages caused by a failure to deliver. The number of suppliers may be restricted somewhat, however, to avoid a number of problems. First, if one's requirements are divided up into a number of smaller transactions, the economics of quantity purchases is lost. Second, multiple transactions cost more in terms of paperwork and cause severe problems in control of goods received. Third, and of particular interest where processes are highly automated, the variability in product quality from one supplier to another can cause a number of problems as materials and components are fed into the process and become part of the product. High-speed machinery is quite sensitive to minute changes in dimensions, textures, and other tangible characteristics of components. Where colors are involved, proper color matching is an extremely difficult process at best and would be enormously complicated by shipments from multiple sources.

The negotiation of contracts for a reasonably assured supply of materials is often the next stage in dealing with the issue of materials. Purchase agreements are written to provide for some assurance to the supplier that the purchaser will buy some proportion of total needs from that particular supplier. Purchasers are assured of having that supply at a negotiated price, one that usually takes into account the quantity purchased over the life of the agreement. To carry out such an agreement, the purchaser issues releases against that order and the supplier provides the specified materials at the negotiated price. When two or more such contracts have been consumated, the operations manager must arrange to receive materials from all contractor sources. The manager must then undertake to manage the materials process, to accommodate the needs of the conversion, and to do so in an efficient manner. Typically, economic order quantity (EOQ) models are developed to assist in this process. The EOQ model will identify an order quantity that minimizes the total cost of the materials acquisition process while considering demand, cost of carrying inventories, and the cost of placing orders.

The process described is probably typical of most industrial organizations. There are companies, however, that do not adopt these practices. In the steel industry, managers of some companies have made speculative purchases of huge quantities of scrap steel, anticipating an increase in scrap prices in some future period. In the wholesale grocery business, some purchasing agents have been instructed to purchase paper products and containers on the open, or spot, market (rather than through a long-term purchase agreement with a supplier) in the belief that during the time that the contract would cover, prices would be depressed by excess capacity and that supplies would be readily available. Each of these practices incurs risk. In the steel company situation, the company will commit millions of dollars of capital in scrap inventories. If prices go down instead of up, the company's cost structure is less competitive than it might have been had they purchased over a period of weeks or months. In the grocery situation, the company runs the risk that suppliers could run short, resulting in severe price increases and inadequate product availability. One additional consideration has to do with customer/supplier relationships. In the long term, suppliers forced to deal with extremely price-oriented customers on the spot market may develop some resentment at pricing pressures and may be insensitive to spot-market customers' needs as the demand begins to absorb available supplies.

Once materials, human resources, and a technology have been brought together, operating a conversion facility is a process of maximizing productivity within a number of constraints. A customer's desired delivery date is one such constraint. Meeting this objective may, in some instances, mean operating on premium time or making use of less-efficient equipment. Similarly, to the manager of the conversion facility, the technology being employed provides additional limits to achievable levels of performance. A batch-oriented facility is not as efficient for long runs as is a continuous process; nor is general purpose equipment as efficient for large batches as might be semiautomated or automated equipment. Human resources also have limitations, and these limitations change with the character of the work force. Less experienced workers need more guidance than those with experience, for example. Older workers may not work at the same pace as younger ones, and they may have more absences owing to sickness.

The objective of the operations manager is to find a solution to this complex problem that maximizes (for cost-containment objectives) output per unit of cost or, conversely, minimizes cost per unit. If the objective is maximum productivity, then the solution needed is one that minimizes time per unit of output or maximizes output per unit of time. More often than not, the operations manager is asked (if not expected!) to seek both objectives. Usually, both productivity and cost objectives can be achieved, within a reasonable range, by the same configuration of technologies, human resources, and materials.

Aggregate Planning

It is extremely important that both the operations manager and the general manager maintain a large-scale perspective on the total conversion process. One system that can help in maintaining that perspective and help in managing the total conversion process is called aggregate planning.[1] The aggregate planning concept involves a consideration of demand forecast for a relatively long period (1 year is often used in examples). Rather than planning the conversion process on orders in hand or on orders planned for the coming weeks, demand is forecast for the entire period. Seasonal patterns in demand are included, as are growth components and other factors unique to the product being considered. Several strategies are then considered: (a) hold the number of employees and the rate of production constant and accumulate inventories to meet the changes anticipated in demand; (b) hold the number of employees constant but shift the rate of production (and the number of hours worked by those employees) to meet the short-term changes in demand; and (c) vary the employment level to meet the changes in demand.

Each of the strategies has advantages and disadvantages. If, for example, employees were difficult to recruit and if training time is extensive, then maintaining a relatively consistent level of work activity for one's work force would be a desirable strategy, even at the cost of accumulating inventories and encountering risk of obsolescence and decline in product demand.

EXERCISE 5–12

- List one or two *additional* advantages and/or disadvantages to strategy (a).
- List two advantages and two disadvantages for strategies (b) and (c).

[1] A comprehensive treatment of this topic can be found in Adam, E. E., Jr., and R. J. Ebert, *Production and Operations Management*, 2nd Ed. (Englewood Cliffs, N.J.: Prentice-Hall, 1982), pp. 340–409.

Although aggregate planning is often discussed relative to continuous conversion operations, it can have application to intermittent or batch-conversion processes and to services. In the case of batch operations, the aggregate long-term plan has a fixed processing technology and a rated capacity. In the short run, the time horizon must be reduced and an optimum solution reached for a period of perhaps a month or two, matching the available capacity over that time period to the demand anticipated. Plans for scheduling operations can then become much more detailed. Linear programming models can help in achieving optimum arrangement of products, machines, and human resources. Gantt charts can also help, as can simulations and various heuristic approaches to optimizing the use of available resources.

As for services, aggregate planning can be undertaken with one notable exception: services, unlike products, cannot be accumulated in the form of finished-goods inventory. In some kinds of service operations, it is possible, however, to arrange schedules in such a way as to force demand to conform to available service agencies or facilities. Physicians, hairstylists and other service providers often require clients to adjust their demands to the availability of the service. When the wait becomes too long, demand shifts to another agency. To deal with this problem in an aggregate sense, the barber will hire another stylist, set up another chair, and schedule the additional customers for a second or third barber. Physicians combine practices and use their colleagues to handle overflow clients on both a short-term and long-range basis.

Management science has also provided some tools for dealing with decisions involving service facilities. Waiting-line models have been developed that can help in determining the economic optimum, that is, the extent to which customers will wait at a service facility before going elsewhere. These statistically based models have been used to determine the length of the line needed before it is advisable, for example, to open an additional checkout register in supermarkets, to open another desk at airline counters, or to staff additional depository facilities in drive-in banks.

The following exercise is designed to help in developing some skill in a relatively straightforward example of aggregrate planning. Although other problems might be much larger in scope, the Rheotherm exercise should help to acquaint you with a very useful tool that is designed to build an integrative perspective and reach well-reasoned decisions to complex problems. Read the problem through carefully, then respond to the exercise questions found at the end of the problem statement.

EXERCISE 5-13

Rheotherm, a small manufacturer of control devices for the air-conditioning industry, has a total of 70 employees in its manufacturing facility. Historical data has shown that productivity for units manufactured in this facility can be calculated on the basis of 2.468 man-hours per unit. The marketing division has estimated that aggregate demand for the year will total 385,000 units. Seasonal patterns in air-conditioning have been typical for the industry and are shown as percentages of total annual production.

Month	*% of Annual*	*Month*	*% of Annual*
Jan.	6	July	12
Feb.	8	Aug.	6
Mar.	9	Sept.	5
April	12	Oct.	4
May	16	Nov.	5
June	12	Dec.	5

Minimum inventory desired by marketing: 16,000 units
Present inventory: 2,500 units

- Develop an aggregate plan that *holds employment (number of employees) constant* and that uses accumulated inventories to meet monthly demand.
- Develop an aggregate plan that *adjusts employment (number of employees)* to meet anticipated monthly demand.
- Develop an aggregate plan that meets demand by *increasing the productivity per employee (number of hours of work per employee).*

For the questions listed, use the following format for each question answered.

Beginning inventory	*Monthly production*	*Monthly demand*	*Number of employees*	*Number of hours/ employees*
Jan.				
Feb.				
Mar.				
April				
May				
June				
July				
Aug.				
Sept.				
Oct.				
Nov.				
Dec.				

ENLARGING THE SCOPE OF MANAGERIAL CONCERN

The foregoing discussion has focused on the management of an ongoing conversion enterprise. Implicit in this discussion has been an assumption that the *existing* technology, materials, and human resources were the scope of concern. In that respect, the discussion has closely followed the pattern of attention of production/operations managers of past years. The more modern view of operations management is broader and must include a consideration of the entire range of conversion, from the point of origin of the elements of the operation to the delivery of products or services to customers. This perspective is especially important to general managers, given the broader range of responsibilities and the need to integrate the scope and nature of operations with the available financial and human resources while pursuing stated corporate or business-unit objectives.

In this expanded scope of concern and interest, we need both to examine the sources of our materials (to reduce risks and to seek optimum conversion) and to consider the use of alternate employment modes in our use of human resources if we wish to seek maximum effectiveness. In each area, strategic decisions are required to shape the outer boundaries of our concern and to achieve the level of cost efficiency and overall effectiveness in the conversion process that will enable the organization to be a lively and strong competitor. Close collaboration between operations and general management will be needed to assure that the planned course of action makes sound operational sense and that it is consistent with the resources, talents, and objectives of the organization as a whole.

Make Versus Buy

Several major factors must be considered in make versus buy decisions. Most frequently, the question as to whether a company should provide its own materials or components arises because of an interest in cost savings, in reducing the risks of shortages in supplies, and in controlling the quality of materials. These concerns can represent relatively small items of cost or gain or they may represent a major shift in the application of resources and talents in decisions predicated not only on cost advantages, but also on considerations of security and competitive advantage. Small scale make/buy issues are usually handled by the operations-management group with little interaction with general management. Large-scale issues and decisions (such as vertical integration) may be of such magnitude that general management and the organization's board of directors will be engaged in the decision-making process.

Several factors might be involved in assessing the problem of the risks of materials shortages. First, there may be a history of interrupted delivery of materials by one or more suppliers. In some cases, delivery failures may be the result of labor problems, inept management, or an insecure system of delivery. Where deliveries are troublesome, some customers may make use of alternative transportation arrangements or may simply choose to incur the cost of carrying a higher level of safety stock in inventory. Where inept management is suspected, the customer may wish to consider making instead of buying in order to reduce the uncertainty and risk of stockout.

A more ominous potential source of uncertainty about sources of materials may be the actions of competitors who succeed in acquiring the more-reliable sources, either through long-term contracts or through organizational merger or acquisition. In this situation, the customer organization may be left with either a very limited source of supply or with those sources that have been found to lack reliability. The decision to make instead of buy under these circumstances may be driven by necessity or survival and may even be justifiable when some cost penalties are incurred.

Potential cost savings are a second major reason for considering the manufacture of components or the supplying of other materials. Profits of suppliers are costs to customer firms and may appear attractive, in and of themselves, in the make/buy decision. A prudent operations manager (or the general manager), however, would want to consider several important factors before undertaking such a purchase: (1) Although potential cost savings offer a positive cash flow inducement, what is the capital requirement needed in order to begin to achieve the positive flow? An analysis of present values of flows of funds would be most helpful to the operations or general manager in determining whether a positive decision is attractive as an investment. (2) To what extent would such facilities be fully utilized in supplying our customer needs? If, for example, we find that the equipment purchased was only partly utilized in supplying our needs, we are faced with two equally uninteresting alternatives: (a) operating at a very low percentage of capacity or (b) engaging in the business of selling those same materials to other customer firms, perhaps even to competitors. (3) A significant question that must be addressed relates to necessary skills and technical knowledge. Does the customer firm have the technical capability to undertake the supply of a particular material or can that capability be readily hired? If the answers are yes, then the analysis of investment and potential returns can again be explored to assure that the decision makes financial as well as managerial and technological sense.

The next exercise is designed to help you practice some of the analytic skills needed to help you conclude make versus buy decisions. Read through the exercise carefully, then prepare the calculations needed to respond to the questions contained in the exercise.

EXERCISE 5–14

The Multi-Magic Form Company, a major converter of paper products, suffered from numerous failures in its system of supplies. Supplier firms failed to make deliveries of paper stock on a timely basis, and additional costs were incurred as a result. In two instances during the past year, the company was forced to acquire paper from a competitor and to pay a $20 per ton premium in order to meet its own customer's delivery dates. The additional total cost was about $2,400 in one instance and about $3,200 in the second. In at least six cases each month, shortages of needed and ordered materials caused the company to meet customer delivery dates by cutting narrower products from wider widths of paper. The scrapped material could be sold as salvageable paper, but at wastepaper prices. These penalties were somewhat less severe than those mentioned earlier, but they totaled $720 in added scrap paper costs each month during the past year.

On investigation, it was found that the supplier had been unable to locate trucks to handle Multi-Magic's shipments and had resorted to less-than-satisfactory common carriers. The supplier offered substantial savings in delivered cost to Multi-Magic if the company would pay its own freight and pick up its merchandise at the supplier's shipping dock. Savings that would result from these lower prices were $7.85 per ton in truckload quantities. Multi-Magic normally purchased 1,200 tons of paper products per month or approximately 60 tons per working day. Full truckload paper shipments, loaded in skids or rolls and wrapped to protect it from damage, normally averaged 20 tons.

The company's traffic manager estimated that good drivers could be readily hired from trucking firms in the area. His best guess was that wages for the drivers would cost about $9.00 per hour as long as the work was steady and did not involve overnight runs. (The supplier's plant was about 150 miles away. The plant could be reached, the truck loaded, and return home in an easy one-day round-trip.)

Trucks and trailers cost approximately $50,000 and $10,000 each, respectively.

- The company's cost of borrowed funds is currently 12% per year. Should the company undertake the investment in trucking and employ drivers to haul its own supplies? Support your answer with your calculations.
- Your operations-management analyst has estimated that the stockouts suffered last year could have been reduced to a less than 1% chance of occurrence if safety stocks of paper inventories had been raised from the present 3,800 tons to 5,000 tons. Storage facilities would have to be expanded (a one-time capital cost of $60,000). The cost of paper stock is approximately $420 per ton in the grades Multi-Magic buys. Should you expand inventories? Support your decision by means of your calculations.

The make versus buy process and the thinking underlying it form the basis of somewhat broader decisions that involve the incorporation of entire segments of the conversion process in one's area of concern. This is the process of organizational *integration*, which is a significant issue that should be undertaken with close collaboration between operations and general management. Integration can extend in two directions: *backward* toward the sources of supply or *forward* toward the customer. Some industries such as basic steel are nearly fully integrated. They own and operate ore mines, coalfields, and limestone quarries. They own the ships and railroad cars that carry the materials to the mills as well as the warehouses and fabrication centers that construct bridges, ships, and buildings from steel manufactured in the company's mills. Our oil industry is similarly fully integrated. Some major petroleum products companies own and operate facilities that range from the exploration for oil and gas to the retail outlet where petroleum products are marketed to consumers.

The integration process can be undertaken from any position in the conversion chain. A producer of raw materials can undertake the conversion of those materials. A retailer can acquire its suppliers, and a manufacturer can undertake integration moves in both directions. As with the simpler make versus buy decision, cost savings, security of supply, and delivery assurance are factors that can suggest the need for integration. In cases such as fast food chains, the need for quality consistency and assurance of raw materials delivery to the consumer is a compelling reason for maintaining control by owning and operating each stage of conversion.

Contract Versus Employ

Decisions also must be made, from time to time, as to whether human resources should be obtained through employment or through contractural arrangements. In some circumstances, the choice seems clear-cut. If, for example, we wish to have our offices painted, we frequently will employ a painting contractor to complete the job as specified in a contract. The painting contractor provides the services as specified and handles all matters related to the employment of the persons who do the painting. When the job is finished, the contractor is simply paid. The contractor and crew then simply move on to undertake another job. In this case, the job is of short duration, is not a normal part of one's own operation, and makes use of specialized skills and equipment. Similar contractors are used to provide a wide range of skilled-trades services: carpenters, flooring installers, carpet layers, plumbers, electricians, interior decorators, and so on. Contractors are also signed for the provision of a number of professional services: legal representation, architectural design, engineering, arbitration of commercial disputes, business management, accountancy, property appraisal, and a very long list of other types of professional assistance.

In very large organizations, however, many of these services are provided by professionals employed by the client company as full time *employees.* In many of these companies, an entire department of such professionals is engaged full time in the pursuit of professional endeavors for their employer. Land development and pipeline companies, for example, may have literally scores of attorneys working full time on the acquisition of properties, the preparation of leases and contracts, and in legislative efforts needed to assist in the pursuit of the development activity. Similarly, in high-technology companies, hundreds of engineers are engaged in design and development activities for their employer.

In a somewhat less glamorous context, some types of services provided on a routine basis for an employer become the focus of analysis for purposes of considering the advantages of contracting. Plant security is sometimes undertaken by employees, and sometimes it is contracted out to professional suppliers of security services (Brinks, Pinkerton, etc.). Building maintenance, once routinely considered as a function to be performed by employees, is now often contracted to firms specializing in janitorial work. Firms that once employed bookkeepers and accountants are now found to make use of contracted bookkeeping and accounting services offered by public accounting firms.

Several factors are considered in the deliberations over contracting versus employment where human services are involved. First, it is quite important to consider the extent to which the activity is a major component in the operation and whether it involves a great deal of specialized personnel. In the case of the services mentioned in the land-development and high-technology manufacturing businesses, the services to be provided by professionals are extensive and highly specialized. More than likely, these services would be best provided by employees rather than independent professionals.

Where the service is one less uniquely related to the industry and is needed less frequently, then the use of an independent contractor would be more likely. As an example, an aircraft manufacturing company might routinely employ mechanical and aeronautical engineers by the hundreds to conduct its normal business. Its need for an engineer to provide the design work for a new storm drainage system for its physical plant, however, is not a *recurring* engineering problem, is probably outside the expertise of its own staff of engineers, and should probably be contracted to an independent firm of civil engineers.

Cost is a second major factor. In recent years, specialized service firms have found a technology for performing services that permits them to negotiate for contracts that provide substantial savings to client companies.

Employers should be careful in considering the contracting of employment because of the effect on labor relations. The legal relationship between a firm engaging in a contract for services and the contractor is covered under contract law, and it is enforceable in courts of law at local, state, and (where appropriate) federal levels. The contract calls for explicit services and for explicit forms of compensation to the contractor. If services are unsatisfactory or if disputes arise over the contract, the contract can be terminated or adjudicated through civil court action. A labor agreement, although nominally a contract, is a special form of agreement between an employer and a collective of employees represented by a bargaining agent. Its legal status is defined by federal law, and its interpretation is carried out under the auspices of the National Labor Relations Board (NLRB) and (in most cases) the federal courts. The difficulties encountered by some employers in working with employees under a labor agreement might tempt them to consider contracting out the work that is needed to a contractor interested in performing the needed work under a commercial contract. There may be very good commercial reasons for considering such a contract, as spelled out earlier (e.g., specialized skills, work not a part of the mainstream of the business, lower costs). These can be used legitimately as reasons for contracting out work, but the employer must be very careful to be able to demonstrate those sound commercial reasons and to show that the contracting out was not simply a means of obviating the rights of designated bargaining-unit employees covered under a labor agreement or engaged in the negotiation of such an agreement.

EXERCISE 5–15

Charlie Jamison was looking over a proposal from the Watchdog Guard Service Company to provide 24-hour protection service for his plant and warehouse. The contract calls for Watchdog to provide two security officers on day and afternoon shifts, Monday through Friday, one officer on day and afternoon shifts on Saturday and Sunday, and one officer on the night shift, 7 days a week. Officers are to be uniformed and armed and are to have the power of arrest as deputy sheriffs. All security officers employed by Watchdog are trained in security officer work and are so certified by the county sheriff's office. The contract calls for a fee of $2,000 per week. Watchdog is to handle all workmen's compensation, life and health insurance, retirement plan costs, and the costs of vacations for its own guards.

In his analysis of the situation, Charlie reflected on his present guard situation. He currently employs one guard per shift and has a security patrol that checks his premises on the weekend. His costs for security are: guard wages, $7.50 per hour; the patrol service, $100 per week. Employee benefits costs average 38% of wages for all of Charlie's employees. Charlie's guards are not armed. Charlie provides uniforms at a cost of $150 per guard per year. The plant has been broken into three times during the previous year while the guards were occupied elsewhere, and $4,000 in stolen merchandise and damage were reported in the last instance. Charlie's insurance company has said that if thefts continue, Charlie might be moved into the next higher risk category, raising his $3,500 annual premium to $4,500.

Charlie's present guards are members of the local industrial union to which his production employees belong. They have not been active in the affairs of the local union, have filed no grievances, and are considered relatively passive as far as their union role is concerned. If placed on layoff status, their contract rights include an opportunity to bid on jobs plantwide and eligibility for a training period of forty-five days to help in learning their new jobs.

- What economic benefits or costs will Charlie incur if he agrees to Watchdog's contract terms?
- What potential problems might he encounter if he engages Watchdog?
- Should he sign the contract? Explain.

ANSWERS TO SELECTED EXERCISES

Exercise 5–3

Costs: The central location of Louisville (probably) minimized total costs of shipment of raw materials and shipments of finished goods to major metropolitan markets in the eastern half of the United States as well as labor costs and total investment in land, plant, production, and transportation equipment.

Effectiveness: Minimizing distance from both sources and markets as well as handling all orders at a central location will permit both consolidation of shipments and paperwork and more rapid overall response to customer inquiries and orders. In addition, the combination of products permits a one-call-handles-everything service capability that has a distinctive competitive edge.

Exercise 5–5

Summer camps offer group activities to youngsters in stated age categories. Counselors who are specialists in swimming, marksmanship, nature study, or various crafts are needed to provide guidance to groups of youngsters. Special equipment such as horses and tack, canoes and rowboats, craft supplies, and special beach equipment are required to effectively carry out this type of group-oriented service.

Package tours offer a service to groups of clients who wish to travel to an area but who lack enough knowledge of the area, its customs, and the mechanics of travel into, through, and out of the selected area. Travel expertise is needed, as are contacts in the area to be visited; a knowledge of the language, where applicable; and a facility with the currency are very helpful. In some instances, package tour organizations have acquired their own airplanes (Port of Call is one).

6

ORGANIZATION AND MANAGEMENT FOR THE GENERAL MANAGER

In dealing with management problems, the general manager has a variety of avenues for management action: he or she can choose or modify the organizational form, can adopt a suitable managerial style, can recruit and select personnel to fit the needs of the organization and its mission, and/or can provide training and development to assist employees in better matching organizational needs. In this chapter, we will examine these actions, in hopes that we can gain a perspective on the overriding need for a match of organizational mission, organizational structure, human resources, and a managerial style that will aid in the accomplishment of long- and short-range objectives. The first two of these types of management action are discussed in the following paragraphs. We will then look at some of the major contingencies that appear to have the most significant effect on the choice of organization and style. Finally, we will briefly discuss some of the issues related to training, development, recruitment, and selection of the organization's human resources.

An organization can be arranged in a wide hierarchical shape with a fairly broad span of control or it can have a narrow, steep triangular form with narrow spans of control and many managerial layers from bottom to top. In addition, managers can choose from a variety of forms of organizational segmentation. Organizations can be arranged to emphasize business functions, customer groups, products, geographic areas, or parts of a conversion process. In some industries, the organizational form is arranged to emphasize the short-run accomplishment of projects in a project-function matrix.

Second, the manager can choose a particular leadership or managerial style and need not, and should not, be confined to a particular style in all situations. This contingency perspective on management style is being found in an increasingly wide range of literature. Managers can choose to structure tasks rigidly or to delegate the planning and organization of work to subordinates. They can also be personally close and supportive of subordinates or can choose to remain relatively aloof and distant. Similarly, managers can choose to delegate broad authority to operating units or can choose to retain a highly centralized managerial control system. The continuum of delegative styles described by Tannenbaum[1] represents an early description of a range of participation rather than a firm prescription for high participation. The leader-behavior dimensions of initiating structure and consideration[2] have been incorporated in the path-goal theory of leadership,[3] a concept that includes environmental factors such as the task, the formal authority system, the primary work group, and subordinate characteristics as important contingencies. Griffin[4] has four different orientations in his contingency matrix: a participative/achievement oriented style, a directive style, a supportive style, and a maintenance style. The matrix describes situations in which each of these styles can be seen as best suited to the type of task and one characteristic of subordinates.

We will examine organizational structure and management style given the contingencies of (a) a selected strategy, (b) a chosen technology, (c) a strategically defined

[1] Robert Tannenbaum and Warren H. Schmidt, "How to Choose a Leadership Pattern," *Harvard Business Review* (March–April 1958), p. 96.

[2] Ralph M. Stogdill, *Handbook of Leadership* (New York: Free Press, 1974), pp. 393–97.

[3] R. J. House and T. R. Mitchell, "Path-Goal Theory of Leadership," *Journal of Finance and Quantitative Analysis* (1974), p. 5.

[4] Ricky W. Griffin, "Task Design Determinants of Effective Leader Behavior," *Academy of Management Review* 4(2) (April 1979), pp. 215–224.

task, and (d) a given set of human resources. With these contingencies as major variables, we should be able to identify managerial approaches and organizational arrangements that will aid us in the accomplishment of the objectives we have set as the focus of our major strategic plan.

MAJOR CONTINGENCIES

Chosen Strategy

The chosen strategy of an organization is an extremely important element in the determination of an appropriate organizational structure and the selection and reinforcement of a managerial style that is consistent with, and supportive of, that strategy. Three elements in the statement of chosen strategy are worthy of particular mention: choice of industry, choice of product/service offerings, and choice of principal means of competition. A strategy statement that identifies the chosen industry as aerospace technology places the entire organization and its human and financial resources in a technological and product environment that, generally speaking, is rapidly evolving and highly turbulent. At another extreme, a statement that identifies the chosen industry as electric power generation and transmission would place the organization in a competitive environment that *generally* is relatively stable, highly regulated, and capital intensive.

An examination of the organizational forms found in each industry offers excellent information on the organizational needs in each industry's environment and can be used as a first-draft approximation of needs given the statement of chosen industry. The aerospace industry is characterized by turbulence, technological advancement, and uncertainty. Organizations in this industry tend to be much more "organic" in character and are marked by a high degree of specialization, which is a means of adaptation to that environment, and by the need for "integrators,"[5] persons or organizational devices that serve to link widely different organizational units. In many aerospace organizations, as in other high-tech types of companies, the matrix organization is used to pull together the skills of functional specialists and direct them toward the accomplishment of specified short-term and medium-range projects.

Organizations that exist in a stable environment with a mature technology and mature products quite often have a distinctly bureaucratically oriented organization. Jobs are formally defined, and written job descriptions are carefully prepared and then reviewed for accuracy in subsequent periods. Communications are more formal, and organizational proprieties are observed more carefully. Organizations of this type frequently have formally prepared and published operating procedures, handbooks, and statements of standard practice.

[5] P. R. Lawrence and J. W. Lorsch *Organization and Environment* (Homewood, Ill.: R. D. Irwin, 1969), pp.137–140.

Although the formality described is a common characteristic of these organizations, the particulars of their organizational makeup offer considerable variety. Some companies are built around an extensively developed and formally defined set of major functions. In these firms, each function reports at or near the top level of the company and is made up of layers and layers of managers expert in that particular function. A geographic or product orientation is often combined with the function to provide units of reasonable size for managerial direction.

One example of this form of organization is found in some companies that manufacture consumer products. The three major functions of marketing, operations, and finance are separated. Marketing is managed through an extensive functional organization that incorporates both geographic sales representation to, and contact with, retail outlets as well as product management that is designed to focus attention on the marketing of a product that has its own unique market identity and need for promotional attention. The marketing function is separated from operations, except at a relatively high level. Operations is made up of a limited number of multiproduct production units, each managed and staffed by persons whose interests, skills, and talents are unique to operations.

In this type of company, the functional organization assures the concentration of talent needed for effective competition in a highly mature product/technology environment. Marketing managers supervise other marketing managers; operations managers supervise other operations managers.

Another organizational form found in stable, highly mature industries is an organization broken down by function and parts of the conversion process. In this type of organization, the operations section of the organization is compartmentalized in accordance with discrete steps in the conversion process. In paper mills, the wood-procurement process is organizationally separated from wood storage and chipmaking. Similarly, the digesters are separated from the bleach room and the machine room, where the paper is actually made.

In addition to these two commonly found types of formal organizations, we can also find large stable organizations that are organized around clearly identified geographic units. Each geographic unit may contain numerous functional specialists, but each unit and function will have carefully defined boundaries.

EXERCISE 6–1

- Draw an organization chart that is separated at the top level by function, then later by product categories. (Material at the end of this chapter may help get you started.) Would you anticipate any difficulty in managing with this type of organization? Explain.
- Draw an organization chart that is separated at the top level by product categories, then by geographic divisions, then by functions.
- Draw an organization chart that is separated at the top by customer groupings,

then by geography, and finally by function. Can you suggest a type of company for which this organizational form might be useful? Explain.

The organization that is found in industrial environments characterized by a high rate of change and a higher level of uncertainty is often much less formal and has a work culture that is much more expertise oriented in decision making. Mechanisms for gathering and disseminating information are extremely important in assuring organizational adaptation and response to changing conditions. Information-gathering responsibilities are often an expected part of job definitions. In addition, market-information specialists and technically expert employees are formally charged with the responsibility for maintaining currency in developments in their respective fields.

The dissemination of information is often facilitated by internal bulletins, by new product-development groups, or by research and development committees assigned the responsibility of maintaining the currency of the organization's technology.

EXERCISE 6–2

Draw an organization chart that contains a functional breakdown and includes the following business functions: engineering, production, sales, advertising, market research, process research, product research, accounting, personnel, purchasing, data processing, payroll, billing, shipping, public relations, treasurer, controller, plant protection, maintenance, customer service. (These business functions need not be at the same organizational level, so group them in a way that seems reasonable to you.)

Describe on your chart an appropriate committee to examine the following categories of issues (one committee for each issue category).

- A competitor has just introduced a line of products that undercuts the price for your major product.
- A change in manufacturing equipment has been announced by your equipment supplier that will result in substantial reductions in man-hours and great gains for the company in profitability, if capital can be raised.
- Your marketing department has received inquiries from customers about the likelihood of your company developing and selling a new product that would result in substantial cost savings for your customers in their own processing costs.
- Your research team has conceived of a process by which your manufacturing technology could be drastically altered. You have been told that further exploration will involve an investment of easily $5 million. Further, adopting the new approach would involve an investment of at least $15 million and would probably mean moving the manufacturing facility to the source of your raw materials.

The matrix organization, mentioned earlier, is used to bring highly specialized functional expertise (normally seen in functional organizations) to bear on projects that have a high visibility, high significance to the organization, and a short to

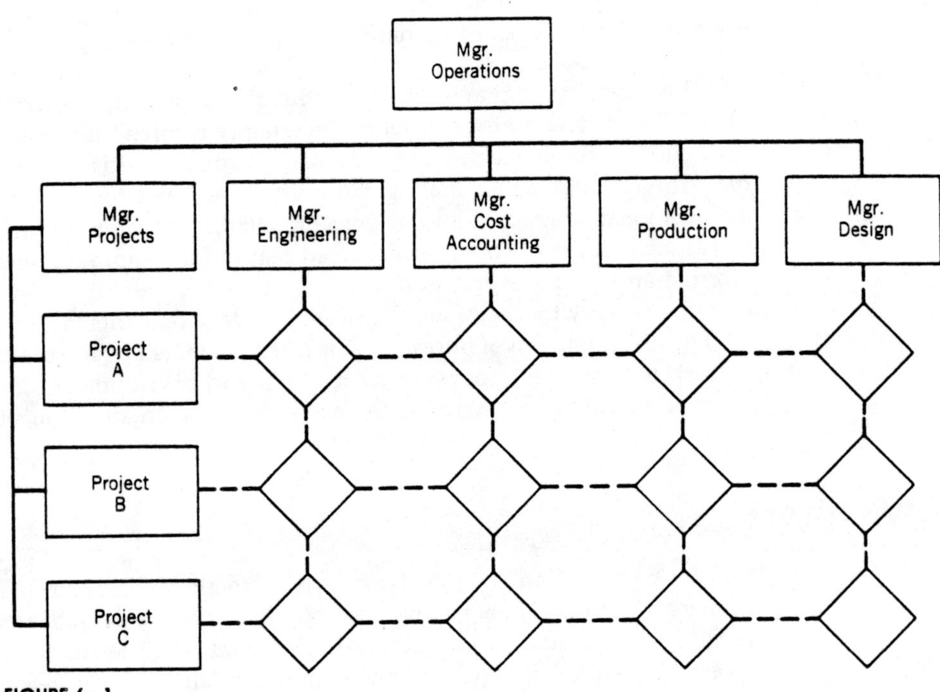

FIGURE 6-1

moderate life. Project managers assigned to a given project serve to provide scheduling, coordination, and project continuity for the life of the project.

Figure 6-1 is an abbreviated matrix organization. Functional managers report to the Manager of Operations, and functional specialists report to *both* the functional manager and to the managers of Projects A, B, and C.

EXERCISE 6-3

For this exercise, the functional departments listed in the preceding exercise should be used. Draw organizational charts that depict matrix organizations to be used in guiding and managing these projects:

- The purchase of land and the construction and leasing of space for a small shopping center.
- The purchase of an invention, its development into production, and its introduction to the marketplace.
- The acquisition (either lease or purchase) and installation of a large-scale computer system for use in financial and managerial accounting.

Thus far we have discussed organizations that seem to be found in environments that are clearly either stable, with relatively low uncertainty, or turbulent and frought with rapid change and ambiguity. The electric-power-generation industry seems to epitomize a stable industry, and aerospace one that is highly turbulent. Although we characterize these industries as either dynamic or stable, subsets of each may have quite different characters. In aerospace, some major product lines are relatively mature and have remained in their present state of development for a number of years. As one example, twin-engined, light-passenger aircraft used for private, corporate, or air-taxi service are little different than similar aircraft produced in the 1950s.

Electric power generation, as an industry, is typified by a very stable technology, and it exists in a most predictable, controlled external environment. This broad description of the industry does not, however, adequately depict either the stage of excitement and the new-product/new-process advancement that is found in power generation through chemical power cells or windmills or the extent of interest seen in the development of fusion-type atomic-power generators. The choice of industry establishes a range of environmental factors and may provide an accurate view of the extent of change for most organizations in that industry. It may not, however, accurately cover the immediate environment for those firms that select products or services at the extremes of stability or turbulence.

Thus, when the choice of product or service offerings is added to the choice of industry, we begin to develop a much more accurate idea of the extent to which products and technologies are undergoing change. The stage of development of our chosen product in its product life cycle is extremely significant. Although this is a concept covered in some detail in Chapter 8, it is important to note that the introductory and growth stages are characterized by a very active competitive and technological environment. Although the mature stage is highly competitive, the number of competitors is much smaller, the technology is highly developed and stable, and products are highly refined. The mature stage represents a stable environment, with a relatively low rate of change. The decline stage is characterized by a high level of uncertainty in customer preferences, a reduction in competitors, and a lower level of predictability in customer behavior.

The choice of means of competition is a third factor of extreme importance in the choice of strategy. Strategic objectives can be accomplished by being an aggressive price competitor; by being a technological leader or a follower; by being competitively nimble and thereby occupying one or more small niches in a competitive structure; by dominating a single segment of a segmented market; by acquiring or merging with other firms; or by other strategic means. Each of these means conveys a *modus operandi* that suggests a type of organization. If one were to adopt the principle means of competition, being an aggressive price competitor, the organization used to assist in the accomplishment of strategic objectives *with that means* should be arranged to assist in that endeavor. Organizational patterns that aid in rapid decisions on pricing would be desired, as would an organization that brings highly focused special attention to cost control and to promotional efforts that bring the competitive price of products or services to the attention of targeted customers.

If the choice of means were technological leadership, we would expect to find an organizational structure that emphasized research and incorporated units designed to assist in the rapid implementation of new products or technologies such as new-product departments or committees or process-development groups.

EXERCISE 6–4

Draw organizational charts you believe would depict organizations that use price competition and those that use technological leadership as a principal means of competitive emphasis.

EXERCISE 6–5

Draw an organizational chart that would aid in carrying out organizational objectives for an organization that has chosen to compete by means of occupying small niches in a large market.

The following statements of strategy and policy are from prominent corporations. As you read them, reflect on their organizational implications, then answer the exercise questions that appertain to each corporation.

Whirlpool Corporation

- "Whirlpool Corporation and its consolidated subsidiaries manufacture and market a full line of major home appliances as well as certain other related products."
- "The Company markets its products for nationwide sale under the Whirlpool brand name and also markets central heating systems and central air conditioners under the Neil brand name."
- "The Company is also the principal supplier to Sears, Roebuck and Co. of many of these products which are marketed under Sears and Kenmore brand names."

Policy Statements

- "Refrigeration sealed system brazing is typical of those fundamental manufacturing processes where careful workmanship helps to achieve Whirlpool Corporation's exacting standards of quality."
- "Water and energy conservation are given high priority in designing Whirlpool products, a positive expression of the Company's sensitivity to energy and environmental concerns."
- "Whirlpool educational programs include the most up-to-date training techniques to increase product knowledge and hone human relations skills."

- "Effectively managing the physical distribution of finished products from Whirlpool factories to consumers is essential for balancing inventory costs with optimum product availability."
- "Whirlpool stands behind its products with a wide array of services that form one of the strongest two-way communications networks between a manufacturer and the consumer found in any industry."[6]

EXERCISE 6–6

- Describe what you believe to be Whirlpool's choice of competitive emphasis. Explain.
- Describe how you believe this would be reflected in the organization chart for Whirlpool and at what level or levels in the company's organization.

FMC Corporation

"As one of the world's leading producers of machinery and chemicals for industry, agriculture and government, FMC participates on a worldwide basis in selected segments of five broad markets: Industrial Chemicals, Petroleum Equipment and Services, Defense Equipment and Systems, Performance Chemicals, and Specialized Machinery. FMC operates 126 manufacturing facilities and mines in 29 states and 15 foreign countries."

Corporate Objectives

- "Incorporate advanced manufacturing systems into FMC plants."
- "Make optimum use of our human resources through greater employee involvement."
- "Improve the cost position of phosphate production at Foret, FMC's Spanish chemical division."
- "Commercialize human antibody and immune regulation products in order to diagnose and treat major diseases."
- "Penetrate the market for electronic oilfield pump control products."
- "Incorporate new technologies into existing products."
- "Obtain a major share of mainland China's pesticide market."[7]

[6] *Whirlpool Corporation Annual Report,* 1983.

[7] *Annual Report, FMC Corporation,* 1983.

EXERCISE 6–7

- To what extent do you see FMC's choice of markets determining the type of organizational form that should be used? Explain.
- To what extent do the statements of corporate objectives have an effect on the organizational form and the management style that would seem to be appropriate? Explain.

Choice of Technology

The general manager not only functions within an industry/product environment, but (as discussed in Chapter 5) also makes a choice of a technology that will meet product-quality requirements and customer needs for quantity and delivery dates. If, for example, the technology chosen is highly advanced, with specialized and costly high-volume equipment, then not only must the order pattern reflect the desire to produce large quantities of similar or identical items, but the entire organization should be constructed around the concept of a large-scale, high-volume conversion operation. Procedures are stabilized to freeze the best operating decisions as standard responses for repetitive operating decision problems. Similarly, the large scale of operations and the necessity for standardized treatment for customers and employees encourages the development of standard practices dealing with personnel matters, credit practices, and customer relations.

The advancement of technology often means that the work of employees becomes highly specialized and compartmentalized to assure that duplication of effort does not occur and that all stations in a multiple-station process are adequately staffed. The specialized compartmentalization that exists at the lowest levels in the mass-production technology often transcends that level and becomes apparent at higher and higher levels in the organization.

Where the choice of technology is that of a simple form, one that uses handtools or simple machines, the organization becomes much more dependent on human factors, and often has a more personal character. In these one-of-a-kind technology organizations, the number of layers from the bottom of the organization to the top is small, thus shortening the social and communicative distance between subordinates and top managers.[8] In this type of organization, the operative level employee has a much greater latitude in tasks and decision making. Task assignments tend to be broader in character and much less rigidly defined.

The more primitive technology has advantages in adapting to specialized customer requirements and in rapid response. These needs call for organizational forms that are designed to achieve quick decisions and to adjust priorities and schedules to accommodate change. The rigid, bureaucratic organizational form is ill suited to these requirements and must give way to a more adaptive "organic"[9] arrangement, one that

[8] Joan Woodward, *Industrial Organization: Theory and Practice* (London: Oxford University Press, 1965.

[9] Tom Burns and G. M. Stalker, *The Management of Innovation* (London: Tavistock Publications, 1961).

makes use of less formal communications, an expertise-based decision-making system, and multidirection communications to maintain cohesion in turbulent environments.

EXERCISE 6–8

Your company, Front-Range Fences, Inc., is in the business of designing and building fences for residences, commercial businesses, and municipal properties. After each job is designed and estimated and the customer has accepted the quotation, construction is undertaken by a crew of builders. Each job differs in terms of fencing materials, height of fence, and the peculiarities of each property. Although some jobs are quite large (e.g., woven-wire fencing around a golf course), most range in cost to customers from $1,200 to $2,500. Power equipment is available to dig postholes and stretch wire, but in many residential properties, proximity to sidewalks, shrubbery, and structures precludes the use of anything but hand tools. Materials range from pickets to cedar planks to split wooden rails and from woven wire to decorative wire, to decorative wrought or cast-iron metal fencing. Gates must be constructed for entrances and driveways, and decorative posts are often built, on-site, to meet customers' aesthetic preferences. Work crews are often three or four fence builders, but rarely more than five or six persons.

- Identify the elements in this particular business that will call for special attention in designing an organization. (See some suggestions at the end of the chapter.)
- Sketch an organization chart for managing this company during the stage in its growth when it employs 20 fence builders.
- Sketch the chart that you think would be appropriate when the organization reaches an employment level of 80 fence builders.

EXERCISE 6–9

Parkview Papers, your paper-manufacturing company, makes specialty papers for custom printers. Your equipment consists of a pulp preparation unit that converts commercial pulps, dyes, and (where needed) bleaches into the materials needed by a 60-inch paper machine, which then produces specialty coated and noncoated papers in weights from 10 pounds to 40 pounds. Coatings are applied by a separate machine that provides the slick, hard, and glossy appearance of entertainment programs and high-quality magazines. The cutting, finishing, and packaging areas receive paper in roll form, cut it into sheets, stack it on pallets, and wrap it for shipment to customers.

Operators of each piece of equipment are highly trained. Normally, because of the length of the training period, they are trained in one area of the manufacturing process and do not migrate to other areas of the plant to move upward in their careers.

Papers of a single color can be manufactured in a variety of weights (and thus thicknesses) in the same manufacturing schedule, by simply adjusting the paper machine. Widths of orders are cut out of stock that covers the entire width of the paper machine. Within a color category, coatings may or may not be applied depending on the customer's needs. Thus, widths, thicknesses, and coating variables can be dealt with fairly readily. When colors change, however, the pulping area and the paper machine must be shut down, washed thoroughly, and restarted with pulp of the new color formulation. In addition, adjusting the color tint is a most painstaking process that is extremely important in order that accurate color matching between batches of colored papers is accomplished. Your marketing organization maintains a modest inventory of standard sizes, weights, and colors to handle small orders, but normally it likes to provide a working schedule that limits color changes to one or two per week. Order backlogs range from 2 to 4 weeks, but the marketing staff is hesitant to quote more than 4 weeks because of pressures for faster deliveries from competitors.

- Consider the technology described above, then think of elements that probably will need to be emphasized organizationally. (See suggestions at the end of the chapter.)
- Sketch an organizational chart that reflects this emphasis.

Human Resources

The last element in our list of contingencies is that of human resources. In many cases, we have only limited choice regarding the human resources to be used in a particular strategy, especially one that involves an existing organizational unit. The literature in organizational behavior lists a wide range of personal variables that may have a bearing on the choice of the managerial strategy employed. Employee need for growth,[10] authoritarian orientation,[11] knowledge of goals and paths to goals,[12] and preferences for directive or consultative managerial styles[13] have all been found to have a bearing on the type of organizational structure and management style used in a given situation.

Although generalizations are somewhat risky, it is reasonable to conclude that employees who tend to be outer directed and who prefer structured situations and a more directive management style will be more comfortable in a somewhat more formalized, bureaucratic organization. Similarly, new employees, or employees whose tasks are ambiguous and who are unclear on the means toward accomplishing

[10] See J. R. Hackman and Greg R. Oldham, *Work Redesign* (Reading, Mass.: Addison-Wesley, 1980); and Ricky W. Griffin, *Task Design—An Integrative Approach* (Glenview, Ill: Scott-Foresman, 1980).

[11] V. H. Vroom and F. C. Mann, "Leader Authoritarianism and Employee Attitudes," *Personnel Psychology* 13 (1960), pp. 125–40.

[12] House and Mitchell, "Path-Goal Theory of Leadership." *Journal of Finance and Quantitative Analysis* (1974). p. 5.

[13] Stogdill, *Handbook of Leadership* (New York: Free Press, 1974), p. 111.

those tasks will be more comfortable in working with a supervisor who tends to structure the work situation, at least until the ambiguity is reduced and both tasks and means are clarified.

Employees who tend to be inner directed, who are comfortable in ambiguous situations and who have a high need for challenge and growth will enjoy a less-structured work environment. Similarly, employees who are thoroughly familiar with the task will prefer to be left to complete their work without unnecessary instruction or guidance from their supervisors. For these persons, a formalized organization and a structuring supervisor will be seen as repressive and restrictive. Attempts at structuring by supervisors will be interpreted as overcontrolling and will frequently be resented.[14]

The manager preparing a strategy for implementation must, one would conclude, consider the general character of the persons with whom he or she will be working. If, in general, they have been comfortable in a bureaucratic environment, it is unlikely that they will easily adjust to a more free-form organizational context with a broader or less-clear range of decision types. The institution of a more-organic organizational environment may call for a degree of preparation and coaching to move subordinates into a different organizational context in a nonthreatening way. In addition, some of these characteristics of subordinates are deep-seated personal attributes, largely unaffected by coaching and preparative efforts.

The normal processes of migration among employees tend to result in individuals seeking an environment they find comfortable. Changing that environment may induce the same discomfort that caused the person to seek out the former environment in the first place. As a consequence, we may find some of our subordinates migrating again, seeking the environment they have found to be most rewarding.

A similar problem exists as we move from the more-ambiguous, less-formal, and more-organic organization to one that is more hierarchical, more formal, and more predictable. Employees find that the boss is less reachable, that more communications are written, and that rules exist where none did before. For some, this formalization is stifling and to some degree demeaning. Social distance between operative and manager has increased because of size and formality, and the operative has lost the sense of personal contact with the organization's leadership.

MANAGING A GIVEN STRATEGY

The person given the task of managing an organizational unit with a given strategy should examine the major contingencies to first determine the managerial structure and style that would be most effective under *ideal* conditions. If, for example, the task is clearly defined, the environment quite stable, the technology well advanced, and the product a mature one, the ideal managerial structure and style would probably be

[14] R. C. Day and R. L. Hamblin, "Some Effects of Close and Punitive Styles of Supervision," *American Journal of Sociology* 69(5) (1964), pp. 499–510.

relatively formalized and bureaucratic. Other contingencies would call for a quite different structure and style, under ideal circumstances.

EXERCISE 6–10

Your first managerial assignment is that of coordinating the activities of a parent's group for a school that is investigating the impact of educational computer applications in primary grades (Kindergarten through Grade 6).

- Describe the structure of the organization you would want to use in this situation. (See some hints at the end of the chapter.)
- Describe the managerial style that you think would be most appropriate.

Although we would all find it relatively easy to choose a managerial style given clear evidence of the major contingencies, the situation is hardly ever that clear, nor does it meet the ideal requirements mentioned earlier. First, evidence on the nature of the environment is rarely so compelling as to clearly indicate its turbulence, ambiguity, or uncertainty. Second, tasks often seem ambiguous initially but frequently become quite clear as learning takes place. Thus, even in a situation where tasks will eventually be highly structured, the situation is seen by participants as quite ambiguous at first. Finally, in situations that we believe will be quite ambiguous, supervisory styles and organizational assignments must be relatively highly structured until such time as goals and paths toward those goals are clarified, even though we may ultimately desire an organization and a managerial style that is organic and participative in nature.

EXERCISE 6–11

Consider the dynamic nature of the situation described in Exercise 6–10 from the perspective of the manager.

- How would you *start out* the management process (i.e., establish a structure and adopt a managerial style) in the coordinating assignment of that exercise?
- Would you maintain that structure and style or gradually change to another as the group began to deal with its task? Explain.

The extent to which the ideal structure and managerial style can be adopted depends, to a very large extent, on the makeup of the individuals with whom the manager is, and will be, working. As mentioned earlier, some individuals strongly prefer a more fluid, organic organization and feel stifled and overcontrolled in the more bureaucratic organization. Other persons prefer the clarity and predictability of well-defined jobs and a formal organizational structure.

THE DENVER PROJECT: DECENTRALIZING THE CORPORATE DATA PROCESSING ACTIVITIES

Ken Mayhew was deep in thought as he gazed across his desk and through the glass partition to the busy machine room. He felt pleased and a bit flattered that he'd been chosen to supervise the new operations decentralization project, an installation and shakedown assignment that would last several months.

In April of the preceding year, Canada and Associates, a consulting systems-design firm, had studied the company's existing data processing (DP) activities in great detail. They reported favorably on the general systems design and on the hardware and software currently in use. They had also complimented the vice president of data processing on the quality of maintenance of the programs and the level of qualifications and training for personnel in both the Systems Department and the DP Operations Department.

The consultants expressed a deep concern, however, about backup capability and the current high operating cost and suggested than an appropriate approach for building capacity as well as providing capability for breakdown or overload problems would be to duplicate the existing configuration of equipment rather than replace it with a larger system. Thus, a separate, intact unit located in the second largest division (Denver) would provide additional capacity and backup capability instead of the major expenditure for radically increasing system power in a single central unit.

The current hardware configuration consists of an IBM 370/168 (2 MB) CPU, 8 (50 MB) disk units, 20 (1600 BPI) tape drives, 4 (2000 LPM) printers, and a stand-alone data entry system with 24 terminals. The operation is currently manned 24 hours per day, 7 days a week. Breakdown time has been minimized by having carefully trained operators and by good service support from vendors. Capacity utilization has ranged in the high 80% to low 90% (over three shifts), and a lengthy list of new applications is backlogged. The existing backlog of new applications is forecast to require approximately 50% additional capacity if entirely implemented.

Current physical facilities are strained. Equipment, supplies, and working space for staff are severely limited, as is space for all departments in the company's headquarters office building.

An alternative to locating the duplicate operation in Denver is that of locating a satellite DP site in New York, the headquarters city. Site costs, problems in securing adequately trained staff, the security of equipment, and the safety of operations staff working around the clock all mitigate against a second location in New York City.

The Wheeled Products Division, located in Denver, expressed considerable interest in locating DP Operations in its administrative building. Several sound reasons were advanced in support of this idea. Space was available, the Denver employment situation was strong, and the division's own DP activity utilized nearly 30% of the capacity of the central computing facility. Data transmission costs could be saved and labor costs reduced. Finally, vendor support in Denver was considered to be exceptionally good.

Ken's concern focused on the staff he must select to install and shake down equipment in order to start up the systems to be run in Denver and on the building of the operations staff that would assume responsibility for the Denver operations once it was operating satisfactorily. Early estimates anticipated that the Denver operation could be running in approximately 8

This case was prepared by the author.

to 10 months. Ken's key operations supervisors are:

1. Ed Snedecor—age 46. Worked 15 years at IBM, has worked with the 360 series equipment since their introduction, prefers shiftwork, likes to recruit his own assistants. He grumbles frequently about lack of adequately trained or motivated workers in the labor market today. Dislikes interruptions in his operationing schedules and is intensely interested in minimizing machine time on his shift. He competes with the other shift supervisors in achieving operating rate goals. Has not expressed much interest in participating in vendor training on new equipment, particularly configurations involving scientific applications or units of significantly greater power. High school plus a year of college.
2. Nancy Jacobs—age 33. College graduate. Started with the company 10 years ago. Began as a programmer, but found operations more to her liking. Has worked in all phases of operations. Excellent troubleshooter. Finds new applications interesting and frequently requests permission to attend vendor seminars or new equipment and management seminars offered through a local university. Nancy is well liked by her subordinates, but she is sometimes seen as too willing to interrupt established routines and schedules to accommodate the requests of users with problems.
3. Carole Larkin—age 47. High school plus 2 years of business college. Carole began her work in operations 25 years ago as a key punch/verifier operator. Carole's performance over the years has been steady and dependable. She has risen from her entry-level job through data entry until 7 years ago when, at her supervisor's request, she attended, over a 12-month period, vendor training programs in operating mainframe, and I/O equipment. Her performance in the program was quite acceptable. She has commented that she found schooling to be quite demanding, often involving study well into the nighttime hours. After completing her training, she worked as an assistant shift supervisor for 2 years, then acted as fill-in supervisor (covering vacations, illnesses, and leaves of absence) for 3 years; she was made shift supervisor 2 years ago. She has performed quite well in her present job. Her subordinates seem to like Carole, particularly her desire to establish and maintain a clear and well-understood work schedule that is followed rigorously. Carole has said, "I'd like to be able to know—even if I'm 20 miles away—exactly what we are currently working on when I get a question on our operation from topside (top management)."
4. Edward Leonard—age 32. Business graduate (UCLA) plus MBA from Pepperdine. Ed was a management trainee with the corporate training program. He has been with the company 4 years and with DP Operations 3 years. His ability to recruit and train new employees is considered to be a great strength. Technically, Ed is still learning about data processing equipment and systems. He has attended numerous vendor training programs and has performed well. When tricky technical issues arise, Ed is inclined to look to vendor representatives or an experienced operator or supervisor for help. Ed has said that he'd like to see the company move toward more sophisticated equipment and sees his future tied to an ability to learn the new equipment from the moment it is installed. Ed's long-term aspiration is to reach executive level, either through DP or through the systems/controller routes.

Ken's specific problem is that he is expected

to choose persons to install the equipment, train and/or recruit the needed staff for operations, and begin the implementation of existing routines.

Ray Johnson, assistant vice president for computer operations, has been most specific about applications to be run at the Denver facility. They include:

First: All operations that affect *only* the Wheeled Vehicle Division.

Next: Routine operations for the corporation that can be accommodated by mail or messenger-delivered I/O (i.e., card decks or paper/magnetic tape and mailed or messenger-delivered checks, documents, and reports.)

Next: Backup operations for the corporation during central facility peak loads or downtime requires telecommunication linkage to meet time deadlines for batched daily runs.

Interactive (real time) operations are explicitely excluded (to hold data transition costs down). Debugging and testing of programs will be confined to the central facility.

EXERCISE 6–12

- Select a team to send to Denver.
- What organizational structure and management style would you suggest for the effective implementation of the Denver Project during the first 3 months? Explain.
- The next 6 months?
- The remainder of its existence under its current assigned role?
- Would you expect your chosen team members to experience any discomfort as you make your organizational and managerial changes? Why?

The "Why Tinker with It?" case presents a situation that to some extent is similar to the one contained in the Denver Project Case. In this situation, however, we may find some individuals either threatened by the assigned project or somewhat unwilling to undertake the job. Read the case, then respond to the exercise that follows.

"WHY TINKER WITH IT?"

Ed Jarvis was puzzled by recent events. As newly appointed manager of system operations maintenance of the company's centralized computer center, he and most of his senior staff had seen the center grow enormously. From a punched-card machine accounting shop used to maintain financial accounting records, the center had expanded to be a complex that incorporated an IBM 3033, several disk I/O units, tape drives for monthly and weekly payroll and accounting routines, high-speed printing capacity, and several remote terminals.

For Ed, the growth had been both challenging and rewarding. Much of the systems design work on the various expansion stages had been done by a project team made up of vendor analysts and company systems analysts and programmers assigned from the Systems Analysis Section, which was headed by Charles Jacoby, an MS (computer science) graduate of Carnegie-Mellon, hired about 5 years earlier. Both Ed and Charles reported to Nathan Ellsberg, vice president of administrative operations. Although Ed hadn't been directly involved in design work, he had been called on to assist in systems review meetings and in the planning and implementation of changes as they occurred. His staff had been selected from operations personnel. All had progressed through each of the stages of transition—learning new routines, taking courses offered by vendors, and seeing their jobs altered as hardware and systems changes were made.

Recently, as a part of his system maintenance activities, Ed had been asked to undertake a review and redesign of the systems used to handle sales and billing transactions. The systems in question had been in use for over six years and seemed overdue for reexamination and modification. The project sounded interesting to Ed—and somewhat at variance with his group's normal assignments. When he asked if he would be able to get help from Charles's programmers and analysts, he learned that they were all engaged in a major project dealing with comprehensive sales/operations forecasting for the corporate planning department, a project given A-1 priority by the president of the company.

Ed reviewed the project with his senior staff and was surprised at their lack of interest. Pete Zifferelli, formerly manager of data control, seemed to exemplify the staff's response when he said, "Hell, Ed, that system's fine—why tinker with it? We haven't had any significant error costs associated with that system since it was debugged over six years ago." Ed had little to rejoin with except a comment to the effect that old systems, although useful, may lack service features that newer systems might have and may be less efficient with respect to service time and space utilization.

Ed's key staff—and a brief outline of their backgrounds-are

Gregory Olson—age 43. BBA, University of California at Fullerton. Employed as accounting clerk at age 27, machine accounting at age 34, most recently shift supervisor of computer room operations. Has had FORTRAN and COBOL programming courses.

Sally Everson—age 36. High school plus a two-year certification in bookkeeping from Valley Community College. Hired as keypunch operator at age 25, senior keypunch operator at 28, supervisor of data entry at 30; most recently shift supervisor of data entry and control. No programming or systems design experience or training.

Edgar Astrala—age 53. High school plus

two years accounting at Bear Creek Vocational Center. Employed at age 27 as bookkeeper. Machine accountant trainee at age 34, machine accountant at age 35, shift supervisor of machine accounting at age 41; has been shift supervisor of computer operations since age 44. No programming or systems design training.

Pete Zifferelli—age 42, BBA University of Akron, MBA Wayne State University. First employed as cost analyst at age 29, senior cost analyst and team leader at age 32, assigned to computer development and installation team at age 34, and data control supervisor at age 37. Has had training in both FORTRAN and COBOL and participated in system design work during the conversion process.

As Ed made a mental review of his senior staff's qualifications, he considered the problem. A nine-month deadline had been tentatively set for the review and redesign project. Some additional funding might be available to cover travel and other miscellaneous costs, but Ed's group was expected to perform the revision project concurrently with their normal activities.

This case was prepared by the author.

EXERCISE 6–13

Individuals with a high need for growth are often found to exhibit an urge to learn new things, to become uncomfortable as the job becomes routine, and to move from challenge to challenge. Their careers are characterized by relatively frequent movement and by a desire for variety and learning. Persons with a low need for growth are often found to desire a stable, predictable work setting. Their advancement is somewhat slower and frequently gives evidence of a lack of interest in new projects or processes.

- How would you characterize the individuals described in the "Why Tinker with It" case?
- What kind of organizational structure and managerial style does the *situation* call for?
- What organizational structure and managerial style would you choose to use in this situation, *with these people?*
- Explain any differences in your answers to these two questions.

PLANNING A NEW MANAGERIAL STRATEGY

In establishing a strategic management plan, the strategist must consider the contingencies covered thus far and must also consider the effect of learning and the establishment of social stability as time passes. Organizations seem filled with uncertainty and ambiguity to new employees. In addition, new jobs cause additional anxiety as do social relationships in new social surroundings. These are transitory uncertainties, however, and cause less difficulty as employees become socialized and become more experienced in their particular jobs. To employees, much of the uncertainty faced in their day-to-day work is resolved through experience. Some uncertainties, however, are not so easily remedied. Those caused by customer buying patterns, by competitor actions, and by changes in products and technologies will not be resolved through the passage of time.

AN IDEAL MANAGERIAL MIX

Consider the following situation: Our manager is faced with the development of a new organization to carry out a research and development project in a newly emerging field, bioengineering. The task she has been assigned is to develop a biological organism and a process that will assist in the decomposition of waste materials in food processing and aid in their conversion to a form of animal food that will have commercial value. The initial organization is expected to have between 20 and 50 persons employed and will be staffed by biological research scientists, chemical engineers, research assistants, and cost analysts.

Generally speaking, this appears to be a situation that would lend itself well to a more informal, organic organizational form. Experts in genetics, biological research, and engineering could, in that type of organization, freely exchange information and thereby contribute to the solution of very complex problems. Decisions needed in each area of expertise would be made by persons with the best information in that field and talents could be moved to areas of need without the interference of formally bounded positions or titles.

The management style that appears to be most appropriate would be participative, consultative, and achievement oriented. The situation offers considerable motivational potential to persons with a high need for achievement. Beyond the motivating effect of the research task, the use of a consultative or participative style adds even more motivating potential, especially for persons with high needs for personal growth.

Organizationally originated rewards such as pay raises, promotions, and formal commendations will have a positive effect on employee satisfaction for many employees in most situations. In the situation we have described, however, the rewards that keep the research labs open 24 hours per day will probably not be pay and compliments from the boss, but the personal rewards that the researchers gain through their work. A sense of achievement, a sense of competence, and the satisfaction of solving complex problems all aid the manager in providing stimulus to these talented people. The social rewards attained through the acknowledgement of one's peers and the sense of contribution to the entire project are also significant rewarding components.

The managerial framework that has been described thus far can be called an "ideal" managerial mix. Given a particular situation, we have been able to plan an organizational structure, a style, and a set of rewards that should offer an appropriate degree of guidance for the work situation and an opportunity for employees to obtain meaningful rewards.

Now, let us describe another situation: Our manager is given the task of operating a 24-hour security service. Four security routes have been established for security personnel to patrol on a round-the-clock basis. Contracts for security services have been written for a 3-year term. Patrols cover the same structures on their routes, but they are required to vary their routes in order to avoid establishing patterns that might permit criminals an undesired opportunity for illegal entry. Officers are required to record the time of the security check for each structure and must submit clock records to verify the regularity of their patrol patterns. In addition to the patrol personnel, a central communications staff is assigned the responsibility of handling all calls both from citizens and patrol personnel.

EXERCISE 6–14

- Develop an organizational structure you believe to be appropriate for the security service situation outlined above.
- Then, select a management style and a set of rewards that you think will be appropriate for employees found in organizations of the type described.
- In what ways does this organization differ from the bioengineering research organization described earlier?

The two examples used here represent situations in which an ideal combination of task, people, structure, and management style work very well to achieve organizational objectives. Other situations, however, offer different challenges. A dynamic, fast-moving organization can begin to peak in meeting challenges. Members of the organization can find themselves solving the same problems over and over. Further, as a technology or a product matures, the excitement brought about by new information and new challenges in the marketplace can begin to dwindle. What had been a challenging job becomes simply more of the same.

Organizations tend to become more stable, more rigid, and more bureaucratic as they grow larger, even if products and the environment do not reach maturity. Persons employed in organizations such as these find themselves increasingly uncomfortable as time passes. Organizational needs have changed owing to shifts in the environment, the demands for managerial control and organizational coherence, or because of product changes. The needs of the individuals who participate in the organization, however, have not.

As these situations develop, managers are faced with several potential consequences. First, if people are sufficiently uncomfortable with the more formal organization, they may migrate to jobs within the organization that seem to have less formality. Second, they may migrate to less formal organizations outside the present employer's firm. Third, they may stay in their present position(s) and be chronically discontent.

Managerial action to address these potentially serious situations can take the form of modifying the organization to permit a degree of informality within the otherwise formal framework. Many of the larger aerospace or electronics firms have adopted this approach. Managers dress less formally, offices have a uniform (and relatively low-status) decor, and employees are urged to use first names rather than more formal types of address.

A second managerial action is to create, either explicitly or implicitly, a department or section as a unit within the more formal larger organization that retains its own informal character. An individual manager may choose to use this approach as a component in his or her own management style, without a formal acknowledgement of organizational differences. Even in a relatively bureaucratic organization, a department manager may choose to develop an "organic" unit, one that is somewhat out of character for the whole company. Employees in that unit may be seen as unconventional or nonconforming, as will their manager.

Other managers might deliberately structure and formally identify a more-organic unit as a planned action to continue the development of new ideas or to continue work toward the solution of complex problems. Bell Laboratories is one such organizational unit. The Hallmark Greeting Cards Company has identified a small group of creative persons who develop humorous ideas for new cards. They are organized as a separate unit and are physically separated from the rest of the company.

Organizationally, management has found this means of supporting the creative work of these persons and preventing the inhibition of the creative process that might occur if the group were included in the same physical space as the remainder of this large company. The effective manager should be able to understand and respond to the generalized needs of the larger organization while accommodating the needs of a particular task and/or group of employees. In the following sections, we will discuss some of the ways of working toward an "ideal" mix of technology, task, structure/style, and people by means of training and development and through the recruitment and selection process.

TRAINING AND DEVELOPMENT

Training and development activities are one means of assisting in achieving a better fit of personal attributes to task, technology, and structure. For some individuals, uncertainty is caused as much by a lack of understanding of the culture and social norms as much as by an understanding of the task. In a classic field experiment, Gomersall and Myers were able to reduce turnover and increase production and learning rates significantly by devoting a two-day period to an extended orientation period for new employees. Once anxiety had been reduced by means of the extended orientation, employees were able to attend to new-task concerns and to achieve much higher levels of production, on a significantly accelerated growth pattern.[15] Skill training has a somewhat similar effect. When uncertainties and ambiguities are reduced as the result of improved performance, employees not only have a lower level of anxiety, but require much less guidance and not nearly as much close supervision. For them, organizational structure has become much less salient as their competence improves and as the boss can move on to other matters. Supervisory training has a similar effect for first-line or aspiring supervisors. Generally, introductory supervisory training programs emphasize the critical elements of planning, organizing, directing, and controlling. To the extent that these programs are effective, supervisors should become more competent at structuring their work, and the work of their subordinates. Fiedler maintains that this structuring is helpful in only some of the situations that managers encounter because some situations do not need additional structuring. Fiedler's position, we should note, is supported by field research.[16]

Our discussion has concentrated on training activities that have the effect of reducing anxiety and of aiding the fit between employee and the task and between employee and the organization by *increasing* structure and predictability. A second way in which training can help is by developing creative skills and thereby building an understanding of, and tolerance for, the less-structured situation and the less well-defined tasks. Development exercises have been designed that aid in encouraging creativity and in developing a tolerance for ambiguity. Brainstorming techniques, normative group approaches to project planning, delphi techniques, and storyboarding are all aimed at providing a means of reducing or eliminating structural or social inhibitions to creativity and of building a tolerance for ambiguity.

RECRUITMENT AND SELECTION

Although training and development offer a means of providing an adjustment to a situation that does not offer a good fit of people, task, structure, and technology, there are some individuals who simply will not or cannot adjust personal needs sufficiently to accommodate the level of structure or the latitude for choice needed by management. Some will transfer to a work setting more suitable to their own needs. Others will quit and look to other employers for a setting better matched to their needs. Given a reasonable freedom for movement between jobs and employers, a migration process will gradually result in employees reaching an accommodation that can be tolerated over a longer term. The natural process described can serve to achieve the type of fit desired by the manager. It does take time, however, and can be accelerated

[15] E. R. Gomersall and M. Scott Myers, "Breakthrough in On-the-Job Training," *Harvard Business Review* 44 (July–August 1966), pp. 62–72.

[16] F. E. Fiedler and M. M. Chemers, *Leadership and Effective Management* (Glenview, Ill.: Scott-Foresman, 1974).

by deliberate transfer, termination, outplacement, and replacement by employees whose personal needs are better suited to the new situation.

The recruitment of individuals who one believes will fit well in a highly structured situation should take into account the kinds and types of positions applicants have had and their expressed reasons for leaving. Job specifications for a highly structured position might include attributes such as "follows instructions," "adherence to standard procedures," or other phrases that indicate the extent to which the incumbent's tasks involve the performance of carefully prescribed work. Phrases such as "analyzes, then develops a plan for action, and executes" or "designs products . . ." or "develops copy appropriate for . . ." are often used for a job that has a much lower degree of structure. In general, the descriptions are much broader, less specific, and make use of words such as "develop," "design," "generate," "analyze," "plan," "create," etc. The recruitment process should seek applicants from organizations that have a character similar to that of the job in question or from applicants *dissatisfied* with the *opposite* type of organization. Bureaucratically oriented applicants might be found in bureaucracies or among those uncomfortable with the lack of structure in a more organic organization.

It is useful to consider that employees who prefer structured organizations and jobs like the predictability of their work and its attendant rewards. Consequently, rewards based on longevity, reliability, and loyalty will have a powerful and sustaining effect. For applicants who enjoy a more free-form organization with a higher degree of ambiguity, the excitement of the task, expanded responsibility and authority, and accomplishment-based rewards tend to have a powerful motivating effect. Advertisements and interviews should stress the advantages of the rewards system for each fit in order to have maximum appeal to those individuals most appropriate for the job/structure/technology under consideration.

Selection should follow similar guidelines. In some cases, the specific knowledge needed for a particular job can only be learned on the job. Given a reasonable level of ability to learn, the selection can then concentrate on the issue of fit, and selection can rest upon the issue of the *best* fit.

As one example to illustrate this type of selection process, a division personnel manager for a large New York-based company sought a division benefits administrator to serve as the principal administrator of the employee insurance program, which covered life, medical, and accidental death. In addition, the benefits administrator would handle all aspects of enrollment-eligibility screening and claims processing for the retirement plan. Benefit plans are unique to each employer. Their eligibility terms, levels of contribution, and claims processes are not only different, but are quite rigid. Although some technical knowledge is needed to understand the general parameters of employee benefit plans, the principal attribute required is that of a person who can meticulously *administer* the plans according to very carefully defined guidelines.

When no experienced benefits administrators were found in preliminary recruitment, the personnel administrator sought candidates in the company's accounting department. The successful applicant was a cost accountant, comfortable with number work, and quite experienced in adhering to specific procedures and standard guidelines. His performance after a relatively short indoctrination period was exceptional. It is interesting to note that this person not only performed at exceptional levels in this job, but within 4 years was promoted to the position of manager of employee benefits for the corporation, a Fortune 500 company, where he served with distinction until his retirement. This, quite clearly, was an individual who worked well in a structured work environment.

Other individuals chafe in bureaucracies and blossom in an environment where creativity, ambiguity, and informality are common. The effective manager will attempt to develop those conditions that best match the needs of the task, the external environment, and the needs of the individuals required to accomplish the work at hand. Where necessary, training can provide one means of easing existing employees into a different situation. Where this transition cannot be accomplished, recruitment and selection can aid in the replacement of individuals who do not find the situation comfortable with persons who match the situation's needs.

The Electronic Data Systems case describes one of the success stories of modern industry: the development by H. Ross Perot of the Electronic Data Systems Corporation. Read the case to obtain a general overview of the material, then reread the case slowly while giving particular attention to the issues of organizational mission, organizational environment, organizational structure, management style, recruitment, and training. Exercise questions are found at the conclusion of the case.

ELECTRONIC DATA SYSTEMS CORPORATION

Throughout its 21 years of operation, Electronic Data Systems (EDS) has relied on a solid teamwork approach guided by strong upper-level management to attain its current strong competitive status. H. Ross Perot, founder and chairman of the board of EDS, has epitomized the American dream with much flare and concurrently with much controversy. While building the EDS empire, his name has been brought before the public for his noncorporation exploits such as his leadership of the War on Drugs and his rescue in 1979 of two EDS employees who were captive in an Iranian jail.[1] Nonetheless, Perot's success with EDS has been formidable.

HISTORY

Perot founded EDS in 1962 with a mere $1,000 investment. He realized that IBM, his then-current employer, was selling hardware to customers but did not show customers how to utilize it properly. "What these customers needed . . . was someone to design, install,

This case was prepared by Deborah Weaver, Monique Hensel, and Jeff Bell under the supervision of Professor Adelaide Griffin, North Texas State University, and Professor Sexton Adams, Texas Woman's University.

and operate their data processing systems for a fee," thought Perot.[2] This was the basis on which Perot acted when he set out to build EDS, and his desire to fill a gap that IBM neglected has rewarded him handsomely.

Electronic Data Systems began by purchasing unused computer time on the computers of other companies, usually operating from different locations each night. Yet beginning in 1964, EDS's revenues doubled each year until 1968, at which time the first public offering of stock was made.

Unique in comparison to other firms in the computer services industry, EDS has emphasized its reputation, financial strength, professionalism, and quality of service—all grounded on five basic tenents:

1 It developed basic philosophies to guide its business:
   - Provide outstanding customer service.
   - Build the finest professional staff in the computer services industry.
   - Deal with each employee as an individual.
   - Recognize and reward excellence.
   - Build a sound record of financial strength.
2 It created the concept of facilities management. In 1962, the computer services industry consisted of software houses. Under the facilities-management concept, EDS becomes the data processing department of a client such as a large insurance company, a bank, or a government agency. Facilities management enables EDS to provide a total, long-term agreement for services involving computers, people, and systems at predetermined prices and with defined, dependable time schedules and desired results.
3 It created the concept of a long-term contract in an industry that was accustomed to 90-day contracts. When EDS entered the market, it was generally accepted that no company could sell a 5-year contract. Long-term contracts provided EDS with the financial stability it needed for continued growth.
4 It formally organized a recruiting group to identify and bring into the corporation the top professionals in the computer industry.
5 It initiated data processing skills-development programs because of a scarcity of experienced, qualified operations and systems engineering personnel.[3]

Since its inception in 1962, EDS has grown to become one of the largest firms in the computer services industry, employing over 11,700 people and with assets in excess of $330 million.[4] In 1975, EDS began offering its services internationally. As of 1983, its international clients include Canada, Kuwait, Belgium, Mexico, Singapore, Spain, Great Britain, Saudi Arabia, Malaysia, and the Netherlands.[5]

Organization

Ross Perot appointed Mort Meyerson president of EDS in 1979. Meyerson wasted no time in reorganizing EDS into specialized groups geared toward addressing specific industry and government needs. The vice presidents of each group report directly to Meyerson. The five groups are illustrated in Exhibit 1, the EDS organizational chart.

Electronic Data Systems executive officers are usually elected by the Board of Directors at the board's first meeting subsequent to the annual meeting of stockholders. However, the board may appoint additional officers as necessary at any time.

Most of the growth EDS has experienced since beginning operations has been internally generated through acquisitions.

EXHIBIT 1
EDS Organizational Chart

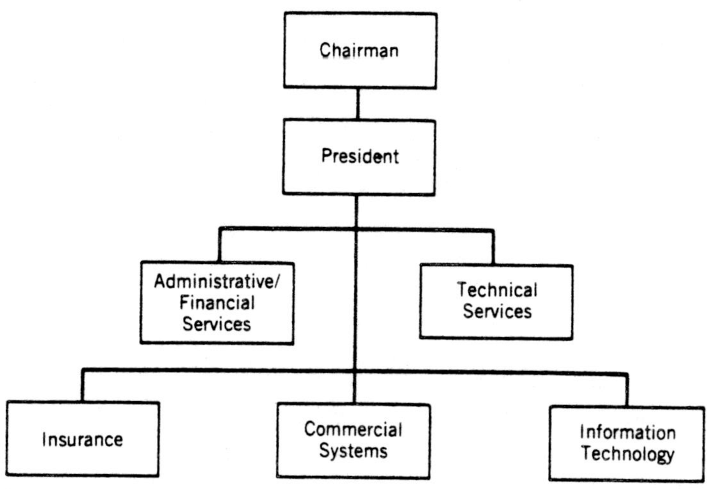

Source: Company records.

H. Ross Perot—Chairman of the Board

A leading factor in EDS's success has been its founder and "general," H. Ross Perot. He prefers to handle matters and tackle challenges by the "one-man, one-job, let's go" approach. In an interview with the *Dallas Times Herald* in September 1982, Perot stated his philosophy on how EDS should be managed.

> *The way we get things done around here is everyone takes a small piece of it and does it. Everybody is talking to everybody else, and somebody is always in charge. That's EDS, that's the way EDS is.*[6]

Through this managerial style Perot has produced a most formidable product—EDS. The company originated in 1962, went public in 1968, and has been diversifying from its data processing base to the production of electronic hardware. A large part of the company's stable growth has resulted from the heavy emphasis Perot has placed on hiring, training, and developing a staff of the highest-quality professionals. Electronic Data Systems is well known for routinely attracting the best talent and providing formal training that is unsurpassed by its competitors. This recruitment philosophy is typified by EDS's early recruiting slogan, "Eagles don't flock—you have to find them one by one."[7]

In 1979, Perot turned over the presidency of EDS as well as many of the day-to-day management responsibilities to Mort Meyerson. But Perot still plays an active part in directing the company he created. He describes his emphasis on teamwork:

> *If you worked for EDS and you called me and I was really busy, it might take me an hour to get back to you. Normally I just talk to you when you call. Anytime anybody has ever been hurt, anytime an employee has had a serious problem—twenty-four hours a day,*

seven days a week—I've known about it and Mort has known about it. We do whatever it takes to deal with it. I think that if there's a secret behind EDS's success, it's that we all just work hard together.[8]

Henry Ross Perot was born June 27, 1930, in Texarkana, Texas, the son of a cattle-and-horse trader and cotton broker in east Texas. Perot attended public schools in Texarkana and took a 2-year prelaw course at a local junior college. He considered his courses to be neither difficult nor interesting. Watching his father transact business with nearby farmers may have been more stimulating to him than his educational experience. He recalls an episode between a nearby farmer who was interested in selling a horse to Perot's father. No matter how interested in buying the horse, his father would remain indifferent to any offer. A few days later the deal was settled and the price his father paid was below the original price.

As a boy, Perot enjoyed selling—Christmas cards, saddles, the *Saturday Evening Post,* and the *Texarkana Gazette.* He established a paper route that demanded he travel 20 miles a day on horseback to deliver the paper. This route was established because of Perot's efforts, thus he received 70% of the price instead of the customary 30%. Later, when the route began to grow and thrive, the newspaper tried to renege on the ratio, but Perot argued against any change.[9]

Perot is considered to be an achiever and an attention-getter.[10] Some in the industry may feel his actions are publicity stunts to promote EDS services. However, Perot insists his intentions are concerned with the crisis at hand. An interview with him in *Esquire* in December 1980 revealed that "Ross Perot thinks about the individual and society—about values, the meaning of loyalty, the secrets of success."[11]

Perot's personality and managerial skills have pulled EDS out of several major crises in prior years. In building EDS, he envisioned the company as a health-insurance industry conglomerate. This dream was realized in the early part of 1979 when an EDS subsidiary bid for a 5-year contract to run part of the Illinois Medicare plan. This contract was estimated at $41.8 million for the life of the contract by EDS. The bid established by EDS was $40 million below that of two large insurance companies—Prudential and Metropolitan. The contract began in April 1979, and two major problems soon surfaced that hindered EDS's execution of the contract. First, 6 months after initiating the job, unprocessed paperwork began to accumulate. The number of unprocessed claims continued to increase, and those claims that were processed often contained mistakes. Second, although comprehensive site-location studies were conducted to arrive at the place most suitable for a central office, the planners failed to look at actual employment statistics in suburban Des Plaines (the site chosen for the Illinois project). In addition, planners did not investigate the fact that the town had almost no unemployment. These two errors produced a quarterly review for the first year of operation that revealed EDS had failed in five major performance standard tests designed to ascertain whether EDS was fulfilling the terms of the contract. Thus, EDS had to pay contractual penalties amounting to $700,000. Outside the financial loss, EDS created poor customer relations among aging Social Security and disability dependents who floundered while waiting for the EDS-created errors to be corrected. Early in 1980, claims were again backlogged; by June 1980, EDS declared that procedures were efficient in processing claims. Perot and his management team were able to convince the administration of the Illinois Medicare plan that EDS had regained control of its data. However, the decision to allow EDS to continue working on the project was due in part to the costly delays of replacing EDS.[12]

Less than a month after the Illinois Medicare episode, another experience served to disrupt EDS. On July 15, 1980, the Texas Board of Human Resources announced its decision to take the expiring Texas Medicaid contract away from EDS and award it to Bradford National Corporation of New York. Bradford was a new low bidder and would take over the contract that EDS had been awarded in 1977. The loss of this crown jewel in EDS's empire was good reason for alarm. A few days after the contract had been awarded to Bradford, Hilmar Moore, chairman of the Texas Board, received a call at his ranch near Richard, Texas, from Mort Meyerson. Meyerson and Perot proposed a visit with Moore at his ranch to discuss the misperceptions that had led to the expiration of their contract. Moore readily agreed to the visit; by the end of their visit, Moore was convinced that EDS should regain the contract. After personal visits to two other board members, the Texas Board was willing to submit the matter for reevaluation by a new set of analysts and actuaries. The new hearing began and the new outside consultants reaffirmed the decision to take the contract away from EDS. The Bradford people celebrated the decision, relieved by the renewal of their original victory. However, 2 days after the second hearing, Moore and two of the three board members announced they were convinced that it would be more advantageous for Texas to remain with Perot and, therefore, the contract with EDS would be renewed.[13]

Mort Meyerson — President

Mort Meyerson joined EDS in 1966 as a trainee and subsequently built EDS's health-care division into the company's largest division. His noteworthy contributions earned him the presidency of EDS as of 1979. Meyerson recognized that EDS had grown in size and scope and that decentralization was necessary to permit more management to make decisions. Thus, EDS was reorganized into essentially three smaller companies with distinct specialties and markets: (1) the Insurance Group, (2) Information Technology, and (3) Commercial Systems. Each of these division is run semiautonomously by EDS executives who have spent most of their careers with the company.[14]

EDS SERVICES

Electronic Data Systems assists the technology world through its computer services segment. It delivers services on a long-term basis, using four elements: communications, hardware, software, and industry experience. Because EDS specializes by industry, it is the largest computer services firm that can provide specialized know-how in banking, insurance, and health care.

Four contract arrangements are available to EDS customers: facilities management, program management, professional services, and turnkey. *Facilities-management* contracts account for almost 50% of EDS's business. In this arrangement EDS essentially becomes the data processing entity for its client institution. This includes such functions as system design, training, programming, implementation, and operation of the systems it installs and develops. The *program-management* contract includes the services of the facilities-management contract plus clerical and/or administrative work. Thus, in this contract, EDS operates the computer systems, runs the communications network, and provides clerical people, underwriters, and adjusters. These services are typically used in health-care services such as Medicaid and Medicare. The *professional-services* contract allows the customer to purchase a highly professional skill such as software by the hour, week, month, or on some other basis. This service is provided to help EDS's customers in a specific area, and it represents only a small part of EDS's business. Because of its specialized nature, the cost for this service is high, usually around $15,000 to $20,000 a month for one person's time. The final type of contract is the *turnkey* arrangement. With this contract, EDS designs a system, installs it, and then turns it over to the customer. These four contract arrangements allow EDS to fill the needs of a wide variety of customers, tailoring the services it provides to the special industry in which the customer is competing. In other words, it is a *total system approach.*

As previously mentioned, EDS is broken into five major groups (see Exhibit 1). The first two areas are known as the support groups and consist of *Administrative/Financial Services* and *Technical Services.* EDS's business essentially consists of the three other groups, each of which is run by its own vice president as a semiautonomous business. The *Insurance Group* services commercial insurance, health care, and state and local governments. The *Commercial Systems Group* includes credit unions, savings and loans institutions, and banks. The *Information Technology Group* services government and international business.[15] Exhibit 2 provides an overview of ED's service groups broken down into its segments.

EXHIBIT 2
EDS service groups

INSURANCE GROUP
- Private Sector
  - Blue Cross/Blue Shield
  - Life Insurance
  - Property and Casualty Insurance
  - Hospitals
- Government Agencies
  - Medicare A and B
  - Medicaid
  - State and Local Governments

COMMERCIAL SYSTEMS GROUP
- Financial
  - Banks
  - Savings and Loans
  - Credit Unions
  - Air Transport
  - Associations
- Small Businesses
  - Business Systems
  - Centurion
- Industrials
  - Manufacturing
  - Retail
  - Distribution
  - Systems Software
  - Airlines
  - Energy

INFORMATION TECHNOLOGY GROUP
- Government Services
- International

Source: Company records.

STRATEGIC PLANNING SYSTEM

The method of strategic corporate planning used by EDS can best be described as an intuitive-anticipatory approach. It is characterized by comparatively short time horizons and reaction times. The planning decisions are based on the experience and intuition of the corporate management of the company.

Electronic Data Systems used a top–down approach to set annual corporate objectives and goals. Perot emphasizes his teamwork orientation in which the corporate objectives are established by Perot and the Chief Executive Officer (CEO). The group vice presidents then review the corporate objectives by Perot and the CEO and add their input. Next the CEO and the group vice presidents discuss the probability of successfully accomplishing each objective until a consensus is reached. Thus, the teamwork that Perot affectionately refers to at EDS is geared to carrying out objectives and goals set by top management.

Mort Meyerson cites the following objectives for EDS during the next 5 years:

1 To increase revenues and profits by 20%

annually and to boost after-tax profit margins to 10% by 1985.

2 To become a $1 billion company in revenues and to become a $100 million company in net income by 1978.

In addition, EDS's corporate policy manual states the following strategic goals for EDS in the long run:

1 To become the most respected computer services firm in the data processing industry.

2 To attract and retain the most outstanding computer professionals and to provide them with the career opportunities they seek.

3 To make EDS an exciting and rewarding place to work.

4 To make a fair profit for the organization, its stockholders, and the people who built the company.

5 To have EDS grow into a large company, yet remain a great company.

These long-range goals and objectives are communicated to lower-level managers who put them into operation. Management believes that teamwork at the functional levels is created by the efforts of these managers to meet company objectives.

DIVISIONS

Support Groups

Electronic Data Systems *Administrative and Financial Group* facilitates the three major service groups in carrying out the routine activities on a day-to-day basis. This group is comprised of three functional departments, each of which maintains and monitors its own operations: Accounting/Finance, Legal, and Personnel and Employee Relations. The Accounting/Finance Department is responsible for all capital expenditures and revenue receipts in addition to analyzing and monitoring these activities. The Legal Department handles all law aspects of EDS's ventures, including customer contracts for services, employee-training contracts, acquisitions, and any other activities that may require legal advice or representation. The Personnel and Employee Relations Department is responsible for handling selection and placement, compensation, health and safety, training and development, employee relations, and labor relations. All three of these departments act as a facilitator for EDS's three customer-service groups.

The *Technical Services Group* operates out of five regional data centers. Three data centers are located in the Dallas area, and additional data centers are located in San Francisco and Camp Hill, Pennsylvania. These five regional data centers integrate smaller computer centers and terminals located throughout the offices of EDS customers. The data centers can process information faster and at less cost through the use of several large computers. Thus, the centers run computers, print reports, microfilm documents, and transfer data from one location to another. The concentration of large computers offers backup capability—a feature small data centers do not have. This convenience is realized when one computer fails to work and processing must be switched to other computers. Another plus of the regional data centers is the sheer volume, or capacity. EDS realize the extreme importance of skilled operations people. It offers an Operations Development Program of 12-to-18-months' intensive classroom and programmed instruction, including on-the-job training. Advanced equipment and capable personnel make it happen for EDS.

Service Groups

With its *Insurance Group,* EDS has created a profitable niche, providing flexible contracts based on customer needs. Eleven commercial insurance companies signed contracts with EDS during the 1982 fiscal year. The contracts included existing customers and new firms. New firm contracts contributed to approximately half of the growth in contract agreements.[16] One of EDS's most recent developments is the Insurance Machine—a computer system designed to help issue and administer life, health, and annuity policies. Also created to help meet the economic challenge of the 1980s in the insurance field is the Universal Life Policy (ULP). Because the ULP pays interest on premiums and allows flexible financial planning, it has become popular among EDS customers.

EDS has been instrumental in cutting the cost of administering health-care programs for 16 years.[17] It developed the first system for processing Medicaid claims that utilized a joint Medicare plan to process hospital claims in addition to processing claims from doctors and other suppliers. During 1982, EDS is trying to carry this same one-system idea to computerize doctors' offices. Using such a system, doctors and hospitals could file claims on computer terminals and thus lower costs and increase the processing of paperwork. EDS recognizes that faster claim processing is a main advantage of this new system. Based on this concept, EDS installed an Electronic Claims System at Massachusetts Blue Shield and a group health-care system for Blue Cross/Blue Shield of Iowa as well as Blue Shield plans in Montana and Puerto Rico.[18]

Nursing homes and hospitals can also trim expenses by using EDS's computer-based systems. For example, a patient-care system can cut information-handling costs by as much as $3,000 per day. In 1982, EDS installed systems in eight hospitals and seven nursing homes. These systems allow health-care professional to direct their attention toward patient care rather than concentrating on paperwork.

Electronic Data Systems involvement in the Blue Cross/Blue Shield programs dates back to 1966. Diversity may be the key to EDS's future, but as of 1983 EDS is still highly dependent on government business in this area. Within the Blue Cross/Blue Shield segment, EDS has set up 10 plans that account for 93% of the current available market.[19] Exhibit 3 highlights the Insurance Group's major account activity during 1982.

EXHIBIT 3
Major account activities of the insurance group during 1982

Medicare

- 70.0 million Claims Processed
- $5.8 Billion Total Benefits Paid

Medicaid

- 79.3 Million Claims Processed in 15 States

Blue cross/Blue shield

- 10 Plans
- 93% of Current Available Market

Source: Company records.

The *Commercial Systems Group* experienced a record-paçe growth in the financial area. In 1982, seven large banks and thrift institutions signed contracts with EDS that range from five to eight years. Electronic Data Systems is the largest processor in banking, serving 650 banks with 10 million accounts in 49 states. Banks in New Mexico, Oklahoma, and Texas have become EDS's customers. These banks add another 180 customers to the company.[20]

In 1982, more than 40 banks purchased the Return of Information System, one of EDS's turnkey contract arrangements. Such an increase in services to the community has required EDS to double the customer base for this product. As with its other service areas, EDS offers a complete range of services to financial institutions based on the inistitution's varying needs. The vice-president of this group feels that EDS's flexibility in providing services greatly assisted the growth in this area.

Electronic Data Systems feels very strongly about keeping pace with rapid changes in the industry. An example is EDS–LINK, which is a breakthrough in electronic funds transfer technology.[21] This new system permits individuals to make deposits and withdrawals across town or across the country at any participating financial institution. The demand for EDS–LINK is projected to be strong, but this remains to be seen.

Banks are not the only segment of financial institutions that are latching on to EDS's expertise in computer services. The strongest growth area of the Commercial System Group can be attributed to new credit union contracts. In 1983, over 3,000 credit unions serving 7 million members used EDS computer systems. One thousand credit unions became EDS customers through the purchase of credit union systems from Western Bradford Trust, Missouri League Data Services, Data Processing of the South, and Financial Data Services.[22] A computer system is available for every size credit union. The newest development is the Cundata 2000—a distributing data processing system that links small business computers in the credit union with large computers at an EDS data center. The Cundata 2000 and the credit union business in general are examples of remote processing through one maser system in Dallas. On-site microcomputers accept and print information while tied to the computer system through a large communication network.

Also within the Commercial Systems Group is the small business sector, which is not considered to be profitable. As of 1983, Meyerson has considered this area to be a research and development effort, although he is openminded and optimistic that a market will develop in this area in the future.[23]

Electronic Data Systems offers a line of minicomputers that are sold through a national network of 40 independent dealers.[24] These minicomputers are designed and manufactured by one of its subsidiaries, Centurion Computer Corporation. In keeping with EDS's flexible services concept, these minicomputers provide tailor-made systems to customers. Thus, a large department store chain can use a computer to predict fashion trends. The same computer can decide what advertising and promotional inserts go to specific customers.

A software maintenance plan based on productivity brings about a savings of time and money. One incentive-based contract, for example, brought about a large change. Four EDS systems engineers replaced 34 of the customer's systems engineers. This type of change takes highly motivated, experienced systems engineers to make it work, but it is a new concept EDS is promoting. Another new idea is a package consisting of computer hardware, software, installation, and maintenance. This package concept has been well accepted because businesses then receive data processing results without the problem of dealing with different vendors.

The *Information Technology Group* has also experienced growth—predominantly in the government and international areas. The largest contract ever made in the computer services industry was offered to EDS by the U.S. Army in April 1982. Project VIABLE is a 10-year, $656 million contract securing EDS's expertise to build and operate five regional data centers to provide data for processing information for 42 U.S. Army bases. This project is in the startup phase as of 1983. Forty-two military posts, each with its own distributed data processing center, will be tied into a network. The number of terminals alone is close to 18,000. Electronic Data Systems is modeling this complex network on the computer and communications network that it built to do the processing for its insurance and commercial data rather than designing a completely new system. Such an approach to building a new system is not new to EDS, and it has been implemented successfully in the past.

The experience with the project will put EDS in a good position to win contracts for similar systems from other government agencies and large corporations. Perot has expressed his belief that the U.S. Army contract was won by beating companies like IBM and Computer Services, a cast of a gnat beating a giant.

The Department of Defense has also signed a contract with EDS for a Defense Enrollment/ Eligibility Reporting System (DEERS). This is a health-care eligibility system for all of the dependents of retired U.S. military personnel.[25] It was created due to continued fraud and abuse present in the current eligibility system. Dependents simply had to display a card when using medical facilities. Under DEERS, dependents are issued a machine-readable plastic card with their thumb print and photograph. DEERS consists of a network of terminals throughout the United States to determine the eligibility for 9 million people. The challenge for EDS in this service area definitely is linked to the contract awarded by the U.S. Army. Management must find and train 300 people by 1983 and a total of 700 persons by 1985 to meet the demands of the U.S. Army contract alone.[26]

In the international market, EDS offers the same sophisticated systems used in the United States. Belgium, Canada, Great Britain, Kuwait, Malaysia, Mexico, the Netherlands, Saudia Arabia, Singapore, and Spain are countries currently using EDS services. EDS is designing and building an audio processing system that is part of the total command and control system for ships of the Royal Saudi Naval Forces. The system will increase communication between land-based command and the fleet at sea. Although this area is rewarding EDS with profits, there is some skepticism as to whether EDS should rely or even offer their services to forces that could very possibly confront the United States in military action.

Another area EDS has penetrated is entry into the market of higher education. A two-year contract has been set up with Pennsylvania State University to design, develop, and install computer systems to process everything from class schedules to payroll.[27] The future potential of this new market is broad and open to much speculation.

FINANCIAL DATA

EDS's fiscal year is from July 1 to June 30. Recessionary pressures limited its revenue growth rate to 12% in 1982 as compared to 21% in 1981. In 1982 both earnings per share and net income increased 24%, compared to a 31% increase in 1981.[28] The return on equity was 26% and the return on assets was 16%. The company's net profit margin was 9%, and the revenue per employee was approximately $50,000.[29] Project VIABLE is expected to provide EDS with $50 million in revenues during fiscal year 1983 and has the potential to add another $320 million in revenues over the 10-year contract period. Pretax profits from the U.S. Army contract are expected to start at about 7% and increase to 10% within 2 years. Electronic Data Systems has also negotiated a $500 million dollar contract with Texas Medicaid.[30] The company will handle all of the data processing activities of National Heritage Insurance Company, an EDS subsidiary, that underwrites certain parts of the Texas Medicaid Program. Texas Medicaid is one of the nation's largest processors of medical insurance claims.[31]

Electronic Data Systems has reduced its cost of revenues as a percentage of systems revenue since the second quarter of the fiscal year 1980. The cost reduction reflects the significant impact of EDS's current pricing policy and increased use of strict cost and contract measures. Increased levels of marketing activities and increased expenditures to support the company's growth have resulted in increases in selling, in general, and in administrative expenses. However, as a percentage of systems revenue, these expenses have been declining since the fourth quarter of fiscal year 1981.

The increased use of long-term debt to finance capital expenditures has caused interest costs to increase. Electronic Data Systems's capitalization of interest costs beginning in fiscal year 1981 has resulted in the elimination of interest expenses in both 1981 and 1982.[32]

Two financial statements in Exhibit 4 and Exhibit 5 highlight EDS's performance as of June 30, 1982.

EXHIBIT 4

EDS consolidated statements of income for the years ended June 30, 1982, 1981, and 1980

(in thousands except earnings per share)	*1982*	*1981*	*1980*
Revenues:			
Systems and other contracts	$503,335	$448,611	$368,627
Interest and other	6,637	6,003	6,034
	509,972	454,614	374,661
Cost and expenses:			
Cost of revenues	378,479	345,160	290,696
Selling, general and administrative	61,111	53,277	41,246
Interest expense	—	—	1,079
	439,590	398,437	333,021
	70,382	56,177	41,640
Provision for income taxes	28,154	22,471	16,585
Income before equity in earnings of unconsolidated subsidiary	42,228	33,706	25,055
Equity in earnings of unconsolidated subsidiary	4,739	4,110	3,835
Net income	$ 46,967	$ 37,816	$ 28,890
Earnings per common share	$ 1.72	$ 1.39	$ 1.06

Source: EDS 1982 Annual Report, p. 26.

EXHIBIT 5
EDS consolidated balance sheets June 30, 1982 and 1981

(in thousands)	*1982*	*1981*
Current assets:		
Cash and temporary investments	$ 18,646	$ 7,447
Marketable securities, at amortized cost	20,391	22,074
Accounts receivable	87,872	75,085
Inventories	6,666	6,743
Prepayments	7,864	6,468
Total current assets	141,439	117,817
Property and equipment, at cost less accumulated depreciation:		
Land	3,922	2,983
Buildings and facilities	26,852	18,112
Computer equipment	17,727	9,821
Furniture and other	13,402	13,186
	61,903	44,102
Other operating assets:		
Investment in unconsolidated subsidiary	25,544	20,805
Cost in excess of net assets of acquired companies, less accumulated amortization of $459 in 1982; $300 in 1981	5,848	6,007
Purchased software, less accumulated amortization of $6,290 in 1982, $2,041 in 1981	18,186	7,807
	49,578	34,619
Investments:		
Land held for investment and development	51,755	49,411
Noncurrent notes receivable, primarily from land sales, and other investments	4,487	8,730
Bonds and notes, at amortized cost	21,030	—
	77,272	58,141
	$330,192	$254,679
Liabilities and Stockholders' Equity		
Current liabilities:		
Accounts payable	$ 21,482	$ 21,820
Accrued liabilities	18,591	21,726
Deferred revenue	5,070	1,742
Income taxes	31,041	22,972
Current portion of notes payable	1,867	3,967
Total current liabilities	78,051	72,227
Deferred income taxes	3,693	3,526
Deferred revenue	11,621	—
Notes payable	32,304	17,229
Commitments and litigation		

EXHIBIT 5 *(continued)*
EDS consolidated balance sheets June 30, 1982 and 1981

(in thousands)	*Typical Breakdowns*	*1982*	*1981*
Stockholders' equity:			
Common stock, without par value; authorized 50,000 shares in 1982 and 1981; issued 29,797 shares in 1982; 29,332 shares in 1981		60,554	50,664
Net unrealized loss on noncurrent marketable equity securities		(688)	(652)
Retained earnings		156,795	124,113
Treasury stock, at cost; 950 shares in 1982; 1,322 shares in 1981		(12,138)	(12,428)
Total stockholders' equity		204,523	161,697
		$330,192	$254,679

Source: EDS 1982 Annual Report, p. 27.

COMPETITION

Company sources cite EDS as a leader in the computer services industry when ranked by net income, second only to Automatic Data Processing (ADP). Although both EDS and ADP are in the computer services industry, they service different target markets. Automatic Data Processing concentrates on small businesses, and EDS concentrates on large businesses. Even though EDS does not have a major competitor that competes across the board with its operations, in each of its main business areas, there is at least one company that competes directly and most effectively with EDS. In the hospital industry, EDS competes with Shared Medical. In the health-care industry, EDS competes with Computer Sciences. The major competitor in the government marketplace is Systems Development Corporation, a subsidiary of Burroughs. Electronic Data Systems main competitor in the banking business is Systematics.[33] Exhibit 6 provides a comprehensive overview of computer industry competition compiled by the Gartner Group of Merrill Lynch.

EFFECTS OF INFLATION

To reduce the adverse impact of inflation and to increase the effective management of operations and capital, EDS emphasizes asset turnover and operating profit margins. It closely monitors return on capital expenditures and cash flow from receivables to manage its assets effectively. Effective control of operating costs and an increase in sales will serve to spread fixed costs while improving profit margins, company sources contend.[34]

LITIGATION

In February 1979, Electronic Data Systems Corporation of Iran (EDSCI) filed a breach-of-contract suit against the Social Security Organization of the government of Iran, the Ministry of Health and Welfare, for breaches of a contract for data processing services. On May 9, 1980, the case went to trial and the EDS subsidiary won an award in the sum of $19 million plus costs and interest. The subsidiary has attached funds in a New York bank to satisfy the award,

EXHIBIT 6
The top-20 in computer service

Providing software and services to computer users has exploded into a $13 billion business. Here are the 20 largest players, ranked by their 1980 revenues as reported by Gartner Group, a leading research firm. Merrill Lynch assisted with the "main service area" information. As defined by Gartner Group, services noted in the table include: processing (1), custom/contract software (2), remote computing services (3), batch services (4) and facilities management (5).

Company	*Main service area*	*Revenues (millions)*	*As % of total revenues*	*% change in revenues 1979–80*
IBM	2	$2,414.5	9.2%	−21.9%
Control Data	3, 4	722.7	19.0	18.6
Computer Sciences Corp	2	560.3	100.0	34.9
ADP	3, 4	505.0	100.0	24.1
EDS	5	408.5	98.7	31.1
Honeywell	3	349.7	7.1	21.0
General Electric (GEISCO)	3	299.3	1.2	19.3
Tymshare	3	211.0	89.5	19.7
System Development Corp*	2, 5	186.8	100.0	14.6
McDonnell Douglas (McAuto)	3	160.7	2.6	−21.9
Bradford National Corp	4	142.7	100.0	18.8
Planning Research Corp	2	127.4	41.5	24.5
Informatics Inc	1, 2	125.9	100.0	12.0
Bocing Computer Services	3, 4	125.0	1.3	30.2
Burroughs Corp	2	132.9	4.3	26.8
General Instrument	2	115.3	14.0	15.2
United Telecommunications	3	115.1	6.0	20.0
Shared Medical Systems	2	105.6	99.1	28.3
Wyly Corp	3	99.0	84.0	13.6
TRW	1, 5	94.2	1.9	32.7

Source: Reprinted in Harold Seneker, "The Growth Industry's Growth Industry." *Forbes,* July 6, 1981.
*Acquired by Burroughs Corp., Jan. 5, 1981. *Source: Garner Group: Merrill Lynch*

and although a federal appellate court upheld the injunction forbidding the transfer of the Iranian funds, EDSCI must pursue its claim before the Iran-U.S. Claims Tribunal in order to collect this award. A claim was filed before the tribunal in January 1982, but as of April 1983 the tribunal has not responded to the claim.[35]

Sportster Incorporated, a 10-year-old chain of sporting goods stores based in Tyler, Texas, filed suit on November 29, 1982, against EDS claiming breach of contract and fraud. Sportster seeks $88,000 in actual damages and $10 million in punitive damages. The suit claims that EDS sold the company a minicomputer system that never worked properly, that EDS was to modify the system as needed for 5 years but abandoned the project, and that EDS personnel made fraudulent claims about the system's capabilities.[36]

On February 16, 1983, EDS filed a breach-of-contract suit to recover $9,000 from each of three former employees. The suits claim that the three former employees breached an agreement to repay EDS for their training as systems engineers. Two employees resigned approximately 1 year after signing their contracts and one employee was terminated. According to EDS's employment contract, each employee must sign a promissory note when hired for training. If she or he resigns or is terminated for just cause within 2 years after training, the employee must repay EDS for the training received—amounting to $9,000 per employee. This suit is currently pending in the courts.[37] Such breaches of training contracts are not new to EDS, however, because once an employee has completed EDS's rigorous training program, he or she possesses highly marketable skills. Because EDS's compensation package is competitive, management is unsure of why there seems to be such a mass exodus from the EDS ranks, although it is a well-known fact that at EDS an employee's every personal move is scrutinized, and not only on-the-job behavior.

INDUSTRY OUTLOOK

The rapid growth of the computer services market can be attributed to the rising number of computer installations, declining hardware prices, growing user sophistication, productivity-improvement efforts, and a shortage of qualified customer-employed programmers. INPUT, a leading international consulting firm, predicts that the $15 billion computer services market will grow at an annual rate of 19% to reach $35 billion by 1985. The firm also comments that "at this pace, the value of computer services—excluding contributions by hardware manufacturers—by early 1984 should exceed that of computer hardware shipments."[38] Exhibit 7 illustrates the value of hardware shipments versus computer services in the United States. EDS Management anticipates computer operations will continue to grow in several specific areas. These areas and their estimated growth are illustrated in Exhibit 8.

Electronic Data Systems management is deliberating about expectations in the computer industry over the next decade, and the challenges they will face. Although they have been successful thus far, several of EDS's top managers are skeptical as to whether such success will continue if EDS does not establish a formalized strategic planning system, especially as EDS has grown so rapidly in recent years. However, these same top managers are aware of Perot's intentions of remaining active in his company, of thus maintaining his militaristic, top-down planning process. The five group vice-presidents have been informally discussing possible avenues for developing a strategic planning system that will meet Perot's approval and yet will also incorporate ideas from lower-level managers who have to live with the day-to-day mechanics of the plans handed down to them.

Another concern of management is centered on an article appearing in the *Dallas Morning News*, "Dallas Life" section, on April 17, 1983. The following quote is the opening statement of Jane Sumner's documentary "How Much Do You Make?":

> *Two things will get you fired at multimillionaire H. Ross Perot's Electronic Data Systems company in North Dallas. One is marital infidelity. The other is talking about how much you make.*[39]

Statements such as this are not uncommon when discussing the reputation EDS has built regarding employee practices on and off the job. Although there are no longer strict requirements on clothes, length of hair, and beards, such topics as proper social behavior and pay secrecy are areas that many EDS employees seem to believe are none of EDS's concern if it does not affect their work performance. Perot feels that EDS's staunch image is a positive factor, but

EXHIBIT 7
Value of U.S. Hardware Shipments versus Computer Services (in billions of dollars)

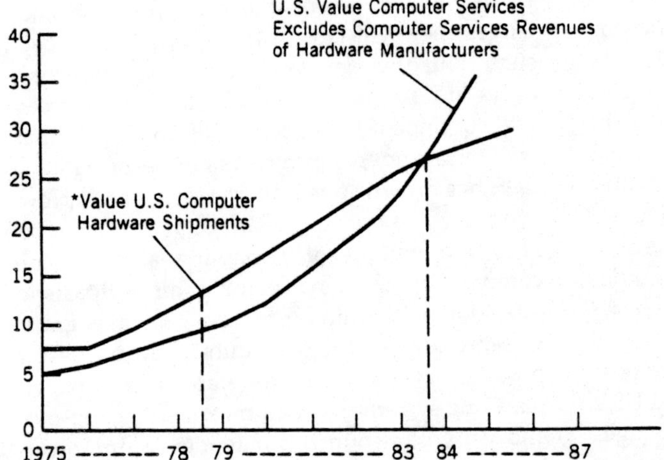

Source Standard & Poor's Industry Surveys, Office Equipment Systems and services, July 30, 1981 (Section 2), p. 22.

EXHIBIT 8
Growth in Computer Operations Fiscal Year 1982

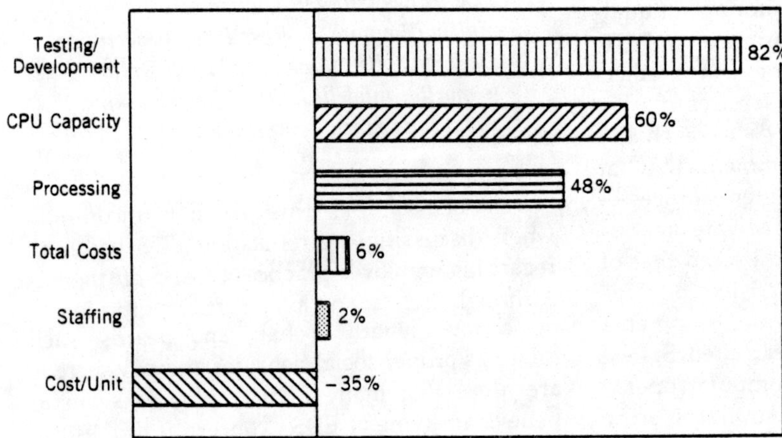

Source: Company records.

some upper-level managers disagree in view if EDS's inability to retain many talented computer professionals once they are trained at EDS. Thus, these managers are also discussing the personality of EDS and what (if any) changes should be made to improve EDS's organizational climate. They plan to bring their comments to Perot's attention for consideration, although they are unsure about Perot's reception of such ideas.

ENDNOTES

1. Scott Parks, "Perot Says He Seeks Results, Not Limelight." *Dallas Morning News,* June 28, 1981.
2. Darwin Payne. *Dallas: An Illustrated History,* Windsor Publications, Inc., 1982, p. 322.
3. *The EDS Story: Past, Present, and Future,* EDS brochure.
4. *Electronic Data Systems Corporation 29th Annual Report,* 1982, p. 2.
5. *The EDS Story.*
6. Mary Don. "Perot: General of EDS." *Dallas Times Herald,* Sunday, September 19, 1982.
7. "H. Ross Perot, as American as Apple Pie." *Dallas Times Herald,* Wednesday, October 20, 1982.
8. Ibid.
9. Arthur M. Louis, "The Fastest Richest Texan Ever." *Fortune,* November 1968, p. 171.
10. "Perot Says He Seeks Results."
11. Ron Rosenbaum. "Ross Perot to the Rescue." *Esquire,* December 1980, p. 62.
12. Ibid., p. 70.
13. Ibid.
14. John Kirkpatrick. "EDS'[s] Growth Obscured by Founder Perot." *Dallas Morning News,* February 2, 1982, p. 1D.
15. EDS President Mort Meyerson's Presentation to Security Analysts in San Francisco, January 18, 1983, pp. 1–4.
16. *Annual Report,* p. 16.
17. Ibid., p. 13.
18. Ibid.
19. Meyerson's presentation.
20. *Annual Report,* p. 9.
21. Marcy Rosenberg. "EDS Planning EFT Network for Texas Bank." *Computerworld,* Vol. 13, March 1979, p. 61.
22. *Annual Report,* p. 9.
23. Meyerson's Presentation, p. 7.
24. Ibid., p. 10.
25. Lt. Col. Gordon W. Arbogast. "VIABLE: The All Army Network." *Government Data Systems,* January/February 1983, p. 10.
26. "EDS Builds on Its Computing Services." *Business Week,* No. 2745 (Industrial Edition), June 28, 1982, pp. 90B, 90F.
27. *Annual Report,* p. 20.
28. *Valueline Selection and Opinion,* August 27, 1982, pp. 736–42.
29. Meyerson's Presentation.
30. Irwin Frank. "Analysts See Growth Potential in EDS." *Dallas Times Herald,* Wednesday, August 4, 1982.
31. *Annual Report,* p. 14.
32. Ibid., p. 38.
33. Meyerson's Presentation, pp. 11–12.
34. *Annual Report,* p. 38.
35. Ibid., p. 31.
36. "Sportster Files Suit Against EDS." *Dallas/Fort Worth Business,* December 20, 1982, p. 6.
37. "EDS Sues 3 Ex-workers for Break of Contract." *Dallas Morning News,* Thursday, February 17, 1983, p. 28A.
38. *Standard & Poor's Industry Surveys,* Office Equipment Systems and Services, July 30, 1981 (Section 2), p. 22.
39. Jane Sumner, "How Much Do You Make?" *Dallas Morning News,* Sunday, April 17, 1983, p. 8.

EXERCISE 6–15

- From your reading of this case, you can describe in two sentences the general organizational strategy of EDS? Prepare for class discussion or as a homework exercise.
- In your estimation, what general organizational form, and what general managerial style would seem to be best suited to this company's chosen environment and task? How well does the company's organizational form and management style match your concept of the ideal?
- Describe recruitment and selection standards and practices you would recommend for this company. Why?
- What types of orientation programs and training/development programs would you recommend for use in this company? Why?

ANSWERS AND SUGGESTIONS FOR EXERCISES

Exercise 6–1

Major business functions include such concerns as marketing, finance, production (or operations). The vice presidents in the functional organization, therefore, would have their responsibilities defined by functions:

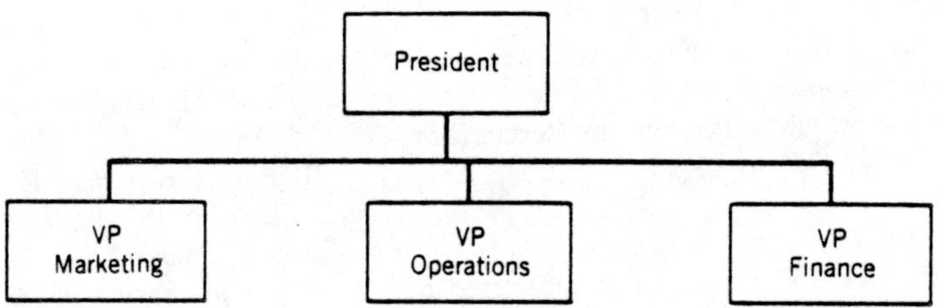

Exercise 6–8

Some things you might wish to consider are:

1 Each job is a one-of-a-kind task requiring close contact between the customer and the company.
2 Problems on the job need to be solved quickly to avoid costly downtime or the loss of valuable materials.
3 Crews are small in size and work in widely separated locations.

Exercise 6–9

The size of this company is not large. In addition, there is a need for a very high degree of specialization and a need for a closely focused supervision by persons intimately familiar with the technical problems in production, color matching, order scheduling, or addressing the specialized needs of customers. This need for close and technically knowledgeable supervision should suggest one form of organization as particularly appropriate.

Exercise 6–10

Hint: Your task is not well structured, and you lack formal authority. You know little about the abilities of the others with whom you will be working. This should suggest something about the degree of formality you will want to recommend.

PART TWO

INTERFUNCTIONAL INTEGRATION—CONCEPTUAL AND ANALYTIC TOOLS

In Part One we examined both the basic tools used by the general manager and the need to integrate the components of each function's concerns into a functional plan or program of action that has internal consistency. Functional managers and general managers need a broader view in order to provide perspectives that maximize the total effectiveness of the function.

In Part Two, three perspectives are offered that provide you with the opportunity to learn how to integrate *across* functions and achieve, as best you can, a maximum effectiveness for the entire organization. To some extent, the chapters in Part Two can be seen to focus on *tools,* which is probably a reasonable way to view them. They provide not only a way to pull together the major business functions, but they also offer you practice in the skills of analysis and synthesis that will aid you in examining more comprehensive and less well-structured problem situations in the material covered in Parts Three and Four.

The first chapter in Part Two deals with break-even analysis, a topic you probably covered to some extent in your accounting work. In Chapter 7, however, you will explore break-even analysis in much more detail and in much greater complexity. You will find that it offers important insights into the working dynamics of cost, volume, and profitability relationships. Chapter 8 on life cycle analysis should also be familiar, at least initially, from your background in marketing. Again, you will find more complexity and more opportunity to explore the integrative nature of this managerial tool than might have been the case thus far in your course work. Finally, Chapter 9 on operational forecasting provides an opportunity to begin the process of forming a basis for projections of sales, costs, and capital needs into future periods in a comprehensive rather than fragmented way.

Carefully studied, the material in Part Two should be most helpful in giving you a full appreciation of the problems and complexities of integration and the management of an entire business unit. In addition, it should be very helpful in providing an opportunity to learn and practice the use of some important tools for managing an integrated business unit, skills that are also needed as a foundation for the study of the process of planning and forming strategies for integrated operations, which will be taken up in Part Three.

7

BREAK-EVEN ANALYSIS

TRADITIONAL BREAK-EVEN CHARTING

Break-even analysis is an application of elementary mathematical tools to business problems. In its simplest form, the break-even chart represents a linear cost function and a linear revenue function. At their juncture, a break-even point is defined. Sales over the break-even point generate profit. Sales below that point result in losses. Figure 7–1 is the classic break-even chart and is comprised of four linear functions on a chart that uses dollars on the vertical axis and units on the horizontal axis. The fixed cost function is described by the horizontal line that runs the width of the chart. (Fixed costs have been described briefly in Chapter 2.)

For traditional break-even analysis, fixed costs do not change (over the range of volume covered) and are, therefore, depicted as a horizontal line. Variable costs in the traditional model change by a uniform amount as volume changes. The variable cost line, therefore, also is depicted as a linear function, but one that starts at the origin and rises by a constant over the range of volume covered.

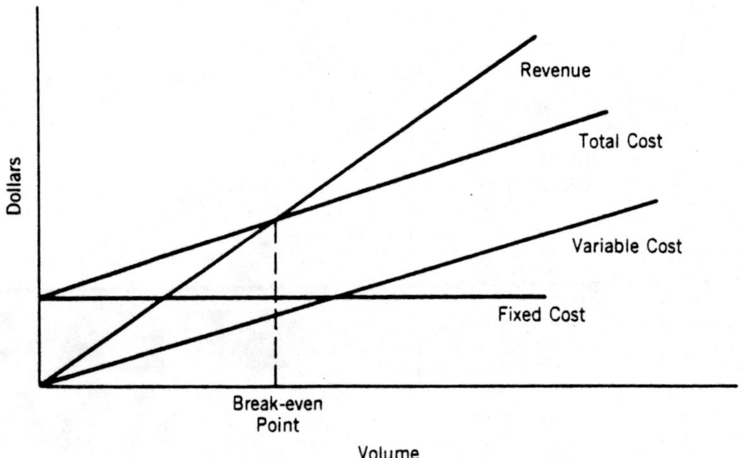

FIGURE 7-1 Traditional break-even chart.

Total cost, the sum of fixed and variable costs, is represented by a line starting at the fixed cost amount, at zero volume, and rising by the amount of variable cost as volume increases. Revenue is represented by a line starting at the origin and increasing by a constant amount for each unit sold.

The mathematical formula for computing the break-even point in the traditional linear model is straightforward.

$$\underset{\text{(in units)}}{\text{Break-even Point}} = \frac{\text{Fixed Costs}}{\underset{\text{(per unit)}}{\text{Revenue}} - \underset{\text{(per unit)}}{\text{Variable Cost}}}$$

An example may illustrate: COOPCO, a small cooperage, manufactures a standard metal-bound oak cask for use in the distillation and manufacture of whiskey. COOPCO's selling and administrative costs total $85,000 per year (a figure held fairly steadily over the past 3 years). Ten craftspersons are employed the year round, at a cost of $125,000. Laborers needed to prepare raw material, move orders through the cooperage, and prepare orders for truck shipment are hired by the shop supervisor on the basis of need. His rule of thumb is that this type of labor is added or deducted purely on the basis of volume. He estimates the cost of this labor at $1.60 per cask, regardless of volume. Materials cost $2.86 per cask.

EXAMPLE

Fixed costs are:	$ 85,000	Selling and administrative expense
	125,000	Craftspersons
	$210,000	Total fixed costs

Variable costs are:	\$1.60	Direct labor per cask
	2.86	Materials per cask
	\$4.46	Total variable cost per cask
Revenue per cask	\$9.75	

$$\text{Break-even point} = \frac{\$210{,}000}{\$9.75 - \$4.46} = \begin{array}{c}\text{39,697 casks per Year} \\ \text{or} \\ \text{3,308 casks per Month}\end{array}$$

EXERCISE 7–1

Refer to the data on COOPCO. Assume that fixed costs increase 15%, materials 21%, direct labor (all categories) 10%, and that selling price is successfully increased to \$10.25 per cask. Calculate the new break-even point per month. (Answer can be found at the end of the chapter.)

The traditional model is a handy tool, one that is sometimes overlooked by practicing managers. Its calculations are simple, and for many situations, its rough approximations can suffice for general planning and preliminary feasibility analysis.

Some businesses (e.g., a CPA or law firm) either lack a convenient unit of analysis or have multiple units in a product line, either of which pose problems in calculating or preparing charts for the determination of the break-even point. In this case, *dollars of revenue* become the unit of volume. *Percentage* of sales dollars becomes the unit of variable cost.

EXERCISE 7–2

Given this data:

Fixed costs \$226,892 per year

Materials 29% of sales

Labor 38% of sales

Selling commission 11% of sales

Discounts and transportation 8% of sales

Calculate break-even point for a week's operation.

EXHIBIT 1
Pikes Peak Forge Company, Inc.
Income Statement, 1983–86

	1983	*1984*	*1985*	*1986*
Net Sales	$1972978	$2075298	$2611349	$3354959
Cost of Sales				
Inventory, July 1	115241	151208	134141	161828
Direct Materials	563186	560823	689727	1069050
Direct Labor	982635	1046865	1127484	1178212
Gas & Electric	41591	46278	47930	58755
Shipping	15989	16576	19908	15947
Total Costs	$1718642	$1820950	$2019190	$2483792
Less: Inventory, June 30	151208	134141	161828	260692
Cost of Sales	1567434	1686809	1857362	2223100
Gross Profit	$ 405544	$ 388489	$ 753987	$1131859
Operating Expenses				
Administrative Salaries	$ 28224	$ 21991	$ 23986	$ 32452
Advertising	1121	139	393	
Auto Expense	4966	3828	6499	4495
Bad Debt Expense	40901	620	30197	
Contributions	742	1709	102	911
Depreciation	38120	39060	52200	51174
Employee Medical Expense	1910	2711	2239	1966
Insurance	37021	34482	22187	46081
Interest Expense	1623	985	1053	
Legal Fees	2683	7479	66113	101753
Licenses	59907	70065	89646	89699
Loss on Sale of Assets	1144	1110		
Miscellaneous Expense	1749	980	4542	5377
Office Expense	3499	4505	4243	5133
Pension Plan Costs		40238	51704	50521
Professional Fees		5554	11104	20363
Rent	55934	55518	48116	44414
Sales Commissions	2716	2040	9648	10669
Store Expense	58389	80335	70803	89948
Subscriptions & Dues	1536	2740	2891	4192
Travel Expense	2865	1132	2208	1837
Total Operating Expenses	345050	377221	499794	560985
Net Operating Profit	$ 60494	$ 11268	$ 254193	$ 570874
Add: Miscellaneous Income	1331	792	4774	21707
Net Income Before Taxes	$ 61825	$ 12060	$ 258967	$ 592581
Provision for Income Taxes	26594	934	126544	289268
Net Income	$ 35231	$ 11126	$ 132423	$ 303313

EXERCISE 7–3

The income statements of the Pikes Peak Forge Company, Inc., in Exhibit 1 have been compiled for analytic purposes. Inspect the cost figures in Exhibit 1 that are found under *Cost of Sales* for 1984, 1985, and 1986. List those items that seem to be essentially *fixed* and the amount you expect them to be in 1987.

EXERCISE 7–4

For those figures listed under *Cost of Sales* in Exhibit 1, that seem to be more closely related to sales volume (i.e., are variable costs); list each together with your estimate of their cost *as a percentage of net sales* for 1987.

EXERCISE 7–5

Repeat the process described in Exercises 7–3 and 7–4 for all of the items listed under *Operating Expenses* in Exhibit 1.

Fixed-Cost Items	*Estimated Amount (1987)*
____________	$____________
____________	$____________
____________	$____________
____________	$____________
____________	$____________

Variable Cost Items	*Estimated Amount (1987)*
____________	______% of sales
____________	______% of sales
____________	______% of sales
____________	______% of sales
____________	______% of sales

EXERCISE 7–6

Total of all fixed-cost items____________

Total of all variable-cost items____________

Calculate break-even point (per year):

____

MORE COMPLEX BREAK-EVEN ANALYSIS

The traditional model for break-even analysis is based on a number of assumptions. Although its simplicity is helpful in rough calculations, we should not overlook these assumptions. We will probably find that hard decisions have to be based on more refined (and more realistic) model development.

Fixed Costs

Each function that comprises the break-even chart should be developed separately and should be studied carefully in order to determine its true shape. The fixed-cost function is depicted as a horizontal line. When we examine the costs that are typically used to make up fixed costs, we find that a constant cost level is not an accurate representation of reality. Some costs undoubtedly remain fixed so long as major capital expansion is not undertaken. Property taxes, interest expense, fire and casualty insurance premiums, security expenses, and building depreciation are unlikely to change unless a change is made in the facility used. Thus, these fixed costs for a shop in one's garage remain fixed until the shop is moved into commercial space. Each major change in facilities carries with it an increase to a new level of fixed cost and the horizontal line found in Figure 7–1 has now become a "step" function.

The "steps" in the function shown in Figure 7–2 become large when we consider other costs that increase in steps as volume increases. Clerical/managerial expenses do not change smoothly as volume increases but "step" to higher levels as the capacity of existing clerical/managerial staff becomes fully utilized and additional staff is hired.

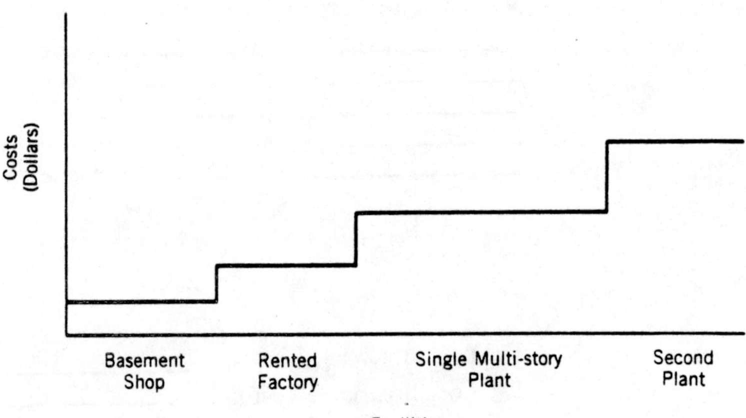

FIGURE 7–2 Step function resulting from expansion.

Smaller "steps" are found in the fixed-cost function as an existing facility moves from a single shift of 40 hours of production per week to multishift operations working 24 hours per day, 7 days per week. As additional shifts are started, supervisory, maintenance, janitorial, factory clerical, equipment depreciation, and many utilities expenses "step" up to a new level that remains relatively constant until the third shift is started, at which time another "step" is taken. The effect of these shift-by-shift additions to fixed costs is a subdivision of major "steps" into at least three minor upward moves in the cost structure. With access to detailed cost information, a competent analyst should be able to approximate the shape of the stepped fixed-cost function by using estimates of clerical and supervisory staff at each level and estimates of indirect labor and other semifixed expenses.

EXERCISE 7–7

Charting Fixed Costs

Construct a fixed-cost function and draw it on graph paper. Use the following table of yearly costs as data for the construction of the fixed-cost line.

Facility	*Selling expense*	*Three-shift capacity in units*	*Depreciation expense per shift*	*Factory supervision & clerical per shift*	*Utilities per shift*	*Indirect labor per shift*
Basement shop	$ 42,000	$ 6,000	$ 700	$ —	$ 1,200	$ —
20,000-square-foot rented space	54,000	28,000	14,200	36,000	8,000	15,000
100,000-square-foot owned factory	178,000	200,000	100,000 (1) 40,000 (2) 40,000 (3)	115,000	40,000 (1) 30,000 (2) 30,000 (3)	45,000
1,000,000-square-foot owned plant	888,000	3,000,000	1,300,000 (1) 450,000 (2) 450,000 (3)	980,000	380,000 (1) 250,000 (2) 250,000 (3)	525,000

Each additional 3 million unit plant will require the same costs as a single plant except that selling and administrative expenses rise by 1.65 multiplier as additional plants are put into service.

Please show fixed-cost functions for all shifts, at all volume levels to 6 million units per year. (Hint: Two sheets of graph paper may be helpful, one for low-volume fixed costs, the second for high-volume fixed costs.)

Variable Costs

In the traditional model, variable costs are depicted as varying in a linear relationship with volume. This relationship assumes a constant unit value for variable costs, an assumption that must be examined in some detail.

Direct materials is a cost item often considered a purely (or nearly) variable cost. Several elements should be considered in developing a more realistic variable-cost function for materials. First, nearly all commercial materials are priced (through negotiation and cost-reduction activities) to offer price discounts for larger quantity purchasers. At the extreme, very small quantities of fabricating steel, for example, are extremely costly on a cost-per-pound or cost-per-ton basis because of the cost of placing the order, handling expenses, and the higher unit cost of shipping small quantities. At another extreme, a manufacturer using hundreds or thousands of tons of steel each year not only achieves maximum economies of ordering and transportation costs, but is also in a bargaining position that may permit other pricing concessions (quantity discounts, freight absorption, or more rigid quality or size specification). Thus, the variable cost function should reflect the price reductions that are available as volume increases.

When the maximum of such concessions has been reached, the line should become linear instead of curvilinear, and it should remain linear through the range of volume until limitations of available supplies are reached. At that point, shipments of materials from remote locations may be needed to avoid a shutdown of the plant. When supplies become scarce, bidding from prospective buyers also causes prices to rise as the remaining available resources are exhausted. The effect of these forces is to cause the straight-line linear function to begin to hook upward, forming a gently S-shaped cost function.

The *price* factors that cause the materials portion of the variable cost function to follow an S shape are accentuated by a similar pattern in materials *usage*. The early stage, where volume is low, cruder technology is employed, and a lower level of expertise in materials management is exercised should result in poorer materials usage and higher unit costs. In the center section of the curve, where adequate supplies exist and scale of operations is large, materials-usage efficiency should be quite high. At the far right, where marginal materials may be acquired from less reliable sources, materials usage is again poorer and unit costs higher. All these factors should result in a variable cost function for materials that takes the general form shown in Figure 7–3.

Labor costs are not materially different. At the low-volume end, both the technology and the labor used are less specialized, and labor is, therefore, more costly per unit of output. As technology becomes more mechanized, labor costs should straighten — or even cause the function to decline — as automated processes become economically feasible. Again, as supplies of available labor become scarce, prices can be raised through competitive bidding or labor can be imported from more-and-more remote areas . . . both factors result in an increasing slope in the variable cost function.

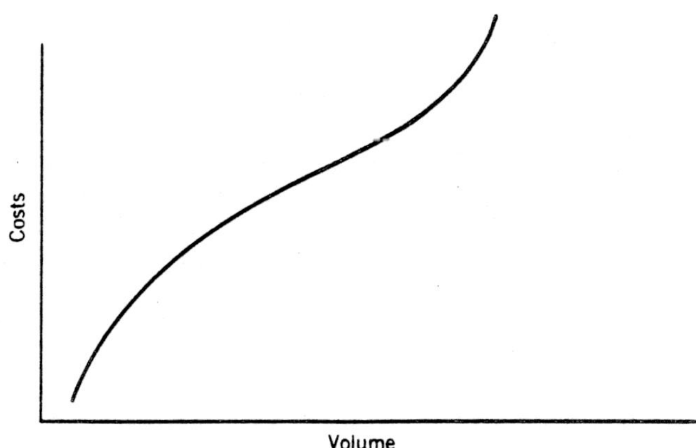

FIGURE 7–3 Variable-cost function showing effects of pricing, supplies availability, and utilization.

EXERCISE 7–8

Consider the following data, then construct and chart a variable cost function with two components: materials and labor.

Materials: Minimum order cost	$50.00
Less than 100 units	$ 8.00 per unit
100 to 1,000 units	$ 6.50 per unit
1,000 to 10,000 units	$ 5.75 per unit

Purchasing has advised that orders in excess of 10,000 units will have to be shipped from the West Coast at a unit price (including freight) of $6.25 per unit for shipments in the 10,000-to-20,000-unit range. East Coast and international suppliers can sell at a price of $7.50 delivered in the 20,000-to-50,000-unit range. General purpose equipment will be used to produce the first 6,000 units of volume. Labor costs for operators of this type of equipment average $11.75 per hour in hourly wages. The production rate at this level of technology is 1 labor man-hour per unit. Between 6,000 and 8,000 units, semiautomatic equipment will be used. Labor rates average $9.50 per hour, and the productivity is 0.8 man-hours per unit produced. Between 10,000 and 30,000 units, fully automated equipment will be used. Labor rates will average $8.75 per hour and productive efficiency will be 0.7 man-hours per unit produced. Between 30,000 and 50,000 units, labor costs will rise to an average of $9.00 (owing to labor market price competition), and efficiency will drop back to 0.95 man-hours per unit produced.

THE LEARNING CURVE

A more rigorously defined representation of the effect of improvements in operating efficiency over a period of time is the learning curve. Typically, the learning curve for manufacturing is based on data gained from cost and performance records taken from manufacturing similar products or performing similar services. As the first item in a series is completed, knowledge and skills gained in the completion of the first unit are applied to the second. Those of the first and second to the third, and so on. Generally, the conventional way of expressing the improvements in operations derived from leaning is a learning rate, expressed in percentage terms. An 80% learning rate means that as the production output doubles, the time required per unit declines to 80% of its preceding level. For example, if a unit required 500 man-hours to produce at first, the second unit would require 400 hours, at an 80% learning rate. At 80%, as the cumulative output reached 4 units (doubling from the *preceding* level), labor usage for the fourth unit would drop to 320 man-hours (80% of the 400 reached at 2 units of output). At 16 units, labor hours for the sixteenth unit would be down to 204.8.

Can you calculate what the labor hours are for the eighth unit? the thirty-second? (Check for the answers at the end of the chapter)

EXERCISE 7–9

If the first unit takes 8,274 man-hours to build, estimate the *total* man-hours needed to build 32 units at a learning rate of 87%. (Hint: You may wish to use graph paper to help.)

EXERCISE 7–10

Now estimate the gain or loss in man-hours that might be observed at a learning rate of 81.5% for producing the same 32 units as in Exercise 7–9.

Parts (A) and (B) of a case on City Hardware, Inc., are now presented. Before reading the case, reflect for a few moments on the material you have been studying in this chapter. Then read each part of the case carefully. When you have completed the first reading, go back to the beginning and study the case thoroughly. Then examine the questions contained in the Exercises that follow the case. Respond to those questions as directed by your instructor.

CITY HARDWARE, INC. (A)

City Hardware, Inc., is a closely held firm, its board of directors consisting of all six of the company's stockholders. Three families control the business: two father–son families and two cousins. All are prominent business and professional men and women and live in major cities throughout the state. The business has been in these three families since its incorporation, and participation has been limited to two members from each family. Control has been maintained even as the new, younger owners have moved away to pursue their own professions.

In February 1973, the board met to discuss the future direction of the firm. Current operations included both a retail hardware store in the downtown central city area and a wholesale plumbing supply division three blocks away in a railroad-siding warehouse. Considerable sentiment existed on the board for a shift of the firm toward becoming exclusively a retail hardware store. Specific items on the agenda included the determination of the firm's future type of operation, possible locations available, and financing necessary for any such changes.

The general manager attended the meeting and presented board members with his evaluation of the firm in a written memo dated February 4, 1973. The following excerpts from that memo present his viewpoint:

> *We draw our trade from a large area encompassing several counties, partly because of the wholesale business we have, partly because of the diversified inventory we carry, partly because we deliver, and partly because of our consumer credit program. It has been expressed by some of our customers that we are high priced, but we usually have what no other business carries. Also, we generally have had personnel who know the entire hardware line, although this is fading fast as our old-time employees retire.*
>
> *Our Wholesale Plumbing Division is presently the most profitable segment of our business, but the firm has not been able to meet its goals of increased profitability from the retail end. As you have suggested, this Division should be the main thrust of the business. There is a real opportunity in the area known as "home-center" operation, catering to the "do-it-yourselfer." If we go to this type of operation we could capture a large share of the market because our existing strength in the hardware business would make us a one-stop center.*
>
> *While we have shown a 43 percent increase in sales for the past year, the figures show that there was not a significant increase in any area except the sporting goods field, and most of that was at the wholesale level and at low margin. Our success in generating new sales has leveled off, partly because of inadequate physical space. We know that a new, modern facility would increase sales again.*
>
> *One of the major obstacles we would have to overcome should we go into a new, more modern operation would be our pricing structure. I would suggest going to a one-price system with a lower margin. I believe we could improve our net profit figure with new homeowners' business that we presently do not have. A real education program would have to be done on our contractor and industrial accounts. But I believe we could convince them to stay with us despite the loss of their "wholesale customer" status. A couple of former contracting customers have*

This case was prepared by Professor Paul Miesing.

told us that they now purchase their hardware elsewhere. They are paying more for their merchandise, but they don't have parking problems to contend with. They figure they come out just as well, taking the cost of the men's time into account. Several contractors make us their first stop in the morning on their way to the job. Our best bet is to move right out where all the building is going on.

As a result of the aforementioned facts and given the goal of increased retail sales and profits, I see no alternative but to make immediate plans to relocate the main base of our hardware operation. The wholesale plumbing business could remain where it is for a few years, but it would simplify operations if we construct a combination facility to house both divisions. The general direction indicated by growth of present customers and potential new customers would be in the northern area of the suburban belt around the city. As previously reported, land costs are high where frontage on the highway is available. However, further inquiry has revealed that land which is a block from the highway can be purchased for around $20,000 per acre. This is considerably under our previous figures. Also, land east on Route 62 costs about 30 percent less than that out north on Route 53. With a building cost of $10 per square foot, a 20,000-square-foot building plus land would run approximately $260,000. Add to this $50–75,000 for fixtures and equipment and $20–30,000 for parking lot paving and we come up with a figure of around $350–375,000 total cost. This would give us the large, high-ceilinged, modern design we've been dreaming about and allow us to go ahead with the full-line "home-center" retail hardware store in a good location. We would keep most of our contractor business with this plan and increase retail sales as well.

We could finance this move one of several ways: (1) raise capital through additional stock sales; (2) raise capital through debentures; (3) sell the present properties and lease the new property; or (4) establish a separate real estate holding operation, so the business can lease the property from the real estate operation. I have had informal discussion with real estate people who feel we could sell the two downtown properties for around $125,000.

BACKGROUND

Located in a mid-Atlantic state, City Hardware has been a respected local name in hardware for nearly a century. The charming store occupies its original high-ceiling building, complete with small bin storages up and along the walls and serviced by aged clerks sliding floating ladders to and fro as they pick items from memory. It was fun just to go in and see this quaint store out of the past.

The firm has shown total wholesale and retail sales of over $1,000,000 annually since 1947 and prides itself on its nickname, "the dependable hardware store." The town in which it is located centers around the major state university and hospital complex, with light and medium manufacturing also providing jobs. Growth in the area has been steady since 1940 and the city–county population totals nearly 75,000. Surrounding counties provide approximately another 75,000 potential customers, most of whom come into town on Saturday to do their shopping. (Census data are shown in Exhibits 1 and 2.)

Residential migration has been along the major traffic arteries, as is characteristic of many cities experiencing growth. Residences along the northern Route 53 area have increased dramatically, and one shopping center and an additional large department store opened to satisfy the growing needs of the area. A second shop-

EXHIBIT 1
Selected area housing characteristics, 1970

	County	*City*	*Total*
Household population	34,361	37,957	72,318
Year-round dwelling units	11,715	14,288	26,003
Seasonal units	23	3	26
Occupied units	10,541	13,647	24,188
One-unit structure	9,093	8,141	17,234
Multiunit and mobile	2,622	6,147	8,769
Owner-occupied units	6,758	6,583	13,341
Median value	$21,100	$20,200	$20,650
Lacking one or more plumbing facilities	1,299	137	1,436
Renter-occupied units	3,783	7,064	10,847
Median rent	$ 122	$ 102	$ 109
Lacking one or more plumbing facilities	732	401	1,133
Crowded units	842	745	1,587
Lacking one or more plumbing facilities	440	66	506
Persons per unit	2.93	2.66	2.78
Persons per occupied unit	3.26	2.78	2.99

ping center, featuring a large national chain department store, is rumored for the near future farther north on Route 53. Growth to the east of the city along Route 62 has been slower, characterized by an increase in commercial businesses (almost all local car dealers, plus two building supply companies) with very little increase in residential dwellings. The interstate highway south of the city and the hilly terrain and high land prices to the west have kept growth slow in those directions. (A map of the area is included as Exhibit 3.)

The retail hardware industry has enjoyed steady growth in the past five years, according to a survey by the Retail Hardware Association. (Exhibit 4 shows relative sales and net income trends for the hardware industry.) Growth has been due primarily to increases in residential housing and leisure time. Home improvement items have experienced the greatest growth, as more homeowners make minor improvements and repairs themselves, citing self-satisfaction and lower costs as their major reasons.

BUSINESS ORGANIZATION

Two separate entities come under the title of City Hardware. The first, the Wholesale Plumbing Division, located on Wood Street, specializes in plumbing supplies and sells primarily to contractors and builders. The personnel are considered extremely knowledgeable, and personal service is highly stressed. Their large variety of supplies and accessories has made City Hardware the major supplier of wholesale plumbing in the area, with 35 percent of the market, but space limitation has begun to present a possible constraint to growth. The present facility has 5,200 square feet of space. It is owned by the company, but current building codes prevent any additions to the building. Also, the building is old, preventing the installation of modern inventory-handling equipment (such as conveyor belts and freight elevators) and necessitating costly manual inventory handling. Their primary competitor, C. J. Lilly Co., is located eight blocks away in a modern one-story building.

EXHIBIT 2
Selected city and county demographics

	1970	*1960*	*Change (percentage)*
Effective buying power			
City	$120,587,000	$ 53,251,000	126.4
County	108,198,000	41,641,000	159.9
Retail Sales			
City	$118,014,000	$ 72,443,000	61.5
County	21,650,000	13,415,000	61.4
Car registrations			
City	13,854	7,479	85.1
County	12,817	7,373	73.8
	October 1971	*October 1961*	
Telephones	45,375	23,250	95.2
	July 1972	*July 1962*	
Water (gallons sent out)	224,539,000	147,290,000	52.4
	December 1971		
Electric meters			
City	15,746	N.A.	—
County	11,086	N.A.	—
	26,832		
	1971	*1961*	
City land value	$ 21,736,970	$ 11,804,130	84.1
Assessed value	77,667,180	40,576,670	91.4
Taxes	3,720,265	1,420,183	162.0
Tax rate	4.70	3.30	42.4
County land value	N.A.	$ 5,342,470	—
Assessed value	$ 52,191,130	18,692,060	179.2
Taxes	3,079,276	725,263	324.6
Tax rate	5.90	3.81	54.9

The Retail Hardware Division is located in the city's downtown area, on the main street. It deals primarily in hardware and repair items, including paint, hand tools, and power tools. It also provides a large sporting goods selection and a china department. Seventy percent of its sales are on a wholesale basis to builders and to small "general store" outlets throughout the state. The remaining 30 percent is in retail sales. The retail and wholesale departments are run by the same personnel out of the same store: Each sales clerk decides whether a sale is "wholesale" or "retail." The store has the reputation of being high in price, but offering personal service and a complete selection. The Retail Hardware facility, also owned by the company, is a three-story brick building. Total store area is 15,000 square feet; the first floor of the building serves as the

EXHIBIT 3
Area map

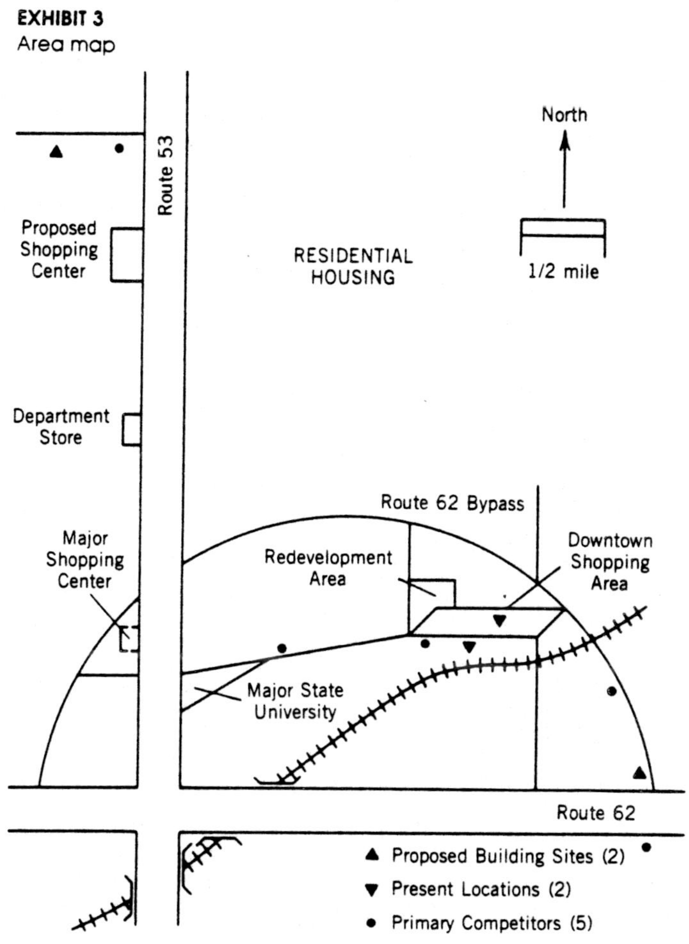

main sales floor and the upper floors serve as storage areas. Most of the basement is also a sales area, housing such departments as sporting goods and china. Because of lack of space, only about 15 percent of the merchandise inventory can be displayed in the sales area. At present, the clerk takes the customer's order and searches the storage area for the desired item. The average search time is 5 minutes.

Just as in the Wholesale Plumbing Division warehouse, the hardware facility has become cramped, and the multistory building cannot be modified for mechanical inventory handling. Under present conditions, merchandise is handled an average of six times by company personnel between the railroad car and the final sales. (Financial statements are included as Exhibits 5 and 6.)

EXHIBIT 4
Trends for the hardware industry

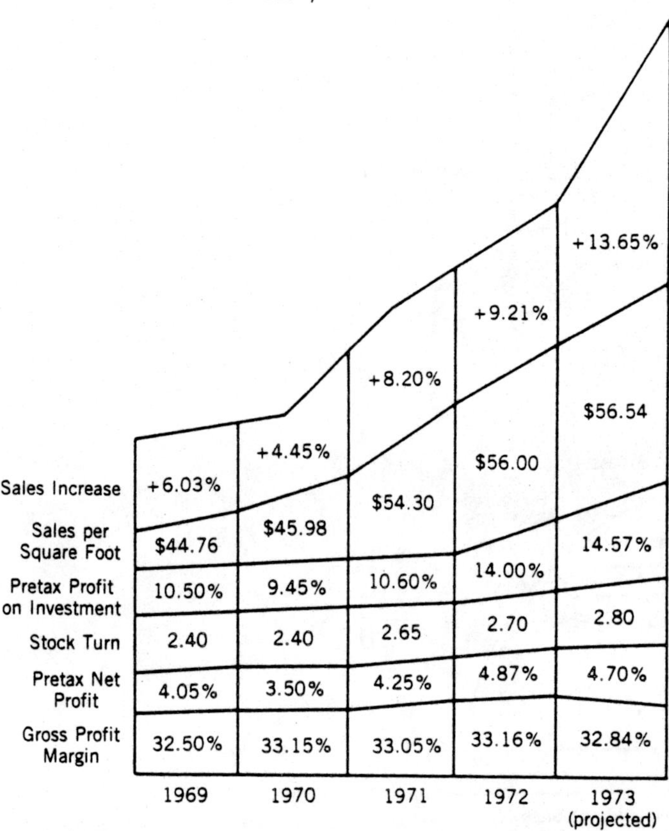

EXHIBIT 5
City Hardware, Inc., Balance Sheets

	1969	*1970*	*1971*	*1972*
Current Assets				
Cash	$ 39,000	$ 33,000	$ 16,000	$ 12,000
Accounts receivable—trade	169,000	154,000	162,000	244,000
Other receivables	7,000	9,000	18,000	4,000
Less allowance	6,000	9,000	10,000	15,000
Net receivables	170,000	154,000	170,000	233,000
Inventories	467,000	405,000	462,000	562,000
Other current assets	2,000	2,000	1,000	1,000
Total Current Assets	677,000	594,000	649,000	808,000

EXHIBIT 5 *(continued)*
City Hardware, Inc., Balance Sheets

	1969	*1970*	*1971*	*1972*
Property, plant & equipment				
Land	19,000	19,000	19,000	19,000
Building & Improvements	98,000	101,000	128,000	128,000
Furniture, fixtures & equipment	26,000	30,000	37,000	38,000
Automobiles & trucks	14,000	15,000	16,000	18,000
Total cost	157,000	165,000	200,000	203,000
Less accumulated depreciation	121,000	123,000	127,000	133,000
Net property, plant & equipment	36,000	42,000	73,000	70,000
Other Assets	3,000	12,000	12,000	4,000
Total Assets	$717,000	$648,000	$734,000	$882,000
Current Liabilities				
Notes payable to bank	$239,000	$ 40,000	$ 70,000	$ 65,000
Accounts payable	44,000	47,000	66,000	245,000
Long-term debt due	—	11,000	12,000	12,000
Other payables	61,000	23,000	26,000	11,000
Total current liabilities	344,000	121,000	174,000	333,000
Long-term liabilities—building	—	134,000	123,000	110,000
Total liabilities	344,000	255,000	297,000	443,000
Capital				
Capital stock	80,000	80,000	80,000	80,000
Retained earnings	301,000	322,000	367,000	386,000
Total	381,000	403,000	447,000	466,000
Less treasury stock	8,000	10,000	10,000	27,000
Net Capital	373,000	393,000	437,000	439,000
Total Liabilities & Capital	$717,000	$648,000	$734,000	$882,000

EXHIBIT 6

City Hardware, Inc. Income Statements Years Ended June 30, 1969 Through 1972

	1969	*1970*			*1971*			*1972*		
		Hardware	*Supply*	*Total*	*Hardware*	*Supply*	*Total*	*Hardware*	*Supply*	*Total*
Net sales	$1,136,000	$636,000	$520,000	$1,156,000	$633,000	$474,000	$1,107,000	$985,000	$601,000	$1,586,000
Less cost of sales	823,000	485,000	390,000	875,000	428,000	346,000	774,000	774,000	455,000	1,229,000
Gross profit	313,000	151,000	130,000	281,000	205,000	128,000	333,000	211,000	146,000	357,000
Operating expenses										
Advertising	$ 8,000	$ 9,000	$ 1,000	$ 10,000	$ 10,000	$ 1,000	$ 11,000	$ 11,000	$ 1,000	$ 12,000
Auto & truck	5,000	2,000	2,000	4,000	3,000	2,000	5,000	4,000	1,000	5,000
Bad debts	10,000	9,000	3,000	12,000	4,000	3,000	7,000	3,000	11,000	14,000
Data processing	—	—	—	—	—	—	4,000	5,000	—	5,000
Depreciation	5,000	2,000	2,000	4,000	3,000	2,000	5,000	4,000	3,000	7,000
Interest	8,000	11,000	8,000	19,000	8,000	6,000	14,000	10,000	7,000	17,000
Repairs	1,000	—	—	—	1,000	1,000	2,000	—	—	—
Salaries	210,000	134,000	33,000	167,000	142,000	53,000	191,000	149,000	55,000	204,000
Supplies & office supplies	5,000	5,000	3,000	8,000	6,000	3,000	9,000	8,000	2,000	10,000
Taxes & licenses	15,000	9,000	7,000	16,000	9,000	6,000	15,000	10,000	7,000	17,000
Utilities (light & telephone)	6,000	5,000	2,000	7,000	6,000	2,000	8,000	6,000	2,000	8,000
Other	26,000	21,000	12,000	33,000	19,000	12,000	31,000	19,000	18,000	37,000
Total operation expenses	$ 299,000	$207,000	$ 73,000	$ 280,000	$211,000	$ 91,000	$ 302,000	$229,000	$107,000	$ 336,000
Pretax income from operation	$ 14,000	$(56,000)	$ 57,000	$ 1,000	$ (6,000)	$ 37,000	$ 31,000	$(18,000)	$ 39,000	$ 21,000

CITY HARDWARE, INC. (B)

MEMORANDUM

To:	Board Members, City Hardware, Inc.
From:	Chairman of the Board
Re:	Future direction of the company
Date:	May 14, 1976

Due to the disappointing results of the past two years, I feel it is necessary for us to meet as soon as possible. Therefore, I am calling a meeting of the Board for Friday, May 21 at 10:00 A.M. The purpose of the meeting will be to determine feasible ways to reverse the current situation. Since the General Manager will not be present, please use discretion in discussing this matter.

Signed,

Mark Taylor, Jr.

BACKGROUND

In the spring of 1973, the Board of Directors of City Hardware, Inc., acting on the recommendations of the general manager, decided to move the company from its long-established downtown location to a new site in the northern suburbs of the city. This move involved relocating the company's downtown hardware store and a wholly owned plumbing supply company—with separate locations and store managers—to a single building. The company based its move decision on the expanding growth to the north.

The firm decided to concentrate on retail hardware sales. As the general manager noted, most residential development of the past few years had occurred in the northern suburbs. He saw sales potential in contractors going to the job as well as home owners who continue working around their homes after construction is completed. Summary financial information for the period preceding the move decision is shown in Table 1.

The move took place just before the onset of the recession–inflation phenomenon which followed the end of the Vietnam War and extended through the Nixon–Watergate era. Although unemployment was high with the economic slowdown in full swing, inflation continued unabated. (See Exhibits 1 and 2.)

PERSONALITIES

Howard Martin began his career as general manager of City Hardware in 1970. He had previously held the same position in a nearby city and was hired by City Hardware on the basis of his character references there. Howard managed the store with a loose administrative style, giving his employees free rein. Both Howard and his wife were quite active in local activities, maintaining a respected personal image within the community. In addition, Howard concentrated considerable time and energy toward qualifying for trips and other business-related benefits. As a result, the Martins were able to visit many places which they would never otherwise have seen.

Board members and stockholders comprise a very interesting group. None of them live in the immediate vicinity of the stores. The majority stockholders are two father-son teams. In addition, two cousins also serve on the board.

The two fathers, most knowledgeable of the group, are no longer active in the organization. Their two sons have taken over leadership. Mark Taylor, Jr.—who, together with his father, controls 45 percent of the company's stock—is president of the company. An MIT graduate, he now owns his own high-technol-

This case was prepared by Professor Paul Miesing.

TABLE 1

Year	*Net sales*	*Cost of goods sold*	*Gross profit*	*Operating expenses*	*Net income*
Hardware					
1969	$660,000	$477,000	$183,000	$211,000	$(28,000)
1970	636,000	485,000	151,000	207,000	(56,000)
1971	633,000	428,000	205,000	211,000	(6,000)
1972	985,000	774,000	211,000	229,000	(18,000)
Supply					
1969	$476,000	$346,000	$130,000	$ 88,000	$ 42,000
1970	520,000	390,000	130,000	73,000	57,000
1971	464,000	346,000	128,000	91,000	37,000
1972	606,000	455,000	146,000	107,000	39,000

ogy corporation in the northern part of the state. Les Hill III and his father own 25 percent of the stock. Like Mark, Les has been a corporate officer for a long time. Les, a graduate of a prestigious eastern university, is now vice president of a major tool-manufacturing corporation.

Primarily because of the physical distance between the stockholders and City Hardware, they interact only with Howard and feel rapport with him in times of success. But in times of losses, misunderstanding and a lack of communication predominate, and their disagreements often become volatile.

Howard has employed older, "handyman" types who are knowledgeable in hardware. Most consider their jobs long-term, although many had problems once they moved to the new modernized store. Traditionally, Howard

EXHIBIT 1
Area housing starts

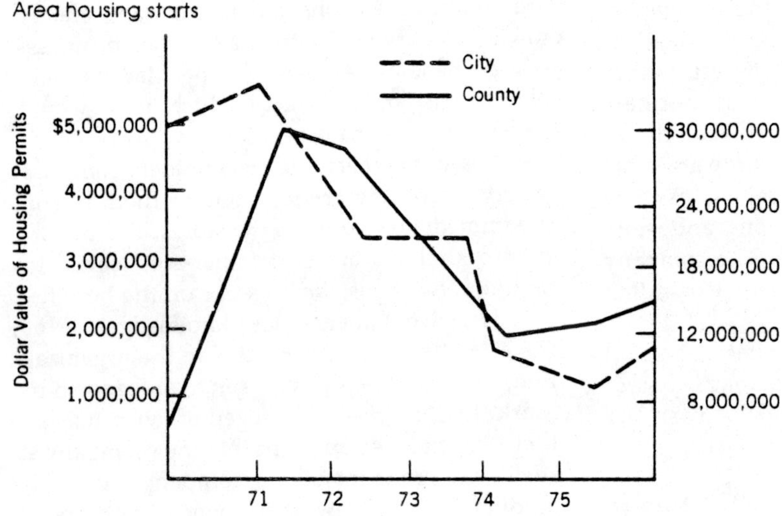

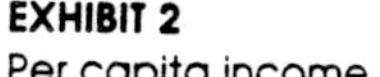

EXHIBIT 2
Per capita income

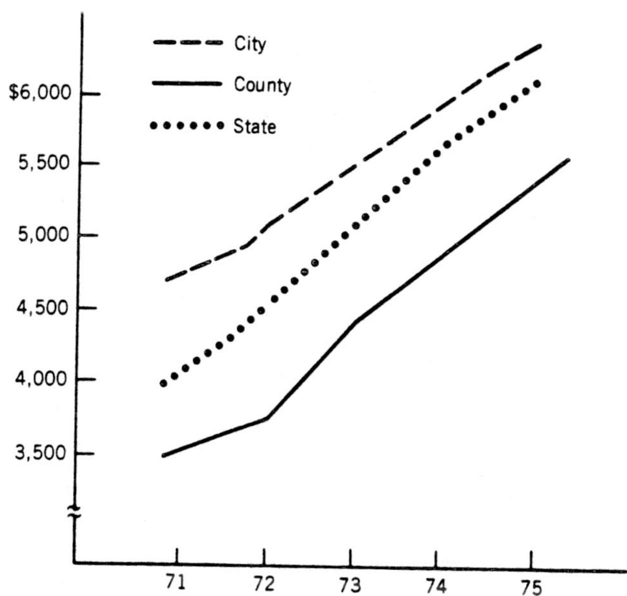

wanted to be an ally to his employees, supporting their side in arguments with the board. Much as Howard tries to remain on their good sides, the employees (as will most employees) still recognize his weak points and take advantage of them.

STORE OPERATIONS

City Hardware's pricing policy is largely set by department buyers (see Exhibit 3), who have overall responsibility for sales as well as buying all inventory items in their departments. Based on a 27 percent to 30 percent markup over cost, prices depend on the buyer's perception of what will move the inventory. A buyer might adjust the price asked of an individual customer in order to make a particular sale.

The management of City Hardware seeks to compete with other local hardware stores, building supply, and plumbing supply houses on the bases of price, personal relationships between customers and employees, broad credit policies, wide product selection, and delivery to retail customers. The company had a reputation of being somewhat high-priced, but also of being a place where you can get almost anything you want. The older salesman have a reputation for knowing the hardware business so well that they are able to listen to your problem and help you solve it. Also, you can get parts for items which haven't been manufactured or offered for sale for some years. Past policies of buying carload lots, formerly facilitated by the railroad siding near the plumbing supply operation, assured this ready supply of parts.

With the new move to the new location, City Hardware management switched to a self-service retailing policy, with fewer salesman on the floor and standard packaged items replacing the old-line bin operation. However, price markups of the downtown location were retained in the new store.

EXHIBIT 3
City Hardware, Inc., Organization Chart

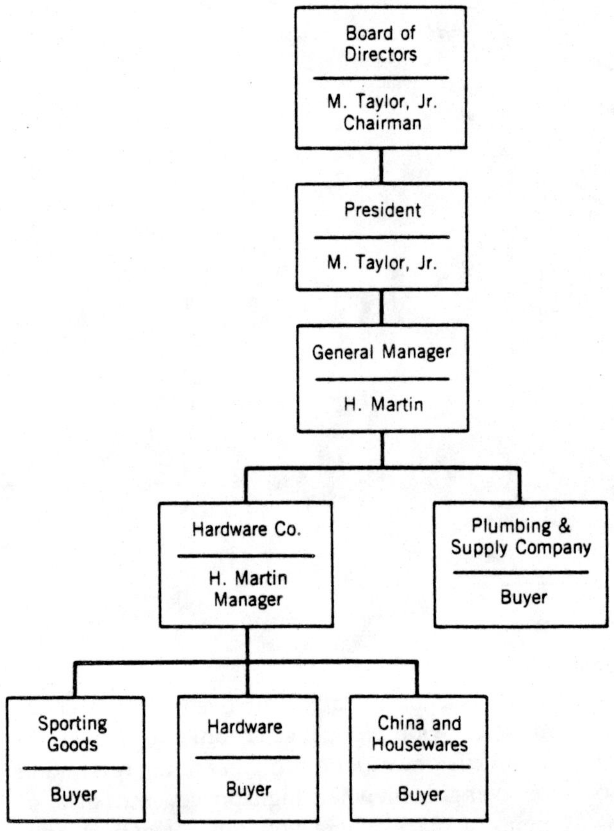

Accounting systems for the company primarily consist of multicolumn journals and a ledger, maintained by an accountant assisted by a bookkeeper. Since total sales maintain a stable dollar level, the management does not feel a need for complex financial or cost-accounting systems.

SPECIFICS OF THE MOVE

In the spring of 1973, when the board of directors approved the decision to move all operations to a new site in the northern suburbs, it was estimated that a three-acre tract of land would probably cost $60,000. Active negotiations began promptly, resulting in the April 1973, purchase of four and one-half acres at a total cost of $229,000. The acquired site is located next to a large building-materials supply store, one block west of the main north-south highway into town. The land purchase was financed with a $45,000 addition to an existing mortgage from a local bank, $4,000 of internal funds, and the issuance of $180,000 in 8 percent bonds to the prior owners of the land.

Les Hill wanted to work with the general manager in developing the design of the new building, especially the office area. Les felt that the offices—especially the general manager's—should reflect the prestige locally associated with the company. Accordingly, he helped to contact a well-known local architect with a reputation based on the homes he had designed. The City Hardware building was his first venture into the commercial building field.

He designed a 22,000-square-foot building (see Exhibit 4), characterized by open steel beams. The center of the sloping ceilings is sufficiently high to accommodate offices on the second floor. This design allows the manager to look down from a gallery outside his office onto the housewares, china, and sporting goods selling area, approximately the size of a grocery store. Mr. Martin could view the hardware selling floor, equivalent in size, from another gallery adjacent to the 1,000-square-foot conference room. The galleries are interconnected,

EXHIBIT 4
New store layout

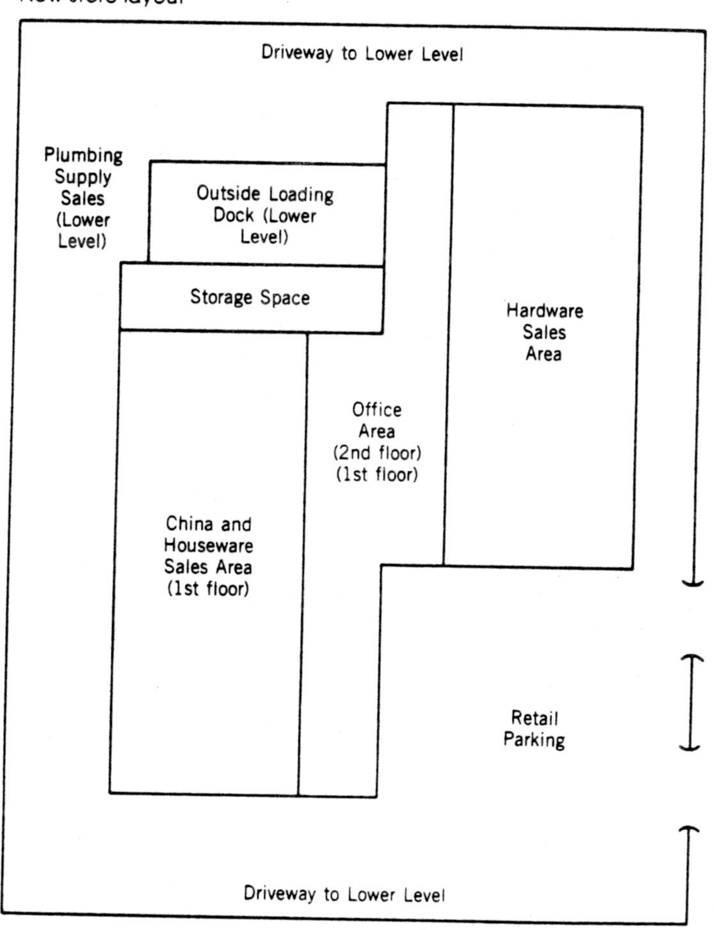

providing access to the various offices and to the stairs. The basement is given over entirely to the plumbing supply operation.

Although Mr. Martin had originally estimated building costs of $220,000 (22,000 square feet × $10) based on an estimate of $10 per square foot, it became evident that costs would run somewhat higher as the actual construction time approached. Since the proceeds from the sale of the downtown store went to pay off a mortgage on the property, two of the board members came forward and agreed to construct the building, which the company would then lease. This plan relieved the company of all obligations except a guarantee for a building construction loan. As of June 30, 1976, however, the old supply company building had still not been sold.

The company ultimately negotiated lease agreements calling for annual rental payments of $109,000 over the next 26 years, the rental of furniture and fixtures adding $21,000 per year, to be renewed annually.

Operations began in the new building on August 11, 1975. (Financial statements are included as Exhibits 5 and 6).

EXHIBIT 5

City Hardware, Inc., Balance Sheets at June 30, 1972 Through 1976

	1972	*1973*	*1974*	*1975*	*1976*
Current Assets					
Cash	$ 12,000	$ 16,000	$ 9,000	$ 15,000	$ 14,000
Accounts receivable—trade	244,000	203,000	156,000	137,000	91,000
Other receivables	6,000	6,000	5,000	3,000	55,000
Less allowance	14,000	12,000	9,000	11,000	7,000
Net receivables	236,000	197,000	152,000	129,000	139,000
Inventories	560,000	510,000	606,000	690,000	471,000
Other current assets	811,000	725,000	769,000	765,000	633,000
Total current assets	811,000	725,000	769,000	765,000	633,000
Property, plant & equipment					
Land	18,000	247,000	247,000	243,000	233,000
Buildings & Improvements	128,000	129,000	128,000	129,000	48,000
Furniture, fixtures & equipment	38,000	46,000	47,000	48,000	62,000
Autos & trucks	19,000	19,000	20,000	20,000	18,000
Total cost	203,000	440,000	442,000	440,000	361,000
Less: acc. dep.	133,000	138,000	141,000	149,000	81,000
Net property, plant & equipment	70,000	302,000	301,000	291,000	280,000
Other assets	1,000	7,000	69,000	7,000	8,000
Total Assets	$882,000	$1,034,000	$1,139,000	$1,063,000	$921,000
Current Liabilities					
Notes payable to bank	$ 65,000	$ 65,000	$ 90,000	$ 135,000	$180,000
Accounts payable	245,000	154,000	191,000	146,000	223,000
L-t debt due	12,000	47,000	51,000	52,000	39,000
Other payables	11,000	16,000	53,000	14,000	60,000
Total Current Liabilities	333,000	282,000	385,000	347,000	502,000
L-t liabilities—bldg.	110,000	291,000	248,000	197,000	59,000
Total Liabilities	443,000	573,000	633,000	544,000	561,000
Capital					
Capital stock	80,000	80,000	80,000	80,000	80,000
Retained earnings	386,000	405,000	450,000	463,000	304,000
Total	466,000	485,000	530,000	543,000	384,000
Less treasury stock	27,000	24,000	24,000	24,000	24,000
Net Capital	439,000	461,000	506,000	519,000	360,000
Total Liabilities and Capital	$882,000	$1,034,000	$1,139,000	$1,063,000	$921,000

EXHIBIT 6
City Hardware, Inc., Income Statements Years Ended June 30, 1973 Through 1976

	1973			1974		
	Hardware	*Supply*	*Total*	*Hardware*	*Supply*	*Total*
Net sales	$874,000	$602,000	$1,476,000	$822,000	$650,000	$1,472,000
Less: cost of sales	676,000	439,000	1,115,000	537,000	467,000	1,004,000
Gross profit	198,000	163,000	361,000	285,000	183,000	468,000
Operating expenses						
Advertising	$ 11,000	$ 2,000	$ 13,000	$ 11,000	$ 1,000	$ 12,000
Auto and truck	3,000	1,000	4,000	3,000	1,000	4,000
Bad debts	2,000	2,000	4,000	11,000	22,000	33,000
Data processing	6,000	2,000	8,000	5,000	3,000	8,000
Depreciation	5,000	3,000	8,000	5,000	3,000	8,000
Interest	12,000	8,000	20,000	20,000	14,000	34,000
Repairs	1,000	2,000	3,000	—	1,000	1,000
Salaries	143,000	75,000	218,000	153,000	80,000	233,000
Supplies and office supplies	7,000	2,000	9,000	7,000	2,000	9,000
Taxes and licenses	11,000	8,000	19,000	13,000	9,000	22,000
Utilities (light and telephone)	7,000	2,000	9,000	7,000	3,000	10,000
Rent	—	—	—	—	—	—
Other	21,000	14,000	35,000	20,000	11,000	31,000
Total operating expense	229,000	121,000	350,000	255,000	150,000	405,000
Pretax income from operation	$(31,000)	$ 42,000	$ 11,000	$ 30,000	$ 33,000	$ 63,000

EXERCISE 7–11

Inspect the income and expense data, then prepare a break-even point calculation (in dollars of revenue), using the mathematical formula approach for calculating the break-even point.

EXERCISE 7–12

One proposal that has been presented to you as advisor to the executive committee at City Hardware is the reopening of a separate wholesale plumbing supply store in a downtown location. The store would be about one-half the size of the new store (Exhibit 4, Part B) and would be staffed by a complement of six employees. It would be located in a moderate-rent commercial area accessible to downtown-area plumbing contractors.

Use data from the case and your own judgment to develop a break-even analysis. Estimate the sales volume needed to break even and the sales volume needed to return a profit after tax greater than the firm's cost of capital. (Refer to Chapter 3 for a refresher, if needed.)

EXHIBIT 6
City Hardware, Inc., Income Statements Years Ended June 30, 1973 Through 1976 *(continued)*

1975			*1976*		
Hardware	*Supply*	*Total*	*Hardware*	*Supply*	*Total*
$669,000	$572,000	$1,241,000	$742,000	$373,000	$1,115,000
414,000	451,000	865,000	540,000	274,000	814,000
255,000	121,000	376,000	202,000	99,000	301,000
$ 12,000	$ 1,000	$ 13,000	$ 31,000	$ 7,000	$ 38,000
3,000	3,000	6,000	3,000	2,000	5,000
3,000	14,000	17,000	6,000	11,000	17,000
8,000	2,000	10,000	10,000	2,000	12,000
5,000	4,000	9,000	5,000	4,000	9,000
20,000	13,000	33,000	17,000	12,000	29,000
—	—	—	3,000	2,000	5,000
164,000	65,000	229,000	185,000	71,000	256,000
8,000	1,000	9,000	12,000	2,000	14,000
13,000	9,000	22,000	16,000	10,000	26,000
8,000	3,000	11,000	24,000	5,000	29,000
—	4,000	4,000	68,000	46,000	114,000
22,000	11,000	33,000	39,000	23,000	62,000
266,000	130,000	396,000	419,000	197,000	616,000
$(11,000)	$ (9,000)	$ (20,000)	$(217,000)	$(98,000)	$ (315,000)

BREAK-EVEN ANALYSIS AND FINANCE

Persons responsible for the financial function in business organizations have reason to pay attention to break-even analysis for several reasons. First, as the scope of operations (i.e., volume) increases, each unit of productive capacity brought into service through adding shifts, increasing the capacity by adding new machinery, or opening new production facilities involves the necessity of providing capital funds or their lease-obligation equivalents.

The startup of additional shifts requires the least outright capital investment but increases machinery and plant utilization, which increases the noncash depreciation expense and accelerates the replacement schedule for capital equipment. Shifts can be started up on a relatively short-notice basis, and they can be readily shut down as demand declines. The second level effects of adding machinery causes an immediate demand for capital funds as well as an increase in noncash depreciation expense. Here, the commitment is for a larger sum. Typically, it is of longer duration than the shift startup, and may require months or years of advance planning in order to obtain "slot" time in equipment suppliers' order backlog listings. The addition of an entire plant calls for a substantial long-term commitment. Not only are the sums larger, but the commitment is for longer time periods. The planning timetable for a major plant construction project can easily cover several years. In the case of nuclear power plants, a timetable of as much as 12 or 15 years is needed in order for the company to comply with all government and regulatory agency requirements.

Financial planning for break-even purposes can be accommodated in very rough terms by calculating the ratio of total assets to total sales, then applying that ratio to revenues to obtain the estimated total capital needed at each level of revenue. Cost of that capital can be developed by means of estimating the interest charges for borrowed funds and the cost of needed dividends (or reported earnings) at varying levels of volume and risk. If realizable volume projections and a firm's cost structure combine to provide for a handsome percentage of profit, the risk to owners and creditors is reduced. Coverage of interest payments is higher, security of stockholder investment is enhanced, and debt-to-equity ratios are improved as substantial earnings accumulate. Thus, as forecasts project operations toward and beyond the break-even point, capital requirements increase, but cost of capital is either lowered or held to present levels.

Example

Bobcat Bushings Company currently has a cost structure as follows: Selling and administrative costs are now $280,000 per year and are not expected to change over the next 18 months. Factory overhead costs include property taxes, casualty insurance, plant security, and fixed factory overhead totaling $180,000 per year. In addition, machine depreciation, utilities, and factory indirect labor and supervision total $460,000 for each shift. Revenue is estimated to be $17.50 per unit of production. Variable costs (materials, labor, and packaging costs) total $6.10 per unit. Capacity is 6,000 units per shift, per month.

EXERCISE 7–13

Calculate the present one-shift break-even point in units per month. (Answer is found at the end of the chapter.)

EXERCISE 7–14

How many break-even points are there for this company? At what volume?

EXERCISE 7–15

Some additional data: James Johnson, sales manager, forecasts this sales-volume array:

Monthly Volume (units)	*Percentage Likelihood*
22,000	5%
24,000	15%
26,000	30%
28,000	40%
30,000	10%

Calculate expected sales volume.

EXERCISE 7–16

Your financial vice president, Harder C. Rockness, tells you that your present total assets (fixed and current assets) are $7.6 million and that new equipment and needs for working capital to support sales will be approximately $2 per unit of productive capacity.

Further, he has said that cost of capital is inversely related to estimated profitability. When profit is 5% or more of sales, the prime interest rate (now 11%) is a close approximation of pretax capital costs. For profits in the 0-to-5% range, he estimates that cost of capital increases in increments to 15%. Below break-even, cost of capital escalates to 25% at a −5% profit on sales figure.

EXERCISE 7–17

Does the forecast volume (Exercise 7–15) require opening a new plant? If so, develop the new total cost structure, including new fixed plant overheads and new *shift-based* overhead costs. Assume that variable costs will be the same as present levels.

Selling and Administrative Costs	________
Old Plant Factory Overhead	
Fixed Overhead	________
Shift-based Overhead	________
New Plant Factory Overhead	________
Fixed Overhead	________
Shift-based Overhead	________
Variable Costs:	

Estimated volume × variable cost per unit

= ________

EXERCISE 7-18

At this sales volume, estimate the new capital required and the added cost of that new capital. (New financing costs should be added to fixed costs.)

EXERCISE 7-19

Now calculate the expected profit and profit on sales, including the cost of new capital in your calculations.

Let us take another example and see if this thinking can be applied to another type of company.

EXERCISE 7-20

Sterling Medical Laboratories is a company operating a chain of medical laboratories in a six-state region. Each laboratory is equipped and staffed to perform comprehensive blood, urine, and sputum analyses. Patients and specimens arrive during daylight hours, but testing can be accomplished 24 hours per day.

During a typical full-capacity shift, 1,260 samples or specimens are processed. Staff for capacity operations in the typical laboratory is comprised of a day shift made up of five persons, an evening shift of three, and a night shift of two people. (Although test processing can be done by only two persons, additional staff are needed to draw blood, bill clients, and prepare reports on the day and evening shifts.) Costs, including fringe benefits, are $15,000 per employee per year; $20,000 per year for the facility (one laboratory); and $2 per specimen for supplies and testing equipment used in the analyses. Revenues are $12 per specimen, charged to the physician or health-care agency who, in turn, bill patients for lab work. Calculate the break-even point for one lab, in specimens per year.

EXERCISE 7-21

At a volume (in a given city) of 5,000 specimens per day, describe the number of operating units (labs), the number of shifts for each unit, the cost structure, and the estimated total profitability.

The Kranken Korrugated, Inc., case is designed to help you develop an understanding of a very complex break-even situation for a manufacturing plant. You may find it helpful to make use of graph paper in charting costs and in visualizing the shape of the cost and revenue functions.

KRANKEN KORRUGATED, INC.*

Ted Jacobs, general manager of the Middletown plant of Kranken Korrugated, wrestled with the financial data presented by Bob Leamons, his accountant. "Bob," Ted said, "why is it that we lose money at eighteen million square feet of corrugated products per month, make money at twenty-two million feet, and then come up with a loss at twenty-four and a half million feet? From all that I learned in my management and accounting courses in college, once we pass the break-even point, we should continue to make a profit . . . and we should make a higher percentage of profit as volume increases. What's going on?"

Bob reflected for a moment, then said, "Well, sir, I'm not sure. I learned the same things, but our results certainly don't reflect what the theory says they should. I'd like to spend some time working on that question . . . if you don't object. We're in the middle of the accounting cycle, so I shouldn't be interrupted too frequently." "Absolutely" said Ted, "I need that information if I'm to do an accurate job of forecasting for the coming year. Can you have some answers in a week?" I think so," said Bob. "Let me take a crack at it and I'll get back to you at least by a week from today."

As Bob was leaving Ted's office, he reflected on the nature of the box business and on the cost system used in Kranken's Middletown plant.

The basic machine used to make the corrugated board (called a corrugator) had a 5-day per week, 40-hour capacity of approximately 30 million feet per month, assuming a very "easy" mix of orders, a mix that maximized operating rates and minimized slowdowns and stoppages for machine setup and/or order changes. A more workable "maximum" was a figure of about 26 million feet per month, based on the typical pattern of orders received by the plant.

The other equipment used to manufacture boxes included slitters, printer-slotters, and closing machines (folder-gluers, folder-tapers, and stitchers). Although an unusual mix of orders might permit this equipment to produce at a 30-million-square-foot-per-month basis, 26 million feet also served as a practical maximum.

From his own cost data, Bob developed the following information of the typical mix of orders for Middletown:

Sales	$2,850,000 per year
Volume	244,635,000 square feet per year
Materials Cost	$1,795,500 per year
Direct-Labor Cost	$600,000 per year
Indirect-Labor Cost	$189,500 per year
Corporate Overhead	$80,000 per year
Factory Overhead	$100,000 per year

* This case was prepared by the author.

At this volume, the plant operated at just under two full shifts of production, 5 days per week. Capacity figures obtained from Henry (Hank) Shekelton, the production manager, were based on the typical mix. Hank's estimate was approximately 14 million square feet for one shift, about 20.5 million square feet for two shifts, and about 26 million square feet for all shifts. Hank said that the lower rate of production for the second and third shifts was the result of the inability of customers to receive shipments at night, the lack of finished goods storage in the plant, and (given the fast production cycle . . . 30 to 50% of orders had less than 3-day lead times) a lack of suitable matchups to make efficient corrugator runs.

Hank, when asked about production costs, said that labor cost averaged 5 cents per 1,000 square feet (MSF) higher for the second shift and 11 cents per MSF higher for the third shift. In addition, higher scrap rates on the second and third shifts caused materials costs to be 37 cents per MSF higher than first-shift rates on the second shift and 52 cents per MSF higher than first-shift rates on the third shift.

Factory overhead included about $70,000 for first shift and overall plant overhead, and the remainder for the second shift. Hank said that third-shift overhead would add another $25,000 to the figures shown for the year.

EXERCISE 7–22

From the data presented thus far, calculate and chart on graph paper the fixed and variable cost curves, then total them to develop a total cost function.

After leaving Hank, Bob decided that a discussion with Randolph Twitchell, Kranken's sales manager, might be useful. Randy was considered to be an experienced (15 years) and excellent sales manager, well acquainted with the dynamics of the Middletown market for corrugated boxes. Bob was particularly interested in the dynamics of prices at various levels of volume. Randy told him that the usual competitive forces and customer preferences dominated the market at levels up to a demand for Kranken of about 23 million square feet per month. (Competitors' volume rates were similarly stabilized at a relatively predictable level.) This represented the outer limits of expected volume for the customers with whom Kranken had supplier contracts. Beyond 23 million square feet in volume, Randy said, his salespeople had to begin to actively solicit spot orders for boxes. The spot market in Middletown was dominated by a large food wholesaler and by several shipping companies. These customers preferred to shop the market for low prices, and they typically placed orders at prices 8 to 12% below the price per MSF that was obtained from contract purchasers. Nearly all of Kranken's current volume was shipped to contract purchasers. Thus, Randy explained, although additional volume was readily available, its price was less attractive, and heavy bidding in the spot market resulted in even lower prices than those he had previously mentioned, reaching 15% below contract prices at 27 million square feet and somewhat lower than that at a 30-million-square-foot level.

Bob asked Randy if the cost of the spot-market business was less than that of contract business. Randy said that it might be if production runs could be lengthened, but that the spot buyers didn't purchase larger quantities, a strategy designed to keep the competitive bidding active. Thus, costs would closely approximate the structure now found in the business produced and sold under supplier contracts.

EXERCISE 7–23

Calculate the revenue function for Kranken Korrugated—draw the revenue function on the chart prepared for Exercise 7–22—up to a volume of 30 million square feet per month.

EXERCISE 7–24

Calculate break-even point(s).

After leaving Randy, Bob decided to discuss the possibility of exploring a project he had heard discussed in casual conversation among managerial personnel. The project involved a $350,000 expenditure for a plant warehouse building, with associated equipment located next to the present shipping area and, thus, directly accessible to the end of production lines. The proposed warehouse would permit expanding second- and third-shift operations by providing a staging warehouse for goods produced at night for shipment and made ready in daytime hours. The presence of this warehouse would involve the following additional expenses:

Depreciation	$10,000 per year
Heat, Light, Power, Taxes	$15,000 per year
Manpower: 2 employees per shift, all shifts, @ $10,000 each	$60,000 per year

It was expected that this warehouse facility would permit expansion of the second shift to reach a volume level of 25 million feet for two shifts and a three-shift volume of 34 million square feet per month.

EXERCISE 7–25

Adjust the cost and revenue structures as needed, then calculate the effect of adding the warehouse on break-even points and profitability. Should Bob recommend that the company spend the $350,000?

ANSWERS TO SELECTED EXERCISES

Exercise 7–1

$210,000 × 1.15	= $241,500
$2.86 × 1.21	= $3.46
$1.60 × 1.10	= $1.76
Total Variable Cost	= $5.22/cask

$$\frac{\$241{,}500}{\$10.25 - \$5.22} = 48{,}012 \text{ casks per year}$$

or 4,001 casks per month

Question *Preceding* Exercise 7–9

At 8 units, 256 man-hours
At 32 units, 163.84 man-hours

Exercise 7–13

Selling and Administrative Expenses	$280,000
Factory Overhead	180,000
Shift Related Overhead (one shift)	460,000
Total Fixed Costs	$920,000

Fixed Cost per Month: $920,000/12 = $76,667

Revenue	$17.50
Variable Cost	6.10

Monthly Break-even Point:

$$\frac{\$76{,}667}{\$17.50 - \$6.10} = 6{,}725 \text{ units}$$

8

THE PRODUCT LIFE CYCLE AND THE GENERAL MANAGER

The product life cycle is a concept that has been in use in marketing thinking for a number of years. In graphic form, the life cycle takes the shape seen in Figure 8–1.

In its overall configuration, the life cycle is a reflection of product demand as the product moves from introduction through saturation into obsolescence.

In traditional marketing terms, the life cycle contains four stages:

- Stage 1 Introduction or Innovation
- Stage 2 Growth

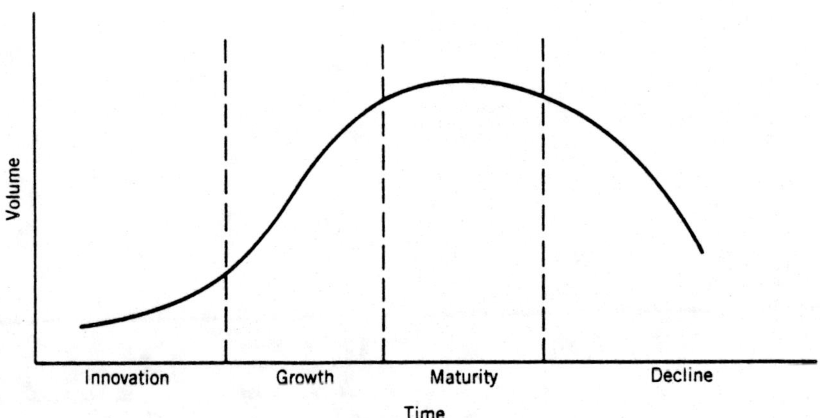

FIGURE 8-1

- Stage 3 Maturity
- Stage 4 Decline

Each stage has implications for marketers. In traditional form, characteristics of products, pricing, channels of distribution, number and size of competitors, and profit margins all differ as products move from stage to stage.

The product-life-cycle concept has most frequently been considered a marketing tool. As we noted earlier, in general management, one rarely deals with issues, problems, or changes in one functional area of business without encountering related problems or issues in other areas of the firm. In this chapter, we will carry the product-life-cycle concept well beyond its typical applications in marketing, and will find that it offers a framework for the much more comprehensive integrated perspective needed by the general manager. More explicitly, we plan to discuss key considerations for marketing, manufacturing (or operations), finance, and research and development in each of the four stages of the classic model.

EXERCISE 8-1

For each of the following products, list the stage you believe the product to be in at the present time:

1. Popcorn ___
2. Home computers ___
3. Cordless telephones ___
4. Solar-powered television ___
5. Spring-wound wristwatches ___
6. Self-programming computers ___

7. Passive-solar homes ___
8. Cabbage-Patch dolls ___
9. Genetically "engineered" organisms ___
10. Claw hammers ___

The *general* model for the product life cycle as a framework for managerial decision making has been the subject of a number of research studies. Its utility as a backdrop for well-reasoned managerial choices is seen in summary form in Table 8–1 and can be found in an extended discussion in Michael E. Porter's *Competitive Strategy*[1]. The product-life-cycle concept, although most helpful as a way of thinking about competitive environments, poses a number of problems, only some of which are readily addressed. Predicting the length of a product's life cycle, for example, requires some insight into the rate of technological development of a particular industry. Consumer taste may be a principal factor in determining the length of successful life for style goods or toys.

In addition, the sense of where one is in terms of a stage of the product's life cycle does not materially aid in determining when the change will begin to take place in that stage as the product moves through the cycle. When does growth begin? When does the shakeout and stabilization process signal the onset of a maturity stage? Ready answers to these questions are not available. We can, however, recognize that there are, in fact, product life cycles of different length and shape, and we can discuss at length the types of considerations that should shape the decisions of general managers who deal with integrative business problems in those product/industry environments.

We will, therefore, concern ourselves with issues of product life per se, issues that cut across all functions and all stages of the product-life-cycle framework. Short-lived, or fad-type, products (hula hoops and pet rocks come to mind) have a cycle *shaped* very much like products that have a long life such as a gas-fired cooking range—but a dramatically compressed cycle. If we were to plot each on a time axis with the same scale, the differences would be very clear (see Figure 8–2).
This, of course, represents a most extreme case of differences in product life. For our purposes, a three-part categorization of product life should serve to guide thinking and decision making as well as extend our thinking beyond that used for the general model seen in Figure 8–1. Products with an expected life of 2 years or less would include unique gift items, style merchandise, and many types of toys. In a second category are products whose commercial life expectancy extends to 10 years before obsolescence, substitutions, or changes in consumer buying patterns result in their demise or near demise. These products might include black-and-white instant-print cameras and film, polyester clothing, electric carving knives, or cordless grass trimmers. Products whose life extends beyond 10 years are common. Blue jeans, large kitchen appliances, household detergents, electric clocks, frozen pizza, and ballpoint pens are examples.

[1] New York: Free Press, 1980, pp. 156–88.

TABLE 8-1
Summary of predictions of product-life-cycle theories

Prediction regarding	*Stage in life cycle*			
	Introduction	*Growth*	*Maturity*	*Decline*
Products and Product Change	Poor quality Product design and development key factors Many different product variations Frequent design changes	Technical and performance variances Reliability very important Product improvements made competitively Good quality	Superior quality Standardization Product change less rapid	Little product differentiation Spotty product quality
Manufacturing and Distribution	Overcapacity Short production runs High-skilled labor Specialized channels of distribution	Undercapacity Move to mass production Scramble for distribution Mass channels	Near optimum capacity Longer production runs Mass channels	Overcapacity Mass production Specialty channels
Buyers and Buyer	High-income buyer	Wider buyer group	Mass market	Customers are

Behavior	Buyer inertia	Consumers will accept uneven quality	Saturation Brand loyalty	sophisticated buyers
Marketing	Very high advertising-to-sales ratio Skimming High marketing costs	High advertising-to-sales ratio Advertising and distribution key for nontech products	Segmentation Service important Efforts to extend life cycle Packaging important Advertising very competitive	Low advertising-to-sales ratio Little marketing
Competition	Few competitors	Many competitors Mergers and casualties	Price competition Shakeout Private brands	Exits Fewer competitors
Risk	High risk	Risks reduced because growth covers mistakes	Cyclicality sets in	
Margins and Profits	High prices and margins Low profits Demand somewhat price inelastic	High profits Moderately high prices	Falling prices Lower profits and margins Stable market structure and prices	Low prices and margins

Source: Adapted from Michael E. Porter, *Competitive Strategy* (New York: Free Press, 1980), pp. 159–61.

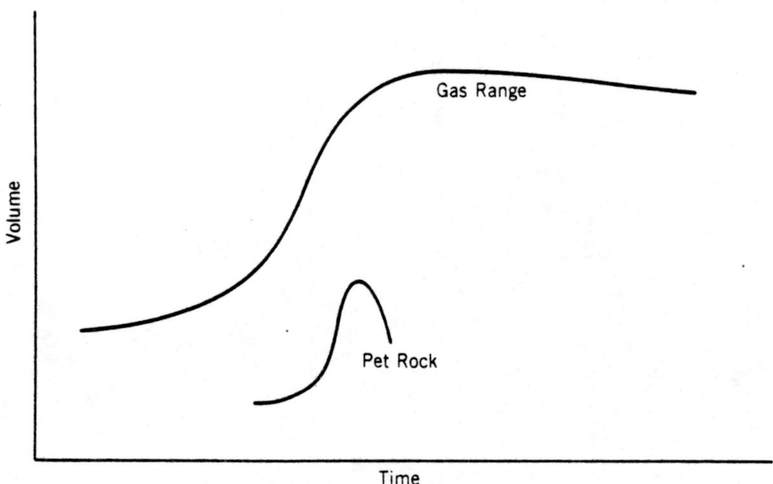

FIGURE 8-2

Each product/customer match, of course, has its own demand pattern. For some products in high demand, the introductory and growth phases are short and growth rates are extreme to the point of seeming explosive. Where a popular new product addresses a large market, volume rises very rapidly to meet overall demand. In other cases, demand builds slowly owing perhaps to the need for customer education or to the breakdown of previous buying habits and patterns. Thus, both the shape and the scale of the product-life-cycle curve are unique to each product.

Figure 8-3 shows several shapes of product life cycles that reflect some of the differences in market size, customer need, or resistance to changes in purchasing. We will deal with short, moderate, and long-lived products in turn. We will consider

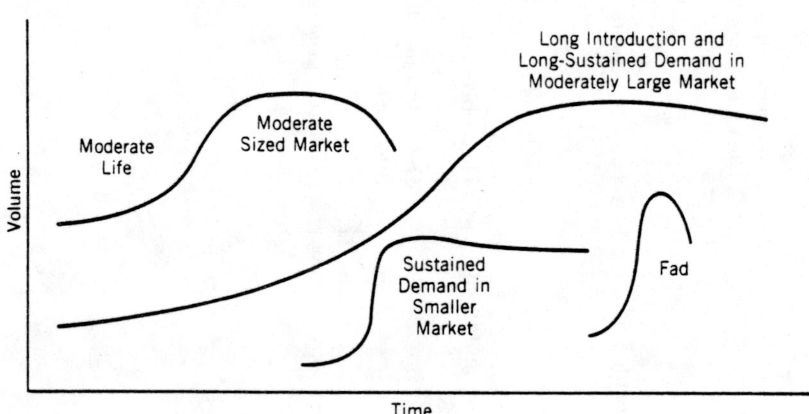

FIGURE 8-3

the product life cycle for each category and will look at the major business functions in each stage of the cycle.

SHORT-LIVED PRODUCTS

Stage 1: Innovation

Products falling in this category are introduced to the market with a very short or nonexistent introductory stage. The product either has appeal or does not. If this product has appeal at all, it should be accepted almost immediately and demand should be both strong and widespread. Because of the instant acceptance of the product, competitors are forced to copy rather than develop competing designs if they wish to attract customers away from the product innovator. In the case of a copyrighted or patented design, competitors may be unable to copy and must suffer as the owner of the copyright legally monopolizes the market for the new product. A toy product of this type is the Holly Hobby line of dolls and doll accessories and toys bearing the Holly Hobby image. A second example is the (illegal) copying of Apple personal computers. Foreign manufacturers shipped copies of patented U.S. designs into the United States as a means of capturing the booming demand for personal computers.

Where designs are not patented or copyrighted, competitors may copy key elements of the design and attempt to capitalize on the attraction of the product introduced by the leader. Again using the toy industry as an example, the introduction of hand-held electronic toys such as OMAR (which at its introduction had a relatively high selling price) spawned the introduction of a wide range of hand-held battery-powered games and toys, many nonelectronic, but all hand-held and electrically powered. For these products, the *concept* of a hand-held electrical/electronic game was more important than the specifics of the game or the patent or copyright that protected the product leader.

Stage 1 for short-lived products, therefore, is not only brief, but it is characterized by attempts at quickly copying leading product features, if possible, and moving quickly into Stage 2. Research and development activity is focused on product intelligence gathering and on rapid adaptation of products to leading design characteristics. Success in this stage is dependent on the ability of adapting a key new element to the largest potential market. Fashion-goods firms are the best examples of this form of product development. Major designers establish a theme or mode that achieves critical acceptance among the knowledgeable. Larger-scale commercial clothing manufacturers, at this point, must adapt the theme or mode to a broad range of garments—keeping the style elements for customer appeal but avoiding the stylistic extremes that might not be desired (or wearable!) by most purchasers.

For purposes of keeping up with, or leading in, style, these manufacturers must adapt the theme, but they must do so in such a way as to convey it to a broader audience. This link in design and/or theme transferability is critical in Stage 1 marketing and product-development work for short-lived products. The spate of products that followed the showing the *Star Wars* series of films offers another example of theme adaptation and transfer. Although the figures and characters were protected by copyright, the *Stars Wars* theme could be found in clothing, toys, glassware, comic books, and a broad range of other children's products.

Stage 2: Growth

For those fortunate enough to own the copyright or patent, the manufacturing problem becomes one of supplying a large demand in a very short time. Several means are available. For manufacturers with extensive resources, the problem is one of conversion of resources and concentration on the product targeted for mass production. Decisions of product-line enrichment are needed in order to convert facilities from the manufacture of less-profitable lines to those of the new star of the line. In other cases, demand is so strong that even large companies cannot fulfill demand in the time needed by consumers. Here, the only way to attempt to satisfy demand is to subcontract manufacture and distribution to other firms, either domestically or worldwide. In this context, it is interesting to note that the designer of the Cabbage-Patch dolls chose to license the product to a major manufacturer and distributor (Coleco) rather than attempting to finance and manage the massive effort required to meet the demand for this spectacularly successful short-lived product.

Marketing short-lived products frequently involves heavy advertising and promotion (to build demand rapidly) and major attention to distribution (to reach the rapidly burgeoning market thus stimulated). The Cabbage-Patch doll craze caused Coleco, the manufacturer and marketer, to devote enormous attention to distribution prior to the holiday season, even to the extent of air-freighting planeloads of dolls from manufacturers in Taiwan and Korea in order to meet customer needs in the U.S. Christmas market. Marketing through established distribution systems can be extremely helpful with short-lived products. Thus, the use of large retail chains or large-scale wholesale distribution companies offers a rapid means of distributing short-lived products to large numbers of high-traffic retail outlets.

Prices typically are high, as marketers capitalize on the novelty nature of the new-product concept and the preemptive position in the marketplace. Given a high price level at the consumer level, attractive discounts can be offered to distributors, thus speeding the movement of the new item to consumers.

Financing the short-lived product can pose problems given the size of the potential demand, the necessity for manufacture and distribution of very large quantities of products for sale, and the risks inherent in marketing products that have a short-lived appeal. Risks are high but so are the potential monetary rewards.

Markups on short-lived products are high (at least initially). The turnaround time for collections of open accounts may require a heavy investment in receivables, inventories of finished goods, and materials needed for manufacture. To whatever extent possible discounts for immediate cash payment can and should be offered and support from suppliers should be solicited. In short, demands for short-term working capital are especially high and all available sources for funds must be tapped to carry the product through the period of peak need.

Stage 3: Maturity

For products in Stage 3, the maturity stage is quite short. Product demand rises quickly, markets saturate rapidly, and residual or secondary demand is relatively low. It is most important, therefore, to assess as accurately as one can, the total demand that is to be expected. First, to fully exploit the demand that does exist and secondly to avoid overmanufacturing and overstocking products for which demand may well not exist in the near future. Because demand drops quickly and does not return, long-term commitments and extensive capital investments (especially investments in highly specialized equipment) are inherently risky and should be avoided.

Stage 4: Decline

Management of the maturity and decline stages requires quite close attention to product demand and a systematic reduction in order or production quantities so that the risk of overstocking is reduced. Contractural arrangements with subcontractors need to be written to permit reductions in quantities or cessation of operations on short notice.

Similarly, collection of open accounts should be monitored closely, as should payments to contractors. As the cycle winds down, both payables and receivables should drop in a consistent and proportionate manner so that resources can be shifted to products at other stages in the cycle.

"HOW ABOUT 'THE MOGUL MASTER'?"*

Tom Parkinson was thinking about the new snow toy he had just designed and built for his children. It was, at the moment, the object of attention of a long, noisy line of youngsters, each waiting for a turn on the snow-packed hillside opposite the Parkinson home. The device the children were riding so enthusiastically was simply a sturdy, well-braced wooden seat mounted at low-chair-height atop a short, stainless-steel-shod ski. With a bit of practice, the children balanced themselves on the seat and flew down the hill, bouncing into the air as they sailed over the irregular surface of the hillside. Some fell off, but the hand grips placed under the edges of the seat enabled them to tumble into the snow easily without undue danger of coming into contact with the toy itself.

As the noise of the playing children drifted across the street, Tom thought, "The kids really seem to like that gadget—suppose I made these toys for sale, wonder if I could turn a profit at it?"

That night he talked it over with his wife, Shelly, and considered what might be involved. In his review, several factors were weighed. First, he had about $50,000 in marketable stocks and bonds that he'd salted away for retirement. Second, he'd recently become disenchanted

* This case was prepared by the author.

with his job as a representative for a hardware manufacturer and had contemplated a change. Third, although he didn't have extensive experience in the field, he was well acquainted with manufacturing methods and processes and had developed a number of friendships among managers in a wide range of manufacturing plants.

As Tom and Shelly talked, the idea began to take shape, "Suppose we put our savings into this toy and began to manufacture it—could it work? Could we make a go of it?" They decided to explore the idea and Tom began to collect information from manufacturers and toy retailers.

Manufacturers were reluctant to undertake the project, primarily because of the low (to them) volume of manufacture and the high cost of setup needed for short production runs. Their cost figures were:

Quantity	*Set-up Cost*	*Materials*	*Labor Cost*
1–20	$ 85	$4.00/unit	$3.50/unit
21–50	$ 85	$3.75/unit	$3.30/unit
51–100	$ 85	$3.60/unit	$3.10/unit
101–200	$125	$3.05/unit	$2.40/unit
201–500	$125	$2.90/unit	$2.25/unit

Retailers were also cautious. Untried toys were a big risk, they said. "They take up floor or shelf space, absorb capital, and have little chance of success without advertising and promotion." "Did you plan on advertising?" they asked Tom.

Tom described the delight of his neighborhood's children to retailers and showed snapshots of children at play with the new toy. After getting assurances from Tom that advertising would be used to encourage sales, several retailers said they'd try his product if he could get the new toys delivered before late January, the peak of the snow season, but now only weeks away. For the customers most likely to be interested, they said, the toy should sell at $19.95 to $29.95, but not higher. Markups to retailers were customarily 50% of retail price.

The considered opinion of the retailers was that if the product caught hold at all, it would be a big seller. Three retailers placed orders for 5 toys each, but they asked Tom for a limited distribution arrangement, restricting him to selling only to these three stores in his home city. With a high rate of success, they estimated sales at 50 units per store for the remainder of the season, with moderate success, 20 units; and with a low rate of sales success, 5 units. They recommended that Tom invest at least $5,000 in newspaper advertising in local and regional newspapers to support sales.

Tom then considered a broader market appeal, and reflected on the seven major metropolitan areas he had traveled in his work as a manufacturer's representative. Each was in the 100,000-to-500,000 population range. Tom estimated that he could identify at least four excellent retail outlets in each city and believed that each was capable of selling twice the volume of the retailers from whom he had received orders in his hometown.

As Tom and Shelly reviewed the situation, they puzzled over the whole project. Should they undertake it? If so, should they sell only in their hometown? Should they go for broke and try for the seven city areas? Finally, they needed a name for the toy. Shelly, thinking of the bumps called moguls in skiing, said "How about Mogul Master?" and the name stuck.

EXERCISE 8–2

- Calculate total manufacturing cost and unit cost at 45 units of production. (Check your answer at the end of the chapter.)
- Calculate total manufacturing and unit cost at 60 units of production.
- Homework Problem A: Prepare on graph paper a plot of unit costs for the volume range beginning at 20 units and ending at 100 units. Calculate and plot in increments of 10 units.
- Homework Problem B: Prepare on graph paper a plot of unit costs for the volume range beginning at 150 units and ending at 500 units. Calculate and plot in increments of 25 units.

EXERCISE 8–3

- What is your belief about the likely life of this product? Long, moderate, or short lived? (See comments at end of chapter)
- Given the answer above, what is the likely life of the product *as far as the Parkinsons are concerned?*

EXERCISE 8–4

- Calculate costs, revenues, and gross profits for sales to three stores at maximum, moderate, and low sales volumes.
- Calculate costs, revenues, and gross profits for sales to 31 stores at maximum, moderate, and low sales volumes. (28 stores in the larger cities, three stores in Tom's hometown.)
- Homework Problem: From your answer to the second question on 31 stores, estimate the capital needed to fund sales at the moderate level. Shipments to retailers are scheduled as one third of the order on January 15, one third on February 1, and one third on February 15. Manufacturers require 15 days to manufacture and deliver and payment of one-half the cost of the order when ordering, with payment of the balance 30 days after shipment and delivery. (Note: Each order must be costed separately where more than a single setup will be needed by the manufacturer. The retailers from whom Tom had received orders were prompt in meeting their bills on net 30-day terms according to the bank's credit reference service.
- (Hint: Work *backward* from delivery dates to determine a payment schedule for manufacturers; work *forward* from delivery dates to calculate cash receipts sched-

ules from retailers. Then, summarize over the manufacturing and selling period to determine the peak capital requirements.

- Can Tom do it?
- If so—how?
- If not—why not?
- What remedies can you suggest?

If his new product sold at maximum volume, Tom thought that he should consider manufacturing the product himself. His knowledge of manufacturing companies suggested that gross profits on manufactured goods of this type and in these volumes was approximately 10% of manufacturer's selling price. Tom and his acquaintances in manufacturing estimated that equipment and buildings for manufacturing could be purchased for approximately $250,000.

EXERCISE 8-5

- Should Tom attempt to find the financing needed to buy the equipment and building? Explain.

A third alternative to be considered by Tom is that of licensing. A major toy manufacturer has on occasion acquired exclusive manufacturing and marketing rights to new toy concepts at a rate of 1% of retail sales.

EXERCISE 8-6

- How many units would have to be sold to generate $50,000 per year in royalty income? (See answer at the end of the chapter.)
- Estimate the number of major cities (100,000 to 500,000 population) to which distribution would be needed in order for Tom to earn $50,000 per year at *moderate* volume? At *maximum* volume?
- Would you advise Tom to seriously consider licensing a manufacturer and marketer? Explain.

PRODUCTS WITH MODERATELY LONG LIVES: 2 TO 10 YEARS

For products with moderately long lives, competition is a much more significant factor . . . at all stages of the product life cycle. Each stage of the cycle is more protracted in time, and competitors have more time to plan, design, and implement competitive actions than is the case with short-lived products. In the innovation stage, patent or copyright protection is still available, but competitors have more opportunity to find alternative designs or features that will have competitive appeal.

Stage 1: Innovation

In the innovation stage, marketing experts have the opportunity to conduct market research on product acceptability and to educate customers in anticipation of larger-scale production, thus preparing a market for product presentation. More effective marketers may thus be able to improve their competitive position, even with products whose characteristics are not superior. It has been said that the IBM corporation's attention to customer education in data processing applications has been materially helpful to their company's sales staff, aiding sales even in those instances where the company's products were technically inferior to those of major competitors. Similarly, their attention to customer-oriented software development and extensive advertising in national media prepared the market for their products and resulted in nearly instant success for their personal computer, even though the product was introduced later than market leaders and at a significantly higher price.

Missionary sales work is called for at this stage in order to explore customer interest, to acquire information on customer needs and buying patterns, and to obtain those critical first sales. An important element in this type of sales work is customer education, informing and educating customers about the company and its products as well as the specific product/application being introduced. Publicity can also be used to describe product advantages and applications well in advance of the actual introduction. In the computer technology field, two examples come to mind. In the first, the Mostek Corporation's new product, called the compu-chip, was the subject of a feature-length newspaper article months ahead of its availability. Its technical features were described as well as its possible applications, advantages over current products, and approximate cost. In a second case, Coleco heavily advertised its remarkably low-priced Adam home computer/printer system well before its introduction in the marketplace, stimulating demand for the product and for Coleco's stock. When news of production delays and quality problems with early shipments reached the stock market, stock prices sagged and unhappy investors were extremely critical of Coleco's management, claiming they had been misled by the early promises.

Providing attentive service to early customers is extremely important in establishing customers confidence, in developing product loyalties, and in obtaining key information about product problems, advantages, and needed changes.

As Stage 1 progresses and as information accumulates on product acceptability and market potential, marketers need to begin the process of planning for long-term marketing attention to the rapidly expanding markets found and developed in Stage 2. Expansion plans should be readied for implementation and should include anticipated channels of distribution, recruitment plans, and the product features to be emphasized in sales and promotional efforts. Implementation should begin when marketing research indicates that customer acceptance is strong and when growth in demand is likely to be sustained.

Production or operations management during the introductory stage must address two major concerns: (1) rapid adaptation to changes in product design brought about by the wishes of present or potential customers and (2) adaptation of product and process design to achieve production or operations efficiencies in anticipation of the need for the higher volume and lower costs needed during the next stages of the product life cycle. Technical product superiority or marketing appeal may have to be shaded to achieve product cost efficiencies, and sound judgement is needed to deal adequately with the tradeoffs in values inherent in these choices.

In operations, flexibility is a critical component. Employees' versatility is essential, and capital equipment should permit easy setup and easy adjustment to meet customer needs for product/service modifications and small-order quantities. As early indicators of product acceptance and market demand are observed, operations managers must anticipate the move to Stage 2 by planning for larger-scale, more-specialized operations with more-specialized tasks and lower-skilled employees. Supervisors and key employees from Stage 1 will serve as a cadre of trainers and supervisors for the expanded operations expected in Stage 2. Personnel specialists should begin planning the recruitment, selection, and training of prospective employees.

Research and development, as we have just seen, has two distinct paths, and is directed toward applications and modifications rather than basic research or the development of fundamentally new products. Market research on customer needs, interests, and market depth is one path; product and process-design work aimed at improving the efficiency and cost performance of operations is another.

Requirements for financial resources during Stage 1 are relatively short-term in nature. Cash is needed to provide support for extensive market research and customer education. Money is also needed for engineering studies, manufacturing analyses, and product-design work. Profits are very low, and Stage 1 products may generate losses. The risky nature of unproven products may obviate the possibility of borrowing, and the firm may have to rely entirely on owner-provided funds for its financial resources. It is readily apparent that with the heavy demands for money for operating expenses and the lack of externally obtained funds, cash management is an extremely important element at this stage of the life cycle.

Capital expenditures need not be a major concern in Stage 1 because product acceptance is not certain. Construction or acquisition of large-scale facilities would be unwise, as would accumulation of large inventories of raw materials and finished goods.

When market size is established, and when product acceptance begins to be sustained, financial management attention must shift to the *planning* needed to acquire capital and employ it in long-term assets to anticipate the enlargement in scale of operations that will take place in Stage 2.

Stage 2: Growth

As Stage 2 begins, physical and technical differences in products are frequently apparent. These serve as the principal means of competitively differentiating products in the minds of customers. Marketers in Stage 2 must seek out the characteristics of products that customers are likely to persist in expecting as demand continues. These product features form the core of the generic "standard" product that will emerge from Stage 2 and enter the maturity stage.

Marketers are very active in stimulating sales and delivering products to rapidly expanding markets in Stage 2. Distribution channels suitable to larger markets are desired, as are promotional forms well suited to large audiences. The rate of growth in Stage 2 for products with moderately long lives is not as rapid as it was for short-lived products. Marketers may choose to develop their own distribution system and may integrate forward as a means of maintaining closer control over marketing while generating greater profit. Similarly, the slower rate of market growth permits the use of push-type promotion, should the choice be made to use existing distributors.

Price competition in the latter part of Stage 2 is intense. Products become physically more similar, and producers of less-popular products may attempt to salvage market position by competing through reductions in prices. Firms that have products with popular features and that have solved the technical manufacturing problems will be able to hold costs down to levels that will sustain modest profits even at the lowered price level. Competitors with less-popular products will suffer from shrinking markets and will be unable to cover costs. Those that have not developed effective operations systems will incur uncompetitively high costs and may suffer financial losses, even to the point of withdrawal from competition.

This shakeout of the uncompetitive has been seen in recent years as numerous manufacturers left the market for pocket calculators. As the market exploded in Stage 2, product characteristics, keyboard styles, and display features all became quite similar. Prices dropped dramatically, and large numbers of suppliers began to drop out of competition, leaving the field to a limited number of large manufacturers capable of mass manufacturing and mass marketing these now-standardized products at significantly reduced profit margins.

A similar process is now underway in the home computer industry. At this time, the "standard" home personal computer (to be used for applications other than entertainment) could be defined by describing it as IBM PC compatible with RAM capacity of 256K, a keyboard styled after the IBM selectric with a keypad, and disc storage capacity of 300 to 500K, and with two discs. Although specifications are both rising and becoming more standardized, prices have been reduced dramatically by several suppliers and a shakeout is now underway.

For operations managers, Stage 2 presents enormous challenges. As demand expands, operations managers must not only satisfy current customers to achieve and hold customer loyalty, but also must plan for, and implement, expansion in facilities, equipment, and personnel. In addition, as standardization of product characteristics occurs, operations managers must seek out techniques to manufacture products efficiently at higher and higher rates of production.

Success in managing growth is critical at this stage. Planning, capital investment analysis, purchasing, and equipment installation must all be managed effectively as operations expand to meet demand. In addition, the recruitment, selection, training, and deployment of personnel are important as scale of operations increases. As the scale becomes larger and technology becomes more highly specialized, the required skill level declines as the scope of each task is reduced. The most effective managers of operations recognize this and adjust task requirements, skill levels, and wage rates accordingly, thereby taking advantage of a principal benefit of larger-scale production technologies.

Financing in Stage 2 calls for implementing the plans for financial expansion developed in Stage 1. The growth in sales and operations must be supported by commensurate increases in financial resources. All available forms of financial resources should be employed but in ways that result in the development of a well-formulated financial structure. Profit generation during Stage 2 is fairly strong for firms that can survive the competitive shakeout. The progressive strengthening of the equity base through accumulations of retained earnings offers a foundation upon which a structure of short-, moderate-, and long-term debt can be added.

Although supplier credit and bank loans can be of considerable help in supporting working capital needs, long-term capital sources such as long-term loans, mortgages, debentures, and stock sales should be employed to provide funds for permanent working capital and for land and depreciable assets. Demonstrated growth and continued profitability in the face of intensified competition make the surviving competitors in Stage 2 appear exciting and attractive investment prospects to investors and creditors.

Given the longer life (2 to 10 years) of the product, success patterns established in Stage 2 offer a stronger basis for estimating financial success. Debt loads, consequently, are higher than in the more risky Stage 1. In additional, fixed assets offer collateral security for lenders to the successful Stage 2 firm. Dividend policy in Stage 2 should be restrictive, owing primarily to the need for funds and the necessity of developing the equity base upon which the debt structure can be built.

Stage 3: Maturity

In Stage 3, the maturity phase, products with moderately long lives encounter numerous problems in each functional area. In marketing, the number of competitors is reduced because of the shakeout that occurs in Stage 2. Similarly, the standardization of products in Stage 2 has reduced tangible, or objective, product differences. Profit margins have been squeezed by competitive pressures, and large-scale marketing and distribution are the norm.

Given that product differences are minimal and that prices are held under closely competitive scrutiny, marketing efforts for current sales emphasize product differentiation, personal sales attention and effort, and customer services. Market research is directed toward the establishment of intangible product characteristics or attributes held in the minds of consumers. The "Pepsi Generation" promotional campaign is one example of a marketing attempt to associate youth, athletic life-styles, and slim bodies with the consumption of soft drinks. "The Marlboro Man" has been used for years as a way of associating a masculine, Western life-style with the smoking of Marlboro cigarettes.

Product-development work is similarly directed toward improving the product characteristics now seen as most significant by consumers. Market intelligence is needed to monitor competitor actions. Marketing managers seek to hold and gain market share in a relatively closed market, capitalizing, where possible, on lapses by competitors. New markets and new applications for products are additional objectives of market research in Stage 3. Market research is also directed at identifying new products as replacements for the current mature star, in anticipation of changes in customer tastes and the onset of product decline.

For operations managers, Stage 3 represents the challenge of scale carried to its extremes. Mass production is the norm, and massive capital investment in technology is justified on the basis of the cost savings accumulated by means of small savings over large numbers of units of production. Operating leverage is high in Stage 3, and fixed costs are covered by attention to operating as close to full capacity as possible. Operations of 24 hours per day, 7 days per week are not uncommon in the production of Stage 3 products. Operations managers must be prepared in this stage to work as close to the capacity of machinery and work force as is feasible and to maximize the utilization of their equipment. Long production runs are desirable because setup time and cost are minimized and because automated processes can be fine-tuned to achieve high production while meeting acceptable quality standards. Attention to the appropriateness of quality standards is important in Stage 3. Achieving a quality standard higher than that demanded by the marketplace results in cost penalties and slower production, factors that are not covered by market prices. Cost accounting and standard costs of manufacturing are most helpful to the operations manager in the process of controlling the cost of operations. In Stage 3, the tools of management science are often quite helpful in balancing production facilities, maximizing the utilization of equipment or personnel, and in minimizing costs of materials and equipment through the calculation of economic lot sizes and/or economic order quantities.

Engineering research is often used to assist in the fine-tuning process. Product flow studies, product cost studies, and industrial engineering analyses can help to achieve lower costs, higher rates of production, or both. As product life reaches the decline stage, careful analysis of capital equipment life is needed to avoid an accumulation of equipment designed to produce merchandise that is no longer marketable. As before, operation at the edges of capacity is needed, but at this part of Stage 3, the concern is operation within the existing life of equipment that may be completely worn out, or nearly so. Conversion plans can be readied, so that facilities can be shifted to other uses and the equipment either scrapped, converted to other uses, or sold on the used-equipment market. As the product moves to Stage 4, contingency plans need to be developed to anticipate the transfer, retraining, layoff, or termination of employees currently working on Stage 3 products.

Financing in Stage 3 is dramatically different than in earlier stages. Profit generation is high and capital needs tend to have been satisfied as the firm moved into Stage 3. In the terms of the Boston Consulting Group (BCG), the firm may be seen as a cash cow, generating excess funds that may be used in a variety of needs. Dividends are expected by shareholders and cash may be used for that purpose. Capital equipment may have a relatively long life, so that cash requirements for replacement may be low while.noncash expenses for depreciation continue to shelter earnings from taxation. Some firms have drained cash from Stage 3 operations to support growing or developing divisions, in a pattern consistent with the BCG strategic framework we will discuss in Chapter 15. Industries that have made this a consistent practice over many years have found themselves unable to meet capital needs as technology changes and, in effect, have drained away their means of meeting competition. Hospitals are one general type of organization that has drained away "profit" to hold down the cost of medical care to patients only to find that they do not have the capital funding needed to pay for state-of-the-art technologies such as the CAT scanner.

The management of cash receipts, therefore, is a major responsibility of financial managers in Stage 3. As the stage continues, cash must be employed productively and, where possible, placed in investment forms that permit conversion to cash as large funding requirements dictate. Stockholder needs must be addressed, but sound judgment and strong will may be needed to avoid dissipating surplus funds during periods of high cash generation.

The moderately long-lived product poses additional problems for financial managers in that they must monitor the impact of the demise or decline in demand for their product on the financial operations of the company. They not only must be concerned about the investment in capital assets mentioned earlier, but also must be alert to the effect of scaled-down operations on debt-interest payments, repayment schedules, and expectations of stockholders for regular dividends.

Stage 4: Decline

As the moderately long-lived product enters Stage 4, the firm must alter its pattern of operations significantly. As volume declines, the scale of manufacturing must be reduced, equipment shifted to other use, dismantled, scrapped, or sold. Layoff or discharge procedures must be instituted to reduce nonproductive labor cost and clerical and managerial employees must be transferred or furloughed.

Marketing managers must examine the costs and benefits of each distribution system to assure that the costs are adequately covered by the value of products sold through those outlets. Low-cost promotion and distribution systems may be used to replace the more-intensive (and expensive!) ones in order to improve marketing cost and profitability performance. For example, mail order or telephone sales may replace personal contact or call frequencies may be reduced to justify continued distribution in low-volume markets. When volume levels become so low as to raise the issue of product discontinuation, marketing managers may consider closeout or clearance sales to empty their inventories of products no longer marketable at profitable levels. Here, too, personnel may undergo transfer, layoff, or furlough to avoid incurring excessive costs. Capital equipment such as salesperson's autos, demonstration equipment, and other depreciable materials associated with marketing the discontinued product may be reallocated, scrapped, or sold.

Financial managers are intimately involved, of course, in the disposition of any capital equipment, and the recovery of capital funds for use elsewhere. In addition, financial managers must monitor the winding-down process to assure that inventories, accounts receivable, and other current assets do not exceed prudent limits. Raw materials inventories not needed for production need to be sold for original value or salvage and accounts receivable must be monitored to avoid unduly high bad debt losses. Outstanding indebtedness should be retired as soon as reasonable in order to avoid an overly burdensome cash management problem caused by low cash receipts and an undiminished need for coverage for interest payments, debt-repayment schedules, and stockholder dividends.

One example of a company that has successfully managed Stage 4 for some of its products is the Boeing Aircraft Company. Boeing's employment in the late 1960s exceeded 120,000, but it dropped to less than 40,000 in 2 years as Boeing's orders for both military and civilian aircraft products dropped very suddenly. When a product line is discontinued, the company's manufacturing facilities are stripped of everything associated with the production of a product line. Huge "garage sales" are conducted to help in clearing miscellaneous items and in converting assets to cash. When finished, the clearance process has emptied massive buildings, liquidated assets, and placed employees on a nonpaid standby basis in anticipation of new orders or new products.

In the following section, we will examine the product life cycle for those sold by a company that supplies specialized fabricated metal products and services the agricultural and construction industries.

SHARPCO, INC.

I want to keep the company profitable, of course. There was a time when I wanted Sharpco to grow as big as it possibly could. Now, though, I place more importance on having some time for my family and myself and on my own health. I suppose I would like to see the company get to where it would furnish a good living for me and my family and only require half the time and energy it demands now. I would like for us to be a little

Sharpco, Inc. case is by Arthur Sharplin of Northeast Louisiana University.

more respected, too. Our competitors are pretty big boys—the Caterpillar dealers and the Fiat Allis dealer—and they have big fine buildings and nice machinery and a good deal of prestige. That doesn't bother me as much as it once did, but I would like to see us upgrade our public image a bit.

The speaker was James Sharplin. He had just assumed full responsibility for the company he had managed for nine years by buying out the interest of his brothers Art and Jerry. Although he felt equal to the task, he knew the complexity of managing a small business and expected that the days ahead would be consumingly difficult. Neither of his brothers had worked full time in the firm for several years, but they had always been there when James needed them. Art had taken care of financial matters, making credit arrangements, establishing accounting controls, and so on, and Jerry had provided technical expertise as well as sound business judgment. Like James, Jerry and Art had often pitched in as working supervisors on particularly difficult or urgent jobs. In the past, the three had made all major decisions as a team, with Art acting as catalyst and coordinator. Now, James would have final responsibility. James knew that he could still call on his brothers—they were not leaving the area—but all three felt that it would be best if he could be fairly independent.

COMPANY OPERATIONS

Sharpco is located on the outskirts of Monroe, Louisiana. The Sharpco plant is about 400 feet from Interstate Highway 20 and is clearly visible from that major east/west thoroughfare, but the nearest interchange is about three fourths of a mile away. Sharpco, Inc., is engaged in four related businesses.

First, the company provides parts and service for crawler tractor undercarriages. The undercarriage for a crawler tractor consists of the heavy chainlike track, that substitutes for the rubber tires on conventional tractors along with the related sprockets and rollers that keep the track in alignment and in the firm contact with the ground. Crawler tractors typically operate in sand, gravel, and dirt; consequently, they wear away all portions of the undercarriage rather rapidly. A typical undercarriage will last for perhaps 1,500 operating hours before it must be completely reconditioned. Usually, this involves building up the metal surfaces that are in contact with one another, replacement of the pins and bushings that hold the tracks together, and the repair of breaks and cracks that occur as a result of vibration and stress. A typical undercarriage reconditioning job may result in a customer billing of \$2,500 to \$8,000. In addition to performing the repairs, Sharpco sells a wide array of undercarriage parts, track chains (called rails), rollers, idlers, and sprockets to customers who do the repair work themselves.

Second, Sharpco designs, fabricates, and sells tree-cutting blades for crawler tractors and digging buckets for backhoes and excavators. The company also makes a number of other specialized tools designed to be pushed or pulled by heavy tractors. This includes such tools as rice-field leveling blades and land-clearing rakes, which are used to push timber into piles for burning once it has been cut. All of these items are fabricated partly from extra-high-strength steel, using specialized welding materials and techniques.

Third, Sharpco provides custom welding services to commercial, agricultural, and industrial customers. This includes repair and fabrication of all kinds of steel items both at Sharpco's plant and at customer locations.

Finally, Sharpco cuts and sells various steel plates and shapes, commonly called angles, rounds, channels, flats, and beams.

HISTORICAL SKETCH

In 1972, at the urging of his brothers Art and Jerry, James Sharplin left his job as welding and undercarriage shop manager for a major Caterpillar dealership and accepted their offer to join them in their construction business. The Sharplins were engaged in industrial and plant maintenance contracting and, in addition, had completed a number of small concrete, steel, and mechanical projects for the U.S. Air Force. After just a few months, James, Jerry, and Art decided to build a shop at the present site of the Sharpco plant and to go into the steel-fabrication business. Only $33,500 in initial investment was available and much of this was in machinery and equipment contributed by the Sharplins. By personally signing the mortgage, the Sharplins along with their wives, were able to buy the necessary land and building materials. The initial 49-foot-by-49-foot shop building consisted of a galvanized, corrugated metal (roofing tin) exterior over a frame made of used steel pipe and pine lumber. Art, Jerry, and James erected the building themselves during breaks between construction jobs. A portable construction shack, purchased for $450, served as the shop office. Because of the shortage of funds, the only equipment available was welding machines, cutting torches, and handtools previously owned by the three brothers.

Sharpco opened for business in early 1973. From the beginning, James managed the shop and Jerry and Art spent most of their time on other endeavors. Sales were slow at first, with the construction company giving Sharpco several small fabrication contracts and a few customers bringing welding jobs to the shop.

Being thinly capitalized, Sharpco could not afford a single unprofitable year. The first year saw profits in the range of $4,000 to $5,000. This was only possible, James says, because he took little salary and "used every method known to man to keep expenses down and sales up."

Because of his experience with the Caterpillar distributor, James was known in the northeastern Louisiana area as something of an expert in the design and construction of large tree-cutting blades for land-clearing tractors.

During 1974, drawing on his previous experience, James designed and built several of these blades for northern Louisiana land-clearing contractors. The blades ranged in weight from 2 tons to about 8 tons and sold in the range of $4,000 to $12,000 each. They turned out to be much more profitable than other types of fabrication. Sales and profits improved in 1974. In addition, a permanent office was added that year.

By the beginning of 1975, Sharpco had a work force of five men in addition to James. During 1975, Art worked about half-time at Sharpco, managing the office and buying and selling steel, a sideline he had gotten Sharpco into in late 1974. Jerry, the most expert of the three in the area of general fabrication, spent about one third of his time at Sharpco. During this entire period, all three brothers did a great deal of physical work in the shop. Also during 1975, a 60-foot-by-75-foot addition was made to the shop building.

The year 1976 was a banner year for Sharpco. Sales grew to $574,000 and profits, after reasonable salaries for the owners, were $40,510. Appendix A includes financial statements for 1976–81.

During 1977, it became possible to take advantage of James's expertise and reputation in the area of crawler tractor undercarriage repair. Sharpco purchased several large machines, which gave the company the capability of repairing undercarriages. From that point on, undercarriage work contributed a major part of Sharpco revenues and profits.

Art had completed his MBA degree in 1973 and moved away to Baton Rouge in 1976 for the purpose of completing his doctoral degree. While in Baton Rouge, he commuted back and forth to Monroe every week or two to consult with James and to help in the management of the firm. James recalls that this was a particularly difficult period for him; but, because he knew Art had long dreamed of becoming a college professor, he didn't object. From 1977 onward, Jerry was totally involved in his construction activity and only infrequently consulted with James or worked at Sharpco.

In 1978, sales exceeded $1 million for the first time. Although steel fabrication revenue declined after 1977, the company prospered and book value net worth exceeded $250,000 by the end of 1980. It was at this point that Art, having completed his doctoral degree and having accepted a full-time professorship at the university in Monroe, suggested to James that James become the sole owner of Sharpco. In the winter of 1981, James traded real-estate holdings and a small amount of cash for the Sharpco stock held by his brothers.

ORGANIZATION

Exhibit 1 gives some idea of the organizational relationships that exist at Sharpco; however, like most small companies, Sharpco has no formal organization chart and all members of the organization routinely interact in ways not suggested by Exhibit 1. For example, Jerry Thompson often assigns work to Peggy Turnage and James Sharplin often bypasses both of them and deals directly with workers. Peggy Turnage is a very trusted employee and frequently accepts customer orders for work and assigns work directly to the welders, operators, and mechanics. Several of the workers are particularly knowledgeable about certain kinds of jobs and certain kinds of equipment. Without significant formality, they often take charge in their areas of expertise, acting as temporary working supervisors.

PERSONNEL

Sharpco employs seventeen persons (see Exhibit 1). Wages are partly based upon an infrequent survey of wages of similar workers in the Monroe area. There is a fairly standard medical-care plan and a week's vacation is given after the first year. Only the assistant shop manager, Jerry Thompson, is allowed a two-week vacation. The workers average about 47 hours a week.

FINANCING

The initial equity investment in the firm was only $33,500. By 1981, this had been supplemented by about $250,000 in retained earnings. Machinery and equipment purchased over the years were financed through borrowing from a small country bank in Delhi, Louisiana. Vehicles and individual pieces of machinery were financed using individual installment notes. All notes were personally endorsed by the Sharplins. Recent financial statements are included in Appendix A.

MARKETING

Sharpco's 1981 advertising expense is expected to be $21,000. This is being spent on a combination of direct mail (15% of total), newspaper (10%), and yellow-page advertising (75%). James Sharplin and Jerry Thompson frequently make sales calls on customers within about 50 miles of Monroe. Primary reliance for advertising, though, is upon word-of-mouth. According to James Sharplin:

> *We make the best land clearing equipment in the South. Our ability to do critical high-strength welding and fabrication is second to none. We also offer high quality undercarriage parts and service at reasonable prices. The word gets around.*

About one third of the steel items Sharpco

EXHIBIT 1
Organization Chart

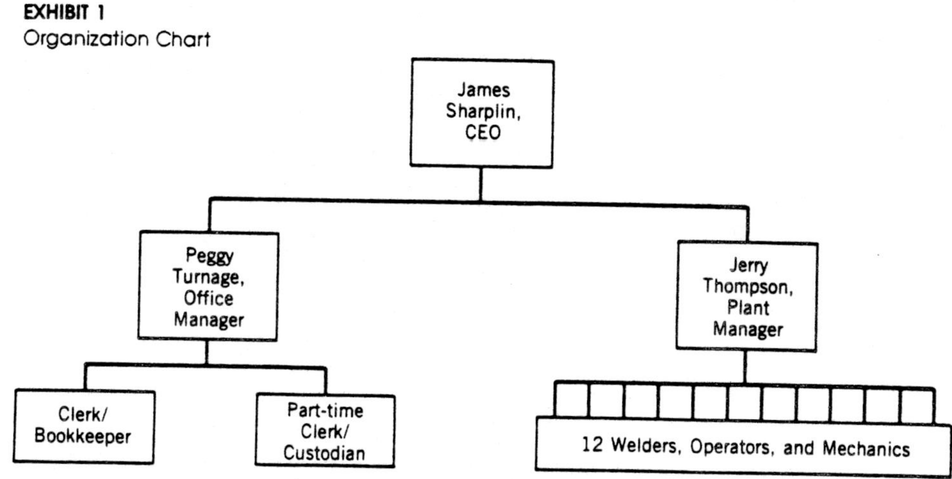

manufacturers are sold to equipment dealers, who resell them. The remainder of Sharpco's sales are at retail.

INTERVIEW WITH JAMES SHARPLIN

The following interview was conducted at 5:30 A.M. on October 16, 1981. The interview is not verbatim; some questions have been omitted and the interviewee was allowed to read and edit his comments.

Q. James, I noticed that sales have been declining over the last several years. What do you think is the reason for this?

A. I think we are in a recession to begin with, and construction activity is really depressed. Many of our sales are to contractors. Also, our dependence on the land-clearing business has created a problem for us. Not only is most of the land in this area cleared up now but many of our major customers like Chicago Mill and International Paper are being prohibited from clearing some of their own land by the environmental authorities. Finally, we decided a couple of years ago to increase our prices at a rate well above the inflation rate. We expected that to cause sales to decrease. I think it has worked pretty well, too. In 1978, we had twenty-eight employees, and I was literally working myself to death. Although we made a good profit that year, I felt that things were just about out of control. I went to Houston to a trade show a few days ago and besides that I took two weeks off last year. I couldn't have done those things in 1978.

Q. Do you think the problem with the land-clearing business will continue?

A. Yes, absolutely! There just isn't much more land to clear in this area, and I think the government will continue to protect the hardwood bottomland. So, a lot of the land-clearing contractors are hanging it up.

Q. How much of your business has been related to land clearing?

A. Our shop revenue last year was just under three hundred thousand dollars. Land-clearing-equipment sales and repairs were well over half of that.

Q. Are you doing anything to make up for those lost sales?

A. Yes. We're changing directions somewhat.

We're shifting to more emphasis on undercarriage work, although we'll continue to keep some welding and steel fabricatiôn activity going. I negotiated an arrangement with a Florida company to furnish us a two-hundred-thousand-dollar inventory of undercarriage parts on consignment. We plan to increase the amount of undercarriage work that we're doing. Previously, we have mainly sold the parts that we installed. Now, however, we are also advertising and selling the parts themselves.

Q. What kind of consignment deal do you have?

A. The best I have ever heard of. To begin with, the prices are about five percent better than those I have been able to get through outright purchases. At the end of each month, I total up the sales of consignment items and then have to pay for these within thirty days. There are no interest charges.

Q. Don't consignment arrangements normally favor the supplier?

A. Yes, and that causes me to wonder. Art mentioned the other day that I might be helping to launder some money from the Florida drug trade. It's a good deal for me, though, and I don't know if I should check that out or not.

Q. What kind off wages does Sharpco pay?

A. Well, I pay the plant manager and the office manager pretty well. But I pay the others what I think I have to pay to keep them. If I make a mistake, I want it to be on the low side. It's easier to raise a worker's pay than to reduce it.

Q. I noticed that steel sales have declined a good bit, by fifty percent in one year. Why is that?

A. Well, the downturn in business activity affected it a good bit. But after Sol's Pipe & Steel started handling new steel and after O'Neal Steel Company bought out Monroe Pipe and Steel, the market just became too competitive. I also raised steel prices about twenty-five percent last year.

Q. How much of your inventory is steel?

A. About half of it—a little over one-hundred thousand dollars.

Q. You mentioned earlier that you have more time now than you did in the past. How many hours a week would you say you work now?

A. I am usually here at about six-thirty in the morning, although once every week or two I have to come in at four or five o'clock to get something for a customer, usually a land-clearing contractor. Those fellows have their tractors running at daybreak. I usually go home at five o'clock now, though, and sometimes even earlier. I don't have to work Saturdays, probably, but I usually do because Saturday afternoon is my best time to get caught up on paperwork.

Q. I noticed you are dressed in blue jeans and a workshirt. Do you still work in the shop?

A. Yes, particularly since I have cut the work force down. There is not a job in the shop that I can't do better than any worker out there.

Q. Do you do that because you enjoy it?

A. I do enjoy it, but I don't do it for that reason. I do it because every time I back away and try to stay uninvolved things get messed up. Just yesterday a tractor was started up without oil in the final drive. If I had not just happened by, this would have cost us six or seven thousand dollars.

Q. Do you consider Sharpco a success?

A. Oh, absolutely! I am just an ordinary guy. I would have been happy to have made service manager at Louisiana Machinery [the

Caterpillar dealer] by this time. That pays twenty-eight thousand dollars a year. Instead, I have my own company, pay myself thirty thousand dollars a year, drive a company car, and nobody tells me what to do. I expect the company to earn me thirty to eighty thousand dollars a year in addition to my salary. The company is worth a lot more than the three hundred thousand dollars book value, too. Even though depreciation on the fixed assets has totaled nearly one-hundred-fifty thousand dollars altogether, they would still sell for more than we paid for them. In fact, I would say that Sharpco has made me a millionaire.

APPENDIX A

SUMMARY OF FINANCIAL STATEMENTS

Sharpco, Inc., balance sheets

	Calendar years				
	1976	*1977*	*1978*	*1979*	*1980*
ASSETS					
Current Assets					
Cash	8,720	8,390	30,962	10,204	19,677
A/R-Trade	83,420	98,994	88,405	82,688	54,394
Reserve for Bad Debts	0	(4,576)	(11,016)	(10,016)	(11,013)
A/R-Other & N/R	2,359	3,688	85	1,650	10,689
Inventory	173,957	199,651	198,027	186,388	181,744
Total Current Assets	268,456	306,147	306,463	270,914	255,491
Fixed Assets					
Improvements	12,307	17,225	16,495	16,495	16,495
Buildings	69,955	81,955	92,176	94,743	104,271
Machinery & Equipment	57,817	108,793	128,518	142,641	133,712
Office Furn. & Equip.	2,090	7,749	9,524	18,149	16,113
Vehicles	23,129	38,475	36,183	30,084	36,223
Total	165,298	254,197	282,896	302,112	306,814
Less: Accu. Depr.	(29,368)	(63,923)	(101,609)	(118,549)	(143,444)
Net Depr. Assets	135,930	190,274	181,287	183,563	163,370
Land	22,000	34,010	34,010	34,010	34,010
Total Fixed Assets	157,930	224,284	215,297	217,573	197,380
Other Assets					
Deposit	0	500	500	500	500
Total Assets	426,386	530,931	522,260	488,987	453,371
LIABILITIES & OWNERS EQUITY					
Current Liabilities					
A/P-Trade	85,314	68,902	49,095	27,236	28,245
Accrued Expenses	8,381	14,865	12,900	8,903	0
W/H & Accrued Taxes	3,901	4,907	3,539	5,909	3,071
Accrued Payroll	0	14,082	0	0	0
Accrued Income Taxes	5,466	0	7,610	2,406	9,363
Notes Payable	81,985	119,658	112,252	85,934	67,747
Total Current Liabilities	185,047	222,414	185,396	130,388	108,426
Long Term Liabilities					
Notes Payable	94,352	138,664	113,932	72,264	38,000
Stockholders' Equity					
Common Stock	33,582	33,582	33,582	33,582	33,582
Less: Treasury Stock	0	0	0	0	(11,316)
Retained Earnings	113,405	136,271	189,250	252,753	284,679
Total Stockholders' Equity	146,987	169,853	222,832	286,335	306,945
Total Liabilities & Stockholders' Equity	426,386	530,931	522,160	488,987	453,371

Sharpco, Inc. income statements

	Calendar Years				
	1976	*1977*	*1978*	*1979*	*1980*
Revenue					
Shop	456,742	510,979	494,329	321,008	295,244
Undercarriage	0	184,497	420,348	431,110	354,564
Steel	115,139	155,224	197,354	194,789	92,048
Miscellaneous	2,261	9,572	8,949	3,112	4,366
Total Revenue	574,142	860,272	1,120,980	950,019	746,222
Direct Costs					
Materials	295,254	404,042	536,919	397,679	332,486
Shop Labor	73,513	166,834	200,205	145,483	92,602
Sub-Contractors	3,276	1,374	2,300	2,894	4,440
Freight	1,107	6,525	5,062	6,812	4,631
Other Direct Cost	196	1,111	975	70	516
Total Direct Cost	373,346	579,886	745,461	552,938	434,675
Gross Profit	200,796	280,386	375,519	397,081	311,547
Indirect Costs	149,328	257,520	318,241	331,599	270,258
Profit Before Taxes	51,468	22,866	57,278	65,482	41,289
Income Taxes	6,958	0	4,299	1,979	9,363
Net Income	44,510	22,866	52,979	63,503	31,926

EXERCISE 8–7

- Define the probable life span and the stage of the product life cycle you believe Sharpco's tractor undercarriage parts and service currently occupy. Explain. (See comments at the end of this chapter)
- Define the probable life span and the stage of the life cycle currently occupied by three-cutting and other specialized tools. Explain.
- Define the probable life span and the stage of the life cycle currently occupied by welding services and steel sales. Explain.

EXERCISE 8–8

- Consider the answer to the questions in Exercise 8–7 and describe the instructions you would give to your sales manager as to the way you best believe marketing efforts should be directed for each of these three product areas.

- What instructions would you have for the person in your firm responsible for the manufacturing function for these products?
- Describe the principal financial concerns you have with regard to these products.
- What direction would you recommend for the company's research and development?

LONG-LIVED PRODUCTS: OVER 10 YEARS

Stage 1: Innovation and Stage 2: Growth

In many respects, the early stages of products that have extremely long lives are similar to those with only moderately long lives. The introduction and growth stages are somewhat more protracted in time than those of short-lived products and product demand grows in Stage 2 to an extent that calls for very large scale production and distribution in the latter part of Stage 2 and on into Stage 3. Repeat orders and continued use indicate a sustained demand.

Stage 3: Maturity

The most significant differences between products with moderately long lives and those with extremely long lives begin to appear in Stage 3. Moderately long-lived products become obsolete when some other product replaces the functions served by the original product or when there is a fairly significant change in product characteristics serving a specific function to the consumer. One product that comes to mind that became relatively obsolete as its functions were served by another product is that of the table or countertop toaster oven. In its introductory growth and maturity stages, the toaster oven was used by small families and single persons to toast bread, broil steaks, and more extensively, to heat precooked frozen dinners and reheat leftover food. The introduction of the microwave oven and its subsequent growth into a widely sold, mass-produced consumer appliance has cut into the market for the toaster oven. The microwave oven does not broil or toast, but it is much quicker in its operation than the toaster oven, has a much wider range of applications, uses less electrical energy, and can cook larger meals. For many consumers, the microwave oven is clearly more useful.

A second example of the obsolescence of a product with a moderately long life is the electric typewriter. Early electric typewriters were little more than motorized manual typewriters. They used a touch-controlled electrical keyboard wired to motorized striker arms that hit the surface of the paper with a metal typeface. A cylindrical platen carried the paper back and forth across the center of the machine, enabling the typeface to strike the paper. Many electric portable typewriters still have this form of construction.

In the early 1960s, IBM introduced a machine that performed the same functions as the older electric machine but did so in a dramatically improved way. The Selectric Typewriter made use of a new technology and performed the printing function by moving a lightweight plastic ball across the width of the paper—instead of moving the paper across the typeface location—and moved the plastic ball in two rotational directions, indexing the ball to enable the type faces engraved on the face of the ball to strike the paper as each key was touched. The number of moving parts was reduced from hundreds to a scant few. The machine could operate at speeds much faster than the older machines, and it could not be jammed. Additional type balls could be purchased, enabling users to type in scientific notation, script, foreign-language characters, and in a variety of type styles. With its introduction, the Selectric Typewriter ushered in a new generation of typewriters, and the older machines were quickly seen as obsolete. Typewriters were still needed and used, but their technical characteristics were dramatically different.

For products that have an extremely long life, the maturity stage is much more protracted. New designs are developed to compete with the dominant product but they fail to adequately satisfy customer needs or are insufficiently attractive to persuade customers to shift their product loyalties. Product usage becomes an accepted part of consumer life-styles. It is not likely to change dramatically unless life-styles change significantly or a revolutionary shift in technology permits the functions of the mature product to be accomplished in an entirely new way or at a very significant reduction in cost, or both.

Home air-conditioners offer an example. Prior to World War II, few buildings of any kind were air-conditioned. Theaters that were air-conditioned advertised with festoons of paper icicles or other icy-appearing decorative trim on their marquees. Changes in housing and an affluent population enabled home air-conditioning to become a luxury to be purchased by the well-to-do in areas where heat and humidity were severe. Later, air-conditioners became widely available in less-expensive homes and with the advent of the window air-conditioner even in rented apartments. This expansion in use over several generations is now reflected in the use of air-conditioning in offices, markets, theaters, homes, automobiles, shopping malls, and large sports arenas. Home purchasers now expect to have an air-conditioned home and specify that feature as a part of their "standard" home specifications. The adoption of air-conditioning as a part of consumer life-style assures a very long life cycle for the air-conditioner as we now know it.

EXERCISE 8–9

- Identify one technological factor that might cause the market for air-conditioning equipment described to drop dramatically. Explain.
- Identify a social or economic factor that might cause the market for air-conditioning equipment to drop very significantly. Explain.

As a second example, the market for horses, wagons, buggies, and streetcars was dramatically affected by the advent of the automobile. Population density and geographic proximity made the trolley and horse-drawn vehicles sufficiently convenient and economically feasible in an increasingly urbanized country. The direct substitution of the auto for the horse and streetcar was one reason for the decline in use of these older forms of transportation. Beyond this direct effect, however, the auto made it possible for people to live in areas much farther from work, stores, and schools than had been the case with horse-drawn transportation. When the population density declined with the development of suburbs, the use of the earlier forms of city transportation was both uneconomic and impractical. Thus the change in life-style brought about by the auto contributed as much to the change in markets for these various forms of transportation as did the auto itself. Indeed, as the shortage of petroleum becomes more critical, the sprawl of urban areas brought about by the widespread use of the automobile is the despair of transportation experts seeking solutions to the need for nonauto urban mass transportation.

A dramatic change in technology is another way in which the market for an established, mature, and long-lived product can be altered. Were we to discover, for example, a process for electronically laundering clothes, consider the impact on the manufacture and sale of home laundry equipment, detergents, commercial laundries, commercial dry cleaning establishments, and numerous other types of businesses, each dealing with products or services related to the cleaning of garments and with extremely long-life expectancies. All would be affected. Some directly, others less so, but all would begin to see the onset of the decline stage. Because of the similarities in moderate and extremely long-lived products well into the third stage of the life cycle, we will discuss only the impact of the latter part of Stage 3 and Stage 4 on each of the major business functions in the following sections.

Marketers in the early and extended portions of the mature stage for long-lived products concentrate heavily on product differentiation, holding and gaining market share in a market dominated by a limited number of large and aggressive competitors. Market research specialists seek product improvements to aid in gaining market share and in sustaining a continued demand. Distribution channels become well established and wholesalers and/or retailers in many cases are assisted or supported by manufacturers.

For success with extremely long-lived products, a substantial "investment" should be made to establish a strong and vigorous distribution network. Considerable managerial attention should be directed to assist distributors and provide help in order to assist in solving problems and to assure that customers receive a competitive level of sales and service attention. Similarly, a substantial "investment" in product-management personnel, in advertising and promotion personnel, and in contractural relationships demonstrates a personal and organizational commitment founded on a belief in the long-term life expectancy of the product. In organizational terms, a stable and formalized infrastructure of organizational assignments, career-oriented personnel, and supplier relationships will sustain the product as it continues to serve customer needs over its extended lifetime.

The expectation of an extended life for a product should encourage thinking about integrating forward toward the ultimate consumer. Capital investments in retail establishments and proprietary distribution systems can be justified with an extended life but only infrequently when product life expectancy is short. Thus, with products for which we anticipate an extremely long life, marketing management may find that partial or complete forward integration is justifiable in terms of maintenance of market share, distribution control, and profitability.

Marketing policies for extremely long-lived products should become stable and relatively formal. The establishment of standardized procedures will greatly aid in dealing with recurring problems and should result in consistent, technically correct, and cost-effective marketing. Training should be provided to marketing and sales personnel to assure that uniform practices are used across product areas and geographic zones.

What has been described is the gradual development of a more bureaucratic, formalized marketing organization that is heavily committed, financially and organizationally, to the wide-scale distribution of a long-lived product. This type of organization is well suited to work in an environment in which the rate of change is relatively slow, where repetitive rather than unique problems are encountered, and where a highly refined technology and managerial expertise are required. These are precisely the circumstances found in the maturity stage for long-lived products.

As with the bureaucratic organization in other contexts, the bureaucratic marketing organization must *ultimately* adapt to long-range technological, market, and social changes. The change process for bureaucratic organizations tends to reflect long periods of stability interrupted by short, convulsive (and often unpleasant!) periods of adjustment. An analogy might be the stability of the earth's tectonic plates that are disturbed on occasion by earthquakes, reflecting the adjustment to meet the pressures of a gradually cooling planetary surface. Bureaucratic organizations are not well equipped to accommodate change given the extent to which they institutionalize duties, procedures, and relationships. The bureaucratic marketing organization has these institutionalized rigidities, but it must find ways to respond to shifts in customer needs, changes in products, and changes in the technologies of the business. In doing so, it must not lose its strengths of technological expertise nor the economic superiority gained by size. The gradual adjustments brought about by relatively minor shifts in customer preferences and by small changes in product characteristics can be accommodated by the bureaucratic organization through adjustments in standard operating procedures and through the complex decision-making processes of the bureaucracy.

The *dramatic* change, that which indeed may cause the product to begin the decline phase, is much more difficult to identify and accommodate. First, the early signals of product obsolescence may be no more threatening than any one of hundreds of attempts at unseating the currently mature star. Second, even as the new product begins to threaten an existing type of product, competitors still see a very large total market and a sizable share of that market still loyal to the older product. As a consequence, they may choose to target for a larger share of a smaller market, hoping that the intruder will most seriously affect competitors' products rather than their own. Finally, the extent of commitment made to an existing mature product is undoubtedly a factor that contributes to the reluctance to abandon a product facing obsolescence, and with good reason. Capital investments and organizational commitments are not abandoned without a thorough analysis of costs and benefits and extensive research on the likely depth of the residual market for the product under attack.

For production and operations managers, the protraction of the life of moderately long-lived products to that of the extremely long-lived product means, as with marketing, the natural extension of the patterns seen in earlier portions of the maturity stage. With the moderately long-lived product, Stage 3 for operations managers means a high degree of specialization in materials acquisition, manufacture, postmanufacture conversion and/or packaging, and distribution to consumers. Operations managers may dedicate specialized equipment to the production of a product or part of a product. Employees are designated to particular products in a plant and job classifications may reflect these special skills and product-oriented duties.

The natural extension of this process involves a further degree of dedication of capital and human resources. For the extremely long-lived product, integration backward is often an attractive alternative in materials management. Backward integration by investments in the chain of supply of raw materials and components can help to assure a supply of raw materials by preventing competitors from acquiring all feasible supplies. Backward integration can also help to assure a consistent quality of materials and can offer the opportunity of lower costs.

Capital is often committed in much larger dollar amounts and for more specialized facilities. Entire factories are dedicated to the manufacture of a product or even one part of a product. In the auto industry, we find transmission plants, body-manufacturing divisions, and facilities devoted to the manufacture of a single component. In this context, machinery becomes even more specialized and refined. Typically, because of the high degree of specialization, operating speeds are extremely high and unit operating costs relatively low.

The paper industry offers one example. Kraft papermills are found in several parts of the country, manufacturing the heavy brown paper that is used for paper grocery bags, multiwall sacks used to hold fertilizer and seed, corrugated boxes, and wrapping paper. The papermills designed to manufacture kraft paper are completely dedicated to the production of this one grade of paper. They draw raw materials from forest areas that produce pine pulpwood (the only wood suitable for kraft paper). Their pulp-preparation facilities cannot bleach the pulp to a white color used in book and printing papers. The paper machines themselves are made for extraordinarily high production rates, ranging to nearly 20 feet in width and operating at thousands of feet per minute, speeds that could only be maintained with the very large orders of paper that come from paper bag or corrugated box plants. In short, this is a totally dedicated capital investment in manufacturing equipment, built entirely for the production of a single product: kraft paper.

In addition to the investment in the papermill, paper companies often invest heavily in woodlands and in the cultivation of pine species especially well suited to use as pulpwood. Forestry geneticists study modifications to the various species of pines to develop strains that can be harvested every 20 or 25 years as a crop.

EXERCISE 8–10

- What is the term used in the latter part of Chapter 5 to describe the process mentioned in the paragraph above?
- What are the desired objectives of this process?
- Extend this process in its *opposite* direction. What types of actions would a paper company undertake to accomplish this extension? Hint: Refer to the discussion of marketing products with extremely long lives (pp. 310–311).
- What would be the objective of this set of actions?
- What are the pro's and con's? Explain in detail.

Financial concerns during Stage 3 of the extremely long-lived product can be complex. For the moderately long-lived product, the organization generates large cash flows, and financial managers must attend to issues of debt-interest coverage, debt-issue refunding, and consistency in dividend payment to income-oriented stockholders. Capital investment has been heavy, but the moderate length of product life suggests that facilities and equipment product-life obsolescence must be considered in any capital investment decision. The extremely long-lived product is not threatened with obsolescence as quickly. The need for very large, dedicated production facilities, distribution, and raw material supply systems suggests that very large sums of capital dollars must be raised and spent to achieve the economies of scale needed to be competitive in markets of this duration.

Relationships with financial agencies, commercial bankers, and underwriters must be maintained in order to have ready access to capital markets and to maintain the confidence of those members of the financial community who can assist in the procurement of large quantities of capital dollars. Cash generation is still very high given the shelter derived from depreciation, a noncash expense, and the financial manager must be concerned not only with paying the costs of that capital (in interest and/or dividends), but in finding alternative investments that generate income while serving as a storehouse of funds for capital needs in future periods. The scale of these needs is very large. It is not uncommon in industries characterized by products with extremely long lives to see investment projects measured in hundred-million-dollar units!

Stage 4: Decline

The effects of obsolescence on organizations involved with long-lived products can be devastating. The companies are extremely large and have highly institutionalized relationships with suppliers, customers, employees, and owners. Totally dedicated facilities are no longer needed and very large physical properties may suddenly have virtually no value. One example might be the decline of the Pullman Car Company, an organization devoted to the manufacture of railroad sleeping cars. Automobiles, the interstate highway system, and air transportation have made the pullman car accommodation for long-distance travelers virtually obsolete. All the physical facilities of the Pullman Company were closed and scrapped or salvaged in other ways. The inability of our steel industry to compete in the international market has had a similar effect on the hundreds of millions of dollars of capital assets once employed in the manufacture of steel. Although still functionally useful, they no longer have market value for the purpose for which they were designed.

In such instances, the long-term relationships with suppliers no longer have either meaning or commercial value, and a domino or ripple effect can cause a large number of commercial organizations to be severely hurt or closed down by the demise of a product or an industry. In recent years, we have seen the competitive obsolescence of a number of industries in the United States as more labor-intensive manufacture began to be undertaken in low labor-cost nations, especially in the Third World. The manufacture of shoes, men's and children's clothing, transistor radios, television sets, and small appliances shifted to plants in foreign locations, so that plants in the United States were closed. The dislocation caused by these long-range changes in the competitive and/or product environment has profound effects on the work force; the demographics of employment; population migration (toward employment in new industries, often involving a major geographic move); and on the character of international trade. The stability and security of the more-rigid patterns found in longer-lived products and the bureaucratic organizations that produce them is shattered as the entire structure becomes outmoded, or un-needed.

Unfortunately, we have not solved the problem of rebuilding and restoring an industry or an economic network once it is no longer useful. Cities in New England have old factories still standing as mute testimony to an industry long since gone. Hundreds of acres of steel-making facilities will be idle or will be scrapped and sold abroad to more efficient manufacturers, leaving little more than industrial ghosts behind. One only has to visit the wreckage of the bustling mining towns of the turn of the century to understand the long-term effects of product demise. If our experience in the West is any example, we can anticipate that many of those who were associated with the dying industry will stay in the homes and neighborhoods of their past and will not leave the area of their former employment for new occupations, new cities, and new neighborhoods. Their children, however, will migrate as jobs dry up and will make the transition to new forms of employment in the Sunbelt or wherever opportunities seem attractive.

In some instances, physical facilities can be converted to other uses. Old railroad stations now are avant garde restaurants, factory buildings serve as shopping malls, and acreage used for factories becomes an industrial park or a residential suburban community. In some instances, because of the highly specialized nature of the capital assets, demolition and salvage is the only reasonably practical way of converting properties to more useful form.

As plants are closed, stockholders must face the prospect of substantial write-offs of the value of these obsolete facilities. Investors will have long since shifted their interests to other securities that offer either more growth opportunities or the prospect of greater assurance of a steady dividend stream. Stock prices in industries with products facing obsolescence, therefore, will drop substantially. Financial managers then find fund raising a most difficult problem and must seek ways of converting assets in order to transfer funds to more promising product areas.

The decline stage for products that have been made obsolete offers some unique problems but also some opportunities. Major competitors and large-scale investors will not sustain interest in a product that is clearly on the decline. Although they may have the funds to sustain operations in this stage, there is not sufficient market depth to support their investment, at least in the scale they find most advantageous. Thus, although a shakeout will occur and many manufacturers will leave the market entirely, we may find the market for products in the decline stage to be left to smaller, more-adaptive competitors. These smaller firms manage to hold customer loyalty in the residual market and have the size, cost structure, and ownership needs such that the profit opportunity in this smaller market continues to be appealing. A large company may retain an interest in the market by maintaining a division of its organization to deal with the smaller market, but it will limit its attentions and funds to that division and will direct more extensive efforts elsewhere.

Marketing in Stage 4 must maintain a highly alert, opportunistic posture. Competitors become desperate in their efforts to hold a position in the market, and each order placed represents a magnified sense of accomplishment or failure given the high stakes in the game of commercial survival. For marketers, identifying the core product that will retain its loyal following and that will provide a lower but sustained level of demand is a critical task. Beyond this, marketers need to identify the factor or factors that engender loyalty to the product. One such example might be found in the firearms industry. Shortly after World War II, the Colt Firearms Manufacturing Company decided to discontinue the Colt single-action army pistol, a gun that had been manufactured since the 1860s. It had been replaced by the military in 1915 and by law enforcement agencies even before that date. The cost of production for these old models had risen steeply because of the design's incompatibility with modern firearms manufacturing techniques. The pistol was clearly obsolete, and, in the early 1950s, used models were sold for a few dollars in pawnshops.

Colt discontinued manufacture in the mid-1950s. Within months, the price for used single-action army Colt pistols began to rise to unheard of heights. Afficionados began rebuilding old guns, replacing barrels, cylinders, and action parts, leaving little but the frame and the grip from the old gun. Within a year or two, copies of the Colt single-action army pistol began to be manufactured by foreign manufacturers, and soon a domestic manufacturer began to build a redesigned single-action Colt pistol, one that could be made efficiently and could be used with more powerful modern cartridges. What was clearly apparent was that a strong, sustained market for "the gun that won the West" (or a facsimile) had been overlooked by Colt when it discontinued production of the old gun. The residual market was not found among the military or law enforcement agents or agencies but instead was made up of hobbyists, collectors, and sport shooters for whom the romance of the older design was irresistable. The Colt company itself reinstituted manufacture of the single-action army Colt pistol and presented this market with a collector-quality series, some made in the older, almost legendary versions, and others in the most modern calibers.

Identifying the appeal of the product in its residual market phase is extremely important. Marketing managers must not only know what the appeal is, but must sustain it, support it, and enhance it to whatever extent is possible. The collector-quality Colt pistol is one example. It was purposely developed to appeal to the interest in firearms history, the lore of the West, and the quality interests of the collector.

Production or operations managers must radically scale down operations in Stage 4 while retaining as much efficiency as possible. Management must become more and more a working management, and may find that the luxuries of industrial engineers, personnel staffers, and administrative assistants are relics of a bygone era (Stage 3!). In many instances, padding in wages and in work practices must be eliminated or the entire business can be threatened by closure. Not only may wages be reduced, but workers and supervisors may have to forego holidays or weekends if the business is to survive. Crewing practices may be completely revised to permit smaller operating staffs, and employees at all levels may be asked to perform multiple duties as a means of addressing problems of understaffing or poor use of employees.

Operations practices related to materials must also be reexamined and revised. Frequently, salvageable materials can be saved for production use. Purchasing practices can be tightened, and demands on suppliers for better values in materials and services can be accentuated. Heightened attention to material usage, scrapple problems, waste, and theft can make significant improvements in the cost of materials.

Management must also select equipment carefully for this stage of production. Although the need for production cost efficiencies is a high priority, order quantities will be smaller and customer needs for special types of products will require more-frequent setups and significantly more flexibility. Movement from single-purpose to multipurpose equipment is desirable, as is the standardization and mass production of those core elements common to all products in a particular class.

EXERCISE 8–11

Let us imagine that you are the production manager for a company that manufactures and sells push-type lawn mowers. Mowers are typically made in three widths: 20 inch, 22 inch, and 24 inch. Mowers have a tubular handle, rubber grips, and rubber-tired wheels. Quality differences are reflected in the use of ball bearings in the higher-priced mowers and in grass-catcher attachments, which can be purchased for each of the three widths. What parts of this type of lawn mower do you think you could produce in mass? Which type might have to be made on equipment better suited to smaller production runs? Explain.

Financial managers have a difficult task during the decline stage. The reduction in scale of operations must be accompanied by a commensurate reduction in financial commitments and scale of financial operations. Flexibility in marketing and operations calls for a balance sheet heavy in liquid assets to make possible the opportunistic acquisition of orders by marketers and equipment or materials by operations managers. Financial managers should encourage the use of fixed assets that are nearly or completely depreciated in order to minimize the risks inherent in investing in machinery for the production of goods approaching obsolescence. In addition, financial managers should view assets in an entrepreneurial frame of mind, considering their alternative use, and they must be prepared to suggest the divestiture of these assets should conditions warrant. In some cases, the state of the used-equipment market may be a strong determinant in the life of the enterprise. An active and aggressive financial manager may suggest liquidation of assets when the market for equipment is especially strong, but recommend against it when the sale of equipment would net little more than scrap value.

In addition to an active and aggressive management of liquid and capital assets, the financial manager can be an especially helpful aid in the marketing of products to loyal, long-term residual customers. Careful, discreet, and considerate treatment of the credit accounts of customers can materially aid the marketing of products in this stage. Careful judgment is required, however, because the recovery of overdue accounts arising from the sale of products in Stage 4 may result in little net gain.

In this chapter, we have used a well-studied concept, the product life cycle, as a medium for interfunction integrative thinking. The product life cycle, as we have seen, provides a rich backdrop for decision making by the general manager. Each product's unique appeal establishes a shape and duration of cycle. As customer tastes change and as competing products become available, product-life configurations are affected, sometimes dramatically. It should be apparent, however, that the effect of the stage of the cycle does not bear on marketing alone. Instead, the functions of operations and finance are directly affected by these changes and, consequently, they require the type of business-unit perspective provided by the general manager. In the next chapter, we will examine another medium for connecting the business functions: operational forecasting. This approach is quantitative in nature, a fact that allows us to be specific about the impact of changes in one facet of the business unit on each of the other parts of the enterprise.

ANSWERS TO SELECTED EXERCISES

Exercise 8–2

Setup cost	\$ 85.00
Materials:	
\$3.75 × 45	\$168.75
Labor:	
\$3.30 × 45	\$148.50
Total cost	\$402.25
Cost per unit	\$ 8.94

Exercise 8–3

Once accepted, winter toys have typically had long lives. Toboggans, runner sleds (or sleighs), and aluminum saucers are examples.

Exercise 8–6

At a retail price of $29.95 for a Mogul Master, $5 million in sales (or 166,945 units) would be needed each year to return a royalty income of $50,000. If the retail price were $19.95, then 250,626 units would need to be sold each year to generate a $50,000 royalty income.

Exercise 8–7

The life cycle for these undercarriage parts is tied to that of the crawler tractor, a product that has been on the market since the 1920s. Although used extensively, a number of machines equipped with large rubber tires have begun to replace many of the functions of the crawler tractor. We may, therefore, be seeing the beginning of the change to a decline stage for this equipment and, consequently, the parts business it supports.

9

OPERATIONAL FORECASTING AND THE GENERAL MANAGER

One of the most important functions performed by the general manager is that of forecasting the entire range of organizational activities, given a particular organizational strategy. For a new company seeking capital, this type of forecast is called a business plan. For an ongoing organization, it can be called an operational forecast. In either case, the forecast involves estimates of sales, costs, personnel, production efficiencies, competitive responses, technological advances, interest rates, capital equipment requirements, and a wide array of other factors that affect all aspects of the entire organization.

The operational forecast involves a tightly integrated view of the organization and its operations. Each major function has direct and indirect effects on the others. In addition, each function may constrain the extent to which the others can expand or enlarge. As management scientists would say in dealing with a problem in linear programming, the general manager's job is to "maximize the objective function within a given set of constraints." The "objective function" is often contained in the statements of strategy within which the general manager is expected to operate. If the strategy statement explicitly considers maximization of profit to stockholders as a strategic objective, then the "objective function" to be maximized would be profit per share of stock. Other "objective functions" might be sales dollars, asset size, product leadership, market share, or return on assets.

The constraining effects of each function are the limits of each in a given planning period. Suppose, for example, that product demand is so strong that sales for a given product could reach $20 million in a given period. That level of sales, however, requires capital equipment, funds for working capital and fixed assets, human resources for production and management, and an adequate supply of materials of proper quality. If any of these factors falls below the level needed to support $20 million in sales, then it serves to constrain sales to a level below that which might be achieved in the marketplace. New companies often encounter difficulty in meeting the needs of an expanding level of sales activity. In most of these companies, as volume builds, financial resources are insufficient to sustain accounts receivable and the necessary inventories and costs associated with the production cycle.

In some of the successful companies associated with microcomputers, difficulty in building production to meet demand has caused delays in meeting customer orders and inadequate customer support. Coleco encountered difficulty in producing enough Adam home computers to meet customer and dealer demands, and then met with an adverse reaction from stockholders when sales volume fell well below projected levels. In 1984, Microsoft Corporation was reported in trade publications to be "spread too thin for its many ongoing projects." The company's problems were exemplified by the release of a spreadsheet program for the Apple MacIntosh that contained a number of major bugs, one of which could cause a complete loss of data when the user tried to store a file by one of several file-storage means! An analyst commented that the promotion of talented programmers (with little or no management experience) into project management positions in charge of major software projects had been a major contributing factor in the company's troubles. In this case, the constraining factor appears to be human resources, especially managerial talent.

The purpose for developing the operational forecast is to provide a well-reasoned plan that will serve to guide management thinking, provide operational goals, and permit management to find solutions to problems well in advance. When completed, the plan should have sales targets, by units, products, geographic areas, and other units of measurement helpful to sales management. The operational forecast provides production/operations managers with the sales forecast needed for planning materials acquisition, employment, capital equipment purchase and installation, inventory levels, and the coordination of all operations-management elements needed to achieve production/operations goals. A table of organization can, and should, be developed out of the operational forecast for assistance in personnel planning, management development, and skill training. Financial managers should find that the *pro forma* income and expense statements and balance sheets will serve to identify sources of funds, applications of funds, and areas of funds shortage or surplus. These documents serve as the framework for financial goals and as the basis for financial management control.

The operational forecast should represent the best informed thinking that can be applied to the complexities of running the entire business. Although forecasts can be based on industry data or on company historical experience, the judgments of managers are required to estimate future costs, sales, production efficiencies, and market conditions in future time periods. Purely mechanical extrapolations of history may serve as a starting point, but rarely will they be as useful or as accurate a view of the future as will a forecast that is carefully built, component by component, with the aid of the judgment of managers at each level of the organization.

FORECASTING AND FORECASTING METHODS

Sales activity serves as a principal means of revenue generation and as a key component that determines the needed level of financial resources, capital equipment, and the work force needed for the accomplishment of organizational objectives. As mentioned earlier, nonsales factors can, however, constrain achievable sales levels. Ultimately, all elements must be considered as a complementary set in order for the operational forecast to be achievable in all dimensions. Thus, one could examine the maximum potential of all of the nonsales elements first to determine what might be called the "feasible space" and then examine sales levels as a derivative of the space left by nonsales factors. This approach can be very useful for startup companies operating in newly developing markets where financial, personnel, and management resources are tightly constrained. This method can serve to keep a fledgling company from outrunning its financial capabilities or from attempting to reach a sales level that cannot be handled by available production capacities.

A direct tactic that is more useful for an established company is to begin with a sales forecast, then determine where constraints may be found that might restrict the attainment of the desired level of sales. Frequently, identifying constraints in this fashion provides the focus for management attention at a point in time early enough that managers can acquire or shift resources to avoid a loss in sales volume. In the following paragraphs, we will examine ways of forecasting sales for the purpose of building an operational forecast. Where constraints are encountered, however, we must either adjust resources to remove the constraint or we must slow the acceptance of orders from customers to avoid the sale of products that cannot be produced within the customer's acceptable delivery time limits.

In general, experts in forecasting suggest that the longer the time horizon, the greater the dependence on more subjective methods in forecasting. Estimating sales for next month or for the next several months can be a relatively mechanical process. Historical data may suffice for the development of a realistic forecast of volume for a planning horizon this short. An examination of business conditions into the next century, however, involves a great number of judgments that incorporate an enormous range of interests, all of which have a bearing on the forecast. In considering methods of forecasting, we will start with those that extrapolate from a base of historical data. The first are relatively crude methods that serve as approximations but may suffice in some situations. We will work through several more complex methods, then begin to examine methods that rely more extensively on judgment.

Extrapolations

In using extrapolative forecasting systems, historical data are required. The forecaster's assumption is that whatever patterns were evident in the past will be evident in future time periods. If sales, for example, followed a linear growth pattern in the past, the same linear path will be found in future sales figures. Several crude systems can be used to approximate the slope of that path, and one (linear regression) can be used to calculate the precise mathematical equation for the line that best approximates the pattern shown in the historical data. Let us start by examining the sales and profit data for a 10-year period in Table 9–1:

TABLE 9–1

Year	*Sales*	*Net profit*
1	14	(4)
2	56	(1)
3	110	7
4	180	6
5	235	14
6	260	27
7	292	31
8	300	46
9	322	73
10	380	79

Simply examining the data is a very important first step. We see that sales have increased every year in the series. The slope, therefore, is positive. We can quickly approximate the slope of the line for the entire 10 years of data by using the equation:

$$\text{Average amount of increase (AAI)} = \frac{\text{Year-10 sales} - \text{Year-1 Sales}}{(\text{Number of years covered}) - 1}$$

$$\text{AAI} = \frac{380 - 14}{10 - 1} = \frac{366}{9} = 40.67$$

EXERCISE 9–1

- Calculate the average amount of increase for net profit for the first 5 years.
- Calculate the average amount of increase for net profit for the last 5 years. Explain the differences between the two answers.
- If you were to use AAI method of estimating the future value of net profit, which figure would you prefer to use: the 10-year average, the first 5 year's average, or the last 5 year's average increase? Why?

In graphic terms, the system described is depicted in Figure 9–1. You will note that in each case, the line that is used to approximate the data begins with the first data point in the series and ends with the last data point in that series. If either of these data points seem above or below what appears to be the general trend of the line, then the slope will be raised or lowered by the value of that particular element of information.

When we examine the three lines seen in Figure 9–1, we see distinctly different slopes. The increase projected into years 11 and 12 by the last 5 years data is much less than that projected by data from all 10 years. Had we used only the first 5 years

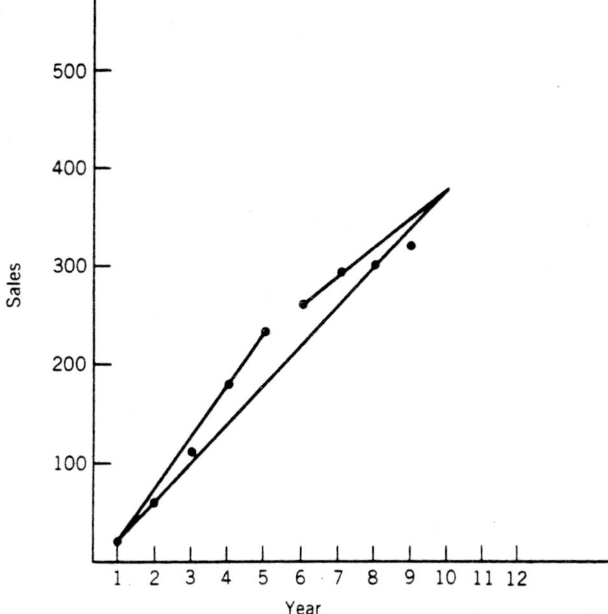

FIGURE 9–1

to forecast, the slope would be so steep that we would have overestimated sales for all subsequent time periods. We should also note that the 10-year line falls below all but one data point in the years between 1 and 10. Each of these lines represents crude approximations of the relationship between sales and time periods 1 through 10 and for some purposes may be sufficient. If, for example, we believe that the most recent time periods are closer approximations to tomorrow's conditions, we may want to select a line based only on the most recent few year's data or we may want to weigh that information more heavily in estimating the extent of change from the present into periods in the future.

A more precise means of determining the relationship between sales and time is to use a regression line, or trend analysis. This approach, called a least squares regression, is found in numerous management science and statistics textbooks. It involves the solution of equations that will find the variables used in the equation for a line ($Y_c = a + bX$), which minimizes the distance between the line and the data points. In effect, it is a *mathematically* perfect fit. The equations used to calculate the least squares regression are:

$$b = \frac{\Sigma\,(xy)}{\Sigma\,x^2}$$

$$a = \overline{Y} - b\overline{X}$$

From the sales data we have used to date:

Year X	Sales Y	$y = (Y - \overline{Y})$	$x = (X - \overline{X})$	(xy)	x^2
1	14	−105	−2	210	4
2	56	−63	−1	63	1
3	110	−9	0	0	0
4	180	61	1	61	1
5	135	116	2	232	4
$\Sigma = 15$	$\Sigma = 595$			$\Sigma(xy) = 566$	$\Sigma x^2 = 10$
$\overline{X} = 3$	$\overline{Y} = 119$				

Then:

$$b = \frac{566}{10} = 56.6$$

$$a = \overline{Y} - b\overline{X} = 119 - 56.6(3) = -50.8$$

and the equation for the line is:

$$Y_c = a + b(X)$$

$$Y_c = -50.8 + 56.6(X)$$

EXERCISE 9–2

- Manually calculate the least squares regression equation for *net profit* for the first 4 years. (Compare your answer with the answer at the end of the chapter.) Hint: With an even number of years, the center falls *between* two years. Therefore, use one-half-year increments for X and x in your calculations.
- Manually calculate the least squares regression equation for *sales* for the 10-year period. Show your calculations and hand in as a homework assignment.
- Check your manually calculated figures by means of a trend-line calculation performed by a calculator similar to the Texas Instruments' Business Analyst II.
- Plot your regression line *for sales* on a graph similar to that in Figure 9–1. Compare the regression line with the line drawn by the AAI approach. Why are they different?
- Use your calculator to calculate the trend lines for *net profit* for the first 5 years and for the entire 10-year period.

The regression line permits us to estimate a value for future time periods by inserting the X value for the desired year in the regression equation. Solving the equation for Y_c will provide us with the trend-line value for the year or years in question. In our example based on 5 years of sales data, an estimate for Year 6 would be calculated as

$$Y_6 = -50.8 + 56.6(6) = 288.8$$

EXERCISE 9–3

- Use the same equation and calculate trend-line values for years 8, 9, and 10.
- Use the 10-year-sales trend-line equation you calculated in Exercise 9–2 and calculate trend-line values for years 8, 9, and 10.
- Use your calculator to provide trend-line values for *net profits* for years 6 and 7 based on a trend line for the first 5 years of data.

The two methods discussed thus far are based on an assumption of linearity: that increases (or decreases) will occur in constant *amounts*. As we saw in Figure 9–1, however, the slope of data often changes and may be found to approximate a *curvilinear* form. If we use a linear model to approximate curvilinear data, our estimates of future values are certain to be over- or understated. We will now demonstrate some examples of attempts to approximate curvilinear relationships.

TABLE 9–2

Year	*Sales*	*Profit*
1	14	(4)
2	19	2
3	31	5
4	47	8
5	68	13
6	96	16
7	135	21
8	180	26

When we examine the sales information in Table 9–2, the growth pattern is quite interesting. Each year there is a positive growth. The extent of growth, however, is not at a constant amount. From Year 1 to Year 2, sales grew by 5. The next year, growth in sales was 12. Between Years 5 and 6, sales grew by 28. A graphic view of the data indicates that the growth in sales is clearly not linear. It appears to *curve* upward as time moves from Year 1 to Year 8 (see Figure 9–2). When a least squares line is calculated, one can see that the trend line falls below the data in early and late years in

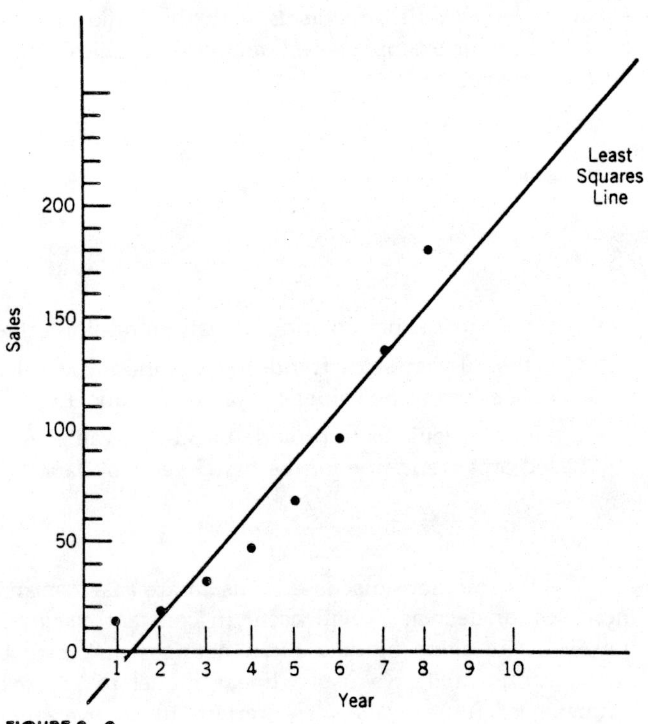

FIGURE 9–2

the series and above the line for Years 3 to 6. If the least squares line were to be used to forecast values for Years 9 and 10, the estimates would be 178.64 for Year 9, and 201.95 for Year 10. If, on the other hand, we were to extend the curve, the estimate for Year 9 appears to exceed the values at the top of the scale . . 350 or more. To find a closer approximation of the curvilinear function that the data seem to demonstrate, several approaches can be considered.

The most precise method would be to make use of computer technology to develop a curvilinear least squares equation and thereby find the most mathematically precise solution. In many cases, however, simpler techniques are available to the forecaster that should provide an acceptable degree of accuracy.

The first of these techniques is to examine the data to determine the *average rate of change* in the data that would be required to cause the value found in the first data period to reach the last value in the set in that number of time periods. In the example based on Table 9–2 data, we need to try to determine what rate of increase will cause a value of 14 to reach a value of 180 in the seven periods of change, that is, 8 − 1 years. One way to arrive at this figure is to examine a table of net present values. The present value (14) is equal to .0777 times the future value (180). If we look in a table of net present values to find the present value of $1.00 in 7 years (the number of change periods we are working with), which is equal to .0777, we should locate the discount rate. In such a table, for 7 periods the value of .0777 is found at a 44% discount rate. This means that if we increased the value of 14 found in Year 1 by 44% each year, compounding the results, we would reach a value of 180 by the eighth year.

A simpler method of reaching the same solution, but somewhat more precisely, is to use a calculator designed to perform present-value calculations. With present value equal to 14, future value 180, and N of 7, the percentage needed to satisfy these conditions is 44.03%. Now let us compare the values obtained by this method to the actual values for the intervening years in order to see the degree of agreement.

TABLE 9–3

Year	*Sales*	*Present-value estimate*
1	14	14.00
2	19	20.16
3	31	29.04
4	47	41.83
5	68	60.25
6	96	86.77
7	135	124.98
8	180	180.01

As can be seen in Table 9–3, the degree of agreement is noticeable, but we still find a substantial difference in the middle of the series: Year 6, for example, has an estimated value that is 7.75 less than the actual amount. The problem is that when we estimate the curvilinear relationship in a set of data from only two data points, the estimate is affected by the extent to which those data points are representative of the rest of the set.

EXERCISE 9–4

What will be the effect on the discount rate in calculations shown if the first figure is *below* the curvilinear function described by the data points and if the last figure is *above* the curvilinear function?

Another means of estimating the curvilinearity of data is to determine a period-by-period average rate of change by calculating the rate of change for each change period and then by averaging the change over the total numbers of periods (see Table 9–4).

TABLE 9–4

Year	*Sales*	*Change*
1	14	0.00%
2	19	35.71%
3	31	63.15%
4	47	51.61%
5	68	44.68%
6	96	41.18%
7	135	40.63%
8	180	33.33%
Average Percentage Change		44.33%

The use of the period-by-period average rate of change is not without faults. In our data, the average rate of change of 44.33% is substantially higher than the value for all three of the last change periods. Its calculation gives as much weight to the high values early in the time series as it does for those in more recent periods, which may be closer in context to the next few years, that is those for which the forecast is intended. For the moment, however, let us examine the results of using these two estimating techniques on historical data, much as we did in Table 9–3. (To minimize distortion from compounding for the period-by-period average percentage of change technique, we will work backward and forward from a value of 57.5, the midpoint between actual sales for Years 4 and 5.)

TABLE 9-5

Actual		Estimate approaches	
Year	*Sales*	*Present value*	*Average percentage change*
1	14	14.00	13.66
2	19	20.16	20.60
3	31	29.04	31.05
4	47	41.83	46.82
5	68	60.28	68.17
6	96	86.77	95.83
7	135	124.98	134.70
8	180	180.01	189.35
9	?	259.25	266.16
10	?	373.40	374.14

For the data in Table 9-5, the average-percentage-of-change method appears to provide estimates that come closer to the actual data for this period. We can check this by determining the total distance between the estimate and the actual and by comparing the two estimation methods.

EXERCISE 9-5

- Calculate the algebraic sum of the distances between the actual sales data and the estimated data for the present-value approach. (Check your answer against the answer at the end of the chapter.)
- Calculate the algebraic sum of the distances between the actual sales data and the estimated data for the average percentage of change method. Which method would you prefer for this data? Explain.

EXERCISE 9-6

- From the profit data found in Table 9-1 plot the data points for net profit on graph paper, then calculate and plot the least squares trend line.
- Use a table of present values to estimate the percentage increase needed to raise profit from the level in Year 2 to the level in Year 8. Show your calculations.
- Use a calculator that can perform present-value calculations to determine the discount rate needed to raise profit in Year 2 to the level seen in Year 8. Carry your answer out to three places past the decimal.
- Calculate the period-by-period average rate of change for profits from Years 2 through 8. Show your calculations.

- Select a method to forecast profits for Years 9, 10, and 12. Forecast profits for those years and defend your method.

What we have just demonstrated and practiced are two methods for attempting to approximate a curvilinear relationship between data and time. Although these are not mathematically precise, they provide us with estimation methods that match trends in the data much more effectively than straight lines and may, therefore, serve to provide a sounder base for our forecasts. It is of particular importance that we examine the data and use several different methods to find the appropriate relationship for the data at hand rather than choosing a single method for use in all situations.

Other Extrapolative Methods Sales forecasts can be developed by extrapolating from data external to the company. If, for example, the company's market share is known, then forecasts can be constructed by developing estimates of market share for future time periods, then by applying that market-share percentage to estimates of the market. This process will result in forecasts of sales that take the total market and the company's share into account. The data in Table 9–6 incorporates information about market size from which market share can be calculated.

TABLE 9–6

Years	*Sales*	*Industry sales*
1	24	237,595
2	29	267,890
3	36	341,675
4	40	377,845
5	48	443,315
6	57	523,655
7	65	589,440
8	72	643,250

EXERCISE 9–7

- Calculate the share of market for each of the years shown in Table 9–6, then select a method for estimating the share of market for Years 9, 10, and 11. Use this method to estimate share of market for those years.
- Industry economists have forecast a growth pattern for Year 9 of 11.5%, for Year 10 of 9%, and for Year 11 of 7%. Use this industry data and your answer to the preceding question to develop a sales forecast for Years 9, 10, and 11.

Other types of data can serve a similar function in the development of a sales forecast, so long as a fairly stable relationship can be found between that particular information and the company's sales over several years. Population, disposable income, capital goods production, automobile production, per capita consumption of a variety of products, all of these might serve as the basis upon which to build an acceptable and defensible forecast. If we were in the automobile accessory business, then data on the production of automobiles would be an obvious choice of information upon which one might wish to build a forecast. Similarly, given the widespread adoption of microcomputers for home and business use, companies involved in software and accessories for microcomputers would be interested in data on sales of the computer itself as well as data on their particular segment of the microcomputer industry. Sources of data include trade publications, industry associations, Department of Labor statistics (which are broken down by geographic regions and in other ways), and research firms that sell data to interested parties.

Seasonality Seasonal patterns of sales are found in a number of industries. Scholastic markets have seasonal patterns that center on the academic school year. Retail stores have a heavy seasonal increase between Thanksgiving and New Year's Day, and food-processing plants' operations are closely tied to harvest patterns for the produce being processed. An examination of the month-by-month sales patterns can reveal the extent of seasonality over a period of years. These patterns can be used in forecasting to take the annual forecast and break it into meaningful components for operational planning. Table 9–7 provides some data that can serve to illustrate this.

TABLE 9–7

Month	*Percentage of sales*
Jan	3.0
Feb	3.5
Mar	4.0
Apr	4.0
May	5.0
Jun	5.5
Jul	6.5
Aug	8.0
Sep	10.0
Oct	12.5
Nov	14.0
Dec	24.0

The seasonal pattern shown in Table 9–7 clearly indicates a heavy pattern of sales in the fall and December. Many retail establishments have seasonal patterns this severe. It is interesting to note that sales in December are eight times as heavy as in the following month. Inventories would need to be built to anticipate the heavy holiday demand, as would staff and the financial base to support this level of sales.

EXERCISE 9–8

Use your forecast for Years 9 and 10 from Exercise 9–7 and develop a breakdown by quarter for each of the two years based on the seasonality pattern found in Table 9–7.

Judgmental Modifications to Extrapolative Forecasts

Thus far we have developed ways of extending historical patterns into future periods by relatively mechanical means. As we gain experience in our markets, however, we may very well find instances where we know that an extrapolation will simply not suffice. Markets saturate, new products emerge to provide a more vigorous competitive atmosphere, economic conditions change, customer tastes begin to shift . . . all factors that might tend to make us wish to adjust our historically developed forecasts downward. In a similar fashion, market information may cause us to adjust our estimates upward. Favorable publicity, a positive consumer-testing agency report, the demise (figuratively!) of a competitor or the competitor's product, patterns in the most recent months (or years) in internal data that seem to indicate an increase in consumer interest in our products, or a deliberate entry into a completely new market are all reasons that suggest increasing our historically based forecast.

The Nissan Motor Corporation in USA case provides an excellent opportunity for us to explore the complexities involved in forecasting in a real-life situation. Nissan Motor has been actively involved in the manufacture and sales of automotive products to the United States and other foreign markets for a number of years. The preparation of a sales forecast for this company must involve judgments about a number of domestic (to Nissan) and foreign elements, each of which may have a significant impact on the forecast. In reading these pages, it might be helpful to note in the margin of the case the positive (+) or negative (−) effect of these factors. When you have completed reading the case, you might wish to develop a summary document that lists the positive and negative factors and then attempt to reflect them by modifying extrapolative or other forecasting approaches you might want to use.

NISSAN MOTOR CORP. IN U.S.A.

In a letter to Nissan's foreign associates abroad introducing its 1978 business report (fiscal year 4/1/78–3/31/79), Katsuji Kawamata, Chairman of Nissan Motor Co., Ltd.; Tadahiro Iwakoshi; Vice Chairman, and Takashi Ishihara, President, stated:

> *The world economy showed some signs of improvement, during fiscal 1978, as a result of the efforts made by many countries to achieve sustained, non-inflationary economic growth. A variety of international economic meetings and trade talks were held in search of greater worldwide cooperation. These efforts, coupled with the appreciation of the yen in relation to the dollar, have produced a more balanced international payments picture. However, unstable factors such as higher-than-expected increases in oil prices and accelerating inflation in some areas still cloud the horizon.*

> *During this accounting term, the Japanese automobile industry experienced a striking contrast between its domestic sales and exports. Domestic sales have been running at high levels as automakers moved to take advantage of relatively favorable economic conditions on the home front. Exports, on the other hand, made a poorer showing with shipment volume remaining below the previous year's levels. This means that the rapid climb of the yen has sharply reduced the price competitiveness of Japanese vehicles and international competition has intensified in the small car segment of the market.*

> *In other words, the automobile industry has entered an age of stiff worldwide competition centering around efforts to produce smaller, lighter and more fuel-efficient vehicles as dictated by the needs for energy and resource conservation. Along with trimmed down exterior dimensions and weight, the movement toward two-box style design and front-wheel drive became widespread during fiscal 1978. In a related move, diesel engine cars were marketed in increasing volumes. Confronted with stringent legislation on emissions and fuel economy, wider application of electronics was also pursued.*

> *In the face of this intensified international competition and the race to develop new vehicles, Nissan has taken steps to further enhance its overall R & D capabilities over a broad spectrum of areas ranging from vehicle quality, performance, and styling to innovative technologies. At the same time, the Company implemented extensive reorganization and personnel changes to provide for more strategic planning from a long-range and global point of view.*

> *At a time when a wide range of problems—such as increases in the price of commodities, unstable oil supply, the continued recessionary mood, pending trade issues and protectionist movements in some areas—overshadow the prospects for improvement in the world economy, stable economic growth is expected to become more difficult. The automobile industry will also undoubtedly meet with ever greater competition in the years to come.*

This case was prepared from published materials by Raymond S. Kulzick of the Graduate Division of Biscayne College to serve as the basis of class discussion rather than to illustrate either effective or ineffective handling of an administrative situation. Distributed by The Intercollegiate Case Clearing House, Soldiers Field Boston, Massachusetts 02163.

NISSAN'S EARLY DEVELOPMENT IN AMERICA

Nissan, manufacturer of Datsun autos and trucks, was a relative latecomer to the American market. In 1957, Nissan Motor Company was persuaded to race Datsuns for the first time outside of Japan at the Mobil Rally in Australia. A Datsun won this 10,000-mile endurance race, generating considerable international publicity. At the same time, Americans were increasing their purchases of small European economy cars—notably the VW Beetle. In October 1957, Toyota (Nissan's major competitor in Japan) founded its first overseas subsidiary in Los Angeles.

Datsun's display at the 1958 Los Angeles Imported Auto Show was received favorably, and Woolverton Motors of North Hollywood, California, was appointed sole distributor of Datsuns in the 13 western states. A total of 52 Datsuns were imported in 1958 out of total imports of over 600,000. 1,290 Datsuns were sold in 1959, including sales of pickups (see Exhibit 1 for Datsun U.S. sales figures).

A CHANGE IN DISTRIBUTION METHOD

In 1959, Nissan sent Soichi Kawazoe to the U.S. to perform an in-depth market survey, and in early 1960 Yutaka Katayama was sent to observe operations at Woolverton Motors.

Dissatisfied with the distributor approach, Nissan opened its own subsidiary (Nissan Motor Corp. in U.S.A.) September 28, 1960, in a suburb of Los Angeles. Nissan's former export manager, Takashi Ishihara (later to become president of Nissan Motor Co., Ltd., the parent firm) was appointed president. The United States was divided into two virtually autonomous regions with Katayama appointed executive vice president in charge of the Western Division and Soichi Kawazoe appointed vice president in charge of the Eastern Division (operating out of Newark, N.J.).

Parker Advertising, Nissan's agency until 1977, prepared its first advertisement in 1961. The initial series concentrated on selling Datsun's engineering superiority and fully equipped "package" price. 1961 also saw the introduction of the 213 sports car, the first car specifically engineered for the American market. Of the 2,629 Datsuns sold nationally in 1962, 817 were pickups.

By the end of 1963, annual parts sales of over $400,000 were supported by an inventory in excess of $350,000. 1963's sales, helped by a rise to 225 dealers, increased dramatically to 4,707 (including 1,983 pickups). In 1964 sales continued their rapid increase to 9,907 units and the dealer network grew to 367. The 410 series, destined to be one of the best-selling, was introduced during that year.

NISSAN BECOMES A COMPETITOR

By 1965, Datsun was becoming noticed. Yutaka Katayama was named president, several expansions were completed—including the third regional office (in addition to the two Division offices), and 55 dealers were taken to Japan on the first Datsun Quality Dealer trip. Parts inventories exceeded $1,500,000. 1965 closed with Datsun sales of 17,937 units—making it the fourth best-selling imported vehicle.

Another important milestone was achieved that year as Datsun's first all-car carrying ship was launched (the fleet would later grow to over 15, nearly all built to Nissan's specifications and leased on a long-term basis). Due to the long distances involved on the Japan/U.S. supply route, Nissan felt it could not rely on common carriers, but should run its own ships.

1966 started off with a much expanded advertising effort with the theme "Drive a Datsun—Then Decide." The new 1600 sports car was introduced and monthly sales exceeded 3,000 for the first time in August. In Japan, Nissan bought out the third largest automaker, vaulting Datsun into first place domestically. 1966 U.S.

sales were 20,939 cars and 8,202 trucks, in spite of supply shortages due to production and shipping limitations and a brief longshoreman's strike.

THE FIRST SUPPLY SHORTAGE

1966 saw the introduction of the 510 series, Datsun's biggest seller, and also a moratorium on new dealers due to severe supply shortages. 1967 saw the introduction of an organized racing program to replace its previous informal one. Over the next several years, Datsuns were to be prominent winners in many international races, increasing the Nissan reputation for engineering excellence.

A doubling of the shipping fleet (to 4 carriers) in 1968 was still not enough to meet demand as supplies continued tight throughout this period. In spite of strikes early in the year at East Coast ports and a 3-month West Coast strike later that year, sales in 1968 moved ahead to 38,788 cars and 17,445 trucks.

1969 saw the introduction of a new advertising theme: "World's Best $2,000 Car." Standardized accounting systems were introduced and sales increased over 50% as dealers rose to 640. A new 5-year marketing program projected annual sales of 300,000 units within five years (versus 86,894 in 1969). Parts inventories continued to expand to over $4,500,000.

1970 saw the introduction of the 240-Z, Nissan's highly successful entry into the high-performance personal car market. Unit sales in 1970 increased to 151,516—a 70% increase over 1969.

REORGANIZATION

By the early seventies, it became apparent that Datsun's dual Division approach to the American market was creating many problems and a complete reorganization was undertaken—effective in February, 1971. Authority was centralized in Los Angeles, while sales offices were split into 3 geographic areas—under central direction.

1971 also saw severe supply problems. A two-month seamen's strike in Japan in April was followed by a 100-day West Coast longshoremen's strike in July. Nissan vessels were diverted to Ensenada, Mexico and Vancouver, British Columbia, to be unloaded. Other dock walkouts later in the year hit East and Gulf Coast ports and arrangements were made to supply Eastern dealers from Quebec and by rail from the West Coast.

These problems were only the beginning, as August saw the imposition by President Nixon of a 10% surcharge on all imported products and later that fall the yen began to increase in value. However, by the end of the year, the surcharge was dropped, and the 7% excise tax on imported and domestic automobiles was repealed. The yen had, however, increased by 17%—forcing a 5% retail price increase on Datsun vehicles. In spite of these problems, sales increased to 185,270 cars and 66,655 trucks during the year.

Three more ships were added to the fleet during 1971 and parts shipments were shifted to containerization to reduce packing requirements as well as damages. A centralized computer system was installed at headquarters to coordinate all parts and vehicle sales. The system provides immediate information on parts availability at all depots throughout the United States.

SALES LEVEL OFF

The price increase in late 1971 reversed the supply shortage, and by early 1972, excessive inventories were piling up. A series of three sales-promotion campaigns were undertaken in an effort to increase sales. Parker Advertising won a national award for the best advertising campaign of 1972 with its "Drive a Datsun—Plant a Tree" promotion. Special mobile vans were introduced to increase dealer service abilities in several key areas and the EPA released its first gas mileage ratings (showing the Datsun 1200 as the best mpg of any car sold in the U.S.). Total sales (cars and trucks) increased slightly to 261,383 units.

As the possibility of gas shortages loomed in 1973, sales of Datsuns increased, and supply shortages were again encountered. The new "Datsun Saves" campaign had already been designed when the new B210 replaced the discontinued 1200 as the U.S. mileage champ. The fall Arab oil embargo increased demand so much that a sales incentive program was shelved. Later in the year, the 240-Z was replaced by the 260-Z featuring a larger engine. Racing parts were available through Datsun dealers and a company-sponsored phone line offered advice on racing modifications.

The procedure for pickup trucks was also changed in 1973. Whereas in the past trucks were shipped fully assembled, contractors were hired at Los Angeles, Seattle and Jacksonville to assemble bodies to chassis which were now shipped separately. 1973 sales beat the five-year goal (set in 1969) one year early by exceeding 319,000 units.

SHORTAGES WORSEN

By 1974, the energy crisis had taken hold. Sales demand was stronger than ever in the U.S. market for Datsun's small, fuel-efficient autos, but the supply situation was another matter. Shortages of oil and other imported raw materials hit Japan especially hard because of its lack of indigenous natural resources. Power and steel were in short supply and Nissan had to struggle to keep its production lines going at all.

Datsun's ships were forced to slow down to conserve fuel, lengthening delivery times for those vehicles that were available. Nissan had to resort to airfreight for some critically needed parts supplies, and prices on vehicles were increased to reflect higher costs of transport.

During 1974 formalized monthly dealer order plans were introduced and new methods of dealer forecasting and planning were developed. The B210 continued to win the best mileage rating (35 mpg) and Datsun set a new five-year goal of 500,000 units. By the end of 1974, Nissan was offering five sedan models, two hardtops, one coupe, two wagons, two 260-Zs and the pickup (which still accounted for about one-third of unit sales). Unit shipments dropped during the year to 183,965 cars and 59,641 pickups.

DATSUN COMES OUT ON TOP

1975 was the year it all came together for Nissan in America. Volkswagen suddenly dropped drastically in popularity (see Exhibit 2 for imported autos *on the road in 1979* by brand and year manufactured) and Toyota and Datsun fought it out for number one. Although in terms of automobile sales, Datsun was still in third place, the large sales of pickups pushed it into first place for total vehicles sold in the import market—331,203 total units (259,807 cars and 71,396 pickups) versus Toyota's 328,918 vehicles (283,909 cars and 45,009 trucks).

1975 was marked by Yutaka Katayama's promotion to chairman of the U.S. subsidiary's board of directors. He was succeeded by Hiroshi Majima, previously in charge of exports to North America and a member of the parent firm's board of directors.

The 280-Z was introduced and Datsun's dominance in racing continued with the winning of three out of four national championships in SCCA competition. In spite of several price increases, sales continued to rise. The B210 was again rated best mileage car by the EPA at 41 mpg. The sales incentive program prepared for Datsun's 15th anniversary year in America was shelved as unneeded, as sales continued to be limited by supply.

THE U.S. AUTOMOTIVE MARKET: 1976–1978

1976 marked a year of change in the American automotive marketplace. While the economy continued to recover from the 1975 recession, buyers abruptly reverted to their traditional taste for larger cars. Imports (mostly subcompacts), which had held 20% of the market in 1975, dropped to 14% (4% of the market is equivalent to 460,000 cars). Total small car demand (both foreign and domestic manufactured) dropped from 51% of the market to 47% while demand for intermediate and full-sized cars rose.

The biggest worry of domestic automakers (as expressed to *Business Week* by Henry Ford II in January, 1977) was that, "Our car sales and employment are being constrained by the discrepancy between the kinds of cars consumers want and the mix of cars it will be necessary to build to meet the fuel economy standards." In fact, first quarter 1977 figures indicated that while overall sales were running at record rates, large cars had further increased their share of market to over 55%. For example, Pontiac large car sales were up by 49%, while small models were off over 20%.

First quarter import sales were up by 30%, increasing their share of market from 14.8% to nearly 17% (an increase of about 100,000 units). However, many of these sales were "purchased" by the use of heavy discounts and promotions. Mazda (produced by Toyo Kogyo) was particularly hard hit by a combination of damage from the 1974 poor mileage achieved by its rotary engine and a move later in 1974 to split its marketing organization into three parts (independently owned) to raise needed cash. The marketing split prevented Mazda from mounting any national advertising campaigns to counteract the rotary image problem.

By the fall of 1977, it was clear that fundamental changes were occurring in the U.S. auto market. Firstly, from a free-market enterprise, the automotive industry had become one of the most heavily regulated in the country. Secondly, the specter of market saturation was finally in sight. Almost one of every two Americans owned a car, while declining birth rates, rising costs of ownership and a reduction in overall purchasing power indicated a permanent slowing in the growth rate of the market.

In addition, U.S. automakers were going to have to compete directly with the imports if they were to survive. This would mean a lower profit per car (smaller cars have traditionally carried lower profits than larger ones), and larger capital investments in new facilities, design, and equipment.

The 1978 model year (fall, 1977) continued the earlier trend. General Motors, after three years of heavy investments (an average of over $3.2 billion per year), introduced their first downsized models while Ford and Chrysler continued to sell their older larger-sized cars. Initially, G.M. sales were off considerably as buyers resisted paying more money for less car. However, a massive education campaign—aimed not only at consumers but also at auto salespeople, reversed that by early 1978. The year ended with G.M. holding an unprecedented 59% of the domestically built auto market (nearly 50% of the total market including imports).

Ford and Chrysler shares continued to drop (to 23.6% and 11.1%, respectively, of the total U.S. auto market)—in spite of Chrysler's introduction in early 1978 of its domestically produced Omni and Horizon subcompacts.

JAPAN/U.S. INTERNATIONAL SITUATION: 1976–1978

As of March, 1976, Japanese exports had increased 23% while imports had only risen 10%. In spite of a growing trade surplus, the Japanese yen did not increase in value substantially against the dollar—leading many U.S. leaders to feel that it was being kept at artificially low levels through Japanese government intervention.

Weak domestic demand in Japan with about 30% of industrial capacity idle, resulted in increased export pressures during the balance of 1976. Japanese exports to the U.S. jumped 40% while purchases from the U.S. rose only 3%.

By 1977, the U.S. suffered a trade deficit of $26.7 billion, of which $8.1 billion was with Japan. Japan's total trade surplus with all nations was over $17 billion—in spite of rapidly rising oil bills.

Through the fall of 1977 and early 1978, after intense pressure from the United States and other allies, the Japanese yen was allowed to float—increasing in value by 22% against the dollar. The domestic Japanese economy remained soft, with unemployment at a postwar high of 2.4% despite Japan's "lifetime employment" policy which keeps at least 1.5 million excess workers on company payrolls.

Although most Japanese firms continued to honor at least the letter of the "lifetime employment" policies—if not the spirit—through voluntary layoffs and early retirements, it was widely predicted that Japan would have to adjust to the gradual phase-out of this system within the next decade. Other industrial nations—notably the United States—were no longer willing to allow the Japanese to maintain stable domestic employment by exporting excess goods when domestic demand softened.

By June of 1978, the yen had appreciated over 25% in the preceding 18 months, but Japanese exports continued to climb. By August, another readjustment had brought the upward revaluation to almost 35% in just 8 months. Japanese firms were able to hold down price increases by partially offsetting exchange losses on sales with lower purchase prices for imported raw materials.

At the end of 1978, the turmoil in Iran had cut off 17% of Japan's oil supplies, dashing Prime Minister Ohira's hopes of increasing domestic demand so that exports could be reduced without a corresponding increase in unemployment. The oil shortfall was likely to increase domestic inflation, dampen investment, and reduce domestic economic growth.

DEVELOPMENTS IN THE IMPORTED CAR MARKET: 1976–1978

In the six months ended September 30, 1976, Toyota sales worldwide increased 16% and profits 60%. Nissan had sales increases of 21% while profits jumped 116%. By June of 1977, overall Japanese auto exports to the United States were up 36% from the prior year in spite of a small exchange rate increase.

Honda, however, led by the mileage champ Civic and hot Accord models, was selling all its factories could produce. Of the total output of 650,000 units, over a third were going to the U.S., and waits of up to 5 months were still reported for the Accord. In addition to the Honda models, Mazda's GLC (45 mpg) was introduced, and by September Ford would be selling its European-built Fiesta. Overall, imports in the first four months of 1977 captured over 18% of the American auto market.

In February, 1977, Nissan started a program at its eight port cities to modify incoming vehicles to better suit American tastes. Customizing production lines are utilized to provide such things as color coordinated side moldings and vinyl woodgrain panels. "We do something to virtually every product line," stated Curtis H. Bartsch, Nissan's national product planning manager.

Worldwide sales in 1977 for Nissan dropped 1.1% in spite of a 6.5% increase in exports due to a decline in domestic demand.

By May of 1978, both Toyota and Datsun had imposed six price increases. Prices on many

American subcompacts were also raised, as the market leaders (such as Chevette) were selling all they could produce. After two straight years of monthly increases, in April, 1978, imported car sales dropped below the prior year. Toyota reported a decline of 12% and Datsun 13%. In July, overall Japanese exports to the U.S. were off by 2.4%.

By the end of 1978, imported cars' share of the U.S. market had slipped to 16.4% from 20.6% in January—mainly because of price increases and stiffer competition. Both Datsun and Toyota entered 1979 with over 10 months of sales in inventories after recording a December that was off by over a third from 1977.

At the beginning of 1979, Nissan Motor Company announced that it had reshuffled 600 employees in the middle management ranks after losing market share to front-runner Toyota in 1978. Nissan officials predicted more drastic moves [might] follow. Nissan's share of the Japanese market dropped from 30.1% to 28.8%. The American market was even worse, as Toyota outsold Datsun by over 100,000 automobiles and even overtook Datsun's top performing pickup truck.

NISSAN'S POSITION WORLDWIDE—1978

Datsun's strong worldwide growth in production, sales and exports from 1969 through 1978 is detailed in Exhibit 3. It is clear that the increase in overall auto sales for 1978 was more than offset by a substantial reduction in truck sales. The export market was hit even harder, with both car and truck sales falling. As of 1978, over 20% of Datsun's total worldwide production was going to the United States and Canada.

Exhibit 4 presents a 10-year summary of Nissan sales, income and employment, while Exhibits 5, 6 and 7 present comparative financial statements for the 1977 and 1978 fiscal years (note that Nissan calls the year ending 3/31/79 "fiscal 1978," contrary to common U.S. practice).

NISSAN IN AMERICA—1978

A survey of imported versus domestic auto buyers in 1977 (see Exhibit 8) clearly indicates an appeal to a different market segment—with gas mileage being the primary concern for import purchasers, while styling and favorable past experiences are the primary motivating factors for domestic car buyers. Datsun's 1978 vehicle line-up, key features, target audiences and advertising themes are summarized in Exhibit 9. An analysis of Japanese price leadership in the subcompact market during 1978 is presented in Exhibit 10.

During Nissan's search for a new ad agency in 1977 (William Esty Company won), all three finalists reached the same marketing conclusions: economy is what gets people into the small car market, but once they are in that market, quality becomes the most important factor. Quality includes not only such things as body fit and good engineering, but also factors such as ease of maintenance, durability and reliability.

About 25% of Datsun buyers are trading in older Datsuns, but the largest portion of buyers are not trading in anything. Market penetration is heaviest in the Western and Southern states, and sales reflect little seasonality—partly because supply is relatively fixed. Datsun dealers now exceed 1,000 with total U.S. employment of over 35,000 people. There are 12 regional sales offices and 11 parts depots strategically located throughout the U.S. stocking over 60,000 different parts.

Incoming cars are quality surveyed by a staff headquartered in the Carson, California, technical center. This includes not only checks of trim, fitting, and options, but also double checks on safety, emission control, and mileage requirements. A product engineering group carries out technical investigations such as inquiries into product failures, establishment of dealer warranty rates and monitoring the quality of U.S. manufactured parts destined for Japan (currently valued at over $11 million).

The future for Nissan Motor Corp. in U.S.A. at the end of 1978 certainly held promise with federally mandated fuel standards due to rise from an average of 18.0 mpg in 1978 to 27.5 mpg in 1985 models, but competition from American automotive companies as well as Nissan's fiercest rival, Toyota, (who had recaptured and held the number one import position from 1976 through 1978) (Exhibit 11) was certain to continue to intensify in the coming years.

EXHIBIT 1
Datsun U.S. sales (in units)

Year	*Cars*	*Trucks*	*Total*
1958			52
1959			1,290
1960			1,640
1961			1,436
1962	1,612	817	2,629
1963	2,724	1,983	4,707
1964	6,504	3,403	9,907
1965	12,625	5,312	17,937
1966	20,929	8,202	29,131
1967			45,491
1968	38,788	17,445	56,233
1969	57,427	29,467	86,894
1970	101,263	50,253	151,516
1971	185,270	66,655	251,925
1972	187,621	73,762	261,383
1973	231,903	87,104	319,007
1974	183,965	59,641	243,606
1975	259,807	71,396	331,203
1976	270,103	80,300	350,403
1977	388,378	99,839	488,217
1978	338,096	94,604	432,700

Source: Nissan Motor Corp. in U.S.A.

EXHIBIT 2
Imported automobiles in operation in the United States by model year, as of January 1, 1979 (thousands of units)

	1973 and Earlier	*1974*	*1975*	*1976*	*1977*	*1978*	*Total*
Primarily Small Economy Models							
Austin	33.1	4.2	11.6	1.0	—	—	49.9
Datsun	607.0	165.3	233.2	260.7	382.6	336.4	1,985.2
Fiat	212.9	62.2	87.0	59.1	62.4	60.0	543.6
Honda	53.3	36.5	92.8	145.5	220.0	273.5	821.6
Mazda	136.7	48.6	57.1	33.5	49.7	74.8	400.4
Renault	94.3	5.6	6.7	6.5	12.8	15.6	141.5
Subaru	49.5	18.7	36.5	47.0	79.5	102.8	334.0
Toyota	859.3	208.0	242.6	337.2	485.7	439.6	2,572.4
Volkswagen	2,864.0	299.2	241.2	197.2	256.8	238.1	4,096.5
Subtotal	4,910.1	848.3	1,008.7	1,087.7	1,549.5	1,540.8	10,945.1
Other Major Noncaptive Makes							
Alfa Romeo	12.2	2.4	5.0	5.0	6.6	6.2	37.4
Audi	82.0	43.8	46.2	32.3	35.4	40.7	280.4
BMW	54.2	13.5	18.3	25.4	28.5	31.4	171.3
Jaguar	39.3	4.5	6.4	7.2	4.3	4.8	66.5
Lancia	—	—	—	—	5.4	2.8	8.2
Mercedes-Benz	202.5	34.5	43.6	42.2	48.2	46.6	417.6
MG	156.4	22.2	24.8	27.2	34.2	26.5	291.3
Peugeot	34.1	6.6	11.2	9.2	9.9	9.0	80.0
Porsche	81.7	19.6	16.0	13.9	19.7	17.0	167.9
Rolls-Royce	6.0	0.6	0.8	1.2	1.1	1.1	10.8
Saab	68.5	11.8	12.9	9.5	12.9	15.6	131.2
Triumph	110.9	16.2	20.0	26.9	28.7	16.4	219.1
Volvo	263.1	48.3	55.6	42.5	46.3	50.7	506.5
Miscellaneous	196.4	5.2	3.6	5.8	4.1	2.9	218.0
Subtotal	1,307.3	229.2	264.4	248.3	285.3	271.7	2,606.2
Captive Makes							
Arrow	—	—	—	29.3	46.5	28.2	104.0
Capri	215.5	69.2	50.8	28.3	22.1	4.0	389.9
Challenger	—	—	—	—	1.8	17.6	19.4
Colt	74.9	37.1	51.5	46.7	69.3	44.3	323.8
Cricket	31.0	—	—	—	—	—	31.0
Fiesta	—	—	—	—	40.0	75.7	115.7
Opel	364.6	50.1	37.4	10.1	28.5	19.1	509.8
Sapporo	—	—	—	—	1.4	12.7	14.1
Subtotal	686.0	156.4	139.7	114.4	209.6	201.6	1,507.7
Overall Total	6,903.4	1,233.9	1,412.8	1,450.4	2,044.4	2,014.1	15,059.0

(continued)

EXHIBIT 2 *(continued)*
Imported automobiles in operation in the United States by model year, as of January 1, 1979 (thousands of units)

	1973 and Earlier	*1974*	*1975*	*1976*	*1977*	*1978*	*Total*
				Percentage Breakdown			
Small Economy	71.1%	68.7%	71.4%	75.0%	75.8%	76.5%	72.7%
Other Noncaptive	18.9	18.6	18.7	17.1	14.0	13.5	17.3
Captive	10.0	12.7	9.9	7.9	10.2	10.0	10.0
	100.0%	100.0%	100.0%	100.0%	100.0%	100.0%	100.0%

Source: Automotive News 1979 Market Data Book Issue, p. 52. As reported in *The Imported Automobile Industry* (Harbridge House, Inc., 1979).

EXHIBIT 3
Production, sales, and exports Nissan Motor Company, Ltd.

Production over the past 10 fiscal years (April–March)

Year	Passenger cars	Total (incl. trucks & buses)
'69	741,174	1,209,620
'70	949,349	1,421,142
'71	1,181,871	1,666,124
'72	1,368,676	1,903,414
'73	1,437,932	1,996,427
'74	1,309,924	1,851,271
'75	1,532,858	2,111,957
'76	1,599,440	2,301,444
'77	1,680,784	2,353,729
'78	1,751,203	2,374,023

Passenger cars
Trucks & buses

(units)

Sales in units over the past 10 fiscal years (April–March)

Year	Trucks & buses	Total
'69	454,211	1,179,661
'70	469,583	1,369,664
'71	484,435	1,662,720
'72	546,481	1,944,636
'73	544,621	1,915,096
'74	538,068	1,877,932
'75	575,527	2,124,799
'76	681,352	2,238,892
'77	582,427	2,383,622
'78	635,622	2,357,137

Passenger cars
Trucks & buses

Exports by area

Area	Units
Oceania	75,785
Middle East	85,446
Latin America	90,436
Africa	94,552
Southeast Asia	117,745
Europe	222,701
U.S.A. & Canada	475,055

Total 1,161,720 (units)

EXHIBIT 3 *(continued)*
Production, sales, and exports Nissan Motor Company, Ltd.

Exports over the past 10 fiscal years (April-March)

Year	Trucks & buses	Total
'69	105,650	301,721
'70	136,445	461,026
'71	170,791	680,989
'72	180,949	703,024
'73	189,059	722,077
'74	239,489	863,322
'75	262,230	975,297
'76	348,529	1,124,328
'77	393,844	1,308,416
'78	326,349	1,161,720

Passenger cars
Trucks & buses
(units)

Source: Business Report 1978, Nissan Motor Co., Ltd.

EXHIBIT 4
Summary financial and employment data Nissan Motor Company, Ltd. (fiscal years ended March 31)

	1978	1977	1976	1975
Net Sales (Millions of Yen)	2,306,685	2,246,393	2,024,624	1,770,198
Net Income (Millions of Yen)	65,465	80,680	85,292	52,214
Dividends Paid (Millions Yen)	17,430	12,966	11,439	8,651
Dividends per Share (Yen)	12	10	10	8
Total Assets (Million Yen)	1,513,823	1,419,931	1,343,530	1,255,607
Capital (Millions of Yen)	76,165	66,544	60,018	54,117
Number of Employees	55,747	54,411	52,577	51,454
	1974	**1973**	**1972**	**1971**
Net Sales (Millions of Yen)	1,429,638	1,270,833	1,176,425	981,812
Net Income (Millions of Yen)	18,801	41,422	48,032	33,693
Dividends Paid (Millions Yen)	8,606	9,340	7,403	6,720
Dividends per Share (Yen)	8	9	8	8
Total Assets (Million Yen)	1,137,742	1,005,063	949,029	886,672
Capital (Millions of Yen)	53,910	53,463	48,061	42,900
Number of Employees	51,612	52,819	51,395	50,430

Source: Business Report 1978, Nissan Motor Co., Ltd.

EXHIBIT 5
Statement of income and retained earnings Nissan Motor Company, Ltd. (years ended March 31) (millions of yen)

	1978	1977
NET SALES	2,306,685	2,246,393
COST OF SALES	1,754,183	1,696,728
SELLING, GENERAL & ADMIN.	460,641	444,075
DEFERRED INSTALLMENT INCOME	−3,039	−1,435
OPERATING INCOME	88,822	104,155
NON-OPERATING INCOME	60,215	69,867

(continued)

EXHIBIT 5 *(continued)*
Statement of income and retained earnings Nissan Motor Company, Ltd. (years ended March 31) (millions of yen)

	1978	*1977*
INTEREST & DIVIDENDS REC'D	52,086	64,796
OTHERS	8,129	5,071
NON-OPERATING EXPENSES	28,957	35,576
INTEREST EXPENSES	23,640	27,844
OTHERS	5,317	7,732
ORDINARY INCOME	120,080	138,446
EXTRAORDINARY INCOME	8,879	8,463
EXTRAORDINARY LOSSES	7,994	5,929
INCOME BEFORE TAXES & OTHER	120,965	140,980
PROV. FOR INCOME TAX & OTHER	55,500	60,300
NET INCOME FOR THE YEAR	65,465	80,680
RETAINED EARNINGS FORWARD	35,647	34,871
INTERIM DIVIDENDS	8,290	6,311
PROV. FOR LEGAL RESERVE	636	631
UNAPPROPRIATED RET. EARNINGS	92,186	108,609
UNAPPROPRIATED RETAINED EARNINGS FOR THE PERIOD	92,186	108,609
APPROPRIATION OF RETAINED EARNINGS:		
LEGAL RESERVE	1,770	1,000
DIVIDENDS	9,140	6,654
BONUS FOR DIRECTORS	240	240
DEFERRED GAINS ON FIX ASSETS	69	68
GENERAL RESERVE	45,000	65,000
RETAINED EARNINGS CARRIED FORWARD	35,967	35,647

Source: Business Report 1978, Nissan Motor Co., Ltd.

EXHIBIT 6
Balance Sheet Nissan Motor Company, Ltd. (as of March 31) (millions of yen)

	1978	*1977*
ASSETS		
CURRENT ASSETS	768,486	755,892
LIQUID ASSETS	591,146	592,478
CASH	72,910	95,063
NOTES RECEIVABLE	344,547	321,992
ACCOUNTS RECEIVABLE	67,612	69,222
MARKETABLE SECURITIES	78,748	78,389
ADVANCES	1,139	1,082
SHORT-TERM CREDITS	27,238	26,722
ACCRUED REVENUE	4,760	4,206
PREPAID EXPENSES	3,522	3,457

EXHIBIT 6 *(continued)*
Balance Sheet Nissan Motor Company, Ltd. (as of March 31) (millions of yen)

	1978	1977
SUSPENSE PAYMENTS	464	400
ALLOWANCE FOR DOUBT. ACCTS.	−9,794	−8,055
INVENTORIES	177,340	163,414
FINISHED GOODS	125,378	104,887
PURCHASED GOODS	12,939	13,526
RAW MATERIALS	6,681	5,847
WORK IN PROCESS	26,944	34,182
SUPPLIES	5,398	4,972
FIXED ASSETS	745,337	664,039
PROPERTY, PLANT & EQUIPMENT	390,800	347,376
BUILDINGS	105,907	99,257
STRUCTURES	16,404	15,619
MACHINERY & EQUIPMENT	134,055	117,928
TRANSPORTATION EQUIPMENT	3,207	3,154
TOOLS, FURNITURE & FIXTURES	24,872	21,426
LAND	64,962	62,567
CONSTRUCTION IN PROGRESS	41,393	27,425
INTANGIBLE ASSETS	1,926	2,031
INVESTMENTS	352,611	314,632
SECURITIES	112,983	99,632
AFFILIATES	70,666	58,354
GUARANTEE SECURITIES	285	414
LONG-TERM LOANS RECEIVABLE	142,594	135,867
LONG-TERM PREPAID EXPENSES	2,481	1,674
OTHER INVESTMENTS	26,495	21,097
ALLOWANCE FOR DOUBTFUL ACCT	−2,893	−2,406
TOTAL ASSETS	1,513,823	1,419,931

Source: *Business Report 1978*, Nissan Motor Co., Ltd.

EXHIBIT 7
Balance Sheet Nissan Motor Company, Ltd. (as of March 31) (millions of yen)

	1978	1977
LIABILITIES		
CURRENT LIABILITIES	714,595	706,807
NOTES PAYABLE	113,305	118,171
ACCOUNTS PAYABLE	144,782	137,936
SHORT-TERM BORROWINGS	157,862	172,382
LONG-TERM DEBT DUE WITHIN YR	27,183	31,873
ACCRUED EXPENSES	114,084	99,110

(continued)

EXHIBIT 7 *(continued)*
Balance Sheet Nissan Motor Company, Ltd. (as of March 31) (millions of yen)

	1978	*1977*
EMPLOYEES' SAVINGS DEPOSITS	67,291	56,026
DEFERRED PROFITS-INSTALLMENT	37,802	34,764
UNEARNED INTEREST	8,648	11,174
PROVISION FOR INCOME TAX	32,432	31,832
OTHER CURRENT	11,206	13,539
LONG-TERM LIABILITIES	150,402	148,589
CORPORATE BONDS, SECURED	11,640	13,228
LONG-TERM DEBTS	75,043	83,051
LONG-TERM DEPOSITS REC'D	19,689	19,273
RESERVE FOR EMPLOYEE TERM.	43,745	32,623
GUARANTEE SECURITIES DEPOS.	285	414
SPECIAL RESERVES	33,673	39,140
PRICE FLUCTUATION	3,373	3,852
ACCUM. SPECIAL DEPRECIATION	18,559	24,900
LOSS FROM OVERSEAS INVEST.	11,741	10,388
TOTAL LIABILITIES	898,670	894,536
STOCKHOLDERS' EQUITY		
CAPITAL STOCK	76,165	66,544
CAPITAL SURPLUS	94,408	62,916
CAPITAL RESERVE	77,136	47,280
LEGAL RESERVE	17,272	15,636
RETAINED EARNINGS	444,580	395,935
SPECIAL RESERVES	23,052	22,984
GENERAL RESERVE	329,342	264,342
NET UNAPPROPRIATED EARNINGS	26,721	27,929
TOTAL STOCKHOLDERS' EQUITY	615,153	525,395
TOTAL LIABILITIES & EQUITY	1,513,823	1,419,931

Source: Business Report 1978, Nissan Motor Co., Ltd.

EXHIBIT 8
The top 10 factors involved in the decision to purchase a new imported or a new domestic car 1977 census of new car buyers by weighted index (average weighted score = 100)

Factors	*Imported car buyers index*	*Factors*	*Domestic car buyers index*
Better Gas Mileage	416.6	Good Past Experience	346.9
In My Price Range	179.8	Liked Styling	268.8
Good Past Experience	174.1	Better Gas Mileage	176.6
Better Quality/Workmanship	173.4	In My Price Range	144.8
Better Overall Performance	158.8	Wanted More Interior Room	103.9

EXHIBIT 8 *(continued)*
The top 10 factors involved in the decision to purchase a new imported or a new domestic car 1977 census of new car buyers by weighted index (average weighted score = 100)

Factors	*Imported car buyers index*	*Factors*	*Domestic car buyers index*
Better Handling/Roadability	151.4	Better Handling/Roadability	98.3
Preferred Smaller Size	150.7	Preferred Smaller Size	96.6
Liked Styling	133.7	Wanted to Try New Make or Model	90.2
Offered Attractive Price	124.6	Preferred Larger Size	87.4
Recommended by Others	93.6	Better Quality/Workmanship	86.3

Sources: Buyers of New Imported Cars 1977 and *Buyers of New Domestic Cars 1977*, Newsweek, Inc. As reported in *The Imported Automobile Industry* (Harbridge House, Inc., 1979).

EXHIBIT 9
Datsun's top car models and target markets for each

Model	*Key feature*	*Target audience*	*Ad-lines*
F-10	Front-wheel drive	Age 18–39 Income $19,000 70% had some college 58% male 59% married	A sporty car that's both economical and fun to drive.
510	Economy	Age 18–44 Income $20,000 70% had some college 55% male 70% married	Best all-around Datsun. The car for people who want more than just economy.
200-SX	Sportscar	Age 20–40 Income $20,000 50% male 50% married	Inexpensive sporty car with SX appeal.
810	Luxury, family car	Age 30–54 Income $25,000 72% had some college 55% male 85% married	World's most underpriced luxury/performance car.
280-Z	Performance	Age 25–45 Income $28,000 plus 85% had some college 65% male 50% married	Best-selling sports car in the world.

(continued)

EXHIBIT 9 *(continued)*
Datsun's top car models and target markets for each

Model	*Key feature*	*Target audience*	*Ad-lines*
Li'l Hustler	Pick-up truck	Age 20–45 Income $20,000 64% had some college 86% male 70% married	America's No. 1 selling import truck, featuring the exclusive "King Cab."
B-210	Low gas mileage	Age 18–40 Income $18,000 65% had some college 50% male 55% married	Datsun's basic car for people who demand lots of economy with extras.

Source: Datsun's Ad-Planner for dealers. As reported in *Media Decisions*, July 1978, p. 69.

EXHIBIT 10
Japanese price leadership in the subcompact market—four rounds of price changes on 1978 models

	Initial Base Price	*Final Base Price*
Corolla	$3,048	$3,498
Datsun B-210	$3,148	$3,488
Chevette	$3,354	$3,734
Pinto	$3,336	$3,536

	Date of price increase	*Percent increase*	*Dollar increase*	*Adjusted base price*
Round 1				
Corolla	12/ 5/77	2.6	80	3,128
Datsun B-210	12/12/77	1.6	50	3,198
Chevette	1/ 2/78	3.0	100	3,454
Pinto	1/16/78	4.0	135	3,471
Round 2				
Corolla	2/27/78	2.0	60	3,188
Datsun B-210	3/ 6/78	1.9	60	3,258
Chevette	3/27/78	2.7	95	3,549
Pinto	—	—	—	3,471

EXHIBIT 10 *(continued)*
Japanese price leadership in the subcompact market—four rounds of price changes on 1978 models

	Date of price increase	*Percent increase*	*Dollar increase*	*Adjusted base price*
Round 3				
Corolla	4/24/78	6.0	200	3,388
Datsun B-210	4/24/78	4.3	140	3,398
Pinto	4/24/78	2.0	65	3,536
Chevette	6/ 5/78	2.6	95	3,644
Round 4				
Corolla	7/10/78	3.2	110	3,498
Datsun B-210	7/17/78	2.6	90	3,488
Chevette	8/ 7/78	2.4	90	3,734
Pinto	—	—	—	3,536

Sources: Automotive News, late 1977 and all 1978 issues. As reported in *The Imported Automobile Industry* (Harbridge House, Inc., 1979).

EXHIBIT 11
Comparison of total U.S. sales Datsun and Toyota

	1975	*1976*	*1977*	*1978*
Datsun				
Cars	259,807	270,103	388,378	338,096
Trucks	71,396	80,300	99,839	94,604
Total	331,203	350,403	488,217	432,700
Toyota				
Cars	283,909	346,920	493,048	441,800
Trucks	45,009	49,823	83,680	94,882
Total	328,918	396,743	576,728	536,682

Sources: Auto sales from *Automotive News 1980 Market Data Book;* Datsun truck sales from Nissan Public Relations Department; Toyota truck sales from Toyota Distribution Department.

EXERCISE 9–9

- From the data contained in Exhibit 1, use an appropriate *extrapolative* technique (only) to develop a forecast for cars (in units) for 1979, 1980, and 1981. Defend your choice of method and the time period on which you based your extrapolation.
- What judgmental factors would you consider in adjusting the extrapolative forecast you have just calculated? Explain.
- Use those judgmental factors to adjust the extrapolated forecast, and justify the degree of adjustment.

EXERCISE 9–10

- From the data in Exhibit 2, calculate the total number of imported autos in operation for each of the years 1974 through 1978. Use this data to develop a forecast of the total for the years 1979, 1980, and 1981 and adjust for judgmental factors you believe to be important.
- Develop a list of judgmental factors that might affect Datsun's market share.
- Calculate Datsun's market share for each year, then prepare a forecast of Datsun's market share for each of the three years 1979, 1980, and 1981, adjusting as you see necessary for judgmental factors. Explain your calculations and adjustments.
- Calculate a forecast of the number of autos that would be sold by Datsun in each of the three years 1979, 1980, and 1981.

Nonextrapolative Approaches

In a number of circumstances, a historical base is not available and extrapolations are not possible. The start-up of a new company is one such situation, as is the introduction of a new product or penetration into a new market area. Situations such as these call for the development of forecasts based on factors other than history. In a start-up situation, estimates of a total market and estimates of the degree of penetration can provide defensible estimates of sales. If the company has early evidence of product acceptance or if customers are seeking out the company to place orders or if the company has few or no competitors, the estimates of penetration may be much higher than if the product is entering a market already occupied by accepted brands. Also, if the product requires educational effort in marketing and needs time to gain acceptance, then penetration will be slow at first, but will gain in intensity as the product becomes known and understood by potential customers.

The knowledge of persons familiar with the market will be of great help. Knowledgeable persons can provide crucial information about decision makers, seasonality in purchasing patterns, typical terms of sale, needs of customers, distribution channels, and pricing patterns. Where this is not known or not available, market research can poll potential customers to gain this information as an early part of the marketing-strategy-development process. In some kinds of marketing, data from the marketing of other products or services can provide guidelines as to the likely number of sales per contact, per mailing, or per thousand in population.

An example of the type of forecasting needed for the introduction of a new product can be found in a system introduced in 1983 that makes the use of an Apple microcomputer to collect, display, and record data fed to it by scientific measurement instruments, or sensors. The system consists of hardware units that plug into the computer, sensors, and a software disk that provides instructions to the computer to monitor and control the data fed from the instruments or sensors. The system has been designed to be sold to science teachers in public and private elementary and secondary schools and to junior and four-year colleges. It permits the screen display and the recording of up to 16 signals and the printing of any combination of those 16 signals in strip-chart form on common dot-matrix printers compatible with the Apple computer.

In demonstrations and trial marketing, the company had found that customers were quite receptive to the new product. In addition, word-of-mouth publicity had resulted in follow-on sales in nearly every instance where demonstrations had been performed. Over 75% of demonstrations had resulted in sales, and it was not uncommon for four to eight units to be sold in the months immediately following a given demonstration.

The company's marketing plan was to concentrate on the 10 states that had the highest number of microcomputers in use in primary and secondary schools. Distributors were to be used—persons or agencies that regularly contacted school systems to provide them with laboratory or audiovisual equipment. Apple knew that approximately 55% of the three hundred thousand microcomputers in schools were Apples and that the remainder were Radio Shack TRS-80s, Franklins (an Apple compatible), and Commodores. Company officials believed that their best chances for sales were in schools that had two or more microcomputers (approximately 35% of these were elementary schools, 63% junior high and high schools.) The numbers of schools with computers were 55,000 elementary schools, 13,000 junior high schools, and 17,000 high schools. Distributors said that they would cover approximately 20% of the elementary schools and 30% of the junior high and high schools. They anticipated a "hit" rate of 10% in elementary schools and a 50% "hit" rate in junior high and high schools.

Let's follow their thinking:

55,000 elementary schools × 55% with Apples =
29,150 elementary schools with Apples

29,150 × 35% (number of schools with two or more computers) ×
20% coverage by distributors × 10% "hits" = 204 units

EXERCISE 9–11

- Carry out the analysis to determine the number of these new products that will be sold to junior high schools and to high schools.
- What will be the effect on your estimate if the coverage is increased to 30% for elementary schools and 40% for junior high and high schools?

EXERCISE 9–12

- Assume that the estimates of sales developed on a national basis in the example for elementary schools and in the first question of Exercise 9–8 are representative. Derive estimates of sales by type of school for the top five computer-using states from the data provided by a market research firm:

State	*Number of Computers in Schools*
California	30,033
New York	20,262
Texas	20,246
Michigan	15,017
Illinois	14,058

We have discussed several different ways of developing a forecast of sales. Extrapolative methods were examined, as were judgments used to modify extrapolations, and methods used to build a forecast when a history does not exist. Each of these methods has application and each should be used where appropriate. No method will offer 100% precision, and all approaches must be based on combinations of data, mathematical or statistical techniques, and the judgments of individuals.

Now we will extend the forecasting process from sales and begin to build the entire expected operational framework of personnel, materials, equipment, and funds in order to develop a multidimensional and comprehensive managerial plan of operations.

ACTIVITY ANALYSIS AND OPERATIONAL FORECASTING

In Chapter 2, we discussed activity analysis as a means of examining the financial health of an organization. We talked about using the relationship between static elements (e.g., assets) and measures of activity such as sales or expenditures for the costs of goods manufactured. Activity ratios such as inventory turnover, the average collection period, and the ratio between total assets and sales were used to begin an assessment of the effectiveness of management in utilizing financial resources.

Activity analysis can also be applied to the other major functions in the business organization. Again, some measure of activity such as sales is compared to a resource or component that management utilizes in converting materials to products or in selling products. Thus, sales per salesperson is an activity ratio and serves as a valuable measure to assess the degree of sales effectiveness. Similarly, productivity —units produced per man-hour—is an activity measure used in production. In office administration, numbers of clerical personnel per $1,000 sales might serve as a measure of activity, as might customer orders per employee for a sales service group or purchase orders per employee for a purchasing department. For many years, Dale Yoder surveyed personnel departments to determine a standard for their effectiveness across the nation. He found the number of personnel professional staff and the total employment for the organization being served, then calculated a personnel staff ratio that served as an assessment of the extent of activity in a personnel department.[1]

In 1970, the ratio was 1 full-time personnel professional per 100 employees in all types of organizations. Manufacturing firms had a ratio of 1 to 110 employees; nonmanufacturing, a ratio of 1 per 90 employees.

The value of activity ratios cannot be overemphasized. They serve to provide guidelines and standards for operational efficiency and also aid in the planning process. If, for example, we have a sales estimate derived from our forecasting in Exercise 9–12, for example, we can estimate from that the number of employees needed for production, the number of sales persons needed to effectively support the sales program, the amount of capital equipment needed (in dollar terms), and the numbers of administrative support staff required in the company's offices.

As we use activity ratios in forecasting, we should remember that some of the components under analysis follow a step function in terms of costs and activity. A new plant will call for a fixed component of costs and staff across a wide range of output. Activity per capital dollar, therefore, will rise while the plant increases its output and will drop significantly as a new plant is constructed and first put into production. Managerial and administrative staff additions have a similar pattern in activity. Although they follow sales activity in the long run, across small increments in business activity their cost factors have a step pattern. Table 9–8 provides a number of pieces of information necessary to develop an operational forecast on the basis of activity analysis.

TABLE 9–8

Sales (last year)	855	Current assets	110
Total assets	280	Current ratio	2.2/1
Net worth	85	Number of salespersons	9
Number of factory employees	39	Number of full shifts in use	2
Number of factory supervisors	2	Factory supervisor costs	28
Number of office employees	6	Profit after 50% tax (last year)	22
Number of executive employees and staff	5	Office costs (½ salaries, materials, and services)	½ 69
Sales costs	135	Executive costs	125
Materials costs	95		

If sales are expected to increase by 12.5% next year, then a number of the elements listed will be expected to increase.

[1] Dale Yoder, *Personnel Management and Industrial Relations*, 6th Ed. (Englewood Cliffs, N.J.: Prentice-Hall, 1972), pp. 16–17.

EXERCISE 9–13

- Make a list of the elements in Table 9–8 you would expect to increase as sales increase. Then, calculate what each of those would be, given a 12.5% increase in sales. (Check your answers against the partial list at the end of the chapter.) Hint: At least 9 will change. Think the problem through very carefully.
- Construct a blocked-out *pro forma* income statement and balance sheet for this company (major categories only — in dollars — of assets, liabilities, revenues, and costs). Will you generate enough capital internally or will it be necessary to seek capital from lenders or by sale of stock?
- Provide a table of organization for the coming year. (A table of organization is a listing of the numbers of persons by category.)
- Calculate the percentage of capacity at which you will be operating.

Using Ratios to Set Financial Targets

In the preceding analysis we have incorporated an implicit assumption: that activity *ratios* will remain the same in future periods as in the past. We are, in fact, extrapolating *activity* in this process. It is not only possible, but highly desirable for managers to examine each of the activity ratios under consideration to determine whether simple extrapolation will be suitable or whether the ratio should be adjusted, judgmentally to deal with the conditions in future periods or to reflect the intentions of management.

An examination of ratios over several periods of business activity often can lead to a number of management decisions relating to the use of assets and the management of costs. If, for example, a manager finds that a ratio such as the current ratio is consistently higher than the average for the industry, questions should be raised about the necessity for the use of these funds and their cost. If funds currently used in current assets could be freed by tighter current asset control or by changes in payment policies, then those funds could be used for the acquisition of capital assets or the repayment of long-term liabilities. Given the cost of acquiring capital in the normal capital markets, these internally developed funds represent the potential for significant cost savings and an opportunity to avoid the dilution of owners' interests. Similarly, if fixed assets are found to be in excess of those used by one's competitors, management may wish to consider the disposition of unproductive fixed assets or give a heightened attention to output in order to increase the percentage of capital assets employed. In the health-care field, hospitals have found themselves operating at or below break-even level for their buildings and equipment. Some have sold off portions of their physical facilities, others have engaged in a variety of marketing campaigns designed to increase patient census.

The ratios of sales to total assets or sales to fixed assets serve as a general guide in determining asset efficiency. In the data provided in Table 9–8, the sales-to-total-assets ratio is 855/280, or 3.05. A figure for fixed assets is not provided. We can calculate fixed assets, however, by subtracting current assets of 110 from total assets of 280 to obtain a fixed-assets figure of 170. The sales/fixed-assets ratio, therefore, is 855/170, or 5.03.

Data made available to us indicate that the ratio of sales to fixed assets for the industry averages 7.05, with the majority of firms' ratios falling between 6.85 and 7.2. To determine how much capital might be freed by more efficient use of fixed assets, we might wish to examine the effects of reaching the industry average, or 7.05. In algebraic form, the path to an answer to this question is:

$$\frac{855}{X} = 7.05$$

Solving for X gives us a fixed asset level of 121.3. At this level of asset efficiency, nearly 50 in fixed assets could be freed (potentially) for use as current assets or for reductions in debt.

EXERCISE 9–14

Use the data contained in Table 9–8 to construct a *pro forma* balance sheet based on the following targets for fixed and current assets:

- Sales/fixed-assets target ratio = 6.84
- Current ratio target = 1.75 (adjust the level of current liabilities to achieve this ratio).
- Use funds freed by this process to adjust long-term debt.
- Calculate the long-term debt/total assets ratios before and after these changes.
- Hint: First, carefully construct a balance sheet based on the data now found in Table 9–8.

For cost control by means of activity ratios, materials costs might serve as one example. Although materials costs as a percentage of sales in the period given in Table 9–8 are 95/855, or 11.111%, a change in the mix of products being produced or a desire on the part of management to reduce materials cost might either increase or decrease the activity ratio and thereby affect the number forecast in the future period. In another case, if a manufacturing plant is currently working at a full one- or full two-shift basis, increased production is likely to push overhead expenses into a new step or plateau in a nonlinear cost function. The activity ratio that served reasonably well at lower levels of production may then be unsuitable for the new production rate.

EXERCISE 9-15

Use the data in Table 9-8 to calculate the answers to the following questions:

- Calculate an activity ratio that deals with employee productivity in manufacturing. Show your calculations.
- Calculate an activity ratio that deals with sales performance per employee. Show your calculations.
- Calculate what an improvement of 5% in factory productivity would mean in terms of staffing the factory given a 15% increase in sales for the coming year.
- Calculate what an improvement of 7% in sales productivity would mean in terms of costs, assuming a 15% increase in sales and an annual cost per salesperson of $22,000.

It is now possible to begin to build an operational forecast based in part on extrapolated information about markets and demand and in part on the operational judgments of managers involved in the major functions of marketing, production and finance. Although each functional manager is solely responsible for some elements in the operational forecast (e.g., sales management should be directly responsible for salesperson effectiveness), he or she shares responsibility for achieving other operational goals. Control of inventories, for example, is financially important in managing current assets. It is also of major significance to salespersons in maintaining adequate stock to assure shipments on a timely basis to customers. Raw materials and components inventories, on the other hand, are of basic concern both to financial managers and to manufacturing management, persons who must maintain a smooth flow of production and minimize costs. Similar paired relationships are needed for effective operational forecasting in accounts receivable, accounts payable, and fixed-asset utilization.

It is not difficult to see that the process of developing a workable and ambitious operational forecast involves the joint efforts of all functional areas and is, therefore, representative of the perspective of the general manager.

We will next construct a detailed operating budget from information provided from Table 9-8 and from functional area managers in finance, marketing, and operations. We will first calculate our estimate of profit and loss for the year, then carry any profit or loss to the balance sheet to derive our estimate of the year-end financial position. When completed, the statements not only represent the composite judgment of the management team, but also serve as standards of performance against which the management team can be measured.

Thus, we will use data from Table 9-8 and information obtained from functional managers to build a fairly simple operational forecast.

DATA OBTAINED FROM MARKETING, PRODUCTION, FINANCE

- Sales are forecast to increase 23.7% over last year.
- Salesperson productivity is expected to increase 7%.
- Factory productivity to increase 2.5%.
- Materials costs (as a percentage of sales) to decrease 3.5%.
- Wages and salaries to increase by 4%.
- Factory supervision to increase by one person.
- Office employees to increase by one person.
- Office materials and services to increase by 10%.
- Number of executives and staff to increase by two persons.
- Current ratio to reach 1.9 by year end.
- Sales to fixed-assets ratio to reach 5.50 by year end.
- Long-term debt will be reduced by 20 at year end.

In preparing the operational forecast, let us first deal with each of these items in question, then develop a profit and loss statement.

- Projected sales: Last year's sales = 855 × 1.23 = 1057.6.
- Sales costs. Last year's sales productivity was 855/9 = 95 per person. Increasing productivity by 7% would mean an increase to 101.65 per person. Total sales of 1057.6/101.65 = 10.4 sales persons needed. Last year's sales salaries = 135/9 = 15 per person. Increasing by 4% (see below) means a salary of 15.6, and a sales cost of 162.86.
- Factory productivity. Last year produced 855 with 39 persons, or 21.92 per person. Increase by 2.5% = 22.471. 1057.6/22.471 = 47.06 employees needed. Wages last year were 359/39, or 9.205. Increasing wages by 4% = wages per employee of 9.573 and total labor cost of 450.5.
- Materials cost. Last year's materials represented 11.111% of sales. Decreasing this expense by 3.5% reduces materials cost to 10.722% of sales, or 113.40.
- Factory supervision. Factory supervision cost 28/2, or 14 per person. This year, wages increase 4%, to 14.56, and the number increases to three persons, for a total factory supervision cost of 43.68.
- Office employees. Last year, six employees cost 34.5, or 5.75 per person. Salary increases of 4% increase this cost to 5.98. Adding an additional person brings office salary expense to 41.86.
- Office materials and services. Last year these cost 34.5. Increasing by 10% brings the anticipated cost to 37.95.

- Executives and staff. Executives and staff cost an average of 25 per person. With a 4% increase in salaries, the cost increases to 26. With an additional two persons, executive and staff costs are expected to reach 182.

From the data we have just developed, we should now be able to assemble a *pro forma* profit and loss statement for the coming year.

Sales Revenues		1057.6
Cost of Manufacture		
Materials	113.40	
Labor	450.52	
Factory Supvr	43.68	
Cost of Manufacture		607.60
Selling and Admin Exp		
Selling Exp	162.86	
Office Exp	79.81	
Exec. & Staff	182.00	
Total S & A Expenses		424.67
Total Costs		1032.27
Profit Before Tax		25.33
Tax @ 50%	12.665	
Profit After Tax		12.665

Development of a *Pro Forma* Balance Sheet

With the information developed from the *pro forma* income statement and the financial targets listed earlier, we can now begin to develop a *pro forma* balance sheet. We will begin by building from last year's balance sheet and deal first with accumulated earnings.

- Net worth. Following normal accounting practice, profit after tax, unless distributed as dividends, will be added to the preceding year's owner's equity accounts as retained earnings. Last year's net worth was 85. Adding 12.665 gives a net worth of 97.66
- Long-term debt. Last year's long-term debt, as one should have calculated by now, was 145. Reducing long-term debt by 20 will give a long-term debt figure of 125.
- Fixed assets. The sales/fixed-assets ratio target for the year is 5.50. If this target is reached, then with sales of 1057.6 and a ratio of 5.50, fixed assets will need to be 192.29.
- Working capital. The level of current assets and current liabilities needed to complete the balance sheet is dependent on three relationships: (a) current assets plus fixed assets = total assets; (b) current liabilities plus long-term debt plus net

worth = total assets; and (c) the target current ratio is 1.9, which means that current assets/current liabilities = 1.9. Although trial and error will ultimately result in achieving the correct numbers to fit into the balance sheet, the use of fairly simple algebraic equations can solve the problem quickly and accurately.

Let current assets = X

Let current liabilities = Y

Let total assets = Z. Therefore,

$$\text{total liabilities} + \text{net worth} = Z$$

Then,

$$\text{(a) } X/Y = 1.9, \text{ or } X/1.9 = Y$$

$$\text{(b) } X + \text{fixed assets} = Z, \text{ or } X + 192.29 = Z$$

$$\text{(c) } Y + \text{long-term debt} + \text{net worth} = Z, \text{ or } Y + 125 + 97.66 = Z$$

Substituting for Y in equation (c), we get

$$\text{(d) } X/1.9 + 125 + 97.66 = Z$$

Then using the equation found in (b) and the one derived in (d), we can solve for X

$$\text{(e)} \qquad \frac{X}{1.9} + 125 = 97.66 = Z$$

$$\text{Subtract} \qquad X + 192.29 = Z$$

$$= \qquad 30.36 = .47368X$$

$$\text{and} \qquad X = 64.09$$

The pro-forma balance sheet derived from these numbers meets all of the target ratios established and reflects the expected results of the coming year's operations.

Balance sheet

ASSETS		LIABILITIES AND NET WORTH	
Current Assets	64.09	Current Liabilities	33.73
		Long-Term Debt	125.00
Fixed Assets	192.30	Net Worth	97.66
Total Assets	256.39	Total Liabilities and Net Worth	256.39

EXERCISE 9–16

As a concluding set of exercises, use Table 9–8 and the following data to prepare a *pro forma* profit and loss statement and a *pro forma* balance sheet.

DATA OBTAINED FROM MARKETING, PRODUCTION, FINANCE

- Sales are forecast to increase 14.6% over last year.
- Salesperson's productivity is expected to increase 5%.
- Factory productivity to decrease .5% owing to the influx of new help.
- Materials costs (as a percentage of sales) to increase 7%.
- Wages and salaries to increase by 2.8%.
- No increase in factory supervision staff.
- Office employees to increase by one person.
- Office materials and services to increase by 8.5%.
- Number of executives and staff to increase by one person.
- Current ratio to reach 2.95 by year end.
- Sales to fixed-assets ratio to reach 5.10 by year end.
- Long Term Debt will be reduced by 10 at year end.

EXERCISE 9–17

From Exercise 9–16, develop specific managerial performance criteria for the managers responsible for marketing, operations, finance, executive/office operations, and for the General Manager.

EXERCISE 9–18

Refer to the Nissan Motor Corporation case presented earlier in this chapter.

- First consolidate the figures found in the balance sheets in Exhibits 6 and 7 to the following abbreviated format:

ASSETS	*LIABILITIES AND OWNER'S EQUITY*
Liquid Assets	Current Liabilities
Inventories	Long Term Liabilities
Property Plant and Equipment	Special Reserves
Investments	Total Stockholder Equity
Intangibles	
TOTAL ASSETS	TOTAL LIABILITIES & OWNER'S EQUITY

- Calculate activity ratios for the years for which data is provided, then establish what you believe to be reasonable targets for activity for 1979 and 1980.
- From your earlier work on the Nissan Motor case and your activity targets established in the preceding question, develop balance sheets for 1979 and 1980. (Please use the abbreviated format described.)
- Will additional funds be needed?

If yes: In what amount? What do you recommend as a source to provide these funds? Explain and justify.

If no: How much is your surplus? To what use would you put the funds not needed for those years? Explain and justify.

ANSWERS TO SELECTED EXERCISES

Exercise 9–2

$$b = \frac{\Sigma\,(xy)}{\Sigma\,x^2}$$

$$a = Y - bX$$

Using half-year increments for X:

YEAR	X	*NET PROFIT* Y	$y = (Y - \overline{Y})$	$x = (X - \overline{X})$	(xy)	x^2
1	2	(4)	−6	−3	18	9
2	4	(1)	−3	−1	3	1
3	6	7	5	1	5	1
4	8	6	4	3	12	9
	$\Sigma X = 20$ $\overline{X} = 5$	$\Sigma Y = 8$ $\overline{Y} = 2$			$\Sigma(xy) = 38$	$\Sigma x^2 = 20$

Then:

$$b = \frac{38}{20} = 1.9$$

$$a = \overline{Y} - b\overline{X} = 2 - 1.9(5) = -7.5$$

and the equation for the line is:

$$Y_c = a + b(X)$$

$$Y_c = -7.5 + 1.9(X)$$

Exercise 9–5

The algebraic sum of distances between the actual sales and the estimated data for the present-value approach is −32.93.

Exercise 9–13

Among the items you should have on your list are:

Number of factory employees
Sales costs
Materials costs

PART THREE

STRATEGY FORMULATION FOR SINGLE BUSINESSES

As we move from the first two parts of this text into the third, our focus of concentration shifts from the *present and short-term future* (i.e., the focus of attention of the general manager involved in *implementing* a plan of action) into the *long-term* future . . . a time horizon extending 3, 5, 10, or 20 or more years ahead.

Although we know that many businesses sell multiple products and engage in several different types of activities, in this part we will concentrate on the development of strategies for single businesses, individual business units for which a strategy can be established. In Part Four, we will examine the complexities involved in strategy formulation in companies where multiple business units must be managed for optimum effectiveness.

THE STRATEGY-FORMULATION MODEL

The process of developing a set of achievable long-range corporate objectives and a workable plan for their attainment (i.e., a strategy) can be seen as that of solving a very large-scale, multidimensional problem. Indeed, problem-solving models and models of the process used to assist in formulating and achieving strategic objectives are quite similar. In both, problems are framed in terms of a gap between some existing state and a desired state. The gap can be closed by the problem solver/manager by a process that involves several separate steps. Information must be gathered that assists in the preparation of alternative plans for problem solution. The information needed must not only relate to the conditions under which the solution must be attempted, but the capabilities of the problem solver or his or her organization to carry out the desired solution. For the gap to be closed, not only must the plan be developed well, but the organization must also be able to execute the plan.

In a model of problem solving based on expectancy-instrumentality theory, a third factor determining the degree to which the gap will be closed is the extent to which the solution to the problem has a positive valence to the problem solver.[1] The problem solver must not only see the problem as his or hers to solve, but must also attach some importance to solving the problem before the process of information gathering, preparation of alternative solutions, choice of solutions, and execution of the choice will be carried out at all, or carried out vigorously.

The information-gathering steps used in the process of developing a business strategy can be described as falling into two broad categories: information unique to the firm (for the most part *internally* oriented information) and information that describes conditions common to all parties involved in that firm's industry (generally *externally* oriented information). Our purpose is to use the information about internal resources to determine what we have to work with in carrying out some plan and to use the information about external conditions to understand the conditions under which we will be working to achieve the desired objectives.

In a very practical way, however, we need to provide some boundaries for our information gathering. In some large companies, where several quite distinct product lines are carried, information that relates to the internal resources

[1] J. R. Lang, J. E. Dittrich, and S. E. White, "Managerial Problem Solving Models: A Review and a Proposal," *Academy of Management Review*, October 1978, pp. 854–66.

of the firm could include that already allocated to product lines other than the one of interest. Similarly, in discussing information relevant to external conditions, a new technology in one product line may affect only that product line and have no relevance to other products carried by the company. An effective way of resolving this problem is the use of the concept of strategic business units. Each unit is a product, a service, or a line of business that has an identifiable group of competitors, a technology, an identifiable market, and factors in the environment that can be identified as bearing directly on that unit.

The use of the strategic business unit as the principal element in the formulation of strategies even for very large multiple business organizations is considered desirable because it is at this level that the transactions between the organization and its constituents (e.g., customers, stockholders, suppliers, employees, etc.) occur. It is also at this level that the trade-offs are made between risks and rewards.[2] For some businesses, the strategic business unit is the entire business. In other cases, several distinct units can be identified even in a relatively small firm. A company such as United Parcel Service is in a single business. It is quite large, but it exists to perform a single service in a single environment. A typical new auto dealership, on the other hand, may be involved in four or more separate businesses. (Examples might include new car, used car, service, commercial or fleet leasing, trucks, recreational vehicles, automotive or truck financing, and other product or service activities.) Each of these businesses has its own customers, technology, competitive structure, and regulatory environmental conditions.

The model we will use for the development and implementation of a strategy is, therefore, designed for individual strategic business units. It involves most of the steps of the model of problem solving, but it is developed for the specific purpose of guiding the development and implementation of the solution of a generic problem for general managers: the formulation of a single business strategy. Figure III–1 is a diagram of the strategy-formulation model we will use in our discussion. As you can see, the model contains a number of discrete blocks that cover separate analytic or action steps to be undertaken. You should also note that the model is circular in its path. Steps follow one another in a sequence designed to aid in a systematic and methodical approach toward the development and execution of a long-range plan of action.

One might enter an organization at any part of the model. Typically, organizations are found in the process of *carrying out* or executing some form of strategy . . . one stated explicitly or one that follows guidelines that are a reflection of an unstated, yet implicitly understood, strategic plan. One might also enter an organization following a reorganization, a process contained in the block labeled, Developing an Organization Structure, a step used to help in

[2] B. Yavitz and W. H. Newman, *Strategy in Action* (New York: Free Press, 1982), p. 19.

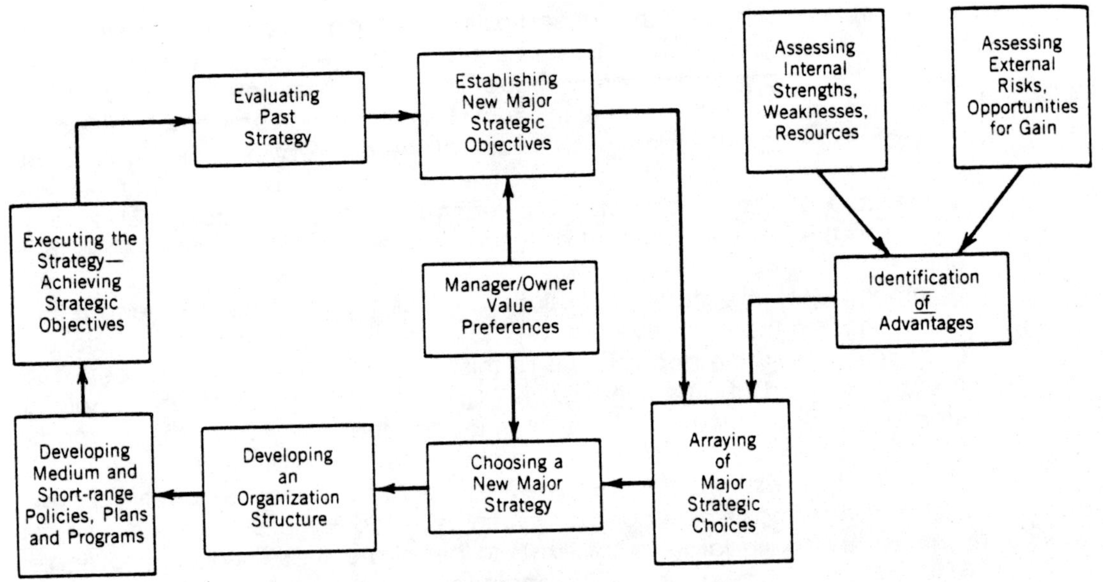

the process of carrying out a new or revised strategy. An understanding of the model, however, should enable the individual to understand the process, and the point in the process in which the organization is currently engaged.

The general manager, at some point or other, must assume the responsibility for evaluation of the effectiveness of a given strategy. If one has been involved in the execution of a strategy for a number of years, it is a matter of considerable importance that the progress of the organization toward the accomplishment of its goals be assessed. If progress has been satisfactory, then perhaps a new set of strategic objectives should be developed. In this case, the strategic plan should be designed to advance the organization from its present state to that established by the strategic objective. The distance between the existing and the desired future state represents the gap to be closed—to use the terminology of problem-solving. If, on the other hand, the present strategic objectives still seem suitable, but performance has not yet reached those objectives, a new plan may be required, one that will be aimed again at closing the gap, the distance between a present state and that desired by the strategist.

From an educational perspective, evaluation is the last stage in the development process in learning. It should be undertaken, therefore, *after* the student has built the knowledge, comprehension, and advanced skills needed to make the evaluation of merit. In the discussions we have completed, we concentrated on building the knowledge and skills required for the successful *execution* of a particular strategy, and thus we could address the evaluation of the effectiveness of the execution of a strategy at this time. In the next few chapters, however, we will build toward evaluation of all parts of the strategy-formulation process by developing analytic skills first, then practicing the skills of synthesis in developing strategic alternatives. We will deal directly with the process of learning about evaluation while addressing the issues involved in choosing a particular strategy, and we will apply that understanding of evaluation while examining the effectiveness of a strategy that has been in place for a period of time.

10

ANALYSIS OF THE EXTERNAL ENVIRONMENT

The process of developing and implementing an organizational strategy for a business unit can be initiated, as we have said, at nearly any point in the process described in Figure 10-1. An experienced strategist might begin at the point of evaluation—to determine the extent of success with past strategies—and then formulate new strategic objectives and move through the remaining steps. For students, however, we believe that the process can be learned best by beginning at an analytic stage and from that stage move to synthesis and evaluation as the new strategy is formulated and chosen from among competing alternatives.

The first of the analytic stages is to examine the environment in which the organization and its competitors are to function. As we examine the external environment, the first set of elements we are searching for are those factors that represent *opportunities* for growth, profit, or the attainment of other relevant long-range objec-

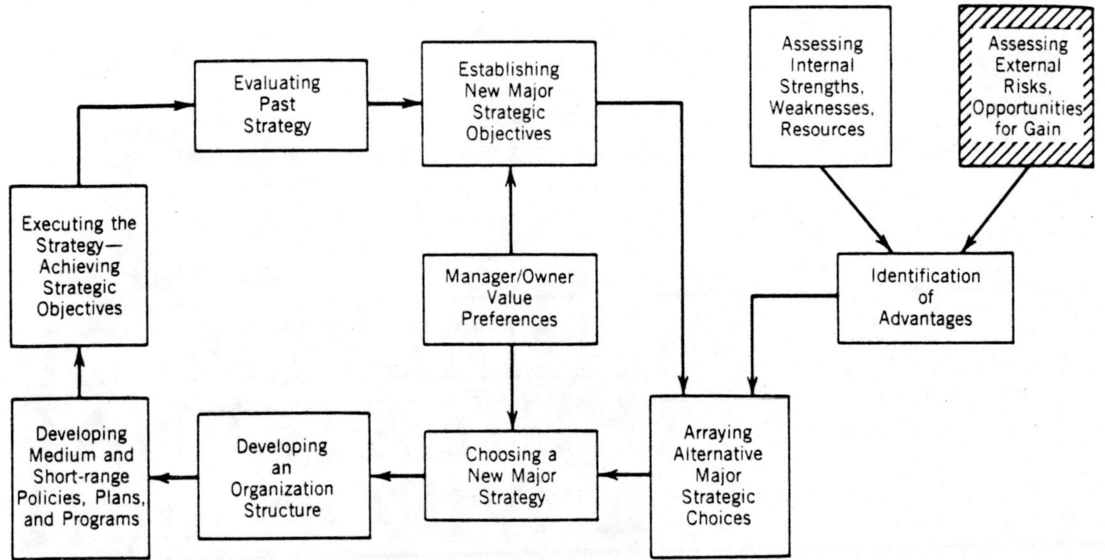

FIGURE 10-1 The strategy-formulation process.

tives of the subject organization and all of its present and potential competitors. Opportunities may arise as a result of growth in a customer group, changes in customer demand patterns, advances in technologies, changes in the demand for substitute products, aggressiveness or passivity in competition, or a host of other factors that we will examine in detail. We should keep in mind, however, that opportunities (as we define them here) are factors that represent the possibility for goal attainment to *all* competitors in a given industry/market.

Our second objective is to develop a detailed list of factors that appear to represent *risks* to our firm or to other firms engaged in the same business. Weather patterns, for example, constitute risks to a number of categories of business. Agricultural businesses, of course, are directly affected by temperature, precipitation, and storm patterns. In many sections of the country, farms located in river basins prosper in the rich soil of the bottomland near the river but suffer in the floods that occur every 5 to 7 years. Timber cutting is affected by snowfall, fisheries by storm patterns at sea, and resort industries by the number of sunny days during the tourist season. In each of these situations, *all* competitors in a particular market segment face the same conditions and the same risks.

Industrial examples might include the effect on all steel mills as auto manufacturers began to downsize their designs. Automobiles that formerly weighed 4,500 pounds (most of which was steel) are now designed to weigh 3,500 pounds. Downsizing by auto makers also had a great impact on the petroleum industry—fuel consumption dropped steadily. Designs for improved fuel consumption for new automobiles sold in the United States were instigated by the auto industry *in response to government-mandated fuel-consumption standards,* another form of environmental action that directly affected the auto industry and indirectly affected many other industries associated with the automobile market. In each of the cases cited, the industry was negatively affected by factors external to the industry.

EXERCISE 10–1

Determine whether the following should be categorized as largely a risk, largely an opportunity, neither a risk nor an opportunity, or both a risk and an opportunity. Explain. (Selected answers are found at the end of the chapter.)

- For the beef cattle business, a long-range weather forecast that predicts 15% lower than normal rainfall in the Midwest.
- For bicycle manufacturing and retailing, the announcement that oil prices in OPEC countries are likely to drop from $26.50 per barrel to near $20.00 in the next 3 years.
- For the river-rafting industry in the Rocky Mountain states, the announcement that a heavier than normal snowfall is anticipated for the coming winter.
- For the paper-carton manufacturing business, the announcement of a complete shake-up in the management of a carton manufacturer whose market share represents about 3.2% of the national market.
- For manufacturers of microcomputer peripheral equipment, the announcement that IBM and AT&T plan to market a completely integrated microcomputer system. (Computer, monitor, printer, modem, and major software for word and data processing, filing, and graphics).
- For the vegetable oil industry, an announcement by medical researchers that animal fats constitute the principal source of threat to human health arising from heart disease.
- Describe in some detail an example where the possibility of an environmental condition change could be a risk to one industry and an opportunity to another.
- Give an example (other than any cited already) where the potential for a government-mandated change can represent a risk to one or several industries and an opportunity to others.

Our examination of the external environment will follow a way of thinking about the environment that has been suggested by several authors. In this approach, the factors to be studied are divided into two broad categories, depending on the extent to which they bear specifically on the organization, or have effects on numerous industries.[1] The first category, that which has application to several industries, can be called the general business environment. The state of industrial development in a given nation; its general economic status; the character and quality of its banking, communications, and transportation systems; the level of education of the work force; and other similar societal characteristics form the basis of the general business environment. The second category, that which bears directly on the organization, can be described as the environment specific to an industry. Each industry has its political heritage, its advocates and critics, its own technology, competitive structure, and a set of competitors, potential entrants, suppliers, customers, and possible substitutes that are unique to that industry. This chapter will address each of these types of environmental factors in turn and will conclude with an in-depth examination of both types of environments and the development of prioritized lists of risks and opportunities presented by each form of environment.

ANALYSIS OF THE GENERAL BUSINESS ENVIRONMENT

Economic, social, political, and technological advancement in the general business environment (and the changes believed likely to take place in these factors during the planning period) are important factors in the environment for any business enterprise. A developing nation, for example, may currently be characterized as having a fairly primitive economy. But strategists planning for developments over a 10- or 20-year period would anticipate changes in the economic status of that country and might anticipate the introduction of modern systems of banking, transportation, and communications. Similarly, as social standards change, the market for a number of products and services has shifted. We will now examine some of the more significant elements in the general business environment and will attempt to understand how changes in any one of these factors might represent a risk to some types of industries, but an opportunity to others.

Economic Factors in the General Business Environment

There are a great number of economic indicators of a general business environment that are important to the strategist. We will develop a short list, but one that comprises most of the more significant components of economic health.

Inflation The rate of inflation in an economy has profound effects on every segment of economic life. With high rates of inflation in the prices for goods, wage rates must be adjusted rapidly in order for workers to have enough money to feed families.

[1] D. L. Bates and D. L. Eldredge, *Strategy and Policy: Analysis, Formulation, and Implementation*, 2nd Ed. (Dubuque, Iowa: Wm. C. Brown, 1984)—Refers to general and specific environmental analyses; J. A. Pearce and R. B. Robinson, *Strategic Management* (Homewood, Ill.: R. D. Irwin, 1982)—Call these the remote environment and the task environment, p. 103.

Financiers must adjust the interest rates for borrowing very quickly, and they will be reluctant to engage in long-term lending. Capital-expenditure projects exceed funding expectations as prices escalate during the duration of the project. The instability of the value of currency results in the use of substitutes for currency that are believed to have intrinsic value. Gold, gemstones, land, and other tangible properties are used as a means of storing wealth during periods of extreme inflation. In the United States, housing has often been sold on the basis of its investment value, a claim that could be justified so long as inflation pushed housing prices to extremely high levels. Thus, although the rate of inflation poses risks for workers and for lenders of money, investors in properties see inflation presenting an opportunity for gain. Brokers and dealers in tangible properties also enjoy the benefits of increased trading during high inflation as nervous investors seek security and gain by exchanging money for property.

Unemployment The level of unemployment in the general business environment is a second key factor in economic health. In modern societies, unemployed workers not only do not generate added value to the economy through their work, but also cause a drain on the economy through government assistance programs expending monies that might otherwise be used to fund projects that might generate revenue. Some unemployment, of course, will arise through natural processes as persons move from job to job throughout the course of their working careers. Other unemployment, however, can be caused by the movement of entire industries to other sections of a country or to other nations. In this instance, not only is the unemployment more dramatic in scale, but it is also likely to affect a broader range of persons, some of whom are much less likely to be able to move to new labor markets or to train themselves for new types of jobs.

A second type of troublesome unemployment is that which remains as a chronic condition. In this type of situation — found for years in the Appalachian Mountain region but now also in parts of New England, Pennsylvania, Ohio, Indiana, and other industrialized Midwestern states — there is a reluctance by workers to move to new labor markets, resulting in large-scale residual unemployment. The consequence is a climate in which the state carries a large welfare burden and where the potential new employer must compete in wage offerings with unemployment benefits and (at least psychologically) with the wages of industries now gone.

Although unemployment can be seen as offering risks to potential employers, it may also be seen as a potential opportunity. Unemployment benefits have limits, and the forces of change can result in employees seriously seeking a change in their type of work and their level of compensation. Younger workers may be more readily persuaded to try a new occupation and to rebuild a working career in that new line of work. For industries that make use of skills that can readily be learned on the job or skills that are new to the industry or the area and that must be learned on the job, a moderately high level of unemployment may mean that their is an oversupply of available labor and that the employer can select good workers for training from a large pool. Similarly, if the work is unpleasant or menial, turnover may normally be very high and workers hard to find. In a labor market characterized by high unemployment, employers have a larger labor pool to draw on and may be able to reduce their turnover somewhat because of the lack of available job alternatives for dissatisfied employees.

At the other extreme, very low unemployment may result in pressure upward on wages, with consequent pressure for increased pricing; constraints on the scale of operations, brought about by limits on the availability of human resources; and the potential for lower efficiencies and poorer quality as more marginal employees are drawn from a dwindling supply of workers.

Interest Rates The prevailing and anticipated interest rates can have a differential effect on the structure of the economy and can thereby directly affect the general business environment for any of a range of industries. In recent years, a high rate of interest (in the United States) for long-term borrowing pushed the rates of interest for home mortgages to levels that priced homes beyond the means of home buyers. The housing industry, both new and resale, nearly shut down. High interest rates also caused industries that had planned large-scale capital-expenditure projects to postpone them. Several effects were felt almost immediately. First, the construction trades were hit by massive unemployment. Second, the real estate industry suffered dramatic declines in income from commissions and persons anticipating a change in residence postponed the move, where possible. In effect, the demand for funds dropped in response to the increase in the price of those funds; the results were reflected in a slump in several major sectors in the economy. Investors or investing agencies that did not have to borrow to obtain funds were able to generate greater income from the effects of the higher rates and thereby could see the higher general rates of interest as an opportunity for gain. When high interest rates continue, capital will shift from areas of lower returns to seek the higher rates of return to be gained through lending.

Extremely low rates of interest, on the other hand, may cause the migration of capital to other, higher-return regions or countries. In addition, these low rates may bring about the recall of high-interest-rate bonds and the consequent disruption of income streams from investment portfolios. Changes in the rate of interest, as we have seen, can have dramatic effects on the general business environment and must be considered carefully as a part of the analysis of economic conditions.

Productivity The general state of industrial or commercial productivity is a significant factor in many industries. In labor-intensive industries, output per unit of time can mean the difference between commercial success or failure. To a large degree, productivity per unit of worker time is affected by the capital investment in productive technology and the state of development in that technology. Where these factors are essentially equal in two regions, the industriousness of the work force can be the principal difference in the relative productivity between the two. It is also worth mention that where wage rates in two economic regions differ, the difference in the cost of production is markedly affected by both factors: wages *and* units produced per unit of time. High wages and low-productivity levels typically mean risks to firms choosing to operate in a particular region. If, however, this is a characteristic of the industry, the high cost of production may mean a significant opportunity for the company that can make use of superior equipment and expertise in production technology as well as have access to lower cost or more industrious workers.

Investment Capital Regions or nations characterized as capital rich are not constrained in the pursuit of new concepts or the expansion of existing facilities. For firms that have a high level of capital intensity (e.g., mass-production industries, electric power companies, institutionalized health-care groups), the presence of available capital is a crucial component in the company's ability to prosper and grow. For other types of industry, where the need for capital is significantly lower, expansion can continue and new ventures can be explored within the limits of a restricted supply of funds. For companies in need of capital, a capital-rich environment presents the opportunity for great gain. Where capital is in short supply, capital intensive industries must either seek capital from other regions or must forego the exploration of the venture. In the less well-developed countries, where capital is not readily available for domestic industry, large foreign corporations have made use of the capital at their disposal to build large facilities. For them, the shortage of capital in that country presented an opportunity for gain.

EXERCISE 10–2

Each of the following conditions in the general business environment represents risks to some elements of the business community and opportunities for gain to others. For each, identify at least two types of organizations or individuals outside of, or within, those regions for whom the specified condition represents a risk, and in addition, two types for which the conditions represent the opportunity for gain.

- A region in the United States has chronic structural unemployment, ranging between 12% and 16%. At least one-half the unemployed are workers older than 45 who were formerly employed in smokestack industries that have now been closed owing to foreign competition. Most of these unemployed own their own homes and do not wish to move to other labor markets to find work.
- Productivity per man hour in a particular economy is notably high. Although wage rates are not as low as in some Third World countries, the level of output is significantly higher than any competing region.
- The legislative branch of government is expected to pass a flat tax bill to be used to derive revenue from private citizens. The flat tax would replace an extraordinarily complex progressive tax that provided tax benefits for hundreds of special interest groups and that was extremely difficult to monitor and administer by the taxing authorities.

- The Soviet Union announces that it will begin the large-scale marketing of gold derived from its gold mines located in Siberia. Gold experts believe these to be the largest underground reserves in the world.
- The Organization of Petroleum Exporting Countries (OPEC) disbands owing to disagreements within the cartel on restricting production and on marketing oil to Europe and the United States.
- The Department of Defense announces that it plans to build a multibillion-dollar space systems repair facility adjacent to the major launch site at Vandenburg and Edwards Air Force bases in California. No other potential sites were discussed.
- A Japanese firm announces that it has developed a completely roboticized auto assembly plant. Company representatives describe the system as requiring approximately 10% of the number of workers as in the company's oldest plant, and 20% of the number of workers in the company's most recently constructed plant. Capital investment is expected to be approximately three times that for a conventional assembly plant. With a roboticized plant, officials said, different models of the same design can be produced interchangeably on the same assembly line, and design changes can be accomplished in about half the time required under the older technology.

POLITICAL FACTORS IN THE GENERAL BUSINESS ENVIRONMENT

To a great extent, the political/legal factors in the general business environment will derive from the dominant political philosophy in the country or region. Examples of the results of different political philosophies can be found in state governments in the United States. The adjoining states of Vermont and Massachusetts, for example, have quite different general business environments as a consequence of the differences in political philosophies of their electorates. Massachusetts can be characterized as politically liberal, socially responsive state with a substantial government and a relatively high state tax burden. Vermont, on the other hand, could be characterized as conservative, with an interest in minimal government interference and low state taxes. Where competing political philosophies are both powerful and quite different (France and Great Britain are examples) the role of government changes rather dramatically as one or the other of the competing parties assumes political control.

The political philosophies that support an extended view of government as an active force in governing and/or controlling economic affairs will enact a variety of forms of government control mechanisms to that end. Laws will be enacted that call for government to regulate employment, control trusts, regulate foreign exchange, monitor environmental and natural resource conservation, and provide for extensive taxation of all forms of commercial activity. We shall next look briefly at some of these types of political influence on the general environment and assess the extent to which each represents a risk or opportunity for commercial gain.

Government Regulation and Enforcement

The presence of extensive government regulation in a business environment has a number of consequences for the conduct of commercial activity. For the most part, government regulation represents a risk because regulations can be changed with little advance notice by individuals unresponsive to the forces of the marketplace. For individuals or agencies with expertise in government lobbying or with specialized knowledge on how to deal with government agencies, however, regulations serve as an avenue of opportunity for gain. As the controls become more complex, these consultants sell their advice or contacts to companies that seek to function in the regulated environment.

The pattern of enforcement of government regulation and law has shown substantial change from one political administration to the next, despite the fact that the laws have remained essentially the same over the years. For a number of years in the 1950s and 1960s, price-fixing enforcement was a focal point for Department of Justice attention. In the late 1980s, insider trading has been prosecuted intensively. It seems evident that not all of our various regulations governing business and commercial activity can be administered uniformly or with equal degrees of intensity. We will, therefore, see periodic shifts in the focus of attention and in the degree of pressure brought to bear on the enforcement agencies to prosecute those in violation of the regulation or law of most interest at that time.

Laws Regulating Employment

A number of different types of laws and regulations can be found that affect employment. Minimum wage laws; child labor laws; laws governing the hours of work, worker safety, employment security, and the employment of various classes of persons are all examples of employment regulation found in the United States. Some of these forms of regulation have been developed through federal law and apply to all states. Others are derived through the states and can be seen to differ depending on the interests of each states' electorate. Numerous examples could be cited to illustrate the effects of these aspects of the general business environment.

One example of the effect of minimum wage laws is found in the reduction in the number of car-wash establishments that follows the enactment of increases in the minimum wage. Car-washes are labor intensive and make use of unskilled labor. Even modest increases in minimum wages result in substantial cost increases to the car-wash operator and often cause price increases that reduce business volume below break-even levels.

For a car-wash operator, the minimum wage laws represent a constraint and a risk because they can be subject to change by legislative action. For the company that develops a highly automated car-wash machine, however, the minimum wage law's effect on the industry presents an opportunity for gain.

In recent years, legislators have sought to make teenagers exempt from minimum wage legislation in order to develop opportunities for employment for a group of potential workers who now have exceptionally high unemployment. State laws regulating the employment of women for many years mandated rest periods, limited the weight that could legally be lifted by women, and in some cases restricted their hours of work. Workmen's compensation laws enacted by the states as early as the 1890s provided for compensation for workers injured or made ill by their work activities.

EXERCISE 10-3

From the following list of types of employment regulation, select three you think present opportunities for gain for an industry or a profession. Describe in detail.

- Workmen's compensation (for job-related injury or illness).
- Laws governing occupational safety and health (OSHA) Occupation of Safety and Health Administration].
- Laws governing the employment of protected classes (minorities, ethnic groups, etc.).
- Laws protecting the security of employee retirement income [(ERISA) Employee Retirement Security Act].
- Laws governing collective bargaining.
- Laws governing the payment of overtime for work over 40 hours per week.

Antitrust Legislation

The United States has maintained a system of internal competition for nearly 100 years with the assistance of legislation that prohibits certain types of competitive activity. The Antitrust Division of the Department of Justice actively prosecutes companies or individuals that act in violation of the Sherman or Clayton Antitrust acts. Concerted actions by a group of competitors, for example, to fix prices, control production, or harm either competitors or customers would be seen as damaging to competition and court action would be sought to seek the cessation of the action and the punishment of the lawbreakers.

This type of regulation is found in the United States, but it is not common elsewhere in international commerce. The Organization of Petroleum Exporting Countries (OPEC), for example, is a consortium of nations engaged in a concerted action for the express purpose of restricting production, raising prices, and (for some members) economically harming its customers. Japanese industry has emerged from the ashes of World War II and been built into seven or eight very large industrial giants, with the encouragement of the Japanese government. These very large companies each produce a wide range of products. They are very active in export trade and are explicitly supported by a government that is intent on maintaining a positive trade balance for the Japanese economy. German industry is similarly organized and contains very large companies and cartels that dominate trade in a particular industry and that are acknowledged and supported by government agencies. State-owned industries are found in a number of countries in the West, an expression of government interest and support for certain critical industries at the expense of competition.

In the United States, the active prosecution of antitrust law presents risks to some types of organizations and opportunities for others. Companies that dominate their market are natural targets for antitrust charges and investigations. Small companies with limited financial resources, however, are afforded the protection of the antitrust law from the very large companies that could afford the losses of destructive competition. The individual firm is also offered the protection of the law from the collusive actions of competitors. This protection has not only been offered to commercial and industrial competitors, but also has been extended into the realm of professional practice, forbidding the "punishment" by associations of competitors of professionals who choose to offer rates below a "standard" fee or commission.

The system of antitrust legislation found in the United States certainly offers protection (and the opportunity for gain) to small, capital-weak companies. We should also recognize, however, that it has the effect of weakening the position (presenting risks) to companies subject to competition from the cartels and giants of foreign competition, especially those financially supported by their governments. The effect of this vulnerability has been seen in the inroads that have been made in several areas of the U.S. industrial economy by competitors from Japan, Korea, and the European Common Market countries. The issue of the trade-off of protection for small competitors within our country for the vulnerability of large and small companies to foreign competition will not be easily resolved.

Foreign Trade

One solution to the encroachment of foreign competition is that of erecting barriers to the entry of foreign-made goods. Although it is generally recognized that these barriers are harmful in the long run, the protection of constituents in the short run may cause government officials to seek to stop the inflow of foreign goods. In years past, the United States maintained a posture of self-sufficiency and sought to keep an industrial base and raw materials in sufficient supply to sustain the economy and a defense system through a period of conflict. The increasing size and needs of our economy and the changes in war technologies have made self-sufficiency a less persuasive argument than might have been the case 40 or 50 years ago. Instead, the United States has maintained a network of relationships with supplier countries to provide its needs through trade agreements in which the United States limits tariffs on imported goods.

The United States has also used international trade as a political tool, encouraging the rebuilding of nations destroyed in World War II as a means of limiting the incursions of the Soviet Union. Foreign industries have been sheltered by a tariff structure in their own economies. As a consequence, industry in the United States has borne the brunt of two forms of action: Its products face fierce competition from foreign-made goods in the United States while tariffs in foreign nations raise their prices to levels that make their products uncompetitive in those foreign markets. For companies operating in the United States, virtually unrestricted competition from foreign competitors represents very real market risks. For exporters, restrictive tariffs have closed many markets or pose the risk of closure.

EXERCISE 10-4

The entry of foreign manufacturers' products into U.S. markets poses great risks for competing U.S. manufacturers. To what segments of U.S. commerce would the entry of these products represent an opportunity? Why? Explain.

EXERCISE 10-5

The presence of tariffs for U.S. goods entering foreign markets represents a restriction or constraint on U.S. exports to those markets. To what firms or industries would this represent an opportunity? Why? Give an example or two.

Environmental and Natural Resource Protection

The degree to which environmental and natural resources are protected by government action varies considerably from country to country and from region to region in the United States. In recent years, conservation of air quality and the promotion of water conservation and improvement of water quality has caused the closure of old power plants, papermills, steel-making facilities, and numerous other industrial enterprises. For their owners, the cost of the improvements needed to meet the new standards for air and water quality could not be adequately covered by the profits expected (especially in the case of older facilities), and the plants were closed. Major steel and paper manufacturers have closed older mills and have made the investment in improved water- and air-pollution-control equipment at locations that will remain competitive and that will stand a chance of recovering the added capital investment.

The industrial processes used in both of the industries mentioned can cause the pollution of air and water. A more recent development among investigators of the Environmental Protection Agency (EPA) is the discovery that metallic contaminants such as cadmium were discarded in common landfill garbage dumps and were found to represent severe environmental hazards. Representatives of the EPA plan to monitor and regulate not only companies engaged in the large-scale manufacture and rebuilding of batteries (a principal source of the contaminant), but also expect to extend the observation and regulation of the disposal of the contaminants to the neighborhood battery shop and garage. Similarly, controls on certain liquid hydrocarbons used for dry-cleaning, which had formerly been placed only on large-scale cleaning establishments, will be extended to all firms that use the hazardous materials. In short, the problems of big companies of 20 years ago are now the problems of even the smallest businesses.

Thus far, we have been concerned with factors that affect nearly all businesses that wish to function in a given region or nation. We will now deal with the more immediate environment of a particular firm in a given industry, the specific industry environment. Before leaving the discussion on the more general environment for businesses, however, we need to examine the *general* environment for a very large business, Chrysler Corporation, as it sought to survive to compete in the 1980s. The Chrysler Corporation case presents an excellent development of the environmental factors faced by the auto industry during a period of extreme stress. As you read the case, note factors that affected Chrysler and all of its competitors. You might want to code them to determine which part of the *general* business environment they represent (economic, foreign trade, regulation, etc.). At the end of the case we have several exercise questions to be used for classroom discussion or for homework assignments.

THE CHRYSLER CORPORATION LOAN GUARANTEE ACT OF 1979

What's good for Chrysler
is good for the country.

As the 1980 automobile year began, one issue emerged that brought together Chrysler's management, the United Auto Workers, Michigan Congressmen, former President Gerald R. Ford, and President Jimmy Carter long enough to successfully defeat a combined force which included the likes of consumer activist Ralph Nader and free-marketeer Milton Friedman. These unlikely sides were formed as Chrysler—the nation's tenth largest industrial company—found itself in a grave situation. A marginal manufacturer in a traditionally cyclical business, Chrysler has historically had erratic profits due in part to its relatively high costs and weak financial structure. But when the market share of the third largest U.S. car maker plummeted from 16.1 percent in 1970 to 9.6 percent for 1979, the beleaguered company was near bankruptcy. Its losses of over one billion dollars in 1979 were the largest in U.S. corporate history,

The research and written case information were presented at a Case Research Symposium and were evaluated by the Case Research Association's Editorial Board. This case was prepared by Professor Paul Miesing of the State University of New York at Albany based on published accounts and public documents, and it is intended as a basis for classroom discussion rather than to illustrate either effective or ineffective handling of an administrative situation.

EXHIBIT 1
New automobile sales in the U.S.

	Total units (000s)	Market share (%) GM	Ford	Chrysler	AMC	U.S. Cars (000s)	Imports Total (000s)	Market Share (%)
1975	8,700	43.4	23.0	11.5	3.8	7,100	1,600	18.4
1976	10,100	47.5	23.3	12.9	2.5	8,600	1,500	14.8
1977	11,200	46.1	22.8	10.9	1.6	9,100	2,100	18.7
1978	11,300	47.7	22.8	10.1	1.5	9,300*	2,000	17.7
1979 (est.)	10,600	45.9	20.1	9.6	1.5	8,300*	2,300	21.6

*Excludes imports produced by foreign manufacturers for U.S. firms, and Volkswagens manufactured in the United States.

and were expected to be followed with a half-billion dollar loss in 1980. (See Exhibits 1 and 2 for industry sales and profits.) Spending from thirty to fifty million dollars a day on cars that would not be available for two years, the company could not generate enough cash to meet its daily operating costs. Only by raising massive amounts of new capital could Chrysler hope to survive. But bankers are reluctant to extend funds to a firm facing such an uncertain future unless the loans are guaranteed by the federal government. Such a proposal was initiated by the Carter Administration, but remained an extremely emotional and controversial issue throughout its subsequent Congressional hearings.

Many of Chrysler's problems were blamed on the skyrocketing costs for meeting tight (and some believed unreasonable) government legislation, costing consumers around ten percent of the price of an automobile. With a billion dollars budgeted for 1979 and 1980 just to meet regulatory requirements, Chrysler claimed that the situation it faced was merely a symptom of excessive government intervention into the affairs of U.S. industry. Their argument continued that, if the company was failing as a result of public policy which required corporations to meet social demands, then federal assistance was justified. Besides, the government had already amply demonstrated its willingness to support the economy through its numerous assistance programs, subsidies, grants, and other policies that aided businesses.

Taking his case to the public by writing in the December 3, 1979, issue of the *Wall Street Journal*, Chrysler chairman Lee A. Iacocca stated that "the unequal effects of government regulation" were unfairly hurting Chrysler. (Exhibits 3 and 4 demonstrate the results of Chrysler's dis-

EXHIBIT 2
Comparative sales and profits for U.S. automobile manufacturers

	Sales ($ billion) GM	Ford	Chrysler	AMC	Profits ($ million) GM	Ford	Chrysler	AMC
1975	35.7	24.0	11.6	2.3	1,151	323	(260)	(28)
1976	47.2	28.8	15.5	2.3	2,903	983	423	(46)
1977	55.0	37.8	16.7	2.2	3,338	1,673	163	8
1978	63.2	42.8	13.6	2.2	3,508	1,589	(205)	42
1979	66.3	43.5	12.0	3.1	2,893	1,169	(1,097)	68

EXHIBIT 3
Comparative expense structures for major U.S. automobile manufacturers (1974–78 average ratios)

	GM	*Ford*	*Chrysler*	*AMC*
Net sales	100.0%	100.0%	100.0%	100.0%
Less: cost of goods sold	85.0	89.3	93.8	90.0
Gross profit	15.0	10.7	6.2	10.0
Less: depreciation selling,	2.1	1.9	1.1	.9
general & administrative	3.7	3.8	4.0	9.0
Operating profit	9.2	5.0	1.1	.1
Add: other net income	1.0	1.1	.1	.8
Less: interest	.6	.7	1.0	.7
Pretax income	9.6	5.4	0	.2
Less: income tax/extraordinary	4.5	2.2	.1	.2
Net income	5.1	3.2	(.1)	0

advantage.) Citing 1965 emission standards as the predecessors for automobile mandates, he claimed that the industry had already reduced pollutant levels by ninety percent and it would cost $250 per car to reach the additional five percent required by 1981. Another example of inane involvement in industry affairs were the safety standards established in 1967, which eventually evolved into forty-four separate and confusing rules. The final imposition of Washington wisdom was 1975's fuel economy standards that demanded doubling the average miles per gallon for the 1985 fleet. Since "regulations amount to a regressive sales tax that hits the smallest company the hardest," Iacocca suggested that "helping Chrysler get through a financial crunch resulting from these regulations is itself a socially desirable thing to do."

EXHIBIT 4
Selected financial statistics for major U.S. automobile manufacturers (1979 year-end)

	GM	*Ford*	*Chrysler*	*AMC*
Total assets (millions)	$32,023	$23,510	$6,653	$1,123
Total debt (millions)	$ 2,094	$ 2,082	$ 4.8B	$ 162
Debt/equity ratio	0.1	0.1	0.4	0.2
Current ratio	1.7	1.3	1.3	1.5
5-year average return on equity	19.8%	15.4%	deficit	1.5
5-year average return on capital	18.0%	12.7%	deficit	2.3
5-year average sales growth	13.2%	12.7%	8.2%	10.9%
5-year cash flow/growth needs	94.9%	90.5%	59.6%	59.5%
Outstanding shares (millions)	289.4	120.2	66.7	31.9
Stock price	$50	$32	$6¾	$6⅞
Dividend	$5.30	$3.90	$.20	$.08
Quality rating (S & P)	AAA	AAA	B	B

Insisting that the company's problem arises from its "need to raise massive amounts of new capital to meet federal law," he made a passionate argument for seeing Chrysler through its temporary crisis:

> *The issue we have raised by going to the government is not free enterprise. We really don't think a loan guarantee to Chrysler is in any sense a reward for failure, nor would it lead to a breakdown in market discipline.*
>
> *Nor is the immediate issue the need for regulatory reform—even though certain reforms are necessary.*
>
> *Rather, the central and critical issue at stake in Chrysler's survival is people and jobs. If government wants to do something about unemployment, if it wants to keep the nation's urban areas and cities alive, if it wants to prevent increased welfare dependency and government spending, if it wants to offset an $8 billion imbalance of automotive trade with Japan, let it approve Chrysler's legitimate and amply precedented request for temporary assistance.*

Iacocca's position was at odds with that of such business leaders as General Motors' Thomas Murphy, Eastern Airlines' Frank Borman, General Electric's Reginald Jones, and Citicorp's Walter Wriston, among others, who stated that government support on such a huge scale would be inimical to a free enterprise system. They shared the "free enterprise" view that corporate managers are responsible to operate their businesses efficiently within environmental constraints and that their performance should ultimately be judged and rewarded by the market place. The government's responsibility to protect the public's interest does not extend to awarding windfalls to owners, managers, creditors, and others merely because they have a large stake in a corporation's outcome. Indeed, any forced distortion of investment flows would lead to lower productivity and fewer jobs over the long-run.

In a Darwinian system where only the fittest are worthy of survival, Chrysler may conceivably wind up as only one of the many thousands of annual casualties of free enterprise, which already include such major corporations as Arlen's Department Store, Equity Funding, Food Fair Stores, Franklin National Bank, W. T. Grant, and Robert Hall. Companies that go bankrupt merely pay the price for its prior management's poor decisions and miscalculations. This would also be true for Chrysler which was out of step when it re-designed big cars for 1974 and 1979, both times caught by surprise with a fuel crisis. Although no one could have predicted the energy crisis, Chrysler insisted on remaining a full-line producer even after American consumers shifted to fuel-efficient cars, only to find later it did not have enough small cars on hand to satisfy the surge in demand. Moreover, periodic economic downturns in no way helped sales.

While some viewed the bailout debates as a test case for future business-government relations, others saw labor unions exerting political pressure to save jobs in an upcoming election year. As evidence of this, an intense lobbying effort was mounted by Chrysler's allies who were attempting to convince the Congress that the aid it was seeking would give the corporation a profitable future and the U.S. economy a valuable manufacturer. Therefore, a one-year reprieve would be worthwhile to the nation.

The bill to approve federal assistance was placed on the U.S. Senate's calendar to follow their year-end debates on the oil companies' windfall profits tax. But for any loan guarantees to be meaningful, legislation had to be enacted before Congress adjourned. If aid were not forthcoming, the company claimed it would go bankrupt by February 14, 1980—St. Valentine's Day. As the long recess rapidly approached, there were fears that a compromise bill would not be agreed upon before the holidays. But Chrysler got its Christmas gift on Friday, December 21, 1979—the last day of the sessions—when Congress passed a multibillion dollar rescue package just minutes before a majority of representatives went home. For the last week of the year, Chrysler's share of the market jumped to 12.4 percent.

The "Chrysler Corporation Loan Guarantee Act of 1979" created an independent, Cabinet-level loan board chaired by the Secretary of the Treasury and including the chairman of the Federal Reserve Board, the Comptroller General, and two other Cabinet officers who are nonvoting members. The board was authorized to grant $1.5 billion of loan guarantees at a charge of one percent per year which must be repaid by the end of 1983. But the company had to allow the government to monitor its operations in detail, audit its books, and even shuffle around top executives if deemed necessary. In addition, Chrysler had to come up with another $2.1 billion on its own while maintaining existing loans owed to current creditors. Of this amount, domestic banks, financial institutions, and other creditors would have to grant $500 million in new loans. Suppliers and dealers were obliged to give Chrysler $180 million in loans and/or stock purchases and states and cities where facilities are located were required to offer $250 million. Chrysler, on the other hand, was mandated to dispose of $300 million assets beyond the $400 million already liquidated and sell $50 million of additional stock. And its nonunion, white-collar employees were compelled to sacrifice $125 million by freezing their wages and benefits for three years and cutting the salaries of top officers.

Perhaps the most sensitive requirement was demanded of the United Automobile Workers. The House version of the bill called for $400 million in extra wage cuts whereas the Senate's bill called for $525 million. The final compromise of $462.5 million—including previously agreed-upon contributions totalling $203 million in wages and benefits—would require new contract negotiations and ratifications by the union members. In turn, the white-collar employees and blue-collar workers would receive $162.5 million in Chrysler stock. The union voted in favor of the proposal on January 5, 1980, and President Carter signed the bill into law two days later.

Immediately afterward, Iacocca announced plans to introduce cars ranging from subcompacts to a new down-sized Imperial. Since Chrysler needs only two good years to survive as a full-line carmaker, the eighteen months immediately following passage of the Act are crucial. But, since the loan guarantees will not be extended again, some feel that Chrysler's inevitable demise had only been postponed.

BRIEF HISTORY OF THE AUTOMOBILE INDUSTRY

The early part of this century saw 181 different automobile manufacturers come—but mostly go. Through consolidation and failure, the industry eventually became dominated by three firms. The evolvement into a concentrated oligopoly began when Henry Ford first revolutionized the then-fragmented industry in 1908 by using an assembly line to bring out an inexpensive car for the masses. His Model-"T" was an instant success with its high reliability and low maintenance cost. That same year, the lesser-known William C. Durant, using a business philosophy of organization and finance, turned the Buick Motor Company into the nation's leading automobile producer by selling eight thousand cars compared to Ford Motor Company's six thousand Model-"T"s. A year later, Durant's Wall Street backers rejected his proposal to buy Ford for eight million dollars. But continued success allowed Durant's holding company to evolve into the General Motors executive offices. Ford was able to maintain half the market with its low-priced, high-volume Model-"T" and low-volume, high-priced Lincoln. General Motors only had twelve percent of the market, but decided to offer a greater variety of automobiles in order to avoid direct head-on competition with Ford.

General Motors added numerous divisions as it grew over the next decade, but Durant insisted on making decisions about Buick without consulting its new president and general manager, Walter P. Chrysler. During the 1920 depression, after Durant and Chrysler had another of their frequent, stormy confrontations, Chrysler left the company to supervise the reorganization of the failing Maxwell Motor Corporation which had gone into receivership. The company was rescued and Chrysler had his name on an automobile by 1924. When the Chrysler Corporation was incorporated on June 6, 1925, it was the last successful entrant into the industry. But its real opportunity opened when Ford, losing market share to General Motors, ceased production in 1927 to design and produce the Model-"A". Chrysler had already pioneered such innovations as high-compression engines and four-wheel brakes, and now its Plymouth was able to take advantage of Ford's absence. The following year, Chrysler purchased the larger Dodge Bros., Inc., although the former Ford supplier had managed to escape a General Motors acquisition bid in 1926. Combined into Chrysler, the new company had one of the largest and most complete car plants in the world. DeSoto was added to Chrysler, and by 1929 the company joined General Motors and Ford as a member of the "Big Three." Thereafter, smaller firms would be unable to compete in the high volume market for the average car buyer.

Automobiles became the largest U.S. business by 1930 and General Motors became its leader for good in 1931, forcing Ford and Chrysler to follow its shift to a marketing orientation which differentiated products and emphasized annual model changes. After Chrysler made costly miscalculations in the mid-thirties as to how much change in appearance the public would accept in one year, the company finally managed to nudge out Ford for the number two spot for 1937 by once again deciding to emphasize research and development. Chrysler eliminated the debt it had acquired for its prior expansions, and in 1946 its reputation for engineering allowed it to repeat its second place finish behind General Motors by capturing a quarter of the automobile market. But Henry Ford II had taken over his grandfather's company after the second World War and immediately recruited the so-called "whiz kids," who reorganized the company and brought professional management techniques to it. Ford's first post-war automobile was introduced in 1949. After the United Automobile Workers struck Chrysler in 1950, the company permanently fell into third place.

The rapid economic growth of the fifties allowed automobiles to become shining examples of free enterprise and the pursuit of happiness. Detroit's chariots typified the "bigger is better" mentality as they continued to grow larger, more comfortable, and conspicuous and came to symbolize mobility, freedom, status, and self-expression. America's romance with the automobile was reflected in billions of dollars in gasoline taxes collected by the Federal Highway Trust Fund. But there were setbacks for the industry as well. Ford's Edsel became a legend in marketing fiascos, and Chrysler's DeSoto was finally dropped. The smaller firms—Kaiser, Willys, Nash-Kelvinator, and Hudson—found it difficult to compete, and so consolidated into the American Motors Corporation. Chrysler then decided to borrow funds to revamp the 1954 model, which was "smaller on the outside and bigger on the inside." Unfortunately, the public preferred General Motors' and Ford's larger cars, and the company's market share dropped to thirteen percent. Only after Chrysler bounced back with its own large car in 1957 did it capture nineteen percent of the market—which has not been reached since.

While Ford responded to a shift in consumer sentiment toward smaller cars by bringing out its highly successful Falcon and Mustang in the early and mid-sixties, Chrysler decided to stay with its higher-priced large cars by continuing to innovate in design, styling, and interior comfort, even introducing high-performance cars into its lineup. It was during this decade of social sensitivity to the quality of life and a struggle to become a "great society" that automobiles fell victim to industry regulations. The "Clean Air Act of 1963" (amended in 1970 and 1977) mandated the amount of pollutants that cars could emit. "Re-tuning" engines to accept emission control devices required an additional ten percent of gasoline consumption. Then, partly as the result of a forty percent increase in motor vehicle-related deaths from 1961 to 1966, and partly the result of a young, obscure Washington lawyer by the name of Ralph Nader writing *Unsafe at Any Speed,* the U.S. Congress passed the "National Traffic and Motor Vehicle Safety Act of 1966." Adding the necessary five-hundred pounds of weight to meet these safety and emission requirements reduced mileage another ten percent. America's honeymoon with the automobile was coming to an end.

Although the automobile industry would continue to grow buoyed by the booming economy of the sixties, the coming collision between energy and the environment would emphasize the shift of corporate decision making from the market to the political arena. The end of the sixties saw an increasingly unpredictable economy with money and materials in short supply. But at the time, few could have realized how the transformation of the industry during the next decade would end in an uncertain future for automobiles and, in the process, force a re-examination of government intervention in the free enterprise system.

TURMOIL IN THE SEVENTIES

On several occasions in the early seventies the government was called upon to decide when a company had become too important to fail. The first of these decisions was in June 1970, when the Penn Central Railroad was denied the two hundred million dollars it claimed it needed to survive. Congress chose instead to let the regulated company go bankrupt and thus become the largest in U.S. history to do so. During the debates, former Senate Majority Leader Mike Mansfield had declared: "I do not believe it is the function of a democratic government to pick up the tab for the failure of [a] private enterprise." Protected from creditors' claims, the profitable segments of Penn Central were able to survive while the government disposed of the remainder. This was done by establishing the "National Railroad Passenger Corporation," or AmTrak, in 1971, to run intercity rail service for passengers.

Chrysler's financial subsidiary found it difficult to re-finance its short-term I.O.U.s after the Penn Central failure caused a softening of the financial markets. Having overproduced and overpriced its restyled intermediate models as a result of misjudging the automobile market which was now swinging back toward big cars. Chrysler went to Washington, D.C., for help. Although Congress rejected the Federal Reserve Board's suggestion to establish special lines of credit that would make it easier for consumers to buy new cars, an internal study had concluded that the Federal Reserve Board had legal authority to directly loan or guarantee such loans to an industrial concern if it felt that failure of the company would imperil the national financial system. As a result, Chrysler's banks were told to loan the company whatever it needed and that the government would cover any losses. Escaping financial difficulties, Chrysler decided to avoid head-on competition with General Motors' Vega and Ford's Pinto subcompacts by instead going after the big-car buyers.

Although Congress had rejected requests for aid by Penn Central and Chrysler, it suddenly reversed itself in 1971 when it narrowly approved $250 million in loan guarantees to the nation's largest defense contractor. Lockheed, with two-thirds of its production going to U.S. military weapons, had lost nearly one-half billion dollars while building the Air Force's C-5A carrier at the same time it was receiving too few orders for its unexpectedly costly L-1011 Tri-Star. In order to obtain government backing, the company had to come up with $245 million worth of credit on its own, pledge its assets and collateral, and open all of its dealings to public scrutiny. Lockheed became profitable and the U.S. Treasury had earned thirty-one million dollars in interest payments by the time their relationship was terminated in 1977.

These precedents became important as large automobiles were battered in the turmoil of the seventies. In 1970, subcompacts had accounted for only three percent of the U.S. automobile market and many of these were imports. By 1973, Chrysler had managed to capture forty percent of this unprofitable market segment with its best-selling Plymouth Valiant and Dodge Dart but had gambled $350 million to replace them the following year by re-styling its more profitable lines. Its timing could not have been worse. With Detroit's 1974 models guzzling a third more gasoline than their smaller and boxier predecessors had twenty years earlier, only General Motors had the foresight to recognize the government's inability—or disinterest—in dealing with the pending energy problem. It re-organized its top management structure to meet the future, and successfully took on new challenges while retaining its strategy of "a car for every purse and purpose": to capture a large share of the small-car market while dominating the bigger car segment.

The oil embargo by the Organization of Petroleum Exporting Countries which lasted from October 1973 to May 1974, vividly demonstrated that the nation's economy and its automobile industry had been operating under the very frail assumption of cheap and plentiful gasoline. The quadrupling of oil prices in three months contributed to the worst economic crisis since the Great Depression. Large numbers of Americans—upset by uncertain gas supplies and long lines at filling stations—began looking overseas to buy their cars. Traditionally capturing fifteen percent of the U.S. automobile market, all foreign cars by now had nearly twenty percent as American car sales had their sharpest slump since the thirties. Although large car sales picked up again shortly after, Ford and Chrysler could not recapture a good share of their markets lost to the imports. Chrysler, once again approaching financial difficulties, responded by firing numerous engineers, designers, and salespeople to cut its overhead costs and reduce its break-even point. This move would later make it difficult to react quickly to market demands and government commands.

Two Congressional debates held in 1974 were to have a bearing on Chrysler and the automobile industry. One was over the possible re-establishment of the Reconstruction Finance Corporation as a lender of last resort. Originated during the Depression to permit the government to act as trustee of ailing companies by eliminating the stockholders, the R.F.C. had made loans amounting to fifty billion dollars during its twelve-year life. Its revival was defeated. Among the proposal's opponents was Senator William Proxmire (D-Wis.), who was then preparing to assume the chair of the Senate Committee on Banking, Housing and Urban Affairs from which he would reign as self-appointed protector of free enterprise.

The other debate studied the feasibility of increasing the industry's "corporate average fuel economy" (CAFE) by forty-five percent. General Motors argued that such legislation was unnecessary since the market was already demanding more efficient automobiles. Although their entire fleet averaged an industry low of 12.2 miles per gallon, General Motors announced that they would be able to substantially increase the mileage on their 1978 cars if safety and emission standards were suspended. Congress refused to go along and passed the "Energy Policy and Conservation Act of 1975" which mandated an 18.7 mile per gallon fleet average by 1980. By 1985, all automobile fleets must obtain an average of 27.5 miles per gallon.

Confident that the public would begin to trade down, General Motors' president Elliott ("Pete") Estes took the risk of downsizing the largest cars for the 1977 model year. These new cars would have interior room, comfort, and driving quality comparable to larger cars, yet would allow General Motors to achieve an industry high of 17.8 miles per gallon. In order to blunt Ford's and Chrysler's introduction of small cars, General Motors also brought out America's first "sub-subcompact," the Chevette, in half the typical three to four years by having its foreign subsidiaries develop it: Opel designed the body in Germany and the engines were made in Brazil. Though the Chevette was not immediately successful as customers began returning to bigger cars, General Motors was poised to introduce its downsized cars. By the spring of 1979, the highly successful front-wheel-drive "X" cars were brought out after four years of development at a cost of $2.7 billion. The compacts were two feet shorter and a fifth lighter than the cars they replaced, allowing them to get twenty-five miles per gallon. By anticipating the market well and correctly responding to it, General Motors should leave the seventies stronger than when they entered it. It introduced a series of small sporty cars (designated the "J"-cars) in the spring of 1981; a year later will come out with a family of smaller intermediates; and by 1983 will have downsized full-size models available. In addition, General Motors has been increasing its capacity for diesel engines, four-cylinder engines, and front-wheel-drive components.

Ford Motor Company not only successfully passed the mid-seventies storm, but 1976 through 1978 were its best years in history. One reason was that then-President Lee A. Iacocca (known as "the Father of the Mustang") felt that he could take advantage of General Motors' downsizing program by staying with big cars in 1976, although this decision was contrary to the many dire predictions of big car sales at that time. Also recognizing that intermediaries and compacts would play a significant role in the future, Iacocca introduced the Fiesta to counter General Motors' Chevette. For his accomplishments, Iacocca was thought certain to become Ford's next chairman, succeeding Henry Ford II who by then had run the company for over thirty years. Instead, the strong-willed Ford ("My name is on the building") felt that Iacocca's talent for developing and selling small cars would not be sufficient to run his company. Ford wanted a successor that also possessed managerial and financial skills. For refusing to accept a secondary rung on the corporate ladder, Iacocca was fired in July 1978, becoming Ford's seventh presidential casualty in two decades. As Ford entered 1978 with over $3.5 billion in cash, it planned to retain its traditional strength in small cars by replacing the highly-successful Pinto in the fall of 1980 with the smaller Escort, its first front-wheel-drive and the first U.S.-built "world car" to be assembled in several countries from parts made in many countries and sold anywhere around the globe.

Chrysler had been pursuing a full-line strategy similar to Ford's but with far less success. Only its strong truck sales, not yet subject to federal fuel requirements, had prevented a cash crisis in 1975. Rather than meet new government standards, the company dropped its trucks in favor of vans and pickups. While General Motors was downsizing its cars, Chrysler—like Ford—stayed with its luxury cars in hopes that customers would rush out to buy the last of the big cars. Chrysler did manage to bring out the smaller and successful Volaré and Aspen in 1976, but buyers were then returning to full-size cars. In attempting to turn the company around, Chrysler's board of directors replaced then-president and chairman Lynn A. Townsend with Eugene Cafiero as president and John J. Riccardo as chairman. One of their first announcements was a five-year plan to spend $7.5 billion to re-model the company's plants and product line by 1979. But delays prevented the redesigned New Yorker and St. Regis from being delivered until later that spring. Then the Shah of Iran was deposed in January 1979, and long gas lines developed by April and lasted until September. Chrysler's habit of shipping cars to dealers before they were ordered had caused its inventory of large cars to swell to eighty-eight thousand cars valued at seven hundred million dollars. Added to the 355,000 cars that dealers already had on hand, the company found itself with a supply good for one to two hundred days out of the three-hundred day sales year. This glut of cars not only cost two million dollars per week in handling and interest charges, but also interfered with the new model introductions.

Buyers by now were demanding fuel-efficient cars. But sales of the immensely popular Omni-Horizons, the first small four-wheel-drive cars made in the U.S. when introduced in 1977, were limited to the 300,000 engines a year that Chrysler had earlier decided to purchase from Volkswagenwerk AG rather than investing one-hundred million dollars to refit an existing Chrysler plant. Although these cars helped Chrysler get the best fleet mileage of the "Big Three" with 20.2 miles per gallon, low-priced small cars continued to remain money losers. Complicating matters, organized labor was lobbying for legislation requiring American manufacturers to include in their fleet average only those cars having at least a seventy-five percent "American content." If passed, this law would effectively exclude from future fleet average Chrysler's high mileage captive imports, such as the Arrow, Challenger, Colt, and Sapporo, manufactured by Japan's Mitsubishi Motors Corp. which is fifteen percent owned by Chrysler.

During the sixties, Chrysler had followed General Motors and Ford overseas by acquiring the failing French Simca and British Rootes Motors, Ltd. Beginning to turn into cash drains at the time large investments were needed, those European operations were finally sold in August 1978, to France's Peugeot-Citroen for three hundred million dollars in cash and fifteen percent in equity for a total value of some $430 million, making the European automaker the fourth largest in the world behind Chrysler. In addition, Peugeot had agreed to assume responsibility for the four hundred million dollars that these operations owed to European creditors. Chrysler holdings in Australia, Latin America, South Africa, and Turkey were also sold shortly thereafter.

To help stem this tide of adversity, Chrysler gave Lee A. Iacocca a one million dollar bonus and a quarter million dollar annual salary to become its president in November, 1978. Given the long lead-time to introduce new cars, Iacocca could not make changes until the company's 1982 offerings. Not only did this challenge represent a fulfillment of Iacocca's aspirations to head a full-line auto company, but it also gave him an opportunity to demonstrate that he had substance to match his style. After bringing along several Ford executives, Iacocca cut inventory costs in half by offering rebates, automatic transmissions, and five-year warranties on large cars. Next, he got out of leasing operations that had cost the company eighty-one million dollars, and saved eighty-five million dollars in insurance premium costs by closing old plants. He also asked suppliers to absorb $150 million in inflationary costs that are conventionally passed along.

In June 1979, Volkswagen, already producing its Rabbit in a Pennsylvania assembly plant acquired from Chrysler, was reportedly looking into buying Chrysler for about fifteen dollars a share, or one billion dollars. This rumor was never verified by any source and was vigorously denied by both firms, who further stated that they would be opposed to any merger or acquisition. Chrysler then began its lobbying campaign in Washington, D.C., for federal relief, relying heavily on Detroit mayor Coleman Young—also the vice chairman of the Democratic National Committee and a strong Carter election backer—to defend this cause. But in July, the government refused to offer Chrysler its billion dollar aid request.

CHRYSLER'S RESCUE PACKAGE

The upcoming 1980 model year was feared to be the worst in a long time for automobiles since the inevitable recession would hit the volatile industry first. (See Exhibits 5 and 6 for economic impacts and trends.) Making matters worse, around twenty-two percent of the cars sold in 1979 had been imports and this figure was expected to rise as high as thirty percent in 1980. As a result, domestic automobile operations were twenty-five percent below their trend line. Such a drop hurts Chrysler because of its large

EXHIBIT 5
Changes in gross national product and automobile production and employment

	Total U.S. real GNP growth (% change)	Automobile production		Automobile employment (% change)
		Industry (% change)	Chrysler (% change)	
1960	2.3	17	34	5
1961	2.5	−16	−34	−13
1962	5.8	23	14	9
1963	4.0	11	43	7
1964	5.3	2	19	2
1965	5.9	20	17	12
1966	5.9	−7	−1	2
1967	2.7	−13	−6	−5
1968	4.4	20	17	7
1969	2.6	−6	−12	4
1970	−0.3	−19	−7	−12
1971	3.0	29	5	6
1972	5.7	6	11	3
1973	5.5	12	14	12
1974	−1.4	−21	−20	−7
1975	−1.3	−10	−21	−13
1976	5.9	28	45	11
1977	5.3	11	−4	7
1978	4.4	2	−6	6

EXHIBIT 6
Selected economic forecasts

	Real GNP growth (% change)			Real spendable income (% change)	
	1979	*1980*	*1981*	*1980*	*1981*
Chase Econometrics, Inc.	−2.5	−1.4	2.7	0.4	3.3
Data Resources, Inc.	−2.3	−1.4	3.3	0.0	1.7
Wharton Econometrics	−2.4	0.0	3.4	0.1	1.8

debts. For instance, a total of $4.8 billion was owed to some two-hundred and fifty banks and other financial institutions, causing the company's net interest payments to jump to $128.9 million in 1978 compared to $74.9 million in 1977 and $52.5 million in 1974. In addition, its long-term debt of $1.2 billion was the industry's largest. Furthermore, the company will be in technical default if its working capital falls below six hundred million dollars. In 1980, $303 million in European loans and another $284 million in U.S. loans become due. As a result of these obligations during an economic downturn, the financial rating services lowered the quality ratings on Chrysler's securities, effectively preventing the company from selling any additional promissory notes.

On August 6, 1979, G. William Miller left as chairman of the Federal Reserve Board to become the Secretary of the Treasury. Three days later, although philosophically opposed to direct government intervention in the free enterprise system, his first public act was to announce that Administration support for Chrysler would be in the public interest. Although tax credits were rejected out of hand, loan guarantees would be considered if Chrysler submitted an acceptable overall financial operating "survival plan." The troubled company, by then losing around seven hundred dollars on every car it sold, submitted its "Proposal for Government Assistance" on September 15 and requested the U.S. Treasury Department to guarantee $1.2 billion of loans.

This request was rejected by the Treasury Department. Although the stated reason was that the amount requested nearly doubled the three-quarter billion dollars which the Administration had indicated it would accept, some believed that past management's continuing association with the company hindered approval while others felt that there was too much controversy for Congress to agree to any bill. The government responded that commitments of help would have to be made by workers, suppliers and dealers, banks, state and local governments, and any others having a large stake in the company. Chrysler was then sent home to reduce its aid request.

On September 20, 1979, Iacocca moved up to become Chrysler's chairman by replacing John Riccardo who had suddenly and unexpectedly decided to retire three months earlier than planned. Facing the toughest selling job of his career, Iacocca once again offered rebates and by the end of September, Chrysler's inventory of unsold 1979 cars had dropped by a quarter to near-normal level and was the lowest of the "Big Three"—but at a cost of ninety-two million dollars in lost profits. In addition, the planned capital expenditures for 1980–1985 had been reduced by $1.1 billion.

Concerned about White House delays in putting together a financial aid package, Chrysler took its argument to Congress in mid-October. Trying to force the Treasury Department's hand, Chrysler executives began testifying before the Senate and House Banking

Committees in early October that federal automobile regulations, gasoline shortages, and an economic recession were the major factors contributing to the company's severe cash shortfall. A revised rescue package was presented to the Administration on October 17, 1979. (See Exhibits 7 and 8 for Chrysler's income statements and balance sheets.) In Chrysler's "modified survival plan," the company reduced its federal loan guarantee request to cover a third of the needed \$2.1 billion, with the remainder coming from outside sources. In this plan, Chrysler detailed how it would remain viable by selling enough cars at prices that could pay for labor and capital—if there are no new gas shortages, the recession is mild and short, and its market share goes up from 10.2 percent to 12.4 percent. Also included were plans for reducing overhead costs by half-a-billion dollars to allow the company to break even with a market share of 10.5 percent. (Exhibits 9, 10, and 11 detail anticipated market demands and cost reduction programs.) But the management consulting firm of Booz, Allen & Hamilton reported to Chrysler that this amount would be insufficient if sales turn down, there is a faster shift to small cars, or Chrysler's market share is less than planned. Any of these situations might necessitate another seven hundred million dollars in contingency funds.

On October 25, 1979, Chrysler and the United Automobile Workers—the country's second largest union with its one-and-a-half million members mostly urban bluecollar workers—agreed to a \$1.3 billion wage pact over the next three years. Alfred Kahn, Chairman of the Council on Wage and Price Stability, immediately condemned the thirty percent wage hike (from \$8.67 an hour to \$11.32 an hour) and benefits over three years as violating the Administration's seven percent wage guideline. (Recommended changes to this guideline may be reviewed by the newly formed Pay Advisory Committee, of which U.A.W. president Douglas A. Fraser is a member.)

Kahn later retracted his controversial statement, and the U.A.W. was the first to make concessions to Chrysler by deferring two hundred million dollars of pension payments (the amount by which it was then overfunded) and delaying an additional \$203 million in wage and benefit improvements over the next two years. The union imposed three stipulations. First, part of the pension contributions must be used by Chrysler to fund "socially desirable" projects, such as saving decaying urban areas in the industrial north or recommending investment sanctions against companies doing business in South Africa. Second, Chrysler's compensation package would have to increase by a third over the next three years so that its workers could reach General Motors' and Ford's already negotiated compensation package of twenty dollars an hour. Third, American workers will finally have a voice at the highest policy-making level of a major company when U.A.W. president Douglas A. Fraser is nominated at Chrysler's stockholders meeting in May 1980, to become one of Chrysler's twenty board directors. Fraser did not expect a conflict of interest to arise by having a labor official represent all Chrysler owners equally or by having a Chrysler director that will remain loyal to U.A.W. members at General Motors and Ford.

While Chrysler's supporters were busy arguing the level of support, there were those that felt that the impact of a Chrysler failure would be mitigated by the "Bankruptcy Reform Act of 1978" that took effect on October 1, 1979. Under the revised Chapter 11, debts would be frozen so that operations could continue. Instead of court-appointed trustees making decisions, existing corporate management would retain control while the company underwent reorganization, saving jobs for workers and paying back creditors quickly. Large creditors could not readily veto a reorganization plan, although it would be easier to force a business into bankruptcy. Chrysler would be able to stay in business, although the company may be

EXHIBIT 7
Chrysler corporation balance sheet October 17, 1979 (millions)

	Actual				*Projections*					
	1976	*1977*	*1978*	*1979*	*1980*	*1981*	*1982*	*1983*	*1984*	*1985*
Cash	$ 168	$ 208	$ 123	$ 150	$ 150	$ 150	$ 150	$ 150	$ 150	150
Accounts Receivable	798	897	848	612	659	795	850	950	1,050	1,150
Inventories	2,354	2,623	1,981	1,815	1,613	1,722	1,814	2,016	2,225	2,462
Other	558	425	610	160	167	170	170	170	170	170
Total Current Assets	$3,878	$4,153	$3,562	$2,737	$2,589	$2,837	$2,984	$3,286	$ 3,595	$ 3,932
Investments, Property, Plant & Equipment	3,196	3,515	3,419	3,678	4,152	5,449	4,784	5,910	6,442	6,737
Total Assets	$7,074	$7,668	$6,981	$6,415	$6,741	$7,621	$8,433	$9,196	$10,037	$10,669
Accounts Payable	$1,351	$1,912	$1,301	$2,283	$1,978	$2,147	$2,308	$2,542	$ 2,822	$ 3,129
Short-Term Debt	172	250	49	16	10	10	10	10	10	10
Long-Term Debt Due Within One Year	69	91	12	123	145	168	184	194	186	152
Other	1,234	837	1,124	—	—	—	—	—	—	23
Total Current Liabilities	$2,826	$3,090	$2,486	$2,422	$2,133	$2,325	$2,502	$2,746	$ 3,018	$ 3,314
Other Noncurrent Liabilities	385	413	381	651	625	623	618	613	613	736
Long-Term Debt (Before New Financings)	1,048	1,240	1,188	1,166	1,096	1,020	928	828	734	666
Net Worth	2,815	2,925	2,926	1,842	1,333	1,738	2,269	2,896	3,775	4,786
Liabilities & Net Worth	$7,074	$7,668	$6,981	$6,081	$5,187	$5,706	$6,317	$7,083	$ 8,140	$ 9,502
Funds to Be Obtained From New Financings:										
Current Year	—	—	—	344	1,220	361	201	(3)	(216)	(730)
Carried F'wd from Prior Years	—	—	—	—	334	1,554	1,915	2,116	2,113	1,897
Total	$7,074	$7,668	$6,981	$6,415	$6,741	$7,621	$8,433	$9,196	$10,037	$10,669

EXHIBIT 8

Chrysler Corporation income and financing requirements October 17, 1979 (millions)

	Actual est.						*Projections*			
	1976	*1977*	*1978*	*1979*	*1980*	*1981*	*1982*	*1983*	*1984*	*1985*
Revenue	$12,240	$13,059	$13,618	$12,415	$13,586	$15,630	$17,811	$19,765	$21,812	$24,142
Costs	11,759	12,863	13,904	13,486	14,059	15,255	17,285	19,110	20,833	22,863
Earnings Before Taxes	481	197	(286)	(1,071)	(473)	375	526	655	979	1,279
Taxes on Income	153	34	(81)	2	9	(18)	10	10	112	283
Net Earnings	$ 328	$ 163	$ (205)	$ (1,073)	$ (482)	$ 393	$ 516	$ 610	$ 867	$ 996
% Return on Sales	2.7%	1.2%	—	—	—	2.5%	2.9%	3.1%	4.0%	4.1%
Funds Applied				$ 143	$ 690	$ 765	$ 714	$ 656	$ 645	$ 373
Funds Generated:										
Profits After Tax				(1,073)	(482)	393	516	610	867	996
Borrowing				(33)	(4)	2	2	2	2	2
Sale of Shares				29	—	40	42	45	47	50
Financing Arranged				510	24	—	—	—	—	—
Change in Deferred Taxes										
Net Funds				3	(68)	(31)	(47)	2	(55)	55
Cumulative Shortfall				$ (707)	$ (1,220)	$ (361)	$ (201)	$ 3	$ 216	$ 730
Typical Financing				334	1,554	1,915	2,116	2,113	1,897	1,167
Total Funds Required				1,493	1,536	1,540	1,590	1,627	1,690	1,740
Cumulative Asset Disposition				$ 1,827	$ 3,090	$ 3,455	$ 3,706	$ 3,740	$ 3,587	$ 2,907
Balance to be Financed				101	496	728	928	1,058	1,091	1,155
From Other Sources U.S.				$ 233	$ 1,058	$ 1,187	$ 1,188	$ 1,055	$ 806	$ 12
Treasury Cumulative Shortfall*										
at 95% Volume				—	$ 1,593	$ 1,994	$ 2,196	$ 2,309	—	—
at 90% Volume				—	$ 1,689	$ 2,258	$ 2,687	$ 3,037	—	—
				—	$ 1,784	$ 2,522	$ 3,179	$ 3,837	—	—

*Revised October 17, 1979, and assumes reduced capital spending; savings of $6 billion over six years; and additional improvements in fixed costs and variable margins for Exhibits 10 and 11.

EXHIBIT 9
Projected automobile sales and Chrysler corporation market share

	1980	1981	1982	1983	1984	1985
U.S. Car Sales (millions of units):						
Chase Automobile	10.5	11.1	11.2	11.4	11.7	11.9
Data Resources, Inc.	10.3	11.0	10.8	11.1	12.9	12.2
Wharton Econometrics	10.6	11.5	12.5	13.0	13.2	12.9
Merrill Lynch	9.7	11.2	12.3	12.5	12.5	12.5
U.S. Treasury Low*	9.3	10.3	10.8	11.4	—	—
at 95% Volume	8.8	9.8	10.3	10.8	—	—
at 90% Volume	8.4	9.3	9.7	10.3	—	—
Chrysler Market Share (%):	10.2	11.1	11.6	11.9	12.1	12.4
Small	11.3	13.2	15.0	16.0	15.5	14.8
Medium	12.9	11.6	10.2	9.7	11.3	12.5
Large	4.6	5.6	4.7	3.6	3.5	4.9
U.S. Treasury Low*	10.5	11.1	11.6	11.9	—	—
at 95% Volume	10.0	10.5	11.0	11.3	—	—
at 90% Volume	9.5	10.0	10.4	10.7	—	—

*Revised October 17, 1979 and assumes reduced capital spending: savings of $6 billion over six years; and additional improvements in fixed costs and variable margins per Exhibits 10 and 11.

EXHIBIT 10
Annual fixed cost reduction program (millions)

	1980	1981	1982	1983
Personnel—reduced salaried employees by 8,500 people	$201.9	$204.2	$204.2	$204.2
Compensation—freeze salaries and benefits of nonunion employees and reduce senior executive salaries	22.2	12.2	12.2	12.2
Facility closings—shut down four plants	69.5	121.5	121.5	121.5
Operating expenses—launch, preproduction, supplies, and service costs	91.6	91.6	91.6	91.6
Marketing—reduce advertising and sales promotions, and sell rather than lease cars to major fleets	137.8	137.8	137.8	137.8
Other	(9.2)	(.5)	(.5)	(.5)
Total fixed cost savings	$513.8	$566.8	$566.8	$566.8
U.S. Department of Treasury adjustments:				
Personnel	$ (3.8)	$ (7.0)	$ (7.0)	$ (7.0)
Facility closings	(14.0)	(18.0)	(18.0)	(18.0)
Operating expenses	(21.0)	(51.0)	(27.0)	(20.0)
Marketing	(26.5)	(40.5)	(7.6)	(21.0)
New fixed cost savings	$448.5	$450.3	$507.2	$500.8

EXHIBIT 11
Variable cost reduction program

	1979–1982		1982–1986	
	Per car	*Per truck*	*Per car*	*Per truck*
Production improvements—new style, design, or performance elements to increase profitability	$174	$ 35	$ 59	$ (52)
New options & equipment changes—making new technology items available for comfort and convenience	55	69	45	40
Design cost reductions—material or component substitutions, parts simplifications, and changes in design to lower material or manufacturing costs	83	37	60	40
Manufacturing improvements—more efficient techniques, facilities, and equipment	82	47	66	65
Component insourcing—building own four-cylinder engines and power train	80	—	48	(10)
Warranty improvements—increased quality and reliability through component redesign, stronger quality control procedures, and additional inspectors	31	56	12	14
Purchasing programs—ensure purchases are made at the lowest cost available	54	52	77	80
Market demand changes—expect greater demand for fully equipped cars, and for luxury and specialty cars	34	34	40	45
Average variable cost savings	$593	$330	$407	$222

	1980	1981	1982	1983	Total
Cumulative variable margin improvements (millions)	$385.3	$759.5	$1008.9	$1223.7	$3377.4
U.S. Department of Treasury adjustments (millions)	(76.1)	(141.5)	(195.0)	(254.5)	(667.1)
	$309.2	$618.0	$ 813.9	$ 969.2	$2710.3

forced to contract and make what the market wants by assembling cars from parts supplied by others. But Iacocca had steadfastly insisted that the nature of Chrysler's operational structure and dealer network would not permit downsizing over the short-run without causing severe disruptions. In addition, he felt that full-lines were needed in order for the company to remain profitable, considering the higher profit margins on large cars, scale economies of volume production, and the variety that dealers needed to effectively compete with General Motors and Ford. Besides, costly government regulations hindered Chrysler's ability to specialize.

Chrysler might be able to avoid re-organization by following American Motors Corporation's strategy of building good cars for specific markets, such as small or family-size cars. Or, by segmenting into high-price, low-volume "niches," Chrysler—always weak in functional business areas such as finance, marketing, manufacturing, and service—could finally capitalize on its traditional engineering strength. Furthermore, consolidation of its Chrysler-Plymouth and Dodge operations would simplify assembly and reduce its parts inventory. Chrysler might even pursue mergers or other types of business combinations or affiliations with another automobile manufacturer or large, financially sound company. Forced by re-organization or initiated on its own, Chrysler must choose a core of business to emphasize and then begin to liquidate its underutilized operations, perhaps selling these facilities to other automobile manufacturers.

Bankruptcy seemed near when Chrysler reported that for the entire first nine months of the year, sales had fallen seven percent from $9.6 billion to $8.9 billion, causing the company to lose $721.5 million so far for the year. On November 1, 1979, previously unsympathetic Secretary Miller surprised Chrysler's management and labor by announcing plans to support a $1.5 billion loan guarantee in Congress, stating that the Administration feared that Chrysler's problems were far greater than had originally appeared. It was made clear that such help would be available only until December 31, 1983.

There were several key considerations which led to this decision by the Administration. First was the fact that automobiles are an important industry, directly comprising five percent of the U.S. Gross National Product and doubling that figure when dependent industries are taken into account: Automobiles use over one-half of domestically produced lead, rubber, and iron; forty percent of all petroleum products and consumer installment credit; over a quarter of all zinc, steel, and glass; and large amounts of aluminum, copper, and plastic. In addition, automobiles also support many ancillary services, such as suppliers and repair shops. It has been estimated that as many as one job of five in the private sector is attributable to the auto industry.

Chrysler's domestic sales of $12.9 billion in 1978 was equivalent to 0.6 percent of the GNP, and $7.9 billion of this amount went to purchase parts, materials, and services from forty thousand domestic suppliers (many of which are small firms that rely on Chrysler's business) with another $2.9 billion spent for wages and salary. Although the extent to which a Chrysler failure would prolong or intensify a 1980 recession is debatable, there certainly would be serious local impacts and economic distress in the older industrial areas of the upper midwest which often bear the brunt of a national recession. For instance, in Detroit—where Chrysler is the largest private employer—a complete shutdown would double that city's already high unemployment rate of eight percent and devastate its economy. Widespread unemployment among Detroit's inner city blacks and other minorities could invariably lead to an increased rate of crime and incidence of violence.

A second justification for government support of a Chrysler bailout is that a bankruptcy could cost more. Neither a failing domestic company nor a profitable foreign corporation contribute to U.S. tax revenues. In addition, since more than a hundred thousand people work for Chrysler and several times that many work for its dealers and suppliers, the U.S. Department of Transportation's worst-case scenario estimates that a complete shutdown could directly add ninety-seven thousand Chrysler workers, 180,000 suppliers, one-hundred thousand dealers, and twelve thousand shippers to the currently six million jobless Americans. An identical number of indirect jobs could also be lost. It is not known how many of these would be permanently unemployed, unable to be absorbed by General Motors, Ford, or other sectors of the economy. According to some government estimates, the cost to taxpayers and to local, state, and federal governments in unemployment compensation, welfare payments, food stamps, other assistance, and the loss of tax revenues might be as high as sixteen billion dollars for 1980 and 1981. (See Exhibit 12.)

Included in the cost to the nation of a Chrysler bankruptcy is the impact on Chrysler's pension fund affecting fifty-two thousand ben-

EXHIBIT 12
Impact of Chrysler failure on U.S. economy (millions)

	1979	*1980*	*1981*	*Total 1979–81*
Loss in personal income tax revenues	$100	$2,400	$3,500	$ 6,000
Loss in corporate profits tax revenues	400	2,400	1,600	4,400
Loss in Chrysler property tax revenues	—	45	30	75
Loss in social security tax contribution	100	1,300	2,000	3,400
Increase in tax expenditures	200	1,300	300	1,800
Loss of government guaranteed pension fund	—	800	—	800
Total loss to government	$800	$8,245	$7,430	$16,475
Change in balance of payments	$500	$2,800	$3,900	$ 7,200

eficiaries and 120,000 employees. With assets of only $1.4 billion to cover $2.3 billion in liabilities, the unfunded pension liabilities greatly exceed the reserves of the Federal Pension Benefit Guarantee Corporation. Formed shortly after Studebaker's bankruptcy fifteen years earlier left forty-five hundred employees with only fifteen percent of their pension benefits, the FPBGC insures employee pension funds and is entitled to use up to a third of Chrysler's book value after liquidation to cover these obligations. Should this amount be insufficient to meet future pension commitments, then the agency itself may be unable to continue its existence without further Congressional appropriations.

A third concern was the significant role that automobiles play in international trade and the U.S. balance of payments. Imports were already increasing their U.S. market penetration thanks to their fuel economy, low purchase price, and the unavailability of domestic small cars. If Chrysler were to go out of business, as much as seven billion dollars would go overseas if General Motors and Ford could not pick up the demand for small cars. Jobs would then follow, reducing the GNP by four billion dollars in 1980 and by six billion dollars in 1981 (or by 0.15 percent and 0.20 percent, respectively) and widening the federal budget deficit by one billion dollars and one-and-three-quarter billion dollars in those corresponding years.

The fourth and final argument for saving Chrysler was that vigorous national competition, and the corresponding benefits of lower prices, product innovation, and efficiency that come with it, requires three significant automobile makers. If the industry were to become even more concentrated in the future, then it would constantly be facing antitrust threats to prevent alleged noncompetitive effects. Such continuous harassment would result in higher costs of litigation to both the companies and the government. Loan guarantees would help Chrysler remain as a third viable competitor in the future, operating on its own resources and being a contributing member to the nation's economic system.

A significant requirement of the bill was that all parties having an economic stake in Chrysler's outcome were to make enough sacrifices to match the government's $1.5 billion backing. At first, most were reluctant to extend themselves further. Even when Chrysler announced its plans on November 28, 1979, to offer $250 million of new preferred stock to these vested interests, no one was willing to accept an equity position. Several Congressmen had other conditions to justify the bailout: Senator Russell Long (D.-La.), Chairman of the Finance Committee, wanted Chrysler to establish an Employee Stock Ownership Plan; Henry S. Reuss (D.-Wis.), Chairman of the House Committee on Banking, Finance and Urban Affairs, suggested that Chrysler produce only mass transit vehicles; and Congressman S. William Green (R.-N.Y.) thought that the government should take its own equity position in the company in exchange for a loan guarantee.

Chrysler's initiatives on Capitol Hill were beginning to pay off as the House of Representatives passed what was essentially the Administration's version of the bill. But as the bill moved to the Senate Committee on Banking, Housing and Urban Affairs, Chairman Proxmire came out firmly opposed to a federal bail-out that would prevent the failure of individual firms:

> *We have a free enterprise economy and free enterprise means the freedom to fail as well as the freedom to profit. Last year, over 6,000 business firms went bankrupt and no one rushed to Washington with a bill to prevent their failure. If we bail out Chrysler, where do we draw the line? On what basis do we say that some firms but not others are worthy of a Federal bail-out?*
>
> *In the last analysis, the only reason we are bailing out Chrysler is that the sheer size of the corporation enables it to deploy enough lobbyists, public relations specialists, dealers and suppliers to bring its claims to the attention of the government ahead of the 6,000 other firms that routinely fail every year.*

On November 29, 1979, the Senate Banking Committee approved a four-billion dollar package consisting of $1.25 billion in loan guarantees and $2.75 billion in outside financing—if the U.A.W. would agree to a three year wage freeze that would save the company $1.3 billion. Senators Richard Lugar (R.-Ind.) and Paul Tsongas (D.-Mass.), who had co-authored this version of the bill, simply felt that the workers were not making enough of a sacrifice. Treasury Secretary Miller retaliated by calling this new imposition unworkable since it would result in the loss of many of the best workers and the impairment of productivity.

The U.A.W.'s rejection of this legislative effort on December 3, 1979, threatened to destroy any rescue package for Chrysler. The workers claimed that tying government aid to a three-year wage freeze would reduce their standard of living by thirty to forty percent at the current rate of inflation. In addition, Fraser felt that re-opening contract negotiations and ratification would conflict with the union's constitution and pose major logistical problems. It would also be politically risky for the union leadership, especially for Fraser who had recommended acceptance of the contract based on his estimate of what it would take to convince Congress that labor was doing its fair share. Fraser had previously rejected the options of buying stock or loaning money to the company out of the union's strike fund.

The compromise that was reached by Congress on the last day it was in session implied that Chrysler was unique among U.S. corporations and, therefore, was entitled to special government treatment. Its long-term ability to compete had come into question since it was the weakest major competitor in an industry undergoing radical transition. Small fuel-efficient automobiles would double their market share by 1985—perhaps eventually capturing forty-five percent—if they could first get through 1980's tight money, high interest rates, anticipated gasoline shortages, high fuel prices, and overall economic decline.

In order to make the kind of automobiles that Americans will want in the future, the industry needs to undergo a complete transformation at a cost of eighty billion dollars through 1985, over half of which would go to meet federal fuel, emission, and safety requirements.

EXHIBIT 13
Planned expenditures by Chrysler Corporation (millions)

	1979	*1980*	*1981*	*1982*	*1983*	*1984*	*1985*	*Total*
Type:								
Tools, facilities, and investments	$ 857	$ 959	$1,137	$1,253	$1,228	$1,334	$1,192	$ 7,960
Engineering research and development	346	367	375	456	465	455	511	2,975
Launch and preproduction	139	261	127	205	253	174	228	1,387
Project expense	104	171	173	188	222	228	214	1,300
Total	$1,446	$1,758	$1,812	$2,102	$2,168	$2,191	$2,145	$13,622
Program:								
Cars	$ 521	$ 655	$ 532	$ 712	$ 954	$ 827	$ 665	$ 4,867
Trucks	83	120	296	383	109	378	584	1,953
Powertrain	345	461	557	452	481	298	167	2,761
Other (e.g., manufacturing improvements)	497	522	427	555	624	688	723	4,041
Total	$1,446	$1,758	$1,812	$2,102	$2,168	$2,191	$2,145	$13,622

General Motors alone will invest fifty billion dollars. Although Chrysler now has the government's backing, it will still have to cut back on its planned $13.6 billion investment plans through 1985. (See Exhibit 13.) Re-tooling will allow Chrysler to replace the Volaré and Aspen in the 1981 model year with 500,000 small, fuel-efficient, four-cylinder, front-wheel-drive automobiles getting twenty-five to thirty miles per gallon. The government rescue should give the company enough time to bring out these new cars (designated as "K"-cars and called the Plymouth Reliant and Dodge Aries) to compete directly with General Motors' current "X"-bodies and Ford's planned Escort by offering 2.2 liter engine with diesel or turbocharge engines as options. Chrysler will be building its own four-cylinder engines by 1980. Such investments will require losing one billion dollars in 1979 and half-a-billion dollars the following year, but Chrysler hopes to earn a billion dollars by 1985.

Around the time that Congress was debating Chrysler's loan guarantees, General Motors reported third quarter operating losses of a hundred million dollars while Ford's domestic car business was on its way to losing a billion dollars for the year, offset only by its financial operations, overseas operations, a large tax credit, and profits from internal sales. By year-end, the automobile industry had temporarily closed thirteen of its forty-three U.S. car plants, indefinitely putting 129,000 employees out of work. Such economic declines make future government policies toward business even more imminent. During the Congressional hearings, several members of the House Committee on Banking, Finance and Urban Affairs offered this dissenting view:

> *Where do we draw the line? What criteria do we use to determine who gets what, when, how much and why, and for what reasons? These questions have not been answered in either a specific or broader context. If we start today with the Chrysler Corporation, who will we see tomorrow? . . . Before we legislate blindly, we must be aware that other companies may be supplicants for the Federal dollar in the future.*

EXERCISE 10–6

From your analysis of the Chrysler case, develop a prioritized list of *economic* factors that affected the decision to pass the Loan Guarantee Act. Explain your reasoning for the priorities assigned. To what extent did these factors represent risks *or* opportunities? For which companies?

EXERCISE 10–7

From your analysis of the case, develop a prioritized list of the *political* factors that affected the decision to pass the Loan Guarantee Act. Explain your reasoning for the priorities assigned. To what extent did these factors represent risks *or* opportunities? For which companies?

EXERCISE 10–8

From your analysis of the case, develop a prioritized list of the *regulatory and/or social* factors that affected the decision to pass the loan guarantee act. Explain your reasoning for the priorities assigned. To what extent did these factors represent risks *or* opportunities? For which companies?

EXERCISE 10–9

Although we typically think of businesses being affected by their environment, consider the extent to which Chrysler actually changed its general environment. List, if you can, the portions of the general environment that it changed, and the persons or agencies who accomplished the change for Chrysler.

The Chrysler Corporation case, which we have just examined, offers an unusual opportunity to see a wide number of societal forces at work in shaping the general environment for companies in a given industry. As we examined that case, we purposely concentrated on the environment in general and did not examine in detail the environmental conditions specific to the auto industry. The effects of a worldwide petroleum shortage, for example, were strongly felt by the auto industry and were an environmental factor of considerable significance. That same shortage, however, also has had far-reaching effects on the petrochemical industry, on the natural gas and coal industry, and on a myriad of industries associated with energy usage or energy conservation. Similarly, an economic recession will have effects on a number of industries, and must be regarded as a component in the general environment of business. Some factors, however, seem to apply to particular industry. The establishment, by Congress, of standards for fuel consumption by autos manufactured for sale in the United States is an environmental factor specific to the auto industry. Government regulations on the operation of nuclear power plants affect that industry directly and have little direct impact on other industries. Next, we will examine the types of factors that tend to affect a single industry. We will develop a number of categories of elements specific to a particular industry and explore each in some detail. Once again, we will be searching for factors that represent risks and those that present opportunities for gain.

ANALYSIS OF THE INDUSTRY-SPECIFIC ENVIRONMENT

The factors that comprise the industry-specific environment can be found to be either risks or opportunities to present or potential participants in that industry. If, for example, the product is currently entering the growth stage in the product life cycle, the opportunities for increased sales are present for all competitors. Similarly, the risks of being shaken out during the growth stage (a factor discussed in Chapter 8) are present for all firms marketing that product. Michael Porter has described five forces that shape the competition in a given industry. They are *buyers—substitutes, suppliers,* and *potential entrants*—who impinge on and interact with the character of the *rivalry among existing firms.*[2] Figure 10–2 depicts these forces and their interaction, which we will now discuss.

Two additional components of environment that are specific to each particular industry are the economic structure of companies in that industry and the prevailing operational/technological requirements. In the following pages, we will discuss a number of components in each of these dimensions of the industry-specific environment and their application to industries with which we should all have some familiarity.

Product Demand Factors

We can begin our analysis of the industry-specific environment by a review of factors affecting demand for the product. The demand for the product may be direct or may be derived from the demand for another product. Demand may be highly sensitive to fluctuations in the business cycle or may be either insensitive to the cycle or follow countercyclical demand patterns. The product may be a convenience good, a luxury, a

[2] Michael E. Porter, *Competitive Strategy* (New York: Free Press, 1980), pp. 3–33.

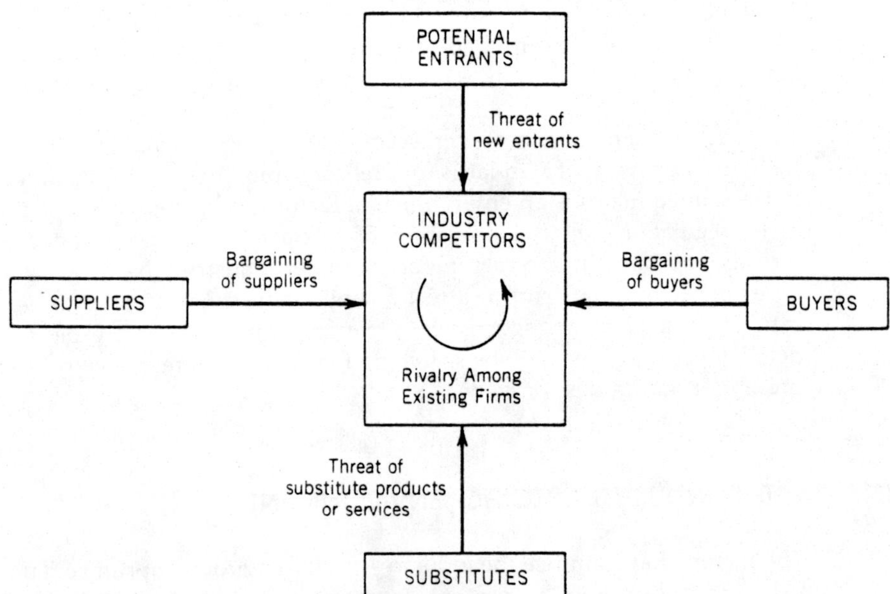

FIGURE 10–2 Forces driving industry competition.* ***Source:*** **Michael E. Porter,** ***Competitive Strategy*** **(New York: Free Press, 1980), p. 4.**

necessity, a postponable purchase, a durable good, a shopping good, or it may represent an item purchased on impulse. Products, in our area of interest, may be readily differentiated by customers or may have the characteristics of commodities. Differentiation, if it exists, is also a factor in many industries. It may be made by customers on grounds of price levels, quality standards or levels, brand names, or technology.

Forces Originating from Buyers[3] Buyers exert pressure in industries by seeking lower prices, higher quality, additional service, and through demands for improved products and services. The forces generated by customers are especially visible when the customer accounts for a high proportion of the company's output. Where customers are purchasing undifferentiated products and where profits are low, conditions are ripe for actual and threatened movement to alternative sources of supply.

Customer structure is also important in and of itself. If an industry is characterized by a limited number of very large customers, then the type of marketing, the specialized knowledge required, and the risk factors involved will be much different than would be the case if customers were widely dispersed. The presence of very large general nonfood retailers such as Sears Roebuck, Montgomery Ward, Penney's, and K-Mart is a distinctive characteristic of all of the industries that supply them with merchandise. Auto parts manufacturers, clothing manufacturers, housewares manufacturers, and a wide range of other types of suppliers must seriously consider the impact of these large firms even if they have chosen to distribute through other outlets. Sears, for example, exerted such power over its suppliers that for all practical purposes they were captive . . . and highly dependent on the fortunes of Sears. Some of Sears's suppliers have sought to develop and market their own lines of merchandise independent of their biggest customer but have found the demands of Sears to dominate their company's fortunes.

A dairy farm operation, for example, might readily shift its purchases from one grain supplier to another as prices change. The grain-elevator-operator's products are not highly differentiated and the dairy operator is under extreme profit pressure. A high-priced ladies' boutique, on the other hand, might find the styling and quality features of one of its suppliers sufficiently distinctive so that it could use those features as one of its own comparative advantages. The boutique, therefore, would not be as likely to change suppliers as was the dairy farmer.

Forces Originating from Product Substitution The availability and relative attractiveness of substitute products is a second major factor affecting demand. In the investment community, a wide range of "products" is used to meet customers' needs for investments. Life insurance, real estate, annuities, savings accounts, stocks, bonds, certificates of deposit, and a host of alternative uses for investor cash offer an extremely interesting internal environment. Although each of these "products" has its own unique appeal, there are many similarities, and the industry has developed mechanisms for dealing with customers' interest in transferring from one to another.

[3] For a more detailed discussion of the topics covered in this section, see Porter, *Competitive Strategy*, pp. 3–33.

The TIAA-CREF retirement organization, which offers retirement plans to educational institutions' faculties, combines several "products" into its offerings. The total plan is designed to provide for retirement benefits. Within the plan, however, members can contribute to an annuity fund, which provides for a guaranteed future return; or to a stock-purchase fund, which offers a higher rate of return at a somewhat higher risk. Members can not only choose between these two types of funds, but can shift their proportions as market forces and their own needs dictate.

In other industries, substitutes can have a dramatic effect. In recent years, shortages, higher prices, and poor quality of wood for wall studding have resulted in the increased use of lightweight, galvanized steel studs for building construction. These studs are straight, uniform in dimension, and reusable. Their introduction has not only had an effect on the wood products industry, but has opened new market opportunities for lightweight steel products.

EXERCISE 10–10

The following is a list of possible factors affecting demand for the products listed at the top of the columns. Note briefly in the spaces provided, your assessment of each factor for that product.

	Spark Plugs	Personal Computer	Coal	Penicillin
1. Direct/derived demand				
2. Sensitivity to economic cycles				
3. Differentiated or commodity				
4. Product life-cycle stage				
5. Substitutes for product				
6. Number of buyers				
7. Type of good				
8. Age/economic status of typical buyer				

EXERCISE 10–11

Now apply the list of factors in Exercise 10–10 to the automobile products discussed in the Chrysler case. Summarize your findings in one or two paragraphs, prepare to hand in your summary or to present it in class.

Forces Originating from Suppliers Suppliers provide a source of pressure in the environment of a specific industry if they tend to be concentrated and if they are larger than the companies they supply. Commercial printers, for example, have little control over the major suppliers of printing paper, that is, companies big enough to be on the Fortune 500 list. Printing paper is *critical* to the commercial printer. It is not something that can be foregone, temporarily (box labels might be one such need the printer could forego, for a time), nor is there an acceptable substitute. Printers will want paper of established grades and will not attempt to print on other materials.

When the customer's industry is not very important to the supplying industry, the supplier can afford to be somewhat indifferent to the needs of the customer. A small-scale manufacturer of electronic equipment who needs a specialized microelectronic chip will find it difficult to get the attention of the major chip manufacturers. For these large companies, orders less than hundreds of thousands of chips are uneconomic and commercially unattractive.

Forces Originating from Potential Entrants The entry of new competitors is brought about by the interest in potential profitability in that industry or in a related field. New entrants' success, however, depends on their ability to overcome a number of points of resistance. Existing competitors, of course, offer resistance to entry through price reductions, aggressive advertising campaigns, and specialized promotional inducements to distributors. The new entrant, therefore, faces an extremely difficult situation in which the new product is compared with known products and suppliers at especially attractive prices and distributed by dealers who have a special interest in staying with an established relationship.

In addition to resistance and retaliation from the industry, the new entrant faces other structural barriers to the attainment of a sustainable position in an existing industry. Brand loyalty, especially in mature markets, makes the introduction of new products particularly difficult. The scale of operations needed for high volume and low-cost (and low-priced) products causes two problems. First, the size of the investment is larger, and the entrepreneur may not, therefore, "dip a toe in the pool" to test the water. Only a plunge will do. Second, the scale of operations called for must make the entry noticeable and is thereby likely to draw a retaliation from the remainder of the industry. In the chemical industry, for example, entry is very difficult because of the capital required, the mature and relatively rigid nature of supplier/customer relationships, and the specialized nature of the technological skills required. In the home construction business, on the other hand, the relatively low level of capital required to build that first home and the ready availability of skilled or semiskilled labor make this an industry that is fairly easy to enter.

Industry Structure and Rivalry among Competitors

The structure of industries varies widely. The steel industry, at one extreme, has for years been characterized by very large, vertically integrated companies. Small companies occupied niches in the steel market and did not attempt to compete head-on with major manufacturers. The vertical integration provided protection for sources of raw materials and for customers through ownership of steel converters and wholesalers. Supplier contracts with very large customers also offered protection against fluctuations in product demand. In recent years, this structure has changed as large companies have closed or scaled back operations significantly. In addition, smaller companies have found attractive niches and seem to be surviving in a changed environment. A much different structure can be found in the personal computer software industry. Here, capital requirements are minimal and thousands of competitors struggle to establish a market position. The software industry is evolving, however, and now has a limited number of larger firms such as Lotus and Ashton-Tate.

An examination of company strategies in an industry can reveal the presence of clusters of companies that pursue similar strategies. Several large highly integrated paper companies, for example, seek large customers in the publishing industry, produce vast quantities of kraft paper (brown paper used in grocery bags and corrugated boxes), and maintain divisions that serve as converters of paper into paper products (bags, boxes, envelopes, etc.). Other paper companies provide tissue and sanitary papers, and yet another cluster can be identified as dealing primarily in the production and sale of newsprint.

Each industry also has its own typical form of distribution. The hardware industry for many years was characterized by small mom-and-pop retail stores. Wholesalers served these retailers, and manufacturers' agents sold products through the two-stage channel. In the 1950s and 1960s, the channels of distribution for both the hardware and the lumber industries changed dramatically. Companies such as Pay & Pak, 84 Lumber, and Handy Dan offered very large-scale discount retailing. In addition, their centralized large-scale buying and distribution systems made the wholesaler obsolete. Today, the large-scale discount store is the typical form of hardware and lumber retailer and distribution is characterized by the presence of these large firms.

Another set of characteristics that should be considered is the distribution of knowledge in an industry and the extent of research conducted in new products, new processes, and new market areas. Where the product is in a growth stage in its life cycle, the research directed toward new processes may be crucial in providing the cost effectiveness needed for survival of the shake out. New-product research is extremely important in emerging industries to establish the means of fitting products and services most closely to the needs of customers. It is also extremely valuable in the maturity stage as competitors strive to sustain sales or to find replacements for products believed to be approaching the decline stage.

Market research is extremely important in several stages in the cycle. As products move from Stage 1 to Stage 2, market research is needed to identify potential markets and product/service mixes seen as desirable by customers. In Stage 2 (growth), market research is needed to assess the most desirable means of expanding toward mass markets. In Stage 3 (maturity), mass marketers seek to find ways of preserving and enhancing market share in stable markets. Given these general requirements, we find that some industries appear to be characterized by leader-follower relationships in market research and that others aggressively pursue independent research activities. In the fast-food industry, for example, some of the major fast food franchisers engage in elaborate and expensive location studies to assure an adequate volume of the right type of clientele. Others follow and locate near the sites of the leader. They are apparently willing to accept a *somewhat* less desirable site in a location the leader has chosen rather than have the opportunity to have the *best* site in a location they have chosen.

Forces Originating from Competitive Rivalry The degree and character of the rivalry between competitors is another characteristic of the industry-specific environment. Several structural factors are believed to contribute to the degree of ferocity of competition. A higher level of competitive action and intensity is associated with a large number or equally balanced competitors. An industry characterized by slow growth may cause frustration among competitors anxious to achieve growth, and may therefore stimulate competitive action. In industries where products are not well differentiated or where a high level of fixed costs exists, conditions are ripe for aggressive competition. The competitive wars between airline carriers in recent years is a good example of this type of situation. Finally, where the company has such specialized resources that exit from the industry may mean liquidation and thereby financial disaster for owners and/or managers, the intensity of competitive pressures for survival is understandably extreme.

The fast food industry is characterized by a high level of aggressive competitive advertising. Competitors are named, competing products belittled, and competitor-identifying characters ridiculed. This type of competitive rivalry is visible to consumers, but it is no more intense than the rivalry carried out in arenas less obvious to the layperson. In industries with a limited number of dominant firms, many executives are personally acquainted with their counterparts in competing firms and may view the competitive relationship on fairly personal grounds. The winning and losing of contracts with important customers and the pirating of key personnel are often the sources of competitive pressures and the strong feelings that are a long-standing characteristic of a particular industry.

In aerospace and high-technology firms, the processes described have existed in an atmosphere of high growth and great commercial opportunity. In this situation, the competitive feelings are somewhat more friendly than is the case when the market has stabilized. In the more mature market, gains and losses are part of a zero-sum game in which one company gains but only at the expense of another. We are now beginning to see this development in segments of the commercial computer industry, and we may see more as the market for computers and computer-related equipment matures.

EXERCISE 10–12

Here is a list of some of the characteristics of the industry structure and competitive practices that can serve as the framework for an industry analysis.

Size and Number of Competitors
- *Presence of dominant firm or firms*
- *Capital requirements*
- *Extent of vertical integration*
- *Clustering by general strategy*

Number, Size, and Distribution of Customers
- *Customer size and power*
- *Geographic distribution of customers*
- *Their interest in integrating backwards*

Typical Channels of Distribution
- *Traditional channels*
- *Emerging new channels*

Extent and Type of Research Activity
- *Market research*
- *Process research*
- *Product research*
- *Distribution or patterns of research dominance*

Competitive Rivalry
- *Open or covert*
- *"Friendly" or "hostile"*
- *Means of expression*
- *Advertising*
- *Recruitment of key talent*
- *Subversion/covert intelligence/etc.*

For this assignment, please work in teams of three to six persons and prepare a paper for presentation in class on the nature of the industry structure and competitive practices in one of the following industries:

Home real estate sales in your city.

Dairy industry in your region.

Legal profession in your city or region.

Home heating and air-conditioning industry.

Institutional health care (hospitals, free-standing emergency-care centers, outpatient service facilities, etc.).

Commercial laundry and dry-cleaning industry in your city.

Laboratory equipment industry.

Computer-related manufacturers.

Mobil-home manufacturing industry.

Other topics assigned by your instructor.

Hint: In addition to searches in your library for information about national industries, reference indexes of industry associations can provide the names and telephone numbers of association offices. Also, conversations with customers, competitors, regulators, stockbrokers, and others with knowledge of an industry will provide an excellent insight into its structure and competitive practices. The research departments of the larger stockbrokerage firms often have profiles of industries that are of interest to their clients. Some of this information, however, may be proprietary and unavailable to the general public.

Industry Economics

The economics of a particular industry were covered briefly in Chapter 2. Reference material is available that offers information on various components of the financial nature of a wide range of industries. Rates of return on sales, assets, and invested capital are listed, as are typical financial ratios. Upper quartile, lower quartile, and median figures provide information about a range of acceptability in financial relationships for a given industry. The structure of assets and the capital structure of the industry can be assessed from the same data. The size of a particular firm cannot be determined through a study of these reported ratios, but should be assessed by means of other industry data. Corporation annual reports and Moody's and Standard & Poor's can provide quite detailed information about individual companies that will serve to give an indication of the size of competing firms.

It is sometimes possible to examine an industry's operating statements to understand better the nature of the relationships between cost elements and revenues. Intuitively, we understand that airline companies, hotels, and hospitals should have high-fixed and low-variable (relatively) costs. Access to the actual figures, of course, would help in specifying the nature of these cost components. A more detailed understanding of the nature of the cost structure might not only help in understanding the industry but might also begin to present information that could describe areas of risk and opportunity. Information on cost of manufacturing, cost of marketing, dollar expenditures on research and development, and the cost of administrative and other overhead expenses can be very helpful to competitors in assessing their own statements and in searching for avenues of improvement.

EXERCISE 10–13

Refer to the chapter Appendix. Examine the data for grocery stores (SIC 5411) and automobile dealers (SIC 5511).

- Discuss similarities and differences in the balance sheets for these two industries.
- From this analysis, what would be your major concerns if you were to consider entering the grocery business? Explain.
- The automobile dealership? Explain.

EXERCISE 10–14

Examine recent reference materials, company annual reports, or other public information to develop your closest approximation of the cost structure for retail department stores (5311). Identify the extent of fixed and variable costs, the gross profit margin, the net profit margin, cost of goods manufactured (as a percentage of sales), marketing costs (as a percentage of sales), and give some estimate of the size of the investment made by serious competitors in that industry.

Operational and Technological Requirements

We conclude our analysis of the industry-specific environment by examining the conversion processes most frequently used by industries. For example, some industries have a highly advanced technology that requires specialized equipment and highly trained, technically oriented personnel. Other industries have technologies that are relatively crude. At the advanced end are the automated production lines that produce wafers of microprocessor chips. These minute devices are incredibly complex, yet are produced by the thousands in factories where clean-room conditions are maintained to prevent product contamination. At another extreme is the forest products industry in which trees are harvested by hand and the most primitive mechanical and power tools are used.

Some industries have a range of available technologies, each one well suited to product types or market-demand patterns. Kraft paper, for example, is made in some papermills in continuous flows of varying grades in order lots of hundreds of tons for paper bag and box manufacturers. In other sections of the same company, however, smaller mills manufacture small lots of specialized papers to be sold to commercial magazine printers, stationery printers, photo developers, and suppliers of mimeograph and photocopying stock. In the smallest segments of the paper industry, craftspersons manufacture highly specialized sheets of handmade papers to be used for artistic endeavors or for the printing of very small editions of poetry or other written work.

Sources of raw materials also offer differences in the industry-specific environment. The oil industry is highly dependent on foreign sources of crude. Other industries rely on highly localized raw materials. Brickyards, as one example, are often located near sources of clay. The difficulty in the transportation of raw materials may call for establishing a plant location in a position central to several of the materials required.

In addition to the problems posed by the availability of raw materials, issues related to their quality also pose industry-specific problems. In high-tech industries, preproduction quality inspections are used to reduce the problems caused by product failures brought about by defective components. In some applications, tolerances are so exacting that inspection is carried out at the supplier's plant and again prior to production at the customer's plant as a way of assuring product quality.

Some of the most significant data that is needed about the industry-specific environment deals with capacity. If the industry is overbuilt, pressures to fill that capacity will be felt in decisions on pricing, on quality, and on geographic market definition. Conversely, an industry that sustains a position of being chronically overbooked may invite competition from within or from foreign competitors who see the long lead times and attractive margins as offering the potential for quick and profitable penetration of an existing market. Information on the extent of capacity and its utilization is not as readily available as other information but may be found in reference materials, in the industry reports prepared for stockbrokerage firms, or may be derived by a careful study of the published reports of major competitors.

The use of human resources is also of concern in the operational dimension. Industries may be highly automated (e.g., oil refining and chemical processing) or highly labor intensive (e.g., clothing and shoe manufacture, assembly, food preparation). Each type of technology carries with it a need for specific forms of human resources. The automated plant requires technologically expert persons to monitor, adjust, and repair expensive equipment. Many of these persons have had extensive education and are sought through searches in national labor markets. Labor-intensive industries call for persons with highly specialized skills, many of which are developed on the job. Typically, recruitment and selection take place on a local or regional basis. In each of these instances, the recruitment, training, personal development, and compensation issues differ because of the needs of the persons required for that particular industry.

As a means of concluding this chapter on assessing the external environment, we will introduce a case that describes the situation encountered by Mary Kay Cosmetics, Inc., a relatively small manufacturer of cosmetics and skin-care products. As you read through the case, you may wish to note first those elements from the general business environment, then those from the environment specific to the cosmetics industry. You may find it helpful to develop checklists for organizing your notes based on the lists of elements in each type of environment that was presented earlier in this chapter. After examining the case, you will find several exercises at its conclusion.

MARY KAY COSMETICS, INC.

INTRODUCTION

Mary Kay Cosmetics, Inc. (MKY), a relatively small manufacturer of cosmetics and skin-care products, markets its wares through an international network of independent sales representatives. Located in Dallas, Texas, the company has five regional distribution centers in the United States, one distribution center in Australia, one in Canada, and one in Argentina. Another distribution center is scheduled to open in Santo Domingo on December 1, 1982. Founded in 1963 by Mary Kay Ash, the company has grown from 9 sales representatives to over 150,000. Starting with an initial investment of $5,500, it has grown to net sales of $235 million in 1981. With a relatively small product line that the independent sales representatives, called beauty consultants, carry with them. Mary Kay Cosmetics, Inc., has a target market of women aged 25 to 44 who are in the middle-and-above income brackets.

Mary Kay — The Woman

The story of Mary Kay Ash's life is, to a large extent, the story of MKY. Mary Kay was born Mary Kathlyn Wagner in Hot Wells, a small town in south Texas.[10] At age 7 she was helping to support her family and her invalid father while her mother ran the family restaurant in a Houston suburb.[7]

Graduation from high school meant the end of formal education, even though she had graduated from Reagan High School in Houston with honors and hoped to attend college. Mary Kay was soon married to Ben Rogers, a marriage that lasted 11 years and resulted in the birth of three children: Marilyn in 1935; Ben, Jr., in 1936; and Richard in 1943. World War II meant months at a time of separation from her husband who was drafted and unable to send home more than a few dollars each month. For a while during the time Ben was in the service, Mary Kay attended classes at the University of Houston, but her college career was cut short by the responsibility of three small children.[22]

Selling for Others

To make ends meet Mary Kay went to work part-time for Stanley Home Products in Houston selling household specialties at parties in homes. She had a natural aptitude for selling and quickly became one of her company's leading sales representatives. Mary Kay learned that people liked to talk to her and that her positive attitude enabled her to overcome most of the obstacles she encountered in sales.[22]

Retirement

In 1953 Mary Kay left Stanley after 13 years and went to work for World Gifts Company in Dallas selling decorative accessories. She moved up in this organization to the position of national training director. After 10 years with World Gifts Mary Kay was working 60-hour weeks and making $25,000 a year. A disagreement over proposed policy changes at World Gifts prompted Mary Kay to "retire" in 1963. She had spent almost 25 years in direct selling and intended to spend her time writing.[20]

Mary Kay carefully avoids discussing her

This case was prepared by Marlene Carle, Robert Carle, Richard Edwards, and Paula Walters, under the supervision of Professor Sexton Adams, North Texas State University, and Professor Adelaide Griffin, Texas Woman's University, as a basis for class discussion rather than to illustrate either effective or ineffective handling of an administrative situation.

age. She comments, "A woman who'd tell that would tell anything."[9] For this reason there are few times when Mary Kay's age is mentioned by writers and reporters who have interviewed her.

Retirement was very unpleasant for Mary Kay. She was unhappy with nothing to do and within a few days after leaving World Gifts, she began writing down all the direct-selling techniques she had learned in her 25 years in sales. After spending 2 weeks on this task, she spent another 2 weeks compiling a list of problems she had encountered in selling, ways of solving these problems, and how she would do things differently in the future if she had the opportunity. Her initial intent was to put this material in a book that would help women sell.[20]

Discovery of the Product

In reviewing and editing the notes she had written, Mary Kay realized that she had prepared everything needed to operate a sales organization. The only thing missing was a product.[7]

Several years earlier, while working for Stanley Home Products, Mary Kay conducted a demonstration of her company's products one evening to a group of approximately 20 women in a home in one of the suburbs of Dallas. The hostess for the party kept the guests after Mary Kay's demonstration to give them little jars of skin treatment and several creams she had prepared from formulas she had been given by her grandfather who had at one time operated a local tannery. The women attending the party were being used to test the formulas. Mary Kay had noticed the beautiful complexions of the women she had met that evening and was anxious to try the skin treatment herself. She took several of the jars, which were of various sizes and shapes and were handed to her in an old shoebox.[20] The creams smelled terrible, but they worked. Mary Kay maintains to this day that her own beautiful complexion is the result of using these creams, which were eventually to become the first of the MKY product line.[20]

THE BEGINNING OF A COMPANY

Soon after the completion of her writing, Mary Kay and her second husband, George Hallenbeck whom she had married in 1963, decided to use Mary Kay's sales and problem-solving techniques and to go into business. George's background included sales and administration. The idea of starting a new business appealed to both of them.[7] The formulas for the skin creams Mary Kay had been given several years earlier were purchased for $500. The woman who owned the formulas had been attempting to produce and market them by herself but had not been successful.[10]

The busy process of organizing their new company was underway. Mary Kay's husband was to be the administrator. He was in the process of planning the physical facilities and caring for other matters regarding the operation of the business while Mary Kay was preparing the final draft of the sales manual, designing and ordering containers, and recruiting salespeople. One month before the business was to open, George died of a heart attack.[7]

Mary Kay discussed her situation with her children. Richard, who was then a 20-year-old insurance salesman in Houston, moved to Dallas and helped his mother start the company in September 1963 with $5,000 capitalization.[6] Richard had attended North Texas State University for a year-and-a-half as a marketing major and was in charge of administration and finance. His mother's duties included training, merchandising, and selling. Six months later Ben, Mary Kay's older son, joined to take care of warehousing and shipping.[7] Ben later became the Vice-President for Merchandising but left the company in 1978.[10]

The new company, Beauty by Mary Kay, opened with two full-time employees (Mary Kay and Richard) and nine women who sold the initial skin-care products.[18] A strategy of MKY from the beginning was that each sales representative was to buy her own products (at approximately 50% of retail), pay for all supplies in advance, and carry a sufficient amount of cosmetics to fill all orders on the spot. The company, therefore, had no accounts payable and no accounts receivable.[20]

Immediate Success

The small staff of beauty consultants was successful both in selling and in the recruiting of new representatives. The number of people added became so large that a system was established whereby some of the beauty consultants became training directors. An incentive compensation plan was devised that enabled beauty consultants who became training directors to draw an override on the commissions earned by the beauty consultants they had recruited and trained.[24] The number of beauty consultants grew from the original 9 to 318 in 1964, just one year after the company began operation. Sales for the first year amounted to $198,514. Second-year sales exceeded $800,000. The growth continued at an astonishingly rapid pace both in the number of consultants and sales, and MKY went public in 1967.[20]

In 1969 it was necessary to add 102,000 square feet to the manufacturing facility in Dallas. A new distribution center was also added in Dallas, and in the late 1960s plans for expansion of sales and distribution centers outside the five-state Texas Southwest were begun.[18] Planning for growth was necessary from the beginning. The company recently purchased a 177-acre site in another area of North Dallas in order to have the land available for future growth.[15]

Expansion

The rapid growth in the 1960s brought MKY to the $6 million sales level and a point where expansion beyond Texas and into the four contiguous states was a logical next step. In the 1970s expansion was first made into the California market with the opening of a branch in Los Angeles designed to serve the western states. The move westward was tremendously successful, and MKY soon had more beauty consultants in California than in Texas. An Atlanta branch was opened in 1972, and a third branch was opened in Chicago in 1975. In 1978 the first office outside the United States was opened in Toronto.[18]

The small regional company of 1970, which had sales of $6 million, grew in the decade of the 1970s to an international company with sales in 1979 of $91 million. In 1980 sales were $166 million and in 1981 they reached $235 million. The sales force now included over 150,000 consultants and training directors.[18]

Annual SEMINAR

One factor that has contributed to the rapid growth of MKY is the ability of the company to instill the spirit of winning and the desire for success in the minds of beauty consultants, training directors, and employees. A major attraction to many of these people is the annual sales meeting, MKY's SEMINAR, which is held in Dallas for three days each August. This spectacle of beauty pageant, Academy Awards' night, and party, also includes the sharing of ideas, classes, the setting of goals, leadership training, and even bookkeeping suggestions. Each person attends the meeting at her own expense. Participants come from all states, Puerto Rico, Canada, Australia, and Argentina. Awards include mink coats, diamond rings, diamond bumblebee pins, watches, luggage, typewriters, pocket calculators, exotic vacations, and the year-long use of pink Cadillacs and Buick Regals. Some 16,000 MKY beauty consultants and training directors have attended the seminar for each of the past two years.[4]

International Operations

Attempts to broaden international operations beyond Canada have led to the opening of a subsidiary in Australia and, more recently, another wholly owned subsidiary in Argentina in 1980. These two companies contributed 3% of the overall MKY sales in 1981. The Australian company appears to have reasonably good prospects for growth; however, the political and inflationary problems in Argentina and the language barrier are forcing MKY to examine this operation carefully before making a decision on whether or not to attempt to expand its efforts in this market.[16] Recruiting is difficult in Argentina, and keeping sales directors in this country is a problem for MKY. As of December 1, 1982, MKY will begin operations in Santo Domingo.

> *In the two [countries] where we have a different language, we have a language barrier that we from the home office standpoint find very difficult to hurdle. . . . We have tried to find someone who not only knows the cosmetic business well, but who is willing to come over here and spend a year to a year-and-a-half learning* our *way of doing business. I don't think we will open any other [foreign] market[s] until we have someone who can speak the languages and is trained here and [can] go there to help us.*[1]

Not only is language a problem, but brochures must be rewritten in Spanish or the foreign language of that country.

Government Regulations and Legal Concerns

The rapid expansion of the business has seen the need for an increase in the number of employees. From the beginning of 1963, with the original two, Mary Kay and Richard Rogers, the company has grown to over fourteen hundred employees.

The beauty consultants and training directors are technically considered to be independent contractors of MKY, not employees of the company. However, this status of independent contractors has been under investigation by the Internal Revenue Service [IRS] since 1978. The Revenue Act of 1978 contained provisions for determining an independent contractor status. With this Act, eligible taxpayers, including MKY, were relieved of all liability for "federal income tax, withholding, Federal Insurance Contributions Act (FICA) and Federal Unemployment Tax Act (FUTA) taxes with respect to their salespersons for any period ending before January 1, 1979."[25] Congress extended the interim relief period until July 1, 1982. Any legislation enacted after the period of interim relief could present a financially adverse effect on the company's future operations. This issue has been magnified as a result of other direct sales companies whose representatives have tried to alter tax deductions.

In 1982 a bill with three provisions was introduced before Congress addressing the status of independent contractors; this was endorsed by MKY and the Direct Selling Association. In a presentation made before the New York Society of Security Analysts on July 22, 1982, Richard Rogers said the bill "would require reporting to the IRS commissions paid to salespeople when those commissions exceed $600 per year. Another provision would require reporting to the IRS sales of product to individuals when their sales exceed $5,000 per person per year. The third provision which is very important to us is called a 'safe harbor provision' which includes several tests which if met would automatically classify a salesperson as an independent contractor rather than an employee."[18] Mary Kay suggested that it would be difficult for her independent contractors to avoid the Internal Revenue Service (IRS) and not report actual commissions because her company provides the needed information regarding each contractor to the IRS, with this information being maintained on a computer system.[1]

In the third quarter of 1982, the issue was resolved, at least for the time being. The IRS ruled in favor of the independent contractor status. Says Mary Kay, "We won."[1] Rogers indicated that an adverse effect could have impacted the company in several ways.

The company presently faces a class action suit with regard to the tender offer and purchase of MKY stock from 1979. "Nothing yet has happened," says Mary Kay. "We think, of course, that it's ridiculous. In 1978 and 1979 we as a company had suddenly realized that our directors weren't meeting the test of a salary requirement except on a secretarial basis. They (women) will take the stable salary rather than a 'maybe' commission."[1] From this, management developed the new compensation plan that has contributed to the success of the growth of the company. "In late 1979, we found '60 Minutes' on our doorstep; and after nine days of filming, we came out smelling like a rose. Since that program, our sales have quadrupled and our numbers have tripled."[1] For most companies a loss of the suit could negatively affect financial operations and future plans. "It's just for $17 million, and we did $458 million last year in 1981. Anyway, we won't lose it."[1]

Growth

Approximately 40% of the fourteen hundred MKY employees are housed in a modern, eight-story office building in North Dallas. This $7 million structure contains approximately 109,000 square feet of office and meeting space and was completed in 1978. The building is now completely free of encumbrance and is a showplace for employees and others; it is a rounded structure of bronzed-gold, glass, and beige brick, filled with plants, flowers, trees, and a color display of woods, rugs, and paintings.[20]

According to management, the continued and rapid growth of MKY has necessitated the expansion of the physical plant and plans have begun to build a new facility that will be a campus. Land encompassing 177 acres has been purchased over the past year and in November 1982 ground was broken for the new building. "Almost every department will have its own building, particularly production, distribution, and administrative facilities. We already have our own print shop and legal counsel. In addition, there will be a child care center and possibly in the future plans are to build a hotel."[1] Estimated cost is $100 million for this five-year project; and, according to Mary Kay it will be paid for from funds generated internally.

Product Line

The initial product line at MKY consisted of skin-care products for women. Since the introduction of this line in 1963, the line has remained relatively stable. Since 1976, there has been a gradual move toward diversification of products and additions to the Mary Kay line. In 1980, the skin-care line was diversified to meet the needs of the different consumers whose skin types were not alike. Colors have been updated to reflect the colors in fashion. The sunscreen has been reformulated and in 1981, MKY introduced the Body Care System. The line has also been expanded to include toiletry items, accessories, and hair-care products. The skin-care products for women still account for 50% of the sales revenue and will remain to be the major income producers in all likelihood.[25] Today the products at MKY are still primarily oriented toward skin care rather than the high-fashion market.

Still, the line consists of only 45 products. Says Dr. Myra Barker, Vice-President for Research and Development, "Our plan is to maintain the present number in our line so that our Beauty Consultants can carry the inventory with them. The best way to service our Consultants is to keep the color line basic when offering the Fashion Forecast for fall and spring." According to Dr. Barker, "This strategy allows the Consultants to sell large numbers of basic colors which sell well to our customers. This allows us to discontinue those colors which don't sell well and provide the necessary flexibility of updating our line. Mary Kay quality is instilled in all employees and products."[2]

An 11-year veteran of the pharmaceutical industry, Dr. Bruce Rudy, former Director, Quality Assurance for the Burroughs Wellcome Company, had primary responsibility for government, technical, and regulatory compliance in the quality-control area. Since joining the MKY organization in January 1981 as Director of Quality Assurance, Dr. Rudy is now serving as Vice-President of Quality Assurance of MKY. "We have one of the strongest quality-control programs in existence. Each batch of raw materials is tested in our labs. They must meet our chemical, physical, and microbiological specifications. Bulk products and finished packaged products are audited on the line, with final testing in the lab. Last week, we were inspected by the F.D.A. which is the primary governmental agency responsible for the cosmetics industry."[30] Says Myra Barker, "We have one of the most sophisticated computer control systems in the industry. Even the FDA was impressed. Our goal is to be the best."[2]

During the past several years, MKY has experimented in the market of skin-care products and toiletry items for men. These are marketed under the product name of "Mr. K." and to date have accounted for 3% of the total company's sales in each of the past three years.[25] "Ten years ago, a man would not have gone into a beauty shop to have his hair done. As time goes on, men will find out that skin is skin. With all the emphasis on youth and keeping trim and fit in this country, skin follows right behind it. For men, skin care is a behind-the-door thing with cosmetics. "I don't have a crystal ball," says Mary Kay, "but it's just one more step to creating the total image, even for men."[1]

"We are faced with the problem of growing too fast. We are constantly reviewing our systems and products for control measures. Typically we are understaffed and have to work a lot of overtime. Give me these problems anyday! They are nice problems to have," reflects Dr. Rudy.[30] [Who goes on to say]

> *"With the building of our new MKY campus, we are phasing in buildings for the new facility. For example, the Glamour Products manufacturing facility is working closely with the engineering groups to ensure that we meet the criteria for a drug company and can be approved by the FDA. We are looking at meeting not only present, but future requirements for the industry and our company."*[30]

Manufacturing, Research and Development

The manufacturing and research and development facilities for MKY are located in Dallas. Products needed in other geographic areas are shipped to the various distribution centers. Raw materials, fuel, and electrical energy are available in the Dallas area at reasonable costs, and there are no plans to relocate any of the manufacturing or research and development facilities at this time, although the company does study energy-related costs. Company officials point out that a continuous research and development program is underway and is geared mainly toward the goal of improving present products; however, only a very small percentage of total income is budgeted for the research and development department.[25]

Management and Philosophy

The primary reason for the success of MKY is the motivating reason for starting the company. "This company was really begun to give women an opportunity to advance, which I was denied, when I worked for others." This opportunity to become successful and the rewards provided for hard work are evident in the slogan, "I can, I will, I must," which Mary Kay instills in all her employees, particularly during the training seminars. "I train the sales force by example and by relationships."[1]

Although the sales force is independent, it maintains a strong and intimate relationship with the mother company. The organization of the sales force is the brainchild of Mary Kay herself. One of the more subtle activities that takes place at the home beauty show is the recruitment of new beauty consultants. A portion of each show is reserved for explaining the MKY sales organization, its compensation, and its incentive plan.

Recognizing a lag in the sales force and a loss of competitive edge in 1978, MKY changed its compensation program.[22] In addition to the markup they receive on the products they sell, sales managers are also eligible for a series of commissions based on their monthly unit sales. To become a sales manager, the beauty consultant must recruit 24 women into the organization to become consultants. The sales manager is then eligible to participate in a training program and later become a sales director. Sales directors spend time on independent sales, but they also manage, train, and recruit other sales consultants. "We expect sales directors to sell a minimum level of $3,000 wholesale products per month, which is $6,000 retail."[1] Mary Kay says that if a sales director falls short of that goal for two consecutive months, then the company contacts that woman to see how they can help. The Chairman of the Board doesn't just want them to "be" minimum. She wants to help them excel. The average sales director will earn $30,000 in 1982. New sales managers will come to Dallas for a week of training and return from time to time during the year for special training programs. The highlight of the year being the SEMINAR. It consists of workshops conducted by outstanding beauty consultants and directors. Used not only during SEMINAR, but also at other times during the year are training materials such as guides, manuals, tape cassettes, flip charts, films, and other materials developed by MKY staff.[11]

The incentive plan is no small contribution to the motivation strategy employed by MKY. This plan allows sales consultants and managers to set goals for themselves whereby they can earn expensive and extravagant prizes for outstanding sales. Not only is the prize itself a motivator, but also its method of presentation serves to provide the recipient of extended measures of recognition from her or his peers. Promotion from sales director to national sales director is also recognized on awards' night during SEMINAR.

Being promoted to National Sales Director is no small task. Each woman must have already proven what she can do. Each person has at least 10 offspring directors who they have brought into the company and nurtured up the ladder. These 10 offspring directors must have women whom they are working with and motivating and are called second-line directors. For example, Shirly Hutton earns $32,000 per month and has 26 offspring directors. Rena Tarbet, who is "Living with cancer for seven years now" is working on her third-million-dollar year in sales.[1]

> *"Richard and I are the parents of the company. company. We are really mother and father figures, which I am given the credit for the success, and really Richard deserves as much or at least half of everything that has been done and then some. When I started the company, I didn't know that Richard had an IBM head. I take care of motivating of the sales force and public relations work. I don't know the financial condition of the company because I don't have to. Richard knows all of that. I ask for a sales report and the number of recruits that we had for each month. That's all I need. I take it from there"*[1]

Communication is considered a high-priority motivational strategy at MKY. Monthly publications with circulations of 150,000 weekly bulletins, personalized letters, and 15,000 telephone calls per month keep sales directors and consultants in touch with the home office.[15] MKY also has a computerized tracking system of keeping up with its complex organization of sales consultants, sales directors, and their respective sales and recruiting data.[20]

Sales Staff

Today there are over 150,000 independent beauty consultants selling MKY products. The company places a great deal of emphasis on the rapport with others inside the organization; however, company policy is very clear on the requirements that must be fulfilled to be a beauty consultant. These requirements are:

- Submit a signed agreement with cashier's check or money order in advance in order to receive the Beauty Showcase, which is the basic sales kit.
- Attend three beauty shows or sales demonstrations.
- Schedule five beauty shows for the first week's activity.
- Attend training classes conducted by a sales director in the area.

The beauty shows are the company's market place and are held in homes with no more than six customers in attendance.

Future of MKY

It would seem that MKY would merge or be acquired by another company. Mary Kay's reply, "All the time, but no thanks. These companies believe they can bring in their male executives and take over this [two-by-four] company and show them how to run it. You can't run a direct sales company like that. We must operate in a different way. Right now we are in the top ten in the cosmetics industry. Richard's and my goal is to be the largest and best skin-care company in the world. I'm sure we are the best. Now we have to concentrate on becoming the largest."[1]

The future of MKY lies in the hands of the National Sales Directors. These NSD's are carbon copies of Mary Kay herself. She constantly feeds into their computers that they are Mary Kay. "Wherever you go, whatever you do, be careful what you do, because you are Mary Kay. You are the future of the company. When I'm not here anymore, you will be taking over. Each of you are in training to be Mary Kay."[1]

Mary Kay's goal is for every single day that passes, she tries to touch as many of these women's lives that she can. "If I see one more woman today become greater than she ever thought she could be by my persuasion that she is great, then it's a good day."[1]

Richard Rogers, 38-year-old-son of Mary Kay Ash, is positioned at the helm of Mary Kay, serving as President and CEO of the company since 1968. He is responsible for setting the tone and direction for the company. In the plans are the building of a new MKY campus.

THE INDUSTRY

Mary Kay Cosmetics, Inc. is a participant and competitor in two basic industries: the cosmetics and personal-care industry and the direct-sales industry, the latter composed of approximately twenty-two hundred direct-sales companies. Among MKY's competitors in the cosmetics industry are Avon, Revlon, Estee Lauder, Gillette's Jafra, Richardson-Vick, Faberge, Chesebrough-Ponds, and Noxell. With well over $2 billion in sales in 1981, Avon, Revlon, and Gillette are the industry leaders. Chesebrough-Ponds's 1981 sales were $1.5 billion. Ranked within the top 10 of cosmetics industry sales, are

MKY with $235 million (net) along with Faberge and Noxell in the same sales category.[28,8] Skin care, which is MKY's niche, is the focus of the competition.

With its appeal to older women in middle-to-high-income brackets who are entering the work force in record numbers, skin care and quality are the targets for a growing number of women according to industry analysts. They have more purchasing power but less time to spend their money. They want health, fitness, and value.[13] Appealing to these women with major marketing thrusts are: Gillette with Aapri, a facial scrub containing ground apricot pits, and Silkience, self adjusting moisture lotion; Richardson-Vick with Oil of Olay moisurizer; Noxell with Raintree Hand and Body Lotion and Noxzema; Chesebrough-Ponds's Vaseline Intensive Care; and Estee Lauder's Clinique as well as a number of products from both Revlon and Avon. Noxell and Chesebrough-Ponds's sell the low-cost products. Avon and Revlon products are in the midprice range, with the Estee Lauder products in the high-price range. Mary Kay Cosmetics' products are in the middle-to-high-price range. With the exception of Avon and MKY, all of these companies sell their products over the counter in department stores, drugstores, discount stores, and super markets.[12]

The cosmetics industry as a whole is seeing a gradual downturn for the first time in its history according to *Forbes's* Richard Stern. What has been classified as a recession-proof industry is now seeing growth that is mainly attributed to inflation. Volume sales are declining and the assumption that growth is eternal is gone. The skin-care-treatment portion of the industry is the only expectation for growth, with perhaps 2% for 1982. Even though the recession is motivating a shift to more reasonably priced products, Avon and Revlon are hurting the most. The industry has survived other recessions because of the increasing numbers of women entering the work force. But, the rate of increase has been declining in recent years.[29] To further complicate the volume of sales, virtually every cosmetic company has sales promotions on the concept of a free gift with purchase. Mary Kay Cosmetics is different. Says Chairman of the Board Ash, "They would love to get out of that business. We don't have to do that. We don't need to."[1]

Both Stern and Mintz of *Sales and Marketing Management* note that Avon's problems stem from a less-captive home market and an inadequate compensation program for sales representatives. Retail outlets such as drugstores, mass merchandisers, and food stores are capturing some of Avon's low-to-the-middle-income market. Avon's reward program of gifts and vacations to outstanding sales representatives has failed to improve productivity, which has been in a decline since 1979.[19]

Other industry analysts speculate that the leveling of sales in the cosmetics industry can be attributed to consumers cutting back on purchases traditionally categorized as luxury items because of inflation and recession; the number of women entering careers is leveling off; and the bulge in the teenage market seen in the 1960s and early 1970s is beginning to decline. The portion of the cosmetics industry that has had some immunity to this decline is the skin-care portion of the industry.

Some analysts believe the biggest threat to the industry, however, is the threat of regulation by the Food and Drug Administration (FDA).

> *If a cosmetic item is regarded as a drug, the industry could be confronted with expensive regulations. These include detailed manufacturing controls, more frequent government inspections, product registrations, labeling requirement changes, and other reviews. The Toxic Substances Strategy Committee, a special White House panel studying cancer, has asked Congress to*

> *review cosmetics legislation and bring the industry under tighter federal control.*[27, p. H28]

Increased regulation would mean higher production costs and higher prices to the consumer. Research and development divisions would require expansion into more scientifically oriented segments. Industry experts suggest that this would especially be burdensome to the smaller cosmetics companies and would, in fact, make it very hard for them to exist.

The other industry in which MKY competes is the direct sales industry. Competition is not only for customers willing to provide their home as the marketplace, but also for recruits for sales representatives, on whom the industry is totally dependent. Competitors include Amway, which sells home products; Shaklee, which has organic, nonpollutant household products; Home Interiors and Gifts; and Princess House, which sells a fine line of crystal and other table accessories. All of these companies apparently understand the importance of acquiring and motivating large numbers of recruits. Use of exciting contests with flashy rewards such as big cars, furs, expensive jewelry, and extravagant vacations is a motivational factor overlooked by none of these companies. Family harmony and devotion to God are emphasized not only by MKY but also by others such as Amway and Home Interiors and Gifts. The latter parallels many of MKY's motivational practices and was, in fact, founded by Mary Kay Ash's former sister-in-law, Mary Crowley.[21]

Another characteristic shared by the direct sales companies is investigation by the IRS regarding the status of their direct-sales personnel. MKY (as do many of the others) claims that their beauty consultants are independent distributors and not employees of MKY. Consequently, MKY pays no federal withholding or employment taxes for any of their 150,000 direct sales representatives. MKY and other direct-sales companies are currently protected from liability under an interim relief act passed by Congress.[25]

Other pressure being exerted by the IRS on direct-sales organizations such as Amway targets individual sales representatives' use of business expenses as tax shelters. In a copyrighted article in the *Fort Worth Star Telegram*, reporters Bowles, McKinsey, and Magmusson claim that Amway recruiters use the advantage of tax shelters as an enticement to becoming an Amway distributor. The pitch is to use the Amway distributorship as an excuse to write off new clothes, Christmas gifts, appliances, long-distance calls, new cars, vacation houses, and expensive vacations. In IRS audits of the tax returns of three hundred Amway distributors in Baltimore last year, all but two resulted in back taxes and penalties being assessed. The average payment was $1,350, not including interest and penalties. Currently one thousand more Amway distributors in Baltimore are undergoing IRS audits. According to Roscoe Edgar, Jr., the IRS Commissioner:

> *"It appears that the tax benefit aspects of many of these activities may be the primary reason large numbers of the people become involved. Promotional schemes, recruitment methods and other information we have on these activities frequently highlight the anticipated tax benefits above all else. This indicates to us that the individuals involved know full well what they are doing."*[7, pp. B1, B3]

EXTERNAL ENVIRONMENT

Economic Forces

There are several factors of the economy that impact on the cosmetics industry in general and MKY in particular, among these are consumer demand, competition, and the general state of the national economy. For one reason or another the once-held assumption of eternal growth for the cosmetics industry seems to have vanished. The supposedly recession-proof cosmetics industry has, for the first time in its history, experienced a downturn in business. According to Jack Salyman of Wall Street's Smith Barney and Allan Mottus, an industry consultant, unit sales have been flat for years, with nearly all of the growth (43%) since 1978 attributable to a 39% increase in the cost of living. The shakeout appears to be focused on the middle market. This leaves the effect of MKY uncertain.[29]

As in any other retail industry consumer demand is the key factor that influences a company's business decisions. Competition to meet the consumers' needs has stiffened considerably in the cosmetics industry, as evidenced by the fact that many companies formerly in totally unrelated businesses now have lines of cosmetics. Clothes designers are a good example. One economic factor that is affecting consumers and industry alike is the present higher cost of borrowing money, the prime lending rate. This makes it more expensive for MKY to produce and sell its products and results in higher cost to the customer.

Technological Forces

If a company is not on the leading edge of industry technology, it will be at a competitive disadvantage. The cosmetics industry is not a high-technology industry in the sense of the product produced. But a company needs the latest technology to be able to produce its product cost effectively, which is instrumental in gaining a competitive advantage. In the cosmetics industry, technology revolves around research into how the skin relates to the rest of the body and how it relates to its environment. Of major concern is the safety and efficacy of the product.[4]

Social Forces

Two keys to the success of the cosmetics industry, factors that greatly influence MKY's business strategy, are population demographics and sociological changes. As noted by Richard Stern of *Forbes*, "The key is the underlying demographics. The industry rode out previous recessions by riding the skirts of ever more working women. More working women meant increased women's spending and more cosmetics to wear to the office. But the rate of increase in the number of working women has declined in recent years." Stern also sees "sociological changes afoot as well. Working women now seem to prefer convenience to ambience, prompting a shift in distribution channel toward more merchandisers, discount drugstores and even supermarkets and away from department stores."[29, p. 162] These changes would appear to enhance the appeal of direct marketing because, from a convenience standpoint, it is much easier to have a product brought to you than it is to have to go get it. Also, the recession seems to have caused a shift in buying habits that may impact the cosmetics middle market significantly. As in other retail industries, consumers of cosmetics have gone to lower-priced goods in an effort to economize or have switched to higher-priced goods for quality.[29] Population distribution is very important to the cosmetics industry in helping determine target markets. There has been a definite change in the distribution of the population. Between 1970 and 1980 the number of people over the age of 30 increased 40%, while total population grew only 11.4%. America is growing older.[12]

Political/Legal Forces

The factors that affect MKY in the political/legal area fall into two categories. First, there are laws that affect the cosmetics industry as a whole. Then there are factors that are concerned just with regulating firms that sell through direct-sales marketing techniques. Mary Kay Cosmetics, like the rest of the industry, is subject to regulation by the FDA and the Alcohol and Tax Unit of the Treasury Department. The Federal Trade Commission (FTC) regulates the company's advertising and sales practices. In addition, the company's marketing, packaging, package labeling, and product content are regulated by many other federal, state, local, and foreign laws.

Of more immediate concern to MKY—and all other companies that use direct sales to market their products—is a 116,000-square-foot warehouse. This building and the eight-story office tower are owned by the company free of encumbrance. The company leases a third building in Dallas that has approximately 450,600 square feet. This latter building houses operations for distribution, printing, data processing, and more warehouse space. Mary Kay Cosmetics' office and warehouse facilities in Atlanta, Chicago, Los Angeles, and Australia total approximately 200,000 square feet and are owned free of encumbrance. The office and warehouse facilities in New Jersey, Argentina, and Canada total about 100,000 square feet. These facilities are leased and there is an option to purchase the Canadian facility. The manufacturing facilities and equipment are at least modern and in many cases state-of-the-art and well maintained.[25] Every machine that comes in contact with an MKY product is disassembled, cleaned, and sanitized at regular intervals.[22]

In the interest of future growth MKY has purchased 177 acres in Dallas at the cost of approximately $6.5 million.[25] The project to develop this land will cost an estimated $100 million according to Mary Kay.[1] "At the present time," believes Richard Rogers, "we have in place facilities to support an annual sales volume of approximately $400 million."[15]

Market Resources

Market resources are the elements necessary to transfer possession of MKY's products to the consumer. The company's two most important market resources are channel of distribution and advertising (although it has taken MKY time to understand and properly utilize this resource). MKY's channel of distribution is comprised of one element, a sales force of 150,000 beauty consultants who operate as independent contractors. The products are distributed via one wholesale sale and one retail sale channel. The products are transferred from the company to the consultant at wholesale, then from consultant to the consumer at retail. The beauty consultant's profit is directly derived from the sale of the product to the ultimate consumer. Her profit is the difference between the wholesale price paid MKY for the product and the price the customer paid for the product. Every consultant can sell products wherever she wishes because MKY does not set territories or sell franchises.[14]

Until recently, advertising was used infrequently in MKY's marketing plan. Historically, most advertising was done by word of mouth, relying on direct sales personnel to spread the word. In the past, when there was an advertising budget, it was set at or below 1% of sales. When national advertising was used, ads usually appeared in magazines such as *McCalls, Redbook, Better Homes and Gardens,* and *Ladies' Home Journal.*[26] Since the appearance of Mary Kay Ash on "60 Minutes" in late 1979, the company's view of advertising has been changing. Gerald Allen, MKY's Administrative Vice-President, said the company learned a lesson in the past two-and-one-half years thanks to "60 Minutes." He considers the show partially responsible for the tremendous growth of MKY's sales force. Mr. Allen also believes the show to have been worth the equivalent of $40 million worth of national network advertising and says, "That made believers out of us."[3] In the third quarter of 1982 MKY launched its first nationwide television advertising campaign. The advertising budget for the third and fourth quarters of 1982 will total $3 million and raise the total advertising budget for the year to $4 million (more than double the budget for any previous year).[5,17]

Research and Development Resources

According to John Beasley, Vice-President of Manufacturing for MKY, "Research and Development is the leading edge" in obtaining the corporate goal of being the finest teaching-oriented skin-care company in the world with sales of $500 million by 1990. Since 1975, the company's research and development staff has grown from 2 to 47. Mr. Beasley also said that, "We go after the top ten percent of the people in the country who have the skills that we're looking for and personal integrity."[4] The company funds research all over the world in an effort to develop new technology. Again, to quote Mr. Beasley, "We [MKY] are having to stretch current technology in establishing some new standards in the industry in the area of cosmedogenicity, the interaction of the product, the environment and the skin-causing comadnes (acne)."[4] Of great importance to the company is that research maintain a fast-response attitude because of the rate at which tastes and fashions change.[15] During a recent interview, Mary Kay Ash indicated that the research and development budget would continue to be approximately 1% of sales as has been the case in recent years.

Results of Operations

In 1981 net sales increased at a rate of 41% compared to 83% for 1980 and 70% in 1979. At the same time, the number of beauty consultants increased 42%, 64%, and 33% in 1981, 1980, and 1979, respectively. During the same period, individual productivity of the beauty consultants declined. In 1979 average annual productivity for a consultant increased 27% compared with an increase of 12% for 1980 and a decrease of 1% for 1981. At the same time, selling and general administrative expenses held fairly constant at approximately 51% of sales. It should also be noted that MKY instituted price increases of 15% in 1981 and 5% in 1980. As a result of all the above-mentioned factors, net income increased from $4.8 million in 1978 to $24.2 million in 1981.[15]

Financial Condition

In 1981 *Business Week* ranked MKY as the twelfth fastest-growing company in the country.[9] When asked in a recent interview her opinion concerning the current financial condition of the company. Mary Kay Ash responded, "I think we're doing great!" However, she also admitted that she let her son Richard Rogers, the President and CEO, handle the financial matters of the company.[1]

With the phenomenal growth in the last three years, MKY's total assets have grown from $36 million in 1978 to $101 million in 1981. Working capital for the same period was $5.7 million in 1978, $2.3 million in 1979, $4.0 million in 1980 and $7.8 million in 1981. At the same time, capital expenditures were increasing faster than both working capital and total assets. In 1981 capital expenditures were $25.3 million compared to $12.5 million in 1980, $4.7 million in 1979, and $2.1 million in 1978.[9] There were approximately 14.3 million shares of common stock outstanding in 1981.[15] This represents a 25% decrease compared to the 19.6 million shares outstanding at the end of 1976.[15,23] The decrease resulted from MKY tender offers in 1977 and 1979. Other information on the company is detailed in Exhibits 1 through 3.

Present Strategic Posture

Strategic posture is determined by the answers to questions such as, "What is our product mix?" and "What is our customer mix?" The most important factor in MKY's strategic posture is its niche in the skin-care-products area of the cosmetics market where larger competitors

EXHIBIT 1
Mary Kay Cosmetics, Inc., consolidated balance sheets (December 31, 1981, 1980)

Assets	*1981*	*1980*
Current assets:		
Cash and cash equivalents	$ 7,953,000	$11,085,000
Accounts and notes receivable	2,715,000	1,109,000
Inventories:		
Raw materials	8,888,000	6,380,000
Finished goods	18,193,000	15,218,000
	27,081,000	21,598,000
Deferred income tax benefits	2,948,000	2,036,000
Prepaid expenses	1,213,000	666,000
Total current assets	41,910,000	36,494,000
Property, plant, and equipment, at cost:		
Land	12,298,000	3,793,000
Buildings and improvements	23,869,000	21,348,000
Furniture, fixtures, and equipment	28,299,000	14,963,000
Construction in progress	4,829,000	3,877,000
	69,295,000	43,981,000
Less accumulated depreciation	10,519,000	7,653,000
	58,776,000	36,328,000
Notes receivable	—	1,087,000
Other assets	290,000	522,000
	$100,976,000	$74,431,000
Liabilities and Stockholders' Equity		
Current liabilities:		
Note payable bank	$ 1,260,000	$ —
Accounts payable	8,061,000	8,900,000
Accrued liabilities	16,659,000	13,063,000
Income tax	5,712,000	4,214,000
Deferred sales	1,321,000	4,363,000
Current portion of long-term debt	1,058,000	1,000,000
Total current liabilities	34,071,000	31,540,000
Long-term debt	2,366,000	3,000,000
Deferred income taxes	2,587,000	1,258,000
Stockholders' equity	61,952,000	38,633,000
	$100,976,000	$74,431,000

EXHIBIT 2

Mary Kay Cosmetics, Inc., consolidated statements of income (years ended December 31, 1981, 1980, and 1979)

	1981	*1980*	*1979*
Net sales	$235,296,000	$166,039,000	$91,400,000
Interest and other income, net	1,485,000	712,000	493,000
	236,781,000	167,650,000	91,893,000
Cost and expenses:			
Cost of sales	71,100,000	52,484,000	27,574,000
Selling, general and administrative expenses	120,880,000	86,998,000	45,522,000
Interest expense	1,014,000	635,000	958,000
	192,994,000	140,117,000	74,054,000
Income before income taxes	43,787,000	27,533,000	17,839,000
Provision for income taxes	19,632,000	12,398,000	8,207,000
Net income	$24,155,000	$ 15,135,000	$ 9,632,000
Net income per common and common equivalent share	$1.65	$1.05	$.65
Average shares	14,662,000	14,442,000	14,720,000

EXHIBIT 3

Mary Kay Cosmetics, Inc., consolidated statements of changes in financial position (years ended December 31, 1981, 1980, and 1979)

	1981	*1980*	*1979*
Source of funds:			
Operations:			
Net income	$24,115,000	$15,135,000	$ 9,632,000
Depreciation	2,866,000	1,987,000	1,569,000
Increase in deferred income taxes	1,329,000	351,000	177,000
Gains on sales of real estate not used in business	—	—	(116,000)
Funds provided from operations	28,350,000	17,473,000	11,262,000
Proceeds from exercises of stock options	1,922,000	1,338,000	164,000
Decrease in notes receivable	1,087,000	120,000	—
Increase in long-term debt	366,000	—	5,442,000
Proceeds from sales of real estate not used in business	—	—	1,182,000
Other	325,000	—	276,000
	32,050,000	18,931,000	18,326,000
Application of funds:			
Additions to property, plant, and equipment, net	25,314,000	12,457,000	4,510,000
Dividends declared	2,851,000	2,458,000	1,764,000
Reduction of long-term debt	1,000,000	1,000,000	5,000,000
Purchase of treasury shares	—	—	9,422,000
Increase in notes receivable	—	—	1,047,000
Other	—	369,000	—
	29,165,000	16,284,000	21,743,000
Increase (decrease) in working capital	$ 2,885,000	$ 2,647,000	$ (3,417,000)

such as Avon are a minor factor.[23] Also, Mary Kay Ash believes that a limited product line maximizes the sales forces' efficiency.[9] Thus, the company's product line is limited to approximately 45 items.[23] Also important is the company's target market. The company perceives its prime market to be women aged 25 to 44 who are in, or a little above, the middle-income bracket, have some college education, and live in suburbia or exurbia.[15,9]

Environmental Research

Environmental research is used to determine if an organization can keep pace with external change. As MKY continues to grow, it must be able to recognize and react to changes in competition, consumer demand, and economic conditions. The company believes that to do this it must be capable of supporting rapid sales-volume growth with consistently high-quality products and reliable service.[15]

BIBLIOGRAPHY

1. Mary Kay Ash. Personal interview given to Paula Walters. Dallas, Texas. (November 16, 1982).
2. Myra Barker. Telephone interview with Paula Walters. (November 22, 1982).
3. Tom Bayer. "Mary Kay Tries Net TV." *Advertising Age* (August 2, 1982).
4. John Beasley. Vice-President, Manufacturing. Published interview. Mary Kay Cosmetics, Inc. (May 1982).
5. Billy Bowles, Kitty McKinsey, and Paul Magmusson. "IRS Questions the Use of Tax Shelters by Some of Amway's Distributors." *Fort Worth Star Telegram*. (November 10, 1982): B1, B3.
6. *Chemical Week*. "Mary Kay Finds Incentives That Pay Off." (May 13, 1981): 50–51.
7. *Chemical Week*. "People." (August 6, 1975): 40.
8. *Chemical Week*. "The Chemical Week 300 Companies: 1981 Divisional Results." (February 24, 1982): 45.
9. Marcia Froelke Coburn. "Direct's Sleeker Sell." *Advertising Age* (March 1, 1982): 50–51.
10. Mitchell Gordon. "Mary Kays Team." *Barron's*. (July 9, 1979): 32, 34.
11. *The Insiders' Chronicle*. "Analysts Caught Off Guard by Mary Kay Profit Spurt." (November 9, 1979): 1, 17–18.
12. Lori Kesler. "Skincare Penetrates New Layers of Profits." *Advertising Age*. (March 1, 1982).
13. Mary McCable English. "Face of the 80's What's Ahead." *Advertising Age*. (March 1, 1982): Section 2, PM–11.
14. Mary Kay Cosmetics, Inc. "A Business Perspective." (1982).
15. Mary Kay Cosmetics, Inc. "Annual Report 1981."
16. Mary Kay Cosmetics, Inc. "Interim Report for Six Months Ended June 30, 1982."
17. Mary Kay Cosmetics, Inc. "Interim Report for Nine Months Ended September 30, 1982."
18. Mary Kay Cosmetics, Inc. "Presentation of Mary Kay Cosmetics, Inc., Before the New York Society of Security Analysts on July 22, 1982."
19. Steven Mintz. "Avon, You're Looking Better." *Sales and Marketing Management*. (April 5, 1982): 52–57.
20. *Nation's Business*. "Flying High on an Idea. (August 1978): 41–47.
21. James Perkins. "Artful Promotions: Key to Direct Selling Success." *Direct Marketing*. (April 1980): 55–58.
22. Paul Rosenfield. "The Beautiful Make-up of Mary Kay." *Saturday Evening Post*. (October 1981): Reprint 2714B82.
23. Howard Rudnitsky. "The Flight of the Bumblebee." *Forbes*. (June 22, 1981): 104–6.
24. *Sales & Marketing Management/Special Report*. "Mary Kay: Some Overriding Reasons for Success." (August 23, 1976): 54–55.
25. *Securities and Exchange Commission*. "Annual Report, Mary Kay Cosmetics, Inc." (Year Ended December 31, 1981).
26. Pat Sloan. "Mary Kay Putting on an Ad Show." *Advertising Age*. (March 24, 1980): 36, 44.
27. *Standard & Poors Industry Surveys*. "Cosmetics and Personal Care Products." (May 20, 1982: H26–H28.
28. *Standard & Poors Industry Surveys*. "Composite Industry Data." (1982): H31–H44.
29. Richard L. Stern. "The Grease Trade Skids." *Forbes*. (October 25, 1982): 161–64.
30. Richard Rogers. Telephone interview with Paula Walters. (November 22, 1982).

EXERCISE 10–15

Identify the principal factors that affect the general business environment for Mary Kay Cosmetics during the 10 or so years prior to 1981.

- Rank these factors and describe which will present the most significant *risks* to Mary Kay in the next 5 to 10 years. Explain your reasoning.
- Now describe those which present the most significant *opportunities* for Mary Kay Cosmetics. Explain your reasoning.

EXERCISE 10–16

Identify the principal factors affecting the industry-specific environment for Mary Kay Cosmetics during the 10 or so years prior to 1981.

- Rank these and describe which will present the most significant *risks* to Mary Kay in the next 5 to 10 years. Explain your reasoning.
- Now describe those which present the most significant *opportunities* for Mary Kay Cosmetics. Explain your reasoning.

EXERCISE 10–17

Consider the list of risks and opportunities you have developed in the two preceding exercises. What rate of change in (a) sales and (b) earnings would you use in a forecast of operations for the next 5 years. Explain.

ANSWERS TO SELECTED EXERCISE

Exercise 10–1 A drought represents a risk for those holding herds through the dry period. The situation also poses a risk for those selling early because of the forecast. An oversupply on the market will cause prices to drop.

For those persons owning wells, irrigation systems, or riverbottom properties, the situation may present opportunities, especially if your competitors do not have these aids to more modern farming.

The carton manufacturer's situation represents a potential opportunity as his competitor's employees are preoccupied with the reorganization. "Sowing confusion among one's enemies" is a well-conceived strategy and may offer a short-term opportunity to exploit markets before the emerging new organization is aware of its risks.

In the longer term, a reorganization in one's competitor's firm may mean the advent of more able managers and competitors. One might well be advised to step carefully and monitor developments closely.

APPENDIX

APPENDIX

	SIC 2842 Polishes & sanitary (no breakdown)		*SIC 2843 Surface active agent (no breakdown)*		*SIC 2844 Toilet preparations (no breakdown)*		*SIC 2851 Paints & allied PDT (no breakdown)*	
	1986 (187 estab)		*1986 (19 estab)*		*1986 (148 estab)*		*1986 (274 estab)*	
	$	%	$	%	$	%	$	%
Cash	58,928	11.6	49,866	7.1	73,734	12.5	96,661	10.0
Accounts receivable	147,320	29.0	193,844	27.6	128,003	21.7	273,550	28.3
Notes receivable	1,524	0.3	702	0.1	11,797	2.0	4,833	0.5
Inventory	125,984	24.8	176,285	25.1	175,193	29.7	296,749	30.7
Other current	27,432	5.4	55,484	7.9	33,623	5.7	51,230	5.3
Total current	361,188	71.1	476,181	67.8	422,350	71.6	723,024	74.8
Fixed assets	79,248	15.6	169,262	24.1	80,813	13.7	126,626	13.1
Other non-current	67,564	13.3	56,889	8.1	86,711	14.7	116,960	12.1
Total assets	508,000	100.0	702,332	100.0	589,874	100.0	966,609	100.0
Accounts payable	71,628	14.1	125,015	17.8	81,403	13.8	163,357	16.9
Bank loans	5,080	1.0	23,177	3.3	12,387	2.1	14,499	1.5
Notes payable	15,748	3.1	34,414	4.9	23,595	4.0	32,865	3.4
Other current	62,992	12.4	89,898	12.8	93,790	15.9	103,427	10.7
Total current	155,448	30.6	272,505	38.8	211,175	35.8	314,148	32.5
Other long term	57,912	11.4	80,066	11.4	66,656	11.3	121,793	12.6
Deferred credits	508	0.1	7,726	1.1	1,770	0.3	1,933	0.2
Net worth	294,132	57.9	342,036	48.7	310,274	52.6	528,735	54.7
Total liab & net worth	508,000	100.0	702,332	100.0	589,874	100.0	966,609	100.0
Net sales	1,195,647	100.0	832,876	100.0	1,000,000	100.0	2,045,702	100.0
Gross profit	474,672	39.7	277,348	33.3	491,000	49.1	660,762	32.3
Net profit after tax	68,152	5.7	28,318	3.4	74,000	7.4	40,914	2.0
Working capital	205,740	—	203,676	—	211,175	—	408,876	—

APPENDIX *(continued)*

	SIC 2842 Polishes & sanitary (no breakdown) 1986 (187 estab) $ %			SIC 2843 Surface active agent (no breakdown) 1986 (19 estab) $ %			SIC 2844 Toilet preparations (no breakdown) 1986 (148 estab) $ %			SIC 2851 Paints & allied PDT (no breakdown) 1986 (274 estab) $ %		
RATIOS	*UQ*	*MED*	*LQ*	*UQ*	*MED*	*LQ*	*UQ*	*MED*	*LQ*	*UQ*	*MED*	*LQ*
Solvency												
Quick ratio (times)	2.8	1.4	0.8	1.8	1.2	0.5	1.8	1.0	0.6	1.9	1.3	0.8
Current ratio (times)	5.0	2.5	1.7	2.6	2.1	1.4	4.1	2.1	1.4	3.7	2.6	1.7
Curr liab to NW (%)	16.6	43.8	91.5	29.6	60.5	78.7	23.7	56.1	139.8	26.3	49.5	95.1
Curr liab to inv (%)	53.1	99.2	192.9	71.9	125.3	180.1	67.9	111.5	175.4	65.2	98.2	150.5
Total liab to NW (%)	22.1	57.1	124.2	51.2	76.4	148.2	32.6	80.0	197.4	36.9	70.1	153.8
Fixed assets to NW (%)	12.2	37.8	59.6	27.8	34.0	68.8	16.6	32.1	59.4	15.2	28.0	53.1
Efficiency												
Coll period (days)	26.5	43.4	56.4	27.7	39.4	54.8	24.6	45.5	62.2	29.9	39.7	50.3
Sales to inv (times)	16.6	9.6	5.7	10.3	8.3	6.2	9.7	6.5	4.6	11.7	7.9	5.6
Assets to sales (%)	32.5	41.4	57.8	27.7	45.3	73.4	34.7	52.2	81.2	32.1	40.2	54.8
Sales to NWC (times)	8.5	6.1	4.1	10.6	7.2	3.5	11.1	5.7	3.1	9.1	5.4	3.9
Acct pay to sales (%)	3.2	5.3	8.1	6.0	7.5	8.9	3.2	6.3	10.7	4.0	6.5	9.1
Profitability												
Return on sales (%)	9.3	4.0	2.0	5.0	3.6	1.2	11.6	6.8	2.0	4.7	2.1	0.5
Return on assets (%)	13.8	8.4	3.5	7.4	5.2	2.6	16.2	9.0	3.4	9.6	5.4	1.6
Return on NW (%)	28.1	13.9	6.4	11.1	11.0	1.6	32.7	17.9	8.4	20.1	10.4	2.4

APPENDIX

	SIC 5411 Grocery stores (no breakdown)		*SIC 5422 Freeze meat provis'n (no breakdown)*		*SIC 5423 Meat/seafood (fish) MK (no breakdown)*		*SIC 5431 Fruit, vegs markets (no breakdown)*	
	1986 (2295 estab)		*1986 (27 estab)*		*1986 (396 estab)*		*1986 (88 estab)*	
	$	%	$	%	$	%	$	%
Cash	42,628	13.6	26,287	10.2	17,548	17.3	28,113	14.0
Accounts payable	13,791	4.4	56,181	21.8	8,825	8.7	14,659	7.3
Notes receivable	2,194	0.7	—	—	1,014	1.0	2,008	1.0
Inventory	108,763	34.7	29,637	11.5	19,779	19.5	38,354	19.1
Other current	13,478	4.3	12,886	5.0	3,956	3.9	11,847	5.9
Total current	180,854	57.7	124,990	48.5	51,122	50.4	94,980	47.3
Fixed assets	69,270	22.1	46,904	18.2	27,894	27.5	55,020	27.4
Other non-current	63,314	20.2	85,818	33.3	22,416	22.1	50,803	25.3
Total assets	313,438	100.0	257,712	100.0	101,432	100.0	200,804	100.0
Accounts payable	42,628	13.6	19,328	7.5	11,766	11.6	26,908	13.4
Bank loans	2,821	0.9	5,154	2.0	609	0.6	803	0.4
Notes payable	11,284	3.6	14,174	5.5	4,260	4.2	5,623	2.8
Other current	35,418	11.3	29,121	11.3	11,766	11.6	28,113	14.0
Total current	92,151	29.4	67,778	26.3	28,401	28.0	61,446	30.6
Other long term	69,270	22.1	42,265	16,4	20,591	20.3	35,743	17.8
Deferred credits	313	0.1	1,546	0.6	101	0.1	—	—
Net worth	151,704	48.4	146,123	56.7	52,339	51.6	103,615	51.6
Total liab & net worth	313,438	100.0	257,712	100.0	101,432	100.0	200,804	100.0
Net sales	1,400,000	100.0	720,000	100.0	531,557	100.0	1,312,500	100.0
Gross profit	302,400	21.6	257,040	35.7	146,178	27.5	354,375	27.0
Net profit after tax	33,600	2.4	40,320	5.6	19,136	3.6	38,063	2.9
Working capital	88,703	—	57,212	—	22,721	—	33,534	—

APPENDIX *(continued)*

	SIC 5411 Grocery stores (no breakdown)			*SIC 5422 Freeze meat provis'n (no breakdown)*			*SIC 5423 Meat/seafood (fish) MK (no breakdown)*			*SIC 5431 Fruit, vegs markets (no breakdown)*		
	1986 (2295 estab)			*1986 (27 estab)*			*1986 (396 estab)*			*1986 (88 estab)*		
	$		%	$		%	$		%	$		%
RATIOS	*UQ*	*MED*	*LQ*	*UQ*	*MED*	*LQ*	*UQ*	*MED*	*LQ*	*UQ*	*MED*	*LQ*
Solvency												
Quick ratio (times)	1.3	0.6	0.3	5.2	1.3	0.7	2.3	1.0	0.4	1.7	0.5	0.2
Current ratio (times)	4.3	2.2	1.3	6.4	2.1	1.1	4.8	1.9	1.0	3.9	1.6	0.9
Curr liab to NW (%)	17.8	47.1	113.3	7.7	29.2	104.0	14.0	38.7	97.2	15.0	36.5	138.7
Curr liab to inv (%)	35.2	73.8	125.7	79.1	149.2	342.0	51.2	128.2	259.3	57.8	131.7	280.5
Total liab to NW (%)	31.2	84.0	207.0	33.9	77.4	131.1	27.1	68.9	174.0	25.3	76.8	189.1
Fixed assets to NW (%)	24.5	55.6	118.3	9.9	75.2	90.2	25.3	62.0	122.8	20.4	85.5	139.4
Efficiency												
Coll period (days)	1.0	2.6	6.5	10.9	18.6	30.6	1.8	6.5	13.3	1.7	2.4	8.8
Sales to inv (times)	24.7	16.8	10.7	48.0	30.7	16.4	68.3	39.0	22.4	59.4	33.6	19.8
Assets to sales (%)	12.7	19.4	32.4	20.0	58.6	66.7	10.3	17.8	27.9	12.8	21.1	28.6
Sales to NWC (times)	31.5	16.2	8.8	31.2	9.4	4.5	41.2	22.0	10.8	34.9	19.7	9.2
Acct pay to sales (%)	1.3	2.4	3.9	0.9	2.2	2.9	1.0	2.1	3.4	1.0	2.3	4.5
Profitability												
Return on sales (%)	3.6	1.6	0.4	7.9	3.9	0.4	5.8	2.8	0.5	3.7	1.4	0.2
Return on assets (%)	12.7	6.6	1.5	22.2	6.8	4.6	26.0	11.3	0.6	11.3	2.8	—
Return on NW (%)	32.8	14.8	5.3	44.2	15.1	6.1	64.4	20.0	1.0	35.0	6.7	0.1

APPENDIX *(continued)*

	SIC 5511 *New, used car dealers (no breakdown)* 1986 (2120 estab)		SIC 5521 *Used car dealers (no breakdown)* 1986 (859 estab)		SIC 5531 *Auto HM sup stores (no breakdown)* 1986 (2073 estab)		SIC 5541 *Gasoline service Sta (no breakdown)* 1986 (1673 estab)	
	$	%	$	%	$	%	$	%
Cash	123,955	7.4	26,447	10.5	23,516	10.8	26,219	14.9
Accounts receivable	137,355	8.2	33,248	13.2	37,887	17.4	22,172	12.6
Notes receivable	5,025	0.3	4,282	1.7	1,524	0.7	830	0.5
Inventory	1,070,364	63.9	117,879	46.8	91,234	41.9	42,056	23.9
Other current	102,179	6.1	8,816	3.5	5,879	2.7	8,270	4.7
Total current	1,438,877	85.9	190,672	75.7	160,041	73.5	99,597	56.6
Fixed assets	97,154	5.8	31,737	12.6	31,790	14.6	38,889	22.1
Other non-current	139,030	8.3	29,470	11.7	25,911	11.9	37,481	21.3
Total assets	1,675,061	100.0	251,879	100.0	217,743	100.0	175,967	100.0
Accounts payable	77,053	4.6	11,335	4.5	39,194	18.0	20,764	11.8
Bank loans	20,101	1.2	5,038	2.0	2,395	1.1	2,464	1.4
Notes payable	309,886	18.5	18,135	7.2	10,234	4.7	7,215	4.1
Other current	599,672	35.8	57,177	22.7	22,645	10.4	21,468	12.2
Total current	1,006,712	60.1	91,684	36.4	74,468	34.2	51,910	29.5
Other long term	128,980	7.7	31,989	12.7	33,315	15.3	29,738	16.9
Deferred credits	—	—	756	0.3	—	—	176	0.1
Net worth	539,370	32.2	127,451	50.6	109,960	50.5	94,142	53.5
Total liab & net worth	1,675,061	100.0	251,879	100.0	217,743	100.0	175,967	100.0
Net sales	6,500,000	100.0	750,000	100.0	491,606	100.0	1,013,245	100.0
Gross profit	845,000	13.0	174,000	23.2	164,196	33.4	182,384	18.0
Net profit after tax	143,000	2.2	37,500	5.0	19,664	4.0	27,358	2.7
Working capital	432,165	—	98,988	—	85,573	—	47,687	—

APPENDIX *(continued)*

	SIC 5511 New, used car dealers (no breakdown)			*SIC 5521 Used car dealers (no breakdown)*			*SIC 5531 Auto HM sup stores (no breakdown)*			*SIC 5541 Gasoline service Sta (no breakdown)*		
	1986 (2120 estab)			*1986 (859 estab)*			*1986 (2073 estab)*			*1986 (1673 estab)*		
	$		*%*	*$*		*%*	*$*		*%*	*$*		*%*
RATIOS	*UQ*	*MED*	*LQ*	*UQ*	*MED*	*LQ*	*UQ*	*MED*	*LQ*	*UQ*	*MED*	*LQ*
Solvency												
Quick ratio (times)	0.4	0.2	0.1	1.9	0.5	0.2	1.6	0.8	0.4	2.1	0.9	0.5
Current ratio (times)	1.7	1.4	1.2	6.2	2.1	1.3	4.4	2.3	1.5	4.2	2.1	1.2
Curr liab to NW (%)	119.7	219.0	347.8	15.4	60.2	164.2	23.5	57.7	130.2	17.7	43.5	100.9
Curr liab to inv (%)	80.1	93.7	106.7	31.5	73.3	110.1	38.4	76.6	125.4	54.0	110.8	200.5
Total liab to NW (%)	137.8	243.4	378.5	30.1	86.2	216.5	34.9	82.9	191.6	28.6	68.9	166.4
Fixed assets to NW (%)	10.2	21.7	42.6	8.4	24.3	62.3	11.4	32.0	72.8	23.2	51.9	108.2
Efficiency												
Coll period (days)	3.2	6.2	10.9	2.9	10.8	30.4	12.4	23.4	40.1	2.6	7.3	17.1
Sales to inv (times)	8.7	6.4	4.6	11.8	7.5	4.1	9.8	5.9	3.8	50.9	31.3	16.5
Assets to sales (%)	18.8	24.4	33.1	19.1	29.5	61.2	29.0	41.7	61.1	10.2	17.9	32.6
Salees to NWC (times)	27.9	17.2	9.9	18.1	8.2	3.8	11.2	5.8	3.3	39.2	19.3	9.1
Acct pay to sales (%)	0.5	0.8	1.4	0.5	1.1	2.6	4.0	6.7	10.9	0.9	2.0	3.7
Profitability												
Return on sales (%)	2.8	1.6	0.7	8.1	3.5	1.0	7.0	3.2	0.9	4.3	2.1	0.6
Return on assets (%)	9.8	5.4	2.3	16.5	8.4	2.2	13.0	6.1	1.8	18.0	7.9	2.5
Return on NW (%)	36.8	19.7	8.7	44.4	19.4	6.1	26.5	11.6	3.4	38.0	15.3	5.4

Dun & Bradstreet Credit Services, *Industry Norms and Key Business Ratios*, 1986–87 (Library Edition), Murray Hill, N.J. Used by permission.

11

ANALYSIS OF INTERNAL RESOURCES AND IDENTIFICATION OF AREAS OF POTENTIAL ADVANTAGE

In Chapter 10, we were concerned with developing an understanding of the environments within which the organization functions. In both the general business environment and the industry-specific environment, our concern is to understand the potential risks facing all present or potential competitors and to seek out areas of opportunity for gain. In this chapter, we seek to understand in detail the resources at the disposal of the strategist and to determine within those resources areas of strength and weakness. When combined with our understanding of the environment, we should then be in a position to identify attributes of our company that offer an advantage in the competition for customers. The shaded blocks in Figure 11 – 1 are the sections of the strategy-formulation model addressed in this chapter. Our objective is to set the stage for the formulation of an array of possible strategies, each designed to address an area of market opportunity by means of the application of any competitive advantage that the company might enjoy, minimizing risks, and avoiding competition in areas where the company is at a competitive disadvantage. We will begin by a rather detailed examination of internal strengths and weaknesses. One must clearly separate these attributes, which *are unique to our organization*, from risks and opportunities that *are common to all competitors in a given environment*.

ANALYSIS OF INTERNAL RESOURCES

A convenient way to begin the analysis of internal resources is to divide these into four broad categories of assets. These are: (a) physical assets, (b) financial assets, (c)

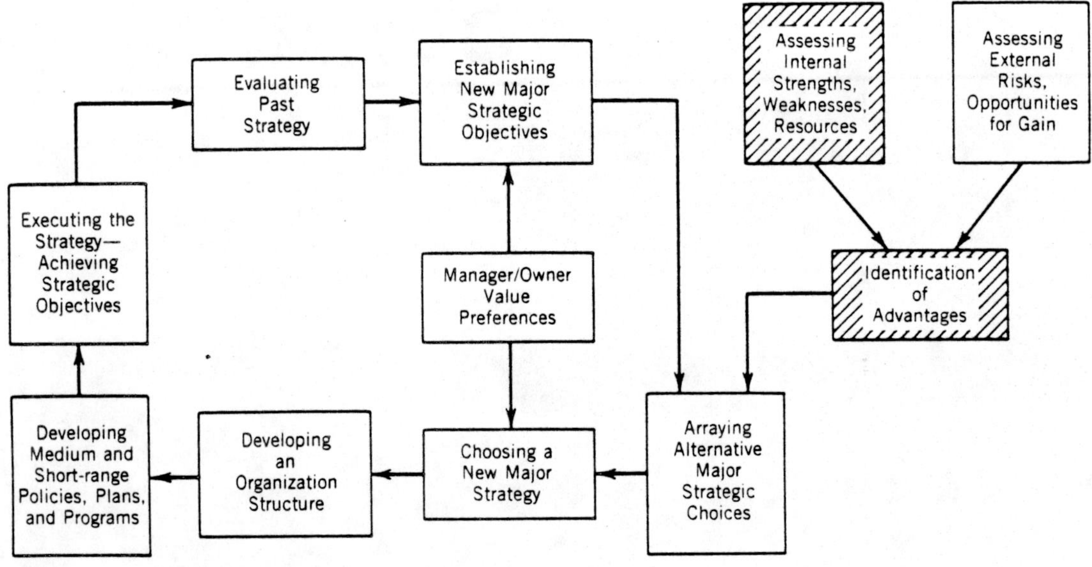

FIGURE 11 – 1 The Strategy Formulation Process.

human assets, and (d) market assets. Each category of asset has a number of elements that should be examined in turn to determine the extent of its strength or its weakness. As we proceed in this process, we will attempt to understand that element and to arrive at some preliminary assessment of its strength.

Physical Assets

Physical assets include all of the elements related to the physical facility and the equipment with which operations are to be accomplished. Factors such as the capacity of the facility, its age, state of repair, annual maintenance, utilities costs, and general configuration are important in this assessment. To provide one example, in some parts of the industrialized East and Midwest, multistory factory buildings were constructed in the 1920s and 1930s. Although they offer the advantage of a smaller square footage of land use and lower heating expense, the multistory construction requires the use of elevators or interfloor conveyors to move products, and thus may be more costly to maintain and service than might be a somewhat more modern single-story plant of equivalent square footage. The strategist possessing a multistory plant in an industry where the standard is a single story may find that the plant and its attendant problems constitute a weakness in a competitive sense.

The location of one's facility is another factor that may present a strength or a weakness. A study of the costs of transportation can aid in the determination of relative attractiveness of location, but generally, a site that minimizes the costs of inbound shipments of raw materials *and* outbound shipments of finished goods is desired. Where bulk materials must be moved, access to water or rail transportation is important. Where finished goods are costly to ship, locations closer to customers may be highly advantageous. Access to interstate highways, rail sidings, or dock locations can be a distinct strength in industries in which specialized transportation needs exist.

A special situation involving location relates to employees. Where transportation costs are a relatively small portion of total cost and where the acquisition of personnel is of extreme importance, a location in which the quality of life is high may be a crucial factor in maintaining competitive strength. In recent years, for example, the location of numerous high-tech companies in California, Colorado, and suburban Boston communities has offered employees of such firms an attractive style of life and plays a major role in the competition for highly talented personnel.

Production equipment should be assessed in several different contexts. First, one should determine whether the equipment can be used for a variety of products or whether it is limited in its application: Is it special purpose or general purpose? Its age and general state of repair should be determined to see that it represents the state-of-the-art in technology, is outmoded, or is obsolete. The presence of either special-purpose or general-purpose equipment does not of itself indicate a strength or a weakness without some intended market in mind. If the market intended is large and cost/price sensitive, then special-purpose high-capacity equipment will be required to meet competition. If, on the other hand, the intended market is small with specialized needs and custom characteristics, then general-purpose equipment may better suit the operational needs of the organization.

EXERCISE 11-1

- Identify two industries in which special-purpose high-capacity equipment is a primary means of production.
- Identify two industries in which general-purpose equipment is a primary means of production.
- Identify two industries in which the cost of shipping finished goods is high.
- Identify two industries in which bulk transportation of raw materials is common.

EXERCISE 11-2

An acquaintance of yours has expressed an interest in developing his hobby of furniture making into a commercial custom-manufacturing furniture business. He has heard of a furniture factory for sale in a town in rural Arkansas, roughly 100 miles from Little Rock and approximately the same distance from Shreveport, Louisiana, the next largest major city in the area. His investigation has revealed that several woodyards in the area near the factory cut hardwood and that most of the former employees of the factory still reside in the community. The plant is a three-story brick structure, built in 1912, heated by gas-fired space heaters. The roof was replaced 23 years ago. A single freight elevator services the floors; however, employees reach the upper floors by means of relatively narrow stairs. A sprinkler system was installed in 1945. The building has been inspected twice yearly by city fire officials since the installation of the sprinklers.

The factory employed 80 persons on two shifts of manufacturing at its peak. It had been built to make wooden kitchen chairs in a limited number of patterns. Most of the equipment in the factory has been replaced twice; however, the varnish and stain tanks and the drying ovens have been in the plant since its construction. On balance, the equipment is about 20 years old and fully depreciated according to accounting records. During its last year of operation, the plant and equipment required the services of two maintenance men.

- Assess the physical assets offered for sale. Indicate those you believe to represent competitive strengths, and those you believe to represent competitive weaknesses. Rank your selections.

Financial Assets

In Chapter 2, we developed an understanding of the tools used to analyze the financial condition of an organization. In our analysis of the financial assets available to the firm, we should make use of the techniques discussed in Chapter 2 to assist in evaluating the asset structure, the capital structure, and the effectiveness of the use of capital. Let us suppose, for example, that our current ratio is 4.2 to 1, our quick ratio

1.9 to 1, our average collection period 25 days, and our inventory turnover 6.2 times. In addition, we have found that total debt as a percentage of total assets is 22%. Generally, these ratios would suggest that the company's financial health is quite sound. The company probably has additional borrowing capacity and its management appears to manage its funds in a conservative and sensible way. We could probably conclude that its financial condition represents a strength in the determination of future strategies.

At least one additional piece of information would be needed to determine financial strength, however, and that is the absolute size of the company. In an industry dominated by giants, a small company is unlikely to be able to compete *on the same basis as* a large company. Its size precludes the acquisition of large-scale capital assets or its ability to market and distribute on a national or international scale. Although its financial health is good, size serves to limit the strategic options. Our evaluation of strengths and weaknesses, therefore, depends to some extent on a knowledge of the characteristics of the industry in general and of the principal competitors in the marketplace.

In addition to the issues of general health and financial size, the availability of credit can represent either a strength or a weakness. If an industry, for example, generally maintains a 2:1 to 1 current ratio and our company has a 4.2 to 1 position, our financial management has either sustained a larger portion of current assets than might be desired or it has foregone the use of additional supplier credit. The following example might serve to help in understanding the assets that might be made available through a restructuring (to reach industrywide average figures) and through the use of supplier credit.

Present Situation

Current Assets	$210,000	Current Liabilities	$ 50,000
Fixed Assets	200,000	Long-Term Debt	82,000
		Owner's Equity	278,000
Total Assets	410,000	Total Lia. & O. E.	410,000

Restructuring to reach a desired current ratio can be accomplished by shifting assets from current to fixed assets through the payoff of long-term debt or by increasing current liabilities and using the funds thus generated to add to fixed assets or to pay off long-term liabilities. Let us look at each in turn.

Shifting Assets

Current Assets	$105,000	Current Liabilities	$ 50,000
Fixed Assets	305,000	Long-Term Debt	82,000
		Owner's Equity	278,000
Total Assets	410,000	Total Lia. & O.E.	410,000

Squeezing current assets to reach a desired current ratio can be accomplished by reducing cash balances, by tightening credit practices, and by reducing inventories. The result, in this example, is to free 105,000 for application to fixed asset purchases.

When the funds are used to pay off long-term debt, the results are:

Payoff of Debt

Current Assets	$128,000	Current Liabilities	$ 50,000
Fixed Assets	200,000	Long-Term Debt	0
		Owner's Equity	278,000
Total Assets	328,000	Total Lia. & O.E.	328,000

In this instance, total assets decline, long-term debt is eliminated, and the current ratio drops from 4.2 to 1 to 2.54 to 1.

The third approach used to achieve a given current ratio is to increase current liabilities and to apply the funds to fixed assets. This increases both liabilities and assets, but it provides funds that might serve as the base for increases in sales volume and profit increases.

Increasing Liabilities

Current Assets	$210,000	Current Liabilities	$100,000
Fixed Assets	250,000	Long-Term Debt	82,000
		Owner's Equity	278,000
Total Assets	460,000	Total Lia. & O.E.	460,000

Here, the current ratio drops to 2.1 to 1, but total debt to total assets shifts from 132,000/410,000, or .322 to 182,000/460,000, or .396. In the earlier two examples (Shifting Assets and Payoff of Debt), the composition of the balance sheet has shifted. In the latter example, the size of the capital base *decreased*. In the final example (Increasing Liabilities), the absolute size of the capital base *increased* as funds were brought in from sources outside the company. Thus, within the limits established by industry practice, companies may have access to resources that may be tapped for purposes of achieving a specific strategy. A company that has managed its funds and its balance sheet composition more conservatively than its competitors may therefore not only be in a stronger position in a static sense, but also has as a potential resource the funds that could be made available through a relaxation of financial constraints *within* the limits of practice used in that company's industry.

Increasing long-term debt to industry levels offers another avenue for capital resources. Although the management of the company may prefer a more conservative, lower-debt (sometimes called, less-leveraged) balance sheet capital structure, the availability of additional capital represents a strength and a potential competitive advantage.

EXERCISE 11–3

The following balance sheet is the most recent statement from the Slaybough Corporation, a manufacturer of metal forgings and stampings.

Current Assets	$ 780,000	Current Liabilities	$ 170,000
Fixed Assets	740,000	Long-Term Liabilities	390,000
		Owner's Equity	960,000
Total Assets	1,520,000	Total Lia. & O.E.	1,520,000

- Use the data in this chapter's Appendix to help you evaluate this balance sheet for general financial health.
- Use the data in the Appendix (use upper quartile figures for the industry) to help you to develop a *pro forma* balance sheet that might indicate the change in the composition of assets and the capital structure used to provide for those assets . . . assuming that management were willing to borrow to the limits suggested by industry upper quartile figures. HINT: Begin by calculating long term and current liabilities

EXERCISE 11–4

The company's sales last year were $4,250,000. Profits were $252,000.

- What evaluation would you make of the financial *performance* last year? Support your comments by comparison data derived from Appendix data. Use as many comparison figures as you think will present an accurate evaluation.
- Assume that the market is not saturated and that sales expansion can take place within the limits of the capital that is available to support sales. What sales and profit estimates would you make for the period following an expansion to the levels of capital assets suggested by the *pro forma* balance sheets developed in Exercise 11–3. Show your figures. Explain your reasoning.
- Use your business reference library to study the size of the firms in this industry. Would you regard the Slaybough Corporation as being a large, medium, or small company in this industry?

Human Assets

Human resources are distinct assets of organizations and should also be examined in detail. Each industry will call for human resources of varying types. Labor-intensive industries often require large numbers of low-skilled workers capable of performing relatively simple tasks and available at low rates of pay. Industries in the United

States that employ labor of this type include crop harvesting, car washing, fast food, and freight handling.

Blue-collar occupations that require lengthy apprenticeships or training programs include skilled artisans (pipe fitters, machinists, tool and die makers, carpenters, bricklayers, steamfitters, etc.) as well as numerous other industrial occupations in which skills are learned on the job through long-term job progression systems. Typically, these skilled jobs are held by persons with long seniority who command wages at or above the level of first-line supervisors. In the high-tech industry of the 1980s, skilled assemblers and technicians capable of performing complex tasks form key components in the existing human resources of their employers.

For any given industry, an assessment of the nonexempt (blue-collar and clerical/technical white-collar) work force should include an examination of the relative productivity of workers, the turnover rate, grievance frequency (either officially, in a unionized facility, or unofficially, in a nonunionized plant), incidence of work stoppages or sabotage, accident rates, and the relative ease of hiring new employees. Other indicators of a healthy labor force include a low scrap rate, a low incidence of damage to equipment, and a low level of pilfering of company supplies and equipment.

The assessment of management capability offers a somewhat less clear-cut set of problems, or standards of measure. One way of beginning this analysis might be to examine the educational qualifications of key management personnel and their work experience. Beyond this initial examination, however, one probably should examine the operating results in key functional areas to obtain some general indicators of performance. The careful analyst will wish to look for the special attributes of high-quality leadership, a strong sense of the mission of the organization, an ability to inspire the confidence and cooperation of others, and an ability to effectively organize and direct the work of others. Finally, the presence of an opportunistic and entrepreneurial outlook on the part of the management team may provide a unique capability for an organization, especially as it faces rapidly changing conditions or a highly competitive and dynamic industrial environment.

In finance, one might begin by asking what indicators are there of *poor* financial performance. These might include such things as extremely high accounts receivable and high bad debt losses, excessive levels of assets not employed in the business, cash shortages, accounts payable at extremely low levels (or at levels that have resulted in penalty terms from suppliers), or failure to anticipate the need for debt repayment.

On the other hand, if a series of income statements and balance sheets indicates a state of stability in the management of assets and the repayment of creditors at levels that seem to be reasonable in light of the company's industry, then we might conclude that the financial management of the firm was in control and properly handled. In addition, our conclusion that we have a competent management team at work in the financial area of the company's affairs would be supported if we see that the financial officers of the company have consistently sought innovative ways of managing funds to maximize returns while maintaining their security.

In production/operations management, a similar process of analysis might first seek evidence of *poor* performance. Late deliveries, high materials costs, high scrap rates, high rates of customer returns for quality defects, accident incidence, grievances, excessive overtime, high machine downtime, and high setup costs are indicators of problems in the management of operations. In some cases, some of these types of problems may be evidence of a lack of smooth coordination between marketing and production. When specifications are unclear or delivery dates unreasonable, production management may be required to manufacture in smaller lots (resulting in high setup costs) or may manufacture products outside the specifications sought by the customer (resulting in a higher-than-desirable reject rate). Experienced operations executives make use of judgmental standards for assessing performance. A scrap rate of 8% may be a "normal" figure in one industry, but high (or low) in another. Some industries publish operations data that provide information highly useful for comparison purposes.

Production/operations that give evidence of high effectiveness not only have impressive statistical performance, but also appear to function smoothly. Interrelationships between portions of the operation are handled easily and work flows steadily through the facility. Communications are timely, crises are rare. In addition, where production/operations management expertise is high, we often see evidence of ingenuity applied to plant layout, scheduling, materials handling, or other areas critical to the efficient flow of materials and the effective use of materials and personnel. The effective operations/production manager will have a sound grasp of the latest equipment in his field and will aggressively attempt to find ways to justify the purchase and installation of new equipment as a means of reaching increasingly demanding standards of operating efficiency.

In marketing, evidence of poor marketing management might be found in high levels of customer complaints, chronic late deliveries, shrinking market share, salespersons who have a superficial knowledge of the product or how to sell it, and "oops" notices that are sometimes found in local newspapers . . . notifying the public of mistakes in quoted prices, shortages of advertised items, or other errors in printed advertising. Poor management of the marketing function can also be found in a mix of product, price, promotion, and distribution that is improperly arranged, or that fails to have a unified, coherent character. Errors in pricing might be found in cases in which orders are accepted at prices that are neither likely to recover the cost of production nor to develop a permanent market position.

Marketing management that is (probably) performing satisfactory would be found in companies in which both market share is stable or growing and the promotion, distribution, and product types offered for sale evince a thorough understanding of the target market and its needs. In this organization, salespersons have a sound knowledge of their own product and organization and of the products and practices of their principal competitors. Promotional activities are keyed to the interests of decision makers and are balanced to achieve a mix of appeals through publicity, advertising, direct-sales work, and promotional activity aimed at the interests and buying patterns of the decision maker. Market research is customer oriented and sales representatives are charged with both the responsibility of soliciting customer comment and opinion and conveying that information to those involved in distribution, dealer relations, advertising, and new product development.

The exceptional marketing company has a growing market share. Customers are loyal and may return for a lifetime's purchases of the company's products. In the exceptional marketing organization, not only is the marketing mix well arranged and highly complementary, but it also contains evidence of creative attention in its details in order to distinguish the company and its products from its competitors and to reinforce its identity in the minds of consumers and decision makers. Products are designed with consumers in mind. The introduction of new products is followed by delivery as promised and customer complaints and suggestions that follow new product introductions are given quick attention and response.

In research and development (R & D), the cost of development, and the quality and utility of new products and processes offer a reasonable means of assessing management's ability in R & D work. Among inventors, the number of patients filed in a given time period serve as an index of productivity. In other instances, an especially brilliant solution to an industry problem may establish its originator or the originator's company as an innovative leader.

Commercial acceptability is another criterion measure that at times might be overlooked. We have all encountered some device or other that was *engineered* to function well, but that in the hands of most mortals simply did not. In the microcomputer industry, the phrase *user-friendly* has become a watchword. Equipment that is technically capable of solving complex problems will fail in the marketplace without attention to the needs of users and the development of documentation, or on-screen assistance, for its effective use. We now have microcomputers that are designed with hardware of great capacity and sold to users for whom a fraction of the capacity would be sufficient to meet the technical demands of their applications. The additional capacity is used to manage the untutored user, that is, to guide the user through the software to a successful application. In some ways, the more powerful microcomputers can be considered analogous to the large and powerful automobiles of the 1970s. In those autos, the additional horsepower served to drive power steering, automatic transmissions, power brakes, seats and windows, and to air-condition the car's interior. Only a small portion served to convey the occupants from point of origin to destination.

A successful R & D program can be built around adaptation and modification of ideas generated elsewhere. In some industries, successful firms are those who find ways to develop less-costly copies of original designs. In some instances, copying brings about successful patent-infringement lawsuits, but in many cases, the adaptation is sufficiently different, so that an infringement case cannot be won. In this form of R & D activity, market and product information is crucial, as is the technical ability to close the gap between a competitor's idea and a production model of one's own.

Process development is of extreme importance in Stages 2 and 3 of the product life cycle. The company that identifies the product that will serve as the industry standard and then develops the lowest-cost production technologies is likely to survive the shakeout that occurs late in the Stage 2 of the cycle. In Stage 3, the scale of operations requires attention to minute detail in production efficiency to generate profits under the intense competition found in this stage. Cost savings in the hundredths of cents per piece when multiplied by the millions of units produced result in substantial savings to the efficient. In the fast food business, where literally millions of meals are served each week, portion control can mean the difference between success and mediocrity in financial performance. Strict attention to the use of tools that measure portions precisely and to the training of counter and kitchen help will result in great savings in materials costs for this very large industry. Process development can extend to the individual worker: Industrial engineers study workers to seek the most efficient methods for the accomplishment of tasks. Similarly, product flow through plant facilities is the subject of intense analysis and managerial attention. One example of this type of production-process technology is the just-in-time system of delivery of components to an assembly plant.

The Master Crafts case offers an opportunity to examine financial and human assets in a company engaged in the construction business. Read the case carefully, then respond to the exercise questions that follow.

MASTER CRAFTS, INC.*

Master Crafts, Inc., (MCI) is a builder of multifamily condominium and apartment structures. Master Crafts has been in business for 25 years and has been a dominant competitor in the four-state western region it serves. In its 25-year history, MCI has constructed 82 projects that encompass over fifteen hundred living units.

Master Crafts projects are notable for distinctive and tasteful exteriors, attractive placement on intended sites, and the livability of their interiors. Tom Jameson and Charles David, the firm's architects (and substantial stockholders) have on several occasions achieved national attention and awards for their designs.

Mike Holder, MCI's chief operating officer, has been associated with the firm for four years. Prior to joining MCI, he had been marketing director for Dongen Properties, a large developer and builder of single-family residences in Arkansas. Mike is an MBA graduate of Louisiana State University and has had a successful career in new home sales.

Bob Rehnquist is MCI's administrative vice president and chief financial officer. Bob has served with MCI since its formation and has moved upward in the organization from bookkeeper to accountant to office manager to his present position. Bob is a graduate of an associates' degree program in accounting at Weber Community College and is a member of the Metro area's Chamber of Commerce. Bob is a director on the board of the State College nearby and also serves on the boards of the Metro State Bank, Metro Rotary, the State's Real Estate Advisory Board, and the Home Builder's Association for the four-state region. Bob's staff includes an accounting department, a cost-estimating department, a cashier, a receptionist, and a secretarial/typing staff.

Jim Edwards, MCI's vice president of construction and operations, is a former carpenter and licensed contractor who joined MCI 10 years ago. Jim has served as lead carpenter and later superintendent of the company's construc-

* This case was prepared by the author.

tion crew. Jim's staff includes 4 project managers, a planning department, and the new superintendent of MCI's 40-man local construction crew. Work done outside the local area is accomplished by subcontractors found in areas near the location of the project.

Marketing activities are undertaken by Mike Holder with the assistance of the firm's two noted architects. The company had very good success in bidding for new projects in its early years, but it has lost business to its competitors more frequently in the past 3 or 4 years. Mike attributes the loss of several projects to developers "ignoring superior design in order to do business with their friends." The dollar value of MCI's bids and those of competitors on projects did not display consistent price differentials. In some cases, MCI was higher in price than its competition, in other cases lower.

Financial results on MCI's projects were mixed. Overall, a modest profit (1 to 1.5% of bid amount) was attained. Table 1 provides data on representative projects over the past several years.

In addition to the inconsistent and none-too-high profit levels, another disturbing factor to Mike was the increasing number of serious complaints from customers. In two instances, civil lawsuits were filed against MCI for alleged faulty construction. Among the complaints were allegations of cracked foundations and sagging structural members, plumbing leaks, foundation settlings, and damage caused by leaking roofs. Most of the complaints had arisen in projects remote from MCI's offices, where projects had been built by subcontractors under the direction of project managers.

Increasingly, MCI has been asked to agree to penalty clauses for delays in project completion. Mike had not been able to determine whether other bidders were asked to agree to these types of contract terms.

TABLE 1
Selected MCI projects, 1976–85

Expected completion date	*Actual completion date*	*Amount bid*	*Requests for changes*	*Total revenue*	*Total costs*	*Profit (loss)*
Jul 1, 76	Jun 15, 76	$1,258,500	$112,000	$1,370,500	$1,285,100	$ 85,400
Oct 1, 76	Sep 20, 76	856,200	0	856,200	891,200	−35,000
Sep 20, 79	Oct 1, 79	1,475,000	120,000	1,595,000	1,450,200	144,800
Feb 1, 81	Feb 8, 81	940,000	45,000	985,000	996,000	11,000
May 1, 82	Jun 3, 82	1,891,000	260,000	2,151,000	2,014,000	137,000
Jun 1, 83	Aug 2, 83	1,265,000	35,000	1,300,000	1,412,000	−112,000
Jul 1, 83	Aug 10, 83	921,000	62,000	983,000	961,000	22,000
Aug 1, 83	Oct 12, 83	1,100,000	125,000	1,225,000	1,260,000	−35,000
Apr 15, 84	Jul 5, 84	813,500	12,500	826,000	818,000	8,000
May 15, 84	Aug 22, 84	650,000	26,000	676,000	667,000	9,000
Aug 1, 84	Nov 6, 84	1,950,000	212,000	2,162,000	2,318,000	−156,000
Sep 15, 84	Jan 30, 85	714,000	19,500	733,500	697,500	36,000
Dec 31, 84	May 10, 85	1,100.000	125,000	1,225,000	1,315,000	−90,000

MCI financial data (000)

Year	*1980*	*1981*	*1982*	*1983*
Cash	$ 32	$ 11	$ 8	$ 76
Uncollected Billings from Contractors	123	196	204	331
Inventories	71	60	81	119
Equipment (net)	122	140	146	157
Buildings (net)	68	64	60	56
Land	50	50	50	50
Total Assets	$ 466	$ 521	$ 549	$ 789
* * * *	*	*	*	*
Contractor Accounts Payable	90	88	70	201
Wages Payable	28	97	72	153
Notes Payable (180 days)	50	40	100	120
Common Stock	120	120	120	120
Retained Earnings	178	176	187	195
Total Lia. & Equity	$ 446	$ 521	$ 549	$ 789
* * * *	*	*	*	*
Billings (Sales Revenues)	$5,903	$4,223	$6,891	$9,432
Dividends Paid	30	30	30	30

EXERCISE 11-5

- Prepare a list of the principal areas of financial strength and weakness in the MCI situation. Explain your choices and your rankings.
- Prepare a list of the principal areas of strength and weakness in human assets in the MCI situation. Explain your choices and your rankings.

Assets in the Marketplace

Although outside the company in a literal sense, several factors unique to each company are found in the marketplace. They are either strengths or weaknesses and can form the basis on which strategies can be built. We should, therefore, consider them internal resources rather than parts of the environment, and we must include them in our assessment of resources at the strategy formulator's disposal.

Products are an extremely important component of internal resources found in the marketplace. Technically superior ones or those with sufficient quality for commercial sale and normal use or items with minimal quality and suitable for only occasional use are examples of different types of product quality. Brand names carry a product-line's reputation to newly introduced products and make the introduction significantly less difficult than if it were to be made without the brand reputation to help pave the way. As one example, General Motors Buick Division has for some time used the advertising slogan, "Wouldn't you really rather have a Buick?" to aid the sale of several new models. Product reputation can have a long-term negative carryover as well. Several car models of Renault have been marketed in the United States in recent years. Despite the fact that these autos have had excellent success in European markets, their acceptance here has been badly dampened by customers' recollections of poor models sold here by Renault in the late 1950s and in the 1960s.

Company reputation is another internal asset. For many years, Sears Roebuck purchased goods from suppliers for private branding under Sears's labels. Although consumers might not have known of a Kenmore brand, they were assured of its suitability for their use by the backing of the Sears Roebuck organization and its various product guarantees. A now somewhat dated slogan that trades on the reputation of a company not on a brand name is, "You can be sure, if it's Westinghouse."

Product warranties are another aid to marketing and can serve to help in the establishment of a strategy. Lee Iacocca, the supersalesman at Chrysler Corporation, built a significant sales effort around the 5-year, 50,000-mile warranty on Chrysler's product line. Although many industries have what might be described as an industry-standard warranty package, a company such as Chrysler has undertaken to use a nonstandard product warranty as a positive factor in its sales effort. Mr. Iacocca not only forced his competitors to meet and exceed his warranties (to 6 years and 60,000 miles), but he made a further move to a 7-year, 70,000-mile warranty in late 1986.

Dealers, distributors, and service personnel can be a strength or a weakness. Where customers have little technical knowledge of products or their applications, dealers serve as product experts and can significantly aid in the marketing effort by finding the product best suited to the needs of each individual customer. In addition, dealers or distributors often serve as the first line of contact with customers having trouble with the product. An attentive and helpful dealer can often turn a potentially detrimental situation into a positive gain by deft handling of the problem and a helpful approach to the customer. Because of the importance of this initial contact for both sale and service, the franchising of dealers is approached most carefully by major manufacturers. Automobile manufacturers limit the number of franchises in a particular area in order to assure that each will have a sufficient volume of business to maintain an active service and repair facility as well as a positive attitude toward the supplying company. Dealers and distributors also serve as a vital source of market information and provide the grist for forecasts of trends in customers' interests.

Finally, the share of market presently held by a company serves as a source of strength or as an area of weakness. If a company is dominant in a particular market, its products have become a part of an established buying pattern for its customers. Competitors seeking to dislodge the company from its dominant position must not only develop a marketing plan that offers the customer a mix that is seen as more desirable, but must also break that established buying pattern. Market share is hard to build, but once built it is very difficult for competition to dislodge. The company with an established share, especially where buying patterns are built on fairly frequent usage, has a real strength that can be used in establishing plans for achieving strategic objectives.

EXERCISE 11–6

The information provided to this point can be summarized in checklist form for use in evaluating cases or other business situations you may encounter.

Develop checklists for the four major areas of strengths and weaknesses, including any subheadings that you find. You may wish to check your list with the partial list found at the end of the chapter.

The following short case provides some information about a small company. As you read through the case, you may wish to note areas of strength and weakness. The checklist that you developed in Exercise 11–6 should be helpful. (Hint: You may wish to have the list typed and duplicated for use in future case analyses.)

THE PERFORATED PAD COMPANY

The Perforated Pad Company (PPC) is in its ninety-ninth year of operation. Through this century, the company has managed to survive increasing competition, a plant site far removed from its customers, a nearly disastrous lawsuit, and the death of its most successful owner. This case looks at the business problems of a small manufacturer through the example of PPC. It considers PPC's history, present situation, and future outlook. It is meant to form the basis for class discussion and not as an example of good or bad management practice.

This case was prepared by William P. Allen as a basis for class discussion rather than to illustrate either effective or ineffective handling of an administrative situation. The case is meant to form the basis for the class discussion and not as an example of good or bad management practice. Prepared in 1975, it reflects the facts of that time, not necessarily those of the late 1980s. The issues presented are as significant now as they were at the time of the case. The approaches learned through a careful study of the case, therefore, can be applied in the business world of today and similar business situations well into the future.

BACKGROUND

The Perforated Pad Company is not the kind of company that knocks the horse-and-buggy days. The horse-and-buggy days are the very foundation of the business. The prosperity of the business in this advanced stage of the motor age is due to the fact that the horse remains very much with us and the buggy hasn't yet become completely a museum piece.

This paragraph, found at the beginning of PPC's product catalogue, points to the company's total dependence on the horse and a Western life-style. Perforated Pad has found its niche in the very large industry serving the horse-and-rider market. During the company's century of operation, the industry and its market have undergone tremendous changes. Years ago, the industry supplied a type of product for a life-style characterized by cattle ranches, cowboys, and the horse and buggy. Today, despite the persistence of cattle ranches in the West, the industry manufactures products primarily for leisure and recreational activities. Its products now emphasize style and appearance where once functional utility was the major selling point. The industry's many manufacturers produce such diverse items as Western fashions, horse medicines, feed supplements, leather products, ranchwear, horseshoe nails, and much more. Within this context, PPC produces a high-quality product for work, show, and recreational riders. Today, it is the largest manufacturer of saddle pads in the country.

COMPANY HISTORY

The PPC was established in 1877 and incorporated in 1882. By 1901, it had a capitalization of $50,000 and produced fronts, blinds, rosettes, pads, patent leather, and felt goods for the harness trade. Bill Goucher started working at PPC in 1933 and soon became the principal owner. In 1953, Bill moved the business from Woonsocket, Rhode Island, to nearby Cumberland, Rhode Island. The new plant consisted of one floor with 2,000 square feet of space. The addition of a second floor in 1956 and the more recent (1971) construction of a warehouse have more than doubled the original area. Today, the two buildings house 20 sewing and stitching machines, a pair of fabric-cutting tables, and various stamping, riveting, and polishing machines. Fourteen women are employed at stitching and sewing; three men perform various production and shipping duties. The office staff consists of two secretaries and the plant manager.

In 1957, Bill brought his nephew, Jim Hachey, into the business. At that time, the company's only major product was saddle pads. Pads are placed under saddles (hence the name) to soften the ride or are used alone for bareback riding. A broad classification of these pads, therefore, distinguishes between saddle pads and bareback pads. The particular saddle pads produced in the late 1950s were made of coarse felt covered on one side by a piece of cotton duck and cut roughly to the shape and size of the pad. To this were added leatherwear patches to protect the fabric from the friction of the saddle. Another type, the English-style saddle pad, fits a different type of saddle and is made of two pieces of soft felt stitched together. The bareback pads have straps and stirrups attached and are made of softer, finer felt.

The period after 1957 saw the expansion of PPC's product line. Pads were now being covered with brightly colored plaid fabric for use by recreational and show riders. Later, acrylic and polyester fur pads were added to the line. Obviously, the market for horse products was changing and PPC was doing what Bill and Jim thought was necessary to meet these changes.

Bill died in 1971. Because Jim had been managing the production and purchasing aspects of the business for several years, Bill's death occasioned no business crisis. Jim's aunt, Mary Goucher, became president and was the principal stockholder. Jim, however, made all operating decisions.

In 1974, horse sheets and blankets were added to supplement the pad line. Blankets are used to keep horses warm in cold weather and they also prevent hair growth. Therefore, because so many horse shows are now held inside during cold months, horse owners find blankets indispensable to the presentation of a clean, well-groomed animal. Sheets are lightweight covers that are used to ward off chills after workouts, to keep horses dry during rain and clean while in the barn, and also to protect their wounds and stitches after surgery.

CHANGE AFTER BILL'S DEATH

After Bill's death, Jim began instituting changes in three areas: facilities and equipment, product lines, and marketing strategy. These changes were motivated partly in response to changing markets, partly because they were overdue, and partly to accommodate new managerial objectives. Taken together, they would seem to enhance the company's production and sales potential.

The most fundamental change, however, was in management's objectives and conception of the business. Often under Bill's direction, profit making seemed secondary to other concerns. An incident that occurred several summers ago points this out.

At that time, PPC was not able to get raw materials quickly enough or in sufficient quantity to satisfy demand. Part of the problem lay in fabric shortages, but the company also lacked sufficient storage capacity to maintain a satisfactory inventory. Orders were pouring in and the backlog at times exceeded 6 weeks. Heated arguments arose between the two men over Jim's practice of using available materials to fill the orders of big accounts. Smaller orders, usually placed by old customers and totaling less than $200 or $300 were neglected. The businesses placing these orders were often owned by old friends of Bill, and Bill would pressure Jim to supply these friends. Jim would counter with demands for more storage and production space, but Bill always said no. Tensions between the two men ran high that summer.

Behind this recurring argument lay two conflicting conceptions of PPC. Bill's major concern was to have the company furnish him with an income stream for his remaining years. Second, he wanted to take care of his friends. Thus, he was against relatively large capital improvements or other changes that would adversely affect his income. In other words, he chose to guard against losses by reducing capital expenditures and risk. Jim, on the other hand, saw many accounts quitting PPC because they could not receive their merchandise quickly. One customer, primarily a large manufacturer of saddle and leather goods, started to make his own line of pads. Other customers, mostly intermediate and small accounts, turned their business over to other manufacturers. Jim knew that the company would soon be in trouble. As Jim saw it, if PPC continued to do only as much business as it wanted through the servicing of old accounts, it would be caught between increased competition and increased production and cost problems. This scissors effect would eventually put the company out of business.

The debate ended with Bill's death. Jim now controlled all aspects of the business. In the years since 1971, his own management style has manifested itself in several ways. We will examine and evaluate this style by investigating the changes Jim has made since 1971.

Production and Purchasing

On a recent visit to PPC, the case writer immediately noticed obvious improvements in the plant's layout. Before, the floor was cluttered with broken-down machines gathering dust, felt rolls piled to the ceiling, and unorganized scrap and old pads. Things are now more ordered, as if each machine and each work area is a neatly defined department. Most of the felt and fabric rolls are stored in the new warehouse and only a few days' supply is on hand in the main building. Several new machines are in operation. An area has been sectioned off for blanket and sheet production. The office is similarly uncluttered and a copying machine has been installed. These changes and additions give the shop an aura of efficiency it has never had before.

Production proceeds through much the same process as before. Felt or fabric is set out in layers on the cutting table. Pad shapes are outlined on these materials by tracing a cardboard pattern on the top layer. The pad shapes are cut out and sent upstairs to the sewing room. Here a variety of transformations occur, most involve either stitching the cotton duck on the felt or sewing two pieces of cloth together. These latter pieces are carried downstairs and stuffed with the felt pads. The stuffed pieces then go back upstairs to be closed and stitched.

A similar simplicity characterizes material purchases. Jim mentally compares his material inventory with his orders, determines what additions to inventory are needed, and places his order. Problems occasionally arise with mills that demand large quantities per order. For example, if Jim wants four different plaids, a mill may require that he purchase an entire mill run for each color. This consists of 2,000 yards or 10 rolls of fabric per color. Neither PPC's volume nor warehouse capacity is large enough to handle such a large addition to inventory more than a few times each year. Jim often avoids this problem by making deals with smaller mills who store the fabric for him and deliver on demand. But he pays, at least indirectly, for this service and can seldom take advantage of quantity discounts.

Thus, production mixes old and new processes and arrangements. The new equipment and warehouse, however, make production more efficient than before, as evidenced by fewer and shorter order backlogs and by a larger volume of sales.

Products and Marketing

Perforated Pad's biggest developments are occurring in new products and marketing strategy. As mentioned, production of horse sheets and blankets began in 1974. These new products bear a profit margin of about $6 per blanket and $4 per sheet compared to an average profit of $2 per pad. Thus far, sales of sheets and blankets have been small, totaling about $35,000 in 1974. Total sales in 1974 were about $375,000. Jim expects much more volume from these newer items as customers become more aware of them. Jim also hopes to add a line of sheets for cattle in the near future.

The most far-ranging change is occurring in PPC's sales strategy. For the past 13 years, the company's primary customer contact came through the travels of one man, Oscar Olson. As PPC's manufacturer's representative, Oscar canvassed Utah, Colorado, Arizona, Texas, Oklahoma, Indiana, Kansas, Minnesota, Tennessee, Kentucky, Louisiana, and Mississippi. He was so well known and so reputable that customers often came to him with their orders. He carried PPC's entire line of products and at his peak brought in 50% of its business. Oscar is old now, however, and lately has concentrated his efforts on only his biggest accounts. Each of these brings PPC approximately $3,000 to $8,000 in sales per quarter. Oscar neglects smaller customers, who may bring $5,000 in sales each year, and he no longer has the energy to hunt out new accounts.

Jim has retained Oscar even though the man has slowed down. Jim says, "Oscar is a good company representative who has contributed much to Perforated Pad's success. I could never tell him we no longer need his services. Fortunately, he has come to me and told me that he wants to retire."

Oscar's place is being taken by two men who will work his old territory, and more. They, too, will serve as manufacturer's representatives and plan to mount an intensive and aggressive campaign to expose PPC's products to as many potential customers as possible. They plan to secure new accounts and recapture old ones lost because of poor service in the past. Specifically, they plan to focus on veterinarian supply houses. These suppliers are beginning to expand their product lines from medicines to numerous other horse products. Perforated Pad presently carries only 2 such accounts, whereas the number of potential customers is more than 75.

Besides aggressive salesmanship, the new representatives plan to present their wares before various assemblages of horsemen and horsewomen. One such gathering is a trade fair, several of which are held each year throughout the Midwest and Far West. At these fairs, each manufacturer sets up a display of products for inspection. A new method of displaying products through live demonstrations on horseback is beginning to be seen at trade fairs. It is also being used at smaller gatherings convened at the behest of the sales representatives.

Perforated Pad advertises in trade journals and other publications, but it relies heavily on its manufacturer's representatives for volume. Jim estimates that 85% of the company's marketing effort is personal contact. At present, Jim's main concern is increasing his product exposure. He feels that if the new men show the products enough, sales will increase. He does not want to become directly or even indirectly involved, however, in the salesmen's selection of territory or technique. He provides them with no marketing support other than product samples and catalogues. As Jim sees it, it is the representative's responsibility to determine who and where PPC's market is. To Jim, a small manufacturer in Rhode Island selling to markets in the Midwest and Far West has to rely on its representatives in the field. Jim says that the industry has always operated this way, and he sees it continuing to do so.

FINANCIAL HIGHLIGHTS

Perforated Pad has not operated profitably in the last few years. As of June 1974, the company had an accumulated deficit (net operating losses and profits occurring since the equity recapitalization of December 31, 1970) of $11,612.87. Annual profit and loss statements contain the following bottom-line figures:

1971	($ 5,365.16)
1972	$ 4,748.48
1973	($12,224.96)
1974 (June)	($ 771.23)

The second half of 1974 and 1975 proved financially disastrous as over $25,000 worth of pads, suspected of containing anthrax, were destroyed and had to be replaced by PPC. Moreover, the federal government prohibited the shipment of any pads of this type for 4 months. Jim estimates this extraordinary business loss at more than $40,000.

Despite this poor financial showing, Jim feels that the company has done well overall since 1971. He points out that Bill's wife, Mary, draws over $30,000 each year as the company's president, yet makes no contribution to the business. Sales have increased from approximately $200,000 in 1965 to over $400,000 in 1975. Gross profit on sales has consistently ranged between 18 and 20%, a level Jim considers good. Furthermore, inventory turnover increased after 1971, providing an indication of greater efficiency since Jim took over.

Inventory Turnover	
1971	13.8
1972	16.9
1973	15.6
1974	16.0 (est.)

Finally, early indications are that 1976 will be a most profitable year.

Thus, despite the poor profit showing, Jim is able to justifiably point out improvements made in the last five years. He is obviously concerned about losses, but realizes that he and several other members of the family live comfortably because of Perforated Pad and will probably continue to do so for many years to come.

EXERCISE 11–7

- Use your checklists for assessing strengths and weaknesses to develop a list of these characteristics of the internal resources of PPC.
- When the list is completed, identify the top five strengths and top five weaknesses and rank them. (No. 1 in each ranking should be the most significant strength or weakness.)
- When ranked, prepare a brief explanation as to the rationale for your ranking of (a) strengths and (b) weaknesses.

IDENTIFICATION OF POTENTIAL AREAS OF ADVANTAGE

The process of analysis designed to disclose the existence of one or more areas of advantage involves a thorough exploration of each of the three components we have just studied. First, we need to know what the general business environment will require of members of an industry as well as the effects of EPA rulings that are likely, for example, to call for the development of new processes, new materials, or new disposal methods for entire industries. The research competence or the engineering talent needed to meet those demands in the general business environment may or may not be found in the affected industry. For those companies that have such talent, the changes demanded in the general environment are less immediately threatening than for those companies unprepared to respond. Similarly, as consumer preferences change, companies with active market and product research units are likely to respond more quickly and more effectively to change than will their competitors. In each of these instances, the presence of specific types of resources serves to provide the basis for an advantage over the company's competition. During the shortages of petroleum fuels in recent years, an advantage was identifiable for some manufacturing plants that had been constructed with furnaces capable of conversion to make use of either fuel oil or natural gas. As fuel oil supplies were threatened, the conversion to gas enabled manufacturing to continue with minimal disruption. Generally, this form of potential advantage is gained by the presence and use of a specific type of asset. Examples can be found in several areas of assets.

Thus far, we have discussed physical and human resources. Other situations might involve the emerging necessity for equipment of specific types. When demand for a limited product line is expanding rapidly, mass-production equipment can be used to manufacture products on a multishift basis. A manufacturer utilizing general-purpose equipment for the production of the same product might find, however, that production expansion was limited by the availability of qualified workers and that the extensive setup costs involved in long-run production on general-purpose equipment resulted in noncompetitive product costs. On the other hand, if demand patterns begin to demonstrate that customers prefer a much wider range of product types and insist on considerable individuality, then mass-production equipment will be much less suitable for the product variation and consequent shortening of production runs than would equipment of a more general-purpose type.

The presence of a long-standing sound reputation may serve to preserve and gain market share during conditions of market shakeout. As the microcomputer industry moves toward maturity, the loss of small competitors has made some customers concerned about the possibility of owning an orphan microcomputer, so that they have gravitated toward the better established names such as IBM and Apple. In this case, the reputation of the company aided it during a change in the industry-specific market.

Financial resources also serve as an avenue for advantage over the competiton during a change in the general business environment or the industry-specific environment. If a revolutionary technological development becomes generally available, for example, the company with capital resources will be able to achieve the earliest slot time for new-equipment delivery and can assure itself of a lead over its competitors in the application of the new equipment. Financial resources also enable a company to purchase equipment and materials opportunistically or to obtain an order from a customer who might be too large for the less well-funded competitor. For routine purchases, the well-financed company can also take advantage of quantity and cash discounts.

The presence of strength in the quality, quantity, and loyalty of one's blue-collar work force can be a great advantage during periods of rapid expansion in demand when new employees must be trained and when hours of work may be extended. Conversely, a company that has a work force that might be considered a weakness may be forced to rely on supervisors for training and for the manufacture of product in excess of the normal work load.

A strong management team can be of enormous advantage during periods of market turbulence and uncertainty. Their ability to cope with change, to anticipate new conditions and demands, and to deal with the emerging conditions will give their employer a distinct advantage over competitors who have less capable management.

EXERCISE 11–8

Consider strengths in the four major areas of assets the strategist uses in planning and executing organizational strategies (physical, financial, human, market).

- List for each of these, three or four types of situation in the general business environment in which a particular form of strength would present the possibility of an advantage for the firm over its competitors.
- Also list for each, three or four types of situations in the industry-specific environment in which a particular form of strength would present the possibility of an advantage for the firm over its competitors.

Distinctive Competence

In addition to the possibility of an advantage that is made available by the presence of internal resources that are especially useful in a given environmental setting, an organization may have a unique ability to cope with one or more situations. Some companies, for example, have a special talent for responding to rapid change in demand. Others may have an ability to manage the manufacturing of a particularly difficult product mix. In the aircraft industry, the Boeing Corporation is able to adjust the scale of its operations to suit the variability of its order patterns, and it has been able to earn a profit at very low levels of sales as well as during periods of high sales volume. IBM is known for the attention paid to customer education and for the extent to which their personnel are schooled in effective marketing techniques. The technical superiority of Digital Equipment Corporation's products has gained them an enviable position in the sales of their VAX line of minicomputers, especially in European markets.

In each of the examples cited, the distinctive competence of the company was not multidimensioned. Further, the areas of competence were particularly helpful in one set of conditions, but they might not be helpful or might not be needed in another. IBM's customer education skills might not be needed in markets where customers are highly skilled experts in computer technology. Digital's technical superiority may be lost on users with minimal knowledge of, or concern with, the technological aspects of their equipment. A salesperson's ability to establish and support long-standing relationships, as another example, might not only be unnecessary in some types of saleswork, but also might actually interfere with the effective conduct of sales activity.

The following case offers an excellent opportunity to study a company in its early years. As you read the case, use the checklists you have developed or make notes on the margins of the case in preparation for exercise questions that follow the case. It will be necessary to assess both categories of external environment and to make an evaluation of the internal resources of the Muse Air organization in order to identify possible advantages and/or distinctive competences.

MUSE AIR

"I told Michael that he didn't know what the hell he was getting into. It ain't no small task to start an airline." This was M. Lamar Muse's first reaction to his son's suggestion to start their own airline. In spite of that, at the age of 60, Lamar Muse has embarked on a new business venture that, in order to be successful, must attract a large percentage of the air-travel market of Southwest Airlines. Thus, after careful analysis by a national graphologist, Henry Miller, to determine its success quotient, he launched his own company, Muse Air.

Lamar is an experienced competitor with over 30 years of diversified management experience as Chief Executive Officer (CEO) of three successful airlines. His career in the airline industry began in 1948 when he joined Tran Texas Airways (now Texas International) as secretary, treasurer, and CEO. He was responsible for accounting matters as well as budgeting and cost control. Muse often appeared before the Civil Aeronautics Board (CAB) as the Trans Texas representative during route and subsidy proceedings.

Later, Muse worked as assistant vice president, corporate planning, for American Airlines, where he handled long-range planning, including equipment and facilities requirements.

In 1965, he held the position of president and CEO for Central Airlines in Dallas. While at Central, which is now part of Frontier Airlines, Muse appeared before the CAB as the company's chief policy witness and financial expert.

Before teaming up with Southwest, Muse was president and CEO of Universal Airlines, an air charter and contract cargo airline in Detroit. Muse left his high-ranked position at Southwest in 1978 after an executive policy dispute over expansion of the airline. Through his guidance, Southwest had prospered. During the 7 years Muse was with Southwest, the airline repeatedly outstripped the bigger national airlines by providing customers with low fares, convenient schedules, and quick turnarounds at close-in airports. When Muse left the company, he signed an agreement not to compete with Southwest for 2 years.

Contrary to what many people believe, it was his son Michael, a CPA and attorney, who originated the idea to start Muse Air. Muse could not assist Michael until his no-competition agreement ran out in September 1980, but he was more than interested. Then, on October 27, 1980, Muse, his son Michael, and their lawyers called a special press conference in Houston. At that time Lamar Muse said that he had, "decided to go for it. . . . Since that time, it's been a lot of hard work."

When asked if it is tough to attract passengers away from Southwest, Muse said,

> *You damn right it's tough, but there is one difference. Ten years ago we had to build and develop the market. Today all I have to do is take it away from them, and that ought to be a piece of cake.*

In response, Howard Putnam, then the president of Southwest Airlines said that he did not mind competition from Muse.

> *We fought for deregulation and believe in free enterprise. If you do that you're asking for competition. It's making us a little sharper. It has got the adrenalin flowing in our people and we have enjoyed having the*

This case was prepared by Lauren Nicholas, Rich Redle, and Tony Romero, under the supervision of Professor Sexton Adams, North Texas State University, and Professor Adelaide Griffin, Texas Women's University, as a basis for class discussion rather than to illustrate either effective or ineffective handling of an administrative situation.

> *challenge. Anytime someone comes into the market with lots of seats, they're bound to get some passengers, and they're going to have to get them from us.*

Asked if Southwest predicted cutting their airfares on similar flights with Muse Air, Putman said,

> *No, we never said that. It was the media that brought up the price war. We don't plan a price war.*

If Southwest changes its mind and decides to cut their rates, Michael Muse said,

> *We're going to match their fares. What else can we do? You can't let your competition carry your passengers cheaper than you do. We're going to advertise what their true intentions are in cutting the fares. We think the effect will be to stimulate the market so much that everybody will be flying full. The bottom line is that we'll make more money with this airplane at lower fares than they will, even with a full load. It doesn't really make much sense for them to do that. That's why we didn't cut the fares, because we think that the fares are where they should be. Our fares are equal to Southwest.*

Muse made another unprecedented move in launching his new airline. Muse Air will be totally nonsmoking.

> *The no-smoking policy was strictly a marketing decision. I'm no crusader. [He quit smoking himself only 7 months ago.] Ten years ago I wouldn't have thought of anything like that. Now I think the majority of people will appreciate being able to fly in clean air rather than a smoke-filled container. It may cost us a little business from the people [who] just think they can't go 50 minutes without smoking a cigarette, but I think there will be many, many more [who] will make an effort to change over to us that wouldn't have otherwise. So far the response has been unbelievably positive.*[1]

Patsy Morgan Prendergrass, president of Amelia Martin Travel Agency in Dallas, confirmed Muse's optimism. "The travel agency is booking Muse airline like crazy. Of our Southwest traffic,. probably thirty percent of the passengers already want to fly Muse Air," she said.

Muse Airline blasted off with a $1 million-plus ad campaign featuring Muse. The theme "Big Daddy Is Back" is supposed to emphasize Muse's reputation and visibility in the air industry. But when asked what "Big Daddy" represents, Muse said, "I don't know. It's something the advertising agency came up with." He also commented that he really did not think it fit his image, but "Hell, if it sells seats . . . but I'll never hear the end of it from my friends. I'd rather be known as the best little airline in Texas rather than the biggest busline," he added.[2]

THE COMPANY

Muse Air Corporation is a newly organized company that provides low-fare, high-frequency scheduled airline service in Texas and plans to expand into the central United States by utilizing the operating strategies developed by Lamar Muse while at Southwest Airlines.

The company commenced service on July 15, 1981, between Dallas's Love Field and Houston's Hobby Airport — the airports closest to the central business districts of those cities — with two new Super 80 aircraft leased for one year from McDonnell Douglas Corporation. Muse Air plans to take delivery of four new Super-80 aircraft and initiate service to additional cities from Dallas and Houston in June 1982.

The success of Muse Air is dependent on a

number of factors, which cannot be assured, including its ability to generate sufficient revenues, to maintain sufficient levels of passenger volume at adequate fare levels, to compete effectively with Southwest Airlines, to obtain fuel supplies at satisfactory prices, and to secure future financing.

The company has not had any experience with its proposed route or rate structure. It does not have any firm basis other than management's opinion, experience, and analysis of publicity-available statistical data on which to estimate the volume of traffic or the amount of revenues these structures will generate. Accordingly, no assurance can be given that such revenues or that load factors will be sufficient to make the company's proposed operations economically viable.

TERMINAL, MAINTENANCE, AND OFFICE FACILITIES AND SERVICES

Muse Air has reached agreements with the city of Dallas, certain airlines, and other parties for the lease of terminal office and aircraft maintenance facilities at or near Dallas's Love Field and Houston's Hobby Airport.

> *The Company leases from the City of Dallas, on a long-term basis, ticket counter space, aircraft departure gates, passenger holding lounges, baggage handling facilities and operations office space adequate to meet the Company's initial needs. In connection with such lease, the Company pays Texas International Airlines for the value of improvements it made at Dallas['s] Love Field, but is no longer using, and subleases from that airline certain other facilities at Dallas['s] Love Field.*
>
> *Muse Air subleases, at Houston['s] Hobby Airport, ticket counter space, an aircraft departure gate, passenger holding lounge and operations office space from Republic Airlines. The Corporation contracts initially with Republic Airlines for the provision of ramp services and general baggage and ground handling at Houston['s] Hobby Airport. Muse Air provides its own ramp services and general baggage and ground handling at Dallas['s] Love Field, as well as its own passenger check-in and ticket counter staffing at both Dallas['s] Love Field and Houston['s] Hobby Airport. They also sublease aircraft maintenance facilities, at Dallas['s] Love Field.*
>
> *Muse Air will relocate and expand its general headquarters and establish its reservations office and flight dispatch facilities in space to be leased near Houston['s] Hobby Airport. The Company currently leases general office space in Dallas, Texas.*[3]

OPERATING AIRCRAFT AND FACILITIES

The company began operations with two new Super-80 aircraft, configured to accommodate 155 passengers in a single-class seating arrangement. The first two Super-80 aircraft are leased from McDonnell Douglas Corporation for a one-year term at a rental of $4 million. The lease of the two Super-80 aircraft will terminate on delivery of the four aircraft being acquired by Muse. These aircraft are being currently operated by other air carriers, including PSA, Swissair, and Austrian airlines.

On April 2, 1981, Muse Air executed agreements with McDonnell Douglas Corporation covering the lease of the two Super-80 aircraft and the acquisition of four Super-80 aircraft. Upon the purchase agreement, a progress payment of $13,175,000 was paid on May 15, 1981. The company has made arrangements to provide the balance of the purchase price, approximately $88 million.

For comparison, their major competitor, Southwest Airlines currently operates with Boeing 737-200 aircraft. The purchase price for these units presently is $13.5 million a piece as compared to a $22 million purchase for the DC-9 Super-80. Southwest recently purchased three new Boeing 737-200 aircraft for delivery in 1982. Although not as fuel efficient, the aircraft "gets more people in the air" said a Southwest executive.

Muse Air believes that the Super-80 aircraft is well suited for the high-volume, short-to-medium haul routes it intends to serve and will be among the most fuel-efficient aircraft per available seat-mile throughout the 1980s. In a 155-seat configuration, the Super-80 aircraft provides an optimal level of capacity for the short-to-medium haul, high-volume markets Muse Air intends to serve. The Super-80 aircraft has wider seats and aisles and consumes less fuel per seat flown than current comparable single-aisle Boeing jets, including the Boeing 737-200 operated by Southwest Airlines, with which Muse will compete. It is estimated that the Super-80 will consume 16% less fuel per seat flown than the Boeing 737-200 aircraft over the Dallas/Houston route. The Super-80 aircraft is also one of the quietest commercial jet aircraft flown today. The substantially reduced noise impact of the Super-80 aircraft on communities surrounding close-in airports such as Dallas's Love Field was an important factor in Muse Air's selection of the Super-80 aircraft.

Lamar Muse has brought many innovations to the U.S. airline industry and plans to make more. His planes will have the lowest operating cost of any aircraft in its class and an increased range of over 2,000 miles. These advantages stem from the new Pratt and Whitney turbofan engines, its larger fuel capacity and a longer wing. "You just can't b-e-l-i-e-v-e it when you take off. It sounds like a glider. No noise at all," Muse said.[4]

Standard also on the Super-80s is a new wide-look interior that provides seats for 155 passengers. The 3-2 seating configuration provides 122 window and aisle seats. Attempts will be made to assign only those seats, unless passengers traveling together request the middle "squeeze" seat. On prime-time flights, the middle passenger will receive a surprise gift from Muse for the inconvenience. "We have elected to give passengers enough room to be comfortable as opposed to being squished up so tight that you can't recline the seat. Each passenger has 20 to 25% more space than the competition," Lamar Muse said. He is attempting to attain a clubcar rather than a cattle car image by offering assigned seating and thus eliminate the indignities of rushing to get the best seat.

He is very concerned with the reserved and sophisticated image of his new airline. Stewardesses now go by the title of in-flight-service-representatives, and Muse's employees do not wear hot pants, but instead model designer clothes for their customers.

BUSINESS

Operating Strategy: As previously stated, Muse Air's objective is to provide "high-frequency, low-fare, single-class jet service in high-density markets not generally exceeding a 500-mile distance." They operate out of Love Field in Dallas presently, but plan to create a large interstate hub at Houston's Hobby Airport and in 1984 to move the company's headquarters to Houston when their present lease is up.

This move is primarily because of the federal regulations that limit Love-based carriers to service within Texas and its four bordering states. Possible noise limitations and night-flight restrictions had no effect on the decision of Muse to move. The city of Dallas, however, feels Muse Air is moving because of their imposed regulations and is trying to keep Muse at Love Field, saying it won't adopt the noise restrictions and that it is trying to keep the airport going.[5]

Currently, Muse plans only to match prices of their competition (mainly Southwest Airlines), not undercut them. But Muse contends that if Southwest lowered their prices to a dollar, he would have to match it. A peak/off-peak fare structure is being used that Lamar Muse began at Southwest Airlines. Peak is regular business hours and fares are $40 versus $25 in off-peak hours. Fares will be lower than the standard industry fare level (SIFL) authorized by the CAB. As of December 18, 1981, the SIFL price is $76.19. Simple operating procedures are used, including cash-register ticketing and expedited check-in and reservation procedures. There is no interchanging of passengers with other carriers by the use of standardized ticketing, reservations, and baggage handling (called interlining), which costs extra money and is used by the larger airlines. High passenger volume will depend on the establishment and maintenance of routes and fares, dependability of service, convenient departure times, airport locations, and name recognition. These factors are of great importance as far as achieving successful operations.

Air-Travel Market: Initial service is between Dallas and Houston with approximately 12 trips each way daily, Muse Air is the first competition Southwest has encountered out of Love Field and Hobby Airport since Braniff relocated to Dallas/Fort Worth Regional Airport in August 1974. The Dallas/Houston market is one of the 10 largest local air-travel markets in the country, representing 76% of total Dallas/Houston air travel between Love Field and Hobby Airport. Annually, 1.5 million passengers are estimated in this market.

The passenger load factor (the percentage of paid seats above cost on average flights) has been increasing monthly; however, November figures show a slight reduction from October results. The present figures are still below original forecasts. Michael Muse indicated that they will begin making a profit when its planes are 50% full, its original projection for this was early 1982. Recent reports from Southwest indicates that their passenger traffic for September 1981 has increased 6% as compared to September 1980. Southwest's revenue passenger miles were up 17% from 1.45 billion miles to 1.75 billion miles for the same period. A passenger mile equals one paying passenger flown 1 mile.

Contrary to Southwest's growth, Braniff International reported its September 1981 traffic as having dropped 25.6% from September 1980. For the first 9 months of this year, traffic dropped 28.7%. The passenger load factor remained the same, reflecting a 28.7% decline in available seats from the paring of some international routes during Braniff's major overhaul.

Routes: Once Muse Air is established, it in-

EXHIBIT 1
Muse Air Air Traffic 1981

Month	*Trips*	*No. of pass.*	*Revenue pass. miles (million)*	*Avail. seats per mile (million)*	*Average pass. flight*	*Average pass. load*
July	425	16,178	3.9	15.8	38.1	24.6%
Aug.	662	27,121	6.5	24.7	41.0	26.4%
Sept.	624	31,887	7.7	23.3	51.1	33.0%
Oct.	620	39,829	9.6	23.2	64.2	41.5%
Nov.	612	39,118	9.4	22.9	63.9	41.2

Source: "Air Traffic," *Muse Air News Release* September 1981, p. 4.

tends to expand beyond the present Dallas/Houston market to include other cities such as Austin, San Antonio, Kansas City (Missouri), St. Louis, Cincinnati, Oklahoma City, Memphis, Chicago, Atlanta, and Pittsburgh. Dallas, Houston, Chicago, and Atlanta would be the four major hubs. Many of these routes have a lot of competition already, but Muse feels there is sufficient traffic to justify entry.

Competition: In the airline industry, passenger traffic is expected to grow over the next 5 years at a rate of 4% annually. The industry is highly competitive, especially since the Airline Deregulation Act of 1978—in whose passenger Lamar Muse was a forceful and persuasive advocate—when pricing structures were changed considerably. Primary competition in the Dallas/Houston market is Southwest, which has been an exclusive carrier there for more than 6 years.

Muse feels the best thing for Southwest to do to compete against Muse Air is to ignore them. If they try to ruin Muse Air, they would undoubtedly succeed. This is what Southwest feels is the reason for their success vis-à-vis Braniff. The latter at their inception tried to drive out Southwest by fighting them in court and lowering prices. Instead, Braniff began to look like a predator and Southwest to look like the underdog; the result was that passengers flocked to Southwest in record numbers. If Braniff had left them alone, Southwest feels they would have failed.[6] Southwest is basically leaving Muse Air alone hoping that they will go under without any help.

Executives from the industry predicted doom for many corporations after the Airline Deregulation Act; instead, quite a few newcomers began popping up, especially in Texas. These upstart airlines cashed in on underserved (or poorly served) markets. New airlines have a lower cost base than the big airlines because there are no union contracts and people happily pour capital into them, which was especially true of Muse Air and New York Air who sold common stock on the public market. The big airlines have been unable to do this recently.

There is a group of other small airlines recently started or in the plans for the near future: New York Air began in December 1980 and lost an expected $1.9 million in their first quarter on revenues of $7 million. In March 1981, they carried 25% of the traffic from New York to Washington, D.C., and New York to Boston, routes previously dominated by Eastern Airlines. New York Air is owned by the Texas Air Corporation, a holding company that also owns Texas International Airlines.

Texasamerica is a new CAB applicant with headquarters at Houston's Hobby Airport. They plan to fly to San Antonio, New York, Philadelphia, and Las Vegas. Lone Star Airways is about to start nonstop flights between Houston and oil cities in the Middle East. Air Colorado is planning to begin operations in June 1982 between Denver and Dallas/Ft. Worth, Los Angeles, Salt Lake City, San Francisco, and Chicago. Their setup will be similar to Muse: low cost, no-frills, all seats the same price, and peak/off-peak fares.

Sun Air was to have begun operations in November 1981 between Dallas/Fort Worth and Houston's Hobby; Abilene; Jefferson County Airport, in Beaumont-Port Arthur; and San Angelo, Texas—and with hopes of adding the Lower Rio Grande Valley in the future. They had three starting delays and a shaky beginning with four presidents in 9 months. This past September, they folded before service even began—at a reported loss of $870,000 to investors.

People Express, out of Newark, New Jersey, began selling stock at $13.50 per share and it was up to $20.00 as of June 1981. They raised $26 million even before purchasing any planes. Midway, out of Chicago, began in November 1979 with $510,000 on revenues of $13.1 million.

Midway, New York Air, People Express, and Muse Air successfully started up operations.

They did so before airline stocks nosedived and before the Professional Air Traffic Controller's Organization (PATCO) strike, which began August 2, 1981. They are at an advantage in the marketplace because they now have something to sell: a name, a certain reputation, facilities, and high-load factors. For the most part, private money should be available to them. They may get less money than they would like at public offerings, but they should sell.

John J. Casey, board chairman of Braniff International considers these new airlines healthy for competition. He says, "Competition grows a market. Just look at what Southwest has done for the Dallas/Houston market." Reasons for these corporations, says Ron Woestermeyer, senior vice president-marketing of Texas International, is that "they see the opportunity to make lots of money; à la Southwest. They feel they can compete effectively with a lower cost structure."[7]

Bigger, established airlines are upset because they cannot compete effectively against the nonunionized upstarts, but they did lower rates to compete and now they are flying nearly full on those competitive routes. Pan Am was having trouble with its mostly international routes so they merged with National Airlines to add domestic routes and enter the competition there in that area. (See Exhibit 2.)

EXHIBIT 2
Who's who in the new breed of airline

Airline	*Home Base*	*Start Date*	*Cities Served*	*Fleet*	*Capitalization (millions)*
Midway	Chicago's Midway	11/1/79	Chicago, Kansas City, MO, Detroit, Washington, St. Louis, NY, Omaha, Philly	(9) DC-9-10s	$27.5m
New York Air	NY's Laguardia	12/19/79	NY, Washington, Boston, Cleveland, Louisville	(7) DC-9-30s	33.2m
People Express	NY's Newark	4/30/80	NY, Buffalo, Norfolk, Boston, Jacksonville	(5) 737-100s	61.3m
Muse Air	Dallas's Love	7/15/81	Houston, Dallas	(2) DC-9 Super-80	110m
Sun Pacific	Ontario, Canada	7/81	LA, San Francisco, Las Vegas, Ontario	(4) DC-9-15s	16m
Sun Air	Dallas/Fort Worth	9/81	Dallas, Abilene, San Angelo	(4) DC-9-15s	12m
Pacific Express	Chicago, Calif.	10/81	San Francisco, LA, Boise, Eugene, OR	(7) BAC 111s	30m
Air Chicago	Midway	10/81	Minneapolis, Atlanta, NY, Pittsburgh	(8) DC-9-10s	50.3m
Trenton Hub Ex. (The) Airline	Trenton, NJ	2/1/82	Chicago, Pittsburgh, Boston		18.5m

Source: Adapted from "Upstarts in the Sky," *Business Week*, June 15, 1981, p. 80.

Business Week also reported:

> *Newcomers can make money with low fares because of low costs and high labor productibility. Employees' awareness that they are in at the beginning of an experiment that could alter the course of aviation history not only contributes to high productivity, but also generates a unity of purpose rarely found in a big organization. Potential problems with this competitive advantage is the possible inability of the new airlines to gain access to capital and to maintain their cost advantages. Established airlines are cutting their fares fast.*[8]

Short-haul markets, those under 500 miles, are where air traffic is growing fastest. In 1980, it grew by 9% while long-haul markets, those over 500 miles, dropped by 5.3%. This may be partly owing to some auto traffic shifting to air. Lamar Muse has long had a theory that, if properly run, a short-haul airline can be competitive with the automobile. If costs can be kept comparable and with the time-saving factor, people will use the airlines.

ADVERTISING

To date, Muse has spent over $1.5 million on advertising, with a hefty reserve allocated for additional expenditures. These dollars have been invested in all forms of advertising, including television, radio, newspaper, billboard, and magazine. An important factor that Lamar feels contributed to the success of Southwest was name recognition. His new strategy is no different.

Muse's advertising agency came up with the "Big Daddy Is Back" campaign. Publicized to be one of the most successful attention-getting campaigns of recent times. It has taken on a head-to-head confrontation with Southwest's "We Love You" campaign that underscores sex appeal as its major theme. Lamar plans to offer what he considers to be style and sophistication, which he believes will appeal to both men and women.

ORGANIZATION

Employees: Muse currently has 224 full-time employees, some of whom were wooed by Muse when they were laid off from larger companies because of the PATCO strike. The employees include 20 pilots/copilots, 38 flight attendants, 96 passenger-service personnel, 20 maintenance personnel, and 50 administrative and clerical workers. Pilots are trained under Federal Aviation Administration (FAA) approved programs to fly the Super-80 aircraft of Muse Air. McDonnell-Douglas has been contracted to train these pilots as well as the maintenance personnel to service the aircraft.

A major aim of Muse Air is to maximize each employee's productivity. Compensation levels are low compared to other airlines, who base their levels on seniority. The company feels that its employees will work hard to insure success of their new company. They are part of it and a failure would reflect, in part, on them—as would success. This gives employees a big incentive. And as Lamar Muse has made others rich (e.g., at Southwest), these employees feel they also have a chance to get rich.

The company intends to provide benefits such as life, health, and accident insurance plans as well as a profit-sharing plan to give employees both incentive and employee identification with the company.

Management: Muse Air has two directors, elected annually by the stockholders. Employees have a stock-option plan that allows them to purchase up to a total of 295,000 shares of common stock of the company. The directors are responsible for the administration of this plan, determining who is eligible, purchase price, and the number of shares available. As of December 1981 no options have been granted.

M. Lamar Muse joined Muse Air October 21, 1980, as the company's chairman of the board and CEO. (Exhibit 3.) As stated previously, past history includes a stay at Southwest Airlines from January 1971 to March 1978 as president and CEO, prior to which he was president and CEO of both Universal Airlines and Central Airlines. He was vice president and chief financial officer of Southern Airways, assistant vice president for corporate planning for American Airlines, and secretary/treasurer for Texas International Airlines. Muse is a CPA.

Michael L. Muse was the founder of Muse Air and has been the president and treasurer since incorporation in January 1980. From September 1978 to January 1980, he was a tax manager at Price Waterhouse & Co. in Dallas. From February 1976 to March 1978, Muse was at Southwest Airlines, most recently as finance and administrative vice president and chief financial officer. Muse is an attorney and a CPA.

Edward Lang became Muse Air's senior vice president of marketing in March 1981. Prior to that he was with Southwest Airlines as vice president of personnel and marketing. Previously, Lang had been an officer with Braniff Education Systems and Alaska Airlines.

James T. Ferguson joined Muse Air in March 1981 as the company's vice-president of flight operations. For more than 33 years, he was with Texas International Airlines, most recently as senior captain, piloting a DC-9 twinjet aircraft. From 1966 to 1968, Ferguson was chief pilot for Texas International at its Dallas crew base.

EXHIBIT 3
Organizational chart

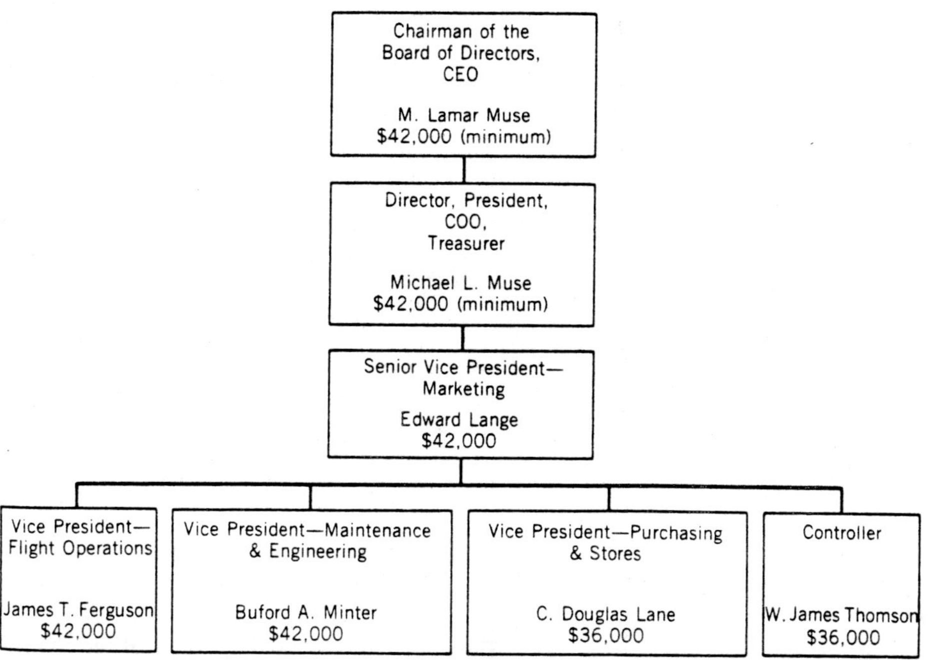

Buford A. Mintor also joined Muse Air in March 1981 as vice president of maintenance and engineering. Prior to that, he was with Braniff Airways for more than 40 years in the maintenance department, most recently as staff vice president of base aircraft maintenance.

C. Douglas Lane joined Muse Air in March 1981 as vice president of purchasing and stores. For the past 5 years, he was director of purchasing for Southwest.

W. James Thomson became the company's controller in March 1981. Also with Southwest for the past 5 years, he was in the accounting and finance departments, most recently as director of treasury operations.

REGULATION

Environmental

There are presently no noise curfews at either Dallas's Love Field or Houston's Hobby Airport. However, a citizens action group has pressured the Dallas City Council to undertake an investigation and study of noise levels at Dallas's Love to determine if operational restrictions should be imposed at the airport in order to reduce noise levels for the surrounding area. The significance of this report is such that the recommendations may set the stage for costly legal battles between the city and the present user of Dallas Love's facilities.

> *Recent litigation in various jurisdictions of the United States has tended to establish liability on the part of airport proprietors for damages when it has been determined that the aircraft noise has severely caused a decrease in property values for the surrounding airport area.*[9]

In April 1981, the consulting firms of Howard, Needles, Tammen and Bergendoff in association with Bolt, Beranek and Newman, Inc., and Pan Am World Services were hired by the city council at a cost of $212,000 to review solutions to the Love Field noise problems. Tentatively, they have recommended that a nighttime curfew be placed on aircraft whose noise level emissions exceed a maximum of 95 decibels. The preliminary report has indicated that there would be major economic losses to the airport, the users, and the region.[10] Among them—air carriers would lose 5 to 10% of daily operations and revenues and 100% of all nighttime departures. Southwest Airlines would probably have to move it's maintenance facilities to San Antonio. Dallas's Love Field and the region would lose a minimum of four hundred airline-related jobs. The report also estimates that Dallas residents would have to pay an extra $800,000 in property taxes because of the aviation-related business and resulting tax revenues that would be lost owing to the curfew. City council support for a curfew at Love Field appears to be slipping at this time owing to political and economic pressures.

Muse Air's operating certificate is subject to all applicable environmental laws and regulations and there can be no assurances that FAA certification would not be revoked if it was found that Muse did not satisfy such laws and regulations.

Government and Agency

Muse Air is subject to the Federal Aviation Act of 1958 under which the CAB and the administrator of the FAA exercise regulatory authority over air carriers. The CAB has jurisdiction over among other things, the issuance of certificates of public convenience and prescribes the routes over which an air carrier is permitted to operate as well as the rates and fares charged by air carriers.

The Deregulation Act amended the Federal Aviation Act and effected significant changes in airline regulation. It provided greater freedom of carriers to enter and leave markets. It reduced

CAB authority to control fares and lessened antitrust exemptions for air carriers. Under the act, the CAB's controls over routes will terminate December 31, 1981, and control over rates and fares will terminate January 1, 1983. At that time, the regulatory supervision of consolidation mergers and interlocking relationships will pass to the Justice Department. On January 1, 1985, the CAB will cease to exist. At the present, though, the CAB continues to possess substantial economic regulatory jurisdiction over passenger airlines. Muse Air's certificate is unlimited in duration but could be altered, amended, modified, or suspended by the CAB if evidence is presented and substantuated that Muse has failed to comply with the economic provisions of the Aviation Act or any condition or limitation of their operating certificate. The CAB is also empowered to review discrimination allegations to prevent unfair methods of competition or deceptive advertising practices, to inspect the carriers' properties and records, and to approve or disapprove certain contracts between air carriers. Presently Muse does not have an interchange passenger agreement with other carriers. An agreement of this type requires, among other things, CAB approval and the utilization of standardized tickets along with means of handling baggage and reservations.

The CAB presently controls the fare structures by means of tariffs filed by the airlines. They have the power to investigate and suspend such tariffs if they find the fares to be unlawful or in restraint of competition.

> *Except for routes where the proponent of the fare carries more than 70 percent of time traffic the Deregulation Act provides that the CAB may not find any domestic fare increase to be unjust so long as it is not more than 5 percent above the average fare rate as set by the CAB. (Rate is calculated by CAB using a formula which reflects the average cost for trunk line carriers.) Fares set less than 50 percent below this average rate are currently not allowed. These average costs are reviewed semiannually by the CAB.*[11]

Muse Air, as are all carriers, is subject to the FAA with respect to aircraft maintenance and operation. The FAA's jurisdiction over such things as equipment, ground facilities, communication, training or other safety-related factors was largely unaffected by the Deregulation Act.

Love Field

The use of Love Field by commercial (common) air carriers was modified in 1979. It was at that time that the International Air Transportation Competition Act was formulated, in part owing to the opening of Dallas-Ft. Worth Airport. The Love Field section of that act provides that a common carrier may provide passenger air transportation to one or more points outside of Texas, but not outside of a four-state region that includes Arkansas, Oklahoma, New Mexico, and Louisiana unless they were doing so on or before November 1, 1979. Service, however, can be permitted to those states providing no interline conditions exist between operating airlines.

Economy

On October 26, 1981, William B. Franklin, chief outlook editor for *Business Week* said, "Interest rates are finally beginning to slide under the influence of a softening economy, and the induced monetary ease of the administration plus the Federal Reserve's policy of the past several months has been that of injecting large supplies of reserves into the banking system." The recent decline, however, comes "too little too late" to stimulate or reverse the present economic trend. The unemployment rate rose to 7.5% in September 1981 and to 8.1% in October. The continued rise in the unemployment rate and the present range is normally associated with recessionary periods. This has lead to corporations as well as individuals looking for ways of reducing their outlays. Many are turning out to be scrooges where expenditures are concerned.

On October 29, 1981, Howard Sharpe, economist for Purcell, Graham and Co., predicted that the economy was in "the worst recession since World War II." He based this on leading indicators that continue to point down. Among them are vendor performance, stock prices, the layoff rate in manufacturing, the number of new business formations and raw material prices.

Current Funding and Financial Operating Atmosphere

A number of new airlines that have entered the market with cut-rate fares as an alternative for competition to the larger and established airlines are seeing setbacks even before getting off the ground. Airline stocks have devalued by 35% since June. "The very weak market conditions, with the added uncertainty of the air traffic controllers' strike still unsettled, are inhibiting new airlines from getting financing," says Michael Derchim, an airline industry analyst, at Oppenheimer and Company, "Investors are avoiding risks right now."

Continued public financing of the upstart airlines will depend on the quality and the money-raising power of an inexperienced management. The airlines that have raised money so far have done so by being managed by big names in aviation.

Several major airlines are suffering losses. (See Exhibit 4.) Eastern reported third-quarter losses of $38.7 million, Republic Air reported a loss of $18.4 million for the same period. Chief Executive Officer Frank Borman of Eastern said the loss was partly due to the air controllers' strike but cited competitive pressures. Delta Airlines, long considered one of the most profitable airlines, reported a 71% decline in earnings for the third quarter. The third quarter is traditionally the strongest period for airline earnings because of heavy summer traveling. Most airlines continue to blame the sagging economy, high interest rates, the air controllers' strike, and price competition as a reason for poor performance.

Sharply curtailed earnings make the straight purchase of aircraft with internally generated funds all but impossible for most carriers. Financing with straight bank loans and equipment trusts are also becoming more difficult as institutions seek to shorten their debt maturities.[12] Equipment-trust financing today normally will not exceed 12 to 12½ years, reports W. Blake Thompson, senior vice president for finance at U.S. Air.

The alternatives to the bleak industry outlook for financing equipment comes in the form of air-frame makers providing additional assistance, creative financing arrangements through foreign companies, and leasing arrangements that take advantage of new lease tax benefits.

Air Controllers' Strike

On August 2, 1981, PATCO began a strike. The members of PATCO were government employees who had signed a no-strike clause in their contract. In the weeks following the first walkoff, negotiations broke down and the return to work order by the president was ignored by most members. This lead to the government firing of the approximately 12,000 remaining members. The effects of the strike are beginning to take their toll. In order to maintain safety with its limited staff of controllers, the FAA has ordered greater spacing than usual between planes. This has sharply cut the capacity of the air-traffic system to handle flights. Compounding the problem has been the resurgence in flying by small general aviation aircraft. Major uncertainties face travelers as new services and routes are being canceled by the FAA, which

EXHIBIT 4
Muse Air Corporation financial data 1980–81

	Sales				Profits				Margins		Return on com. equity		
Company	3rd qtr. 1981 $mil	Change from 1980 %	9 mo. 1981 $mil	Change from 1980 %	3rd qtr. 1981 $mil	Change from 1980 %	9 mo. 1981 $mil	Change from 1980 %	3rd qtr. 1981 %	3rd qtr. 1980 %	12 mo. ending 9/30/81	PE ratio	Earnings per share 12 mo.
American Airlines	1,106.6	6	3,110.6	9	14.4	10	37.1	NM	1.3	1.2	−5.3	NM	−1.32
Braniff International	306.6	−20	946.0	−16	−19.3	NM	−84.0	NM	NM	4.5	NM	NM	−8.09
Delta Airlines	891.3	6	2,727.1	13	7.6	−71	83.1	−3	0.9	3.1	13.0	9	6.42
Eastern Airlines	902.1	5	2,834.5	11	−38.7	NM	−39.2	NM	NM	NM	−15.0	NM	−2.53
Frontier Airlines	152.2	24	436.3	26	11.0	86	24.3	90	7.2	4.8	28.7	5	3.87
Northwest Airlines	527.3	9	1,417.1	16	17.5	0	13.6	890	3.3	3.6	2.3	35	0.90
Ozark Airlines	88.4	15	286.1	38	1.2	NM	12.9	NM	1.3	NM	30.5	4	2.30
PSA	117.8	9	327.8	2	16.0	78	20.5	0	13.6	8.4	10.0	8	2.36
Pan American	947.7	−5	2,669.2	−9	48.2	152	−185.5	NM	4.9	1.9	2.0	18	0.16
Piedmont Aviation	148.2	16	443.5	28	10.2	18	23.3	114	6.9	6.7	29.6	6	4.24
Republic Airlines	368.2	73	1,093.2	89	−18.4	NM	−39.6	NM	NM	NM	−36.6	NM	−1.87
Trans World	1,466.5	5	4,028.9	7	74.0	5	73.5	123	5.0	5.0	8.1	9	1.93
UAL	1,363.8	1	3,924.7	5	7.2	−54	−5.5	NM	0.5	1.2	2.6	19	1.00
U.S. Air	268.1	7	816.1	16	7.1	−54	38.4	−9	2.6	6.2	20.8	3	3.83
Western Air	293.6	7	826.6	11	−7.3	NM	−17.4	NM	NM	NM	−16.9	NM	−2.20
Industry Composite	8,975.4	5	25,887.8	9	130.8	−30	−44.4	NM	1.5	2.2	0.7	12	0.15

Source: Standard & Poor's Compustat Services Inc.

above all must insure safety in the skies. Adverse weather conditions also add to the lengthy delays in departure times. Airline executives are beginning to show their frustration. "I am thinking of switching to the Gum Ball Business," fumed American Airline President Robert Crandall.[13] His comment, though in jest, is indicative of the current operating conditions facing all airlines. J. Lynn Helms, President Reagan's FAA administrator, indicates that the small general aviation craft have began to swamp the air-control system in an apparent effort to avoid airline delays. More travelers began flying in air taxis, chartering planes, or taking the corporate jet. Such planes are operating at 125 to 130% above normal. The strike has been abandoned, but the government has maintained the fired status of the PATCO members. Estimates are that it may be as long as 2 to 3 years before all routes and services will be resumed to prestrike conditions.

Fuel Costs

The cost for commercial jet fuel has risen sharply since 1973 when costs were around 15¢ per gallon. The past dependence on foreign petroleum products and the instability of the Mideast countries has lead to shortages and substantial price increases. Producer price index's for commercial jet fuel (kerosene base) have risen from a January 1979 level of 340.2 to 896.7.[14] This represents an increase of 163.6% (or .652¢ per gallon) increase to the present-day price of $1.052 per gallon. Although there is a current stabilization in the petroleum industry, Muse admits that "We are at the mercy of the producers" as far as price goes. "The only thing about it is, so is everybody else."[15]

FINANCIAL OPERATIONS

The company has obtained commitments from First National Bank of Dallas and Continental Illinois Bank and Trust Co. of Chicago to provide senior secured debt for $57.5 million subject to the airline meeting earnings and working capital requirements, among which the company must report an operating profit during March and April 1982. Working capital must be maintained at a level not less than $3 million for a period from August 1, 1981, through April 30, 1982, and stockholders equity must not be less than $30 million for the same period. The loan commitments from these institutions provide for a 12-year amortization schedule with a balloon payment at maturity and the payment of ³⁄₈ of 1% commitment fee. Repayment of the loan commences in the second year of the loan at an annual interest rate of 2% above the respective banks' prime rates. Additional financing will be from McDonnell Douglas, who on receipt of $13.2 million from Muse, will make available $17.7 million for the purchase of their aircraft. Muse has the option of utilizing the monies for purchase or leasing the aircraft. If purchased, the financing will be amortized over a 12-year period. If leased, the amount will apply to a 15-year lease agreement.

Presently the airline has no long-term debt. (See Exhibits 5 and 6.) In order to generate some leverage, Muse is evaluating the use of these commitments versus the potential benefits now offered by the new tax benefits introduced by President Reagan.

The tax breaks, which make leasing much more attractive, allow for companies that do not show a profit to turn over their investment tax credits and depreciation allowances to a profitable company. In doing so, the carrier gets a substantial break on the lease price, and what is more, they can bid up the sales price charged to the profitable company whereby an immediate increase in cash flow can be realized.

Hans Plickert, an analyst with E. F. Hutton and Co., figures the per-share leasing benefits "will be measured in dimes rather than dollars. It will certainly help the airlines

EXHIBIT 5
Muse Air Corporation (a development stage company)

Statement of Operations

	Three Months Ended September 30		Nine Months Ended September 30	
	1981	*1980*	*1981*	*1980*[a]
REVENUES:				
Passenger	$ 2,417	$ —	$ 2,417	$ —
Other	39	—	39	—
Total operating revenues	2,456	—	2,456	—
EXPENSES:				
Fuel and Oil	1,554	—	1,587	—
Flight operations excluding fuel	1,398	—	1,453	—
Maintenance	429	—	515	—
In-flight service	251	—	308	—
Station operations	416	—	445	—
Marketing	1,276	—	1,323	—
Insurance, taxes, and administrative	412	5	637	9
Depreciation and amortization	71	1	90	1
Total operating expenses	5,807	6	6,358	10
OPERATING INCOME (LOSS)	(3,351)	(6)	(3,902)	(10)
Interest income	606	13	1,211	14
NET INCOME (LOSS)[b]	$(2,745)	$ 7	$(2,691)	$ 4
Weighted average common and common equivalent shares outstanding	2,950	31	1,863	31
Net income (loss) per share	$ (.93)	$.22	$ (1.44)	$.12

[a]From date of incorporation (January 30, 1980) through September 30, 1980.
[b]No provision for federal income taxes has been made in these statements as the company does not anticipate any income tax expense for the period ending December 31, 1981.

cash position." But he sees little effect in the market. Plickert states that "the market is not terribly responsive to such balance sheet considerations."[16]

Most airlines are considering the benefits; however, little action is expected until the IRS clarifies the new law. The concern here is that the IRS could require carriers to capitalize leases, thus increasing their reported debt.

Muse currently has about $15 million in assets made up of cash and certificates of deposits. It is estimated that this working capital is sufficent to cover operation into the second half of 1982.

PROJECTED SALES

Muse expects the number of flights per week to average 154 until delivery of the four new

EXHIBIT 6
Muse Air Corporation (a development stage company)

Balance Sheet

	September 30, 1981	*December 31, 1980*
ASSETS		
Current:		
Cash and certificates of deposit	$11,926	$325
Prepaid aircraft lease costs	3,029	—
Accounts receivable	898	—
Other	634	1
Total Current Assets	16,487	326
Flight and ground equipment, at cost, less reserves[a]	18,019	110
Unamortized certification costs	48	57
Total Assets	$34,554	$493
LIABILITIES AND STOCKHOLDER'S EQUITY		
LIABILITIES		
Current:		
Accounts payable	$ 836	$ 19
Accrued liabilities	272	—
Unearned revenue	226	—
Total Current Liabilities	1,334	19
Convertible subordinated debentures	—	190
STOCKHOLDERS' EQUITY		
Common stock and paid-in capital	35,906	410
Retained earnings (deficit)	(2,686)	4
	33,220	414
Less stock subscription	—	130
Total Stockholders' Equity	33,220	284
Total Liabilities and Stockholders' Equity	$34,554	$493
SHARE DATA:		
Common stock issued and outstanding ($.10 par)	2,950	350
Book value per share	$ 11.26	$.81

[a]Includes aircraft progress payments of $13,838 at September 30, 1981 and $100 at December 31, 1980.

planes in July 1982. Aircraft availability is presently estimated at 95% per plane, with total availability for the two aircraft considered to be 90.25%. Current schedules have been established that indicate 65% of the flights to be prime time. Muse had expected the average load factor for 1981 operation to exceed 38.3%. However, through September they have achieved only a 28.35% load factor. Originally, Muse had projected losses of $2.5 to $3 million for 1981, but third-quarter results indicate they will far surpass those figures.

CONCLUSION

The future of Muse rests not only in Lamar Muse's past experiences and reputation, but also in Mike Muse's ability to carry on those talents. As Mike puts it, "Lamar spends three or four days a week in the office and he is a good spokesman for the company." But, Mike does not hesitate to add, "I run the company." Muse expects his airline to start making a profit in early 1982. Analysts claim the sooner the better as Muse takes on $75.2 million long-term debt in July 1982 for the financing of four new planes.

When asked about future plans for the new equipment, Mike states, "We are not sure how we will utilize the airplanes but eventually we plan to serve Atlanta and Chicago out of Houston Hobby."

The question is, can he do it without Big Daddy?

NOTES

1. "Big Daddy Keeps Watchful Eye on Flock," *See Magazine,* September 1981, p. 10.
2. "Is Big Daddy Really Back?" *D Magazine,* November 1981, p. 132.
3. "Muse Air Prospectus," *E. F. Hutton & Company, Inc.,* April 1981, p. 14.
4. "Upstarts in the Sky," *Business Week,* June 15, 1981, p. 78.
5. "Dallas Courts Sue Muse Official," *Dallas Morning News,* November 17, 1981, p. 1A.
6. "Is Big Daddy Really Back?" p. 135.
7. "Upstarts Hit a Downdraft," *Business Week,* October 26, 1981, p. 186.
8. "Upstarts in the Sky," p. 81.
9. "Muse Air Prospectus," p. 21.
10. "Proposal Bans Night Flights at Love Field," *Dallas Morning News,* October 24, 1981, p. 1, 11a.
11. "Muse Air Prospectus," p. 21.
12. "Upstarts Hit a Downdraft," p. 186.
13. *Wall Street Journal,* November 3, 1981, p. 1.
14. *Producers Price Index,* January 1979, October 1981.
15. "Upstarts in the Sky," p. 28.
16. "Heard on the Street," *Wall Street Journal,* October 8, 1981.

EXERCISE 11–9

- After reading the Muse Air case carefully, prepare a ranked list of environmental factors that represents risks and opportunities presented by the general business environment. Limit your list to the top three to five risks and the top three to five areas of opportunity.
- Prepare a ranked list of environmental factors that represent risks and opportunities presented by the industry-specific environment. Again, limit your list to the top three to five risks, and the top three to five areas of opportunity.
- Develop a statement of a paragraph or two in length that describes Muse Air's potential advantages or its distinctive competences. Support your choices with persuasive logic or argument based on your answers to the first two questions in this exercise.

ANSWERS TO SELECTED EXERCISES

Exercise 11-6

Physical Assets
- *Capacity*
- *Age*
- *State of Repair*
- *Etc.*

Financial Assets
- *Debt Percentage*
- *Asset Balance*
- *Etc.*

Human Resources
- *Skill level*
- *Special talents*
- *Etc.*

APPENDIX

APPENDIX

	SIC 1521 1-family hsg. constrn (no breakdown) 1986 (2342 estab)		*SIC 1522 Residential constrn (no breakdown) 1986 (886 estab)*		*SIC 1531 Operative builders (no breakdown) 1986 (1223 estab)*		*SIC 1541 Indl bldgs & warehses (no breakdown) 1986 (1733 estab)*	
	$	%	$	%	$	%	$	%
Cash	33,601	17.2	86,889	16.1	115,210	11.0	105,638	18.6
Accounts receivable	36,727	18.8	136,001	25.2	100,547	9.6	220,931	38.9
Notes receivable	2,344	1.2	10,794	2.0	26,184	2.5	5,679	1.0
Inventory	16,605	8.5	32,381	6.0	140,347	13.4	15,902	2.8
Other current	31,452	16.1	87,969	16.3	245,083	23.4	75,537	13.3
Total current	120,730	61.8	354,033	65.6	627,370	59.9	423,687	74.6
Fixed assets	41,025	21.0	89,588	16.6	200,046	19.1	74,401	13.1
Other non-current	33,601	17.2	96,064	17.8	219,946	21.0	69,857	12.3
Total assets	195,356	100.0	539,685	100.0	1,047,362	100.0	567,945	100.0
Accounts payable	22,271	11.4	82,032	15.2	58,652	5.6	138,011	24.3
Bank loans	2,540	1.3	7,556	1.4	16,758	1.6	4,544	0.8
Notes payable	12,307	6.3	24,826	4.6	100,547	9.6	20,446	3.6
Other current	35,750	18.3	94,985	17.6	226,230	21.6	89,167	15.7
Total current	72,868	37.3	209,398	38.8	402,187	38.4	252,168	44.4
Other long term	27,350	14.0	73,937	13.7	200,046	19.1	46,571	8.2
Deferred credits	586	0.3	2,698	0.5	5,237	0.5	2,272	0.4
Net worth	94,552	48.4	253,652	47.0	439,892	42.0	266,934	47.0
Total liab & net worth	195,356	100.0	539,685	100.0	1,047,362	100.0	567,945	100.0
Net sales	538,810	100.0	1,215,482	100.0	1,300,000	100.0	1,729,522	100.0
Gross profit	138,474	25.7	285,638	23.5	275,600	21.2	337,257	19.5
Net profit after tax	35,023	6.5	70,498	5.8	71,500	5.5	77,828	4.5
Working capital	47,862	—	144,635	—	225,183	—	171,519	—

RATIOS	*UQ*	*MED*	*LQ*	*UQ*	*MED*	*LQ*	*UQ*	*MED*	*LQ*	*UQ*	*MED*	*LQ*
Solvency												
Quick ratio (times)	2.3	1.0	0.4	2.0	1.1	0.5	1.3	0.5	0.1	2.1	1.3	0.9
Current ratio (times)	3.5	1.7	1.1	3.3	1.6	1.2	3.3	1.6	1.1	2.7	1.6	1.3
Curr liab to NW (%)	15.7	58.7	161.2	18.3	66.8	189.0	14.0	62.3	202.8	36.3	94.2	206.3
Curr liab to INV (%)	71.7	140.9	337.2	78.9	162.8	436.1	50.6	97.6	179.5	129.9	304.1	606.3
Total liab to NW (%)	33.7	91.6	223.5	38.6	105.4	256.6	40.5	120.5	309.3	48.5	116.2	239.9
Fixed assets to NW (%)	15.6	43.2	99.3	9.4	28.2	81.2	8.6	35.1	110.0	13.6	29.9	57.5
Efficiency												
Coll period (days)	8.8	23.7	48.9	14.2	35.2	64.3	5.5	21.5	63.3	27.7	47.0	71.9
Sales to inv (times)	107.4	28.6	7.6	118.1	26.2	7.1	13.2	3.8	1.7	238.3	79.7	27.4
Assets to sales (%)	17.7	33.0	65.6	21.5	36.1	86.0	40.2	78.2	175.2	21.3	30.9	45.6
Sales to NWC (times)	25.4	11.1	5.0	21.8	10.1	3.8	14.1	5.1	2.2	22.0	11.9	6.5
Acct pay to sales (%)	1.5	3.8	7.4	1.8	5.3	11.5	1.2	3.8	7.6	3.2	7.3	12.2
Profitability												
Return on sales (%)	11.6	4.9	1.5	11.4	4.3	1.1	11.2	4.7	1.0	6.9	2.8	0.9
Return on assets (%)	23.0	9.6	2.4	18.6	6.7	1.6	9.4	4.2	0.7	14.7	6.6	2.2
Return on NW (%)	59.7	23.5	7.4	49.8	20.5	5.8	34.8	14.7	2.8	34.8	16.6	6.1

APPENDIX

	SIC 4463 Marine cargo handlg (no breakdown) 1986 (77 estab)		*SIC 4469 Water trans svs nec (no breakdown) 1986 (418 estab)*		*SIC 4511 Certificate air tran (no breakdown) 1986 (173 estab)*		*SIC 4521 Ncertificat air tran (no breakdown) 1986 (168 estab)*	
	$	%	$	%	$	%	$	%
Cash	96,387	9.1	36,273	11.0	706,940	11.2	61,418	10.9
Accounts receivable	275,390	26.0	43,198	13.1	1,205,584	19.1	100,297	17.8
Notes receivable	10,592	1.0	2,638	0.8	37,872	0.6	5,071	0.9
Inventory	15,888	1.5	64,303	19.5	347,158	5.5	43,387	7.7
Other current	106,978	10.1	13,520	4.1	353,470	5.6	41,133	7.3
Total current	505,235	47.7	159,933	48.5	2,651,023	42.0	251,307	44.6
Fixed assets	262,680	24.8	90,684	27.5	2,272,306	36.0	173,548	30.8
Other non-current	291,278	27.5	79,142	24.0	1,388,631	22.0	138,613	24.6
Total assets	1,059,193	100.0	329,759	100.0	6,311,960	100.0	563,469	100.0
Accounts payable	85,795	8.1	23,083	7.0	776,371	12.3	71,561	12.7
Bank loans	6,355	0.6	2,968	0.9	56,808	0.9	2,254	0.4
Notes payable	37,072	3.5	15,499	4.7	277,726	4.4	22,539	4.0
Other current	142,991	13.5	52,432	15.9	1,022,538	16.2	91,845	16.3
Total current	272,213	25.7	93,981	28.5	2,133,442	33.8	188,199	33.4
Other long term	207,602	19.6	81,780	24.8	2,152,378	34.1	145,375	25.8
Deferred credits	1,059	0.1	1,649	0.5	82,055	1.3	1,690	0.3
Net worth	578,319	54.6	152,349	46.2	1,944,084	30.8	228,205	40.5
Total liab & net worth	1,059,193	100.0	329,759	100.0	6,311,960	100.0	563,469	100.0
Net sales	2,172,445	100.0	461,491	100.0	2,750,000	100.0	891,406	100.0
Gross profit	734,286	33.8	198,903	43.1	918,500	33.4	358,345	40.2
Net profit after tax	184,658	8.5	30,920	6.7	134,750	4.9	33,873	3.8
Working capital	233,022	—	65,952	—	517,581	—	63,108	—

RATIOS	UQ	MED	LQ	UQ	MED	LQ	UQ	MED	LQ	UQ	MED	LQ
Solvency												
Quick ratio (times)	2.5	1.2	0.7	2.0	0.8	0.3	1.4	0.8	0.5	1.5	0.9	0.5
Current ratio (times)	3.7	2.3	1.2	3.5	1.8	1.1	1.7	1.3	0.9	2.3	1.3	0.9
Curr liab to NW (%)	9.8	47.7	98.1	14.3	44.4	108.7	47.3	81.3	157.5	26.9	57.3	135.9
Curr liab to INV (%)	146.8	369.3	491.5	54.8	101.7	213.1	211.9	472.2	840.4	137.6	224.5	518.5
Total liab to NW (%)	32.8	67.9	130.4	33.2	95.7	221.9	117.5	198.8	394.9	58.8	138.2	306.8
Fixed assets to NW (%)	35.9	83.9	125.3	35.6	73.5	164.4	77.5	163.8	254.8	56.1	106.6	221.9
Efficiency												
Coll period (days)	31.8	43.1	77.3	9.4	22.2	51.8	24.6	34.0	44.1	19.7	31.3	43.6
Sales to inv (times)	87.7	54.5	16.4	21.1	9.5	4.5	61.7	30.6	17.7	49.3	22.1	8.6
Assets to sales (%)	40.0	87.9	146.4	37.7	70.5	123.1	45.5	78.1	108.9	36.0	54.2	101.9
Sales to NWC (times)	11.5	4.6	2.3	13.9	6.6	3.4	26.5	13.8	8.0	18.0	8.4	4.9
Acct pay to sales (%)	1.8	3.3	6.8	1.3	2.8	6.1	3.7	5.9	9.9	2.3	4.1	8.1
Profitability												
Return on sales (%)	18.3	7.6	0.7	12.2	4.3	0.6	6.9	3.3	0.4	9.1	3.8	0.6
Return on assets (%)	13.6	4.4	1.3	14.4	5.8	0.4	5.5	3.1	(0.1)	18.8	8.0	0.2
Return on NW (%)	27.7	12.3	3.9	27.4	14.5	1.9	20.5	10.5	0.5	42.5	23.7	3.7

APPENDIX

	SIC 3462 *Iron & steel forgings* *(no breakdown)* *1986 (61 estab)*		SIC 3465 *Automotive stamping* *(no breakdown)* *1986 (124 estab)*		SIC 3469 *Metal stampings nec* *(no breakdown)* *1986 (504 estab)*		SIC 3471 *Plating, polishing* *(no breakdown)* *1986 (444 estab)*	
	$	%	$	%	$	%	$	%
Cash	138,954	7.7	191,168	9.9	71,036	11.2	45,784	14.9
Accounts receivable	400,621	22.2	590,883	30.6	173,785	27.4	85,730	27.9
Notes receivable	9,023	0.5	3,862	0.2	3,806	0.6	2,765	0.9
Inventory	330,242	18.3	403,577	20.9	106,554	16.8	18,744	6.1
Other current	73,989	4.1	71,447	3.7	28,541	4.5	13,827	4.5
Total current	952,829	52.8	1,260,937	65.3	383,721	60.5	166,850	54.3
Fixed assets	492,656	27.3	322,475	16.7	152,220	24.0	79,892	26.0
Other non-current	359,115	19.9	347,578	18.0	98,309	15.5	60,533	19.7
Total assets	1,804,600	100.0	1,930,991	100.0	634,250	100.0	307,275	100.0
Accounts payable	187,678	10.4	382,336	19.8	76,110	12.0	27,655	9.0
Bank loans	45,115	2.5	28,965	1.5	8,880	1.4	4,302	1.4
Notes payable	83,012	4.6	71,447	3.7	23,467	3.7	12,906	4.2
Other current	182,265	10.1	274,201	14.2	74,207	11.7	43,019	14.0
Total current	498,070	27.6	756,948	39.2	182,664	28.8	87,881	28.6
Other long term	366,334	20.3	285,787	14.8	106,554	16.8	49,779	16.2
Deferred credits	19,851	1.1	7,724	0.4	1,903	0.3	615	0.2
Net worth	920,346	51.0	880,532	45.6	343,129	54.1	169,001	55.0
Total liab & net worth	1,804,600	100.0	1,930,991	100.0	634,250	100.0	307,275	100.0
Net sales	2,840,202	100.0	5,113,187	100.0	1,300,000	100.0	605,921	100.0
Gross profit	761,174	26.8	1,339,655	26.2	430,300	33.1	266,605	44.0
Net profit after tax	127,809	4.5	204,527	4.0	55,900	4.3	35,749	5.9
Working capital	454,759	—	503,989	—	201,057	—	78,969	—

RATIOS	*UQ*	*MED*	*LQ*	*UQ*	*MED*	*LQ*	*UQ*	*MED*	*LQ*	*UQ*	*MED*	*LQ*
Solvency												
Quick ratio (times)	2.1	1.0	0.7	1.5	1.0	0.7	2.5	1.4	0.8	3.5	1.6	0.9
Current ratio (times)	3.9	1.7	1.2	2.5	1.7	1.2	4.3	2.2	1.4	4.4	2.2	1.2
Curr liab to NW (%)	21.9	46.5	106.8	42.1	79.4	140.9	19.1	43.6	93.4	16.8	40.8	93.0
Curr liab to INV (%)	95.6	147.2	290.6	114.6	164.2	241.3	82.3	152.0	262.9	129.0	284.9	496.2
Total liab to NW (%)	38.9	82.1	213.0	55.8	126.3	220.0	28.4	72.1	157.2	22.3	68.6	173.9
Fixed assets to NW (%)	38.7	62.6	106.8	26.1	54.9	150.5	30.6	59.8	106.8	30.1	57.0	122.1
Efficiency												
Coll period (days)	44.7	54.4	60.6	32.9	42.3	52.1	34.0	43.8	59.3	31.7	44.9	58.8
Sales to INV (times)	13.1	8.5	5.7	17.5	10.8	8.8	24.3	13.0	8.2	67.7	35.5	15.4
Assets to sales (%)	54.1	72.1	91.0	31.5	39.9	52.0	35.9	47.5	67.4	32.2	44.6	66.9
Sales to NWC (times)	10.0	5.1	3.1	15.2	9.2	5.7	10.7	6.4	3.7	11.6	6.5	4.1
Acct pay to sales (%)	3.0	5.8	9.9	4.2	6.1	11.1	2.3	4.6	8.4	1.8	3.2	6.7
Profitability												
Return on sales (%)	6.9	3.8	1.1	6.4	3.7	2.8	8.3	3.7	1.1	10.6	4.7	1.3
Return on assets (%)	9.2	4.7	1.8	16.5	10.1	4.9	11.8	6.2	1.5	14.3	7.8	1.8
Return on NW (%)	27.1	6.3	2.4	39.1	19.7	12.8	23.1	10.9	2.9	29.3	14.2	3.0

Source Dun & Bradstreet Credit Services, *Industry News and Key Business Ratios*, 1986–87 (Library Edition), Murray Hill, N.J. Used by permission.

12
ARRAYING AND CHOOSING STRATEGIES

As we continue to move through the strategy-formulation sequence, we have completed a three-part analytic process and can now begin to prepare strategic plans designed to achieve long-range objectives. (See the shaded area in Figure 12–1) The analysis in the preceding two chapters provides a detailed depiction of the business environment in which the organization is to function. In addition, our discussion has shown how the general manager/strategist assesses in detail his or her organization's strengths, weaknesses, and the potential areas of advantage in a chosen environment. Following these carefully developed analytic steps, you should begin to synthesize: to prepare a list of possible long-range courses of action, that is, strategies.

The choice of strategy must be made not only with an awareness of the analytic data previously mentioned, but also with an understanding that the plan must accommodate the existing and predicted dynamics of a competitive environment *and*

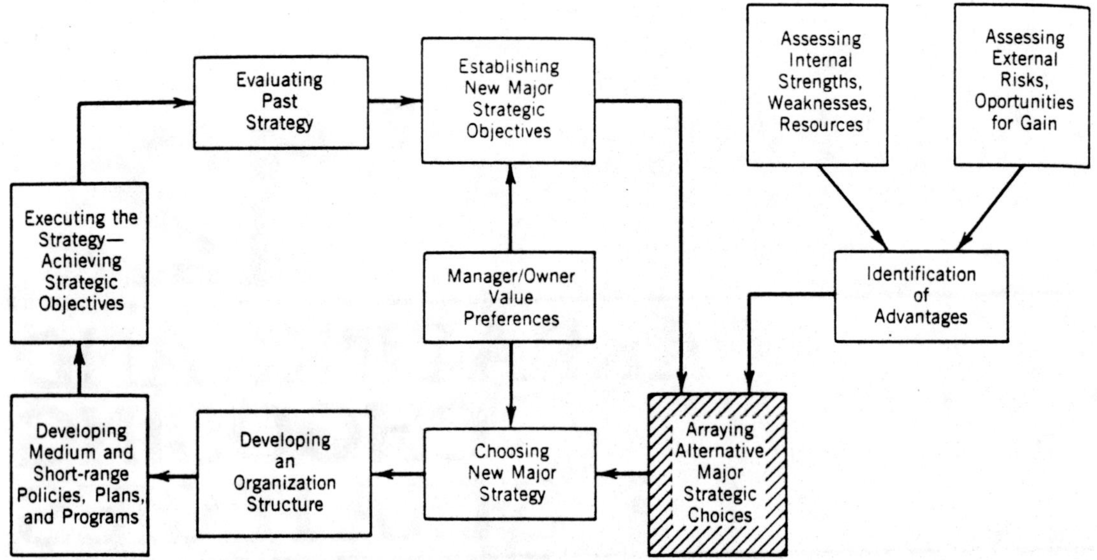

FIGURE 12–1 The strategy-formulation process.

the risk preferences of the strategist and his or her constituency. In the following analysis, we will make use of two types of contingency approaches as frameworks for arraying strategies. The first of these considers the company's relative strength and the market's attractiveness as two principal independent variables. Two models that use these variables will be discussed. As we examine each framework, we will describe strategies that seem appropriate for each set of conditions.

The second approach involves an application of the product life cycle as a framework for strategy selection. The strategies for each stage of the life cycle that are suitable for various levels of strength or risk preference will be described. As in previous chapters, exercise questions will help you to develop a more comprehensive understanding of the material and its application. Case material will be used to permit you to apply the new information to real-life business situations.

STRENGTH/ATTRACTIVENESS AS STRATEGY-SELECTION FRAMEWORKS

The Directional Policy Matrix

The directional policy matrix is used extensively in Europe and can be adapted for both single-business and multibusiness strategy-selection applications.[1] In this chapter we will consider the framework for its application to single-business situations. The matrix uses two axes and contains nine cells. Relative attractiveness is scaled on

[1] D. E. Hussey, "Portfolio Analysis: Practical Experience with the Directional Policy Matrix," *Long Range Planning,* 11 (August 1978), pp 2–8.

an axis labeled, *Business Sector Prospects.* Organizational strength is scaled on an axis labeled, *Competitive Capabilities.*

The matrix (see Figure 12–2) provides an array of action orientations for the strategy formulator that is based on relative strength and the degree to which the situation appears attractive.

BUSINESS SECTOR PROSPECTS

COMPETITIVE CAPABILITIES	Attractive	Average	Unattractive
Strong	Leader A	Leader Growth B	Cash Generator C
Average	Try Harder D	Proceed with Care E	Phased Withdrawal F
Weak	Double or Quit G	Proceed with Care Phased Withdrawal H	Disinvest I

Source: Adapted from D. E. Hussey, "Portfolio Analysis, Practical Experience with the Directional Policy Matrix," *Long Range Planning*, 11 (August 1978), p. 2–8

FIGURE 12–2 Directional Policy Matrix.

Let us examine the implications of each prescription, moving from the situation in Cell A (at the upper left of the matrix)—where the company competitive capability is high and the prospects are attractive—toward the lower right, Cell I—where competitive capability is low and prospects are not attractive.

Cell A (Capabilities: Strong/Prospects: Attractive) *Leader.* This strategic direction suggests an aggressive posture toward holding *and gaining* market share, an active practice of investing earnings and other sources of capital, and an active research and development program directed toward both product and process improvement.

Cell B (Capabilities: Strong/Prospects: Average) *Leader and Growth.* The *Leader* direction is suggested at the extreme of company competitive capability in a market that is of average attractiveness. Where competitive capability is not quite as high, a *Growth* form of strategic direction is suggested. In this mode, capital investment should be made in amounts sufficient to *maintain* market share and thereby to enable the company's product to grow with the market. Outside funding sources probably will not be utilized extensively.

Cell D (Capabilities: Average/Prospects: Attractive) *Try Harder.* This strategic direction is suggested for situations in which market prospects are very attractive but where competitive capability is only average. Improvements in competitive capability should move the situation into the *Leader* direction found in Cell A. Among other actions, strategists may wish to consider extraordinary capital expenditures, concentrated marketing attention, or additional attention to R & D as a means of trying harder and thereby improving competitive capability.

Cell C (Capabilities: Strong/Prospects: Unattractive) *Cash Generator.* This direction is suggested for situations where competitive capability is high but market prospects are relatively unattractive. One example might be the situation in which a product begins to move out of the maturity stage of the product life cycle and begins the process of decline. In this situation, cash flows from this product should be diverted to other more promising applications. Capital investment should be minimized and attention directed toward minimization of costs and maximization of profitability for the remaining life of the product.

Cell E Capabilities: Average/Prospects: Average) *Proceed with Care.* It is suggested in the situation in which prospects are moderately interesting and competitive capability is only average in strength that one proceed with care. In this situation, investments must be made with caution. Investments in large-scale or longer-range projects are probably unwise because neither the potential gain nor the competitive risks involved can justify these kinds of commitments.

Cell G (Capabilities: Weak/Prospects: Attractive) *Double or Quit.* This strategic direction suggests an aggressive screening of prospects to determine which should be backed vigorously and which should be abandoned. It focuses limited resources on projects that have attractive prospects and permits the weaker firm to find a niche in an attractive market.

Cell F (Capabilities: Average/Prospects: Unattractive) *Phased Withdrawal.* This direction is recommended for a situation wherein a company has only average competitive strength in a market that is relatively unattractive. In this situation, profits are unlikely to be significant. The objective of this approach would be to minimize losses, to avoid investing more heavily in an unattractive market, and to ease investment into other projects as conditions permit.

Cell H (Capabilities: Weak/Prospects: Average) *Phased Withdrawal* and *Proceed with Care.* These directions are recommended for the situation in which market prospects may be moderately attractive but where the company's competitive position is weak. As the discussions for Cells E and F suggest, these strategic directions permit the firm to use caution to avoid losses and, where conditions warrant, shift resources to more promising project areas.

Cell I (Capabilities: Weak/Prospects: Unattractive) *Disinvest.* This strategic direction is suggested by a very unappealing situation in which the company's position is weak and where market prospects are poor. In all likelihood, losses have been apparent for some time. Human and capital resources salvaged from this situation can be redirected toward situations of greater promise for commercial success.

EXERCISE 12-1

Your new high-tech company is facing exciting times. The new optical storage device your R & D department has developed has generated over 7 months' backlog of orders for your production facility and you have stirred the interest of customers and competitors both nationally and internationally. Your first product, an advanced optical reader, has been very well accepted, and it continues to establish new sales records each month. The R & D team working with the optical reader has accumulated a lengthy list of product improvements to be incorporated in the first major modification of the product since its introduction 27 months ago.

Because you are now completing the second stage of your strategic business plan and have not prepared plans for a third stage of financing, your funds are somewhat limited. Monies generated from the optical reader appear to be sufficient to sustain the inventories and receivables needed to maintain the growth rate now experienced. Capital funding for product improvements, however, would require funding from some other source. The monies budgeted for optical storage have been sufficient for the development of the product to date, but little remains.

Your financial vice president has assured you that, based on the acceptance of the company's products to date, third-round financing could be achieved in 6 to 9 months in amounts in the $10 to $20 million range. He has also said that the company's bank has expressed an interest in establishing a line of credit at 12% for as much as $500,000, a debt that would nearly match the $525,000 in owners equity.

Earnings before tax have been negative until this past year when a profit of $210,000 was recorded.

Your marketing manager is delighted at the degree to which the company's products are achieving acceptance among the professional buyers for the companies who are your prime customers. He worries, however, about the potential size of the market. It is, in his opinion, a multibillion-dollar annual market as both devices are designed to replace existing processes or equipment. If, he reasons, the company cannot supply the demand, other larger companies may see the potential as sufficiently attractive to decide to develop, manufacture, and market the devices. Rumors in the trade publications indicate that this process may have taken place.

- From what you have just read, what cell in the directional policy matrix do you believe most accurately describes the company's situation? Why?
- Give examples of information that would call for an upward revision in your estimate on the company's *competitive capability*. Explain your reasoning.
- A downward revision? Explain.
- What information about the industry would suggest that your assessment of the *business sector prospects* is too low? Explain.
- Too high? Explain.

EXERCISE 12-2

Based on the information provided and the directional policy matrix, describe the type of strategy statement you would develop to help in guiding yourself and fellow executives for the strategy planning period.

- First, how long a planning period would you use? Why?
- What will be the major components in the strategy statement?
- What factors would cause you to revise this strategy?

EXERCISE 12-3

Consider the major U.S. auto manufacturers.

- Place Ford, General Motors, and Chrysler on the matrix. Suggest strategies for each. Be specific and explain your reasoning.
- Place Toyota, Honda, Renault, and Volkswagen on the matrix. (You may wish to use reference material to obtain information about each company.) Suggest strategies for each. Be specific and explain your reasoning.

Boulton's Strength/Attractiveness Framework

Boulton's framework considers several types of controlling strategic objectives and a ranked array of strategies for their achievement.[2] It is seen in Figure 12–3 and uses *Industry Attractiveness* and *Business Strength Relative to Competition as* its principal situation variables.

In the high-strength/high-attractiveness triangle (in the upper-left corner), we find two types of objectives based on the degree of aggressiveness or strength of the company. *Seek to Increase Share* is an objective suitable for an extremely strong company or an aggressive company with moderate strength. In the broad band that

[2] William R. Boulton, *Business Policy: The Art of Strategic Management* (New York: Macmillan, 1984), pp. 48–50.

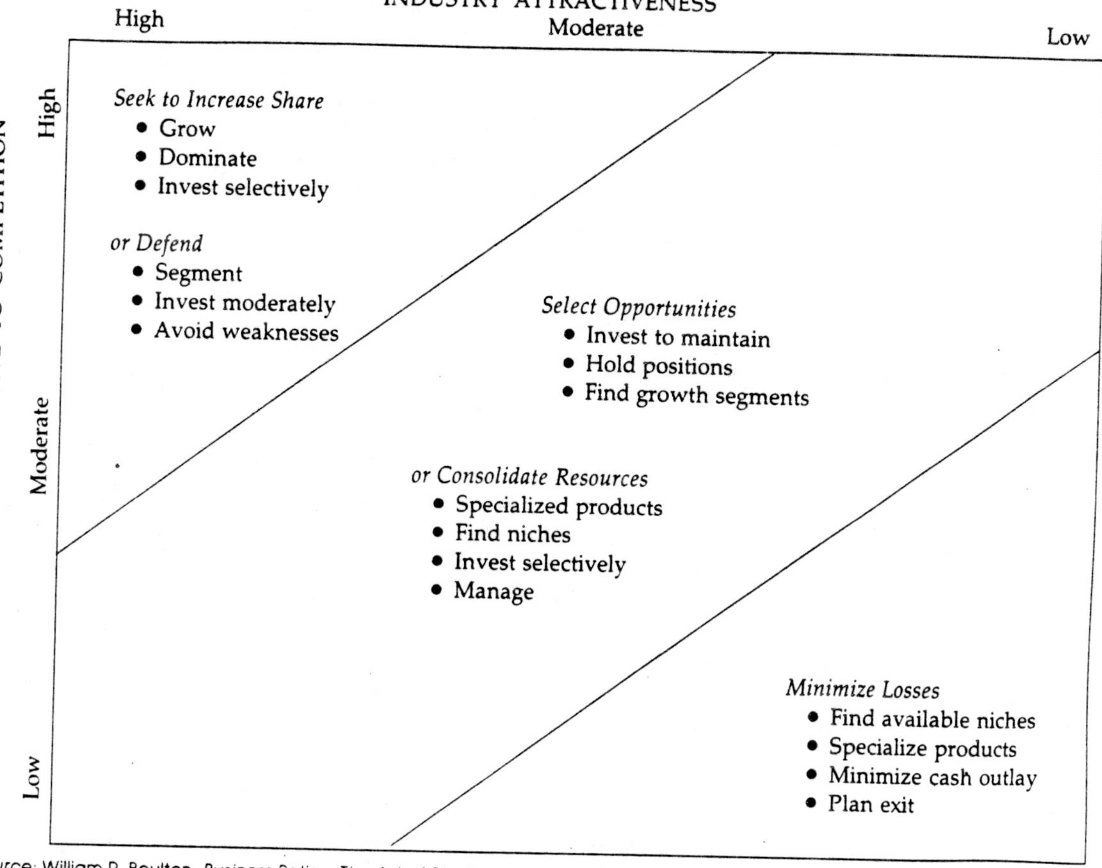

Source: William R. Boulton. *Business Policy: The Art of Strategic Management* (New York: Macmillan, 1984), p. 49.

FIGURE 12–3 Boulton's strength/attractiveness matrix.

runs from the low-strength/high-attractiveness situation (seen in the lower left to the high-strength/low-attractiveness corner in the upper right of the diagram), two broad objectives are also found. Again, these objectives appear to depend on the relative strength or the degree of aggressiveness chosen by the strategy formulator. *Select Opportunities* is an object suitable to a situation in which attractiveness is high or where strength (or aggressiveness) of the company is at the upper end of the range for this category. *Consolidate Resources* seems appropriate for situations where the attractiveness of the industry is at the low end of the range for this broad category or where company strength or aggressiveness is low.

In the third category, represented by the low-strength/low-industry attractiveness triangle (seen in the lower right corner of Figure 12–3), the object in all cases is to minimize losses. A somewhat stronger company or one that is more aggressive would tend to use the strategies higher on the list than would the weaker or less-aggressive company. As market attractiveness declines, both strong and weak companies will be more inclined to adopt loss-minimizing strategies lower on the list.

Strategies designed to increase share of market would include action components such as increasing investment, increasing market research and marketing intensity, intensifying advertising and other promotional media, and engaging in aggressive pricing designed to capture market share, even at the expense of short-term profits.

The strategies designed to defend market share would suggest more caution in investment and would call for an alert analysis of position to avoid weaknesses. Segmentation could serve to identify a vacant or underserved niche in the market, to identify a specialized niche that is not the target of very large competitors, or to develop a distinctively high-quality product that has appeal to a small percentage of customers across a wide market.

Some of the strategies used to defend one's position in a highly attractive industry market can also be used to seek selected opportunities in markets of moderate attractiveness. Here, stronger or aggressive firms identify areas of opportunity for growth or invest to maintain positions in these areas. Weaker or less-aggressive firms identify specialized products or underserved market niches for selective investment in a market of moderate-to-low attractiveness.

As market attractiveness dwindles, the strategies suggested become progressively less ambitious. Stronger firms seek to minimize losses by identifying available niches or by developing specialized products. Weaker firms minimize cash outlays and seek avenues for an exit from the industry.

The Canadian Casting Company, Ltd., case offers an opportunity to apply some of the thinking outlined in the two analytic frameworks discussed thus far. As you examine the case, please assess, to the best of your ability, the relative attractiveness of the precision casting industry. It may help to examine library reference material about this industry to better understand the number and size of competitors and the size and growth rate of the industry itself. You should also critically examine the strengths and weaknesses of the company and then be prepared to respond to the exercise questions at the conclusion of the case.

CANADIAN CASTING COMPANY LIMITED

In July 1980, Mr. Peter Johnston (45), President of the Canadian Casting Company Limited (CCC), Ancaster, Ontario, was deeply involved with a review of his current operations and with plans for expanding the company's facilities and personnel. CCC had grown rapidly in the four years since he had taken it over, for the second time, so that now all aspects seemed to be "bursting at the seams." This had created some very real problems, not the least of which concerned the role of Mr. Johnston himself. How much more of the load could he carry with the existing setup, how much further could he extend himself, and in what direction should he take the company?

Canadian Casting Company (CCC), as its name implied, was engaged in the casting of a wide variety of intricate parts, requiring a high degree of precision and quality, for an equally diverse number of industries.

THE CASTING PROCESS

Investment casting, the process utilized by CCC, is also known as the "lost-wax" process or "precision" casting. The concept is said to have been developed initially in China some 4–5,000 years ago and trade literature described it thus:

> *The term investment refers to a cloak, or special covering apparel, in this case a refractory mold, surrounding a refractory-covered wax pattern. In this process a wax pattern must be made for every casting and gating system; i.e., the pattern is expendable.*

This case was prepared by Professor W. H. Ellis of McGill University as the basis for class discussion rather than to illustrate either effective or ineffective handling of an administrative situation. All names have been disguised.

A number of variants of the process exist, but they have the following points in common:

1. Disposable or expendable patterns are used.
2. Molding is done with a fluid aggregate or slurry.
3. The aggregate is hardened in contact with the pattern, providing precise reproduction of the pattern.
4. The aggregate is bonded with an inorganic ceramic binder.
5. The mold is heated to drive off all wax.
6. Pouring is performed with the mold preheated to a controlled temperature in order to pour thin sections which would not otherwise fill out.

CERAMIC-SHELL MOLDS

A variant of investment molding is ceramic-shell molding. Such molds may be made by alternately dipping the pattern in a coating slurry and coating with silica or other refractory. A shell of ¼ in. or more thickness may be built up in this way. The pattern is then melted out, and the mold processed as described previously.

Further details on the . . . investment precision casting process . . . are shown in Exhibit 5.

COMPANY BACKGROUND

Following his graduation as an electrical engineer from a well-known Canadian university, Mr. Peter Johnston joined a large firm specializing in electronics. "Electronics were my life at the time," remarked Mr. Johnston, who added that having seen a radio at an earlier age, "by

EXHIBIT 1
Canadian Casting Company Limited balance sheet as at March 31

	1980	*1979*	*1978*	*1977 (5 months ending March 31)*
ASSETS				
CURRENT				
Accounts receivable	$ 646,209	$ 406,205	$260,469	$ 11,654
Loans receivable	4,505	13,871	—	1,313
Inventories	760,997	383,595	228,643	39,740
Prepaid expenses	14,619	25,671	14,082	—
Rent deposit/subscriptions receivable	—	—	—	4,500
	1,426,330	829,342	503,194	57,207
FIXED	1,736,335	458,633	344,037	230,081
OTHER	5,186	7,527	9,869	13,469
	$3,167,851	$1,295,502	$857,100	300,757
LIABILITIES				
CURRENT				
Bank indebtedness	$ 557,435	$ 254,539	$162,712	$ 87,735
Accounts payable and accrued charges	409,567	219,832	148,733	41,134
Income taxes payable	40,172	4,620	114,840	—
Long-term debt due within one year	81,692	61,130	21,250	6,250
Deferred income taxes	3,163	6,900	—	—
	1,092,029	547,021	354,535	135,119
LONG-TERM DEBT	1,225,221	316,792	284,152	159,560
DEFERRED INCOME TAXES	135,927	51,780	30,138	127
	2,453,177	915,593	668,825	294,806
SHAREHOLDERS' EQUITY				
CAPITAL STOCK	5,500	5,500	5,500	5,500
RETAINED EARNINGS	709,174	374,409	182,775	451
	714,674	379,909	188,275	5,951
	$3,167,851	$1,295,502	$857,100	$300,757

the time I was eleven, I started working night and day studying it." By 1971 Mr. Johnston had risen to the position of chief engineer of the company's communications division.

"At that point, I looked at myself. I had studied on my own, had my engineering degree, had worked on electronics all my life, and having achieved the position of chief engineer, I said 'where do I go from here at the age of 36?'" Mr. Johnston continued, "I have had a certain number of goals in life even when I was very small. My main goal was to do some kind of

EXHIBIT 2

Canadian Casting Company Limited statement of earnings and retained earnings for the years ended March 31

	1980	*1979*	*1978*	*1977 (5 months ending March 31)*
SALES	$2,824,637	$1,980,304	$1,280,843	$11,668
COST OF GOODS SOLD (Schedule)				
Inventory, end of period	1,989,162	1,482,677	833,163	5,614
GROSS PROFIT	835,475	497,627	447,680	6,054
EXPENSES				
Advertising and sales promotion	25,997	16,151	16,075	683
Amortization—deferred expenses	2,342	2,342	3,600	220
Amortization—leasehold improvements	—	—	—	298
Automobile	15,294	11,597	13,427	—
Bad debts (recovery)	(1,453)	10,442	2,000	—
Commissions	88,142	59,973	25,026	—
Delivery and Freight out	5,494	12,226	5,297	—
Depreciation—automobile	1,808	2,584	—	—
Depreciation—machinery & equipment	—	—	—	1,550
Depreciation—office furniture & equipment	2,987	2,243	1,342	75
Directors' fees	—	700	12,500	—
Donations	50	500	100	—
Dues and subscriptions	1,695	617	379	—
Equipment rental	—	—	10,362	—
Factory expense	—	—	—	175
Interest and bank charges	27,481	9,937	20,437	—
Interest on long-term debt	52,609	20,040	14,757	—
Loss on disposal of fixed assets	—	832	—	—
Management fees	2,890	3,175	39,652	—
Office salaries	113,002	74,076	21,845	—
Office supplies and postage	8,827	7,588	4,097	—
Professional fees	21,661	22,212	11,838	1,000
Rent	—	—	—	1,123
Sales discounts	11,278	10,704	6,472	—
Telephone	10,471	8,301	7,675	—
Travel	7,710	3,265	3,624	352
	398,285	279,505	220,505	5,476
EARNINGS FROM OPERATIONS	437,190	218,122	227,175	578
OTHER EARNINGS				
Rental income	18,238	—	—	—
EARNINGS before income taxes	455,428	218,122	277,175	578
INCOME TAXES	120,663	26,488	44,851	127
NET EARNINGS	334,765	191,634	182,324	451
RETAINED EARNINGS, beginning of year	374,409	182,775	451	—
RETAINED EARNINGS, end of year	$ 709,174	$ 374,409	$ 182,775	$ 451

EXHIBIT 3
Canadian Casting Company Limited statement of changes in financial position for the years ended March 31

	1980	1979	1978	1977 (5 months ending March 31
SOURCE OF WORKING CAPITAL				
From operations				
Net earnings	$ 334,765	$191,634	$182,324	$ 451
Items not requiring an outlay of working capital				
Depreciation	134,238	61,318	42,056	1,625
Deferred income taxes	84,147	21,642	30,011	127
Amortization—deferred expenses	2,342	2,342	3,600	—
Amortization of leasehold improvements	—	—	—	298
Loss on disposal of fixed asset	—	832	—	—
	555,492	277,768	257,991	2,501
Increase in long-term debt	908,429	32,640	124,592	—
Issue of common shares	—	—	—	5,500
Loan payable—shareholder	—	—	—	115,810
Loan payable	—	—	—	43,750
Sale of fixed asset	—	1,285	—	—
	1,463,921	311,693	382,583	167,561
USE OF WORKING CAPITAL				
Additions to fixed assets	1,411,941	178,031	156,012	—
Purchase of fixed assets	—	—	—	232,004
Purchase of other assets	—	—	—	13,469
INCREASE IN WORKING CAPITAL	51,980	133,662	226,571	(77,912)
WORKING CAPITAL, beginning of year	282,321	148,659	(77,912)	—
WORKING CAPITAL, end of year	$ 334,301	$282,321	$148,659	$ (77,912)
REPRESENTED BY				
Current assets	$1,426,330	$829,342	$503,194	$ 57,207
Current liabilities	1,092,029	547,021	354,535	135,119
Working capital	$ 334,301	$282,321	$148,659	$ (77,912)

innovation, to do experiments, and if I wanted to do that in the future, I had to have a foundation of some kind that I could control, that I could utilize, like having the people, the facilities and the resources. I said, 'Okay, this is where my electronic career ends.' I have got to where I am and there wasn't much that I could go on in this company."

The electronics firm had a division that made investment castings, but had been operating at a loss of about $250,000 annually for five or six years. The company had decided to cease the casting operation and to dispose of it. Mr. Johnston stated that "just at that time, I started thinking of my own career. I had heard about the investment casting plant, so I walked over there and said 'Well, maybe I'll take a chance on it,'" and subsequently made arrangements for its purchase in November 1971.

Some five years later, early in 1976, Mr.

EXHIBIT 4
Canadian Casting Company Limited schedule for the years ended March 31

	1980	*1979*	*1978*
COST OF GOODS SOLD			
RAW MATERIALS			
Inventory, beginning of year	$ 232,105	$ 102,972	$ 25,598
Purchases	533,327	435,598	286,746
Freight and duty	15,132	19,197	7,954
	780,564	557,767	320,298
Inventory, end of year	481,544	232,105	102,972
	299,020	325,662	217,326
DIRECT COSTS			
Direct labour	803,938	594,918	404,589
Payroll levies	85,345	57,923	37,016
Contract labour	62,691	49,074	16,210
Tools and dies	525,413	261,271	138,082
	1,477,387	963,186	595,897
MANUFACTURING EXPENSES			
Amortization—leasehold improvements	5,579	5,077	4,535
Amortization—jigs and fixtures	4,650	4,650	4,650
Depreciation—machinery and equipment	72,312	46,764	31,529
Depreciation—building	46,902	—	—
Electricity and heating	79,493	66,432	33,094
Insurance	4,042	8,989	1,338
Plant maintenance and repairs	22,933	20,011	2,998
Production costs	—	—	5,889
Rent	37,371	26,744	15,933
Shop supplies	45,270	23,753	13,474
Taxes	22,166	17,228	18,029
	340,718	219,648	131,469
	2,117,125	1,508,496	944,692
WORK IN PROCESS			
Inventory, beginning of year	118,411	113,875	14,142
	2,235,536	1,622,371	958,834
Inventory, end of year	227,428	118,411	113,875
COST OF GOODS MANUFACTURED	2,008,108	1,503,960	844,959
FINISHED GOODS			
Inventory, beginning of year	33,079	11,796	—
	2,041,187	1,515,756	844,959
Inventory, end of year	52,025	33,079	11,796
COST OF GOODS SOLD	$1,989,162	$1,482,677	$833,163

EXHIBIT 5

Canadian Casting Company Limited, the casting industry and processes

Ceramic molding

Ceramic molding is an offshoot of the investment-molding process. Reusable patterns are used for this process, as in sand molding. The molding aggregate consists generally of a slurry composed of refractory grains and ceramic binder. In one process, silica grains plus ethyl silicate, water, alcohol, and a gelling agent such as HCl are used. The slurry is poured around the pattern and allowed to gel in about 4 to 7 minutes. The pattern is then removed. The mold is fired by igniting the alcohol in the aggregate. After the mold has cooled, it is assembled and if desired, preheated before pouring. In another process of the same type, the refractory grain slurry is bonded by calcium and ammonium phosphates. These processes may be used for making cores as well as molds.

Certain advantages characteristic of the investment and ceramic casting processes are:

1 Casting high-pouring temperature alloys to accurate dimensions. The metallic-mold processes are not suitable for steel and other alloys which must be poured at high temperature. Accuracy of ±0.003 in. per in. is possible in some castings. Machining on castings of many difficult-to-machine alloys is reduced or eliminated. Elimination of machining is one of the great virtues of the process.
2 Castings of great exterior and interior intricacy may be achieved.
3 Thin sections may be cast, even in the high-pouring-temperature alloys, because of the heated molds. Wire forms down to 0.002 in. in diameter and 2 in. long have been cast.

Source: Heine, Loper, and Rosenthal, "Principles of Metal Casting" (New York: McGraw-Hill, 1967), pp. 36–39.

Johnston's partner, Lester Greenfield, while discussing the company, said "Look Peter, we each own half of the company and the way I see it now, the business is doing so well, you and I can relax and even if you want to, you can retire in a year or two." At the same time, the Federal Business Development Bank (FBDB) approached Mr. Johnston with the remark, "Hey, look, you are doing well, how about permitting FBDB to invest 30%?" Mr. Johnston very quickly informed the bank officials that he was not interested in diluting his holdings with additional shareholders.

Coincidentally, Mr. Greenfield suggested that he, Mr. Greenfield, change his role from being a passive, silent partner to an active position of running CCC, saying to Mr. Johnston, "Let me take over, you run the production part and I will look after the management of the company."

Mr. Johnston pointed out that the business and customers were built upon a close relationship which required comprehensive technical knowledge, beyond the pure casting technology. He commented to Mr. Greenfield, "To run a business like ours is not a matter of mass producing the components. Pure administration alone is not really the normal way of operating this business. For example, you can't sit down and do time studies, these are all jobbers, each part is different." Following further discussion, a meeting of the Board of Directors was held at which time Mr. Johnston was outvoted by the combination of Mr. and Mrs. Greenfield, both of whom were directors. Mr. Johnston was promptly told to step aside as President of the company.

The dialogue that ensued was thus:

Johnston: Fine, I'm fired. I am going to leave the company, but let's make a decision right now at this meeting. We are going to have a sell-out agreement set here and now. You have the option. You can buy me out or sell it to me, at whatever price you come up with, I don't care.

Greenfield: Oh well, we'll have a buy-out agreement, and I will buy you out. I will give you $75,000 cash in 90 days and I'll buy you out.

Johnston: Right! I'll take it and I'll leave the company, but with one stipulation. I am free to do whatever I want to do.

This stipulation was received with something less than enthusiasm by Mr. Greenfield. A compromise was finally reached granting Mr. Johnston's decree but on the added condition that Mr. Johnston guarantee the $220,000 in loans outstanding at the time. Mr. Johnston believed that he had no choice. He commented as follows on the situation that developed over the ensuing six months.

In a very short time, by the beginning of 1977, Mr. Greenfield and the company were in deep financial trouble. I found out why. Once I left, my partner didn't really know the processes and yet insisted on controlling everything. He took a stopwatch, went inside and started timing everybody and insisted that everyone work faster. He insisted on it because he thought that if the current production methods could make so much money for the company, by pushing the workers a little bit more, he could increase the output correspondingly. Well, the operators disagreed. They disliked someone standing behind them and timing them. He didn't go through the foremen, the supervisors or the production managers. He went directly down to the production level and said "You can go faster than that." The workers replied "Sure, we can go faster, but it may not be good." "Do it anyway!" The workers did as they were told with the result that the rejection rate soared to 85% compared with the normal rate of 12%. Mr. Greenfield himself would put the castings in the box, even if they were of doubtful quality.

After about six months of this, Mr. Greenfield asked the accountant to contact me, to see if I would buy the company back. Following a third refusal, we agreed to terms and arranged a joint meeting with a lawyer and an accountant to complete the transaction.

On arriving at the meeting, Mr. Greenfield announced that he was not going to sell and turned around and walked out. By August 1977, the bank took over and liquidated the company.

In this six-month interval after leaving the company, Mr. Johnston had started once again to build up a related casting business. By the time the liquidation proceedings had been completed on CCC, Mr. Johnston's new operation was underway, serving different customers and markets. Now Mr. Johnston was able to merge the two functions and again took over CCC's complete facilities. When word of CCC's demise reached many of the long-standing customers, "They flocked to my office—from Florida, Hughes Aircraft in Tucson, Lockheed from somewhere else, Pratt and Whitney, Boeing—they all came in here. They sat here and said, "Now Peter, what are you going to do? We need castings."

It is the custom in the investment casting industry that the customer retains ownership of the tools required for the production of the specific products of the individual companies. With the liquidation under Mr. Greenfield, customers had to obtain a release from the creditors in order to transfer the material to Mr. Johnston's new operation. Customers then came to Mr. Johnston, "Peter, we need the castings now. Can you get them fast?"

"They sat here for weeks until we could get the investment casting process started again. We worked here day and night, trying to get things done. We had a hard time in that period because these big customers cannot stop their production. Often they might have as many as 5,000 people waiting on a production or assembly line for one small casting piece."

Commenting further, Mr. Johnston added, "Companies like Boeing are so big and yet they couldn't do much about it. Whenever they can, they take a tool to somebody else in the States, but a lot of them cannot do this type of casting. We finally got it going. For four and a half years, I worked sixteen hours a day, day in and day out, but we got the volume up to about $1.2 million in our first year."

In the intervening years since Mr. Johnston's reentry to the management of the company, sales more than doubled by year-end 1980 to $2.8 million with net profits of $334,000 (Exhibits 1 to 4).

COMPETITION

In Canada, a total of 10 companies were reported to be engaged in the Castings, Precision Investment, Lost-Wax process, compared with some 235 in the United States. It was Mr. Johnston's view that "in reality, there wasn't that much competition because there aren't that many good ones who can produce premium quality products. So really, the competition was not that great. For example, there are parts that we make now that can only be produced by six companies in the world, not just in North America and CCC is one of them."

He added, "Now when you get that kind of technology, people will buy from you and they push you to produce it. This is the kind of industry we are in and the kind of company we operate. But you have to keep up with recent developments. You have to have new ideas. You have to produce technology that other people don't have, or can't catch up to you with. Then you are always in the forefront. If you stay in the top ten, you are O.K. In fact, I would like to stay in the first two if I can, but that takes time."

"It's not too bad though. We started production again in 1977 so in less than four years of production, we have already got into the top ten," Mr. Johnston commented.

PRODUCTION

On initially taking over the casting plant in November 1971, Mr. Johnston remarked that there "were no orders left and seven people to run the operation, including myself."

Coming from an electronics background, investment casting was indeed a "foreign field." However, with an engineering degree and an innovative desire, Mr. Johnston "went in there and worked on the process, first in department number one, then number two, and so on until I understood the whole process. I did everything in the whole plant."

CCC faced a difficult introductory period of approximately eight months with "no orders and seven people to pay." . . .

MANAGEMENT PHILOSOPHY

Management philosophy at CCC involved many of what might be termed the usual aspects of management—how to manage people, external and internal communications, service to customers and general policies. Mr. Johnston added, however, that "I have found out one thing that perhaps people haven't thought about much and that is the internal atmosphere, the atmosphere you try to generate in your own company. This is all the responsibility of the president himself. Nobody else can set it. If I want a certain atmosphere in the company, I'll make sure I set it up myself."

Elaborating further on this facet of his management philosophy, Mr. Johnston believed in the manner management dealt with the people. In a small company it was possible to know everybody and care about what they were doing. If Mr. Johnston saw something not being done correctly, it was his practice to pick up the casting and calling the individual aside, would say, "You can do better than that. I will show you how to do it." The correct procedure was then demonstrated to the employee and repeated until the employee attained perfection. "They know that I didn't crucify them. They are learning something. If you do enough of this, people will respect you and also, they care. Once a person makes a mistake, they know it. All I say is, 'That's a mistake, and now let's do it properly.'"

It was Mr. Johnston's philosophy never to "put a person down," and [he] insisted that all his managers followed a similar philosophy. "If somebody does something wrong, the first thing for me to do is to go and help to do it the right way."

Teamwork was also regarded highly as a component of Mr. Johnston's management philosophy. "People have to work together, and I insist on it in the company."

Although the managers in CCC had their titles and clearly defined responsibilities (Exhibit 6), this did not preclude Mr. Johnston from imparting to them that "every job in the company is your job. If I am shorthanded in here, you come and help me; if you are shorthanded, then I go on the line. Every problem is yours. Once you have that atmosphere, the people know it is crucial that we have to work together as a team and more than that, they all know each other's job well enough that they can step in if anything happens."

Through the medium of regular formal and informal meetings, attempts were made to ensure that this "teamwork atmosphere" prevailed and moved down the line to the direct labour, ensuring that they were happy with the company. This, in Mr. Johnston's view, avoided a lot of problems, including union problems. "You treat them like human beings. We make a point of never pushing people around. If one

EXHIBIT 6

Canadian Casting Company Limited, organization chart (1980)

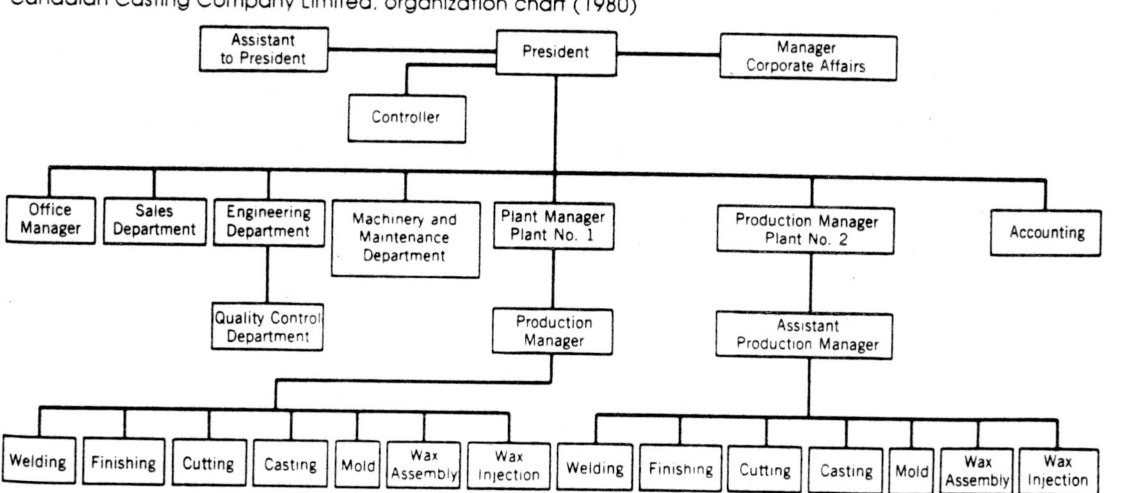

does ten pieces a day and another does two, we leave the latter alone, knowing that this is their individual speeds. We want it that way because in this business quality is everything, not the speed of production."

In addition to creating the "team atmosphere," bonuses were awarded every six months, "depending on the whole company's performance, not the individual—the whole company's. At the end of every six months, I work out the figures, sales against the number of employees and determine what the bonus will be."

Mr. Johnston recognized that this was easier to do with 100 to 120 employees and expressed the opinion that some other criteria would have to be developed when CCC became substantially larger. At this point in time, "It works out fine, maybe one of the reasons being that all the people know and trust me."

As an illustration of the team atmosphere that was apparent in the early stages of the company's operation and has continued throughout, Mr. Johnston recalled the production of the first castings.

"Because customers were waiting for their orders we had worked into the evening and at nine P.M. we poured the first casting. The production manager said, 'Fine, now let's stop and call it a day.' The men got cleaned up and walked into my office where I was still working, carrying two bottles of whiskey. I didn't know it, but they had had these bottles hiding inside for a week, waiting for this particular moment. We drank until midnight. So they do sort of care for the company."

A LOOK TO THE FUTURE

In keeping with his product philosophy Mr. Johnston believed that there was virtually no end for the demand for investment precision castings with which CCC was directly involved and producing. Demand was increasing and with expected improvements in technology that Mr. Johnston foresaw, "we are forecasting for nearly $6 million by 1983 and should reach sales up to $30–40,000,000 a year easily before too many years pass by."

In addition to the expansion of the casting part of the business, Mr. Johnston considered that the next area of development might be into machining. "Certain castings have to be machined before being used. Right now, the customer asks us to do it but we don't have the means to do so."

In looking into the future, Mr. Johnston was concerned also as to the physical location, certainly of parts of his operations, should continued expansion take place. CCC sales were in the United States, the United Kingdom, Germany, France with contacts in Hong Kong, Israel, and Spain—"whoever deals in aeroplanes or electronic equipment."

Not the least of his concern about the future growth of CCC was the role he himself should play. "I worry about that a lot. Although I have ten management people under me running the company, I have yet to find one who can run the whole show. Finding people is very difficult. I am looking for good people all the time. I'll be glad to take every day off and let somebody run the show for me."

EXERCISE 12–4

Please refer to Figure 12–2, which describes the directional policy matrix.

- Place CCC on this matrix.
- Prepare a paragraph or two in which you describe the reasoning that supports your choice of position on the Business Sector Prospects axis.

- Now prepare a paragraph or two to support your choice of position on the company's Competitive Capabilities axis.
- Given your placement on the matrix, prepare a statement of strategic objectives for CCC, and develop several statements of strategy which can aid in guiding your managers in the functions of Marketing, Production/Operations, Finance, and Research & Development.

EXERCISE 12–5

Use the strength/attractiveness framework of Boulton found in Figure 12–3. Analyze CCC's relative competitive strength and the industry attractiveness, then place a mark on the diagram seen below to indicate your best guess as to the company's position.

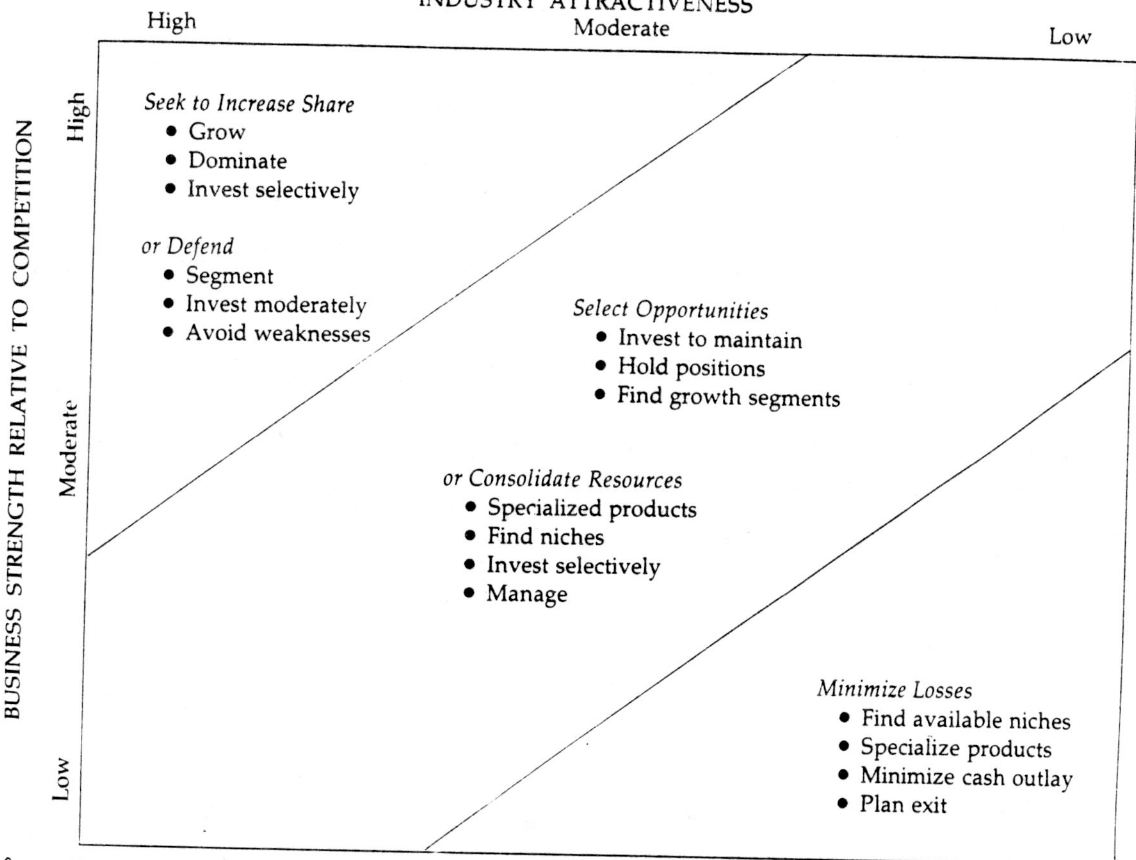

Source: William R. Boulton. *Business Policy: The Art of Strategic Management* (New York: Macmillan, 1984), p. 49.

- Prepare a paragraph or two that supports your choice of position in the diagram relative to competitive strength.
- Prepare a paragraph or two that supports your choice of position in the diagram relative to industry attractiveness.
- Given your placement on the diagram, prepare a statement of strategic objectives for CCC and develop several statements of strategy that can aid in guiding your managers in the functions of marketing, production/operations, finance, and R & D.

Next we will examine another major framework used in arraying strategies, the product life cycle. As we proceed, we will not only develop a rationale for strategy selection, but will discuss the implications for strategy implementation inherent in each stage of the life cycle.

The Product Life Cycle as a Framework for Strategy Selection

In Chapter 8, the product life cycle was discussed at length as a concept that can be quite useful in relating the functional area concerns of the general manager. In that chapter, the movement of the product throughout its life cycle was reflected in a series of organizational and managerial changes that were needed as management sought to achieve commercial success through the series of stages in the development of the product.

The organizational adaptation process is explored thoroughly by Miles and Snow,[3] who discuss an organizational "adaptive cycle" that seems quite similar to the dynamics of the first three stages of the product life cycle as it might apply to a company or an industry. The adaptive cycle describes the ways in which organizations cope with environmental conditions by dealing with three major problems: the *entrepreneurial* problem of determination of the product/market domain, the *engineering* problem of choices of technology for production and distribution, and the *administrative* problem, in which issues of stabilization and renewal are the focus of attention.

The product life cycle has served as a major construct in arraying strategic choices for a number of years. In a key article on the use of this framework, Hofer developed an extended theoretical perspective of its application to strategy formulation.[4] More recently, Anderson and Zeithaml found that the evidence of empirical studies on strategy selection and the product life cycle supported its use as a major contingency variable in the process of formulating or selecting an appropriate strategy.[5]

[3] Raymond E. Miles and Charles C. Snow, *Organizational Strategy, Structure, and Process* (New York: McGraw-Hill, 1978), pp. 13–30.

[4] C. W. Hofer, "Toward a Contingency Theory of Business Strategy," *Academy of Management Journal,* 18(4) (1975) pp. 784–810.

[5] Carl R. Anderson and Carl P. Zeithaml, "Stage of the Product Life Cycle, Business Strategy, and Business Performance," *Academy of Management Journal,* 27(1) (1984), pp 5–24.

We will use the concept of the product life cycle to explore in some detail the types of strategies that seem to be needed as a product *and its industry* move from the inception stages of a product/service concept through a period of growth in customer acceptance and quantities produced to a stabilization or maturity stage and, finally, to a stage of product decline or demise.

The framework within which we will explore these strategic choices, however, deserves some discussion. First, we will utilize the classic product life-cycle diagram broken into its four stages. In the classic diagram, the vertical axis is typically labeled *volume.* In our case, although volume is implicit in the shape of the curve (as in the classic model), two major characteristics of the firm serve as secondary and tertiary components in this contingency perspective. The first (as in the models described earlier) is that of the company's competitive strength. Where the company has the competitive capability, (e.g., financial resources, product patents, productive facilities, expertise, etc.), its management may wish to consider strategies significantly more ambitious than those undertaken by weaker firms.

Second, each firm's key strategists and their constituencies have different preferences for risk. In some cases, a company with substantial competitive strength may be directed by a strategy team that is relatively risk averse. They may, therefore, choose to adopt the strategic posture of a somewhat weaker company as a means of reducing exposure to business risk. Similarly, a weaker company may have a management team willing to take somewhat higher than normal degrees of risk. As such, the company may undertake strategies more suitable to a company with a stronger competitive position. As we examine the life cycle diagrams (Figures 12–4 to 12–8), therefore, we must select as appropriate those strategies that meet the *controlling* contingency rather than simply one of the two suggested here.

Innovation Stage 1 in the product life cycle is characterized by a high degree of uncertainty. In the first half of this stage, industry activity focuses on *innovation,* the creation of ideas and working prototypes of product concepts. The second half can be called a new product *implementation* phase, in which industry attention is directed toward the introduction of new products to early markets and in which R & D, marketing, and operations personnel seek to prepare a technology that will enable the new product to be effectively produced and marketed. Figure 12–4 depicts the section of the product life cycle dealing with Stage 1 and contains a number of broad categories of business strategy seen as appropriate for this stage and for the strength and risk preferences of a given company and its strategists. Although the classic shape of Stage 1 in the product life cycle serves as a backdrop in this diagram, the vertical axis here is scaled for competitive strength and/or risk preference.

In the innovations phase of Stage 1, critical components in strategy formulation include an emphasis on product research and on intelligence gathering. In the implementation phase, critical components include an emphasis on process research and the extent of investment in plant and equipment. Four variables seem to provide a framework for each class of strategy in this model:

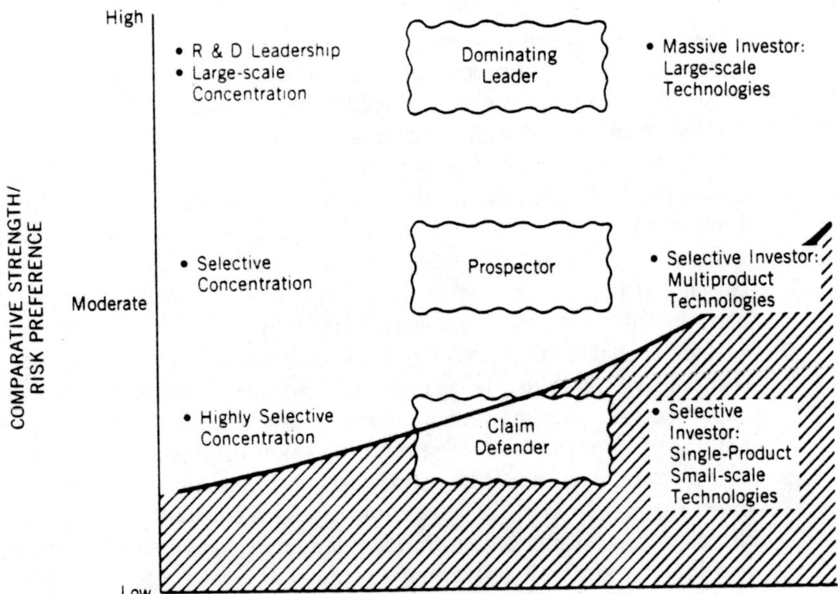

FIGURE 12–4 Developmental-stage strategies.

- The width of the product/market *domain* chosen by the strategist.
- The focus of research and development activities: the balance between product and process or between fundamental and applied research.
- The degree of investment of resources. Investments will be described as ranging from massive through moderate to selective, limited, little, or none.
- The operational mode of the company as a competitor. Similar to the generic strategic postures of "Overall Cost Leadership," "Differentiation," and "Focus" of Porter,[6] the descriptive labels of *Dominating Leader, Prospector,* and *Claim Defender,* which we will use, may help to capture the sense of the ways that companies act to carry out a strategy in this stage and in other stages of the life cycle.[7]

At the top of the diagram, where comparative strength/risk preference is highest, the Dominating Leader firm seeks large product/market segments in its strategy. This type of company concentrates its research and development on new-product research. Research is guided to emphasize high-quality products, innovative product

[6] Michael E. Porter, *Competitive Strategy* (New York: Free Press, 1980), pp. 34–46.

[7] The latter two terms are adopted from the modes of action of *Prospector* and *Defender* described by Miles and Snow, *Organizational Strategy*.

designs, and the aggressive pursuit of low-cost production and distribution. The Dominating Leader firm seeks to establish a superior position among competitors to structure the industry to its own advantage.[8] Investment in research may be relatively heavy in order that concepts reach critical decision stages and market entry sufficiently early to obtain advantages in gaining production and marketing knowledge, customer loyalty, and cost savings.[9]

In the implementation phase of Stage 1, the Dominating Leader firm will solicit external capital with the express intent of achieving substantial gains in market share through massive investments. Gains are most likely through concentrated attention to product design, product quality, or product positioning actions.[10]

In a somewhat less-aggressive posture, the Prospector seeks profitable product/market opportunities across a broad range of possibilities. While research emphasis is also directed toward new product concepts, a range of potential technologies are often developed by the Prospector. Investment will be moderately heavy to selective, reflective of strength, risk preference, and commitment to the product, however, rather than to a deliberate campaign for market domination.

The Prospector's actions during the implementation phase of Stage 1 will involve attention to the development of flexible productive capability that will enable the company to exploit a number of promising products, each with relatively short lives. Because of the need for flexibility in addressing a number of product concepts, highly skilled employees aid in achieving the rapid movement from product to product or from stage to stage in short-lived products. Multiple technologies serve to meet market needs with a lower risk than would be the case with a heavy investment in a single technology and heavy investment is postponed until product success is likely.[11]

At the lower levels of strength or risk preference are the Claim Defenders, organizations that seek a narrow product/market area of interest. The Claim Defender has severely limited resources, is not interested in larger markets, and focuses its attention on the domination and exploitation of a selected market segment. Research and development and selective investments depend on resources and risk preferences and are directed toward improvements in processes and in increasing efficiency as a means of gaining and holding the dominant position.

To implement Stage 1 strategies, the Claim Defender addresses the issues of stability, efficiency, and security through selected investments, attention to product design, and process efficiency. Growth is not an overriding concern. The development of a highly refined single technology and the use of vertical integration are sometimes used to achieve these ends.[12]

[8] Porter, *Competitive Strategy,* p. 230.

[9] Porter, *Competitive Strategy,* p. 232.

[10] Charles W. Hofer and Dan Schendel, *Strategy Formulation: Analytical Concepts* (St. Paul.: West, 1978), pp. 163–64.

[11] See Miles and Snow, *Organizational Strategy,* pp. 58–59, for a more detailed explication.

[12] Miles and Snow, *Organizational Management,* pp. 40–41.

EXERCISE 12-6

Your Fortune 200 manufacturing company's R & D has apparently come up with another winner. In a project that has been in the laboratory for over 3 years, the scientific team has developed a preservative compound for reducing or eliminating the staining of fabrics by a wide range of organic compounds. The new compound apparently serves to keep the staining agent from penetrating the fibers. Thus, stains by foods, blood, grass, oil, and grease, for example, could be removed by light cold-water washing to free the particles from the woven fabric.

Your company has been an active producer and marketer of commercial chemicals for over 50 years. If new products such as the new compound demonstrate both commercial viability and a substantial market potential, the company's strong financial and operations position assure full support for large-scale manufacture and distribution. The most recent product of a similar type, a gelling agent, has developed into a $250 million per year product that has captured over 70% of its intended market. Generally, management has moved very quickly to support promising new ideas and has found capital funds, personnel, and marketing talents needed to move rapidly into the marketplace in a highly competitive manner.

With the information provided and Figure 12–4:

- Describe the general category of competitor you believe the company to be. Explain your reasoning.
- Based on your assessment of the company and the potential you believe this product to have, describe the broad category of strategy you think this company should employ. Explain why you believe this will be suitable for the situation described.
- Draft some strategic guidelines for marketing, manufacturing, finance, and R & D that are consistent with the overall strategy you have recommended.

Growth Stage 2 in the product life cycle is a period of dynamic change in products, competitive structure, and means of competition. The number of competitors expands rapidly in response to high demand and product choices first expand to test market attractiveness, then narrow rapidly as customers settle on generic configurations of product features. Competitors scramble for market share and for the external capital needed to supply the funds for the heavy investment in capital assets and distribution systems needed to serve very large and far-flung markets. In operations, process technologists seek means of meeting demands for products from mass markets and core technologies are chosen to achieve production and cost targets. In the latter phases of the growth stage, cost pressures from narrowing profit margins and an increasingly quality- and feature-conscious marketplace exert demands on operations staff. Organizationally, the rapid growth in demand requires organizational expansion, the opening of new production facilities, and the rapid employment and training of large numbers of employees new to the company and possibly the industry. Management must not only deal with these expansion-oriented problems, but also must set the stage for the latter phases of growth, where technologies, organizational structures, and organizational practices become more stable, routine, and formal. The shakeout that occurs in the latter phase of the growth stage offers risks to the uncompetitive but opportunities to companies positioned to be able to acquire the assets, personnel, or customers of the unsuccessful.

We will now describe in somewhat more detail the strategic components needed for success following the three broad patterns of strategic response discussed for Stage 1. Figure 12–5 offers a visual summary of suggested approaches.

In Stage 2 the Dominating Leader will invest heavily in the development of distinctive products and in the battle for the largest manageable market share. Promotional and advertising activities will be aggressively pursued. Both product and process R & D will be undertaken. The former to gain and enhance product leadership; the latter to move as quickly as possible into a position of cost leadership in support of aggressive pricing, which can aid in the growth of market share.

The aggressive Dominating Leader may also seek additional market share by means of concentric diversification. In concentric diversification, a common thread links product offerings. In market-oriented diversification, the offerings will reflect the needs of an identified customer group. In production- or materials-oriented concentric diversification, the common thread will be a production technology,

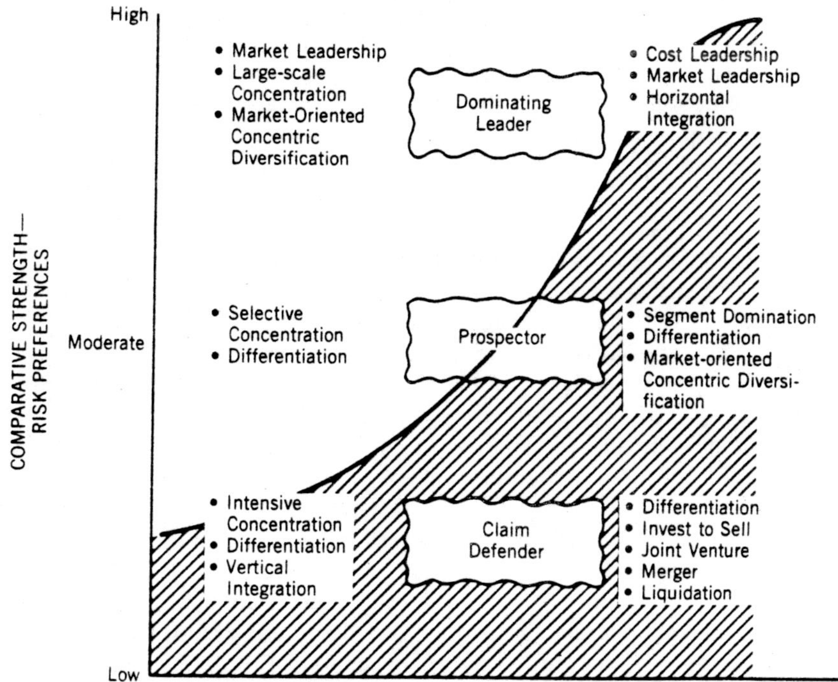

FIGURE 12–5 Growth-stage strategies.

unique production skills, or a common type of material. Given the interest of the Dominating Leader in controlling its markets, a customer-oriented form of concentric diversification is more likely.

Horizontal Integration is another means for the Dominating Leader to gain market share. Although subject to scrutiny on antitrust grounds, the acquisition of another firm in the same industry offers a way to gain cost efficiencies or to expand geographically. This strategic approach may be particularly useful for stronger competitors as the industry approaches the latter, or shakeout, phase of Stage 2 when unsuccessful companies face increasing losses in market position and heavy financial drain.

As the shakeout process becomes apparent in the late portion of Stage 2, successful companies will have shifted the focus of research activities toward process research and will seek efficiencies not only in operations, but also in service and distribution. The learning or experience curve may be used by the Dominating Leader to anticipate cost savings and price on the basis of anticipated rather than current actual costs, thereby placing extraordinary pricing/cost pressure on competitors. Although the market will have chosen a set of products that offer appealing distinctive features, the Dominating Leader will have selected or determined the product that has appeal to the largest segment of the total market. Its identity will be well established, even to the point of serving as the standard of comparison for all other products in the industry. Although the dominant product will be quite evident in its size and presence, others will have been developed to suit other identifiable segments in the market, and the process of differentiation of products will be well under way.

The Prospector in Stage 2 considers a wide range of potential product/market combinations as offering the opportunity for gain. Its R & D activities will involve a high emphasis on environmental and market scanning as well as on the development of appealing product/marketing mixes to address specified market segments. Although not interested in dominating the *industry*, the Prospector utilizes creative marketing and product development to present unique differentiable products to identified segments of the market in which it might hold a very large share.

Advertising and promotion are used more selectively than with the Dominant Leader. Once the target segment is identified, the prospector seeks to grow with that segment and to occupy a significant and profitable position, capitalizing on the unique properties of its products while appealing to a narrowly focused target market. Although the Prospector may be neither capable of, nor interested in, acquiring another company as a means of capturing market share, concentric diversification offers a means of expanding sales to a limited market with a moderate addition to marketing and capital resource investments. As with the Dominating Leader, the diversification would take the form of market-related product offerings.

As the shakeout becomes apparent, the Prospector seeks to consolidate its position in its identified market segments. Product differentiation and carefully developed appeals to its customers are designed to reinforce brand loyalties and resist the appeals from products in other segments. Process-oriented research is needed for the Prospector to maintain profitability in an intensively cost-conscious marketplace.

As pressures for cost-reduction or market-share erosion increase, the Prospector may find it helpful to join forces with other firms. Joint ventures offer the opportunity to share complementary resources and to develop a dominant position in more than a single segment of the market. Mergers also have that characteristic, but may offer the advantages of financial strength, geographic market coverage, or economies of scale in manufacturing, distribution, or administration—all of which serve to resist the competitive efforts of the dominant leader or leaders.

At the lower end of the strength/risk scale, the Claim Defender has constraints on its choices of products and markets and is much more vulnerable to the shakeout that occurs as products move to the mature stage. Resources for research and marketing must be used selectively to identify small segments or niches in the marketplace that may be unappealing to larger or more-ambitious companies. Once identified, the target market is served by a concentration strategy by the Claim Defender. The limited product development research must address very specific needs of this customer group, and promotional appeals must be carefully tailored to the target group to build the loyalty that will be needed to survive the shakeout. Process research is needed to arrange a core technology best suited to the unique requirements of the product, the size and frequency of orders, and the need for customization. The Claim Defender becomes an intensively concentrated specialist in the provision of products to its segment. Because of its vulnerability, the Claim Defender may (if capital is available) integrate vertically to reduce costs, to assure sources of supply and to reduce risks in distribution.

As the growth pattern unfolds, the Claim Defender may find that its position is deteriorating. The success of Dominating Leaders, unanticipated shifts in consumer preferences, or unmet needs for resources may erode the competitive position of the Claim Defender. A particularly vulnerable Claim Defender may wish to invest in plant, equipment, and markets with the intention of selling to another investor or organization before being shaken out. If the planned invest-to-sell strategy has not been considered, either the joint venture or the merger give the Claim Defender, as they did to the Prospector, the opportunity to share talents, resources, and economies of scale.

EXERCISE 12–7

Identify three products you believe are in the growth stage of the product life cycle.

- Select one of the three and describe one or more types of strategy suitable for a small, talented, but financially weak company to use in manufacturing and marketing its products.
- Develop strategic guidelines, which you believe to be consistent with your recommended general strategy, for the company's marketing, financial management, production, operations, or R & D activities in coming years.

Early Maturity The early maturity phase of the product life cycle (Figure 12–6) is characterized by a continuation of growth (at slowing growth rates) by the clear delineation of market segmentation and by product positioning. Competitors frequently consolidate positions that were hard won during the shakeout phase of the preceding stage in the life cycle. As this phase nears its end, the lack of growth and early signs of decline signal a period of profit taking, or harvesting. As in the two preceding stages, strategic choices are not only governed by market and competitive conditions, but also by relative strength and risk preferences of competing organizations.

The Dominating Leader organization will continue the aggressive posture in its strategies seen in earlier stages. It will continue to search for improvement on its own records and will also seek superiority over industry standards in all of its activities. The Dominating Leader will attempt to initiate innovations and to exploit opportunities presented by the weaknesses of its rivals. It will meet the competitive moves quickly and may retaliate with countermoves to minimize any potential gains of its competitors.[13]

[13] Arthur A. Thompson, Jr., and A. J. Strickland, *Strategy Formulation and Implementation: Tasks of the General Manager* Rev. Ed. (Palto, Tex.: Business Publications, 1983), pp. 158–59.

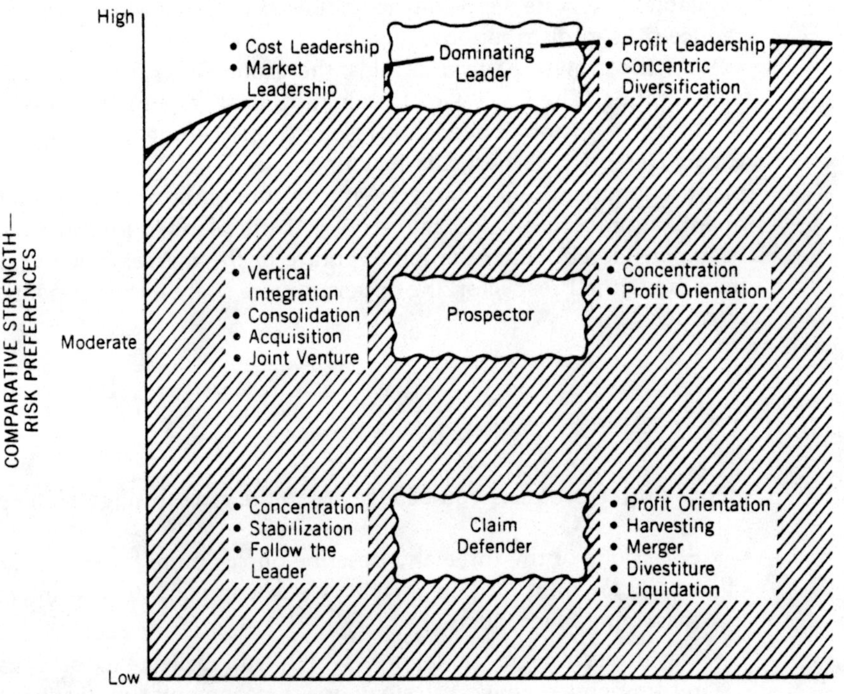

FIGURE 12–6 Strategies for early maturity.

The Dominating Leader will pursue cost leadership, and as a consequence will adopt a variety of measures designed to sustain this strategy. Research and development costs will be minimized and the scale of operations will be large in order to take advantage of economies of scale in purchasing, manufacture, and distribution. Product standardization and attention to process engineering offer manufacturing cost advantages and will be pursued. The successful achievement of cost leadership coupled with an aggressive and reactive marketing strategy make the Dominating Leader a formidable competitor and continue to aid the Dominating Leader firm in increasing its large market share. Concentric diversification may also be employed as a means of increasing sales in markets chosen by the Dominating Leader.

For Prospectors, the early maturity stage is a time for selective investments aimed at capitalizing on an increasingly differentiated market. Positions gained in the shakeout are held and maintained and firms may choose to integrate vertically not only to reduce risk, but also to convert cost centers to profit generators. Small competitors may be acquired as a means of developing additional profitable market position without directly confronting the Dominating Leader firm. Joint ventures that offer the Prospector the opportunity of sharing complementary resources may also be undertaken as a way of achieving goals without all of the competitive tools that would otherwise be needed. For the Prospector, the functions and issues most influential in strategy formulation within the organization concern marketing and R & D.

As the early maturity stage nears its end, the Prospector will continue to selectively invest but will also seek high efficiency in the utilization of assets and begin to be concerned with profit maximization. Sales-mix changes, product pruning, cost or asset reduction programs, or the systematic examination of alternative plans for the improvement in return on investment and cash flows are all actions that might be considered as means of improving profitability. The funds thus generated may be diverted into other, more-promising lines of business or they may be returned to stockholders for their own reinvestment on an individual basis.

The Claim Defender organization will seek product/market niches that offer an opportunity for concentration and stabilized demand. Limitations on resources dictate a small market segment and, for some, may preclude the opportunity for vertical integration. The Claim Defender firm will become expert in its field and will reduce risks by becoming dominant—however, in a limited marketplace. Claim Defenders will adopt a more cautious set of stability strategies, strategies that may involve no change, a consolidation of position, or at most a cautious expansion.[14]

For the Claim Defender organization in the first portion of early maturity, marketing, applied research, production issues and talents form the nucleus of strategy formulation. Later, as growth slows, production and administrative talents and issues seem to dominate discussions.[15]

As with the Prospector, the Claim Defender organization will begin the process

[14] Wheelen and Hunger, *Strategic Management*, pp. 45–46.

[15] Miles and Snow, *Organizational Strategy*, pp. 42, 74–75.

of harvesting as the growth curve flattens, and it will examine investments with caution, focusing on maximizing returns from its carefully defined small-market position. The typical pattern involves cost cutting, a reduction in promotional expenses, production- and maintenance-budget cuts, price increases, and attention directed toward short-term cash flows.

In pursuit of survival, the Claim Defender organization may follow one of two quite different approaches: In the first, it may adopt a distinctive image in support of its position in the marketplace. With limited resources, however, the Claim Defender may choose as another approach to follow the lead of dominant firms in its niche and adopt their product and marketing practices rather than seek its own identity.

As the pattern of growth slows, the Claim Defender may find its position weakening as stronger firms gradually gain market share. The strategist may consider merger with, or sale to, stronger companies as means of avoiding significant losses in capital. Although sale or merger is not always easy in conditions where growth is slow, economies of scale in production and distribution may offer attractive inducements to stronger companies. Dominating Leaders seeking control over the market or Prospectors seeking to establish a strong position in smaller segments are likely candidates for merger or sale.

EXERCISE 12–8

Your company has survived and thrived in the explosive growth in the digital voltmeter market. You are well capitalized, occupy a market position that accounts for nearly 60% of industry sales, and believe that the heavy investments the company has made in this product will be well justified. Although the market is growing, the rate of increase has slowed noticeably in recent years.

- Identify this type of competitor. From the information in Figure 12–6 and the text material, array two or three types of strategy that might be helpful to this company. Under what conditions might one be preferred to the others? Explain for each.
- Select any two and describe how the strategic guidelines for marketing, operations, finance, and R & D will be either similar or different for the two general strategies.

Later Maturity The later portion of the maturity stage in the product life cycle (Figure 12–7) is marked by a stagnation in market growth and the onset of market shrinkage as customer consumption patterns change or as product substitution begins. Brand loyalties remain well established and the large companies that have survived the earlier shakeouts now find that revenues have begun to decline. Although the general market is stable and characterized by relatively low profit margins, segments may continue to grow and may be quite profitable. In addition, the

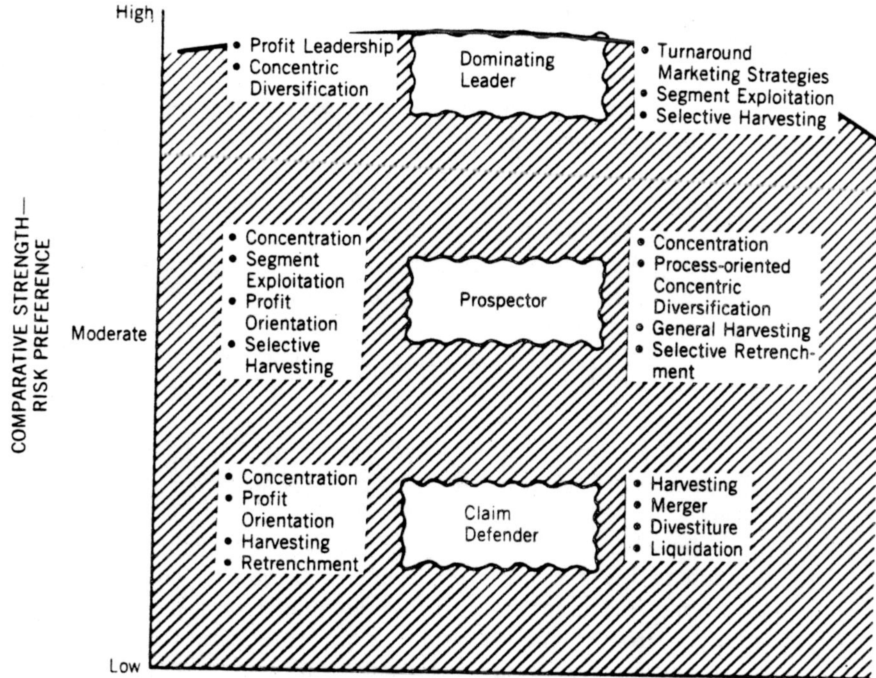

FIGURE 12–7 Strategies for later maturity.

size of market offers the opportunity for considerable profit generation and is, therefore, still attractive to the efficient producer and marketer.

The Dominating Leader firm is in an excellent position to harvest profits from the markets it is serving through cost cutting and by limiting capital expenditure. Prices will be maintained, if not increased, and promotional expenses will be held to a level that is designed to sustain market position. The Dominating Leader may also be in a position to sustain or expand its market position through concentric diversification, selling products that support the principal product in the marketplace and that further reinforce its dominant position. Its investments will be made selectively, in search of growth segments in its markets or for product-line expansion projects through concentric diversification. As market share begins to decline, the Dominating Leader may employ turnaround strategies to regain market share through a variety of sales-enhancing marketing ventures. Product improvements, new applications for existing products, increases in promotional expenditures, and significant price changes are sometimes suggested as means of rejuvenating a flagging market.

As the market decline becomes an industrywide factor, the Dominating Leader will continue to aggressively exploit profitable segments of the market. In areas of decline, it may engage in selected harvesting activities that may include pruning the product line and liquidating excess capital equipment, but it will do so in order to devote talent and resources to profitable segments. Where possible, price increases will be used to increase revenues. When more general harvesting becomes necessary owing to market shrinkage, costs will be cut to an absolute minimum and expenditure for promotion will be focused only on areas of potential market gain.

As the Mature Stage continues, the Prospector will continue its market concentration strategy, but may also seek to exploit any growth opportunities in its markets. It might pursue a concentric diversification strategy, but it would do so in search of profit opportunities that might make use of its production technology or its expertise in dealing with a particular type of material. In stable segments, the Prospector will begin harvesting. Investments will be most selective and marketing and promotion expenditures will be made to sustain a sales level in a relatively stagnant market.

In the late phase of this stage as decline becomes apparent, the Prospector will accelerate the harvesting strategies used in the earlier phase and may begin the processes of retrenchment as profit opportunities diminish. Retrenchment would include cost cutting, cutbacks in hiring or even the layoff of personnel, reductions or elimination of capital expenditure projects, and where possible, the sale of surplus assets.

The Claim Defender is often the first to feel the effects of the lack of market growth or the beginning of decline. In a weaker competitive position, the Claim Defender will have fewer of the advantages of scale of operations or distinctively superior product characteristics. As a consequence, unless the Claim Defender is especially nimble, it may find itself losing market share to its more aggressive and stronger competitors. The Claim Defender, therefore, must be more cautious in its investments and must begin the process of harvesting at an earlier time in this stage than might be the case for the Prospector or the Dominating Leader.

The Claim Defender should seek to preserve market share, but should avoid excessive expenditures for operations, marketing, or promotion. It may have a very strong position in its own segment of the market, and may find that this segment has less sensitivity to substitution or obsolescence than others. The Claim Defender, therefore, may find its market share holding or even growing as the industry declines more rapidly in general than in the small segment occupied by the Claim Defender. Although this is an attractive prospect for the Claim Defender in one sense, its very attractiveness may make the firm the object of the interests of the Prospector or the Dominating Leader, companies with talent and resources superior to the Claim Defender. The Claim Defender may well wish to consider divestiture or merger in the latter phase of this stage of the life-cycle at a time when other companies have an interest in acquisitions and before the entire market deteriorates. As a last resort, of course, the weakest firms unable to compete or to find a purchaser may be forced to consider liquidation of their interests in this product.

EXERCISE 12-9

For a number of years, your company has been involved in the artistic production, manufacture, and sale of stereo records. Your company is not large, but it has had a high degree of success in its line of accompaniment records used by solo performers. The recording industry trade journals have expressed great interest in the recent advent of computerized sound recording equipment, a technical development that offers great precision in reproduction and nearly unlimited life. The equipment needed for this type of recording is quite expensive and is likely, therefore, to be adopted only by companies capable of investing in the tens of millions of dollars for each digitizing studio.

- Refer to Figure 12–7 and the text and identify the category of competitor this situation presents. Explain your thinking.
- Array two or three types of strategy that might be helpful to this company. Under what conditions might one be preferred to the others? Explain for each.
- Assume that a financial angel has arranged to provide as much financial assistance as might be needed to make use of the new technology. Would this change your thinking? Explain.
- Would this alter your thinking about your assessment of this company as a competitor?
- Would this lead you to consider other strategies?

Decline The decline stage in the product life cycle (Figure 12–8) presents a dramatic drop in sales volume, a second shakeout of competitors, and a highly intense period of activity as competitors seek to either identify the surviving niche (and dominate that niche) or find a means of leaving the industry to pursue other interests.

Several factors determine the extent to which the market, despite its decline, will be seen as favorable. The first is the cause of the decline and its speed. In some industries, (calculators come to mind) the effect of the entry of new products is catastrophic. The electronic calculator virtually destroyed the market for mechanical desk calculators and slide rules. Further, the destruction was as rapid as the entry of the new products. A second factor is the extent of market segmentation. If a high degree of brand or product loyalty has been developed, the conversion to new products will be significantly slower than if that were not the case. Third, the prospect of damage caused by the retaliation of competitors during a shakeout can make a declining market less attractive than if competitors find the exit process less painful. Multiproduct organizations that can shift resources and personnel to other lines of business may find the demise of a product line significantly less troublesome than might be the case if that were their only line of business. Finally, the extent to which competitors are likely to engage in price wars can make the declining stage in a product's life more or less attractive.[16]

The dramatic change in the size of the market can result in something of an inversion in market structure. Large dominant firms may not find the small residual markets sufficiently attractive to warrant their investment and management atten-

[16] D. L. Bates and D. L. Eldredge, *Strategy and Policy: Analysis, Formulation, and Implementation*, 2nd Ed. (Dubuque, Iowa: Wm C. Brown, 1984), pp. 146–47.

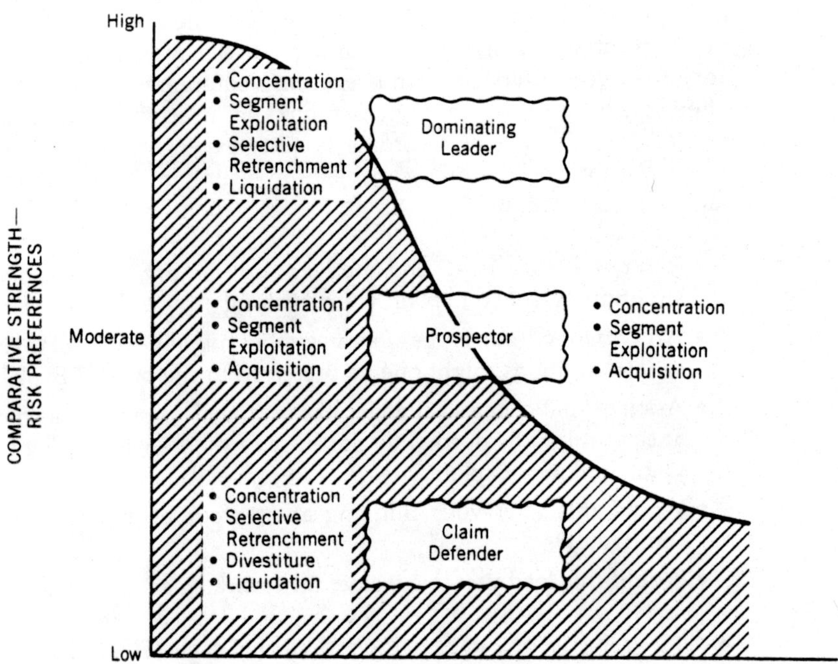

FIGURE 12–8 Strategies for industry decline.

tion. Therefore, they may exit the industry at an earlier time in this stage than will firms that continue to find small segments commercially interesting and profitable. The smaller firms, as a consequence, will find their relative competitive strength significantly enhanced as the result of (a) their specialized knowledge, reputation, and brand loyalty in smaller market segments and (b) the exit of the giants. In effect, the decline stage represents a very significant risk to the dominant firms because of the size of their commitment to this industry. As this risk becomes apparent, they may choose to divest or liquidate rather suddenly rather than ride the decline to a more gradual and more expensive cessation of operations. One example that comes to mind in recent years is the sudden departure of the Woolco discount stores from competition during a time of decline in major discount-house sales volume brought about by intense competition for discount-house trade by other major retailers such as the Target Stores of Dayton-Hudson and a rejuvenated effort by very large retailers such as Sears and J. C. Penney, Inc. The competitive dynamics of the decline stage can be quite dramatic, therefore, and warrant careful attention by competitors at all levels of strength and risk preference.

The Dominating Leader in the Decline Stage will seek to capitalize on its major strengths through concentration. It will improve production and distribution efficiencies and seek to milk the residual markets to the maximum extent possible. It will attempt to emphasize product quality and features to maintain its hold on a loyal market following. The Dominating Leader will invest in aggressive marketing and attempt to make it clear to customers and competitors its commitment to the product and market. It will also ease the exit of competitors by offering to manufacture parts or to assume responsibilities for long-term servicing agreements.[17] As the decline becomes inescapably clear, the Dominating Leader will follow the harvesting strategies described earlier, prune unprofitable operations, and sell off idle assets. Advertising expenses will be minimized, operating budgets held to minimal level, and new capital investment halted. Given the scale of operations and the recognition of general market decline, divestiture of intact operations is not likely, at least on any large scale.

To the Dominating Leader, the extent of investment in product or service offerings and the consequences of a decline in sales and earnings on stockholder relations and confidence often place the company in a position of concealing its intentions of liquidating its interests until the last feasible moments. An earlier announcement undoubtedly would seriously hinder its attempts at harvesting profits and might result in serious losses in sales and personnel during the period leading to the actual time of exit. Thus, we observed in 1985 that IBM had an active advertising campaign under way for the PC Jr at the time that it announced its decision to stop production of that particular personal computer. Woolco announced its decision to close all of its discount outlets a scant 2 months prior to closure, a time that permitted the sale of existing inventories and the orderly replacement of personnel, but little else.

The Prospector can continue to search for arenas of commercial profitability. Prospectors can search for and exploit growth segments in a smaller market, and can (as with the Dominating Leader) emphasize quality and product features as a means of appealing to what might be called loyalist markets. In the firearms industry, companies that retained older manufacturing technologies (e.g., cut rifling and milled parts) advertised this fact as a product-quality attribute during a period when competitors had changed to highly automated and much more modern technologies such as sheet-metal stamping, investment casting, and hammer-forged barrel manufacture. These loyal customers often provide the basis for a continuation of product life but at volume levels well below that of the industry in its mature stage. To the Prospector, the possibility of volume decline is somewhat less significant and of less imminent danger in its impact than is the case with the Dominant Leader. In its search for commercial profit opportunity, the Prospector may wish to attract markets abandoned by Dominant Leaders or underserved by weaker firms. Prospectors may not only wish to seek these markets, but may also want to consider the purchase (often at distress prices!) of idle assets and the employment of key personnel furloughed by companies abandoning their markets. In this way, the commercially alert prospector may enhance its market position by attracting those residual segments of its competitors' customers and may find its market share and its absolute volume growing rather than declining during a period of general decline in industry volume.

The Claim Defender, without the resources of the Prospector, will be unable to

[17] Porter, *Competitive Strategy*, p. 268.

capitalize on the exit of competitors by expanding its markets or its capital base. Instead, the Claim Defender must continue to search for productivity and efficiency to remain viable, and to emphasize product features and quality as a means of retaining its loyal customer following. If it is successful, it may find a graceful and relatively profitable exit from its industry through divestiture of an intact operation to a prospector interested in a sustained position in small markets.

Because of its lack of financial strength, the Claim Defender is much more vulnerable to a decline in sales than its competitors and must maintain a tight control on costs, marketing expenditure, and idle assets. In this sense, it must follow many of the same practices as the Dominant Leader but for different reasons. It must adopt a harvesting mode at an earlier point in the life of the product, and must face the problems of liquidation somewhat ahead of the stronger Prospector firm that is firmly established in a market with a longer residual life.

EXERCISE 12–10

As the last survivor of 19 manufacturers of gas cooking ranges in New England, your firm has found its sales gradually declining, despite a relatively constant (albeit very small) share of the national market for gas ranges. Profits have ranged from 2 to −4% of sales over the past 5 years. Return on investment was 7.8% in the best year in that period.

Your stock's price is: Bid $41, Asked $41½ in the over-the-counter market. Assets are nearly fully depreciated and have little salvage value. Book value of net worth is approximately $46 per share. Your customers, largely building contractors, on the average have purchased your ranges for 9 years.

- Refer to Figure 12–8 and the text and identify the category of competitor this situation presents. Explain your thinking.
- Array two or three types of strategy that might be helpful to this company. Under what conditions might one be preferred to the others? Explain for each.
- Our company's owners have been characterized by an extreme degree of caution. A number of influential stockholders are widows and other large blocks of stock are held in trust for minor children. Does this information affect your choice of desired strategy? Explain.
- Recommend a strategy for this company and develop the guidelines needed for functional areas (marketing, finance, operations, R & D) for the coming years.

As we close this chapter on strategy formulation for single-business enterprises, the Rolm Corporation case is provided to enable you to examine a company involved in the vigorous competitive struggle that followed the deregulation of the communications industry. As you read through the case material, consider and reflect on the major variables involved in the strategy array and selection process: position on the product life cycle, company relative competitive strength, and company risk preference. When you have completed reading the case, prepare to answer the questions found in the exercises at its end.

ROLM CORPORATION

M. Kenneth Oshman sat behind his large oak desk in the ROLM Corporation headquarters in Santa Clara, California, contemplating his next move. Robert R. Maxfield and Walter Lowenstern, the two remaining founders, sat opposite him. Each man fingered a copy of a survey recently published by the Marketing Programs and Services Group entitled, "Communications in the 1980's: Interconnect, New Competition, and Automated Office Product Migration."

The survey, published in October 1980, reinforces the founders' fear that new technology in the telecommunications industry had left tradition PBX systems "virtually stuck, for the most part, with 'first generation' PBX systems incapable of successful migration to an integrated automated office environment."[1] ROLM had experienced substantial growth in its 11-year history, and this strategy is expected to dominate ROLM's future planning.

As they contemplated how to continue to grow at their heretofore rapid pace, the founders' minds wandered back over the marketing success that ROLM had experienced.

TELECOMMUNICATIONS-MARKET DEVELOPMENT

The principal markets ROLM has entered in telecommunications are:

1 The large metropolitan areas dominated by Bell operating companies.

2 Independent telephone companies that buy and lease equipment to their customers.

3 Organizations that buy PBX (Private Branch Exchange) equipment directly from manufacturers and then install and service the equipment themselves.

4 Largely undeveloped international markets.

Many potential users are still quite uninformed about product offerings and to the fact that there are alternatives to Bell and GTE. Manufacturers are still guessing about users needs, however, because the marketplace has been so dominated by Bell that sufficient research was never conducted about alternatives. ROLM has identified cost savings, flexibility, convenience, and ability to upgrade systems as primary decision factors for the purchase of switching systems.

As might be expected, competitive forces are beginning to surface as the vastness of the $2 billion retail market in the United States is explored. Exhibit 1 indicates the competition that faces ROLM in 1980. Western Electric, a Bell operating company, represents the most significant hurdle with over two thirds of the market. ROLM currently has a 15% penetration in the switching-system market potential of the total retail sales estimate.

ROLM is becoming increasingly aware of new strategies that must be developed to maintain its competitive position (second to Bell in

This case was prepared by P. Awa, P. Hennessey, G. Stewart, C. Pepkin, and J. Thompson, under the Supervision of Professor Sexton Adams, North Texas State University and Professor Adelaide Griffin, Texas Woman's University.

EXHIBIT 1
Competition in the telecommunications industry

Western Electric Company, Inc.	(Bell System)
GTE Automatic Electric	(General Telephone)
International Telephone & Telegraph	(ITT)
Northern Telecom	Stromberg-Carlson
Siemens	Plessey & Phillips
L. M. Erickson	OKI
Hitachi-Fujitsu	NEC
Wescom Switching, Inc.	Intecom
IBM	Xerox
Datapoint	Redcom Industries
Lexor Corporation	Olivetti

Source: Marketing Programs and Services Group, 1980.

sales of switching systems). The market for switching systems is maturing, growing at only 13% annually for the next 2 years with more declines in the next 5 years. By 1982, forecasts have indicated that 70% of all offices will have replaced their old, electromechanical PBX's with the new, electronic models. "The good news is that every office needs a PBX. The bad news is that it needs only one," stated Dick Moley, vice-president of marketing for ROLM.[2]

Since its introduction to the telecommunications field in 1975, ROLM has been instrumental in developing a competitive marketplace where none had existed. Bell Telephone had, to this time, controlled markets by federal licensure. All switching systems (i.e., transferring calls between stations), facsimile transmitters, and word-processing/computer communications were developed by AT&T to complement their existing equipment. Without competition, the Bell System continued to utilize electromechanical switching systems, although computer applications were being developed by independent firms to someday capitalize on deregulated markets. ROLM was among the first to recognize the marketing possibilities of internal switching devices that could be purchased for cost savings over traditional equipment. In 1973, ROLM began development of a PBX that could satisfy user needs by offering cost savings, flexibility, and expanded capabilities.

The Carterfone[3] decision in 1968 brought about competition to the Bell System by allowing others to manufacture telecommunications switching systems and making it illegal for Bell to hinder new-product introductions. ROLM was ready with a sophisticated first generation (voice only) system to offer large companies for private use as well as selling to interconnect companies (independent telephone companies) who would then sell and service the equipment to users. Second generation (voice and data communications) systems are still being developed by firms in the marketplace. Bell, with its *Dimension* and *Centrex* telecommunications system, represents the major competitive hurdle. However, deregulation is forcing Bell to set up separate profit-making divisions for its switching systems.

Sales figures since 1972 to ROLM are given in Exhibit 2 to indicate the changing pattern for growth ROLM has pursued by the expansion of its products and services. ROLM's Computerized Branch Exchange (CBX) has been the most successful product development with over 5,000 now in operation in the United States ROLM's competitive advantage, utilizing computer technology for switching calls was a dra-

EXHIBIT 2
ROLM Corporation—sales by division, 1972–80

Division	*1972*	*1973*	*1974*	*1975*	*1976*	*1977*	*1978*	*1979*	*1980*
MIL-SPEC	2.4	3.6	6.1	10.0	12.5	12.6	18.0	26.9	42.3
CBX				1.3	7.8	22.3	37.8	72.2	118.0
ROCO	—	—	—	—	—	—	—	12.0	40.4
TOTAL	2.4	3.6	6.1	11.3	20.3	34.9	55.8	111.1	200.7

Source: ROLM Annual Report, 1980.

matic introduction to a market that had just become aware of the advantages of electronic circuitry.

A PBX is a switching system for telephones that interfaces between a commercial telephone customer and both public and private telephone networks. Usually located on the customer's premises, the PBX consists of: (1) stations or telephone extensions that are connected directly to the system, (2) attendent consoles, and (3) trunk lines that connect the switching system to the public telephone network or to private networks. The PBX generally routines incoming calls to attendent positions from which they may be extended to station users, allows for station-to-station calling without the use of the telephone network, and permits station users to access the telephone network for outgoing calls. ROLM's CBX systems are designed for businesses who often utilize special service trunk lines such as WATS, foreign exchange and tie lines, and typically experience significant telephone expense.

Being at the right place at the right time has characterized ROLM's executive posture. Most planning discussions are focused on who is doing what in the industry. Though the technical nature of the industry is paramount to manufacturers' successes, many other factors must be weighed. Data must be maintained on business trends for the separate markets that ROLM must pursue. It will be through constant monitoring of user needs and feedback from current customers that growth can continue. Considerable risk taking will be involved for ROLM as it has not developed the extensive information systems that are maintained by their larger competitors. Even more uncertainty is expected in marketing office-of-the-future products.

Further growth is anticipated. GTE, the largest independent telephone company, has chosen ROLM's CBX as standard equipment for its customers. The telecommunications division has been estimated to grow at a 30% rate for 1981–83.[4] This growth, if profit levels are to be continued, will be needed to finance expected operating requirements and expansion plans.

Some of the applications of ROLM products are provided to illustrate the developmental efforts that, in 1980, cost the company 6.8% of revenues.[5]

Feature	*Description*
Toll Restriction	Restricts the calls that can be made from an extension to specific local exchanges or area codes.
Route Optimization	Automatically selects the most economical route available for a user's call.
Call-back Queuing	Spreads the demand for special service trunks by establishing priority waiting list, calls user back when

	trunk is available, and in most cases, automatically dials the desired number. When coupled with Route Optimization, routes traffic to optimal and/or less extensive routes.
Call Detail Recording (CDR)	Records information such as the calling and called number, duration of call, trunk used, date and time of day.
Remote Moves and Changes	Allows changes in customers' system such as a telephone's extension number and class of service to be made through the computer memory without an installer visiting the user's location.
System Monitoring	Allows the system to be monitored for defects and feature usage from remote locations.
Centralized Attendant Service (CAS)	Ties together a number of CBX locations in such a manner that they may operate independently of each other while maintaining a central answering point for incoming calls to all locations.
Automatic Call Distribution (ACD)	Receives, concentrates, queues and uniformly distributes a high volume of incoming calls to answering attendants.
Satellite Operation	Connects two or more nearby CBS sites to provide sharing of expensive toll facilities.
CBS Management Reporter	Stores and processes call data as completed and provides telephone cost and usage reports from a terminal connected to the CBX.
ROLM Analysis Center (RAC)	Offers a selection of extended cost, call-detail, and traffic reports to help customers reduce communication costs.
TACL Programs	Provides traffic analysis and traffic engineering statistics for optimal network design.

Competitors are still trying to catch ROLM in features while still providing cost savings. Completely integrated simultaneous voice-data transmissions are now being offered by Northern Telecom and Intercom. Many of the other features are now being seen in competitive machines. Japanese manufacturers are steadily entering the marketplace. Because telecommunications production is not a highly capital intensive industry, ease of entry to the market is most commonly seen by companies already engaged in computerized technology.

Although ROLM is experiencing great success with its first generation applications, innovation by competitors has forced ROLM to respond with many attempts at upgrading its original introduction. Second-generation data-transmission systems as seen by ROLM management will have to be integrated into current CBX technology. The costs of putting a completely integrated voice-and-data system onto the marketplace is currently seen as being unnecessary for ROLM's current plans.

MIL-SPEC DIVISION

Although 78.7% of 1980 sales for ROLM were in Telecommunications, the ROLM idea began with the MIL-SPEC operations. Walter Lowenstern, one of the founders and primary moving force, describes the period.

> *Ken [Oshman] and I have toyed with the idea of a voice scrambler for possible police applications. A vehicle locater, such as the one I had worked on at Sylvania, was also looked into. The idea that finally clicked was ruggedizing a NOVA computer for military applications. Investors were quickly found when such an innovative application was developed. I feel sorry for the police—they still don't have a decent voice scrambler.*[6]

Initially, ROLM grew slowly. Military computers designed to withstand severe environmental conditions were the only products. During 1969, investors were easily found for computer-oriented companies and ROLM was able to begin a small staff that in 11 years would eventually grow to over 3,700. From a tin warehouse, the company would occupy in 1980 a total of 440,000 square feet in lease for 1981 through 1997 and 320,000 square feet in three buildings owned by the company. 125,000 square feet is now reserved for expansion.

ROCO DIVISION

ROLM sells its telecommunications products in the United States directly to end users through the ROLM Operating Companies (ROCOs) as well as to independent distributors of telephone equipment (interconnect companies) who purchase and reoffer the products to their own customers. ROCO sales represented 23% of telecommunications revenues, with 58% being sold to interconnect companies and 20% of revenues generated from independent telephone companies by ROLM's own sales force.[7] The remaining 5% comes from international sales. ROLM had licensed Plessy Communications of Great Britain to expand the European market. However, contract deficiencies by Plessy had caused a revocation of their license in 1980. ROLM currently has no organized European effort owing largely to differences within each country in telephone systems and technology. Licensing is by each country.

The ROCOs are made up of seven wholly owned subsidiaries with 24 sales offices in 13 states. Service is usually provided under separate agreements by ROLM.

ROCO began by acquiring their major "direct" distributors. In 1980, ROLM added 4 more ROCOs, bringing the total to 7. These were ROLM Colorado, ROLM Intermountain, ROLM Texas, and ROLM Atlantic. Exhibit 3 shows the overall company structure.

During the past fiscal year, the ROCO's accounted for 20% of ROLM Telecommunications sales. ROLM's 1980 Annual Report states, "We believe the ROLM Operating Companies play a key role in providing ROLM's Telecommunications Division with the broadest and most effective distribution network in the independent telecommunications industry."[8]

Additional markups that had been charged by these companies are now received by ROLM. The contribution of ROCOs are planned to increase to meet growth objectives.

Another acquisition of one of its distributors is scheduled for 1981. Its New York City location would increase ROCO revenues by 25%.

Perhaps the largest problem facing ROLM in its acquisition of these distribution chains in-

EXHIBIT 3
ROLM Corporation Organizational Chart, January 10, 1981.

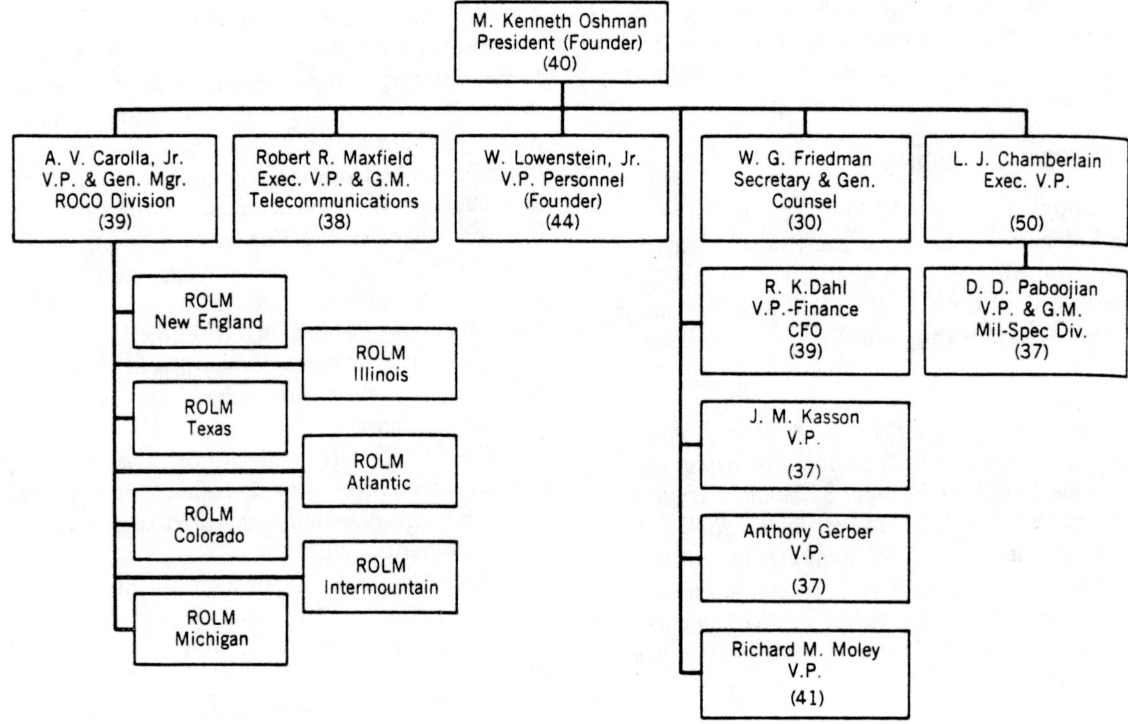

Source: ROLM 1980 Annual Report.

volve personnel. Sales and service are necessary to fully exploit the market potential. Oshman has stated that finding technical personnel to service the digital equipment is extremely difficult in most major metropolitan areas. Sales personnel are more readily available but finding any with experience in selling telecommunications systems is virtually impossible. Corporate executives have voiced concern over the need for more training in benefits received from the products they have developed.

Competition for the work force needed by ROLM will be intense in the coming decade. Engineering personnel of all kinds are desired in computer applications, the construction industry, and manufacturing. The current shortage has affected many firms' plans for product introductions because sufficient cannot be accomplished.

ROLM MANAGEMENT

Richeson, Oshman, Lowenstern, Maxfield (ROLM) began the idea during poker games held after work when all were employed by GTE Sylvania. Each one had attended Rice University in Houston and also received advanced degrees from Stanford University. This close-knit group would move from daydreaming over beer to making strategic decisions that would tie up millions of dollars and thousands of employees. Many of the employees now at ROLM are still surprised with the youth and brains in the company.

Dennis Paboojian, general manager of MIL-SPEC, recalls what ROLM was like in the beginning.

> *When I joined the company in 1972, I felt like an outsider. I had really joined a high-achieving group that could go till 10:00 P.M. every night when we could get an order. There was a different spirit in the company then. There was a spirit of pulling together.*[9]

As might be expected, the founders have not come up with all the splendid ideas that have contributed to meeting the growth objectives of ROLM. One of Paboojian's most memorable occasions was when everyone was sitting around a table discussing whether or not to enter the CBX market. He remembers bringing up the idea as an alternative for growth and then voting against it. Other members of the management group, however, had decided to enter the market and success was found immediately by the acceptance of products introduced from these executives.

Ken Oshman gives a good picture of where the firm has been:

> *I remember calling everyone into the conference room weekly to review not only sales but all prospective sales, and saying, "If we are lucky, we will sell ten computers this quarter." We were in the computer business a year before we decided we could afford a line printer instead of the teletype we were using. Now, I don't know most of the employees, there are no more beer busts till 10 P.M. and my work week is trying to put the pieces together from the past week.*[10]

Bob Maxfield had joined ROLM when it was being formed . . . , "Might as well, I don't have anything else to do." Bob had known the "very bright" engineer at Hewlett-Packard who was recruited to develop the CBX product line. He had also inspired Dick Moley to market the product that would soon become the mainstay of the company.

It was the very businesslike Bob who remembers when he and Ken (in tennis shorts, smoking a cigar) interviewed their first draftsman.

The management staff is very interested in future needs of the company to accommodate the growth desired. Investors will be acquired by increases in stock prices expected. Exhibit 4 shows some of the activity experienced by ROLM in its stock.

EXHIBIT 4
Stock splits

1974	3:1
1976	2:1
1978	2:1
1979	2:1
1980	2:1

Source: Value Line, 1980.

The considerable growth of ROLM has benefited many investors in its 11-year history and is recommended to risk takers who want a stock that may experience price increases. ROLM tries to finance operations by stock offerings. Today, less than 16 million of 40 million authorized are outstanding. Stock holdings of 9.3 million shares in 1975 have increased to greater than 15 million in 1980.

The founders and several key investors, including members of the board, own a significant amount of the stock. Prices have ranged from $1.75 a share in 1976 to $41.50 in 1980. ROLM stock began trading on the New York Stock Exchange (NYSE) in 1979. The future potential for ROLM to investors is largely dependent on how well ROLM succeeds in its growth strategies. Investors must hope that growth pains do not handicap earnings and the ability to finance acquisitions and other needed expenditures.

In an effort to maintain its rapid growth, ROLM is targeting an even larger market: the so called office-of-the-future. Oshman had . . . signed an agreement in January 1980 with Convergent Technologies, Inc., giving ROLM the right to manufacture that company's work station. It is anticipated that growth into marketing facsimile transmitters and "intelligent" copiers will be the next step. Finally, ROLM has indicated that word-processing systems may be developed as well as more computer applications for specific user needs.

ROLM executives are convinced that their new thrust will transform ROLM into a multibillion corporation by the end of the decade. Already, the company's 2-year-old office automation group has a research and development budget of $5 million, or one quarter of the total corporate R & D budget. ROLM will also continue to acquire technology from outside in order to hasten a larger market position in office automation. Though not a division yet, office automation rates as a top priority with Oshman.

Additional strategies for growth encompass adding a stream of new attachments and applications for its CBX products to keep its momentum going. The CBX, which can already store and forward simple messages from one terminal to another, most likely will be upgraded so that users can do such tasks as text editing and maintaining personal schedules.

ROLM will be facing strong competition from such giants as IBM, Xerox, AT&T, and Northern Telecom in the related markets that they wish to pursue.

PERSONNEL/PRODUCTION

The youthful management team at ROLM has managed to acquire many high-caliber employees. Most alarming to top management has been the large increases in employees in the last 2 years and the subsequent loss of contact with day-to-day matters. Instead, it now takes a major planning effort to add additional employees because of the nature of the area in which ROLM is located, Silicon Valley, California. (See Exhibit 5.)

Walter Lowenstern, in charge of personnel and human development has recognized the problem for years:

> *It used to get so bad that we would get Memorex employees in during lunch who were* demanding *that we hire them at exorbitant rates. I'm sure some of our employees were doing the same thing. Memorex has since moved to Dallas, Texas, to escape the lack of loyalty offered by workers in Santa Clara.*[11]

Median incomes in 1980 for Santa Clara were $24,000, or over 40% higher than the national average. Unemployment is below 5%. In 1971, 300,000 people were employed in Santa Clara. Today, over 700,000 people have employment in the area, the majority having involvement in the semiconductor industry of which Santa Clara is the undisputed capital.[12]

Many production employees are involved in routine tasks. To afford respite for those employed in these occupations annual sabbaticals are promoted at ROLM to have employees get involved in either long travel stints or personal interests.

The individual production groups for MIL-SPEC and Telecommunications utilize centralized decision-making systems. ROLM has grown under the very close scrutiny of the founders and continuance of this practice is expected.

New production facilities are being completed to handle the requirements for Telecommunications while gearing up for automated office-of-the-future systems.

EXHIBIT 5
Silicon Valley, California.

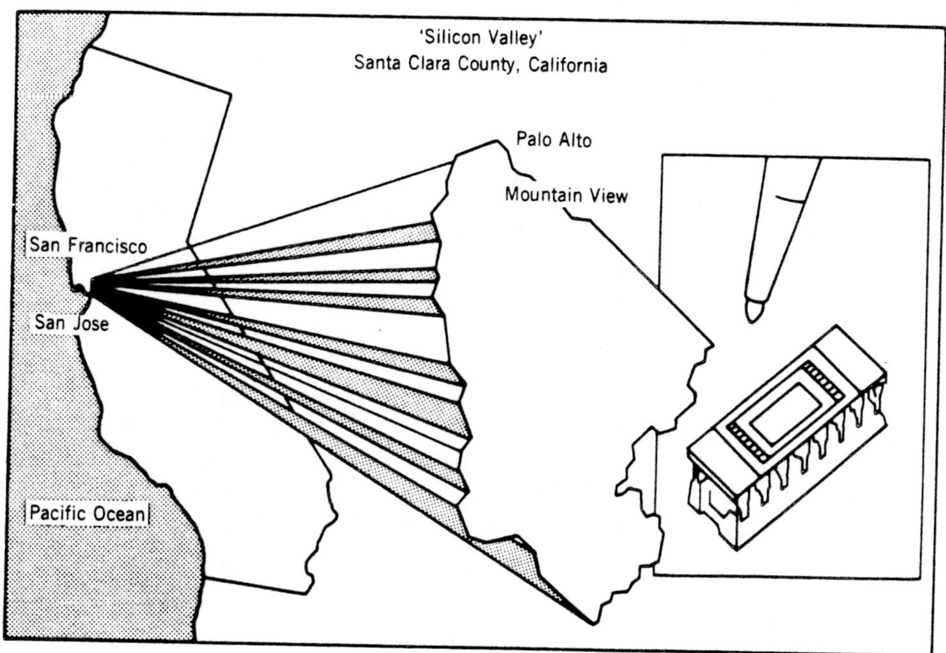

In January 1980, Oshman stated in a press release that Robert Maxfield and Leo Chamberlain, who 6 years ago left Time-Data Corporation to become general manager of MIL-SPEC, were promoted to executive vice presidents to centralize planning activities. Dennis Paboojian, employed by ROLM in 1972, was made general manager of MIL-SPEC. Oshman comments:

> *This decision was necessary because of the company's rapid growth and the number of operating and staff functions which were reporting directly to me. The new organization will allow the top management team to be less involved in the day-to-day operating decisions, to share responsibility, and to focus on long-range plans.*[13]

Employee growth figures as well as net sales per employee (Exhibits 6 and 7) to provide a glimpse at some of the organizational problems that might exist are given.

GOVERNMENT REGULATIONS/LAWS

The communications industry has been under regulation since 1885 when the states, beginning with Indiana, started regulating rates on local telephone service. By 1910, when the Interstate Commerce Commission was granted regulatory authority over interstate phone service, most states were regulating interstate service. Then, the Communications Act of 1934 shifted federal telephone regulation to the newly created Federal Communications Commission (FCC) and at the same time paved the way for AT&T to become a regulated telecommunications monopoly.[14]

Recently, federal regulators have been intent on promoting as much free enterprise as

EXHIBIT 6
ROLM Employee Growth

Source: ROLM Annual Report, 1980.

they can in this industry. The most significant legal action affecting new telecommunications firms was the FCC's Carterfone Communications Corporation decision in 1968. This decision stated, "The Bell System could not prevent or hinder privately owned telephone systems from being connected to their networks."[15]

In 1976, the Consumer Communications Reform Act of 1976 was introduced. Among other things, the act stated, "The FCC may not hold that prices charged by a carrier for a communication service are unjust, unreasonable, or non-compensatory if the price equals or exceeds the incremental costs of providing a communication product or service."[16] This could permit established communications common carriers to provide products or services through existing facilities at prices significantly below those required to be charged by competitors such as ROLM.

EXHIBIT 7
ROLM Net Sales per Employee

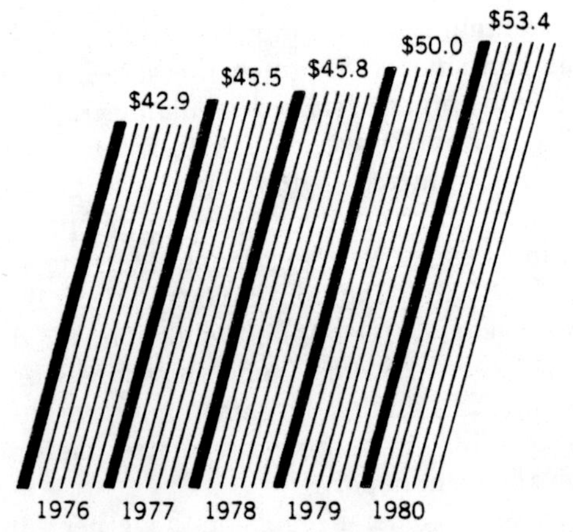

Source: ROLM Annual Report, 1980.

In June 1978, representative Lionel Van Deerlin (D-California), chairman of the House Subcommittee on Communications, introduced the Communications Act of 1978. This act would repeal the Communications Act of 1934, terminate the FCC, and create an entirely new Federal Agency — the Communications Regulatory Commission. It also would permit wide competition in interstate telecommunications.

In April 1980, the FCC issued an order that called for the deregulation of the terminal equipment portion of the telecommunications industry. The order provides that after March 1, 1982, the regulated telephone companies of the Bell System and GTE will no longer be permitted to provide terminal equipment directly to customers. As a result, the two giants will market their equipment through separate subsidiaries that do business with their respective manufacturing subsidiaries.

In response to this activity, a ROLM employee recently stated:

> *These orders by the Federal Communications Commission and new legislation still pending in the House may negatively affect the operations of ROLM. There is a fear that the Bell System and GTE could become more price competitive if there are no safeguards built into the legislation to guard against the two companies use of their financial, marketing, and operational strength to subsidize competitive operations.*

ROLM Corporation and its companies have filed petitions for reconsideration of the FCC order.

FINANCE AND ACCOUNTING

ROLM accounts for income recognition on a completed contract basis for both product lines. Income from sales of MIL-SPEC components and CBXs, which are sold to external interconnect companies, is recognized at the time of shipment. Income from the sale of CBXs through the ROLM operational companies is recognized at cutover. A time line indicating the major milestones in the life of a contract and its definitions are displayed in Exhibit 8. Cash deposits are received from customers as these milestones are reached.

Since keeping costs down is an objective of the company, the revenue and the cost of producing the CBX is monitored. ROLM tries to maintain a 60% standard gross margin in ll CBXs. The management information system is designed to monitor this gross margin. Any exceptions are analyzed by financial analysts and the results are forwarded to the responsible parties.

As mentioned earlier, ROLM has exhibited phenomenal growth since the introduction of its CBX in 1975. Exhibit 9, a five-year financial summary, and Exhibit 10, a comparison of the quarterly financial data for 1980 and 1981, illustrate this growth. During this period sales increased from $20.4 million to $200.7 million —an increase of almost 1,000% in only 4 years. After the first two quarters of 1981, ROLM finds itself with $137.4 million in sales—an increase of 158% over the same period in 1980.

Likwise, net income has increased by 1,372% from 1976 to 1980 and by 149% from the second quarter in 1980 to 1981.

To aid in financing its growth, ROLM offered 1,200,000 shares of common stock to the public on August 26, 1980. In the prospectus, the management group outlined the need for the $41.6 million offering.

EXHIBIT 8
ROLM Corporation contract milestones

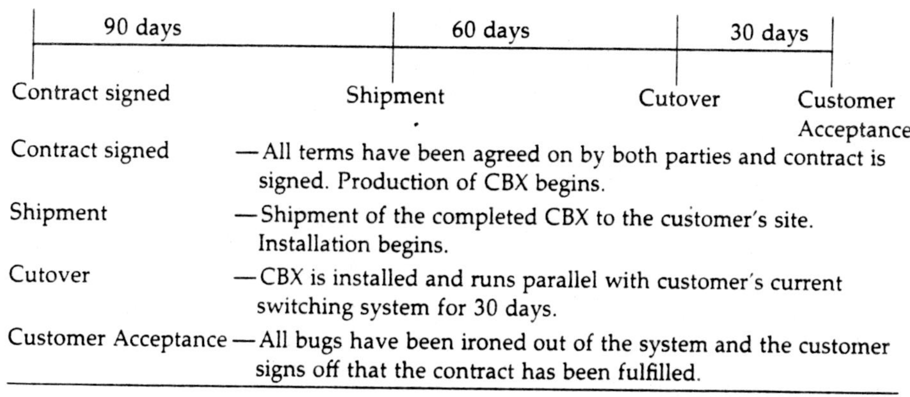

Contract signed —All terms have been agreed on by both parties and contract is signed. Production of CBX begins.

Shipment —Shipment of the completed CBX to the customer's site. Installation begins.

Cutover —CBX is installed and runs parallel with customer's current switching system for 30 days.

Customer Acceptance —All bugs have been ironed out of the system and the customer signs off that the contract has been fulfilled.

EXHIBIT 9
ROLM Corporation financial summary for the five years ended June 27, 1980 (thousands—except per share amounts)

	1980	*1979*	*1978*	*1977*	*1976*
Net Sales	$200,729	$121,092	$55,815	$34,913	$20,357
Cost of Sales	95,306	59,817	29,753	18,505	10,627
Product Development	13,379	7,032	3,824	2,943	1,861
Marketing, Administrative and General	58,474	31,085	14,364	9,563	5,369
Provision for Income Taxes	16,230	11,510	3,960	1,907	1,236
Net Income	$ 17,340	$ 11,648	$ 3,914	$ 1,995	$ 1,264
Earnings per share	$ 2.17	1.49	0.53	0.29	0.23
Common and common equivalent shares	7,995	7,810	7,326	6,880	5,484

Source: ROLM 1980 Annual Report.

EXHIBIT 10
ROLM Corporation 1980 and 1981 quarterly financial information (thousand—except per share amounts)

1980	*Fourth quarter*	*Third quarter*	*Second quarter*	*First quarter*
Net Sales	$62,564	$50,919	$45,970	$41,276
Cost of Sales	29,679	24,604	21,028	19,995
Product Development	4,162	3,640	3,001	2,576
Marketing, Administrative and General	18,746	14,168	14,189	11,371
Provision for Income Taxes	4,822	4,115	3,747	3,546
Net Income	$ 5,155	$ 4,392	$ 4,005	$ 3,788
Earnings per share	$ 0.64	$ 0.55	$ 0.50	$ 0.48
Common and Common Equivalent Shares	8,020	8,010	7,947	7,909

1981	*Fourth quarter*	*Third quarter*	*Second quarter*	*First quarter*
Net Sales			$70,831	$66,563
Cost of Sales			34,320	30,110
Product Development			4,681	4,689
Marketing, Administrative and General			20,205	21,072
Provision for Income Taxes			5,580	5,154
Net Income			6,045	5,538
Earnings per Share			$ 0.35	$ 0.34
Common and Common Equivalent Shares			17,385	16,397

Source: ROLM 1980 Annual Report.

The proceeds will be used to finance the cost of additional manufacturing, product development, and administrative facilities currently being constructed or the construction of which is scheduled to commence during the current fiscal year, to purchase land that will be available for other construction in future years and to repay $9 million of short-term borrowings expected to be outstanding at the time of receipts of these proceeds. These borrowings were incurred to finance working capital requirements.

Management has noticed that return on assets, asset turns, and inventory turns have declined over the last several years. Also, cost of goods sold as a percentage of sales has increased; however, management has not expressed any concern over these statistics, citing them as a "natural outcome of a growth strategy."

Consolidated balance sheets for ROLM Corporation are provided in Exhibit 11.

ROLM OUTLOOK

The founders' minds returned from their wandering as Oshman's phone rang. On the end of the line was the production manager who was again complaining about not being able to complete the schedules given him.

We'll be down to talk to you about it later. Everyone here is aware of the circumstances. See what you can work out in the meantime.

Getting back to the business at hand, Oshman inquired, "Our momentum is carrying us

EXHIBIT 11
ROLM Corporation consolidated balance sheets (thousands)

Assets	*December 26, 1980*	*June 27, 1980*	*June 29, 1979*
Current Assets			
Cash and Cash Equivalents	$ 28,367	$ 3,411	$ 1,913
Accounts Receivable	36,885	30,441	19,442
Inventories	51,858	37,421	24,812
Prepaid Expenses	2,218	1,759	1,380
Total Current Assets	$119,328	$ 73,032	$47,547
Net Property, Plant and Equipment	60,327	44,553	16,541
Total Assets	$179,655	$117,585	$64,088
Liabilities and Shareholders' Equity			
Current Liabilities	$ 15,662	$ 16,314	$ 8,880
Accrued Expenses	32,168	25,059	18,683
Total Current Liabilities	$ 47,830	$ 41,373	$27,563
Long-term Debt	27,002	26,049	6,541
Common Stock and Paid-in Capital	54,915	11,838	8,999
Retained earnings	49,908	38,325	20,985
Total shareholders' equity	104,823	50,163	29,984
Total Liabilities and Shareholders' Equity	$179,655	$117,585	$64,088

Source: 1980 ROLM Annual Report.

forward in the short run but I don't expect it to carry us past 1982, do you?"

Bob Maxfield answered first, "I see a bright outlook for MIL-SPEC because of its increased acceptance for industrial uses. These include the petroleum industry and even agriculture. Increasing R & D in MIL-SPEC might give us long-range benefits we hadn't considered before."

Lowenstern commented to both, "Risks are smaller with MIL-SPEC, I'll agree, but what about our plans to attack the automated office? It's a whole new ballgame!"

Oshman turned and replied, "All of us want to continue with our growth plans. To commit the resources we'll need definite strategies before I'll allow any changes to current practices. I want a detailed planning package on July 1, 1981, to check against where the marketplace is going as indicated by the Market Programs and Services Group. I believe they've hit the nail on the head."

Lowenstern replied, "Let's check with Chamberlain to get his input. I suggest we have a two-day session out of the office to go over the main points of our planning requirements. We could have it the week of the twenty-third."

With that, Maxfield and Lowenstern left Oshman to work out the details of the meeting. If ROLM were to survive as an independent entity as envisioned by the founders, planning would be a crucial ingredient.

BIBLIOGRAPHY

1. Marketing Programs and Services Group, *Telecommunications in the 1980's: Interconnect, New Competition and Automated Office Product Migration* (Gaithersburg, 1980), pp. 1–2.
2. "Rolm's Leap into Office Automation," *Business Week:* February 16, 1981, p. 78.
3. ROLM Corporation News Release, No. 81–601, February 5, 1981.
4. Value Line, 1980.
5. Prospectus for Stock Offering, August 1980.
6. ROLM Employee Newsletter, Special 10-Year Edition
7. ROLM Corporation, 10K Report, 1978, p. 7.
8. ROLM Corporation, 1980 Annual Report.
9. Ibid.
10. Ibid.
11. *Dallas Morning News,* "Trouble in Semi-Paradise," March 10, 1981.
12. Ibid.
13. ROLM News Release, January 10, 1980.
14. "Compromising the Regulatory Restraints," *Business Week,* November 6, 1978, p. 30.
15. Ibid.
16. Ibid.

EXERCISE 12–11

- Describe and explain your assessment of the position on the product life cycle for ROLM's major product/service offerings.
- List the company's major competitive advantages and describe its likely role in the marketplace (i.e., Dominant Leader, Prospector, Claim Defender). Explain your reasoning.
- What is your assessment of the company's willingness to undertake risk? Support your assertions, if possible, with evidence from the case.
- The company has recently undertaken a strategic "new thrust." (See several

paragraphs under the subhead, ROLM Management.) What type of general strategy is this? Explain.

- Given your analysis thus far, what comments do you have about management's choice of strategy.

EXERCISE 12-12

If you were asked to serve as a strategy consultant to ROLM, what would you recommend as a desirable general strategy? Explain your recommendation in detail as a written memorandum or prepare for a verbal presentation in class.

As a second part of this set of recommendations, develop strategic guidelines for marketing, R & D, production/operations, and financial management.

13

IMPLEMENTING A CHOSEN STRATEGY

In Chapter 12 we developed the notion that external conditions and the strengths or weaknesses of our organization are major contingencies that must be considered in selecting an array of potential strategies for the firm engaged in a single business. We made use of the product life cycle as a general framework, against which strategies for Dominating Leader, Prospector, and Claim Defender firms could be examined. In this chapter, we will continue to follow the model seen in Figure 13–1 and will address the first steps in the implementation of strategies, the establishment of organization, and the broad policies needed to guide management action. (See shaded areas in Figure 13–1.) We will once again make use of a contingency approach and will examine those factors that have been found to call for different organizational forms and practices in one set of circumstances than in another. We will be following the leadership of Chandler who in 1962 made clear the wisdom of the concept that

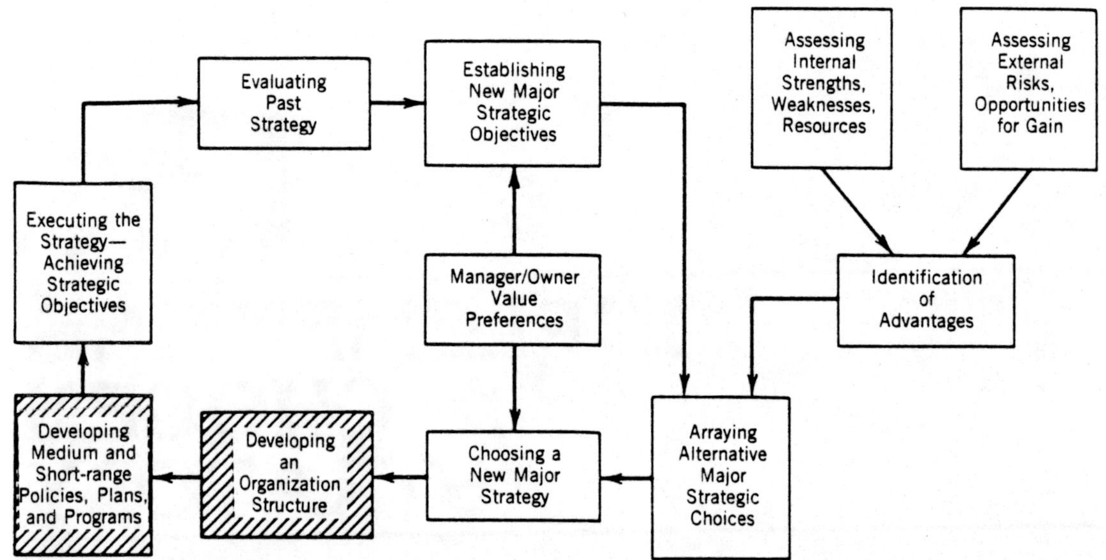

FIGURE 13–1 The strategy-formulation process.

organization structure *follows* strategy.[1] We will also examine some of the research concerning the contingencies of environmental change on organizational design. We will then describe some of the typical organizational forms and their advantages and disadvantages.

Following this descriptive introduction, we then move through the product-life-cycle diagram, much as was done in Chapter 12, and propose some organizational forms for Dominating Leaders, Prospectors, and Claim Defenders. In addition, general suggestions will be made as to appropriate degrees of centralization or decentralization of management decision making and the general characteristics needed for staffing each of the major functions in the organization.

MAJOR CONTINGENCIES AND ORGANIZATIONAL DESIGN

Growth and Size

Organization theorists have long held that organization design is dramatically affected by increases in size. Chandler, among others, held that as an organization's growth objectives were sought (thus following a growth strategy), the type of organization would evolve from a simple unifunctional organization to a multifunction, single-product form and from that to a multidivisional form capable of dealing with

[1] A. D. Chandler, Jr., *Strategy and Structure* (Cambridge, Mass.: MIT Press, 1962), pp. 13–14.

the problems of multiple products.[2] The work of Chandler has been explored by a large body of research. Galbraith and Nathanson,[3] following an extensive review of theoretical and empirical research, describe a model of the dynamics of growth through stages. The entire model deals with development through multibusinesses to the global multinational firm; thus it carries us beyond the scope of the single business. The early stages of the model seen in Figure 13-2, however, deal explicitly with the single-business firm, and serve to provide a graphic guide to changes in organization form as the organization increases in size and complexity. In its origins, the organization makes use of the simple (or entrepreneurial-organization) form in dealing with a single product or service. Functional responsibilities are shared and departmentalization in minimal. As the volume of business increases, the need for specialization and departmentalization becomes increasingly apparent. Administrative responsibilites are separated from operations and functional assignments are made to clarify roles and responsibilities. Coordination, or *integration,* (in the terms of

[2] Chandler, *Strategy and Structure,* p. 362.

[3] J. R. Galbraith and D. A. Nathanson, *Strategy Implementation: The Role of Structure and Process* (St. Paul, Minn.: West, 1978).

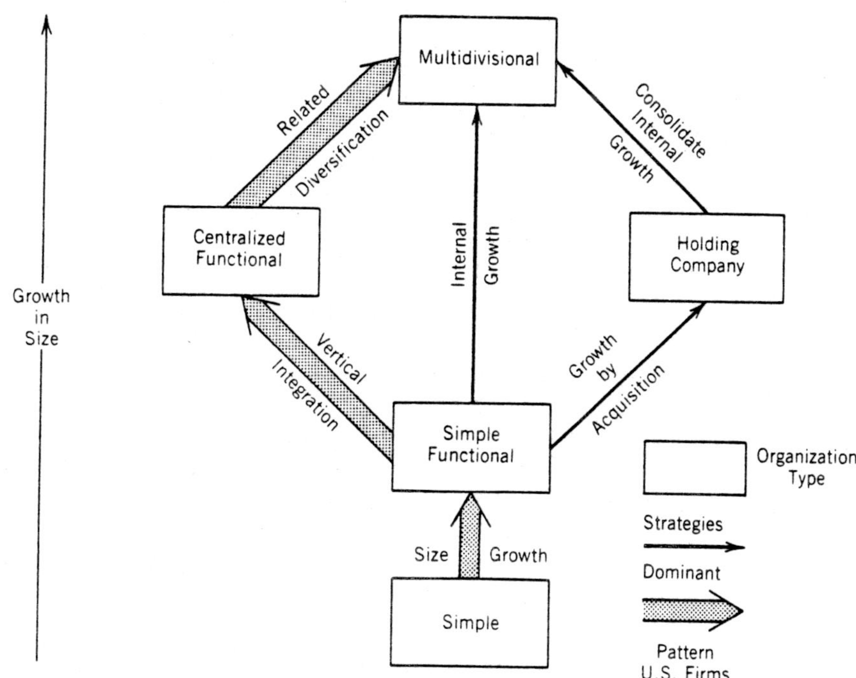

FIGURE 13-2 Organization evolution through growth—single-business companies. Adapted from J. R. Galbraith and D. A. Nathanson, *Strategy Implementation: The Role of Structure and Process* (St. Paul, Minn.: West, 1978), p. 115.

Lawrence and Lorsch)[4] is handled initially by the sharing of tasks and a high level of multidirectional, informal communication. As increases in volume bring about departmentalization into functional subdivisions, much of the responsibility for coordination shifts to the formally defined administrator.

The simple functional organization can grow through internal development into a very large corporation. The coordinative mechanisms that served the smaller functional organization become less capable of dealing with the scale of operations and with the refinements of functional specialists' interests and concerns. Geographic divisionalization helps to deal with the scale of operations and subfunctionalization assists in coordinating the work of highly specialized functions.

As the scope of marketing and manufacturing extends beyond the personal control of the single manager, for example, that person may choose to name persons to be in charge of these respective functions within geographic areas. Thus, a marketing manager may be asked to direct marketing in a sales territory, a state, or a multistate region. Similarly, as multiple manufacturing facilities are established, managers may be assigned the responsibility for operations at that location.

In addition to the geographic expansion, however, subspecialties will also be needed. In operations, specialists in facilities planning, order scheduling, industrial engineering, quality control, or information systems, for example, will be needed as volume increases. Intermediate level managers will be employed to coordinate the activities of these specialists and to integrate their efforts with those of other members of the operations function.

A similar subfunctional development can be found in other major functions. In marketing, marketing research, advertising, merchandising, promotion, public relations, and product development, specialists may be needed as organization size increases. In finance, financial accounting, cost accounting, data processing, construction accounting, stockholder relations, bank relations, cash management, still other specialists will be needed. As with operations, the use of intermediate-level managers assists in integrating these activities *within* the functional organizational form.

Growth through related diversification can also lead to a multidivisional form. In some organizations, product managers are assigned the responsibility for marketing a particular product within the otherwise functional organization. In other instances, where manufacturing technologies differ but where the marketing can be consolidated, manufacturing is separated organizationally but products are marketed through the same distribution channels. Once again, a functional organization is maintained, with some divisionalization used to focus attention on the areas that require specialized product-oriented attention.

In American industry, the empirical evidence indicates that the predominant growth pattern is that depicted by the heavy arrow in Figure 13–2.[5] In this path, the early functional organization evolves into one that makes use of vertical integration to

[4] Paul R. Lawrence and Jay W. Lorsch, "Differentiation and Integration in Complex Organization," *Administrative Science Quarterly* (June 1967), p. 4.

[5] Galbraith and Nathanson, *Strategy Implementation*, p. 114.

assure sources of supply, to capture markets, and to increase profit potential. These organizations will maintain a highly specialized functional character. The operations function is often divisionalized by sequential portions of the conversion process. The steel and paper industries are examples of vertically integrated organizations. In steel, the operations function is departmentalized by raw materials (limestone, ore, coal), primary (iron) production, BOF (steel) production, blooming/slabbing mills (semifinished steel), and a variety of product-oriented production operations such as merchant bar mills, structural steel mills, hot rolled strip, cold rolled strip, galvanized strip, or tin plate strip mills.

Despite the departmentalization, the vertically integrated organization described is nonetheless a functionalized organizational form. As a result, the vertically integrated company will be highly centralized in nature. As this organization seeks to balance its operational resources, it may seek to make use of its strengths in one segment of its integrated operation and sell its products to others in its industry. Paper companies with excess papermill capacity will market paper or pulp to other converters. Steel companies with excess conversion and marketing capacity may purchase "foreign" steel for conversion and sale from companies with available steel making capacity. New related products may be added to the product line to support the primary product or to make use of an effective distribution and marketing organization. Ultimately, this may lead to the multidivisional organization, once again divisionalized to provide the specialized attention needed by either the technology of operations or the specialized demands of customers.

EXERCISE 13-1

Your company, Bonny-Belle Sportswear, has grown from its earliest days, when you, three family members, and a co-worker founded the company. Now, your organization employs 75 people. The marketing group, under the direction of your brother, contains 15 persons. It has 5 people in sales service (3 for inside sales, 2 for order expediting). Nine sales representatives cover three regions: Boston and New England; New York, Philadelphia, and Washington; and the coastal southeast—from Richmond, Virginia, south to and including Florida. The production shop operates on two shifts—approximately 25 persons plus a supervisor per shift—and has cutting, sewing, pressing and finishing, and shipping departments. In the office, your sister, who serves as chief accountant, has payroll, invoicing, accounts payable, and general ledger departments. She handles the duties of cashier.

- To what stage of organizational growth has the company developed?
- If it has passed through more than a single stage, describe each stage. Explain your reasoning.
- Do you see any variance from the general organization form described? Explain and describe the variation or variations.

On the opposite side of the model, the functional organization can grow through the acquisition of companies in the same industry. Initially, these acquisitions may be permitted to operate as semiautonomous units in a holding company relationship. Should there appear to be advantages to be gained through the elimination of duplicative services, consolidation may be needed. The organization that had been a holding company will now be configured as a multidivisionalized organization, sharing key executives and some major business functions and services.

Organizations may be seen to move rapidly through a sequence of strategies and their needed structures or may remain in one stage for extended periods of time. Attainment of one stage does not necessarily mean that a company will remain at that stage. As events evolve, the organization may move backward to an earlier organizational stage. If, for example, a multidivisionalized firm finds a division unprofitable and divests, it may revert to the earlier centralized functional form.

In conclusion, we can see that the natural processes of organizational adaptation to growth and the complexities of size lead to a sequence of changes in organizational form. As Figure 13-1 indicates, changes can occur in different patterns, however the sequence found most frequently in American industry (the bold directional arrows in Figure 13-2) seems to show a change from simple organizational forms through vertical integration to a centralized functional organization and then through related diversification to a multidivisionalized organization.

EXERCISE 13-2

Refer back to the organization described in Exercise 13-1. If Bonny-Belle Sportswear continues to grow, how would you expect the organization to change? Please be specific and describe the changes you anticipate.

Environmental Change

Three field research studies offer insights and guidelines into the relationship between organizational structure and environmental factors. The first, a field study conducted in Great Britain in the late 1950s, examined the effect of technology on organization configuration. Generally speaking, the study found three general organizational shapes that could be linked to particular technologies. Where the technology was relatively simple and where *small lots or one-of-a-kind* products were produced, the organization tended to be relatively shallow (fewer layers) and relatively broad (wide span of control). In *mass-production* technologies in which technological complexity is high, organizations tended to have a larger number of layers and moderate spans of control at the upper and middle levels, with significantly wider spans of control at the bottom of the organization. In *process* technologies such as the paper, oil, or chemical industries technologies are advanced and the number of layers in these organizations is much greater than in the other two forms of technology. In addition, spans of control tend to be relatively narrow throughout the entire organization.[6]

EXERCISE 13–3

- Consider the social dynamics of organizations. In what ways would you expect the organizational structures described to be reflected in the relationships of persons employed in those organizations? Why?
- Which would you expect to appeal to persons who enjoy independence? Why?
- Which would you expect to appeal to persons who enjoy a relatively predictable work environment? Why?
- In which organization would you feel closer to, or more a part of, the strategic direction of the company? Why?

A second study, published in the early 1960s, found that two general organizational types represented different reactions to environmental change. In stable environments with established industries, organizations were found to be much more formal, had clearly delineated hierarchical forms, vertical communication patterns, and centralized, hierarchical decision making. This organization was labeled a *mechanistic organization,* a name that has come to be used to include the bureaucratic concepts of Max Weber and the structuring management principles of Fayol, Mooney and Reiley, Follett, and Urwick.[7]

In environments in which technologies and markets changed rapidly, companies adopted an organic organization in which roles were less clearly defined and organizational relationships both less formal and less rigid. In the organic organization, communication patterns are multidirectional and decision making tends to be decentralized and based on the influence of expertise as opposed to position in the hierarchy.[8] The organic organization is flexible and adaptable. Although the mechanistic organization seeks to maximize efficiency by departmentalization to achieve functional accountability and centralized authority. The organic organization seeks to achieve effectiveness through the encouragement of the maximum use of human resources.[9]

[6] J. Woodward, *Management and Technology* (London: HMSO, 1958).

[7] J. L. Gibson, J. M. Ivancevich, and J. H. Donnelly, Jr., *Organizations.* 5th Ed. (Plano, Tex.: Business Publications, 1985), pp. 488–89.

[8] Tom Burns, and G. M. Stalker, *The Management of Innovation* (London: Tavistock Publications, 1961), pp. 119–125.

[9] Gibson et al., *Organizations,* p. 492.

EXERCISE 13-4

- List two or three industries that you consider to be relatively unstable, uncertain in direction, and in which a high rate of change is the normal state of affairs.
- Select one and describe how an organic organization form might be of help in meeting the specific conditions you believe exist in that industry.
- What would be the consequences if a company attempted to use a relatively mechanistic system in that environment? Explain.

EXERCISE 13-5

- Consider the case of a major university or a state agency. Explain why a relatively mechanistic, or bureaucratic, organization is believed to be well suited to dealing with this type of environment.
- What would be the consequences of making use of an organic organization form for one of these organizations?

The third field research study, published in 1967, examined the performance of firms in industries characterized as having high, moderate, or low levels of environmental change. The study found that organizations adapted to technological and market change by means of two related processes: (1) *differentiation*, a form of specialization used as a means of dealing with turbulence in the environment and (2) *integration*, the mechanism needed to pull together the disparate specialties that differentiation created.

Organizations that performed well in a stable environment (container manufacture) tended to be less differentiated, relatively centralized, and required less attention to integration than firms in more turbulent or uncertain environments. The primary methods used to integrate differentiated functions in these container industry organizations were direct managerial contact and the organizational hierarchy. The high-performing organization in a moderately dynamic environment (the food industry) made use of individual integrators in research and marketing, temporary cross-functional teams, and extensive direct contact among affected managers.

The better-performing organizations in uncertain environments (the plastics industry) tended to be very highly differentiated and, as a consequence, required a significantly greater attention to integration. Differentiated units or functions were integrated through such organizational mechanisms as integrative departments or permanent cross-functional teams at several levels of management. Direct managerial contact and the hierarchy were used less extensively than in organizations in environments that were more stable and certain.

Decision making in companies in the food and plastics industries (moderate and high levels of environmental change) tended to be much more decentralized than was the case in the container industry. Indeed, in the moderately dynamic environment, the high-performing food company displayed higher levels of influence in decision making at low levels in the organizations than at the upper levels.[10]

EXERCISE 13-6

For each of the following industries, indicate the types of integrating mechanisms one might expect to find in the organization, explain why, and provide some illustrative job or department titles for the integrating person or department:

- Electric Power Generation
- Commercial or Industrial Building Construction
- Clothing Manufacture
- Consumer Electronics Manufacture and Sales
- Hospitals
- Ethical (Prescription) Drug Manufacture and Sales
- A Restaurant
- Toy Retailers

ORGANIZATIONAL TYPES

The Simple Organization

The simple organization has very little structure and is typically used to accomplish a single function (see Figure 13-3). Examples might include an artisan's shop, a real estate agency, or other types of organizations in which the operatives act as agents of the owner or director. In prebureaucratic political organizations, members of the political head's official family served as extensions of the power of that person's office. In law enforcement, the officer or agent represents the full power of that agency and can act on its behalf. In its simpler form, operatives fall under the direct supervision of the owner or manager, and they derive their general and specific instructions from the owner rather than from formalized descriptions of duties. To some extent, the office of the president of the United States functions in this fashion. Key subordinates serve at the personal instruction of the president and carry a substantial portion of the influence of the president in their dealings with agencies outside the White House. Duties of incumbents will shift markedly from day to day and from president to president. The simple organization is often found in entrepreneurial situations in which the organization's needs change rapidly and the duties of

[10] Ibid, Lawrence and Lorsch, *Organization and Environment*, pp. 142-43.

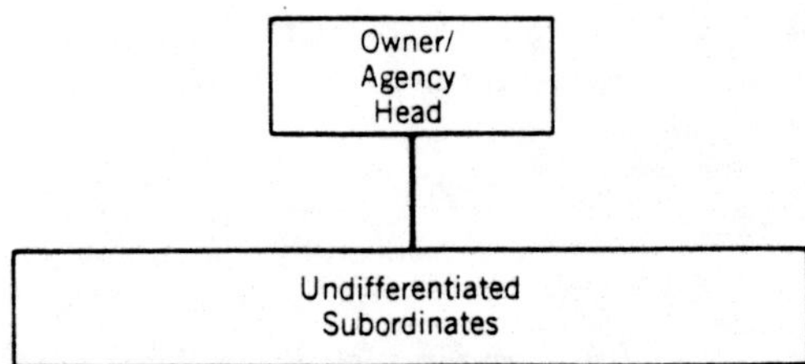

FIGURE 13–3 Simple organization.

operatives and the entrepreneur must adapt to the needs of the organization. Coordination and task assignment will be handled personally by the entrepreneur, a factor that provides great flexibility and rapid response, but one that is necessarily limiting owing to the availability and capabilities of the owner. Relationships will tend to be largely patriarchal and personalized.

Advantages The advantages of the simple organization include ease of control, adaptability to changing market and organizational needs, rapidity in decision making, and informality in relationships.

Disadvantages The disadvantages of the simple organization include difficulty in dealing with complexity in the environment, the large scale of the operations, and a tendency to overload the owner/manager. In addition, managers tend to focus on here-and-now issues rather than longer range problems, and they often fail to develop other managers.[11]

The Functional Organization

The functional organization represents a division of labor, or departmentalization, of the organization by divisions into identifiable specialized portions of the entire task (see Figure 13–4). Business functions include Marketing, Operations, Finance, R & D, Personnel Administration, and a variety of other specialties. Within each major function, other specialties are also found. In a personnel department, for example, labor negotiations, wage and salary administration, employee benefits administration, and personnel planning represent specialized areas of functional concern to the operations of the overall department. A large personnel department is quite frequently organized in such a way as to include subdepartments along the lines of these specialties. In a similar fashion, the manufacturing function may contain such specialized departments as industrial engineering, scheduling, and facilities planning as well as process specialties such as sheet metal fabrication, machining, welding, engine

[11] J. A. Pearce II and R. B. Robinson, Jr., *Strategic Management* 2nd Ed. (Homewood Ill.: R. D. Irwin, 1985), pp. 323–24.

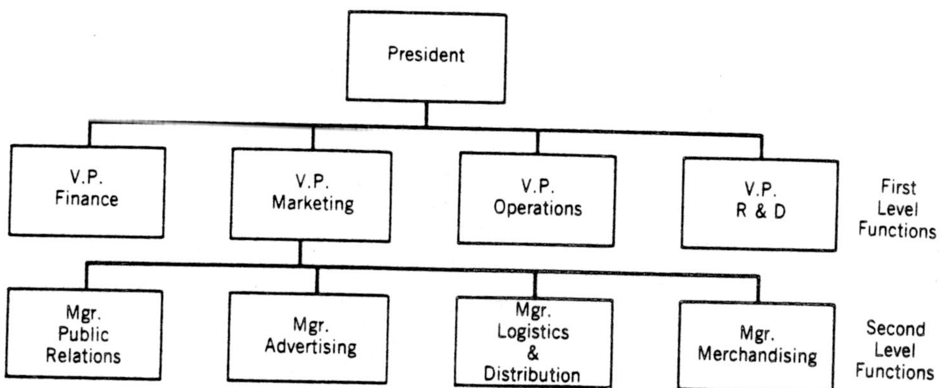

FIGURE 13-4 Functional organization.

rebuild, dynamometer testing, painting, and assembly. (These examples were taken from a vehicle maintenance facility in the organization of a major military base.) Similar forms of specialization and functional departmentalization can be found in marketing, finance, and administrative offices. In each case, the departmentalization is based on areas of specialized knowledge, experience, or training and on a task assignment that focuses on that function as the primary orientation of the operatives. Specialized, shared facilities often can become part of the functional organizational arrangement. As one example, a library, a media center, a computer center, or an athletic facility can serve as an *organizational* function for organizations such as colleges or universities or for larger corporations. Although they are not directly involved in the processes of the mainstream of the organization's activities, their facilities serve as important adjuncts to the main thrust of organizational direction.

EXERCISE 13-7

Sketch an organizational chart that utilizes a functional design and incorporates the following job titles:

Sales Service Supervisor
Accounts Payable Clerk
Shift Supervisor — Manufacturing
Plant Manager
Office Manager
Sales Representative
Office Receptionist
Chief Accountant

Payroll Clerk
Warehouse Clerk
Warehouse Laborer
Machine Operator—Manufacturing
Forklift Operator—Manufacturing
Forklift Operator—Warehouse
Janitor—Office
Janitor—Factory
Maintenance Worker
Supervisor—Maintenance and Janitorial
Invoicing Clerk
Machine Adjuster
Factory Labor
Factory Scheduler
Warehouse Supervisor
Factory Superintendent

Advantages The functional organization provides clarity in task assignment and the opportunity for specialization to meet the advanced and changing needs of technology. It also offers a layering of specialized management attention that provides concentrated expertise in areas of special importance to the organization. Control of strategic decision making, that which must involve cross-functional interests, is maintained by top management.

Disadvantages The most significant difficulty encountered by functional organizations relates to problems encountered as the organization increases in size. The multiple layers of management in large organizations and the separation by functions often creates an organization that is slow to respond to cross-functional problems. The formal cross-functional decision-making authority resides at the top. Decisions affecting the lower levels of two functions must move up through both functions to the top, then back through the same layering to operative level. In many functional organizations, ladders for cross-functional communication are established to deal with relatively routine needs.

The functional organization tends to encourage narrow specialization, can promote suboptimization, and may be the source of difficulty in sharing interests and concerns—or outright conflict. Finally, although the layering of functional specialists provides for a high level of expert managerial attention to problems in each function, it also offers little opportunity for functional managers to fully appreciate the important elements in other functions or to practice the skills required to integrate across several functions.

The Divisional Organizational Structure

The problems associated with organizational growth in the functional organization can result in the establishment of a divisionalized structure. As the number of distinctly different products is increased, functional specialists may find that the skills developed in manufacturing or marketing the first product do not transfer well into a different technology, channels of distribution, or target customer group. An organizational arrangement that enables functional specialists to focus their attentions on the unique technologies and problems of a single product/market, therefore becomes increasingly important. Similarly, as the geographic distribution of the company's markets expands, the logistics of managing widely separated sales territories, manufacturing facilities, and distribution centers becomes burdensome if handled on a centralized functional basis.

The product or geographically divisionalized organization evolves naturally from the smaller functional organization as the organization seeks to broaden its offerings and grow in size. Its arrangement (seen in Figure 13–4) often takes the form of a product or geographic identification immediately below the level of the chief executive and key executive staff. Within the product or geographic divisions, the organization may be arranged by product, geography, or function (see Figure 13–5). Divisionalization can also be used to provide specialized service to different identifiable customer groups. In some industries, departmentalization for service to individual consumers, institutional customers, military organizations, or original-equipment manufacturers may be the means of meeting each customer group's unique requirements for products, delivery, or specialized marketing. In the case of fleet-vehicle sales, while the product may be essentially identical to that sold to the general public, the needs of the fleet owner and the mix of appeals to the purchaser will dictate a different type of sales presentation and a different form of marketing than would be the case in a sale to an individual customer.

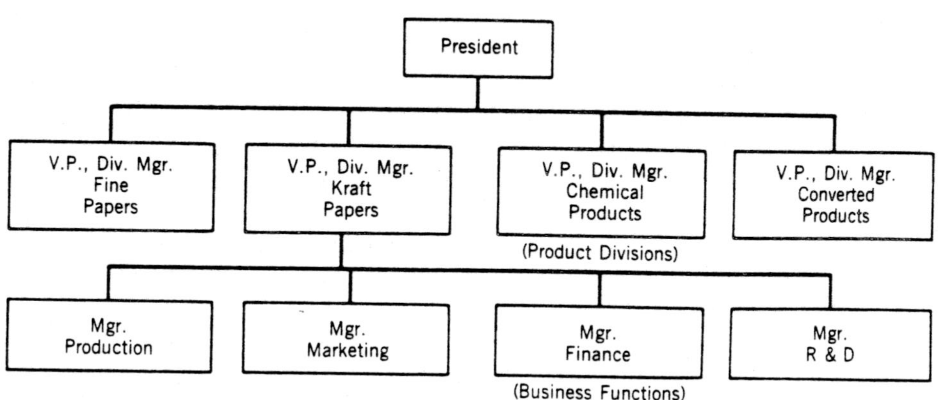

FIGURE 13–5 Divisionalized organization.

EXERCISE 13-8

Your organization manufactures five closely associated products: innersoles, outersoles, counters, heels, and inner liners for shoes. You have been selling these products throughout the country and internationally through six geographic regional offices: New York, Atlanta, Chicago, San Francisco, London, and Tokyo. Your operations include: marketing, manufacturing, R & D, personnel administration, financial accounting, managerial (cost) accounting, and data processing. Sketch the following organizational structures:

- An organization by product at the first level below the president, then by geographic division, and finally by function.
  - Where would you expect coordination and integration needs to be in this organization? Explain.
- An organization by geographic region at the first level below the president, then by product, and finally by function.
  - Would the coordination and integration needs be different in this type of divisionalized organization? Explain.

Advantages The divisionalized organization is particularly well suited to growing organizations. As products or geographic areas are added, new product or geographic divisions can be added to accommodate the need for supervision and control. When the number of product divisions becomes quite large, groups of products are clustered under the management attention of group executives. In addition to the ease of dealing with growth, the product or geographic division permits a meaningful delegation of decision making to levels appropriate for the decision involved. Responsibility for performance can be clearly delineated, and the development and implementation of strategies can be accomplished by persons most knowledgeable about the unique circumstances of that operating unit. Functional specialization can be retained in the divisionalized organization while providing the training and proving ground for managers needed at high levels in the organization.

Disadvantages The disadvantages of the divisionalized organization relate to the degree of delegation. With a high degree of delegation, problems in the interpretation and execution of corporatewide policy can exist. In addition, competition for resources between divisions can result in suboptimal performance and intraorganizational conflict. The divisionalized organization may also have difficulty in negotiating transfer prices for goods and services "purchased" from within the organization. Further, the allocation of large overhead expenses among operating divisions can be the source of conflict, distortion of operating results, and misallocation of capital and managerial resources.[12]

[12] Pearce and Robinson, *Strategic Management*, p. 326.

Simultaneous Organizational Forms

Several types of organization structures can be described as simultaneous structures because they explicitly incorporate two types of structure. In most, a functional structure is combined with either a product or a project management form. The result is one of several types of organizations used to provide the high level of technical expertise of the functional organization to bear on the problems of one or more products or projects. The resulting matrix of influence has caused the most widely discussed simultaneous organizational form to be described as a matrix organization. The matrix organization (Figure 13–6) is often a fairly permanent organizational system for assigning functional specialists and project leaders to tasks in which project accomplishment is the typical pattern of organizational operations. Thus, although a particular task may last a few weeks or months, the basic framework of the matrix is relatively permanent, and it is used for a succession of other projects. Other, very similar forms are the task force and the project team. These, however, are organizations formed on an *ad hoc* basis to meet relatively infrequent needs for an assemblage of functional specialists. In all of the forms of simultaneous organization, the balance of influence can be arranged to favor functions or to lean more heavily

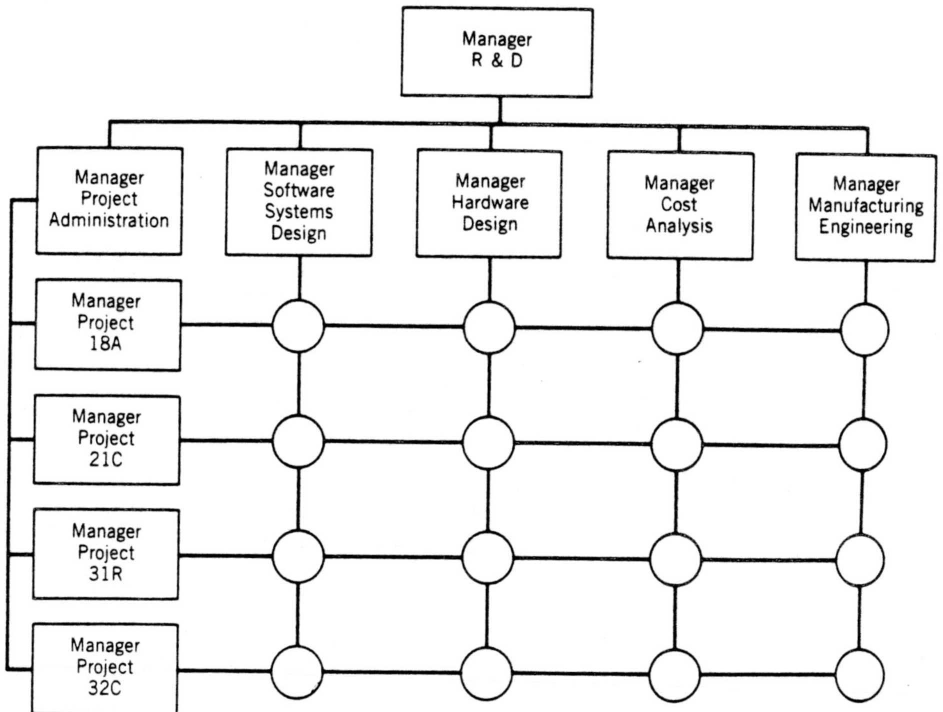

FIGURE 13–6 Matrix organization.

toward product or project authority. The choice of influence will depend on the circumstances and the task. Where a high degree of functional coordination and a responsiveness to market demands are needed, the influence patterns are likely to favor the product or project over functions.[13]

Project duration is a key ingredient in both design and influence. Generally speaking, shorter-duration projects will favor the use of task forces or project teams. Although short-term direction may reside with the task force leader, long-term career direction and supervision will remain with the function. As products become established and market demands clarified, product-oriented organization forms and product divisions become the predominant form and functional specialists find relatively permanent assignments within the product division.

Duration of projects is also a determinant in the influence pattern within the more permanent matrix organization. First, longer-term projects may involve the assignment of functional specialists to sites remote from functional headquarters for extended periods. Functional supervision, under these circumstances, is at best difficult. Second, the high visibility and importance of some longer-range projects may suggest that the dominant authority be that of the project leader. Under these circumstances, the head of a particular function may serve to assist in the selection of appropriate functional specialists and as an advisor and monitor of functional performance but be without direct supervisory control of that functional specialty.

EXERCISE 13–9

Your construction consulting company has a set of functional departments:

Engineering:
- *a Site Layout*
- *b Drainage and Piping*
- *c Architectural—Building*
- *d Heating, Ventilating, Air-conditioning*
- *e Sanitation*
- *f Structural*

R & D:
- *a Materials Research*
- *b Construction Technologies and Methods*
- *c Energy Technologies, including Solar*

Marketing:
- *a Consumer Behavior*
- *b Market Analysis and Assessment Research*
- *c Direct Sales*
- *d Product Assessment and Aesthetics Research*

[13] Galbraith and Nathanson, *Strategy Implementation*, pp. 70–74.

Finance:

a Internal Financial Management
b Institutional Relations
c Customer Servicing—Financing
d Financial Planning and Forecasting

Construction Operations:

a Site Superintendents
b Purchasing and Materials Logistics
c Work force Planning and Acquisition

Your consultation project list and the functional specialists needed, (abbreviated, e.g., as F[c], which stands for Finance: Customer Servicing—Financing) are:

Project No. 1. Duration 22 months. Needed: R(c), M(a), F(c,d), C(a,b,c).

Project No. 2. Duration 40 months. Needed: E(b,e), M(b,c), F(a,c,d), C(a,b,c).

Project No. 3. Duration 6 weeks. Needed: E(a,c,f), R(a,c), M(a,d), F(d).

Project No. 4. Duration 7 months. Needed: M(b,c), F(b,c), C(a,b,c).

Project No. 5. Duration 6 days. Needed: E(c), R(c), M(d), F(a).

- Draw an organization chart utilizing simultaneous organization forms that will accurately and reasonably arrange the functions and project responsibilities outlined.
- Did you use more than a single type of simultaneous organization form? Explain your reasoning.

Advantages The various forms of simultaneous organization offer great flexibility in meeting customer and product needs while retaining the expertise of a large functional department. They can assist in reaching quick decisions and focus attention on product or project timetables and performance in large organizations. The simultaneous organization offers a wide diversity of application problems to functional experts and serves as an excellent training ground for prospective general and strategic managers.

Disadvantages The deliberately created dual influence pattern of the simultaneous organization is inherently a breeding ground for organizational conflict. As a consequence, project managers and the leaders of functional departments must be prepared to deal with enormous problems of coordination, integration, and conflict resolution. For the functional specialists, career development is complicated by multiple reporting relationships and the prospect of working most closely with a person relatively unfamiliar with the niceties of one's specialty. Performance appraisal and reward systems—given the complexities of the interactions between one or more project supervisors, functional supervisors, and individual specialists—are extremely complex and may be the cause of misallocation of rewards and problems in the motivation of key specialists.

We have summarized some of the contingencies bearing on organizational design. We have also described some of the typical organizational forms and have attempted to list some of their advantages and disadvantages. We shall now make use of the product life cycle/strategy-selection framework of Chapter 12 and suggest organization forms that seem suitable to both the environmental conditions and the chosen strategy.

STRATEGY AND ORGANIZATIONAL STRUCTURES

Structures for Developmental Stage Strategies

In their earliest form, all companies in the developmental stage will probably make use of the *simple* organization. This organizational form is well suited to the entrepreneurial character of the problems faced and the uncertainties in technology and the marketplace. The Claim Defender will probably change from this relatively organic organizational form to a small scale and somewhat primitive functional organization toward the end of the developmental stage. The Claim Defender will be highly selective in concentrating on a single product/market combination and will attempt to be expert in serving that narrow market. Its small size, however, will not justify the employment of a large staff of narrow specialists.

Development Stage Staffing Needs: The Claim Defender.

General Manager: More experience in sales/marketing, greater willingness to take risks, and higher tolerance for ambiguity than average.[14]

Marketing: Market developers and marketing generalists.

R & D: Information gatherers, adapters.

Production/Operations: Small-scale single-technology specialists.

Finance: Finance and accounting generalists.

The Prospector, although also beginning this stage of the life cycle with a *simple* organization form, will begin the process of functional specialization and product or customer departmentalization as it addresses small segments of its markets. Given a multiproduct technology, it probably will utilize functional specialists in finance, administration, and production/operations as well as a customer or product departmentalization in marketing. Generally, the Prospector will adopt a *functional* organization with product or customer departmentalization within the marketing function. Should the technologies of two market-related products be different, then produc-

[14] A. K. Gupta and V. Govindarajan, "Business Unit Strategy, Managerial Characteristics, and Business Unit Effectiveness at Strategy Implementation," *Academy of Management Journal*, 27(1) (1984), pp. 25–41.

tion/operations may also be split on a product basis. In its operation, however, the Prospector organization must retain an entrepreneurial character in order to seek out and capitalize on market opportunities. Thus, although functional assignments will be made for clarity and to make use of expertise, the effective Prospector firm will probably be viewed as highly organic, with the informality, multidirectionality in communications, and shared decision-making characteristic of that type of organization.

Development Stage Staffing Needs: The Prospector.

General Manager: More experience in sales/marketing, greater willingness to take risks, and higher tolerance for ambiguity than average.[15]

Marketing: Market developers, marketing generalists.

R & D: Product-development specialists.

Production/Operations: Multiproduct production specialists.

Finance: Financial and accounting generalists, investment analysts.

The Dominating Leader firm, with greater resources, is most likely to move to a *functional* organization form very quickly in order to make use of a larger staff or more-narrowly assigned specialists, especially in R & D, market research, and process technology. In its search for dominance in its industry, management is likely to retain a higher degree of centralized control than in either of the other two organizations. Because of the highly functionalized nature of its design, the Dominating Leader firm is likely to adopt a somewhat mechanistic character as a means of providing coordinative integration and direction to its newly formed and extensive functionaries. The large-scale technology acquired late in the development stage probably will mean the adoption of process departmentalization within the production/operations function. Similarly, as marketing moves toward large-scale marketing and distribution, departmentalization of this function by geography or by customer group may be needed.

Development Stage Staffing Needs: Dominating Leader.

General Manager: More experience in sales/marketing, greater willingness to take risks, and higher tolerance for ambiguity than average.[16]

Marketing: Product/market-development specialists.

R & D: Product-development specialists.

Production/Operations: Specialists in building large-scale production technologies.

Finance: Specialists in acquiring large-scale venture or equity capital.

[15] Gupta and Govindarajan, "Business Unit Strategy," pp. 29–30.

[16] Gupta and Govindarajan, "Business Unit Strategy," pp. 29–30.

EXERCISE 13–10

Your new company, Xena Computer Auxiliaries, has been highly successful in achieving a substantial amount of venture capital in order to begin the marketing of your digitalizing analysis equipment. The product enables a medical diagnostic laboratory to permanently capture the subtleties of color shading and the shapes of microscopic tissues in digital form, a process that not only permits electronically duplicated and transmitted data, but that also enables the pathologist to electronically enhance images and separate tissue types by color for more precise diagnosis.

The venture capital firm has provided you, an experienced general manager, as the person charged with the responsibility for overall direction of the firm as well as the employment and direction of marketing and production staff. The venture firm anticipates growth in sales of 50% or more each year, and it is very aggressive in its search for highly profitable companies that take leadership positions in new markets.

- Describe and draw the organization structure you would expect to utilize for the next 1 to 3 years.
- Describe the types of individuals you will seek to fill key positions in your organization. What will your general directives be to new staff?
- Describe the general character of organizational relationships in this company, both currently and as the company continues to grow.

Structures for Growth Stage Strategies

Claim Defenders will continue to maintain a small-scale *functional* organization. As volume increases, a somewhat higher degree of functional specialization may be required. Generally, however, the demands on the organization will be similar to those in the latter part of the developmental stage. As volume increases toward the end of the growth stage, the Claim Defender may need to provide some *geographic departmentalization* in marketing and distribution but will do so within the functional framework. Because of the firm's vulnerability, its limited resources, and the functional organizational design, the organization will maintain a relatively mechanistic character in this section of the life cycle.

Growth Stage Staffing Needs: The Claim Defender.

General Manager: More experience in sales/marketing, greater willingness to take risks, and higher tolerance for ambiguity than average.[17]

Marketing: Marketing generalists.

R & D: Information specialists, adaptors.

Production/Operations: Small-to-medium-scale single-product production specialists.

[17] Gupta and Govindarajan "Business Unit Strategy," pp. 29–30.

Finance: Financial and accounting generalists.

Prospectors may find that although the functional organization provides the expertise needed for growth, the demands for concentration and product differentiation may require a greater degree of emphasis on product-oriented management. A shift from a small and relatively organic to a larger and somewhat more mechanistic organizational system, therefore, may occur. To some extent, the need for adaptation required in the developmental stage of the life cycle has now been replaced by a need for concentration on selected product/market segments.

Product departmentalization in marketing may provide the degree of product attention needed to achieve distinctiveness in the marketplace. If production technologies are distinctive, then a *product-oriented departmentalization* in production may also be required. As growth continues, the functional character of the organization will be retained, and *product departmentalization* of a more permanent nature (brand managers, perhaps) will be needed to provide sustained attention to the special needs of market segments. *Geographic departmentalization* of both operations and marketing may be required within the functional organizational structure as volume increases significantly in the later portion of the growth stage.

Growth Stage Staffing Needs: The Prospector.

General Manager: More experience in sales/marketing, greater willingness to take risks, and higher tolerance for ambiguity than average.[18]

Marketing: Market-development specialists, brand managers.

R & D: Product-development and process-development specialists.

Production/Operations: Medium-scale, single-product production specialists.

Finance: Financial and accounting generalists, acquisition specialists.

The Dominating Leader firm will continue to make use of a relatively mechanistic *functional* organization as it concentrates on the domination of large segments of a given industry's markets. *Geographic departmentalization* may be needed in both marketing and production in order to deal with the scale of operations and with horizontal integration. If market-oriented concentric diversification is involved, then marketing for all products would probably be managed through the existing marketing organization. In manufacturing, however, *product-oriented departmentalization* may be required, especially if the production technologies of the new product offerings are distinctively different. Coordination in this type of functional organization may require the use of integrative departments (e.g., sales service departments, order-expediting departments, etc.), especially if customers demand specialized product adaptations of unique delivery requirements.

Growth Stage Staffing Needs: Dominating Leader.

[18] Gupta and Govindarajan, "Business Unit Strategy," pp. 29–30.

General Manager: More experience in sales/marketing, greater willingness to take risks, and higher tolerance for ambiguity than average.[19]

Marketing: Market development specialists, specialists in channels of distribution.

R & D: Product-development specialists.

Production/Operations: Specialists in building to, and operating, large-scale production technologies.

Finance: Specialists acquiring large-scale venture or equity capital, acquisitions specialists.

EXERCISE 13–11

Your medium-sized development company has been actively participating in the commercial and residential growth in the Denver metropolitan area. You have chosen to undertake projects that involve moderate acreage and capital investment, and you have been particularly successful in the construction of specialized medical-delivery care centers (such as outpatient surgery centers and emergency-care facilities) and the construction of research laboratories for medical and commercial organizations. In addition to these two principal lines of development, your company has recently built two small manufacturing complexes that required some of the same technology in ventilation, air quality, and waste disposal as the other development projects. The manufacturing developments, in relative terms, are very much smaller than the other two areas of interest. Your central office contains persons responsible for site selection, land acquisition, architectural design, facilities engineering, construction accounting, financial accounting, subcontract negotiation and relations, and marketing.

- Draw an organization chart that represents what you believe is a sensible arrangement of duties for this company. Explain your reasoning.
- Will your organization be relatively mechanistic or relatively organic in its communication and decision-making patterns? Why?
- In what ways will you expect your organization form to change if you continue to be successful and to grow with the continued development of the Colorado Front Range region? Will the organization become more or less mechanistic as it grows? Explain.

Structures for Maturity Stage Strategies

In the maturity stage of the product life cycle, the Claim Defender will maintain the relatively modest scale of operations and will continue to use a *functional* organiza-

[19] Gupta and Govindarajan, "Business Unit Strategy," pp. 29–30.

tional structure to enable its limited resources to be focused on its tightly defined target market. In the somewhat higher volume Claim Defender organization, *geographic departmentalization* can aid in managerial control, but major decisions will tend to be made on a centralized basis. Following the lead of larger and more-aggressive competitors may call for the use of limited-life *simultaneous* organizations such as task forces or project teams. With these exceptions, the organization will tend to maintain a relatively mechanistic character to achieve cross-functional coordination and control by central management.

Maturity Stage Staffing Needs: The Claim Defender.

General Manager: Somewhat less experience in sales/marketing, a lower willingness to take risks, and a lower tolerance for ambiguity than average.[20]

Marketing: Marketing generalists.

R & D: Information specialists, adaptors.

Production/Operations: Small-to-medium-scale single-product production specialists.

Finance: Financial and accounting generalists.

The Prospector firm has stabilized its search for profit opportunities in the mature stage of the product life cycle and will continue to employ the *functional* organization in early maturity. Smaller firms may utilize a functional organization throughout the entire organization. Larger companies may use the functional organization in their primary product divisions. In secondary product areas, brand managers (in marketing) or process managers (in manufacturing) serve to provide specialized assistance.

In the larger Prospector firms as the maturity stage continues, the size of secondary divisions may suggest the use of *product divisions*, with responsibility for manufacturing, marketing, and division profitability residing with the executive in charge of each division. Typically, the financial function and other corporate functions where the economics of scale are substantial (e.g., purchasing, traffic, commercial and investment banking) will remain as central office functions, much as is the case with companies as large as General Motors. Thus, although decentralized in many operating decision areas, major strategic decisions—including acquisitions and capital resource allocation—are made through central administration in a fairly formalized and mechanistic atmosphere.

Maturity Stage Staffing Needs: The Prospector.

General Manager: Somewhat less experience in sales/marketing, a lower willingness to take risks, and a lower tolerance for ambiguity than average.[21]

[20] Gupta and Govindarajan, "Business Unit Strategy," pp. 29–30.

[21] Gupta and Govindarajan, "Business Unit Strategy," pp. 29–30.

Marketing: Marketing generalists, brand managers, market-development specialists.

R & D: Information specialists, adaptors.

Production/Operations: Medium to large-scale single-product production specialists.

Finance: Financial and accounting generalists.

Dominating Leader firms will enter the mature stage in aggressive pursuit of market and cost leadership. In many instances, these companies will maintain a highly centralized and somewhat mechanistic *functional* organization as a means of maintaining tight control of all cross-functional activities at the top while providing a high degree of specialized attention to each function. Departmentalization, when it occurs, is often the result of growth in geographic area served, through a proliferation of brands, or in the expansion into several production facilities.

As the scope of operations begins to encompass national or international markets and a multiplicity of production locations, some single-product businesses find it prudent to decentralize and to provide both coordination and major decision making on operational matters at lower levels in the organization. Frequently, production and sales responsibilities are integrated at a geographic regional center. Functional departmentalization occurs below the level of geographic manager, as might further geographic breakdowns. In some cases, a brand or product breakdown is the basis for divisionalization in a single-business company, with geographic and/or functional departmentalization below that level of the organization. The scale of operations and the widely dispersed nature of its activities suggest that a highly formalized and somewhat mechanistic organizational environment will predominate. The organizational themes of leadership and domination also would suggest a relatively high degree of accountability to central administration and a high level of strategic decision making by top management as well.

Maturity Stage Staffing Needs: The Dominating Leader.

General Manager: Somewhat less experience in sales/marketing, a lower willingness to take risks, and a lower tolerance for ambiguity than average.[22]

Marketing: Marketing generalists, brand managers, advertising and promotion specialists.

R & D: Consumer-behavior specialists, process-technology specialists, new-product specialists.

Production/Operations: Large-scale operations specialists, process-control specialists, industrial engineering specialists.

Finance: Finance generalists, cash-management specialists, investment portfolio managers.

[22] Gupta and Govindarajan, "Business Unit Strategy," pp. 29–30.

Decline Stage Organizational Structures

As the industry moves into a decline stage, the Claim Defender firm is especially vulnerable. Although it will maintain a *functional* form early in the decline stage to provide the focused attention to customers and markets required of a concentration strategy, it must also be flexible enough to meet the demands of competitors and to face the problems of selectively eliminating products or unproductive markets. Its manner of operations, therefore, will shift from a relatively mechanistic type of organization to a much more adaptive, collaborative organic form. As it faces divestiture or liquidation, the organization may revert to the *simple* organization used in its earliest days, with limited functional identification and with a high level of task flexibility and sharing of duties.

Decline Stage Staffing Needs: The Claim Defender.

General Manager: Greater experience in sales/marketing, a greater willingness to take risks, and a higher tolerance for ambiguity than average.[23]

Marketing: Marketing generalists.

R & D: Few or none.

Production/Operations: Small-scale specialists, operations generalists.

Finance: Finance generalists, cost-benefit analysts.

The smaller-scale Prospector firm enters the decline stage as a *functional* organization and will continue in that mode throughout the stage. *Simultaneous* temporary organization forms such as project teams or task forces may be established to deal with problems of acquisitions or selective retrenchment.

Larger Prospector firms enter as *divisionalized* forms and must face reformulation issues as unprofitable divisions are dropped and more promising operations acquired. As the stage continues, the organization will be scaled downward in size to accommodate the general decline in the market and will probably revert to a *functional* framework, at least in primary divisions, with product emphasis in marketing and manufacturing to meet specialized needs.

Decline Stage Staffing Needs: The Prospector.

General Manager: Greater experience in sales/marketing, a greater willingness to take risks, and a higher tolerance for ambiguity than average.[24]

Marketing: Marketing generalists, market analysts.

R & D: Few or none.

Production/Operations: Production generalists.

Finance: Finance and accounting generalists.

[23] Gupta and Govindarajan, "Business Unit Strategy," pp. 29–30.

[24] Gupta and Govindarajan, "Business Unit Strategy," pp. 29–30

The Dominating Leader enters the decline stage in a *divisionalized* form. As the pressures of volume decline become more apparent, selective retrenchment can be undertaken by means of cutbacks in products or unprofitable geographic divisions. Given the relatively precipitous nature of the liquidation by large competitors, the *divisionalized* form will be maintained until such time as the liquidation decision is made. The organization, in all likelihood, will then revert to a functional organization structure until such time as new products offer sufficient need for departmentalization in a new venture.

Decline Stage Staffing Needs: The Dominating Leader.

General Manager: Somewhat less experience in sales/marketing, a lower willingness to take risks, and a lower tolerance for ambiguity than average.[25]

Marketing: Marketing generalists, new product-development specialists.

R & D: New product-development specialists.

Production/Operations: Operations generalists.

Finance: Finance and accounting generalists, cash-management specialists.

EXERCISE 13–12

The Sure-Set Shingle Company, your family business for over 80 years, is facing a significant decline in its industry, the wood shingle business. Several factors have brought about this decline: First, supplies of the clear cedar needed for roofing and siding shingles have declined dramatically. Prices, raised by both a shortage of supply and significant increases in lumber industry wages, have increased by 150% in 5 years. Competition from asphalt and fiberglass shingle manufacturers has increased, and new patterns and technical advantages have priced wood shingles nearly out of the reach of most homeowners. Although commercial use of wood shingles has increased somewhat with the advent of Victorian styling in smaller office buildings, the entire market for wood shingles had declined 20% each year for the past 3 years. There are several other competitors for the wood shingle business in the United States. Your firm is the smallest survivor of a once quite large industry. Your facilities for shingle manufacture are ill suited to making other products, and the family's financial resources are limited. You have been selling shingles in New England and the Southeast regions of the United States and have had sales offices in Chicago and Memphis for the past 15 years. These offices have recorded declines in sales volume for 2 years in a row, and at this time, sales barely cover the salary and operating expenses of the staff in those locations. The Southeast region has had the best performance, probably owing to general economic health and to a continuing interest in more traditional building styles and materials. Although New England has a

[25] Gupta and Govindarajan, "Business Unit Strategy," pp. 29–30.

similar tradition of using wood shingles, new construction is nearly nil, and the majority of sales have been through contractors involved in restorations of older homes.

- What type of organization should this company be using at this time? Explain.
- As the decline deepens, should this organizational arrangement change? In what ways?
- Describe the degree of mechanistic or organic character you would like to see in this situation. Why? How might you help to see that your chosen style is carried out?

The Lovelace Medical Foundation case offers an opportunity to examine a long-range plan for the delivery of health-care services to older residents of the State of New Mexico and to develop the forecast of organizational needs for personnel. From this forecast and the expressed intentions for service deliveries, organization charts can be developed that represent a design intended to meet the type of strategy, the tasks involved, and the growth in the organization. As you read the case, consider those factors that have been shown to be contingencies in our discussion of strategy formulation and organizational implementation. Make notes and prepare to respond to the exercise questions at the end of the case.

LOVELACE MEDICAL FOUNDATION: PLANNING FOR GERIATRIC/GERONTOLOGY SERVICES

The Lovelace Medical Foundation (LMF) is a large, multispecialty, multisite group practice serving the Southwest. The Foundation is staffed by 96 physicians practicing at the main site, three metropolitan satellite clinics, and three associated group practices located in smaller communities within the state. The main site includes outpatient clinics, an acute care hospital, an extended care facility, and a health maintenance organization. Outpatient care only is offered at the satellite clinics and the associated group practices.

On March 23, 1982, the Board of Governors of LMF approved a study to be conducted on the implementation of a geriatric/gerontology program. The main objective of this study was to plan a program of services by LMF for elderly adults and to plan a method by which

This case was prepared by Debra A. Thomas, Health Systems Evaluation Program, Lovelace Medical Foundation; Associate Professor Howard L. Smith of the University of New Mexico; and David J. Ottensmeyer, M.D., Chief Executive Officer, Lovelace Medical Foundation, as a basis for class discussion. It is not designed to present illustrations of effective or ineffective handling of administrative problems.

that program might be optimally implemented by LMF. The specific goals of this study included:

1 Analysis of the feasibility of a program of geriatric or gerontologic health-related services for elderly people (i.e., determine whether such a program is feasible).
2 Analysis of the content of a program which might provide geriatric or gerontologic health-related services to elderly adults (i.e., determine what alternative programs might be considered for implementation).
3 Development of a short-run program, and contingency alternatives, which analytically appears to be the optimal opportunity for LMF to capture a longer market share of older adult patients in view of existing or readily obtainable LMF plans and resources (i.e., develop a program and plan for implementation of the program).
4 Development of a long-run plan for providing geriatric or gerontologic services that will guide the implementation of the short-run program and that will facilitate decision making surrounding the area of services to the aging.

The accomplishment of these objectives would help to formally substantiate the belief that there is sufficient opportunity for a group practice such as LMF to become a leader in providing health services to older adults. It would also create a method for immediately organizing resources to form the program.

A consultant was contracted to undertake the feasibility analysis. The analysis included intensive interviewing of: (1) community persons interested in the aging; (2) public administrators responsible for delivering social and medical services to the aging; (3) private providers delivering geriatric and gerontologic services or conducting research on the aging; (4) educators associated with professionals who serve the elderly; and (5) key staff members of LMF (e.g., department chairmen). Additionally, extensive research into the literature was conducted on existing models of service to the elderly. A specific market analysis was not undertaken because: (1) it would be too costly, requiring a sample of some 400 respondents from the community; (2) it would be too time consuming; (3) its findings would only present *speculation* on whether aging adults *might* use the program; (4) the proliferation of reimbursement patterns would necessitate further market analysis once a final program was in place.

The consultant was given two months to complete the study and was asked to submit recommendations at the end of that period. That analysis and recommendations were based upon the following information.

DEMOGRAPHIC ANALYSIS

Much of the optimism in the health field over geriatric medicine and gerontology programs centers on an aging national population. Actually the population is both aging and becoming younger as a result of the past World War II baby boom. In reviewing demographic data for New Mexico, certain 1980 census data are relevant (see Exhibits 1–3). As with much of the U.S., all counties within the state showed increases in their population of 65 and over. Similar to national trends, females constitute a majority of the over-65 population. A substantial portion (about one-third) of the over-65 population resides in the metropolitan area where LMF's main site and satellite clinics are located.

Ethnicity is an important consideration (see Exhibits 4–6). The 1980 census data indicate that there is a sizeable Hispanic population (especially in counties served by LMF) and a fairly large Native American population among the elderly. These ethnic groups utilize the extended family in maintaining independence longer than other ethnic groups.

New Mexico is considered to be a poor state with one of the ten lowest per capita incomes in the United States. Census data indicate that noninstitutionalized elderly live in owner-occupied housing (see Exhibits 7–9). Households are usually two-person dwellings and household type is a family household. There may be fewer alternatives to the elderly within this state since there is a paucity of retirement of congregate housing for the aging.

PREVIOUS STUDIES OR PROGRAM PLANS

Internal Studies

The concern for improving the delivery of geriatric medicine by LMF is not a recent or novel idea. In 1978, for example, the Office of Development at LMF explored the offerings of other medical centers across the country. It was found at this time that few medical centers on group practices were specializing in geriatric medicine (i.e., had formed departments of geriatric medicine) or gerontology. This may have been a stimulus to the formation of a preliminary geriatric marketing plan by the Marketing Manager at LMF in September 1981. Meanwhile, the Medical Director of LMF formalized a Gerontology Task Force in 1981. In view of these events it is clear that interest in a program offering and extending geriatric services is not new to LMF. This prior planning deserves analysis at the point for the purpose of identifying: (1) existing advisory and staff expectations about geriatric services; (2) assumptions (both correct and incorrect) about the scope of the program that LMF might implement; and (3) factors which have prevented LMF from progressing with more purposeful activities.

On March 20, 1981, a large management consulting firm submitted its final report on programmatic planning at LMF. That report sought to identify high-priority programmatic opportunities for which LMF should plan and to help educate key LMF staff members in the steps of the planning process. The final report recommended that aging—encompassing programs of gerontology, home health care, day care and nursing home care—was a programmatic opportunity worthy of further planning.

The following rationale explained why consultants prioritized aging as an opportunity for further study:

> *Rationale: The predicted growth in the aging segment of the population will generate a demand for services directed to the needs of older individuals. Those needs will not be for medical services only but also for assistance in coping with problems of living. Older people will probably have strengthened political influence and increased financial resources and there will almost certainly be a market for specialized programs to deal with the problems of aging in New Mexico. A programmatic thrust in aging could attract significant numbers of new patients who would require more medical services than a younger group. Making services accessible to the aging through home care and day care could help to establish Lovelace's position as a system of convenient health care services. Aging individuals may be suitable candidates for programs of wellness, and a Medicare HMO could be marketed as well.*

On June 30, 1981, the Medical Director formally notified the Gerontology Task Force (an *ad hoc* internal committee) of LMF about its specific purposes which can be summarized as:

1. Explore the feasibility and range of services which a center for the care of the elderly might provide.
2. Provide short run (1–2 years) and long-run projections for utilization.
3. Develop a strategy for staffing and determine the interface with [the] University of New Mexico.

4 Provide fiscal projections.

The Task Force included a wide variety of physician and non-physician personnel in its membership. As well, the Task Force sought active participation from a group of community consultants with expertise in medical and social programs for the aging.

The recommendations of the Task Force were clearly stated:

1 Recruit and hire a geriatric specialist.
2 Start a four- to six-bed day hospital.
3 Consider a multispecialty facility to include a day care center for the elderly.

Even though an explicit set of recommendations was given, the report indicates that total concensus was not obtained.

The Task Force did address all of the purposes outlined by the Medical Director but clearly emphasis revolved around the issue of whether a geriatric specialist was needed. In the area of caseload projections and financial impact, the Task Force relied on the estimates put forth in the consultants' final report, yet those estimates were never clearly detailed as to how they were formulated. This raised a number of questions. Where did the estimates come from? What relationship was assumed between costs and revenues? What standards were used for estimating productivity of the providers? What sort of patient caseload would be generated? What types of reimbursement would the patients be using? How would the scope of the program offered by LMF affect the caseload and revenues? To what extent would net revenues be generated by the program? How many years would it take to capture capital costs or initial operating deficits? In sum, the Task Force did not demonstrably address the issues of patient load and financial impact.

The Task Force concentrated extensively on the issue of the geriatric specialist—a physician with specialized training in geriatrics—as the head of a special program for the elderly. No clear concensus was expressed for the addition of the specialist although the Task Force in the end recommended hiring a physician who would not function as just another primary care provider but who would be responsible as a teacher and an administrator and who would promote the concept of wholistic care. The lack of support of an additional provider who would possibly duplicate the work already being done by the departments of General Internal Medicine and Family Practice, who would reduce the patient load or revenues flowing to those departments, or who might be paid at a rate higher than the primary care physicians was understandable. The issue of the geriatric specialist as a provider was downplayed and relegated to an administration, outreach, consultation, research and education perspective.

The Task Force reviewed the literature on models of care and concluded that even though little was published on the topic the most promising avenue was a day hospital. On the basis of available literature the Task Force should have expressed the conclusion that no substantial information is available which supports (or invalidates) the use of special clinics by the aging. Nonetheless in considering a possible model for care, a day hospital was selected. There was very little justification given other than it would provide for multidisciplinary assessment and rehabilitation for patients not needing hospitalization.

On September 11, 1981, the Marketing Manager submitted a proposed Geriatric Marketing Plan to the Director of Community Relations to LMF. That plan outlined strategies which might be pursued as outreach to the geriatric community of Albuquerque. The Geriatric Marketing Plan did not provide specific but only general marketing approaches. It was noted that the marketing effort *must* coincide with program efforts if the geriatrics/gerontology concept is to succeed over the short run (i.e., 1–3 years).

External Studies

The 1980 State Health Plan prepared by the Statewide Health Coordinating Council of the Department of Health and Environment clearly addresses the problems of insufficient institutional programs for the aged, that is, the need for more skilled nursing home beds. Yet the realm of public services for the aged is much less clear in that report:

> *Although institutionalization is needed for a small segment of the elderly, other types of continuing care services are required by those elderly who remain in the community. These services can range from a boarding home to homemaker services. The presence of these services within an area may bring about the postponment* [sic] *or the prevention of costly institutionalization for many individuals . . . these services are provided by home health agencies, aging programs, state government and some proprietary agencies. These is no methodology to determine the adequacy of the current services or to make a statement as to what mixture of services is required in what areas of the state. Nevertheless, as the number of elderly continue to increase so will the demand for community based services.*

Reference was made to the House Memorial 51 Task Force which was conducting a study at the same time that the State Health Plan was being formulated.

The Long Term Health Care Study of the House Memorial 51 Task Force reviewed:

1. Available resources to serve the aging.
2. Needs of the aging.
3. Elements that comprise a comprehensive system of care.
4. Main issues in long-term care.
5. Legislations introduced in 1979–1980.
6. A set of recommendations and findings regarding care of the aging in the state.

This report was prepared by the State Health Planning and Development Bureau of the Health and Environment Department in conjunction with the State Agency on Aging.

One of the main features of the Long Term Health Care Study is the presentation of a conceptual framework (see Figure 1) for delivering and planning future services to the aging in the state utilizing a continuum-of-care concept. This concept involves the offering of comprehensive services at the level complementary to the aged person's ability to function. Several points are worthwhile in this model. Gerontology services are misutilized when any level on the continuum is not available or when the services are not linked in a systematic manner. Hence, it is in the State's and aged person's best interest to fill gaps in the continuum-of-care.

The importance of the continuum-of-care is reinforced by the first recommendation of the Long Term Health Care Study for improving services to the aging:

> *RECOMMENDATION No. 1: That the state support, in its program planning and implementation, the concept of a continuum-of-care that meets the physical, social and emotional needs of each individual; that the implementation include development at the state level of a comprehensive service system that allows for individual movement within the various levels of care within the health, behavioral health and social service categories; and that services be provided on a need basis rather than on an income basis, with a sliding fee scale established to pay for services.*

The Long Term Health Care Study divides its analysis of needs (i.e., resources and programs) for the elderly into two categories—health services and social services. Following

FIGURE 1
Continuum of service

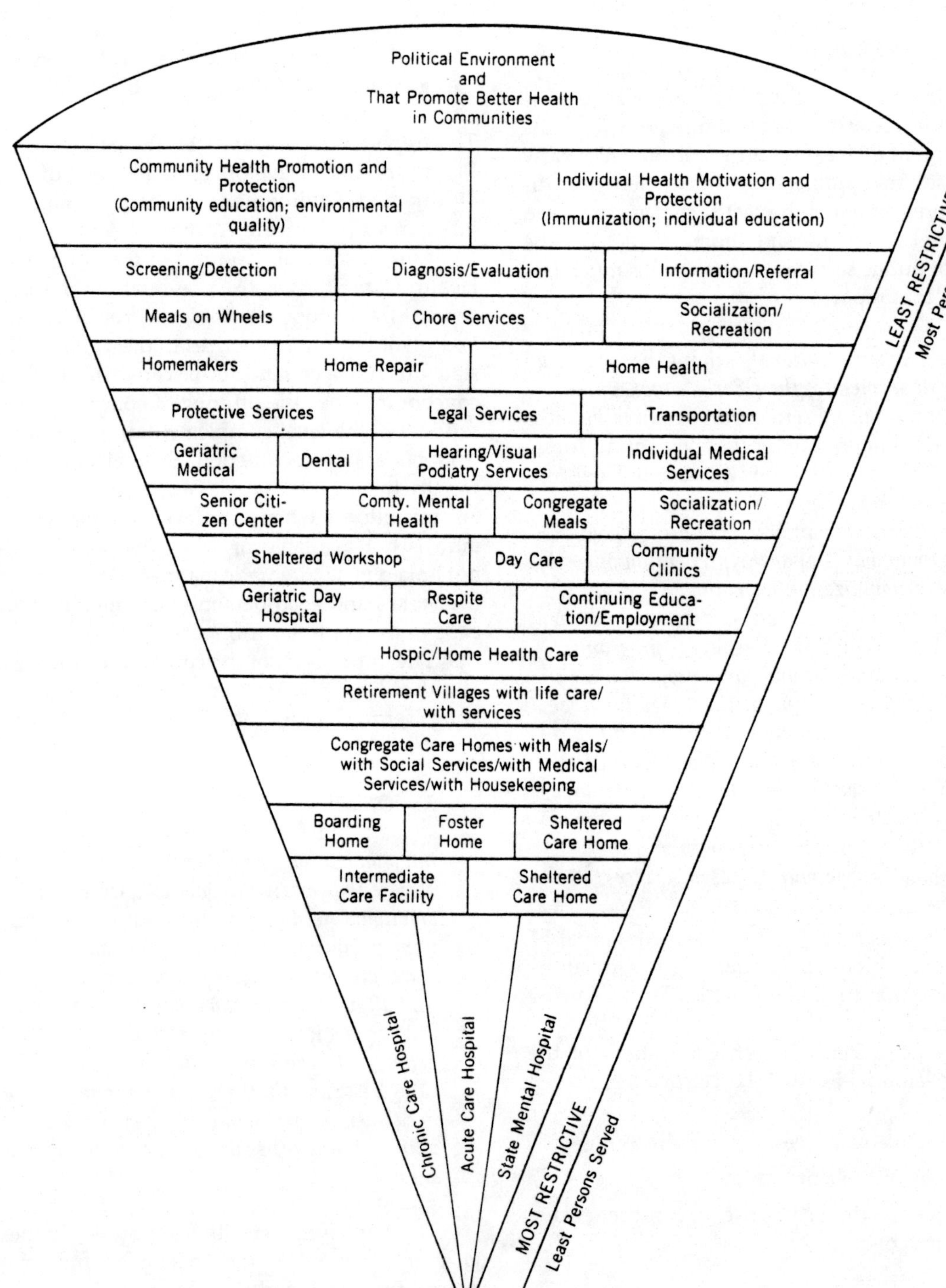

Source: Long-Term Health Care Study House Memorial 51 of the 1979 New Mexico Legislature.

are the summary recommendations for the health services:

> *Health Clinics:* Clinics have been implemented in a number of rural areas to help answer the need for primary care in medically underserved areas. There is a need for clinics in other uncovered areas of the state. Clinics may be staffed by nurse practitioners or physician assistants. At present, Medicare payment cannot be made for these services. Medicare payment should be made to allow payment to this staff when they work under the supervision of a physician.
>
> *Hospital Day Care:* Some nursing homes are implementing day care programs. Such a program was not seen as a need although many reporting programs to the survey did indicate a need for more socially oriented day care centers. There is not sufficient information to compare these two programs although it can be surmised that the medically oriented program will cost much more than the socially oriented one.
>
> *Geriatric Specialists:* The need for gerontologists was noted by a few programs. Special emphasis of this need was made in the Governor's Conference on Disease Prevention and Health Promotion. New Mexico has no geriatricians and it has very few trained gerontologists working in programs for elderly. The University of New Mexico has a gerontology section but it does not have a department that can readily reach across training of physicians, nurses, therapists, psychologists, educators, etc. Since the elderly population is the most rapidly growing group, the need for more persons specialized in care of elderly is also growing. Persons with more knowledge about the elderly would contribute to the quality of care and would also be effective in modifying negative ageism attitudes that exist.

The social services areas of need listed in the Long-Term Health Care Study that are pertinent to LMF include day care, outreach and service hours:

> *Day Care/Respite:* Respite is temporary care of persons needing assistance in order to provide families or guardians periods of respite from the 24-hour need/demand for service. Respite may be on an hourly or daily basis or it may be for several days or weeks at a time. Two short-term respite alternatives are sitters and day care services for frail elderly. Day care centers for frail elderly are not widely available. These are socially oriented programs which coordinate with available health resources. Medical information is required for each client. Special diets are provided. Health-oriented services, such as exercise and reality orientation, are provided along with recreation and arts and crafts opportunities. Day care is a viable alternative to institutionalization and the daily cost per client is about one-fifth the daily cost of an Intermediate Care Facility. All Districts see a need for day care and other respite alternatives.
>
> *Outreach:* All Districts expressed a need for expanding outreach services to reach more people and to recruit them into programs. While some outreach is provided in most programs, this service becomes secondary to the provision of direct services to known clients. If the state wishes to reach all people in need, it will be obligated to expand its outreach capabilities. This is a service area which could be expanded with volunteers.
>
> *Expansion of Services to Seven Days a Week:* Most programs, outside of those that provide either crisis or institutional services, only operate five days a week, eight hours a day. A number of programs, however, should be expanded to cover a seven-day week. The nutrition program is one exam-

ple. Meals are served once, or at the most, twice a day during the work week. Diet needs, however, should be met three times a day, seven days a week. Peoples' need for food and good nutrition is not lessened by the calendar or by the clock. Weekends are lonely periods of time for older persons, particularly for those who are relatively immobilized and without assistance. They need transportation and opportunities to be with other people as much on the weekends as on other days of the week.

Furthermore, the Long Term Health Care study recognized the need for retirement housing.

> *Low Income Retirement Center/Congregate Housing:* Some elderly and disabled can carry out the activities of daily living but need to live in an area where nursing services are available, if required, and where other housing should be available as an alternative to the housing need of elderly and disabled persons and it should be available for persons with all levels of income. Retirement housing does not exist in many areas of the state.

The preceding thoughts on areas of medical and social service need were included in a New Mexico State Legislature requested study that *assessed* the system of services delivered to the aging. A specific *plan* on aging has been prepared by the State Agency on Aging entitled, "State Plan on Aging, Fiscal Years 1981 - 1982." Most of the direct services to the aging are provided by State Agency on Aging (SAoA) projects—mealsites, senior centers, Foster Grandparent programs, Retired Senior Volunteer Programs, and Volunteers In Service to America (VISTA). SAoA services are basically coordinative and supplemental (in terms of funding) as opposed to [those] directly concerned with building an empire of state-funded services. Basically the problem is one of limited resources and extensive needs. The SAoA and AAA's can only fund so many services. They can and do function, however, as primary coordinators of programs by public, private and third-sector organizations involved in serving the aging.

At this point, there are no multispecialty group practices providing geriatric medicine or gerontology services in the State. Even within the metropolitan area where LMF's main site is located, there are no specific clinical services being offered. The State's only medical school does have one geriatrician who is involved in an ongoing longitudinal research program of the aged and offers essentially no clinical services. Therefore in terms of specific clinical services there are no geriatricians, and only a few physicians indicate that they cater to the aging adult. The hospitals and medical centers in the State have not entered into this market segment as of this date.

Plans for gerontology programs or geriatric medicine specialties are not normally publicized until after a program has been organized and ready for implementation. Thus, competition in this area of medicine may be forming, but there is no method of acquiring this information. Programs of this nature do not generally require health systems agency approval. According to one public agency director two national nursing home chains are investigating the possibility of implementing outpatient services in their facilities.

Other considerations to be made in the analysis were interviews conducted with members of the medical staff at LMF. Opinions of several members of the medical staff would prove critical as their endorsements of or lack of support for the plan would mean its success or failure.

The consultant's interviews exposed certain attitudes that would merit consideration. The Chairman of the Department of Internal Medicine commented that "geriatrics was not a valid medical discipline" and that "elderly patients shouldn't be singled out for special program efforts." The Chairman of Family Medicine felt that too many programs had been started at LMF without passing the "acid test" of being at least self-sufficient within a reasonable time period.

THE PLAN

After a two-month analysis of demographics, existant models of geriatric/gerontology services, competition, public program plans and services, in-house resources, planning parameters, and feasible alternatives, the consultant submitted his plan for geriatric/gerontology services to the LMF Board of Governors. The report called for both a short-run implementation plan and a long-run implementation plan for a Senior Services Program at LMF. The overlying consideration was that of developing an initial program that would be most compatible with LMF's mission as stated by the Board of Governors on February 13, 1980:

> *The mission of the Lovelace Medical Foundation is to satisfy the health needs of people and institutions by providing comprehensive health care services, based on group practice, in a responsible and efficient manner, at a reasonable cost, and in accordance with standards of excellence, in recognition of the need for growth and job satisfaction of our personnel.*

Once a health care service was in place and the program was financially viable, then further programmatic expansion could take place.

The entitling of the program—The Senior Services Program—merits some explanation. The use of the terms aging, geriatrics, gerontology or variations on their themes could be more detrimental than beneficial because of the negative connotations that might be associated with the aging process. In contrast, the term "Senior" clearly identifies the program as serving the needs of the aging—regardless of their physical, mental or financial status. It is a term that invites further investigation into what services are offered. By using the connotation of Senior Services, those groups and associations (i.e., Senior Citizen clubs) are readily able to identify with the program. As well, public agency administrators or external LMF health care providers are able to locate the program they are concerned with compared to the numerous other LMF programs.

A separate department was not recommended because it segregates the aging patient from other patients. While this does allow specialization, it alters the physician's (and other providers') performance attitude, and perception of the aging patient. The Program would be housed within an existing LMF primary care department recognizing that aging patients have special needs or problems to be addressed (e.g., anxiety over health, finances, and payment). To meet the diverse needs of the aged population integration with various departments within LMF would be necessary.

Brief overviews of the short-run (i.e., first two years) and long-run implementation plans follow.

Short-Run Implementation Plan

GOALS

Provide primary care and limited social services with backup medical referral for the aging adult.

Integrate existing LMF medical, administrative, and social services in meeting the health needs of aging adults.

Develop contractual and coordinative associations with public agencies and community organizations in meeting the health needs of aging adults.

Collaborate on the formation of an LMF marketing plan to the aging adult in Bernalillo County.

Undertake a semiannual evaluation of performance to assess the development of the Senior Services Program.

OBJECTIVES:

Year 1	*Year 2*
Provide 750 primary care visits by a geriatric nurse practitioner at the main site clinic.	Provide 1500 primary care visits by a geriatric nurse practitioner at the main site clinic.
Provide 80 half-day health screening clinics at the satellite clinics.	Provide 100 full day health screening clinics at the satellite clinics.
Provide 100 health screening clinics in the community.	Provide 150 health screening clinics in the community.
Contract or formalize agreements with public agencies or community organizations to refer patients (from a population base of 200 people).	Contract or formalize agreements with public agencies or community organizations to refer patients (from a population base of 200 new people over and above Year 1).
Provide 24 seminar/lectures to community groups on the Senior Services Program.	Provide 36 seminars/lectures to community groups on the Senior Services Program.
Provide 400 primary care visits by Physician Director or other LMF primary care physicians.	Provide 2400 primary care visits by Physician Director or other LMF primary care physicians.

Monitor (i.e., record the nature, volume, cost and revenues) the following program activities:

Nutritional Counseling Services
Psychiatric Counseling Services
Physical Therapy Visits
Geriatric Nurse Practitioner Seminars to LMF Staff and Senior Adult Groups
Social Services Seminars to LMF Staff and Senior Adult Groups
Referrals to LMF specialists

Administratively coordinate with the Department of Community Relations on the advertising/marketing needs of the Senior Services Program.

Revise plans for additional Program personnel depending on quantity of services offered and quantity of services planned for the future.

Administratively coordinate with the Lovelace Health Plan (HMO) to determine the precise impact of the Medicare demonstration on the Senior Services Program. Revise budget and revenue projections as necessary.

Report semiannually to the Chief Executive Officer and to the Board of Governors on the progress and accomplishments (or lack thereof) of the program.

PERSONNEL:

Year 1	*Year 2*
1 FTE Program Coordinator	1 FTE Program Coordinator
1 FTE Secretary/Clerk	1 FTE Secretary/Clerk
1 FTE Geriatric Nurse Practitioner	1 FTE Geriatric Nurse Practitioner
1 Physician Director (25% time)*	½ FTE Nurse (Master's level) Specialist
	1 Physician Director (80% time)

Note: *The Physician Director's time includes time devoted to primary care for adult patients at LMF and for minor administrative/coordinative responsibilities associated with the Senior Services Program.

FTE Social Services Staff Position (to be defined on the basis of Year 1 evaluation).

STRUCTURE:

The Senior Services Program represents a program management function based on integration. The Physician Director is essentially a figurehead. The Program Coordinator performs as a program manager—a matrix organization is therefore defined by the new Program. The Coordinator will be responsible for integrating: (1) primary care services and referral services provided by the Physician Program Director, the geriatric nurse practitioner and the LMF medical staff; (2) LMF social services directed toward Program patients; (3) marketing plans directed toward the Program; (4) evaluation of Program and personnel performance; and (5) public and community concerns. There are difficulties with this liaison role because the Coordinator must rely on personal contacts, expertise, and ability to negotiate through compromise with line departments (i.e., medical and ancillary departments).

BUDGET:

	Year 1	*Year 2*
Program Coordinator	$20,000	$22,500
Secretary/Clerk	9,300	10,000
Geriatric Nurse Practitioner	21,000	23,000
Physician Director	15,000	60,000
Nurse Specialist	0	10,000
Social Services Staff Member	0	16,000
Fringe Benefits:		
Non-physician (18%)	9,054	14,670
Physician (10%)	1,500	6,000
TOTAL PERSONNEL	75,854	162,170
Travel Costs (estimated 5000 miles per year)	1,000	1,000
Office Space:		
Program (1 room 10 ft. × 15 ft. at $17.05/sq. ft.)	2,558	2,558
Clinic/Exam Rooms		
(Year 1—2 rooms 10 ft. × 10 ft. at $17.05/sq. ft.)		3,410
(Year 2—4 rooms 10 ft. × 10 ft. at $17.05/sq. ft.)		6,820
Supplies (office) and Duplication	2,850	3,175
TOTAL	$85,672	$198,740

PATIENT LOAD AND REVENUES:

The patient load for the Senior Services Program is scaled down in the first year to recognize the start-up problems associated with a new program. It is estimated that a geriatric nurse practitioner will provide 750 primary care visits at LMF while the Physician Director will provide 450 visits. This patient load was estimated backwards from the average physician load in the Department of Internal Medicine. Basically the geriatric nurse practitioner will only be spending approximately 25 percent of total time the first year in seeing clinic patients and the physician around 25 percent of time in the clinic. The second year the expectations are that twice as many primary care visits will be covered by the nurse practitioner. The physician will provide 2400 primary care visits in the second year. It must be remembered that the nurse practitioner and physician are committed to patients who are more time-consuming (perhaps as much as twice that of regular patients). Thus productivity may seem low, but the severity of the patient problems is higher. The initial load of patients will be derived from existing LMF patients who are referred to the nurse practitioner, from the health screening clinics and from the formal arrangements with public agencies/community groups for services.

SERVICES DELIVERED:

The Senior Services Program has the responsibility of delivering the following services:

Primary Care
Referral
Planning
Marketing/Advertising
Evaluation
Developing Contractural Arrangement
Social Service Support
- Psychiatric
- Discharge Planning
- Nutrition

Physical Therapy

The Senior Services Program is meant to eventually generate enough patient referrals that it reaches a point of self-sufficiency (by Year 2). The initial two years of the Program are designed to formulate the concept and begin building a patient base. Since an increased amount of social services will be necessary in the short run in order to justify the program and its marketing, the front-end costs will be moderate, though not discouraging given the potential long run (2–3 years) program perspective. Once the Program reaches stability—where the physician and two nursing personnel are being paid for by primary care revenues—further expansion may be possible for the social services area and consideration may be given to separate clinic facilities.

A Long-Run Plan

The staging of the long-run plan follows in ranked order:

Time (after physician director is incorporated)	*Program Element*	*Major Goal*
1–2 years	Expand social services components (outreach, nutrition, social work counseling)	Provide nutrition and mental health education and counseling to LMF patients and to the Albuquerque Community
1–2 years	Develop day care hospital (4–6 beds)	Serve the social needs and limited medical care of needs of day patients
2–3 years	Inclusion of psychiatric counseling as an effort equal to social day care	Improve outreach to aged with behavioral dementia, and substance abuse (e.g., alcohol problems)
3–5 years	Develop plans for integrating associated group practices in a system of aging care	Horizontally integrate services
3–5 years	Expand continuum of care consistent with LMF financial viability for retirement center.	Vertically integrate services

In terms of the expansion of social services

it was recommended that the coordination between the Senior Services Program and existing LMF social services be expanded through the addition of personnel to the Senior Services Program. Precisely which personnel (and number) are appropriate can only be determined according to the patient load for the Senior Services Program. It was anticipated that full time equivalents of the following personnel will be added during the first 2 years of the long run plan:

Staff Person	*Responsibility*
Nutritionist	Provide nutrition counseling and education at LMF, and at clinics
Nurse/Health Educator (possibly integrated with nutritionist until demand proves financially supportive)	Provide broad spectrum health education to LMF groups concerned about aging. Provide limited seminars, discussions and clinics at public and nonprofit organization functions
Social Worker	Provide supportive services to LMF patients and their families. Act as a referral agent and ombudsperson

Question: If you were a member of the Board of Governors at LMF how would you respond to the consultant's recommendations?

EXHIBIT 1
Percentage of population aged 65 and over by county, 1970–1980

	1970		*1980*	
County	*Population over 65*	*Percent**	*Population over 65*	*Percent**
Bernalillo	19,262	6.1	34,000	8.1
Sandoval	1,259	7.2	3,421	9.8
Chaves	3,900	9.0	7,213	14.1
Cibola (Valencia)	2,272	5.6	4,536	7.4
McKinley	1,901	4.4	2,778	4.9
Dona Ana	3,698	5.3	6,943	7.2
Luna	1,194	10.2	2,625	16.8
San Juan	2,573	4.9	4,759	5.8
Sante Fe	4,272	7.8	6,803	9.0

Source: Census data, Bureau of Business and Economic Research, University of New Mexico.
*Percentage of total population in each country.

EXHIBIT 2
Number (percent) and distribution by sex of persons aged 65 and over 1980

County	Total population	Number (%) aged 65 and over	Number (%) male	Number (%) female
Bernalillo	419,700	34,000 (8.1)	14,011 (41.2)	19,989 (58.8)
Sandoval	34,799	3,421 (9.8)	1,689 (49.4)	1,732 (50.6)
Chaves	51,103	7,213 (14.1)	3,160 (43.8)	4,053 (56.2)
Cibola (Valencia)	61,115	4,536 (7.4)	2,040 (45.0)	2,496 (55.0)
McKinley	56,449	2,778 (4.9)	1,254 (45.1)	1,524 (54.9)
Dona Ana	96,340	6,943 (7.2)	3,042 (43.8)	3,901 (56.2)
Luna	15,585	2,625 (16.8)	1,252 (47.7)	1,373 (52.3)
San Juan	81,433	4,759 (5.8)	2,029 (42.6)	2,730 (57.4)
Santa Fe	75,360	6,803 (9.0)	2,804 (41.2)	3,999 (58.8)

Source: Preliminary census data, Bureau of Business and Economic Research, University of New Mexico.

EXHIBIT 3
Percentage change for New Mexico population aged 65 and over

Year	Percentage of Total Population
1950	4.9
1960	5.4
1970	6.9
1980*	9.0
1990*	10.8
2000*	11.8

Source: Annual Report, New Mexico Selected Health Statistics 1979, State of New Mexico Health and Environment Department.
*Projected.

EXHIBIT 4
Percentage racial distribution by county, 1979

County	Total white non-Hispanic	Hispanic
Bernalillo	57.0	38.2
Sandoval	23.6	36.8
Chaves	66.8	27.7
Cibola (Valencia)	34.1	49.7
McKinley	23.3	13.7
Dona Ana	46.4	50.3
Luna	51.4	46.0
San Juan	52.4	11.6
Sante Fe	33.7	63.3

Source: Annual Report, New Mexico Selected Health Statistics 1979, State of New Mexico Health and Environment Department.

EXHIBIT 5

Number (percent) and distribution by Spanish origin of persons aged 65 and over, 1980

County	Total number of Spanish origin	Number (%) white	Number (%) non-white
Bernalillo	8,316	5,784 (69.6)	2,532 (30.4)
Sandoval	738	442 (59.9)	296 (40.1)
Chaves	737	538 (73.0)	199 (27.0)
Cibola (Valencia)	1,624	1,144 (70.4)	480 (29.6)
McKinley	396	165 (41.7)	231 (58.3)
Dona Ana	2,433	1,748 (71.8)	685 (28.2)
Luna	411	300 (73.0)	111 (27.0)
San Juan	453	275 (60.7)	178 (39.3)
Sante Fe	2,985	2,222 (74.4)	763 (25.6)

Source: Preliminary census data, Bureau of Business and Economic Research, University of New Mexico.

EXHIBIT 6

Number (percent) and distribution by race of persons aged 65 and over, 1980

County	Total aged 65 and over	Number (%) white	Number (%) black	Number (%) Indian	Number (%) Asian and PI
Bernalillo	34,000	30,392 (89.4)	427 (1.3)	487 (1.4)	108 (0.3)
Sandoval	3,421	2,564 (74.9)	53 (1.5)	501 (14.6)	6 (0.2)
Chaves	7,213	6,807 (94.4)	164 (2.3)	34 (0.5)	6 (0.1)
Cibola (Valencia)	4,536	3,428 (75.6)	18 (0.3)	589 (13.0)	15 (0.3)
McKinley	2,778	920 (33.1)	25 (0.9)	1,590 (57.2)	14 (0.5)
Dona Ana	6,943	6,111 (88.0)	89 (1.3)	33 (0.5)	28 (0.4)
Luna	2,625	2,467 (94.0)	39 (1.5)	7 (0.3)	1 (0.0)
San Juan	4,759	3,361 (70.6)	20 (0.4)	1,189 (25.0)	3 (0.0)
Santa Fe	6,803	5,876 (86.4)	23 (0.3)	135 (2.0)	5 (0.0)

Source: Preliminary census data, Bureau of Business and Economic Research, University of New Mexico.

EXHIBIT 7

Number (percent) of household type for persons aged 65 and over, 1980

County	Total	Family household	Nonfamily household	Group quarters: noninstitutional
Bernalillo	34,000	23,489 (69.1)	9,744 (28.7)	767 (2.2)
Sandoval	3,421	2,706 (79.1)	642 (18.8)	73 (2.1)
Chaves	7,213	4,922 (68.2)	2,047 (28.4)	244 (3.4)
Cibola (Valencia)	4,563	3,148 (69.4)	1,387 (30.6)	1 (0.0)
McKinley	2,778	2,109 (75.9)	619 (22.3)	50 (1.8)
Dona Ana	6,943	4,907 (70.7)	1,886 (27.2)	150 (2.1)
Luna	2,625	1,913 (72.9)	672 (25.6)	40 (1.5)
San Juan	4,759	3,190 (67.0)	1,450 (30.5)	119 (2.5)
Sante Fe	6,803	4,449 (65.4)	2,070 (30.4)	284 (4.2)

Source: Preliminary census data, Bureau of Business and Economic Research, University of New Mexico.

EXHIBIT 8
Number (percent) of persons in household for persons aged 65 and over, 1980

			Two person household	
County	*Total*	*Household*	*Family household*	*Nonfamily household*
Bernalillo	25,345	8,913 (35.2)	15,910 (62.8)	522 (2.0)
Sandoval	2,486	604 (24.3)	1,857 (74.7)	25 (1.0)
Chaves	5,188	1,944 (37.5)	3,168 (61.1)	76 (1.5)
Cibola (Valencia)	3,588	1,326 (37.3)	2,185 (61.4)	47 (1.3)
McKinley	2,196	585 (26.2)	1,591 (72.4)	20 (0.1)
Dona Ana	5,216	1,757 (34.3)	3,366 (64.5)	93 (1.8)
Luna	1,908	633 (33.2)	1,249 (65.5)	26 (1.4)
San Juan	3,683	1,393 (37.8)	2,250 (61.1)	40 (1.1)
Santa Fe	5,053	1,920 (38.0)	3,030 (60.0)	103 (2.0)

Source: Preliminary census data, Bureau of Business and Economic Research, University of New Mexico.

EXHIBIT 9
Number (percent) in occupied housing units for persons aged 65 and over, 1980

County	*Total household under 65*	*Total household 65 and over*	*Number (%) owner-occupied for 65 and under*	*Number (%) renter-occupied for 65 and over*
Bernalillo	3,685	21,660	15,469 (71.4)	6,191 (28.6)
Sandoval	354	2,132	1,809 (84.8)	323 (15.2)
Chaves	432	4,756	3,654 (76.8)	1,102 (23.2)
Cibola (Valencia)	450	3,108	2,724 (87.6)	384 (12.4)
McKinley	375	1,821	1,348 (74.0)	473 (26.0)
Dona Ana	721	4,495	3,352 (74.6)	1,143 (25.4)
Luna	183	1,725	1,351 (78.3)	374 (21.7)
San Juan	467	3,207	2,678 (83.5)	529 (16.5)
Santa Fe	548	4,505	3,247 (72.1)	1,258 (27.9)

Source: Preliminary census data, Bureau of Business and Economic Research, University of New Mexico.

EXERCISE 13–13

The proposed staff level at Year 2 is that which might be needed to provide a given level of service to the age 65-and-over population in the counties served.

a Assume that this level of market penetration will increase by 100% by Year 5, an additional 50% by Year 10 (1993), and by another 20% by the year 2000.

b Also, assume that non-whites require 50% of the care as whites, because of the support of their families. (Hint: You may wish to convert these patients to full patient equivalents.)

- Develop growth projections for the age 65-and-over population for 1988, 1993, and 2000—based on data in the case.
- On the basis of this projection, and the programmatic changes recommended in the case, build a table of organization for each of these 3 years (1988, 1993, and 2000). (Note: The table of organization is a listing of positions to be filled and your estimate of the number of persons required for each).
- From this data, develop organizational structures you believe will serve this organization. Draw each structure, label positions, and explain your reasoning for the structure and its ability to support the service strategy you find in the case material.

POLICY RECOMMENDATIONS—STRATEGY IMPLEMENTATION

The myriad of businesses, products, services, and unique environments that one might encounter in the practice of general management would suggest that prescriptions for policies that support one's chosen strategy be difficult to identify and articulate. Fortunately, a recent empirical research study conducted on data drawn from the profit impact of marketing strategies (PIMS) data base provides solid evidence on which a number of sound but necessarily generic recommendations can be made.[26]

Several comments should be made about the applicability of this individual study to general prescriptions for policy direction. First, the data base contained only 11 companies identified as in the introduction stage of the PLC. Only three of the four stages of the product life cycle, therefore, provided data for identifiable policy direction. Second, although the data bank is large (1,234 companies), it is drawn from a single industry—industrial-products manufacturing. The applicability of a particular policy recommendation should be considered with some thought to the extent to which that recommendation, drawn from the industrial-products-manufacturing field, has merit in the business at hand. In general, most of the recommendations seem intuitively sound and can serve as a very reasonable basis for the development of similar statements or directives tailored to one's own industry.

The suggestions that follow are derived from the empirical evidence taken from the regression of a number of strategically important variables on Return on Investment (ROI) and a second set of regressions on *share of market*. These data seem particularly appropriate to the consideration of strategy implementation for Dominating Leaders concerned with market share as a major theme in strategy as well as

[26] Carl R. Anderson and Carl P. Zeithaml, "Stage of the Product Life Cycle, Business Strategy, and Business Performance," *Academy of Management Journal* 27(1) (1984), pp. 5–24.

Prospectors and Claim Defenders, organizations more immediately concerned with ROI than with market share as such.

Policy Recommendations for Claim Defenders and Prospectors—Intent: Build and Sustain ROI During the Growth Stage in the Product Life Cycle

- Maintain tight control on capital investment, to obtain maximum sales revenues from invested funds.
- Seek products that provide a maximum opportunity to add value. (Value added is the difference between cost of materials incoming and sales revenues.)
- Initiate and sustain continued pressure for high productivity in both manufacturing and sales.
- Monitor and control expenditures for product research and development to levels below those of the competition.
- Resist requests for customization of product offerings.

Policy Recommendations for Dominating Leaders—Intent: Build Market Share During the Growth and Early Maturity Stages in the Product Life Cycle

- Emphasize quality of products and service to customers.
- Pursue a broad product line in your chosen industry.
- Integrate backward when possible.
- In marketing, promote through extensive advertising.
- Emphasize product research and development.

Policy Recommendations for Claim Defenders and Prospectors Throughout the Entire Maturity Stage and for Dominating Leaders in the Late Maturity Stage—Intent: Maximize ROI and Harvest Profits

- Maintain control over investments in productive capacity to hold investment/sales down and utilization of facilities up.
- Continue to seek products in which a high value can be added or screen existing products to emphasize high value added.
- Emphasize high employee productivity (perhaps through extensive application of advanced equipment, methods, and high standards) and provide higher than average compensation.
- Emphasize high-quality products and service to customers.
- Minimize product research and development and customization of products.

As the industry declines, all categories of competitors face problems of reductions in facilities, product lines, employment, and divestiture or liquidation. Only three major policy recommendations are listed. Note that for all three categories of competitors (Claim Defenders, Prospectors, and Dominating Leaders), the degree of importance of each is greater than in preceding stages.

Policy Recommendations for All Three Categories of Firms in the Decline Stage—Intent: To Maximize ROI and Harvest Profits

- Screen product lines and select product offerings based on the highest levels of value added.
- Aggressively trim investment in productive capacity to keep investment/sales revenue down and utilization of available capacity up.
- Maintain sustained high pressure for high employee productivity.

EXERCISE 13-14

Review the recommendations for policy direction listed above, then prepare some directives that you might give your marketing, production, and financial executives. Prepare a single statement for each executive in the following situations:

- Growth Stage
  Claim Defender
- Early Maturity
  Dominating Leader
- Decline
  Prospector

14

EVALUATING SINGLE-BUSINESS STRATEGIES

To this point, we have built (in Parts One and Two an understanding of the working knowledge and skills needed by the general manager to be effective in implementing a given strategy. In Part Three, which we are now concluding, we have been concerned with developing a working understanding of the processes of strategy formulation and have made use of a model (Figure 14–1) to help in outlining the major steps involved in developing and implementing such a strategy for a single business. In all three parts, we have been building skills and knowledge, both needed before we can be effective in the processes of evaluation. In this chapter, we will be concerned with the evaluation of strategies in two contexts. First, we will be concerned with the evaluation of a prospective *new* strategy. Here, evaluation is a part of the processes involved in the choice of strategy marked by the shaded block in the lower right center of Figure 14–1. Our evaluation in this context includes an exami-

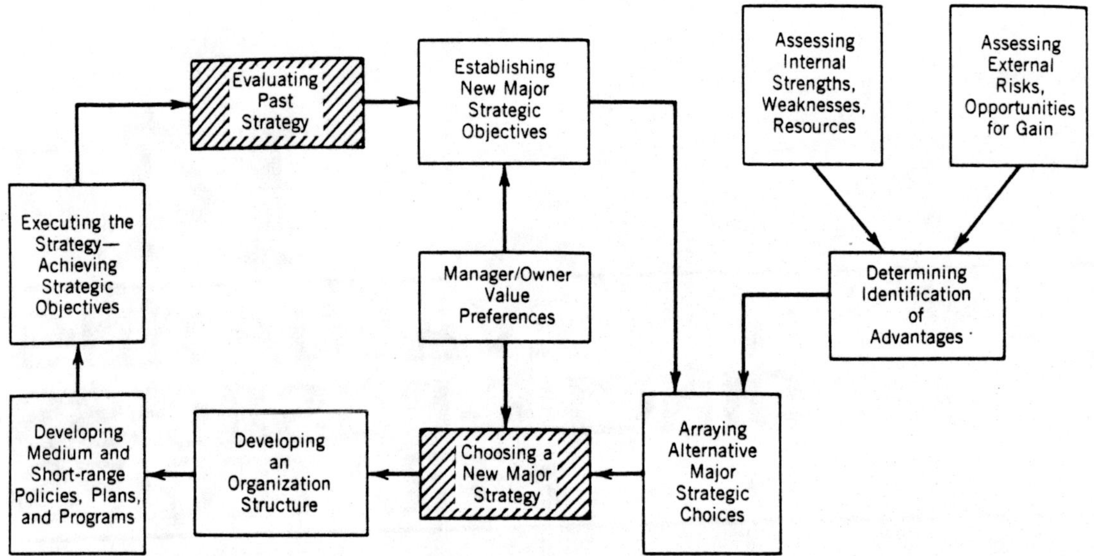

FIGURE 14-1 The strategy formulation process.

nation of the strategic plan to assure ourselves that the plan represents a good means of achieving desired objectives given the existing environment and organizational resources.

The second context is somewhat more complex because it involves not only an evaluation of the strategic plan, but also an assessment of the extent to which the organization has been functioning effectively. This evaluation process is that which is found in the upper left of Figure 14-1. Typically, this is the type of evaluation that is required in sizing up an existing situation. Although the sizing up is usually a *first* step for an experienced general manager, strategist, or organizational consultant, it is presented here—near the end of this book—because it requires knowledge and skills in both strategy formulation and implementation, areas that are only now developed to workable levels.

In this second type of evaluation, we will need to determine the strategy chosen by earlier generations of managers, either from explicit statements identifying selected strategies or, more likely, from the *actions* of the organization and its leaders over a period of time. Components of the strategy must be examined to assess the strategy's suitability given the circumstances of the time. Finally, organizational performance must be studied to determine the extent to which the organization has functioned efficiently and the extent to which it has been effective in achieving several kinds of objectives.

EVALUATION OF NEW STRATEGIES

The evaluation of the array of strategic choices should be the last step involved prior to choosing a strategy for implementation. The strategist at this point in the process must examine alternative strategies in light of a number of different criteria in order to rank choices in terms of desirability and ultimately to choose one or more for implementation and execution. This evaluation also serves to audit the process, to assure that the system of strategy formulation has produced a strategy that will meet the needs of the organization and its constituents.

The first set of criterion measures is that of fit with a selection framework.[1] In Chapter 12, several selection frameworks were described. The directional policy matrix of Hussey (Figure 12–2), the company strength/industry attractiveness framework of Boulton (Figure 12–3), the strategies derived from empirical analysis of profit impact of marketing strategies (PIMS) data, and the product life cycle framework found in Figures 12–4 through 12–8 are examples of these contingency models. In each, a general, or generic, description is provided for a type of strategy. In the directional policy matrix, a general strategic direction of "Proceed with Care" is prescribed for a situation that involves average business-sector prospects and average company-competitive capabilities. In the Boulton framework, where the strategic objective is to minimize losses, the general prescriptions include "Find Available Niches," "Specialize Products," "Minimize Cash Outlay," and "Plan Exit." In the product life cycle framework, prescriptions such as "Selective Concentration" or "R & D Leadership" are used to describe the thrust of the general strategy of the firm.

Our first task, therefore, is to examine the strategies suggested in light of one or, better yet, several of these frameworks to assure ourselves that our choice of general direction is suitable given the particular contingencies at hand. With the general strategy identified, it is important to begin the process of developing a statement of general strategy in terms that have working meaning in the operations of the firm. This statement should contain several very significant elements:[2]

1 The statement of general strategy should clearly identify the domain sought, that is, the chosen industry and the product/market segments that will be the focus of the interests of the company. Some companies are deeply committed to a particular industry. For them, there is little choice of industry. The niche (or several niches) they choose to address, however, can be of crucial importance in the development and implementation of operating strategies.

[1] Richard P. Rumelt, "Evaluation of Strategy: Theory and Models," in Dan E. Schendel and Charles W. Hofer, Eds., *Strategic Management: A New View of Business Policy and Planning* (Boston: Little, Brown, 1979), pp. 199–200.

[2] B. Yavitz and W. H. Newman, *Strategy in Action*, the Execution, Politics and Payoff of Business Planning (New York: Free Press, 1982), pp. 22–31.

2 The advantage to be utilized in serving the selected domain. In Chapter 10, we identified the elements that distinguished one competitor from another. As a strategy is developed, one or more components of that comparative advantage should serve as a principal means of separating the company from its competitors as it addresses the needs of customers in the chosen market. For very large competitors, the scale of operations may offer cost advantages. For smaller firms, attention to specialized needs of customers, unique product attributes, quick responsiveness, or attentive customer service may serve as significant means of differentiating offerings from one's competitors.

3 The strategic thrusts to be undertaken to achieve the desired objectives in a chosen period of time. In most cases, resources are not unlimited, and decision makers must select from several potential actions the course that is likely to achieve the desired objective in a reasonable and satisfactory time period. Where several thrusts are selected, the sequencing and timing of actions can aid in achieving objectives and may avoid undue exposure to financial risk. A company interested in the full development of a new geographic area, for example, might first begin by exploratory marketing, providing products at penalty transportation rates as a means of testing and developing the new market. Extensive investment in plant and equipment might be delayed until the market seems to be proven. In other cases, extensive investment might be needed to capture a market position or to prevent its capture by a competitor well in advance of the development of the market. This type of strategic action is sometimes found in the acquisition of raw materials in vertical integration or in the purchase or lease of theater or major grocery or department store sites in new shopping centers.

4 The target results to be expected. The statement of the results expected from a general strategy serves to add a dimension of specificity to the strategy that is helpful in focusing attention and marshaling resources. Investors and managers also find the statement of desired specified results useful in making decisions about the extent of their own commitment. These expectations also serve as the core of the personal and organizational objectives of the strategists. For effective implementation, these strategic goals require that managers identify appropriate measurement criteria and express the desired results in terms of those measurements. Market share, for example, might be stated in terms of a percentage of a total market or in terms of share of a specified niche. Profitability might be stated in any of several ways: on sales, on assets, on stockholder investment, on market value of owner investment. Growth might be stated in absolute or in relative terms. In any case, the objectives must be phrased in measurable terms. In the case of subjective criterion measures (customer satisfaction, employee morale, industry leadership, etc.), measurement techniques such as consumer panels, surveys, or independent expert opinions may be used to assess that particular result in acceptable form. In some instances, surrogate measures might suffice. An inverse relationship between employee grievances and morale might be posited, for example, in order that a target for morale might be stated in terms of lower levels of grievances. Similarly, product quality might be assessed in terms

of numbers of complaints, percentage of waste, or product failures in a testing program.

Following this clear statement of the general strategy, we should begin the process of developing the operational strategies that will guide divisional or functional managers in the performance of their duties. These substrategies are frequently narrower in scope than the general or master strategy. They may involve an individual division or may differ in terms of their impact on material, monetary, or human resources. Strategies may also be classified as to purpose (e.g., growth) or may relate to specific functions or products/markets.[3]

As one example, a Dominating Leader firm in the early maturity stage may have as general strategies profit leadership and concentric diversification. Strategies that might help in the implementation of these two general patterns of operation might be:

- In marketing . . . "Aggressively seek to develop and dominate market segments which maximize total profitability within existing investment levels." In its execution, this strategy would mean that the marketing staff would examine "the existing mix, accentuate marketing efforts in areas of highest *total* profitability, and seek product/market offerings that would also fill areas of production capacity. At such time as capacity were filled, products of lesser profitability might be pruned or additional capacity added through subcontracting to continue to press for segment domination while maximizing profit and capital utilization.
- In manufacturing . . . "Maximize productivity per capital dollar, while meeting the delivery and quality requirements of our customers. Minimize production and materials costs per unit, while meeting quality requirements of our customers." In execution, this would suggest that existing capital equipment would be utilized to its fullest. Tight control on purchased materials, waste, labor cost, and unit cost of production would be the dominant theme in production management.
- In research and development (R & D) . . . "Find processes which further reduce the cost of production while holding additional capital investment to a minimum. Seek additional new products, related to the present product mix, which will enhance and capitalize on our dominant position in the marketplace." In practice, the R & D function will be split into an applied, engineering-oriented process R & D group and a very applied, product-oriented group seeking to quickly find products to augment an existing strong product position.
- In finance . . . "Maximize the productive use of available capital. Minimize the cost of capital while maintaining the level of financial risk at appropriate levels." In application, this strategy suggests strong cash management operations, and a careful review and screening of fixed assets to assure their productive use.

[3] G. A. Steiner, J. B. Miner, and E. R. Gray, *Management Policy and Strategy*, 2nd Ed. (New York: Macmillan, 1982), pp. 20–21.

Nonproductive fixed assets may be liquidated to divert funds to productive applications. The financial manager will also be involved in an aggressive search for low-cost funds and a careful balancing of risk and capital costs in order to maintain an adequate supply of capital to meet organization needs. The manager of the financial function will need to orchestrate the development of a mix of short- and long-term debt sources and a strong base of stockholder funds to sustain the organization through a lengthy maturity stage.

EXERCISE 14-1

The following characteristics face you as a strategist:

1 Your firm is ranked twenty-eighth in size in your industry, an industry that contains 349 listed companies.

2 Your sales have grown at a rate of 7 to 9% per year over the past 5 years. Profits have ranged from 6 to 9% on sales after taxes.

3 Your board of directors has maintained a conservative position in the financial structure of the company. You now have nearly no long-term debt and a current ratio of 4.6 to 1. Your stockholders have come to expect a regular $2.50 per share dividend and, typically, have not expressed an interest in rapid growth in stock price. Most have held their interest in the company for more than 5 years.

4 Your company manufacturers and sells abrasive disks used with power equipment in the finishing and refinishing of wood, metal, and plastics. Industry growth has stabilized at 4 to 6% per year, closely related to industrial growth nationally.

5 Your company has been particularly helpful to the auto refinishing industry and has developed a number of products specifically designed to help body shops in the repair of autos. In that particular market, your company occupies a significant (65+%) share of the market.

- Place this situation in at least three of the frameworks found in Chapter 12. List the general strategies suggested by each.
- Select two of these three and prepare a statement of general strategy that you believe satisfies the criteria outlined above.
- When the preceding step has been completed, begin the development of the operating strategies you think will be of help to functional or division managers (if appropriate) in planning their activities over the next several years. List several operating strategies for each general strategy. (Hint: You may wish to refer to Chapter 12 and other earlier chapters for some thoughts on the types of directions that might be found helpful by subordinate managers.) Keep in mind that strategies should guide action over an extended period of time. Policies tend to be

narrower in scope, and tactics are shorter time-horizon approaches used to reach limited objectives.

As operating strategies are developed, it might be useful to consider the evaluation criteria of Tilles.[4] The first five of Tilles's six criteria relate to an evaluation of strategies *prior to* implementation. As a consequence, they serve as an additional check on the quality of the desired strategy, prior to its implementation. Tilles's criteria are:

1 *Internal Consistency.* The extent to which each of the operational strategies are consistent with the general strategy and each other. In single-business organizations, especially where a single individual is the strategy formulator, consistency is rarely a problem. In larger organizations, where strategies may be developed out of highly politicized processes, strategic inconsistency can be found.[5] Strategies chosen should not only be consistent in and of themselves, but they should also be consistent with the operating philosophies and managerial styles of owners and managers.[6]

2 *Consistency with the Environment.* The extent to which operational strategies and the general strategy address relevant issues in the external environment. The suggested set of strategies should address areas of opportunity and minimize risks, to whatever extent possible.

3 *Appropriateness in Light of Available Resources.* The strategic set (general and operational strategies) should seem appropriate in view of the resources presently or prospectively available to the firm. In reviewing strategies, it is useful to think carefully of monetary resources, materials, capital equipment, managerial talent, and human resources needed for manufacturing and marketing.

4 *Satisfactory Degree of Risk.* Several measures can be considered. First, the expected risk to be undergone should be balanced by an appropriate rate of return. Extensions of an existing strategy are probably less risky than new ventures and can probably be offset by lower levels of expected return. Entirely new ventures, on the other hand, may have little history and a high risk and probably require a significantly higher rate of return.

5 *Appropriate Time Horizon.* The successful attainment of strategic objectives requires that they be set in a time schedule consistent with their scope. A major aqueduct and water-supply system for a major metropolitan area may require a time horizon of 20 or more years. Similarly, the development of nuclear power plants requires a time schedule of 12 to 15 or more years to accommodate the interests and needs of all of the parties benefiting from, or affected by, the power facility and its potential hazards. Other strategies, of course, have a substantially

[4] S. Tilles, "How to Evaluate Corporate Strategy," *Harvard Business Review* (July–August, 1963).

[5] Rumelt, "Evaluation of Strategy," p. 199.

[6] Steiner et al., *Management Policy*, p. 241.

shorter time horizon. The development of a concentrically diversified product line may require only 6, 12, or perhaps 24 months. In the software business, revolutionary new products may emerge even more quickly and strategic horizons must be adjusted accordingly.

EXERCISE 14–2

Examine the operational strategies you developed for Exercise 14–1.

- Evaluate these strategies in terms of the five criteria of Tilles.
- If any of the five criteria are not addressed by your operating strategies, what modifications do you believe might be needed and/or helpful? Explain.

The Outdoor Outfitters, Ltd. case describes a situation faced by a small regional retailer of outdoor products. As you read the case, make notes so that you can respond to the exercise questions that follow it.

OUTDOOR OUTFITTERS, LTD.

The early seventies witnessed an explosion of interest in outdoor activities such as camping, backpacking, canoeing, and hiking. This trend substantially increased sales of recreation vehicles, including four-wheel drives, campers, and trail bikes. But Outdoor Outfitters, Ltd., a small chain of mountain equipment suppliers, was determined to carry only ecologically safe and sound items—those that are noiseless, nondestructive, and self-propelled. They furthered this image by sponsoring free outdoor country and blue-grass music concerts and other events. A recent catalog of Outdoor Outfitters, Ltd. carried this message:

> *WE HAVE COMPLETED OUR REMODELING!!!*
>
> *Over the past few months, Outdoor Outfitters, Ltd., has been expanding (thanks to your patronage). During that time the store was a mess and service was a little . . . confusing, at best. But that's over with now.*
>
> *We have enlarged and remodeled our showroom. The walls and display fixtures are done with some beautiful locally milled poplar boards and our stone work with local rip rap. We're ready for business now, so stop in and take a look at our new store.*
>
> Our People—*Outdoor Outfitters, Ltd., is staffed by individuals who have been*

This case was prepared by Professor Paul Miesing of the State University of New York at Albany as a basis for class discussion and is not intended to illustrate either effective or ineffective handling of an administrative situation.

involved in outdoor activities for years. We actively use the equipment we sell and can give competent advice on its selection and usage. Educating the public is one of our main concerns and with this in mind, we sponsor educational seminars and trips throughout the year.

Our Products—*The companies . . . whose products we carry manufacture some of the finest outdoor recreation equipment in the world. From the Appalachians to the Himalayas, the products we handle have been tested and refined by generations of outdoorsmen.*

The term "leisure goods" is appropriate to recreation equipment since they are used in one's spare time. Hence, sales depend on the excess time available to the potential purchaser. While the work week has remained constant at forty hours since World War II, the average work year has been reduced by longer vacations and additional paid holidays. Now up to one-third of the average American's time can . . . be considered "free" or unoccupied. Much of this time is spent with the family, and leisure is now considered a necessity by many.

Recreation expenditures also depend on the money available to the potential buyer. As shown in Exhibit 1, sales of these items generally keep pace with disposable income. Of these expenditures, approximately twelve billion dollars a year is spent on sporting goods, with camping, skiing, and fishing equipment purchases equalling nearly one-half billion dollars each. Although growth for this industry is expected to surpass the economy as a whole, it should not match the rate experienced in the sixties and early seventies due to the dampening effects of inflation. (See Exhibit 2.)

Typically, buyers of leisure-oriented goods search for and demand information, are emotionally involved with their purchase, and have the option of postponing it. And since these goods satisfy needs for self-fulfillment and self-expression, there is little brand loyalty. Instead, purchasers are tremendously influenced by friends, experts, and magazine editorials. Furthermore, since first-time purchasers also tend to fall in the nineteen- to twenty-four-year-old age group and are extremely fearful of making a

EXHIBIT 1

Outdoor Outfitters, Ltd., Disposable Income and Recreation Expenditures

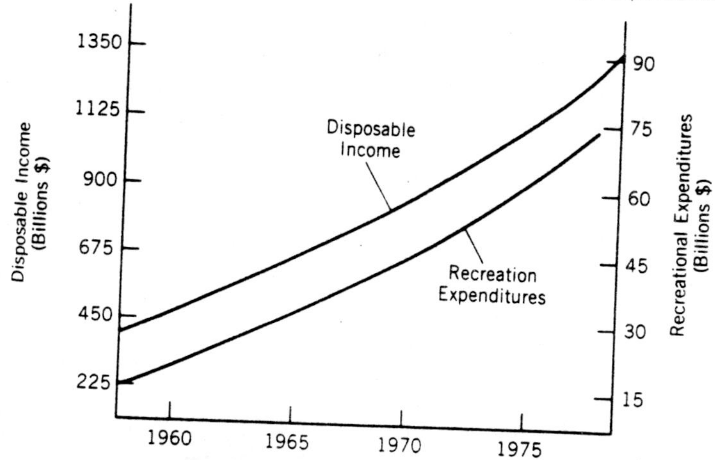

EXHIBIT 2
Outdoor Outfitters Ltd., financial statistics for selected firms for 1977

	5-yr. Avge. ROE	*1-yr. Avge. ROE*	*5-yr. Avge. ROC*	*1-yr. Avge. ROC*	*Net profit margin*	*5-yr. Avge. sales*
AMF, Inc.	13.3%	12.9%	8.9%	9.7%	3.3%	8.8%
Brunswick	12.3	10.9	9.5	8.6	4.0	11.1
Fuqua	5.3	10.5	4.9	7.3	2.7	10.2
Recreation Industry Median	12.7	13.3	9.5	10.1	3.8	10.9
All Leisure Industry Median	15.1	17.5	11.1	12.7	5.4	1.2

wrong choice, these individuals are avid comparison shoppers, take longer to decide, and are price conscious. In short, the "right" equipment is usually one that is economically painless yet chic. On balance, the net result has been larger sales of quality and durable items, with the weakest sellers being the inexpensive ends of the lines.

In addition to time, money, and psychological fulfillment, demand for recreation equipment is also influenced by available "support" facilities, such as the mountains and streams of the nearby environment. Jefferson City, a middle-sized university town and headquarters for Outdoor Outfitters, Ltd., is well suited for this since it is situated close to many national parks and national forests.

The area also draws thousands of visitors each year, being a major tourist and recreational center. This attraction is reflected in the town's annual general merchandise sales (including variety and general stores) of around fifty million dollars, with an identical amount attributed to department store sales. In addition, the median age—heavily influenced by the student population—is twenty-eight for males and thirty for females, with approximately one-fourth of the work force considered as professionals and one-half as white-collar.

Outdoor Outfitters, Ltd., was started in 1972 as the outgrowth of an M.B.A. thesis at the State University in Jefferson City. Having experienced several setbacks during 1973, it was sold by the founder in 1974. The company then began to reach a very good average annual growth rate as several additional stores were gradually opened along the foothills of the nearby mountain range, with Jefferson City serving as the center for these distant operations. However, sales at the Jefferson City store began to level off during the renovation in 1976 and 1977. Although some momentum was lost at this branch, it did not prevent the company as a whole from mountaining its above-average growth rate.

The location of the Jefferson City store was well suited. The only local store carrying specialized recreation goods (except for several discount and general department stores), it was set in off the main thoroughfare through town: accessible, yet isolated. The store itself was somewhat disorganized, but this appearance only emphasized the casual atmosphere of the place. In fact, a recent survey by top management as to how they might improve operations was answered by approximately one-half of the store managers. (See Exhibit 3.)

With knowledgeable sales help, there was originally little need for direction by the managers. But the increase in size also brought about an increase in complexity, and so the acquirers decided to organize the operations by geographic area (see Exhibit 4) and centrally manage the branches so as to achieve scale econo-

EXHIBIT 3

Outdoor Outfitters, Ltd., excerpts from a questionnaire on improving operations

1. Once a customer has decided to buy backpacking equipment, why does the customer buy *our products?* Why does the customer buy from us and not from the competition?
2. What do you think the trend for the future will be—more or fewer customers?
3. Through your observations on the sales floor, how do new customers find out about Outdoor Outfitters, Ltd.?
4. What is the direction you see Outdoor Outfitters, Ltd., moving in?
   What would be your "ideal" direction? If there are differences, what do you perceive to be the motivation for our direction?
5. Please list new product areas Outdoor Outfitters, Ltd., should consider.
   Please list product areas we are into which you think we should get out of.
   Please list product areas which are reasonable considerations for a backpacking shop which you think we should not consider.
6. Other than new product areas, what PROJECT AREAS do you think Outdoor Outfitters, Ltd., should consider? (e.g., teaching, rental, publications, environmental lobbying).
7. Please list things you think Outdoor Outfitters, Ltd., does well—for the public and for in-store operations. Please list your gripes.
8. Do you feel that Outdoor Outfitters, Ltd., is doing an effective job of service to the customer? If not, why not?
   How would you go about improving service?
9. What complaints do you hear most frequently from customers? What complaints do you most often have?
10. What are the praises you hear most often from customers? What praises do you most often have?

EXHIBIT 4

Outdoor Outfitters, Ltd., Organization Chart

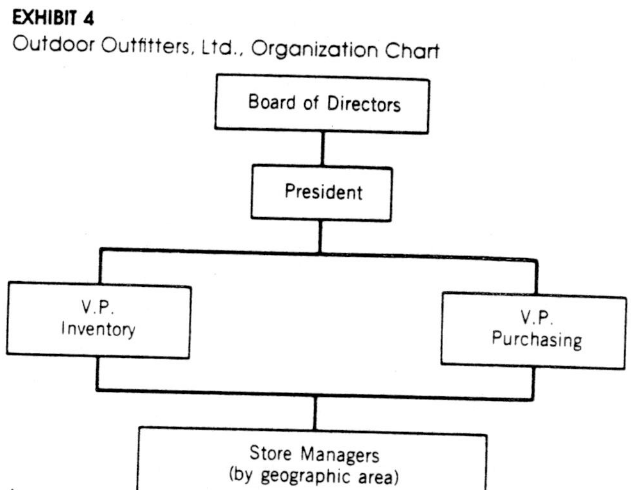

mies and greater purchasing power. The local managers retained the authority to stock, promote, and staff their branches within the budgetary guidelines. In addition, all of the managers would attend monthly meetings which—among other things—determined the inventory to be purchased.

One aspect of this reorganization included a formal inventory control system, whereby items would be ordered monthly based on the prior year's sales. Actual stock levels were then recorded from sales tickets for the past week. Management planned to check this running tabulation periodically for accuracy of item, code number, color, and size, and to readjust any discrepancies. Examination of four random sales days revealed that, whereas the other branch stores averaged four-and-a-half recording errors per day, the Jefferson City store averaged nine recording errors per day over the same period. (See Exhibit 5 for relative productivity estimates.)

Management also attempted to coordinate the stores with inter-company store transfers of merchandise. The company's purchaser relies heavily on reports from the manufacturers' representatives on which items are selling well, so he would determine each store's requirements and make allocations as he saw fit. Imbalances between local supply and demand required special shipping arrangements between branches, causing both delays and unnecessary expenses. Although the other stores averaged seven-and-a-half such transfer requests per week, the Jefferson City branch made eleven-and-a-half inter-store transfer requests per week.

Special order requests also boosted costs. Generally under fifty dollars each, every special order requires fifteen minutes of processing time, both going out and coming in. In addition, costs add up for shipping and handling, telephone, administration, errors—and occasionally the cost of a customer failing to pick up a special order. As a result, management is considering instituting a service charge for special orders, or perhaps offering a discount to customers willing to switch preference toward items in stock. But so far, the sales help is reluctant to either request deposits for special orders or recommend substitutions.

The Jefferson City store sales projections for 1978 have been lowered by ten percent and profits by twenty percent based on early figures (at a time when other local businesses expect increased sales of ten percent). The store's president wrote a recent memo, excerpted here:

> *Our current sales staff at the Jefferson City store consists of young, part-time individuals. As such, they continue to demonstrate an independence not welcome considering our recent setbacks. They are arrogant and impolite to customers. Their work pace is slow, and they avoid responsibility, claiming an unfamiliarity with our established procedures. They are obviously unaware of*

EXHIBIT 5
Outdoor Outfitters, Ltd., relative productivity of Jefferson City store

	Jefferson City store	*Average for other branches*
Number Part-time Employees	9	7
Number Full-time Employees	2	2
Annual Man-hours	7,000	6,000
Sales per Man-hour	$32	$24

the costs involved for their practices. They continue to recommend items to our customers that they enjoy rather than attempt to sell what's on hand. This only leads to expensive imbalances in our inventory, inter-store transfers, and special orders. In addition, they are sloppy and careless in their recording of items sold, further throwing off our inventory control. I really don't think they take this business seriously. Finally, they have demonstrated resistance to our improved system of operations and sabotage every new procedure we attempt to introduce. In short, they apparently do not have our interests at stake but only their own. With this in mind, I suggest we immediately replace the Jefferson City sales staff with more experienced full-time professional salesmen.

All of these problems are now coming to a head. Management is contemplating further expansion by diversifying into such items as sportswear, cross-country skis, and even snowmobiles. In order to better implement this planned growth, management feels it needs to tighten the reins in on the operations so that the various stores will be better coordinated. This need was particularly evident when the Jefferson City store introduced sports-shirts. Resentment from the sales help resulted in low sales, even though they might have earned a high commission on them.

EXERCISE 14–3

Identify the general strategy that was followed by Outdoor Outfitters, Ltd., in its operations from 1974 to 1977.

- List the principal elements which lead you to this conclusion.
- What operational strategies did the company use to help in achieving its general strategic objectives?
- Use the processes discussed thus far to evaluate this strategy.

  How well does it fit one or more of the strategy selection frameworks?
  Is the general strategy complete? If not, what elements would help to clarify the general strategy and to specify its objectives?
  How well does the strategy fit Tilles's evaluation criteria?

EXERCISE 14–4

Now examine the statement contained in the last paragraph of the case, and the recent actions of management.

- Does this suggest a change in strategy? Why?
- Evaluate these actions of management, using any of the evaluative tools which you believe might be helpful.

EXERCISE 14–5

You have been asked to serve as a strategy consultant to Outdoor Outfitters, Ltd.

- Prepare an analysis of the situation faced by Outdoor Outfitters and suggest a general strategy based on that analysis.
- Prepare a statement of the general strategy that you believe will be helpful to top management and to the managers of each of the retail stores.
- Prepare drafts of operational strategy statements that will be helpful in guiding functional and divisional managers at Outdoor Outfitters.
- Test this set of strategy statements by means of the evaluative tools described thus far in this chapter.

POST-IMPLEMENTATION EVALUATION OF STRATEGIES

The approach toward strategy formulation that has been developed is that of a contingency perspective, that is, that organizations can and should be responsive to internal and external forces in developing and achieving long-term organizational objectives. In this, the approach is consistent with an open-systems view of organizations.[7] As Steers has pointed out, "Organizations have stated purposes, communication systems and other coordinating processes, and a group of people who are willing to cooperate on the tasks necessary for goal attainment." Following a brief review of relevant literature, Steers notes, "Several common threads run through these various definitions of organizations. Most importantly, organizations are viewed as collectivities of people working together for common goals. Inherent in such a definition are the related notions of a goal orientation and a systems perspective."[8]

The view of organizations as systems considers that organizational goals or tasks are accomplished through transformations or conversion processes. The environment provides various types of inputs required, a transformation is accomplished, and outputs needed or required by the environment are produced by the transformation. Figure 14–2 is an abbreviated graphic description of the open-systems model of organizations. The organization must not only achieve desired goals, but must also find ways of adapting to the availability of resources and to the changing interests and needs of the environment for output.

One highly simplified example might be the conversion or transformation of students in an educational system. The environment (our society) has a need for an

[7] D. Katz and R. L. Kahn, *The Social Psychology of Organizations* (New York: John Wiley, 1966). See also, F. E. Kast and J. E. Rosenzweig, *Organization and Management: A Systems Approach*, 4th Ed. (New York: McGraw-Hill, 1985).

[8] R. M. Steers, *Organizational Effectiveness: A Behavioral View* (Santa Monica, Calif.: Goodyear Publishing, 1977), p. 12.

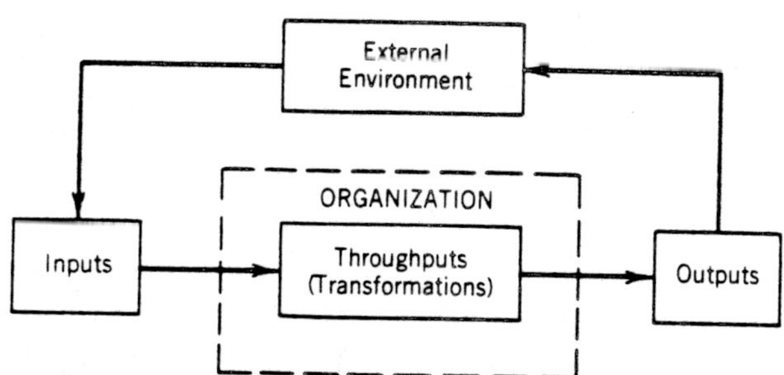

FIGURE 14–2 Open-systems model of organizations. Adapted from R. M. Steers, *Organizational Effectiveness: A Behavioral View* (Santa Monica, Calif.: Goodyear Publishing, 1977), p. 11.

educated citizenry. It has expressed a willingness to provide buildings, space, and tax revenues to fund a system of public education. It also provides higher education programs to produce well-educated instructors and a guaranteed supply of students (through compulsory education). Within the school system, students move through 13 levels of instruction: kindergarten through twelfth grade. At the conclusion of this conversion, or transformation, process, the environment expects that students are able to read and write, are reasonably competent in mathematics, are prepared to enter vocational training or the job market, or are ready for higher education. As the supply of students diminishes or expands, the school system is expected to adjust. Similarly, as the need for new courses (e.g., in computers or in driver education) is expressed by parents and taxpayers, the school system is expected to adapt in terms of its "product" offerings. The school system accomplishes its objectives, but does so in response to the availability of resources and the needs of its clientele.

For our purposes, the evaluation of an organization should make use of both major components: the extent to which goals have been accomplished and the degree to which the organization has been adaptive in relationship to its environment. In addition, it is important that the evaluation cover both short- and long-range time perspectives. Yavitz and Newman[9] observe that strategy formulation and review follow three quite different patterns, depending on environmental conditions.

- In a situation where environmental change is relatively predictable, a fully detailed strategic plan can serve as a control mechanism for the organization's entire life. The authors refer to this type of strategic plan and control system as a "Cook's Tour," or "Place a Man on the Moon."
- A second type of strategic planning and control model is one in which the objective and its importance are evident but the means for achieving the objective are largely unknown. The Lewis and Clark expedition is cited by the authors as a historical example. Modern weapons system development might serve as a

[9] Yavitz and Newman, *Strategy in Action*, pp. 113–21.

modern-day equivalent. In both cases, the objectives are known and are considered achievable. Neither the means nor the timetable, however, are known, and crucial decisions on direction and resource utilization are required on a daily basis.

- The third type of model described by Yavitz and Newman involves decentralized incrementalism. The example cited is that of homesteading the American frontier. Individual homesteaders decided the extent of their interest in moving West and determined the point at which they had achieved their individual objectives. Decisions were not only made on an incremental basis, but were affected by the experiences of others. This approach has been referred to as "muddling through" by Lindblom,[10] and has been supported by the concept of "logical incrementalism."[11] The incremental approach is probably most useful in situations in which both the rate of change and uncertainty of that change are high. In the late 1980s, the microcomputer industry is likely to be characterized this way. Not only will the goals of organizations be set on a highly individualized basis, but the experience of others in the field is likely to have a major effect on the daily decisions of competing firms, decisions that are likely to be short rather than long-range in nature.

Our evaluation process, therefore, will be conducted first at a macro, or strategic, level and will examine the ability of the organization to find and implement *strategies* that are consistent with their strengths, weaknesses, risk preferences, values, and the environmental conditions in which the organization functions.

The second level of evaluation involves an assessment of effectiveness at an *operational* level. Although operational evaluation will be covered in some detail later, four major categories of evaluation criteria are used in this process:

1. The accomplishment of strategic and operational goals, including employee and member satisfaction.[12]
2. The extent to which the organization can command scarce resources.[13]
3. The efficiency of the conversion or transformation processes.[14]
4. The ability of the organization to respond and adapt to the needs, interests, values, and competitive forces in the external environment.[15]

First, we will examine the evaluation of adaptation and goal accomplishment at

[10] C. E. Lindblom, "The Science of Muddling Through," *Public Administration Review* (Spring 1959).

[11] J. B. Quinn, "Strategic Change: 'Logical Incrementalism,'" *Sloan Management Review* (Fall 1978).

[12] Steers, *Organizational Effectiveness*, pp. 12–13.

[13] E. Yuchtman and S. E. Seashore, "A System Resource Approach to Organizational Effectiveness", *American Sociological Review* 32 (1967), pp. 891–903.

[14] J. L. Gibson, J. M. Ivancevich, and J. H. Donnelly, Jr., *Organizations*, 5th. Ed. (Plano, Tex: Business Publications, 1985), p. 35.

[15] Steers, *Organizational Effectiveness*, p. 46.

the strategic level. Then, we will examine the evaluation of much more detailed elements involved in the adaptation, the attainment of transformation efficiencies, and the achievement of operational goals.

Evaluation of General Strategic Performance

At this level of analysis, we wish to examine the organization and its environment while maintaining a perspective of long-range strategy formulation and execution. We should consider the organization in open-systems terms, and we must review and evaluate the processes described in Chapters 10 through 13. Figure 14–3 provides a graphic depiction of the organization and its relationship to its environment that may help you in visualizing this evaluation.

In strategic terms, the organization adapts by first identifying critical elements in the external environment. Identifying risks and opportunities enables the organization to develop product offerings targeted to market needs. It also may provide an assessment of the importance of changes in technologies as well as the extent of environmental provision of inputs: work force, money, materials, and equipment or technology.

The information derived in this step must then be used to make a choice of strategy in order to begin the decision processes required to begin implementation. The organization's structure must be adjusted for maximum strategic impact and organizational policies and programs must be developed, selected, and executed.

Finally, the result of this process of adaptation and achievement is the accomplishment of strategic objectives. As we review Figure 14–3 and the stages in the strategic process, we see that a number of questions can be used for purposes of evaluating execution and goal accomplishment at the strategic level:

1 To what extent has management been able to assess the nature of the general and industry-specific environment with reasonable accuracy?

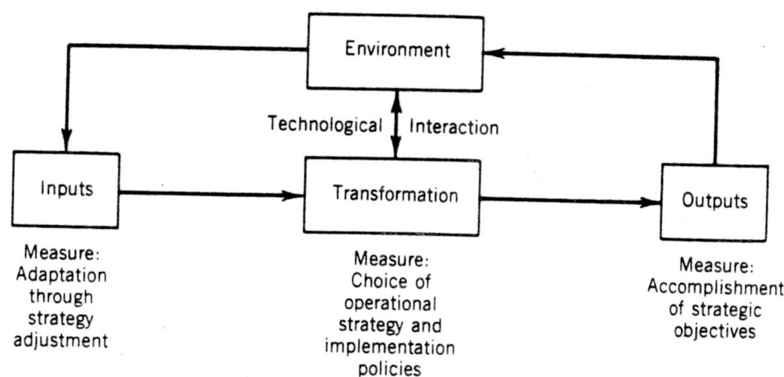

FIGURE 14–3 Execution and goal accomplishment at the strategic level.

2 To what extent has management been able to assess with reasonable accuracy the nature of the internal resources and weaknesses of the organization?

3 To what extent has management been able to identify and adopt a strategy appropriate to the organization's circumstances at the time of its adoption?

4 Were the organizational structure and the policies and programs selected for implementation appropriate to the choice of strategy?

5 To what extent were strategic objectives achieved?

EXERCISE 14-6

Turn back to Exhibits 12-4 through 12-8 and review the factors to be considered in the choice of strategy.

- What elements in the internal environment might tend to move a company *down* on the scale in terms of the typology of strategic modes (e.g., Dominating Leader, Prospector, Claim Defender)?
- What elements in the external environment might move a company *up* on that scale?
- What factors in the values system of key managers might tend to affect the placement on the scale? Explain how these affect placement.

EXERCISE 14-7

Your company, Enterprise Technology Associates, has begun to see the fruits of a lengthy development process for its holographic imaging equipment. The industry has a relatively small number of competitors, but sales have begun to increase significantly. Your company has chosen to address the application of holographic (three-dimensional) imaging as a device to provide realistic training for law enforcement officers. As it has now been developed, a holographic image of an armed criminal can be made to appear and to move realistically in a target-range setting made to look like a typical urban alley or residence. Instead of target images popping up (but not moving) from behind doorways, this new device permits an image of an assailant to appear to move—running, walking, crawling—from point to point in the decorated range setting—wheeling, turning, kneeling, or taking a hostage should that be a part of the practice combat scenario.

Your company has a unique combination of technical talent. One principal is an expert in laser technology (required for holographic imaging). The second has spent a lifetime in law enforcement and is a nationally recognized expert in combat marksmanship techniques.

The two principals have divided the management tasks. The technical expert has assumed responsibility for R & D and manufacturing. The other expert has assumed responsibility for establishing relationships with law enforcement agencies and is presently training a number of marketing representatives. In addition to these two individuals, an accountant has been hired to supervise and perform all accounting, billing, account collection, secretarial support, and financial matters. Strategic decisions are the responsibility of a four-person executive committee comprised of the two principals, the firm's corporate attorney, and its banker. The technical expert serves as the corporation's president.

You have been approached by a number of engineers and marketing experts who have expressed an interest in the cinematic capability of your patented projection equipment to consider other markets and applications. With more financial backing, you might consider expanding to other specialized markets for holography. You have decided, however, believing that your limited resources can be best utilized in serving a smaller market in a superior fashion.

- Identify the stage of the life cycle for this product and the strategic mode of this company. Explain your reasoning.
- Describe the generic strategy employed by this company. Is it consistent with the situation? Explain.
- How is the company organized? Do you find this organization appropriate for the company's situation and planned strategy?

EXERCISE 14-8

Following a presentation he had made to a local ventures group, the company's president was approached by a representative of a large regional venture capital firm. The representative suggested that in his opinion the technological capability of the company's equipment could make a significant impact in the entertainment field. His group would be interested in exploring the financing of a venture into holographic entertainment and could provide capital in the range from $5 million to $50 million, nearly 1,000 times the present capital base of your small company. In addition, he would provide experienced and expert financial advisors and professional marketing and general managers to help in staffing and operating the new venture.

- Assume that you accepted the venture capital. Does this change the situation? In what way? Explain.
- Will the mode of strategy change, that is, might the company move from Leader to Prospector, or Claim Defender to Leader? Explain.
- Will the type of strategy appropriate to the new situation differ from that used in the past? Explain.
- Select a mode, a strategy, and a structure that you believe will be best suited to the new situation. Explain your reasoning.

EXERCISE 14–9

Turn back to the situation described in Exercise 14–7. Enterprise Technology Associates receives a telephone call from the law enforcement expert at 1:30 A.M. and you are told that the other principal, the president, was fatally injured an hour earlier in an auto accident.

- Does this change the situation? Explain.
- Does it call for a different mode of operation, that is, a change from Prospector to Leader, Claim Defender to Prospector?
- Recommend a mode, a strategy, and an organizational structure that you believe will be of help in implementing the chosen strategy. Explain your reasoning.

It should be apparent from the exercises we have just concluded that one measure of effectiveness for organizations is the extent to which their strategists can formulate new objectives and adopt and implement new strategies, strategies that serve to guide the organization in adapting to changes encountered as events unfold.

Goal Accomplishment

The descriptions provided in Chapter 12 for modes of strategic thinking (Dominating Leader, Prospector, and Claim Defender) each contain the essence of strategic objectives framed in terms of a role. In addition, the generic strategies of concentration, vertical integration, profit maximization, differentiation, and others each carry an implicit strategic objective. If, for example, our generic strategy were to be selective concentration, we would expect to ask ourselves after this strategy has been in effect for a reasonable time, "Are we concentrated, and are we concentrated selectively?" If we were to find that we have scattered our product offerings across a broad range of markets or have chosen the largest market segment instead of one that provides for a tightly focused marketing effort, we would have to conclude that we have not achieved our strategic objectives. To operationalize the strategic objective of selective concentration, the general manager might choose as a policy directive to limit (perhaps arbitrarily) the number of markets served and their size as one means of establishing a strategic control mechanism. Measures of achievement for selective concentration could include a maximum number of product/markets served and a specified penetration level in each (i.e., no more than three product/markets and no less than a 30% share in each market). Additional objectives might include a profitability measure for each in order to assure that the search for concentration would be to achieve high levels of profit on sales and/or investment within the limitations of organizational resources.

In an examination and evaluation of a given business's performance at the strategic level, we may find that it has not achieved what might reasonably be expected of a company in those circumstances. Problems might have arisen in choice of strategy, in execution, or in the failure of management to adequately specify the task objectives to be measured and the performance level expected.

EXERCISE 14–10

- Select general strategies for Dominating Leaders in the early development, late growth, and early maturity stages.

  Describe strategic objectives and suggest measures for each.
- Select general strategies for Claim Defenders in the late development, early maturity, and early decline stages.

  Describe strategic objectives and suggest measures for each.
- Select general strategies for Prospectors in late development, late maturity, and late decline stages.

  Describe strategic objectives and suggest measures for each.

Once again as we examine a situation we should make use of the questions posed earlier (see pp. 601–2) and the strategic frameworks found in Chapter 12 to help in determining the extent to which the organization is effective in the strategic dimension: first in establishing a good strategic choice, next in initiating the institution of the strategy, and finally, in executing the strategy in the accomplishment of strategic objectives. We will now examine the detailed shorter-range strategies needed to deal with operational issues in strategy execution.

Evaluation of Operational Strategic Performance

The evaluation of operational strategic performance can reasonably make use of a process that follows an increasing degree of specificity. The process begins by an examination of the apparent suitability of the operational strategies and policies themselves, then examines the effectiveness of operational organizational performance by major functional areas, and concludes with a detailed examination of univariate and multivariate measures of effectiveness.

The first step in the process of examining operational strategic performance, therefore, is to assess the quality of the chosen operational strategies and policies. The general question to be asked is, "Do the operational strategies and policy guidelines serve to guide managerial and operative personnel in directions that will result in the attainment of the general strategic objectives?" If a general strategy for the organization is to adopt a Claim Protector role, for example, then operational guidelines that would permit entrepreneurial actions by managers would not be consistent with the general strategy. Similarly, operational guides that serve to slow market response time in an active competitive market would not be consistent with the general strategies of market dominance across a large market (Dominating Leader) or with aggressive dominance in a smaller segment of the market (the Prospector role).

EXERCISE 14-11

Select any two general strategies from the product-life-cycle strategy-selection framework found in Figures 12-5 through 12-8.

- For each of two different functional areas of the organization, draft operational strategy and policy statements you believe will be consistent with the general strategy. Be prepared to explain your reasoning.
- Now draft two operational strategy and policy statements (this time in different functional areas) you believe to be inconsistent with the general strategy. Be prepared to explain your reasoning.

The preceding step is designed to examine the choice of operational strategies and policies. We are concerned with the extent of congruence between general and operational strategies, and our standards are largely judgmental. As we move to the next, somewhat more detailed assessment, we will begin to explore more objective means of evaluating organizational performance in a multifaceted performance model. In this process, we seek to assess organizational effectiveness, a concept that not only addresses the extent to which the organization accomplishes tasks, or goals, but also the degree to which the organization adapts, survives, and thrives in its environment. Steers[16] concludes his review of the literature by identifying five major facets of organizational effectiveness:

1 Adaptability and Flexibility.
2 Productivity.
3 Job satisfaction.
4 Profitability.
5 Resource acquisition.[17]

For our own operational use, some elaboration on these five measures seems appropriate. First, adaptability and flexibility can often be assessed by means of the measurement of market share. As market needs shift, organizations that are responsive to customers and clients will maintain the flexibility needed to adjust their product/service offerings. Market share is especially revealing as a measure of adaptability and flexibility during periods of market change in which market expansion, contraction, or segmentation are most pronounced.

The most responsive and adaptive organizations will not only respond to customer needs, but also will actively search for new products and new processes that will enable them to anticipate or even create customer interest. The search for new technologies can result in improved products, lower costs, and improved services. A

[16] Steers, *Organizational Effectiveness* (Santa Monica, Calif.: Goodyear Publishing, 1977).

[17] Steers, *Organizational Effectiveness*, p. 175.

composite measure called development will serve to assess the extent to which the organization is involved in new product development and process research.

Another need for elaboration involves the topic of productivity. As developed by Campbell,[18] the single word *productivity* delineates at least two elements involved in transformation: (1) production, or numbers of products made, services performed, or other kinds of transformations and (2) the efficiency of those transformations. We should therefore replace the single measure of productivity with two, production and efficiency.

Our list, therefore, will contain seven effectiveness measures:

1 Market share—especially during time of market expansion or market change.

2 Development—probably evaluated best by the extent of leadership or rapidity in responsiveness in both product and process research and development activity.

3 Production—extent of attainment of transformation goals: responsiveness to customer demands, minimal numbers of stockouts, backorders, and so on.

4 Efficiency—measures of performance per unit of time, per unit of personnel, or per monetary unit where possible.

5 Satisfaction—of major constituencies: employees, customers, stockholders, suppliers.

6 Profitability—A variety of profitability measures were discussed in earlier chapters.

7 Resource acquisition—especially during periods of short supply. Measures might include stockouts, emergency orders of materials, premium prices paid, or excessive materials inventories.

If we examine Figure 14-4, we see that effectiveness measures are placed at points appropriate to the systemic element involved. The resource acquisition mea-

[18] Steers, *Organizational Effectiveness,* p. 40.

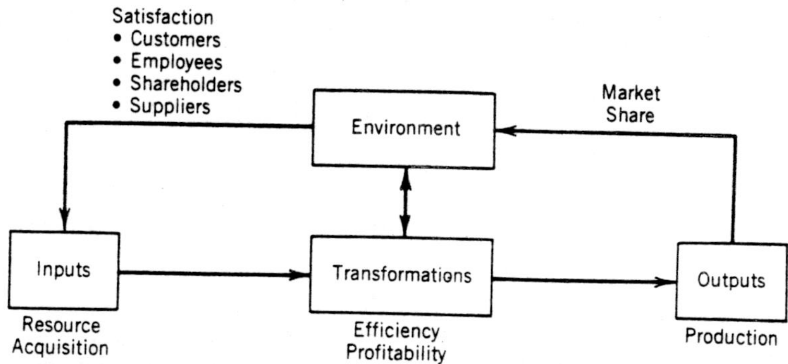

FIGURE 14-4 Evaluation of execution and goal accomplishment at the operational level.

sure, of course, would be placed at the inputs. Satisfaction is a measure that can assess the ability of the organization to acquire and hold resources. As examples, job satisfaction may lead to retention of employees; shareholder satisfaction may aid in achieving stability in stock prices and support for management action.

Production, or the extent of attainment of production goals, serves as a measure of output in the systems model of the organization.

Efficiency and profitability are clearly internal transformation measures, assessing the extent to which resources are optimally used.

EXERCISE 14-12

Your organization is a public utility that provides electrical power to residential, industrial, not-for profit, and government customers in your 25-county service area. Fifty-five percent of your power is provided by your coal-fired and nuclear power plants. The remainder is purchased from other adjacent power-system companies and a manufacturing plant that generates electrical power for its own uses.

- Select four of the seven effectiveness measures previously identified (see Figure 14-4) and list at least two means of operationally measuring these characteristics.
- Which of these measures can or should be used in snapshot fashion? Why?
- Which should be taken over a period of time? Why?
- Which should be compared with industry or key competitors? Why?

EXERCISE 14-13

Your organization is a private elementary school. You provide accredited and licensed educational services to students in Kindergarten through grade 8 to a service area approximately 10 miles in each direction from your school complex.

- Select four of the seven effectiveness measures previously identified (see Figure 14-4) and list at least two means of operationally measuring these characteristics.
- Which of these measures can or should be used in snapshot fashion? Why?
- Which should be taken over a period of time? Why?
- Which should be compared with other schools, or key competitors? Why?

Each of these criterion measures may be assessed by means of a number of critical indicators. Let us examine several, to explore some of the scales or index that might be suitable.

Production Production is the measure of output, the result of the transformation process. For the organization, production represents the extent of accomplishment of its principal goal.

Although we typically consider production to be a measure of manufacturing, brokerage firms, real estate agencies, auto dealerships, and insurance agencies, among a number of types of organizations, consider dollars of transactions to be production. For these organizations, sales representatives produce by selling services or products. The specific measure used to assess production, therefore, will be industry-specific. Tons of steel or paper produced serve as output measures in the steel and paper industries. In electrical power production, thousands of kilowatt hours may be an appropriate output measure. In the garment industry, thousands of dozens of garments may be the choice of measure. In the box industry, millions of square feet of board serve as a unit of production. In service industries, dollars of billings often are a measure of business output. Advertising agencies, law firms, public accounting firms, cinematic productions, travel agencies, and other service companies all use dollars of revenue as measures of output. In annual reports of major companies, most production figures are reduced to dollar equivalents. More revealing data, however, may be reported in some of the preceding units in industry-association data banks or in the internally developed reports used for management control within the organization.

EXERCISE 14–14

Identify, if you can, the unit of production utilized by the following industries:

1. Natural Gas Production
2. Farming
    - 2.1. Soybeans
    - 2.2. Hogs
    - 2.3. Grapes
    - 2.4. Eggs
    - 2.5. Chickens
    - 2.6. Dairy (milk)
3. Rental Housing
4. Lumber Mills
5. Cement Manufacturers
6. Life Insurance Agencies
7. Stock Brokerage Firms
8. Furniture Manufacturers
9. Floor Coverings Manufacturers

10 Plastic Film Sheeting Manufacturers

11 Telephone Service Companies

Efficiency Gibson and his coauthors define efficiency as "the ratio of outputs to inputs. This short-run criterion focuses attention on the entire input-process-output cycle, yet it emphasizes the input and process elements. Among the measures of efficiency are rate of return on capital or assets, unit cost, scrappage and waste, downtime, occupancy rates, and cost per patient, per student, or per client. Measures of efficiency must inevitably be in ratio terms; the ratios of benefit to cost or to time are the general forms of these measures."[19]

Ratios can be constructed that permit an evaluation criterion for comparison with other organizations. In examining the economic health of various countries, for example, the number of hours of work represented in the purchase price of common articles (a suit of clothes, an automobile, etc.) is sometimes used as a global standard-of-living measure. In other, much more specific types of transformations, however, more detailed measures might be employed. To assess the efficiency of a pulp digester in the paper industry, for example, the ratio of tons of pulp derived from tons of wood chips provides a measure of technological efficiency. Kilowatt hours per ton of coal might assess the technical efficiency of a power plant. The financial efficiency of power plants of differing types (e.g., nuclear, coal, oil) could be measured by holding production constant, then assessing the profit per dollar invested with each type of fuel employed. Managers might then be able to examine the relative profitability of generating power with each form of technology.

Market Share Product-by-product market-share analyses will help to determine the extent to which various components in the product line are achieving market acceptance or are falling from favor by customers. The organization that maintains a constant or growing market share while its product mix changes provides evidence of flexibility and adaptiveness in meeting market needs. Product-by-product market-share information may be available through industry associations or through purchased market survey services. When these data are not available, market research may reveal market-share information on a one-time basis.

Other indicators of the adaptability of the organization include the use of the backup matrix (discussed in Chapter 5) to aid in covering for the absence of operative and middle-level personnel as well as to determine the presence of managerial resource plans that define the patterns of the succession to be followed in the event of the death or incapacity of one or more executives. In addition to these systems for adapting to changes in the work force, a number of organizations have developed plans for dealing with strikes, commercial-product failure crises, and a variety of natural disasters. Although the plans are only the first step in response to these environmental factors, their use may mean a more effective and timely response than might be possible through plans developed in a purely reactive way.

[19] Gibson et al., *Organizations*, p. 35.

Development Development is an assessment of the degree to which the company is actively seeking to *anticipate* market needs. This can be measured by the extent to which product- and process-development expenditures are made (often relative to sales) or by a somewhat less-objective assessment of the degree to which the company's products and processes have been successful in anticipating or even stimulating demand. Customer, dealer, or sales representative opinions often are tallied to provide judgmental measures. Objective assessments can be made from published data, often in the organization's annual reports or in data from industry associations.

Satisfaction The satisfaction of major constituencies can be assessed through their loyalty, or the extent to which they continue their association with the organization. Loyal customers continue to buy the company's products year in and year out, often through family generations. New models are accepted by these customers not because of knowledge of the new product, but instead because of a familiarity with the type of product offered under that brand and their past experience with products carrying that brand. Customer satisfaction for products that do not involve repeat purchases can be measured by customer complaints, product returns, or by customer-satisfaction surveys.

Employee satisfaction may be measured by means of satisfaction surveys (e.g., the Job Descriptive Index)[20] or indirectly through measures of employee turnover, absenteeism, or grievances.

Resource Acquisition Shareholder loyalty, a valuable resource in times of need for support or for additional capital, can similarly be assessed by means of turnover statistics. Shares traded as compared with shares outstanding offers a measure of daily or annual turnover. In addition to this objective measure, the support of stockholders for management action as expressed in actions by boards of directors and the willingness of shareholders to permit management to vote their shares by proxy also serve to give important indicators of shareholder satisfaction.

The financial community serves as a supplier of funds. Their backing of management actions and their willingness to provide financial support to management's plans serve as indicators of satisfaction. Other vendors (materials, supplies, services) express their satisfaction by extending credit (especially in difficult times) and by offering preferential treatment in times of short supply.

EXERCISE 14–15

For this exercise, work in groups of four to six persons.

- Identify an industry that you find of interest and for which you are confident that public information is available.

[20] P. C. Smith, L. M. Kendall, and C. L. Hulin, *The Measurement of Satisfaction in Work and Retirement* (Skokie, Ill.: Rand McNally, 1969).

- Select the largest six companies in that industry and prepare an evaluation of the operational effectiveness of each. Information should be drawn from a wide range of sources. Annual reports, Moody's, Standard & Poors, library references, articles in the business and popular press, and opinions of dealers, distributors, competitors, and customers are all potential sources. You will probably find it useful to reach agreement within your group on the categories of information and specific measures to be gathered and used in the evaluation.
- Assign a separate company to each person in your group. Be prepared to present your evaluation of one or several companies in class.

Before reading Overseas National Airways, Inc. (ONA) case, you may find it helpful to review the major topics covered in this chapter. When the review is finished, read through the ONA material, then respond to the questions found at its end. You will probably find that your analysis will proceed more smoothly if you answer the questions in sequence.

OVERSEAS NATIONAL AIRWAYS, INC.

The extensive reorganization of Overseas National Airways, Inc. (ONA), which had taken place in late 1977, was the subject of a thorough review by ONA's management early the following year. The company, which was a major U.S. charter airline and which had worldwide operating authority except for Japan, Australia and New Zealand, had encountered some severe turbulence in the events of recent years. In addition to some earlier aircraft accidents, three serious crashes between 1975 and 1977 had destroyed two DC-10 aircraft and one DC-8. Because of these accidents and large financial operating losses, and in the face of increasing competition in the airline passenger industry, ONA's major stockholders had brought in new leadership in 1977.

Mr. Edward Ory became chairman of ONA's executive committee in April 1977. A complete reorganizational plan was developed during mid-1977. The plan called for ONA to divest all auxiliary and diversified activities. Moreover, the plan was to standardize to DC-10 aircraft operation and to dispose of all other aircraft and spare parts.

These moves would involve a drastic reduction in personnel and scope of operation. In October of 1977, Mr. G. F. Steedman Hinckley resigned as chairman of the board of directors of ONA after 18 years as chief executive. Following the election of Mr. Ory as chairman of the board of directors, the company proceeded to implement the reorganizational plan in November and December of 1977. The fleet of DC-8 aircraft and spare parts was sold. While this resulted in an accounting loss, the company's cash flow was improved for indebtedness commitments and future cash requirements. This move left ONA operating two DC-10-30 jet aircraft, down from a fleet of 21 jet aircraft in 1975. In addition, ONA still subleased out to other operators four DC-8 and one

DC-9 aircraft which it had on lease. Drastic reductions were also made in the number of employees from about 900 to 361.

A third DC-10-30 aircraft was on order from McDonnell-Douglas Corporation for delivery in June of 1978. It was expected that this aircraft would be placed in service in time for the summer peak season in air passenger charter. With this in mind, ONA was projecting a near break-even operation for 1978 (as compared to a loss in excess of $12 million in 1977), and an expected profit of about $2.5 million in 1979 and $5.6 million in 1980.

A consulting firm which had undertaken a thorough study of ONA after its reorganization had reported to ONA's insurance companies that the transformation had appeared to be successful and that when the third DC-10-30 was delivered to ONA in June, the company should be as well organized and managed as any charter airline. While this was very encouraging to ONA's management, Mr. Ory and his staff were also concerned with the changing conditions in the air charter market and were continuing to review all available options.

COMPANY BACKGROUND

Overseas National Airways, Inc., was organized in 1950. From its base in California it began charter flight operations with a fleet of five DC-4 aircraft. The outbreak of the Korean conflict in 1950 greatly expanded ONA's operations, flying cargo and military personnel between the United States and Japan. This was followed later by participating in the evacuation of Dutch nationalists, from Indonesia, the immigration of Hungarian refugees, and transport of supplies to the French in Viet Nam, as well as other charter flight operations.

In 1958, ONA pioneered the transatlantic charter market with a fleet of DC-6 aircraft. The following year, ONA received one of the largest U.S. military air transport service contracts ever awarded to a single carrier. Twelve DC-7's and another DC-6 were required for military passenger operations, both domestic and international, over the Atlantic and Pacific oceans for military contract flights. This large contract, however, proved to be ONA's undoing. The company had been low bidder on the contract and had found that it couldn't make a profit. Consequently, ONA went into bankruptcy and suspended operations in 1963.

Two years later, ONA was refinanced and resumed commercial flight operations utilizing the DC-7 aircraft. Two DC-8 jets and four DC-9 jet aircraft were also ordered, with the two DC-8's being delivered in mid 1966. The Civil Aeronautics Board awarded ONA in 1966 long-term authority for transatlantic charter operations, including tour flights. The transatlantic market developed into the largest tourist flight market for ONA and other charter airlines, as well as a principal market for all of the scheduled passenger airlines of the world. Passenger charter flights to London, Paris and Rome were initiated in 1967 and the CAB certificate was extended to include the Caribbean and Hawaii. In 1968, ONA acquired a fleet of 8 Lockheed L-188 Electra's which were modified for military and domestic cargo operations. By 1969, ONA was operating a fleet of 21 aircraft in commercial passenger and cargo as well as military contract flights. A considerable amount of military business involved passenger and cargo airlift between the United States and other bases in Viet Nam.

The first two DC-10 wide-bodied jet aircraft were acquired by ONA in mid 1973. At that time, the Electra cargo aircraft were sold. Additional DC-8 aircraft were acquired during 1975. Then in November 1975 and January 1976, two DC-10 aircraft were lost in serious accidents. Later in 1976 the DC-9 aircraft were taken out of service, and three DC-10-30's were ordered, two of which were delivered in May and June of 1977, with the third to be delivered in June of 1978. By 1977, the emphasis had shifted more from military to commercial business, with predominantly passenger operations. The following table shows amounts of ONA's net operating revenues attributible to airline services during recent years.

financing problems, according to the *Wall Street Journal.*

MARKETING

Flights between United States and Europe over the North Atlantic were ONA's primary market.

($000)	*1977*	*1976*	*1975*	*1974*	*1973*
Commercial:					
Aircraft Leasing	$ 1,657	$ 2,632	$ 4,520	$ 4,460	$ 2,584
Passenger	67,885	52,467	53,543	47,056	38,395
Cargo	492	9,825	9,977	6,406	6,247
Total	$70,034	$64,924	$68,040	$57,992	$47,226
Military:					
Passenger	$ 9,963	$10,988	$13,200	$ 7,765	$ 5,165
Cargo	—	7,005	8,414	15,757	21,509
Total	$ 9,963	$17,993	$21,614	$23,522	$26,674

Some diversification had been attempted in recent years. ONA had owned the Delta Queen Steamboat Company, which owned and operated the riverboat "Delta Queen" for pleasure cruises on the Mississippi River. ONA had also owned Great Ocean Cruise Line, Inc., a nonoperating company which had contracted for the construction of another riverboat, the "Mississippi Queen." Both of these subsidiary companies had been exchanged by ONA for stock in the Coca-Cola Bottling Company of New York, Inc., in 1976, after the latter had made an unsuccessful attempt to acquire ONA. The Coca-Cola stock was later sold by ONA for $3.4 million, most of which was used to repay bank loans that had funded the riverboats. ONA had also owned Chippewa Land Company, Ltd., which owned land and buildings in California. Chippewa was sold in early 1977 at a loss of about $350,000.

Alaska International Industries, Inc., had also tried to acquire ONA. However, that attempt was "deferred indefinitely" because of

In addition, during 1977, 11% of the company's total revenues came from flying Islamic pilgrams from several African countries to Saudi Arabia during the Haj, or the Moslem holy season. The best nontransatlantic markets were the long range ones: Hong Kong, Tahiti, Rio de Janeiro, Lima, and South Africa, which were all emerging as off season charter destinations.

Most of ONA's charter business was sold through about 20 established wholesale tour agencies who contracted for their flight services twice a year, generally at the rate of about $12.65 per mile for the DC-10 aircraft. Due to the increasing volume of civilian tour travel, ONA had sold out nearly all of its available flight time for the entire year 1978, to fully utilize its present two DC-10 aircraft and after May to utilize all three DC-10 aircraft, for an average daily utilization between 11 and 14 hours. In addition, ONA contracted with the U.S. military for transport of military personnel around the world on a flexible basis, which amounted to approximately 20% of ONA's business. From time to time, foreign airlines were also seeking additional aircraft for charter flights over their routes as seasonal peak traffic occured for them, such as Moslem travel to Mecca during the Haj.

ONA marketing operations were concentrated at its New York headquarters at the JFK International Airport, with sales offices in San Francisco, Detroit and Germany. Other offices in various cities had been closed down as a result of the reorganization, but it was believed by management that the three sales offices plus the headquarters would be sufficient for DC-10 operation.

FLIGHT OPERATIONS

Passenger revenue miles for ONA were about 2.14 billion in 1977, holding fairly steady since 1973 despite the change in fleet configuration. Cargo ton miles, however, had declined steadily and by 1978 ONA was out of the charter cargo business (see Aircraft Operations Statistics, Exhibit 1).

The Director of the Flight Operations Department was Captain Marshall, who was a long-time pilot and experienced flight captain. The flight training managers, pilots and flight engineers reported to the director of flight operations. A number of ONA flight crews had been retired or separated during the recent reorganization, reportedly those who were the least qualified. The pilots union contract allowed for dismissal of any crew member who did not meet ONA standards on all training and proficiency requirements. Crew qualifications were considerably higher in ONA than average U.S. scheduled airlines operating DC-10 aircraft. The ONA DC-10 captains all averaged over 22,000 total flight hours.

The flight operations manual had been revised for DC-10-30 operations only, and the newly printed manual had been approved by the Federal Aviation Administration. Emphasis on operating discipline among flight crew personnel was strong.

Training was an important part of ONA's flight operations. The transition from DC-9 and DC-8 aircraft to exclusively DC-10 required considerable transition training on the part of flight crews. ONA obtained the American Airlines ground-school curriculum built around slides and tapes which American furnished. All of the training manuals were upgraded to the DC-10-30 series aircraft that ONA operated. ONA established very high standards for its flight training, and a federal safety inspector assigned to the company attended all the ground training classes along with ONA crews. Arrangements had also been made with United Airlines to provide DC-10 cockpit procedure training and DC-10 flight simulator training. All of the flight personnel realized that the future of the company and the success of the new operation depended upon a greatly improved safety record.

Each DC-10 required a cabin staff of 10 attendants. Training for these attendants was largely on a classroom basis, with some involvement in the aircraft when they were available at JFK airport between flights and during maintenance. The trainees would fly as crew members for observation only for their first major flight and then would gradually be integrated into the cabin crew as experienced improved their ability. ONA employed about 150 flight attendants, all of whom had been with the airline for an extensive period. Consequently, the need for additional training was not great.

Flight control was an impressive part of ONA's operations. This included crew and flight scheduling, flight dispatch, and worldwide communications. A licensed airline dispatcher and maintenance engineer were both on duty 24 hours a day 7 days a week to provide and maintain constant flight watch of every segment of every flight. No ONA flight could be initiated from any part of the world without dispatch clearance and an approved flight plan by this central flight operations dispatcher at JFK airport in New York.

ONA used the United Airlines computer which was directly connected to ONA flight control center through a keyboard and display printer for flight planning of all flights everywhere in the world. When a flight was contemplated, whether domestic or international, there were more than 20 separate pieces of flight plan informatioin typed into the UAL computer on a terminal located at flight planning dispatch center of ONA at JFK airport. Within a matter of seconds, the computer would print back the entire flight plans with the best routes to fly, upper winds between any two points, the most economical speed to fly, the flight time between all checkpoints, the weight of fuel consumed at each checkpoint, the remaining fuel aboard, the ground speed to be expected, time at each checkpoint, the alternative airport, the fuel at arrival, the most economical power setting, and the most economical and safe fuel load, etc.

The computer flight plan was checked by the dispatcher, and then on signal command, the computer typed a copy of the flight plan message on a teletype circuit to any enroute station in the world requested by the controlling dispatcher, plus a copy for the captain of the flight, wherever he may be located in the world.

The U.S. Weather Bureau's principal weather station in Maryland was connected directly into the United Airlines computer. Weather and upper wind reports from all over the world were fed into the computer on a continuous basis. This weather and wind information and forecasts were constantly passed on to the aircraft crews in flight, and were immediately available to the flight planners and dispatchers. All flights operations dispatch personnel were extremely capable and experienced. Flying a worldwide operation would not be possible without the availability of present-day communications facilities.

MAINTENANCE

ONA had a highly qualified and experienced maintenance organization. The DC-10 line maintenance was being performed by ONA personnel at JFK airport in New York for the 250 hour and 750 hour services. All 1500 hour and 3000 hour major DC-10 heavy maintenance services were being done by United Airlines under contract. ONA had maintenance contracts with United Airlines for both major airframe maintenance services and 100% spare parts exchange program. This arrangement eliminated time out of service for accessories, rotatables and time components. All replacement parts were immediately available from UAL on an exchange basis. In addition, ONA had approximately $4 million invested in DC-10 maintenance spare parts other than engines.

ONA also had a contract with General Electric for all of their heavy engine maintenance and overhauls. Daily engine parameter monitoring data were fed into a GE control computer on a daily basis, and continuous monitoring of all engine operating data was conducted by GE. When a flight terminated at any place in the world, the engine log of monitored parameter data were [*sic*] telexed back to ONA at JFK and fed immediately into GE's computer. Oil spectro-analysis was made at each 250 hour engine service as an additional control over all engine operations. GE engine reliability on the ONA DC-10 aircraft had been excellent.

Maintenance for ONA's DC-10 aircraft was also performed by Pan-American, Lufthansa, BTA, UAL, Continental, and other experienced major airlines as required in various places in the world by ONA and under ONA maintenance personnel supervision. ONA presently had one maintenance engineer based in Los Angeles, two in Detroit, and four in Frankfurt, Germany. All of these engineers were highly trained and experienced with DC-10 aircraft, which had so many double and triple systems that maintenance dispatch reliability of those aircraft was phenomenal as compared to the older generation of DC-8's. ONA had also adopted a special stringent and conservative tire and wheel inspection and maintenance to avoid tire failures and reduce the risk from abortive takeoffs from tire failures. ONA had closed its maintenance base in Wilmington, Ohio, following the recent disposal of its fleet of DC-8 aircraft.

ACCIDENTS

ONA had experienced one major accident with propeller driven aircraft just two years after it began doing business. In 1952, at Oakland, California, a DC-4 aircraft on a training flight was struck by another aircraft in mid-air collision, resulting in a total loss of the aircraft. The next major accident did not occur until 17 years later. In 1969, an ONA DC-9 landing at Sacramento, California, from a military cargo flight suffered a broken fuselage due to a premature wing spoiler deployment during landing. Although there was major damage involved, it was repairable. The next year, in 1970, a DC-9 in vicinity of the Virgin Islands was diverted toward an alternative airport due to bad weather. The aircraft ran out of fuel and ditched at sea with a load of passengers. Twenty-three passengers were killed, and the aircraft was a total loss.

At Bangor, Maine, in 1973, three tires in succession blew out on a DC-8 taking off, and the takeoff was aborted. The aircraft caught fire, which burned through the wing. Although there was major damage, the aircraft was repaired.

The first ONA DC-10 was lost in November of 1975. During a takeoff from JFK airport in New York, seagulls were ingested into the engine, resulting in engine fire. Number three engine disintegrated, the takeoff was aborted, and the main landing gear collapsed. All passengers and crew were safely evacuated, with 32 passengers injured. The engine fire spread to the entire aircraft, which was a total loss.

The Second ONA DC-10 was lost in January of 1976 at Istanbul, Turkey. The aircraft touched down 45 feet short of the runway overrun during a night instrument landing, breaking off the landing gear. All 364 passengers and 13 crew members were successfully evacuated. However, the aircraft sustained major damage resulting in total loss.

The following year, at Niamey, Niger, Africa, a DC-8 cargo flight touched down 1750 feet short of the runway during a night approach on instruments. After the impact, the aircraft rolled over. It was totally destroyed and the two crew members were killed. The cause of that accident had not yet been determined.

All of the accidents had been covered by insurance. However, in order to avoid future accidents and qualify for continued insurance and air charter certification, ONA had reviewed all of its operating procedures and modified them for increased safety provisions. Management believed that standardization on DC-10 aircraft would facilitate an improved safety program and reduce or eliminate future accidents.

ORGANIZATION AND PERSONNEL

Prior to joining ONA, Mr. Ory's experience had been principally in investment and transportation management and had included more than two years (1974–1976) as president of U.S. Banknote Corporation in New York. He had spent more than 14 years managing private investments and was still a partner in a New York investment firm. Mr. Ory was a graduate of the U.S. Merchant Marine Academy and had served as a licensed deck officer on the S.S. America.

Later he had become Controller and Assistant to the President of Grace Line Steamship Company.

Following the reorganization in late 1977, ONA was structured in five operating departments, each of which was directly responsible to the president, Mr. J. W. Bailey, who had previously been president under Mr. Hinckley and now was responsible to Mr. Ory.

The five departments were:

Financial division with 17 total employees.

Maintenance division with 50 total employees.

Flight operations division with 231 total employees.

Passenger services division with 20 total employees.

Marketing division with 17 total employees.

In addition, there was an insurance department and a labor relations department reporting directly to the president.

All of the key personnel in ONA were considered to exceed the normal requirements in credentials and background experience for their respective positions. Notwithstanding the drastic reductions that had recently been made in the number of employees, the morale and spirit of those remaining was considered to be very high.

FINANCIAL SITUATION

Operating revenues of ONA had reached a peak of nearly $90 million in 1975 and had declined to just under $80 million in 1977 (see Exhibit 2).

The company entered 1978 with a relatively strong cash position (see balance sheets, Exhibit 3). Minimum annual payment of principal on the company's long term debt was $3.66 million in 1978 and $3.52 million in each year 1979 through 1982. Although the balance sheet reflected the aircraft equipment at cost, management believed that with rising prices the DC-10's might be worth as much as $20 million more than the book value.

The company had recently disclosed, in a report filed with the Securities and Exchange Commission, that it had made $3.1 million in questionable payments from 1971 through 1976. The report said that payments and allowances to domestic and foreign passenger charter operators and uncollected money owed by the charter operators amounted to $1,675,000 through 1975. Additionally, charter flight commissions that exceeded the 5% allowed by the Civil Aeronautics Board (CAB) rules, together with discounts below tarrif levels, amounted to $945,000 through 1976. ONA had previously disclosed payments of $420,000 involving the company's flight operations between foreign points. ONA also said that it gave less than $10,000 a year in facilitating payments, such as money given customs officials to expedite clearance of goods.

The charter transactions, according to the report, constituted rebates, excess commissions and failure to collect the full tariff filed with the CAB. Most of the payments and allowances were made under an understanding with the charter operators of their agents that if all seats on a flight weren't filled the charter price would be reduced proportionately.

All of the payments mentioned were not accurately disclosed on ONA's books. While those payments wouldn't require additional payment of income taxes they might require adjustment of loss carryovers. In 1976 the CAB had brought charges against ONA in connection with the payments. The proceeding was settled in 1977 with the CAB agreeing that it wouldn't bring further action against ONA if the company discontinued any illegal practices discovered by the director's committees. ONA also paid the CAB $50,000 to settle possible civil penalties that could have been imposed.

The largest single stockholder of ONA was Louis Marks, Jr., a venture capitalist and member of the Marks Toy family. Mr. Marks owned 20% of ONA stock. Marline Resources Company, which was controlled by Mr. Marks, owned an additional 15.5% of ONA stock. The third largest stockholder was Dan W. Lufkin, a Wall Street entrepreneur and former investment banker. Messrs. Marks and Lufkin had controlled ONA for about 15 years. Together with several members of management, they owned about 49% of ONA stock. The other 51% was owned by the public and was traded in the over-the-counter market. Price quotations for ONA stock in 1976 and 1977 were:

1977 Range	*1st Quarter*	*2nd Quarter*	*3rd Quarter*	*4th Quarter*
Low Closing Bid	2¼	2½	3⅛	3¼
High Closing Bid	3¾	3⅞	4¼	5⅞
1976 Range				
Low Closing bid	6	5	3¼	34
High Closing Bid	9¼	7⅜	5½	4½

THE AIR CHARTER INDUSTRY

Charter air passenger transportation served primarily pleasure as opposed to business travelers. As such it is generally seasonal in nature with the greatest traffic occuring during the summer months. Since the tourist travel is also dependent upon economic prosperity to some degree, the industry is also somewhat cyclical. U.S. passenger miles and revenue are shown in Exhibit 4, both for commercial charter operations and for scheduled international and domestic operations.

The air charter industry was highly regulated by the Civil Aeronautics Board of the United States. An airline was permitted to fly only to those areas where it held operating certificates from the CAB. However, a charter operator could fly on any schedule of his own choosing between the authorized points.

The marketing of a certified supplemental (charter) airline was completely different than a scheduled air carrier. The charter airline did not make any direct sales efforts to the public nor any direct advertising to the public. All sales were made through a network of established travel agents. There were thousands of well-established travel agencies in the United States who relied on small local travel agents in each city, town, or community to generate interest and business from their general area public to take low cost travel tours all over the world. This kind of charter tour business had been built up in the United States primarily since World War II. The increased standard of living and affluency had created a strong demand for vacation and convention travel both domestically and abroad.

There were approximately 250 large travel tour agencies in the United States who promoted and generated charter tour business, all fed by thousands of small agencies. These wholesalers would plan, promote and schedule package tours for twelve months of the year by bidding for transportation, hotels, meals, guides, etc., on a highly sophisticated and organized basis, usually twice a year, utilizing smaller widespread travel agencies to sell volume travel business for them at rates less than

50% cheaper than a vacationer or conventioner could provide for themselves individually by traveling at conventional airline and hotel standard rates.

COMPETITION IN AIR CHARTER

The increase in air charter business has not gone unnoticed by scheduled airlines, who were also experiencing increased traffic over the primary tourist routes, the greatest of which was the North Atlantic route. In 1977, the total charter revenue of the domestic trunk and international trunk airlines in the United States totaled about the same as the supplemental or charter airlines in the United States (see Exhibit 5).

Scheduled carriers serving the United States were authorized to perform charter flights on their routes without prior approval. Off-route charters could also be performed without prior approval by U.S. and most foreign scheduled carriers, although in the case of U.S. scheduled carriers there were restrictions as to volume, frequency, and regularity.

There were more than 40 carriers (both domestic and foreign) authorized to operate scheduled and/or charter services on the prime commercial routes between United States and Europe over the North Atlantic. These carriers included 11 scheduled U.S. carriers and 6 U.S. supplemental carriers. Beginning in 1977 the scheduled carriers began to offer large fare discounts within the United States, based on deregulation by the CAB and encouragement by the Carter Administration. Low fares began also to appear on the North Atlantic and Hawaii routes. The Sky Train that began between London and New York on a very low fare basis had prompted other transatlantic carriers to cut their fares. All of these reduced fares by the scheduled carriers added to the competition faced by the charter airlines.

The competitive impact of those very low scheduled fares had been offset to some extent by the efforts of the CAB to liberalize United States charter regulations to enable the supplemental carriers to compete more effectively with the low fares on the scheduled airlines. The result had been to reduce the advance purchase period requirement of some charters and to eliminate that requirement for others. Also reduced were the minimum size of charter groups from 40 to 20 in most programs, to eliminate the minimum stay requirement and to permit sale by tour operators of a greater percentage of the charter flight seats up to the day of departure. Further proposed liberalizations of charter rules had been resisted by many of the foreign governments. However, the United States had been making a strong and continuing diplomatic effort to gain acceptance of the new rules by the foreign governments.

The Civil Aeronatics Board had publically expressed that for years that air charter carriers were the only source of low fare air transportation for the price-conscious traveler and should not be allowed to be driven out of business by the recent rash of scheduled low fares. The CAB added that distinctions would remain between charter and scheduled services because of continuing differences such as requirements that charter tickets must be sold by charter operators and charter flights could be cancelled for non-operational reasons including inadequate sales. The liberalized charter system proposed by the CAB would allow discount pricing and one-way ticketing without requiring advance purchase or minimum group size. It would also replace advance booking charters. The CAB proposal followed a policy established in 1977 to drop unnecessary restrictions on charter airlines.

Another development that might help offset intensified competition from the scheduled carriers was the decline of charter operations of the scheduled carriers. In 1976, the scheduled carriers accounted nearly half of the charter passengers in the transatlantic market as compared to only 37% in 1977. This decline was thought by the industry to be due to the fact that a number of the scheduled carriers had been selling their excess narrow-bodied aircraft and had reduced the number of aircraft devoted to charter activity. It was believed in the industry that no scheduled carrier in earlier 1978 currently had wide body aircraft dedicated to the charter market, which increasingly demanded such equipment to operate profitably.

There were, however, three other developments that might further heighten competitive pressure on the charter market by the scheduled carriers. First, some scheduled carriers had been offering unusually high commissions to travel agents on individual ticket sales. Second, the rights of scheduled carriers to operate charter flights off their regular routes were recently expanded by the elimination or reduction of various limitations on the volume, frequency, and regularity of such off-route charter flights. Third, the CAB had under consideration a proposal that would authorize part charter services on scheduled flights. Although in the past the CAB had rejected various part charter proposals, if it were to approve the scheduling of part charter groups on scheduled flights at charter rates it would heighten the competitive impact on the charter airlines.

There were four major participants in the U.S. Air Charter Passenger industry. They are shown below together with their revenue passenger miles in 1977.

Capitol International Airways	$2.205 billion
Evergreen International	146 million
McCulloch	20 million
ONA	2.142 billion
TIA (Trans-International Airlines)	3.095 billion
World Airways	2.373 billion
Total	$9.981 billion

While these air carriers were mostly involved in passenger operations, they did carry some freight. In addition, there were two major freight charter airlines in the United States: Tigers International and Seaboard. Comparative financial data for some of the charter airlines and scheduled air carriers are shown in Exhibit 6. Tigers International, which operated the Flying Tiger Line (originating from the Flying Tigers in China during World War II) provided scheduled air freight service to key cities in the U.S. and Asia and freight charters on a worldwide basis. Flying Tigers previously purchased some of ONA's DC-8 jet aircraft in order to serve new U.S. domestic markets that were added as a result of air freight deregulation approved by Congress late in 1977.

Capitol International Airways operated a fleet of DC-8 jets. It did not have any wide-bodied jet aircraft. In 1977, Capitol's revenues were slightly greater than ONA's, reflecting a sharp growth over 1976 (see operating summary, Exhibit 7). Capitol had a relatively low level of long term debt (see balance sheets, Exhibit 8). Capitol Airways had been founded by Jesse F. Stallings, who in 1978 was the president, chairman and chief officer and also a major stockholder.

Trans-International Airways (TIA) was one of several operating subsidiaries of the Trans-American holding company. TIA was the largest U.S. air charter line for passengers, with over three billion revenue passenger miles in 1977. Its passenger services were handled by a fleet of wide-bodied jet aircraft. TIA earned $9.5 million profit on $199 million revenue in 1977 and had total assets of $162 million. Its financial resources were backed by its parent company, Trans-America, which had total assets of $1.26 billion and consolidated net income in 1977 of $169 million.

World Airways, Inc. operated a fleet of 747's, DC-10 and DC-8 jet aircraft. In terms of revenue passenger miles it was slightly larger than ONA, and its aircraft operating revenues were near $100 million in 1977 (see Exhibit 9). World Airways for several years had owned as a subsidiary First Western Bank and Trust Company which was sold in 1974 to Lloyds Bank, Ltd., for $115 million. The gain from the sale of the bank resulted in a profit of nearly $16 million after taxes. World Airways then had a very large amount of funds invested in marketable securities (see balance sheets, Exhibit 10). World Airways stock was traded on the New York Stock Exchange, but 82% of it was owned by Edward J. Dailey, who was president and chairman of the company.

RECENT DEVELOPMENTS

During the first quarter of 1978, several events were of serious concern to ONA's management. Although the reorganization of the company had been proceeding smoothly, ONA received notification in February that due to a strike at the McDonnell-Douglas plant the third DC-10, which was scheduled for delivery in May of 1978, would not be delivered on time but would be delivered later that year, perhaps in October. Such a late delivery would entirely miss the most profitable summer peak season during which time about two-thirds of the company's annual profit was made. Loss of the revenue from this aircraft for which charters were already booked could significantly reduce the operating results below the planned break-even operation for 1978.

Additional pressure from competition due to deregulation was also of increasing concern to ONA's management. Congress had deregulated domestic airline operations to a large degree in November 1977, and the CAB was proposing further deregulation of the airline industry, both charter and scheduled, which would adversely affect ONA's competitive position in international operations if the legislation were to pass. Moreover, the foreign exchange rate was a matter of concern. The increasing pressure against the dollar in foreign markets proved to be a disadvantage to ONA's profitable operations.

Although ONA supported aviation regulatory reform, certain proposals pending before the Senate essentially would destroy the vital distinction between supplemental and scheduled air carriers. ONA was opposed to the following proposals:

1 To permit a supplemental to get scheduled authority and a scheduled carrier to get supplemental authority.
2 To freeze the "unrealistic" definition of off-route charter trips as that term was applied by the Board on January 1, 1977.
3 To allow scheduled carriers to charge fares after July 1, 1978, as much as 10% more or, immediately, 35% less than the standard industry fare level. ONA believed that the permissible range of fare change should be no more than 5% added nor less than 30% deducted from the standard industry for coach service, because it was important to restrict the ability of scheduled carriers to offer uneconomic and preditory fares which are subsidized by economy and first class service. The pending legislation did not provide the protection that ONA felt was required to the charter industry.

ONA supported the various proposals which would make air service more competitive, including empowering the Civil Aeronatics Board to issue interstate and overseas charter authority to an applicant filing after June 30, 1981, merely on a determination of fitness. ONA believed, however, that charter authority should be a certificate and not a license.

ONA also believed that supplemental air carriers provided the consumer with the lowest cost air transportation, provided the U.S. government with a rate yardstick vis-à-vis foreign and U.S. flag scheduled carriers, provided a competitive spur to the international air transport association cartel, and added the most responsive backup military airlift capability. It was believed to be in the public interest to insure that the supplemental or charter carriers continued to provide those benefits. The supplemental airlines had provided those benefits because they were a distinct class of air carriers whose sole business was to offer low cost charter air transportation. It was believed that there was no economic way to provide air transportation at a lower cost than charter because the air carrier got paid for operating the aircraft based on 100% load factor, whereas the scheduled carriers accepted the load factor risk which averaged 55% and had significant selling and marketing expenses which resulted in higher fares.

ONA management was continuing to evaluate its operations and was considering all options available to it, including the sale or lease of its DC-10 aircraft. ONA had recently received an offer from another airline to purchase its third (undelivered) DC-10. ONA's management believed that the sale of that aircraft and the sale of its present two DC-10 aircraft could result in a significant gain to the company.

Another item of concern for ONA's management was operating costs, fuel cost in particular. In commenting on the situation, Mr. Ory observed that airlines had a very high fixed cost. "Jet fuel is about the only variable cost we have." "In fact," he said, "most costs in any business tend to be fixed. Charter is becoming less important with more direct flights between points added by scheduled airlines. Charter is a cyclical business on a worldwide basis. We have a plan to stay in business with the DC-10 fleet, but the delay in the delivery of our third DC-10 together with the competitive pressure of deregulation and various pressures on profit are causing us to re-evaluate our position."

EXHIBIT 1
Overseas National Airways, Inc., aircraft operating statistics

Aircraft operating statistics	*1977*	*1976*	*1975*	*1974*	*1973*
Aircraft days operated:					
DC-10-30	434	—	681	728	424
DC-8-63	937	1,164	584	673	1,187
DC-8-61	788	1,276	916	432	296
DC-8-20/30*	—	1,966	1,415	547	14
DC-9-30†	—	1,189	1,557	1,820	1,968
L-188 cargo	—	—	—	2,285	3,526
Average daily utilization (block hours):					
DC-10-30	12.3	—	9.7	10.1	12.0
DC-8-63	11.1	8.7	9.2	11.2	12.0
DC-8-61	9.6	9.3	10.0	10.2	10.0
DC-8-20/30*	—	2.2	3.9	4.2	8.6
DC-9-30*	—	9.6	9.7	9.7	9.3
L-188 cargo	—	—	—	5.3	5.9
Passenger revenue miles (000):					
Commercial	1,866,244	1,620,595	1,659,117	1,492,760	1,959,373
Military	276,389	330,198	349,163	319,295	227,682
Total	2,142,633	1,950,793	2,008,280	1,812,055	2,187,055
Cargo ton miles (000):					
Commercial	3,063	17,132	19,943	21,192	22,385
Military	—	28,806	41,722	84,042	106,233
Total	3,063	45,938	61,665	105,234	128,618
Number of employees (end of year):					
Flight	213	268	447	399	507
Non-flight	148	321	536	433	541
Subsidiary companies	—	—	105	106	135
Total	361	589	1,088	938	1,183

Source: ONA Annual Report.
*The DC-8-20/30 aircraft were removed from service during 1976.
†The DC-9-30 aircraft were retired and the related cargo operation was discontinued during 1976.

EXHIBIT 2

Overseas National Airways, Inc. five year financial summary (dollars in thousands except for per share data)

	Year ended				
	1977	*1976*	*1975*	*1974*	*1973*
Operating revenues:					
Charter revenues	$ 78,340	$ 80,285	$ 85,134	$ 76,984	$ 71,316
Aircraft rentals	1,657	2,632	4,520	4,460	2,584
Total	79,997	82,917	89,654	81,444	73,900
Operating expenses:					
Flight operations	72,778	86,109	81,159	71,364	69,414
Marketing, general and administrative	6,725	7,025	6,313	5,896	6,186
Depreciation	3,385	2,901	3,378	4,072	4,841
Total	82,888	96,035	90,850	81,332	80,441
Operating income (loss)	$ (2,891)	$ (13,118)	$ (1,196)	$ 112	$ (6,541)
Otheer income (expenses):					
Interest and debt expense	(4,260)	(2,052)	(683)	(793)	(1,345)
Capitalized interest and debt expense	—	1,512	—	—	267
Interest income	374	597	1,277	1,146	955
Gain (loss) on disposition of equipment	(3,092)	10,913	2,523	1,991	1,987
Other–net	(137)	(90)	(36)	2	(1,287)
Total	(7,115)	10,880	3,081	2,346	577
Income (loss) before taxes, discontinued business and cumulative accounting changes	$ (10,006)	$ (2,238)	$ 1,885	$ 2,458	$ (5,964)
Federal income taxes (benefit)–deferred	(208)	513	(518)	(585)	1,347
Income (loss) from operation of discontinued business	—	(152)	161	33	45
Loss on disposal of discontinued business (net of applicable Federal income tax of $760,000)	—	(1,975)	—	—	—
Cumulative effect of changes in accounting principles	(2,640)	—	—	392	—
Net income (loss)	$ (12,438)	$ (3,852)	$ 1,528	$ 2,298	$ (4,572)
Income (loss) per share of common stock:					
Continuing operations	$(4.20)	$(0.74)	$0.59	$0.81	$(1.93)
Discontinuing operations	—	(0.92)	0.07	0.02	0.02
Cumulative changes in accounting principles	(1.13)	—	—	0.17	—
Net income (loss)	$(5.33)	$(1.66)	$0.66	$1.00	$(1.91)
Dividend payable per share of common stock	—	—	0.50	—	—
Average number of common shares outstanding	2,330,801	2,317,929	2,305,370	2,305,370	2,394,344

Source: ONA Annual Report.

EXHIBIT 3
Overseas National Airways, Inc.,.balance sheets December 26, 1977 and December 31, 1976

Assets	*1977*	*1976*
Current assets:		
Cash including marketable securities of $6,200,000 in 1977	$ 9,649,000	$ 4,876,000
Cash and marketable securities securing surety bonds for advance charter deposits	2,665,000	2,021,000
Accounts and notes receivable (net of allowances of $1,422,000 in 1977 and $952,000 in 1976)	8,434,000	3,398,000
Expendable parts, materials and supplies	—	1,202,000
Prepaid expenses and other assets	591,000	972,000
Non-operating assets and investment in subsidiary held for resale	3,363,000	549,000
Total current assets	24,702,000	13,018,000
Security deposit	1156,000	2,930,000
Equipment, at cost:		
Airframes, engines, parts and assemblies	64,089,000	11,068,000
Airframe overhaul costs	—	3,786,000
Other property and equipment	2,575,000	3,782,000
Total	66,664,000	18,636,000
Less accumulated depreciation	4,082,000	6,611,000
	62,582,000	12,025,000
Progress payments on flight equipment	9,771,000	29,229,000
Total equipment—net	72,353,000	41,254,000
Non-operating equipment held for resale	—	5,640,000
Developmental and pre-operating costs, net of amortization	—	1,128,000
Noncurrent receivable	222,000	—
Total assets	$97,433,000	$63,970,000

Liabilities and shareholders' equity	*1977*	*1976*
Current liabilities		
Accounts payable and accrued expenses	$12,251,000	$13,744,000
Advance charter deposits	2,665,000	1,750,000
Progress notes payable and current maturities of long term debt	8,987,000	17,546,000
Total current liabilities	23,903,000	33,040,000
Long term debt:		
Senior	38,976,000	2,307,000
Subordinate	19,229,000	1,650,000
Total long term debt	58,205,000	3,957,000
Other liabilities	1,158,000	503,000
Commitments and contingent liabilities		
Shareowners' equity:		
Common stock par value $1 per share; shares authorized, 10,000,000 in 1977 and 5,000,000 in 1976; issued, 2,456,830	2,457,000	2,457,000
Additional paid-in capital	25,560,000	25,425,000
Accumulated deficit	(13,252,000)	(814,000)
Total	14,765,000	27,068,000
Less 126,029 shares of treasury stock at cost in 1977 and 1976	(598,000)	(598,000)
Total shareowners' equity	14,167,000	26,470,000
Total liabilities and shareowners equity	$97,443,000	$63,970,000

Source: ONA Annual Report.

EXHIBIT 4
Overseas National Airways, Inc., U.S. passenger airline miles and revenue (all figures in millions)

	Scheduled domestic		*Scheduled international*		*Commercial charter*	
Year	*Revenue passenger miles*	*Passenger revenue*	*Revenue passenger miles*	*Passenger revenue*	*Revenue passenger miles*	*Passenger revenue*
1970	104,156	$ 6,246.4	27,563	$1,380.4	6,044	$182.4
1971	106,438	6,736.4*	29,220	1,480.0*	7,772	218.7*
1972	118,138	7,564.8	34,268	1,706.5	7,783*	212.2
1973	126,317	8,379.4	35,640	1,894.9	10,161	279.5*
1974	129,732	9,757.5	33,186	2,121.7	9,016*	312.1
1975	131,728	10,113.1	31,082	2,230.1	6,885	287.3
1976	143,271*	11,855.3	33,717	2,411.0	6,647	291.2
1977	156,609	13,487.6	36,610	2,785.7	8,352	359.9

Source: FAA Statistical Handbook of Aviation.
*Revised.

EXHIBIT 5
Overseas National Airways, Inc. U.S. air carrier data, 1976 and 1977

	Domestic trunks		*International trunks*		*Local service*		*Supplementals (charter)*	
	1976	*1977*	*1976*	*1977*	*1976*	*1977*	*1976*	*1977*
Passenger Revenue (Scheduled)	10,239	11,365	2,412	2,790	1,387	1,616	—	—
Charter Revenue:								
Civilian							291	370
Military							107	114
Total	215	238	248	251	32	46	298	484
Freight Revenue (Scheduled)	721	824	381	425	71	83		
Mail Review (Scheduled)	183	217	85	88	18	39		
Subsidy Payments	—	—	—	—	70	67		
Operating Profit	469	514	134	222	90	129	−.06	6.6
Net Income	275	379	171	160	51	84	2.6	−2.8
Long-term debt	3,841	3,316	1,311	1,257	514	567	133	103
Stockholder equity	3,224	3,684	747	883	319	380	213	198
Revenue Passenger Miles (Billions)	131.4 Sched.	141.3 Sched.	33.7	36.6	12.1	13.5	6.7 civilian 1.6 military	8.4 1.6

Source: "Airline Industry Economic Report," Civil Aeronautics Board, Vol. X–4, February 1978.

EXHIBIT 6

Overseas National Airways, Inc., airline statistics comparative financial data 1977 ($ millions)

Airline (FY)	1977 Revenue (E)	1977 Net income (est)					Net income % revenue	1976 Net worth	Net income % net worth	1976 Long-term debt	L/T debt % NW
		Mar Q	Jun Q	Sep Q	Dec Q	Total (E)					
American	$2.230	$ 1	$36	$59	$(21)	$ 75	3%	$610	12%	$416	68%
Braniff	770	7	10	11	7	35	5	189	19	242	128
Continental	655	1	7	17	3	28	4	157	18	328	209
Delta	1.720	22	34	31	223	110	6	542	20	357	65
Eastern	2.005	19	3	9	9	40	2	339	12	566	167
KLM	1.130	(9)	17	40	(9)	39	3	311	13	429	138
National	495	2	3	3	3	11	2	195	6	141	72
Northwest	1.045	12	27	32	23	94	9	666	14	122	18
Pan Am	1.890	(24)	18	67	(9)	52	3	352	115	727	207
Seaboard	135	5	1	1	2	9	7	42	21	59	140
Tigers Intl	480	1	7	8	8	24	5	239	10	698	292
TWA	2.300	(54)	31	67	4	48	2	377	13	908	241
UAL	3.260	(23)	31	76	2	86	3	800	11	932	117
Western	690	2	2	9	1	14	2	117	12	110	94
World	109	(1)	1	3	1	4	4	107	4	18	17
ONA	80	(3)	(3)	2	(2)	(2)	(8)	25	(32)	21	84

Source: ONA Company Report.

EXHIBIT 7
Overseas National Airways, Inc., five year operating summary of capitol international airways
(in thousands of dollars)

	1977	1976	1975	1974	1973
Commercial Revenues:					
Transportation revenues:					
International	$64,827	$38,488	$26,177	$31,677	$27,327
Domestic	9,692	7,253	7,034	8,547	7,034
Maintenance	889	433	468	354	1,357
Other revenues	—	—	—	—	—
Aircraft renals	13	1,161	1,859	255	—
Total Commercial	75,421	47,335	35,538	40,833	35,718
Military Revenues:					
International:					
Fixed annual contracts	1,228	1,041	5,274	2,968	4,116
Individual service orders	4,172	3,515	3,459	3,885	5,630
Domestic	171	103	61	528	789
Total Military	5,571	4,659	8,794	7,381	10,535
Total Revenues	$80,992	$51,994	$44,332	$48,214	$46,253

	Years ended December 31				
	1977	1976	1975	1974	1973
Operating revenues	$80,992	$51,994	$44,332	$48,214	$46,253
Operating income (loss)	348	1,447	536	(1,730)	2,145
Nonoperating income (expense):					
Interest, principally on long-term debt	(382)	(606)	(959)	(1,195)	(1,306)
Gain on sale of aircraft	—	2,536	2,414	2,127	—
Other, net	378	238	110	(75)	(49)
Income before federal income tax and cumulative effect of change in accounting principle and retroactive application of Statement of Financial Accounting Standards No. 13	344	3,615	2,101	(873)	790
Provision (credit) for federal income tax	45	723	519	(209)	188
Income before cumulative effects of change in accounting principle and retroactive application of Statement of Financial Accounting Standards No. 13	299	2,892	1,582	(664)	602
Cumulative effect of change in accounting principle	705	—	—	—	—
Retroactive application of Statement of Financial Accounting Standards No. 13	—	—	—	—	(555)
Net income (loss)	$ 1,004	$ 2,892	$ 1,582	$ (664)	$ 47

Source: Capitol Annual Reports.

EXHIBIT 8

Overseas National Airways, Inc., consolidated balance sheets of Capital International Airways

Assets	*1977*	*1976*
Current assets:		
Cash (including certificates of deposit of $2,500,000 in 1977 and U.S. Treasury Notes of $1,400,000 in 1976)[a]	$ 3,483,622	$ 1,742,327
Accounts receivable:		
U.S. Government	552,911	180,155
Commercial and other	11,639,458	798,771
Federal income tax recoverable	190,333	—
Maintenance parts and supplies, at average cost	1,688,495	1,467,589
Prepaid expenses	1,186,020	858,814
Total current assets	8,740,839	5,047,656
Property and equipment, at cost	49,068,739	47,581,318
Less accumulated depreciation	25,868,907	21,744,024
Net property and equipment	23,199,832	25,837,294
Deferred charges and other assets	3,096,502	913,623
	$35,037,173	$31,798,573

Liabilities and stockholders' equity	*1977*	*1976*
Current liabilities		
Accounts payable	$ 9,849,918	$ 6,168,828
Unearned transportation revenue[a]	583,260	1,207,008
Accrued expenses	2,512,722	1,170,858
Federal income tax	—	931,985
Long-term debt due within one year	1,091,864	1,834,054
Total Current Liabilities	14,037,764	11,312,733
Long-term debt due after one year	3,092,966	4,184,830
Deferred federal income tax	4,887,515	4,286,513
Commitments		
Stockholders' equity		
Common stock, $1 par value 7,000,000 shares authorized, 3,072,000 shares issued	3,072,000	3,072,000
Additional paid-in capital	664,375	664,375
Retained earnings	9,282,553	8,278,122
Total Stockholders' equity	13,018,928	12,014,497
	$35,037,173	$31,798,573

Source: Capital Annual Reports.
[a]Excludes deposits in escrow of $3,654,000 in 1977 and $2,083,000 in 1976.

EXHIBIT 9
Summary of operations of World Airways, and subsidiaries

	Year ended December 31 (in thousands of dollars)				
	1973	1974	1975	1976	1977
Revenues:					
Commercial transportation	$ 60,608	63,922	64,981	50,193	77,505
Military contracts	20,833	19,891	28,207	18,664	16,586
Aircraft leasing	6,735	7,700	10,785	13,075	14,403
Maintenance	5,771	6,187	6,339	6,871	6,196
Net gain (loss) on disposition of assets	6,859	7,070	(25)	971	2,660
Interest and dividends	2,629	7,453	7,737	6,362	7,030
Total	103,435	112,223	118,024	96,136	124,380
Expenses:					
Operating	77,137	75,818	78,040	70,094	89,957
Selling, general and administrative	11,679	11,578	10,316	10,153	10,033
Depreciation	8,103	6,942	6,749	6,606	6,642
Aircraft rentals	7,084	11,443	11,076	10,423	9,493
Interest	2,743	2,488	2,545	1,666	1,789
Total	106,746	108,269	108,726	98,442	117,914
Income (loss) before income taxes, discontinued operations and cumulative effect of accounting change	(3,311)	3,954	9,298	(2,806)	6,466
Income tax expense (credit)	(2,059)	(1,288)	1,822	2,964	2,882
Income (loss) before discontinued operations and cumulative effects of accounting change	(1,252)	5,242	7,476	158	3,584
Discontinued operations	2,254	15,990	—	—	—
Cumulative effect of accounting change (net of income taxes of $1,863,000)	—	—	—	3,018	—
Net income	1,002	21,232	7,476	2,176	3,584
Retained earnings at beginning of period	66,366	67,368	88,600	96,076	98,252
Retained earnings at end of period	67,368	88,600	96,076	98,252	101,836

Source: World Annual Reports.

EXHIBIT 10

Overseas National Airways, Inc. balance sheets of World Airways, Inc. December 31, 1976 and 1977

Assets	*1976 Consolidated*	*1977 Consolidated*
Current assets:		
Cash	$ 2,576,000	$ 777,00
Short-term investments, at cost, plus accrued interest (market value $33,739,000 in 1976 and $80,003,000 in 1977)	33,219,000	80,062,000
Accounts receivable, trade (U.S. Government and other; $2,191,000 and $7,312,000 in 1976 and $1,349,000 and $7,741,000 in 1977, respectively)	9,503,000	9,090,000
Notes receivable, current portion	1,471,000	1,446,000
Prepaid expenses and other current assets	4,524,000	6,481,000
Total current assets	51,293,000	97,856,000
Investments, at cost (market value, $51,292,000 in 1976 and $23,103,000 in 1977)	52,854,000	23,103,000
Operating equipment, at cost:		
Flight equipment	105,800,000	97,176,000
Other	3,786,000	3,867,000
	109,586,000	101,043,000
Less accumulated depreciation	39,510,000	38,982,000
	70,076,000	62,061,000
Note receivable	1,249,000	—
Deferred charges and other assets	296,000	1,720,000
Total assets	$175,768,000	$184,740,000

Liabilities	*1977 Consolidated*	*1977 Consolidated*
Current liabilities:		
Current portion of notes payable	$ 2,102,000	$ 3,845,000
Accounts payable	7,250,000	10,699,000
Accrued payroll	1,506,000	1,917,000
Income taxes payable	1,058,000	9,628,000
Deferred flight revenue	3,101,000	4,452,000
Other current liabilities	3,066,000	1,781,000
Total Current Liabilities	18,083,000	32,322,000
Long-term portion of notes payable	18,178,000	17,103,000
Accrued airworthiness reserves—flight equipment	4,069,000	3,631,000
Deferred federal income tax	22,821,000	17,133,000
Deposits securing lease rentals	300,000	675,000
Minority interest in partnership	5,061,000	3,036,000
Total liabilities	68,512,000	73,900,000
Commitments and contingencies		
STOCKHOLDERS' EQUITY		
Capital stock, $1.00 per value; Authorized: 15,000,000 shares; Issued: 10,000,000 shares	10,000,000	10,000,000
Retained earnings	98,252,000	101,836,000
	108,252,000	111,836,000
Less cost of 200,000 treasury shares	(996,000)	(996,000)
	107,256,000	110,840,000
Total liabilities and stockholders' equity	$175,768,000	$184,740,000

Source: World Annual Reports.

EXERCISE 14-16

- Identify the general strategy followed by ONA prior to 1977. Use the terminology for strategy identification and evaluation described in Chapter 12 and earlier in this chapter. Prepare your responses for submission as a homework exercise or for presentation in class. Support your assertions with data or logical and persuasive argument.
- Prepare an assessment of operational effectiveness for ONA for the period prior to 1977. Use data in the case, and supplement your evaluation by data derived from library sources. Prepare for a written homework assignment or for presentation in class.
- Identify the general strategy that appears to be adopted in mid 1977 by Mr. Ory, ONA's new management. Prepare a critique of this choice. Use the evaluative standards and terminology developed thus far.
- What operational strategies and policies has Mr. Ory established? Please support your response with data from the case.
- What operational strategies remain to be put in place? Which would you institute first? Why?

PART FOUR

STRATEGY FORMULATION—MULTIPLE BUSINESS ORGANIZATIONS

In Part Three, we were concerned with the development and implementation of strategies for single businesses. The strategy formulation process involved a number of analytic stages and provided a framework for a sustained search for improvement in organizational performance during changing internal and external conditions.

Early in the development of the single-business strategic framework, we found that even small businesses find themselves concerned with segments of their operations that have unique competitive environments or unique pricing patterns. In some cases, the business may be involved with products or services at different stages in the product life cycle. Although we recognized the presence of multiple business situations, we concerned ourselves with only the single-business firm for purposes of developing the framework. In this part, we will explicitly discuss strategy formulation and execution in multiple-business situations.

The extension of single-business strategy formulation to multiple businesses should not be considered a simple extrapolation. The corporate general manager is interested in achieving desired levels of *corporate* performance and is interested in business-level strategic performance only to the extent that it enhances performance at corporate level. Thus, the successful corporate strategist will *optimize* business-unit performance across multiple units to achieve desired corporate objectives. Maximization of individual unit performance for one or several units, on the other hand, might lead to less than optimum performance or might obviate the opportunity for growth in promising areas of opportunity.

As one example, let us suppose that one of our divisions has developed a highly profitable new toy that is sweeping the country. We might be tempted, in this situation, to use the cash generated to develop new toys and to expand the division. If toys were our entire business, this rationale might be a satisfactory way of dealing with our new product's success. If, on the other hand, other divisions in the corporation have highly promising longer-lived products in the introductory or early expansion phases and are desperately in need of cash to expand sales, then the corporate management may choose to milk cash from the cash-generating division in order to sustain and build the divisions with greater long-term potential.

Effective management of cash is only one rationale for multiple-business strategy formulation. Marketing efficiencies might suggest the development of multiple businesses needed to manufacture and sell a related product line to a category of customers or through a specific type of outlet. The Coleman corporation, long-time manufacturer of gasoline lanterns, has engaged in the manufacture and sale of tents, canoes, coolers, and other equipment used in camping and outdoor activities.

In another example, American manufacturers of automobiles have found that the search for supplier or manufacturing efficiencies has led to the construction or purchase of plants used to make batteries, sparkplugs, window glass, and sheet steel. These plants not only sell products to the auto builder, but also market them to commercial customers through conventional channels of distribution.

In this concluding part, we will discuss these types of multiple-business situations and examine means of planning, executing, and evaluating strategies that seem appropriate for organizational growth and prosperity.

Chapter 15 deals with multiple businesses without considering the additional complexity of a multinational environment. We will discuss product rationales for constructing a multiple-business corporate strategy, process related reasons for multiple businesses, and a variety of financial rationales. In Chapter 16 the multinational firm and its strategic complexities will be examined. This type of organization often not only has multiple businesses to optimize, but also must do so in social, economic, and cultural settings that may differ markedly. In each of these cases, the complexities involved in the single-business strategy-formulation process are enlarged by orders of magnitude at the corporate level.

In Chapter 17, we will explore some of the more-recent developments of concern in strategic management and will conclude with observations regarding some emerging trends in management and organizations at the strategic level of interest and concern.

15

MULTIPLE-BUSINESS STRATEGIES

In Part III, we concerned ourselves with the process of analysis, formulation, implementation, and evaluation of strategies for single-business situations. In a few instances in Chapter 12, we noted the situation for strategists in which a desirable choice of strategy might well be to concentrate through vertical integration or to broaden the product line to reduce risk or enhance marketing effectiveness. In both cases, our concern was clearly the enhancement and protection of the single-business product line.

Paine and Naumes consider broad strategic alternatives that can serve to assist in the decision process that bridges the single-business and multiple-business strategic choice. Four of their eight alternatives are clearly related to single-business strategic operations: (1) penetration and saturation of existing markets; (2) stability, or continuing and improving an ongoing strategy, including the possibility of adjusting the organization's distinctive competencies; (3) integration, to protect sources of supply or markets; and (4) expansion of the field of strategic interest from local to regional to national or to international markets.

Two alternatives clearly are directed toward multiple-business situations: (5) diversification through internal growth or acquisition and (6) reallocation of resources from one component of the corporation to another.

The last two of the eight alternatives listed can serve in either single or multiple-business situations. They are: *flexibility*, designed to enhance the organization's ability to accommodate change or to take advantage of opportunities and *divestiture*, that is, to terminate the corporation's association with a line of business and to free capital for other enterprises.[1]

It should be apparent that although organizations often begin as single-business enterprises, they may find that the pursuit of the single business, even if very successful, may involve a higher-than-desired degree of risk. Organizations may wish to integrate—to reduce risk of sources of supply or markets—or may wish to diversify—to reduce the risk of declines brought about by the natural life of products. Similarly, a multibusiness organization may wish to divest divisions to focus attention and resources on more profitable enterprises, and they may, therefore, shift back from a multibusiness strategic posture to that of a single-business enterprise.

Thompson and Strickland have developed a framework for strategy selection that incorporates "9 Basic Alternatives of Corporate Strategy."[2] This framework, depicted in graphic form in Figure 15–1, offers the strategist an opportunity to examine the relative desirability of single- or multiple-business strategies in a four-cell matrix, the dimensions of which are the familiar competitive position and market growth. Although this strategy-selection framework can be used to help in selecting appropriate strategies for single businesses, it may also be seen to be a means of determining when to shift from single- to multiple-business strategies to achieve desired strategic objectives.

It is important, however, to remember that the entire corporation's activities should have coherence and should be focused toward identifiable strategic objectives. The corporate strategy, therefore, serves to guide and constrain the strategies selected for each of its business units. Several components of the corporate strategy help to direct, set, or shape the strategies of each business unit. The corporate portfolio describes the *domain* of each business unit. Corporate inputs can build a *differential advantage* for the business unit. Corporate strategic thrusts determine the *strategic thrusts* of each unit, and corporate expectations help in establishing the *targeted results* expected of each business unit.[3]

[1] F. T. Paine and W. Naumes, *Organizational Strategy and Policy*, 2nd Ed. (Philadelphia: W. B. Saunders, 1978), pp. 112–20.

[2] Arthur A. Thompson, Jr., and A. J. Strickland, III, *Strategy Formulation and Implementation: Tasks of the General Manager*, Rev. Ed. (Plano, Tex.: Business Publications, 1983), p.

[3] B. Yavitz and W. H. Newman, *Strategy in Action, the Execution, Politics and Payoff of Business Planning* (New York: Free Press, 1982), p. 70.

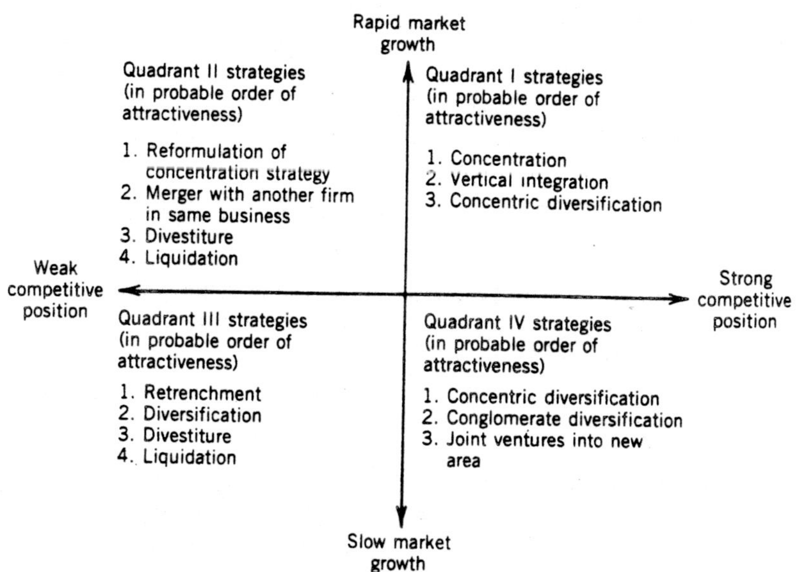

FIGURE 15–1 Strategic choice matrix. Source: Arthur A. Thompson, Jr., and A. J. Strickland III, *Strategy Formulation and Implementation: Tasks of the General Manager*, Rev. Ed. (Plano, Tex.: Business Publications, 1983), p. 154.

We will now consider the deliberate development of multibusiness strategies. First, as the corporation integrates vertically to reduce risk, opportunities for multiple-business strategies appear through imbalances in productive or marketing capacity. The general manager seeking optimum return on available resources may find that the establishment of a second or third business not only satisfies the primary reason for integration (e.g., security of sources of supply or markets), but also provides significant added revenue with little additional investment. Next, we will examine the various types of multibusiness strategic situations that can evolve from a search for exploitation of comparative advantages. These advantages might include specialized equipment, a unique location, managerial expertise, or access to scarce materials. Finally, we will look at several popular portfolio models of financial rationales for the assemblage of conglomerates, a form of multiple-business situation found among very large commercial enterprises.

RISK REDUCTION AND MULTIBUSINESS STRATEGY FORMATION

The concentration strategy used to capitalize on success for single businesses involves a degree of risk. Concentrating on one product means concentrating one's risk in a single product's success or failure. Productive resources focus on that product, and all personnel become specialists in that particular product's unique attributes. Because of the concentration, the organization's entire prospects rely on very specific raw materials, sources of manufactured components, and identified target customers.

A common response to this identified risk is the adoption of a vertical integration strategy. As discussed earlier, vertical integration may involve the purchase or acquisition of the sources of materials critical the productive success. This process, referred to as *backward* vertical integration may involve the acquisition of resources needed for basic production, transportation, and processing of raw materials.

Forward vertical integration is the process of acquiring the intermediate operations that extend from one's own organization toward the marketplace and target customers. Forward integration reduces risks by assuring transportation, distribution, and marketing effort.

Decisions on integration forward or backward involve a careful analysis of costs and benefits, or marginal investment and marginal net profit improvement. Other considerations, however, may suggest integration even at a net added cost. Competitors' interest in acquiring sources of supply may threaten the very existence of supply sources. Limits on the absolute availability of resources might dictate supply acquisition in order that limited sources be reserved for the company's use at present prices rather than at inflated prices in some future time period. Reliability of supply is also a major consideration. Although absolute levels of supply may not be in question, work stoppages, transportation problems, or overbooking by producers can result in delays in shipments that can be very destructive.

EXERCISE 15–1

Prepare for either discussion or as a homework assignment the reasons (other than purely economic) why *forward* vertical integration might be considered desirable. Explain your reasoning in detail. (Hint: You may find it helpful to follow the reasoning used on backward vertical integration.)

EXERCISE 15–2

Your company manufactures work clothing. You purchase denim and cotton duck materials from cotton mills located in the Carolinas and ship it via common truck carrier to your clothing manufacturing plants in Mississippi, Tennessee, and Kentucky. Then you manufacture and sell your unbranded products to a number of retailers and work-uniform service companies, organizations that offer clean uniforms: distributing, collecting, laundering, and redistributing clean work clothing on a weekly or biweekly basis.

- What steps might be taken to integrate backward? Why might your company be interested in doing so? Why not?

- What steps might be taken to integrate forward? Why might your company be interested in doing so? Why not?
- Describe the steps you would want to undertake to conduct the analysis of either one of the decisions needed in the preceding two questions.

Vertical integration in and of itself does not necessarily mean that the company has entered into another business. To be sure, the acquiring firm must be involved in the aspects of the new company that relate to the acquisition and conversion of materials. It may not, however, actively market the new acquisition's products and may reserve its entire production for its own use. If, for example, the acquisition of a parts supplier who fills only a portion of your requirements reduces suppliers from eight to seven sources of supply, your involvement in that supplier's business is solely that of providing for your own needs. On the other hand, if your company acquires a supplier who has substantial sales to customers other than your firm and if your firm cannot make use of all of the capacity of the supplier, then you may find yourself involved in the full range of activities in the acquired business. A perfectly balanced integrated manufacturer would have very little or no excess capacity in any stage of its operations, from raw material acquisition through distribution to retail customer. In practice, this is highly unlikely. As a consequence, integrated manufacturers often find themselves facing the unhappy choice of operating well below capacity or seeking customers for the products that can be produced by the available capacity. In the steel industry, companies with rolling mill capacity in excess of primary steel production will purchase "foreign" (made elsewhere) steel to balance capacity. The "foreign" steel was sold, we should note, by a company that had more steel-making than rolling mill capacity.

EXERCISE 15–3

Give some examples of imbalances in capacity and opportunities for multiple-business operations in *forward* integration in the following industries:

- Automobile manufacture.
- Forest products manufacture.
- Wheat production.
- Shampoo manufacture.
- Gravel mining.

Vertical integration is a natural extension of a concentration strategy. It focuses attention on a single line of business and reduces risks of supply and market attack by competitors; however, it increases the risks associated with the life of the product. As a consequence, we most frequently find integrated operations in industries with long-lived product life cycles.

The high degree of product-oriented risk involved in concentration may call for action steps that increase the organization's flexibility. Three areas of flexibility have been suggested: (a) flexibility of the company's logistic resources and systems, (b) flexibility of management structure and processes and (c) creativity and flexibility of the managers themselves.[4] These adaptability components, all of which lead to a form of corporate nimbleness, can materially offset the risks inherent in the company's product, or line of business. The Boeing Company, involved in a line of business in which products have a high degree of known obsolescence, has been able to thrive in good times and bad, largely on the basis to the flexibility components referred to earlier.

Other organizations can offset product-related risks by a deliberate choice of *diversification*. For some organizations, diversification not only offers a means of balancing risks, but also may make use of the particular strengths of the firm. Thus, the type of relationship that products have to the principal product offerings of the firm should be considered and chosen in a way to maximize the advantage to the company. *Concentric* diversification involves in one case the addition of products that have a common theme or meaning to a given customer group. The Hartz Mountain line of products encompasses a wide range of items, from consumable foods for fish or birds to leashes and brushes for dogs and cats. The product line, however, is entirely devoted to pet supplies. In most cases of this type, the concentric diversification strategy is designed to take advantage of strength in product-name identification or market position for one or more products.

Established marketing channels offer another opportunity for concentric diversification. The strength of an organization's relationship to its marketing channels offers an opportunity to diversify into products that have no intrinsic relationship to those of the company but that are needed or used by customers served by the same channels. A jobber providing a line of nonfood housewares to retail grocers, for example, might expand to add a line of paperback books or magazines to be offered to the same retail outlets. Broader product lines are often found in less-highly populated areas, where a small number of suppliers serve the country stores that sell a very wide line of merchandise to customers in rural areas. In an urban example, many large supermarkets have diversified to include prescription drugs to their retail-grocery customers.

EXERCISE 15–4

Provide three or four specific examples of lines of product-oriented concentrically diversified products. Describe the nature of the general product line.

What problems are posed for materials acquisition and manufacture in expanding through concentric diversification? Explain.

[4] Frank T. Paine and C. R. Anderson, *Strategic Management* (Chicago: Dryden Press, 1983), p. 276.

EXERCISE 15–5

Your company produces and sells high-quality hybrid seed corn to corn producers in an eight-state region in the U.S. Midwest. The brand name is well known and has sustained a high reputation for quality and improved product offerings over a 25-year company history. The profitability of your company's operations has held at sustained high levels. Growth, however, has tapered off in recent years and sales are expected to increase in coming years on the average only at the rate of population growth in your eight-state region. You are considering the possibility of concentric diversification as a means of increasing sales.

- Describe some of the products you think might lend themselves to this strategy.
- For the products you have chosen, describe the problems involved in the production, financing, and marketing of these concentrically linked products. Prepare to discuss your answer in class or to hand it in as a written assignment.

A diversified line of products can also be based on a common production technology. General-purpose equipment, of course, is deliberately designed to provide product-line flexibility. Even where specialized technologies are employed, the imaginative application of that technology offers the opportunity for a distinctive entree into new product/market arenas. The manufacturers of the Timex line of timepieces had developed expertise in high-precision small-metal-equipment manufacture while supplying proximity fuses for artillery shells. Expertise in mass-production metal-parts manufacture and investment casting enabled the Ruger Firearms Company to become successfully established in a very stable and highly competitive mature market for sporting and law enforcement firearms. Both of these examples involve changes in the definition of the company's business. Instead of considering itself in the armaments business, the first organization said it was in the business of manufacturing precise metal assemblies and considered the timepiece to be simply another precise metal assembly.

EXERCISE 15–6

Your company operates as a high-volume mail order house. Each year, you produce six multicolor catalogs, ranging in size from 250 to over 1,000 pages. Two years ago, you installed a high-quality multicolor high-speed printing press to accommodate the company's need for printing capability. This press is operated one shift per day for approximately 3 weeks each time a catalog run is made, but it stands idle during the remainder of the year. Your press crew is made up of highly skilled operators who prefer to work the press or maintain it rather than perform other work in your production facility. Because of the difficulty in recruiting experienced and skilled printers, you have been reluctant to place the press crew on layoff status. Instead, you have considered the possibility of using your excess press capacity to print materials for other companies on a contract basis.

- What kinds of printing might you consider? Why?
- Select one as a likely prospect. How would you organize your company to engage in printing for this group of customers.
- Explain some of the problems you might have in
  Production
  Marketing
  Finance

In addition to market and technology-linked bases for diversification, sources of supply, specialized expertise, a location or locations, or an established reputation and name may offer the opportunity for successful diversification. For example, a forest-products company that had an established position as a purchaser of pulpwood in areas where aspen were plentiful held a commanding position for acquiring aspen and beginning the production of flakeboard, a wood product used in mass-produced cabinets and furniture. AT&T, a giant firm long known for its prominence in the communications field has made a concerted effort to enter the computer industry and, in support of that move, has established AT&T Credit Corporation to assist in the financing of its microcomputer line. The successful entry of this computer will undoubtedly be based on the technological reputation of AT&T's Bell Laboratories and on the company's size and long-established name. An unknown company attempting to battle with the computer giants of today would be unlikely to survive.

Finally, by-products of the principal line of business often become of sufficient economic importance to be considered a line of business. The steel industry for many years supplied cooking gas to local or regional gas-distribution companies. The gas is generated as a by-product of the operation of steel's coke ovens, as is the chemical benzene and other coal-tar products. The paper industry has found markets for shredded bark, a by-product of the wood-preparation process in papermaking. Another example from the paper industry is bagasse—the fiber residue from sugarcane processing—which is a major raw material for paper manufacture in areas that lack a supply of pulpwood. In each of these cases, the value of the by-products is such that each producer finds itself engaged in a by-product business that has its own competitors, pricing ingredients, and unique environmental conditions.

EXERCISE 15-7

Identify at least three products (other than those already mentioned) that you know to be by-products in a manufacturing process. Indicate the major product line.

HAPPY VALLEY STABLES, INC.

Ken Johnson, manager of the Happy Valley Stables, located in north-central Ohio, puzzled over ways and means of increasing revenues. The stable boarded over two hundred pedigreed race and breeding horses at peak times in each season. Although boarding fees were not inexpensive ($150 and up per month per horse), the stable's expenses were high. Owners often were inexperienced in the care and maintenance of their animals and depended on Ken to know how to manage the complete care of their horses, including attention to shoeing and all medical matters. Owners typically expected their animal to be fully ready to resume training when released from Ken's care.

In support of the stable's operations, Ken contracted to have hay raised on over 100 acres of the stable's fields. His hay production typically far exceeded the stable's normal needs. The stable's animals also required grain, water, and pasturage. In support of the stable's requirements for grain, Ken contracted with a local feed mill to mix feed in tonnage quantities to meet his horses' varied needs. He also retained the full-time services of both a veterinarian and a farrier. Pasture maintenance required a full-time crew of eight, while stable hands were needed year-round to attend to the care of the highly individualized needs of the stable's temperamental charges.

In reviewing the options for additional revenue, Ken reflected on the fact that at peak periods all stalls were occupied and a limited number of horses were kept out of covered quarters. During the summer, horses were moved from pasture to pasture, to rotate usage and thereby to allow pastures to renew themselves. Although a limited number of animals might be accommodated during off-peak periods, the stable was operating at, or very close to, capacity as a boarding stable.

EXERCISE 15–8

Discuss any alternatives you think Ken might reasonably consider that would involve diversification. Explain your reasoning and consider the impact on the stable's finances, marketing, and operations.

PORTFOLIO MODELS FOR MULTIBUSINESS STRATEGY FORMATION

The types of multibusiness organizations we have discussed thus far have been constructed by modifying a single-business approach. Generally speaking, the vertically integrated business extends its strategic mission forward or backward (whichever the case may be) to become a fully integrated producer and marketer of an intrinsically related line of products. Thus, a lumber mill might integrate forward by acquiring or building wood-products manufacturing plants, and it might integrate backward by acquiring sources of wood in order to become a fully integrated wood-products company.

The horizontally integrated firm builds from a single-business orientation to the multibusiness strategic posture by extending the line of products laterally. The fully integrated wood-products company mentioned might acquire paper-manufacturing facilities and integrate horizontally by adding paper products to its line. The mission of the organization would have then become that of the production, manufacture, sales, and distribution of forest products, which is a broader definition than that used for the organization that concerned itself only with products made of wood. Is such a firm really diversified? One could argue that the extent of relatedness of the corporation's businesses is so close that, in fact, they are really in a single business. Others could argue that wood products and paper products have quite different competitive and market environments and that they are, indeed, highly diverse enterprises.

Pitts and Hopkins describe two methods of evaluating the degree of diversity in multiple-business organizations. A simple count of the number of businesses is one. In our example, we might include paper products, wood products, bark, and the surplus capacity of any of several stages of production: pulp, paper, semifinished wood products (slabs, planks, etc.), and rough-finished products such as crate and pallet lumber. A second method is the extent of diversity in the logic underlying the strategy of each business. Three types of relatedness are suggested: nonrelated, related to one or more others, and all businesses have some factor of relatedness. Pitts and Hopkins recommend that when comparing diversified and nondiversified companies, a simple count of the number of businesses is satisfactory. When comparing among diversified companies, however, a careful examination of the logic underlying the strategies of the various business is suggested.[5]

EXERCISE 15-9

Make use of the business reference services found in your library. In any two of the following industries, identify one company you believe is nondiversified and another you believe is diversified. Compare the extent of diversity of two companies for presentation in class. Explain your reasoning.

- Automobile manufacture.
- Glass manufacture.
- Forest products.
- Aerospace products.
- Mass communications.
- Furniture manufacture.
- Petroleum-product production.
- Retailing.

[5] R. A. Pitts and H. D. Hopkins, "Firm Diversity: Conceptualization and Measurement," *Academy of Management Review* 7(4) (1982), pp. 620–29.

EXERCISE 15–10

Work in groups of five or six students. Identify and compare two diversified companies in any one of the industries mentioned in Exercise 15–9. Use the method that compares the strategies of each business unit. Refer to the business reference services in your library (as in the preceding exercise). In addition, you may find it helpful to interview (in person or by telephone) marketing strategists in the business units in order to obtain a perspective on how they operate in their respective businesses.

Where businesses are clearly related, as in the wood-products/forest-products examples, a corporate strategy is needed that both accommodates and capitalizes on the operational or market synergies between and among the business units. In businesses that are not related, the corporation may still be able to capitalize on the synergy of shared management expertise, corporate purchasing power, and the ability to generate or raise capital funds. In those companies that lack market or operational relatedness, the portfolio models of corporate strategy seem most appropriate.

Portfolio models are derived from the notion that each unit generates or has needs for cash in relation to its position in the product life cycle. Given business units at different stages of the life cycle, the cash generators of maturity can provide cash to units in the development and growth stages. The portfolio approach, therefore, is helpful in allocation of cash among units while pursuing a corporate mission.

The Boston Consulting Group Four-Cell Matrix

The most popular portfolio model is that devised by the Boston Consulting Group (BCG). The BCG model is displayed in a matrix in which market growth rate and relative competitive position (relative market share) are the two principal dimensions.

Each unit is depicted by a circle. The size of the circle is adjusted to reflect the proportion of assets employed. Figure 15–2 illustrates a portfolio of business units that is balanced by concentrating assets in areas of market strength and by maintaining a balance between cash-needing and cash-generating business unit categories. (In Figure 15–2 note that business growth rate is measured as the percentage change in the market's sales or unit volume over the two most recent periods. Relative Competitive Position is calculated by dividing business unit sales by the sales of the largest competitor and displaying the result on a logarithmic scale. Also note that although the selection of the center points is arbitrary, a relative market share of 1.5 and a market growth rate of 10% are frequently used.)

Stars are business units that have a strong competitive position in a rapidly growing market and offer the greatest opportunity for the corporation. They require a large investment to sustain their growth and thus are often in need of cash from other units in the portfolio.

Problem children are business units in rapidly growing, attractive markets that have a relatively small share of that market. Their lack of market share often suggests that the corporation may need to make a substantial investment in that unit in order to build the share and thereby move the unit toward *star* status. If the organization's management does not believe that star status can be achieved, the unit may be

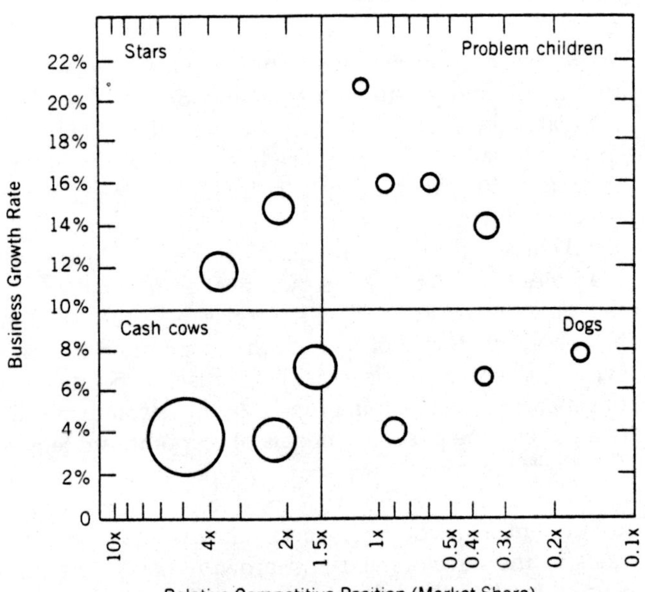

FIGURE 15–2 Boston consulting group four-cell portfolio matrix. Source: Barry Hedley "Strategy and the Business Portfolio," *Long Range Planning* 10(1) (February 1977), p. 12.

divested or liquidated in order that cash can be reallocated to units with better long-term prospects.

Dogs are business units that have relatively small shares in more slowly growing markets; they are seen in the BCG approach as offering only limited prospects for success. Dogs are candidates for cash generation by extensive cost cutting and liquidation of unneeded assets or by divestiture of the entire business.

Cash Cows are business units that have a large relative market share in a market with only modest growth. Investment needs are limited and cash generation is high. Cash, therefore, can be reallocated to star or problem children units.

The portfolio depicted in Figure 15–2 is *balanced* in that the cash-hungry dogs and risky problem children in the right-hand side of the matrix are offset by successful stars and cash generating cash cows. An imbalance in a matrix might mean a higher degree of hard-to-manage risky enterprises than desired or a situation in which needs for cash far outstrip the capability for cash generation. In each case, strategic decisions are needed to either convert problem children to stars or to either clean up or divest business units that appear to be dogs.

EXERCISE 15–11

In our table, data is presented that describes the key information on business units contained in the Consolidated Corporation's business unit portfolio. From this information, prepare a complete BCG portfolio matrix diagram.

Business unit	*Total invstmnt*	*Co. sales*	*Largest co. sales*	*Market sales '84*	*Market sales '85*
A	10.20	56.00	72.00	981.00	1,175.00
B	26.10	187.00	63.00	1,297.00	1,504.00
C	89.80	488.00	1,210.00	9,722.00	10,431.00
D	4.10	22.00	89.00	461.00	483.00
E	122.10	627.00	281.00	1,980.00	2,121.00
F	46.20	340.00	400.00	1,781.00	1,840.00
G	18.90	110.00	61.00	461.00	720.00

EXERCISE 15–12

Prepare a list of at least four recommendations for strategic action based on your analysis of the information contained in our table. Please rank your recommendations in order of their importance for executive action. Explain and justify your recommendations. Prepare for classroom presentation or to hand in as a written assignment.

The BCG matrix has served as a helpful first step in examining collections of business units and evaluating their relative contributions to corporate objectives. The simplicity of the matrix, unfortunately, is the source of some of the criticisms of the BCG approach. Although business sales growth is relatively easy to calculate, defining the market may be quite difficult, especially when substitution of other products may be encountered or when the specific revenue or unit figures needed are found in consolidated accounting reports.

The labels applied to each of the four cells represent oversimplified (and in some cases disparaging) value judgments. Dogs, for example, may represent an opportunity for consistent and steady cash generation with careful management.[6] The implications of these labels are not insignificant for managers in multiple-product corporations. To a hard-working manager, hearing one's life work labeled a *cash cow* or *dog* can be less than stimulating, if not downright demoralizing.

[6] C. Y. Y. Woo and A. C. Cooper, "Strategies of Effective Low Market Share Businesses," *Proceedings, Academy of Management*, (:Academy of Management, August 1980), pp. 21–25.

Of equal significance is the fact that a careful evaluation of the importance of business units must involve an examination of all of those elements so painstakingly detailed in Chapters 10 and 11. Technological factors, unique competencies, environmental attributes, strategic advantages of reputation, location, and customer loyalty are only some of the factors that must be considered in addition to the two dimensions used in the BCG matrix.

The General Electric Nine-Cell Matrix

Two dominant portfolio models have incorporated the criticisms of the BCG four-cell matrix. In a multibusiness adaptation of the business planning matrix, General Electric Company and McKinsey & Company incorporate a wide range of qualitative factors related to industry attractiveness and business strength. Components of business strength include not only relative market share, but also technological strength, marketing knowledge and strength, profitability, technological and managerial capability, and ability to meet the competitive demands of the marketplace for price and product quality.

The dimension labeled *industry attractiveness* not only includes growth rate (as in the BCG matrix), but also market size, competitive structure, seasonality/cyclicality, industry profitability, technological demands, economies of scale, and unique social and human environmental conditions.

To place business units in this matrix, a weighted and scaled subjective evaluation score is calculated by weighting each factor in the two principal dimensions. (Weights must total 100%.) Subjective ratings of each factor range from 0.0 (low) through 0.5 (medium) to 1.0 (high). A total score is achieved by multiplying the weight times the rating for each factor, then summing to achieve a weighted total score. The two scores are then used to place the business unit in a nine-cell matrix as in Figure 15–3. Each unit is depicted by a circle to represent that unit's market and a pie-shaped segment to represent the company's share of that market. Once placed, the prescriptions from the business planning matrix are used to suggest strategic action steps. Invest to grow (I), Evaluate or manage selectively (E), and Disinvest, or harvest (D).[7]

EXERCISE 15–12

Ajax Incorporated, your conglomerate, has business units operating in several different environments. The following information is provided on six of the principal units in Ajax.

[7] J. H. Grant and W. R. King "Strategy Formulation: Analytical and Normative Models," in Dan E. Schendel and Charles W. Hofer, eds., *Strategic Management: A New View of Business Policy and Planning* Boston: Little, Brown, 1979, p. 117. Also see, J. A. Pearce II and R. B. Robinson, Jr., *Strategic Management*, 2nd Ed. (Homewood, Ill: R. D. Irwin, 1985), pp. 250–53

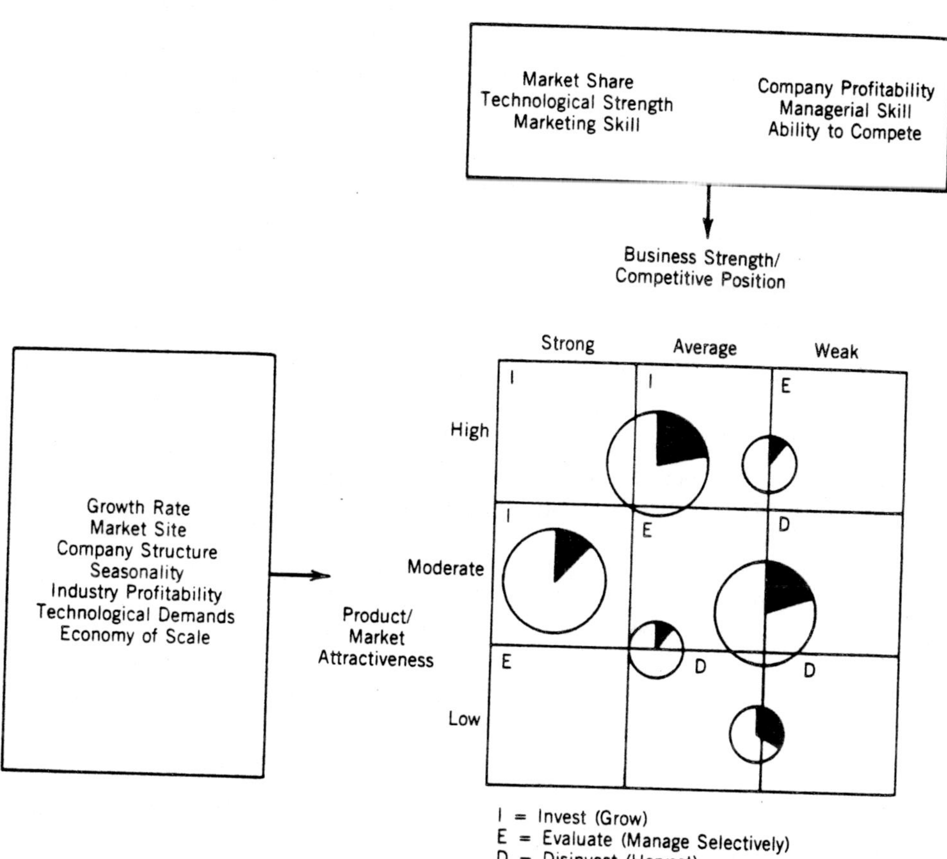

FIGURE 15–3 General Electric nine-cell portfolio matrix.

BUSINESS UNIT A

Industry Attractiveness

- Market Size — estimated $20 billion/year
- Projected Market Growth — estimated 13 to 15% next year, higher in succeeding years
- Technological Requirements — moderate
- Industry Profitability — estimated at 13%
- Competitive Structure — 12 majors, 250 minors
- Economies of Scale — significant opportunities for cost saving
- Seasonality/Cyclicality — limited
- Social/Human Factors — moderate regulation

Business Strength
Relative Market Share—2.2%
Competitive Capability—moderate
Marketing Knowledge and Capability—excellent
Competitive Position—fair
Technological and Managerial Expertise—generally quite good

BUSINESS UNIT B
Industry Attractiveness
Market Size—$125 million
Projected Market Growth—estimated at 16% or more
Technological Requirements—very high
Industry Profitability—18% on assets after tax
Competitive Structure—two principal competitors, three other very small ones
Economies of Scale—insignificant at present
Seasonality/Cyclicality—moderate
Social/Human Factors—environmental and social concerns, some bad press to date
Business Strength
Relative Market Share—$55 million
Competitive Capability—very strong
Marketing Knowledge and Capability—fair
Competitive Position—three competitors, all smaller
Technological and Managerial Expertise—excellent

BUSINESS UNIT C
Industry Attractiveness
Market Size—$400 billion
Projected Market Growth—4.5%
Technological Requirements—high, capital intensive
Industry Profitability—6.2% on invested capital
Competitive Structure—12 very large, 40–50 small
Economies of Scale—very pronounced
Seasonality/Cyclicality—no seasonality, 3- to 5-year cycles (+—20%)
Social/Human Factors—environmental restrictions, regulations on new construction
Business Strength
Relative Market Share—$22 billion
Competitive Capability—moderate to good
Marketing Knowledge and Capability—satisfactory
Competitive Position—fourth in size, moderate
Technological and Managerial Expertise—satisfactory

BUSINESS UNIT D

Industry Attractiveness

Market Size—$5.5 million
Projected Market Growth—estimated 40 to 50%
Technological Requirements—very high
Industry Profitability—poor
Competitive Structure—four principal competitors
Economies of Scale—nil
Seasonality/Cyclicality—unknown
Social/Human Factors—unknown

Business Strength

Relative Market Share—$1.3 million
Competitive capability—excellent
Marketing Knowledge and Capability—fair, at best
Competitive Position—satisfactory
Technological and Managerial Expertise Excellent

BUSINESS UNIT E

Industry Attractiveness

Market Size—$760 million
Projected Market Growth—10% forecast
Technological Requirements—moderate
Industry Profitability—13% return on assets
Competitive Structure—100+ competitors, all small to moderate in size
Economies of Scale—some possibilities; investment needs moderate
Seasonality/Cyclicality—high seasonality; peak in summertime
Social/Human Factors—positive social/environmental

Business Strength

Relative Market Share—$28 million
Competitive Capability—good
Marketing Knowledge and Capability—excellent
Competitive Position—fair
Technological and Managerial Expertise—satisfactory

BUSINESS UNIT F

Industry Attractiveness

Market Size—$400 million
Projected Market Growth—0% or less
Technological Requirements—very low
Industry Profitability—14 to 18% on assets
Competitive Structure—3 principal competitors, 26 moderate, 150+ small shops
Economies of Scale—good potential; investment moderate
Seasonality/Cyclicality—high seasonality
Social/Human Factors—not significant

Business Strength
Relative Market Share—$8 million
Competitive Position—Not strong
Technological and Managerial Expertise—Not strong
Competitive Position—Not strong
Technological and Managerial Expertise—Not Strong

- From the information contained in pages 652–6, construct a nine-cell GE planning grid. Identify by means of circles and pie-shaped segments each of the six business units in A through F. Describe and justify the weights you attach to each factor in terms of your own risk preferences, values, and corporate mission.
- When your matrix is complete, describe a strategic plan of action that will be based on the matrix you have developed. Rank your action steps in order of importance.

The General Housewares Corporation case is included so that you can study a realistic multiple-business situation and begin the process of establishing a *corporate-level* plan of action designed to achieve corporate goals. As you read through the case, be prepared to conduct an analysis of each line of business as if it were a separate business unit. When you have read the case carefully, prepare answers to the questions at the end of the case.

GENERAL HOUSEWARES CORPORATION

General Housewares Corporation manufactures and markets cookware, giftware, and leisure furniture for the home to a large group of retailers and consumers in the U.S.A. and Canada. The company was formed in 1967 by combining ten separate companies into three autonomous divisions, namely, the Cookware Group, the Giftware Group, and the Leisure Furniture Group. Each group is operated as a profit center, subject to financial control by Corporate Management. GHC stock was listed on the American Stock Exchange beginning in 1973, and by 1978 sales had grown to over $60 million.

This case was prepared by William C. Scott, Ph.D., Indiana State University, and Robert A. Hayes, Director of Industrial Engineering, Cookware Group, General Housewares Corp., as a basis for class discussion rather than to illustrate either effective or ineffective handling of an administrative situation.

STRATEGIC POSITION-PRODUCT/ MARKET EMPHASIS

Products

There is a major product line within each of the three division groups. The Cookware Group (53% of sales) manufactures, imports, and markets top-of-the-stove, oven, and specialty cookware in a broad range of price, color, and design, fabricated out of porcelain on steel, cast iron, and aluminum. The Giftware Group (25% of sales) manufacturers and markets a variety of decorative and novelty candles, and it imports coffee mugs, canister sets, serving pieces, kitchen storage items, and related accessories for the home. The Leisure Furniture Group (22% of sales) manufactures and markets seating, dining, patio, and accessory furniture of a leisure nature fabricated out of wrought iron, aluminum, and rattan.

Approximately 2% of sales for Cookware, and 55% of sales for Giftware are from import products sold under GHC labels. One problem facing the Company with this arrangement of having commission agents in foreign countries is that, at any time, shipments can be affected by foreign laws and government regulations, customs duties, tariffs, quotas, strikes and/or the inability to inspect the products prior to shipment, damage or destruction while in transit, delivery delays, and currency fluctuations.

During 1978, new product development has accounted for 8% of sales in the Cookware Group, 15% of sales in the Giftware Groups, and less than 1% in the Leisure Group through changes in color, style, shape, or pattern. As a result of product development, 25% of corporate products are modified annually, and 36.5% of 1978 sales came from products less than three years old. Current backlog of orders, as a measure of market activity, is increasing with the Cookware Group having approximately 9.6% of total sales ($3.9 million), Giftware Group having approximately 1.3% of total sales ($0.2 million), and Leisure Group having approximately 31.7% of total sales ($4.1 million) committed to production for 1979 shipments.

Maintaining product line vitality from the standpoint of sales volume, market share, and profit has been a prime responsibility of GHC management. Anticipating and meeting the changing needs of the consumer is an ongoing practice across all groups through a disciplined approach to product mix. This approach dictates that a potential product must be complementary to an existing GHC product, must be compatible from a distribution standpoint, must have uniqueness through changes in fashion or design, must represent consumer functional satisfaction, must provide the potential for a high margin and satisfactory asset return, and, finally, must have the potential to develop into a sizable business.

Markets

General Housewares markets products in a low to high price/quality range. These products are targeted to a broad range of income levels and consumer preferences. Cookware products are sold nationally and in Canada to approximately 3400 customers. During 1978, the ten largest customers accounted for 27% of total cookware sales of $32.4 million and the loss of this Group's largest customer would result in a reduction in net sales of approximately $4 million. Cookware sells directly to most major retail and wholesale distribution organizations, including general merchandise chains, mail order houses, department stores, mass merchandisers, variety and premium stamp outlets. These sales are promoted through 112 manufacturers' representatives and in four major metropolitan markets by company marketing managers. Prospective customers can see GHC products in showrooms maintained either by the company or its representatives in most principle market cities.

The Giftware products are also sold nationally and in Canada to approximately 10,400 customers of which the ten largest customers represented 25% of total (1978) giftware sales of $15.2 million. Loss of the largest customer would reduce net sales by approximately $1.5 million. Giftware is sold to most major retail and wholesale distribution organizations in the United States through 80 manufacturers' representatives. Showrooms are maintained in most principal market cities.

Leisure Furniture products are sold nationally to approximately 5000 customers with the ten largest customers accounting for approximately 32% of total (1978) furniture sales of $13.1 million. Products are sold directly to general merchandise chains, department stores, mass merchandisers, and furniture store chains through the use of 21 manufacturers' representatives and selected wholesalers who sell to many smaller retail outlets. The Leisure Furniture Group also maintains showrooms in most major market cities.

Since General Housewares is a young corporation, it does not have a corporate competitive advantage based on brand image. Any competitive advantage exists within a group's brand image and must be based on price and quality of the products.

PERFORMANCE GOALS

Performance goals are applicable at both group and corporate levels. Return on sales is a major corporate goal which is also evaluated for each group. A second measurable goal, which is related to the first, is cost. Costs are reported as both costs of goods sold and selling, general and administrative expenses on Exhibit 1. A third goal, applicable to the total corporation, is the restructuring of long-term debt. Other goals exist.

EXTERNAL ENVIRONMENT

The impact of the external environment continually becomes more important as a factor affecting the formulation of strategy. The effect of inflation on raw material cost and other constraints imposed by suppliers have generated increased attention of management. The ban on the exporting of rattan wood from the Philippine Islands, FDA regulations on porcelain enamel components, increased steel and aluminum costs, shipping delays, and longer lead times on deliveries have emphasized the need to seek additional sources of supplies in addition to established suppliers.

Government

The impact of environmental regulations has made several of the company's manufacturing facilities subject to regulation by various local, state, and federal agencies. The increasing impact of EPA, OSHA, EEO, AAP, and other regulatory sanctions must be dealt with in the future and treated as a cost of doing business in our society. On the other hand, government support has been received in the form of import restrictions.

Market

Changing market conditions and consumer demands are developing which are affecting each operating group. Even though the products made by GHC are distributed nationally and are targeted to all income levels, changes in demographic concentration, associated freight costs to point of sale, rising income levels, and changes in buying patterns due to age, social class, and housing styles are requiring new efforts for increased market penetration. Since design features, including price and quality, are the predominent requisite for sales success, and competing companies do not have significant product differences, new product development is an invaluable attribute. Also, mature products must be evaluated for their contribution to profit to determine if upgrading is necessary in order to shift those products into new life cycles, or to discontinue them.

One difficulty is that there are no relevant data concerning "total market" in each of the three operating groups due to the many varied suppliers of comparable products both domestic and foreign. These suppliers range from small "mom and pop" shops in candle-making to large manufacturers who import cookware under brand name labels. Positioning in the marketplace is based upon changes in total sales on a yearly basis. Professional Trade Associations attempt to determine market growth or decline but have to rely on member input for statistics, thus non-member activity is neither known nor monitored.

Industry

The individual companies that compete with GHC vary from small, one-owner establishments to foreign and domestic companies which manufacture similar to substitute products. Some of these manufacturers are larger than GHC and have greater financial resources or are divisions or subsidiaries of large diversified companies. There are no sizable barriers into the markets served by General Housewares. The technology, equipment required, distribution channels, raw materials, and market availability do not pose significant constraints for potential competitors.

In contrast, competitive conditions have caused some industry consolidation. The cookware operation, porcelain-on-steel, in Terre Haute, for example, is the sole survivor of 17 companies in the United States that were in porcelain-on-steel operation after World War II. The majority of the closings of these companies have been attributed to decreasing profits, effect of imports, lack of aggressive marketing practices, and lack of scheduling flexibility to meet customer demands. The entire porcelain-on-steel, aluminum, and cast iron industry has recently suffered from foreign competition from Third World countries that are exempt from import taxes. This has allowed retail pricing for these products to be less than manufacturer's cost domestically. Foreign imports of porcelain-on-steel products alone have increased 153.8% from 1977 to 1978. Reaction to this penetration of the U.S. domestic market was recognized at both the Corporate and Group levels, since the Cookware Group President is also a Corporate Vice-President. Responsibility for possible solutions was delegated to the Group President who, with the United Steelworkers Union and Senator Birch Bayh, testified before the International Trade Commission petitioning for relief. General Housewares has received a favorable ruling from the International Trade Commission for relief from foreign imports. Relief, yet to be approved by the President, would increase duties on imports or impose quotas on import volume. The impact of foreign duty-free competition has resulted in a decline in 1978 sales (down 7.5% from 1977), higher 1978 inventories (up 8.3% from 1977), and a downward trend in production, profits, employment, and wages. The single most important effect, however, has been the decreased usage of asset capacity, which has been reduced 20% due to the effect of imports.

Foreign competition has made larger inroads in the recent past as well as the emergence of changes in product composition from domestic competitors. This is especially prevalent in the Cookware Group where porcelain on aluminum, non-stick surfaces, micro-wave cooking technology from domestic competitors, and porcelain-on-steel cookware from foreign suppliers are causing great problems in marketing channels and profit structure. Recognizing the possible long-term impact of foreign competition, heavy debt structure, levelling of sales, growth in product composition from domestic competitors, environmental controls, and inflation, at both the manufacturer and consumer level, the directors of GHC sought a change in direction of the Business Strategy.

The above environmental complexities and their effects on the corporation have resulted in a recent emphasis to be placed on environmental scanning to gather externally based information. Foreign competition, environmental protection requirements, export bans on raw material imports, domestic competition through technological change and economic conditions have forced a new dimension of management strategy planning upon the corporation. The need to monitor the external environment more critically and consider alternative actions has been recognized.

COMPANY RESOURCES

Financial Structure

The general financial condition for GHC is shown in Exhibits 1, 2, and 3. The short-term obligations are high enough to place restrictions on year-end inventory levels, which creates the need for increased control procedures on inventory levels.

The impact of long-term debt has improved but was still considered high in 1978. General Housewares has been encumbered with a heavy long-term debt structure since its formation in 1967 due to the use of long-term debt financing for acquisitions and fixed asset additions and the subsequent refinancing of this debt. At the present time, General Housewares has completed a $22 million finance agreement providing for 15-year long-term debt, partial re-payment of preferred stockholders, and sufficient short-term debt to allow the discontinuance of the factoring of receivables.

Organization and Management

General Housewares maintains a flat organization structure at both the corporate and the group levels. Each group operates as a separate profit center subject to policy direction and financial control by corporate management. (See Exhibit 4—Organization Structure.)

Each group has its own centralized administrative, product development, marketing, sales, and control functions. The Cookware Group management and staff are located in Terre Haute, Indiana, where they supervise the production of domestic porcelainized steel products in Terre Haute, and a cast iron and cast aluminum foundry in Sidney, Ohio.

The Giftware Group is headquartered in Hyannis, Massachusetts. They operate a decorative and novelty candle manufacturing plant and supervise the importing of other related accessories which are sold under the General Housewares brand, plus other imports of design coordinated items for the kitchen in the form of ceramic coffee mugs, canister sets, and coordinated serving and storage items.

The Leisure Furniture Group is located in Atlanta, Georgia. It supervises a wrought iron and aluminum furniture manufacturing plant in Birmingham, Alabama, and a rattan furniture plant in Lexington, Kentucky.

Corporate Management, headquartered at Stamford, Connecticut, is relatively young (average age 42) with average service of 5.3 years. The President and three Vice-Presidents have backgrounds in finance, engineering, and marketing. There have been very few administrative changes since the corporation was established and relatively few changes in the Group level.

Management compensation is based upon performance through a salary base with modifications for bonus and incentive for key management personnel at the corporate and group levels. Under the current compensation plan, officers and other key management employees of the company may earn additional compensation ranging from 50% to 75% of salary base depending upon the achievement of predetermined profit and cash flow objectives budgeted in General Housewares' Business Plan for the year.

Strategy decisions at all levels are made within a prevailing attitude of risk aversion, i.e., only outcomes with significant chance of success and with little or no risk of financial loss are chosen. This is due to the current financial-based problems faced by the corporation. Decision-making is decentralized within each group and extends down to the functional operating level at each plant. Check and balance of decision-making is only to assure that local goals and objectives are served in the best interest within the context of the decision made and that such decision at any level of any operating group is not in violation of corporate policy.

Decision-making as a whole is done in a reactive posture to counteract specific events in the marketplace and/or external environment, rather than in an aggressive mode with problems foreseen or predicted and alternate strategies developed before the problem develops. Information about the external environment that is utilized is usually obtained informally as it happens to come to the attention of company employees. There is no formal program of reviewing information about the market or other environmental factors.

There is very little social orientation other than that which is legally necessary or "politically" favorable (non-governmental sense). This is due to the very limited number of administrative personnel which, at the corporate level, wear many different hats in order to carry on the daily business of the company. This lack of social obligation and/or exposure extends downward through all groups of the company.

Personnel communication upward, downward, and across organizational lines is emphasized and encouraged from both a practical viewpoint, due to the relatively small number of salaried personnel within the company, and the functional viewpoint of information transfer across each operating group.

The company has a total of approximately 1500 employees of which nearly 300 are clerical, salaried, or administrative positions. Seventy-five percent of the 1200 production personnel belong to labor organizations. The United Steelworkers Union is the largest recognized union (46%), with the Allied Molders (9%), Metal Polishers (12.5%), and Teamsters Unions (8%) having smaller representation. On the whole, the labor climate is favorable with the company being virtually strike free.

Operations

The plant operations within the three operating groups of General Housewares Corp. are labor intensive and are located in older plant facilities that are upgraded on a continuing basis and maintained in good condition for the particular operations for which they are used.

The Cookware Group operates in two factories owned by the corporation with over 650,000 square feet of floor space; the Giftware Group operates from one factory owned by the corporation with approximately 45,000 square feet of floor space and one leased factory with almost 30,000 square feet of floor space. The Leisure Furniture Group operates in three leased factories with over 150,000 square feet of floor space.

Production equipment ranges from older stamping presses with zero book value to new, high technology furnaces requiring moderate capital investment. General Housewares does not, in general, utilize automation in the direct manufacturing process but does have extensive material handling capability through conveyor networks. All equipment, however, is of sufficient capacity and durability to satisfy production requirements.

Due to the financial structure of the firm in relation to its debt position, raw material, in-process and finished goods inventories are rigidly controlled and lead production requirements by a relatively short period of time.

There is virtually no vertical integration in General Housewares Corp. due to the relatively low cost and available supply of raw materials from outside sources. The basic raw materials used are steel, iron, aluminum, wax, wood, sand, clay, and various oxides. The company has neither the financial base, technology, nor share of the market to undertake vertical integration either forward or backward in the foreseeable future.

Manufacturing process controls are not used extensively at any location in the area of statistical quality control, i.e., sampling inspection, incoming and outgoing quality levels, percent defective charts, etc. Most controls are unique to the particular operation under consideration and, thus, are designed to fit that operation. Other controls are "learned" controls that are handed down from operator to operator in the normal course of their work and more or less reflect the state of the art in the manufacture of the product.

Accounting cost controls, however, are quite prevalent in the form of direct labor, indirect labor, and material variance reports and ratio analysis.

There is almost no internal research and development done within the corporation. Any development work is under contract to established firms and is in the form of design features, packaging, shape or pattern changes and color arrangement. Product component composition such as enamel frits, steel, iron, clay, oxides, wax, and wood are purchased on the open market from commercial sources and are not required to be of a specialty nature.

Marketing

Cookware Group product lines range from a complete line of top-of-stove and oven cookware, including saucepans, casseroles, and fry pans in porcelain-on-steel, cast iron, and cast aluminum to large food canners and roasters packed in a variety of patterns, shapes, and sizes. Complementing these products are cast iron utility trivets and decorative hooks for serving and hanging the products. The Leisure Furniture Group products include wrought iron patio furniture and rattan indoor dining and living room furniture and accessories. Individual units such as chaise lounges, love seats, and rocking chairs complement formal seating groups. The Giftware Group produces a wide variety of decorative and novelty candles of varying sizes, shapes, and colors that satisfy both seasonal and everyday consumer requirements. Complementing the candles are candleholders, coffee mugs, food storage containers, and hostess soaps.

Individual product life cycles across the operating groups of GHC varied from failure in the introduction stage to continued success at maturity with some "Bread and Butter" produces approaching the saturation stage with the resultant erosion of profit margin to sales revenue. There was a concerted effort to enter new products or modify existing products into new life cycles in order to bolster profit margins in light of changing market preferences, domestic and foreign competition, and little change in technology. Thus, the marketing strategy reflected this move by trying to develop new markets, identify new product voids and find uses for existing products with some modifications.

General Housewares utilizes merchandising concepts that help the retailer plan his programs for maximum turnover and better profits. Such merchandising includes colorful consumer-oriented packaging, point of purchase displays, informative product labels and literature and helpful product information that enables the retailers to develop a more powerful sales technique.

Seasonally planned advertising (approximately 2.6% of sales dollars in 1978 and 2.2% of sales dollars in 1977) is placed in national magazines, TV, radio spots, storyboards, and retail displays to help retail activity.

EXHIBIT 1

General Housewares Corp. consolidated statement of operations and retained earnings

	For year ended December 31, (000's)				
	1978	*1977*	*1976*	*1975*	*1974*
Net sales	60,825	60,417	54,149	54,158	56,207
Cost of goods sold	42,579	41,375	36,530	37,803	40,067
Gross profit	18,246	19,042	17,619	16,355	16,140
Selling, general and administrative expenses	12,959	12,562	12,167	11,944	11,966
Operating income	5,287	6,480	5,452	4,411	4,174
Interest expense	1,631	1,637	2,036	2,484	3,195
Income before income taxes, cumulative effect of accounting changes and extraordinary credit*	3,656	4,843	3,416	1,927	(7,019)*
Income taxes	1,816	2,422	1,708	963	249
Net income for the year	1,840	2,421	1,357	1,827	(7,268)
Retained earnings, end of year (from January 1, 1976)**	5,607	3,778	1,357	—**	—

*Provision for loss on disposition of assets and write-off of intangible assets, income taxes and extraordinary credit, ($7,998,000). Income before provision for loss on disposition of assets and write-off of intangible assets, income taxes, and extraordinary credit, $979,000.

**Deficit on 12/31/75 of $4,026,000 eliminated by a charge to capital in excess of par value with stockholder approval.

EXHIBIT 2

General Housewares Corp. group sales and profits

	1978	*1977*	*1976*	*1975*	*1974*
Cookware Group					
Net Sales	$32,457	$35,078	$32,206	$32,937	$30,342
Operating Income* (Loss)	4,549	6,374	6,303	6,884	5,466
Return on Sales %	14.01	18.17	19.57	20.90	18.01
Giftware Group					
Net Sales	15,205	13,973	11,700	10,919	12,174
Operating Income* (Loss)	1,677	1,249	797	212	(549)
Return On Sales %	11.03	8.94	6.81	1.94	(2.57)
Leisure Group					
Net Sales	13,163	11,366	10,243	10,302	13,691
Operating Income* (Loss)	106	389	180	(450)	418
Return on Sales %	0.81	3.42	1.76	(4.37)	3.05
Total Corporate					
Net Sales	60,825	60,417	54,149	54,158	56,207
Operating Income* (Loss)	6,332	8,012	7,280	6,646	5,335
Return on Sales %	10.39	13.26	13.44	12.27	9.49

*Income before corporate expense, interest, income taxes, cumulative effect of accounting changes and extraordinary credit. The Corporate Expense item accounts for the difference in Operating Income between Exhibits 1 and 2.

EXHIBIT 3
General Housewares Corp. consolidated balance sheet

	For year ended December 31, (000's)				
	1978	*1977*	*1976*	*1975*	*1974*
ASSETS					
Current Assets:					
Cash	2,974	998	826	993	1,694
Marketable securities at cost	—	—	—	—	4,068
Accounts receivable	7,544	10,422	8,742	6,246	7,190
Inventories, including raw materials and work in process	9,686	8,943	8,991	9,393	13,738
Prepaid taxes	293	351	560	—	—
Other prepaid expenses	109	110	210	495	647
Total current assets	20,606	20,824	19,329	17,127	27,337
Property, Plant and Equipment, at cost:					
Land	250	250	240	225	225
Buildings	1,381	1,295	1,017	951	920
Machinery and equipment	11,006	9,944	9,277	9,076	8,723
	12,637	11,489	10,534	10,252	9,868
Less—Accumulated depreciation	6,769	6,067	5,232	4,583	3,915
	5,868	5,422	5,302	5,669	5,953
Other Assets	482	—	78	296	397
Total assets	26,956	26,246	24,709	23,092	33,687
LIABILITIES AND STOCKHOLDERS' EQUITY					
Current Liabilities:					
Notes Payable	—	—	—	—	11,714
Current maturities of long-term debt	160	1,333	1,333	1,468	1,406
Accounts payable	3,494	2,828	2,752	3,040	3,098
Accrued liabilities	3,136	3,545	3,426	3,162	2,596
Income taxes payable	657	1,757	1,401	—	—
Total current liabilities	7,447	9,463	8,912	7,670	18,814
Deferred liabilities	413	254	360	517	326
Long-Term Debt	10,840	8,278	9,612	10,953	12,421
Stockholders' Equity:					
Preferred stock	1,015	2,434	2,434	2,434	2,434
Common stock	667	665	664	664	664
Capital in excess of par value	967	1,374	1,370	854	4,881
Deficit	—	—	—	—	(5,853)
Retained earnings from January 1, 1976*	5,607	3,778	1,357	*—	—
Total stockholders' equity	8,256	8,251	5,825	3,952	2,126
Total liabilities and equity	26,956	26,246	24,709	23,092	33,687

*Deficit on 12/31/75 of $4,026,000 eliminated by a charge to capital in excess of par value with Stockholder approval.

EXHIBIT 4
General Housewares Corp. organization structure

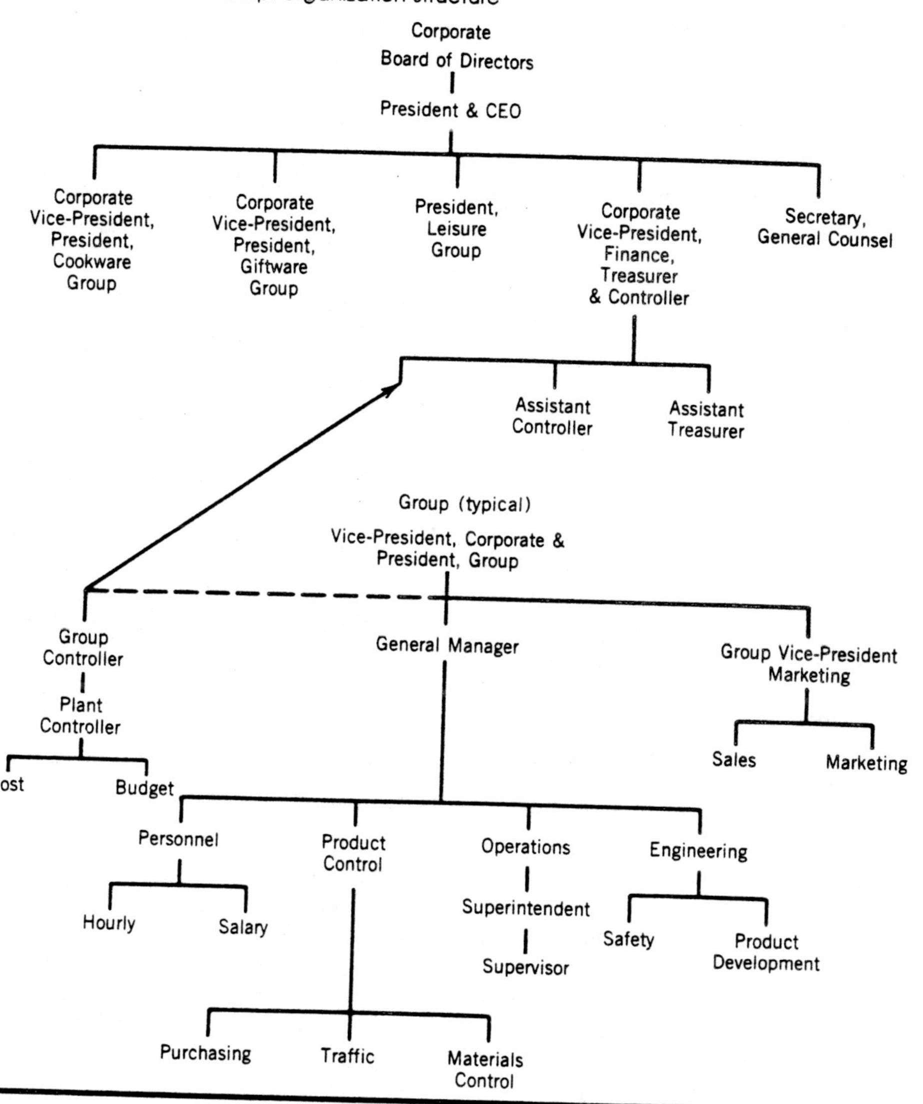

EXERCISE 15–13

From your reading of the case and where necessary from information contained in your reference library prepare answers to the following questions:

- Provide a brief list of strengths, weaknesses, risks, and opportunities for each of the business units mentioned in the case.
- Prepare a table of information that will enable you to apply the GE nine-cell matrix to the General Housewares Corporation's situation as of the date of the case.
- Prepare the complete matrix.
- Develop and present a set of recommendations based on the analysis you have just completed.
- Is this sufficient? Would you feel comfortable as president of the company with these recommendations? Explain.

The GE nine-cell matrix, as we have seen, offers a number of advantages over the somewhat simpler BCG four-cell matrix. Its two major dimensions, however, still call for the analyst or strategy formulator to identify a position at a point in time, and they do not easily account for categories of business units that may be at present in a relatively unattractive situation but that are *about to become* very attractive. Similarly, a static analysis might suggest that an organization is presently strong at a point when it is about to enter a decline phase. These criticisms led Hofer to develop a matrix that incorporates concepts of product/market evolution into a portfolio model for corporate strategy analysis and development.

Hofer's Product/Market Evolution Portfolio Matrix

The Hofer matrix is built on three levels of competitive position (Strong, Average, and Weak), and six degrees of product/market evolution, stages in the product life cycle. These are Development, Growth, Shakeout, Maturity, Saturation, and Decline. In the Hofer matrix, market size is designated by a circle. Business unit share is depicted by a shaded pie-shaped segment of the circle. The matrix, shown in Figure 15–4, is representative of a corporate portfolio that has business units in a range of competitive positions, in nearly all stages of the product-market evolutionary cycle, and in units that have varying shares of their respective markets.[8]

As we examine this matrix, we should be able to compare our assessment of operating units in the BCG matrix to the business units depicted in Figure 15–4. The unit labeled G in the lower right of Figure 15–4, for example, has a relatively small share of market in a declining industry. The unit's position is weak. Clearly, this

[8] C. W. Hofer, "Conceptual Constructs for Formulating Corporate and Business Strategies," Boston, Intercollegiate Case Clearing House, No. 9–378–754, 1977.

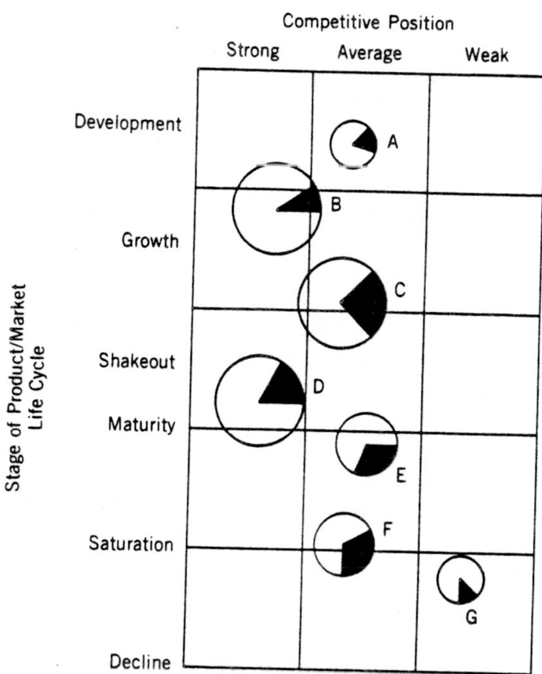

FIGURE 15-4 Hofer's product/market evolution portfolio matrix. *Source:* **Adapted from C. W. Hofer, "Conceptual Constructs for Formulating Corporate and Business Strategies," Boston, Intercollegiate Case Clearing House, No. 9-378-754, 1977, p. 3.**

business unit would be seen as a *dog* in BCG matrix terms. The two larger circles, with relatively large shaded segments found in the lower center of the matrix labeled *E* and *F* appear to fit the classic description of the *cash cow*.

EXERCISE 15–14

- Place each of the remaining business units (A through D) in the BCG matrix. Explain your reasoning.
- Provide recommendations for action steps for units A through D. Explain your reasoning.
- Would you recommend different action steps for units D and F? Explain why or why not.

EXERCISE 15-15

- Refer to Exercise 15-12. Based on your understanding of the product life cycle, place each of the six business units in appropriate stages of the product/market life cycle. Use the categories found in the Hofer model depicted in Figure 15-4.
- Prepare a complete Hofer fifteen-cell matrix for these six business units.
- Develop suggestions for strategic action for each of the six units.

The Hofer fifteen-cell matrix, like the GE nine-cell model, offers advantages over its simpler predecessors. Graphically it offers the strategist an opportunity to view a number of business units collectively in a coherent framework. Like its earlier forerunners, the Hofer model provides a mechanism for describing assemblages of business units that would fit strategies suitable for the corporation. If, for example, all units in the matrix were clustered in stages of the product/market cycle in which profit generation is maximized, the *corporate* strategy revealed would be that of focusing on profit generation. Similarly, if the focus were on growth stage business units, the corporate strategy depicted would be that of emphasizing growth. In both of the preceding situations, the corporate strategy would be maximized for the corporation where the business strength is high and where market share is large.

Figure 15-5 is a representation of an ideal portfolio for a corporation pursuing a growth strategy. As you can see, each unit has a relatively large share of its market and units are concentrated on the growth and early maturity stages of the product/market life cycle.

EXERCISE 15-16

Prepare a Hofer fifteen-cell matrix to represent an ideal corporate strategy for *maximizing profit*. Explain your reasoning.

The Hofer fifteen-cell matrix provides, as we have seen, an excellent framework for depicting both actual and ideal strategic configurations of business units. This matrix together with the strategic prescriptions related to stages in the product/market life cycle (see Chapter 12) can be very helpful in establishing one's present position and in determining reasonable action plans for achieving strategic objectives. The prescriptions found in Chapter 12, however, are based on at least one variable not mentioned in the Hofer model—preference for risk.

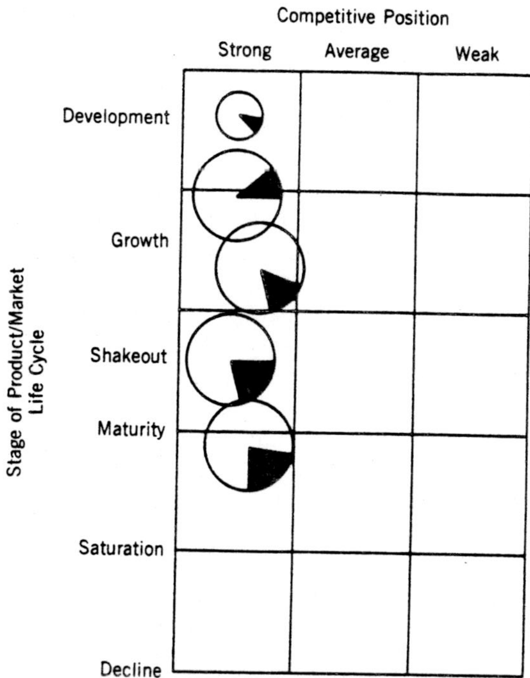

FIGURE 15–5 Corporate ideal growth strategy. *Source:* **Charles W. Hofer and Dan Schendel,** ***Strategy Formulation: Analytical Concepts*** **(St. Paul, Minn.: West, 1978), p. 183.**

Risk Preference and Corporate Strategy Formulation

In Chapter 12, we noted that the degree of tolerance for risk is a significant determinant in the choice of strategy for single-business strategists. In the multiple-business strategy-formulation system, risk preferences again have a significant effect on the type of strategy chosen. If we consider the state of product/market evolution, we have high degrees of uncertainty about the viability of the product/market early in its development stage and late, as the product/market moves into its decline. In the middle stages, uncertainty exists, but not about the viability of the generic product and its market. Uncertainty instead focuses on the specific competitor, its products, and its ability to build and sustain market share during periods of intense competition among large and aggressive competitors.

The extremely risk-averse corporate strategist, therefore, might not engage in businesses until they had moved well into growth stages in which market viability is more apparent and predictable. Market share would be extremely important, so the risk-average strategist would seek to gain market share very quickly through contractural terms in sales contracts with very large customers, intensive marketing, or the acquisition of, or merger with, customers or competitors. Market share and strength of competitive position would continue to be extremely important through the shakeout, maturity, and saturation stages. The risk-averse manager, as the business unit and its product/market approach decline, would seek to minimize losses and would, therefore, be likely to seek to divest the unit early in decline, or near the end of the maturity stage, before the onset of decline. The Hofer matrix for an extremely risk-averse manager would find all of the corporation's holdings concentrated in the four cells at the left-center of the matrix (see Figure 15–6).

The portions of the matrix in Figure 15–6 that are *not* occupied by the business units of the extremely risk-averse corporate manager offer possible arenas of opportunity for managers with a higher tolerance for risks of various types. The manager who believes his company is nimble enough to respond rapidly to changes in customer interest might be quite willing to start, or to stay with, a smaller market share in growth and maturity stages of the product/market life cycle. Similarly, the same risk-tolerant manager might feel confident of the business unit's ability to develop and market new products and may, therefore, wish to invest more heavily in development-stage products than his or her risk-averse counterpart.

Differences would also be apparent near the end of the life cycle. Managers with experience in managing declines may be able to continue to generate cash as more

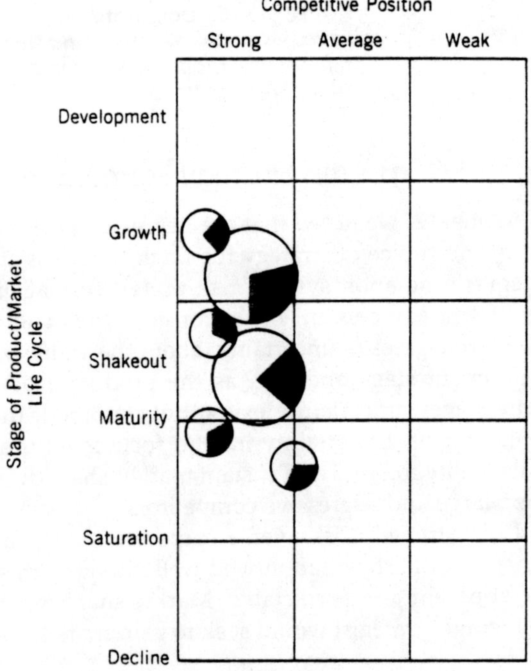

FIGURE 15–6 Risk-averse corporate strategy.

timid companies liquidate. Their expertise in cost containment and liquidation may mean a continuation of profitable and cash-generating operations well beyond the term of interest of the more risk averse.

The development of a *working* portfolio of business units for a strategist who is not averse to risks would, however, probably need to include companies that generate the cash or provide the backstop of financial security needed to avoid financial collapse in the event one or more risky enterprises failed. In addition, the length of product/market life cycles would be chosen so that a sustained maturity stage in one might offset a shorter-term decline stage in another. For developmental risk takers, cash generators are needed to sustain research and development while market interest is built. Thus, the prudent corporate strategist who is a risk taker will maintain a mixed portfolio: One that is built on a stable base of cash-generating business units, the portfolio will engage in developmental risks in which research and development skills are a competitive advantage and on operating risks in which skills in cost control and managing declining businesses are competitively superior. Figures 15–7 and 15–8 are representations of each of these types of corporate strategies.

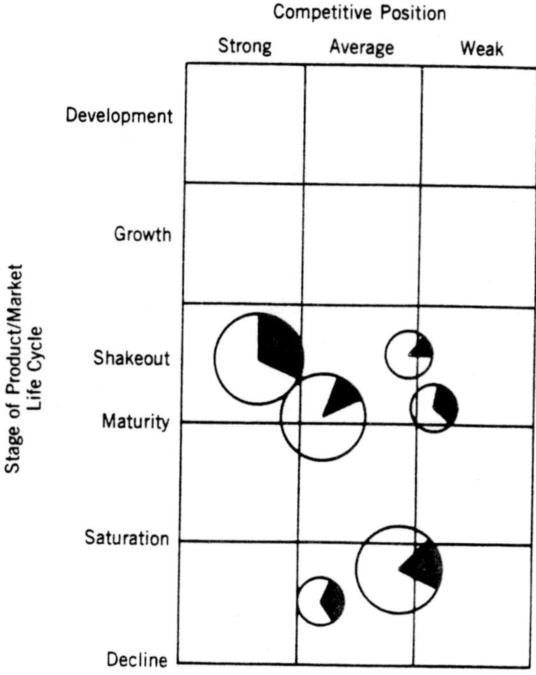

FIGURE 15–7 Operational risk-taking corporate strategy.

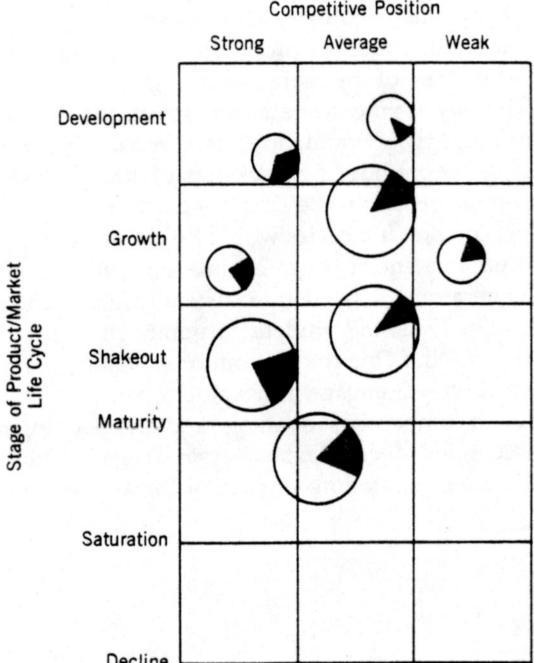

FIGURE 15-8 Developmental risk-taking corporate strategy.

EXERCISE 15-17

Refer to Exercise 15-15. Let us suppose that we have operational expertise superior to our competition in business units A and C and developmental expertise superior to our competition in units B, D, E, and F. We are not unwilling to take risks, but do not wish to destroy the corporation in the process. Develop a strategic plan for the six business units in the corporation designed to:

1. Emphasize profitability. Explain your reasoning in detail. Be prepared to present your thinking as a verbal presentation in class or as a written assignment.
2. Emphasize growth. Explain your reasoning in detail. Be prepared to present your thinking as a verbal presentation in class or as a written assignment.

"MAGIC MONEY" AND GROWTH

We have just discussed a variety of ways of examining the construction and management of a portfolio of business units. As was mentioned earlier, a variety of rationales can be presented that support the acquisition of multiple business units as an outgrowth of the development of a single business. The conglomerate, the type of corporate form most typically associated with portfolio models, may develop as a dominant single-business organization that finds little growth potential in its own industry and seeks investment opportunity in other fields. The successful corporation's financial strength, top-management expertise, and attraction to the investment community give it an opportunity to be especially appealing to the owners and managers of other companies.

To investors a growing and profitable company that dominates its industry presents an attractive investment. Stock prices for companies of this type not only represent an assessment of the past record and present value of the company, but also investors' expectations of future success. As a consequence, the stock price rises to levels that will result in what might be considered abnormal ratios of stock market price per share to corporate earnings per share. For some companies, recent growth and a promising future may result in price-earnings ratios of 60 or 70 to 1, or even more.

In contrast, a company struggling to maintain or improve market position may have suffered in terms of growth or reported earnings. Investors, responding to their understanding of the reported figures, may undervalue this type of company even though its products, facilities, management, and prospects are quite healthy. Stockholders in this company own stock that can be liquidated through sale in the open market but that will do so at a price that does not adequately represent the present or future value of the company.

When we bring these two situations together, we have a perfect opportunity for a mutually advantageous acquisition or merger through exchange of shares of the acquiring company for shares of the acquired company. The stockholders of the acquired company have the opportunity of exchanging undervalued shares of stock for stock that is highly valued. The acquiring firm is able to "buy" assets with stock that might be considered overvalued. The acquired firm also has the opportunity to have access to additional financial strength and managerial expertise.

Management contracts offered by the acquiring firm often provide for a continuation of employment in a financially more secure corporation for the management. With the use of these contracts, the acquiring firm does not need to provide operational management initially and can sustain the operation of the acquired company with little (if any) interruption.

As the acquired company's statements of operations are consolidated with those of the acquiring company, the consolidated report will show significant increases in sales and earnings, increases that are primarily the result of the acquisition. The investment community, seeking high-growth investments, can once again overvalue the acquiring firm's stock, setting the stage for yet another round of merger and/or acquisition. Acquisition, it seems, can continue without cost, fueled by the "magic money" of stock-purchaser expectations and willingness to gamble on anticipated earnings and growth.

The spiral, of course, will ultimately stop. Several factors can bring about a cessation in growth. First, the acquiring firm can lose in the bidding for other firms.

Second, investor caution may bring about a decline in the stock price and thereby make future acquisitions less attractive. Finally, as management contracts reach the end of their term, the acquiring company is faced with a management succession problem and with the difficulties of managing an unfamiliar technology in an unfamiliar environment.

The decline in the conglomerate's fortunes can cause as dramatic a drop in stock price as had been the rise. The management of conglomerates, faced with cash-draining subsidiaries or divisions in which they have little familiarity, have had to divest entire divisions and to liquidate assets in order to maintain solvency. This, of course, is recorded in consolidated statements as a decline in sales or as a reduction in sales growth, either of which has a dampening effect on stock-purchaser interest in the company's stock.

In reflecting on the growth and decline in the fortunes of some of the country's largest corporations brought about by the acquisition of companies, following the pattern mentioned here, it seems evident that the ambitions and confidence of top managers have in some instances caused their companies to pursue unrelated diversification and short-term growth well beyond the organization's ability to sustain itself in the long run. Boise Cascade, Ling Temco Vought (LTV), and the Mobil Corporation are only some of the very large corporate conglomerates that have found themselves in great difficulty following extensive expansion into diverse lines of business.

The Hewlett-Packard Corporation case which concludes this chapter, describes some of the components and managerial energies that have been important to the success of one of the country's best-known electronics-products manufacturer.

In preparing the case for discussion in class or to submit as a written analysis, make use of library reference material, the materials contained in earlier chapters of this text, and the discussion of portfolio models in this chapter in order to help in your diagnostics and your answers to the exercise questions found at the end of the case.

THE HEWLETT-PACKARD CORPORATION

In May 1978, one day before his 65th birthday, Bill Hewlett resigned from his position as Chief Executive Officer of Hewlett-Packard, the company he had helped found in 1939. He was appointed Chairman of the Executive Committee and joined David Packard, Chairman of the Board of Directors, in semi-retirement. John Young, who had succeeded Bill Hewlett as President and Chief Operating Officer in November 1977, was promoted to the vacated C.E.O. position. For the first time in its 39-year history, H-P was to be directed by an executive who had

This case was prepared by Professor Roger M. Atherton of the University of Oklahoma. It was prepared as a basis for class discussion rather than to illustrate either effective or ineffective handling of an administrative situation.

been developed from within the organization rather than being led by its original, almost legendary founders. It had become John Young's responsibility to manage the rapidly growing company as it headed deeper and deeper into the unfriendly territory of computational technology, where the competition was both bigger and tougher than in H-P's traditional businesses—electronic test and measurement, medical electronic equipment, and analytical instrumentation. The question raised by the trade press, Wall Street analysts, and some employees was whether John Young could provide the needed strategies and leadership in this more hostile environment for continued successful growth.

STRATEGIC CHANGES

Electronic Office Systems

By 1981 H-P had become the world's second largest minicomputer manufacturer, exceeded only by Digital Equipment Corporation. In October 1981, the *Wall Street Journal*[1] reported that H-P had decided to expand from their traditional base of data-processing equipment for business, factory, and scientific purposes into the word-processing and office terminal field dominated by IBM and Wang Laboratories. John Young indicated that H-P's strategy would be to place computer power in the form of interactive, information-processing networks directly into the hands of all office professionals, specialists, and managers, as well as secretaries and the data-processing staff. To implement this strategy, H-P introduced 27 new office products, including two new minicomputers, new word-processing terminals, improved computer terminals for creating graphic representations of numbers, new low-cost disc memories, and four new data communications products to tie all these elements together. Electronic mail and electronic filing packages were due to be introduced within a year. Combined with its previously announced products such as laser printers and a low-cost personal computer, these new products gave H-P a fully integrated office system. For the first time, H-P had the potential to penetrate the full spectrum of business computer uses.

Although in 1978 and 1979 Hewlett-Packard had enjoyed an average annual growth rate of 45% in electronic data products revenues, that growth rate dropped in 1981 to 17%. According to *Business Week*,[2] a growing number of their data processing customers had begun to purchase equipment from such companies as Wang Laboratories, Datapoint, and Lanier Business Products, which offered systems aimed directly at the automated office. Growth in the market for conventional minicomputers had slowed to 25%, so that H-P needed to tap into the market for the larger so-called super-minis and the market for office systems, since both were expanding at about 40% a year, if it wanted to continue its healthy growth rate.

A major target for H-P's thrust into office systems would be manufacturing companies. H-P had focused its efforts in minicomputers on this market segment, which accounted for 40% of the company's business computer sales. H-P wanted to offer these same customers systems that integrated everything from measurement instruments and data collection terminals on the factory floor to word processors in the front office in a single data processing network.

The office market presented H-P with new marketing challenges. Minicomputer makers traditionally sold to data processing departments, but to sell office equipment they would have to identify a whole new set of buyers among their large corporate customers. H-P had developed plans to expand its business computer marketing force by 25% and service force by one third. It also intended to go after new customers in financial services, retailing, and other non-manufacturing sectors, John Young has indicated that H-P would not aggressively go after new customers in these other areas except as there were spare resources to do so. These markets were seen as highly opportunistic sectors of the market, where perhaps some additional business could be picked up, but they were not seen as part of the basic strategic program.

Whether H-P could win sales outside its own manufacturing customer base remained to be seen. But few industry watchers doubted the company's new products would appeal to a large proportion of their regular customers. One competitor believed that if they could execute their strategies and followed them up with service and support, there was no question that H-P would gain market share at the expense of word processor vendors with narrower offerings. Conversely, a Wang Laboratories vice president indicated that H-P didn't concern them that much because H-P's strength was selling to data processing managers. Wang and IBM had much more experience selling directly into the office.

The office automation market was expected to triple to $36 billion by 1990, according to a market research report released in October 1981, by International Resource Development, Inc. No doubt the major contenders would compete fiercely to dominate the market while the multitude of small firms, which had just entered the new market, would have to scramble to survive. But in 1981, no single company had managed to secure for itself a corner on the market. *Electronics*,[3] a major trade journal, predicted that the main contenders would be IBM, AT & T, Xerox, and very possibly Wang and Datapoint. It also indicated that DEC and H-P had the background for especially good chances of success. The unanswered question was whether Hewlett-Packard could manage this new growth and whether the company could manage to remain technologically competitive in this new business and their traditional businesses at the same time.

Electronic Calculators

In sharp contrast to the rapid-growth market in electronic office equipment, the market for electronic hand-held calculators was largely saturated. Texas Instruments had been the pioneer in hand-held calculators and dominated the market for years, until low-priced Japanese models had taken over the lower end of the market. In 1981–1982 the different calculator makers were attempting to develop specific market niches that they believed would provide opportunities for further growth. The big Japanese producers had added gimmicks like solar calculators and games such as boxing matches and electronic cube puzzles. Casio was trying to get more business by driving prices still lower. It was also offering low-cost printer calculators that could fit in a shirt pocket. At the high-priced end of the market, companies were developing—or were already producing—products that could compete in the newly-formed hand-held computer market. This market had only developed recently when Tandy (Radio Shack), Casio, and others introduced their pocket computers. In fact, *Business Week*[4] even questioned whether there was still a market for calculators with $300 price tags since the Japanese and Radio Shack had begun to sell hand-held computers that cost less. One consultant asserted that hand-held calculators would replace programmable calculators in the following three to five years. Other experts felt that the market might flatten out, but that the market for programmable calculators would die slowly and hard.

The essential difference between hand-held calculators and computers is the way the units are programmed. On advanced calculators, programs are written by pressing a series of fixed-function keys in the order needed to step through calculations. Hand-held computers, however, use a conventional programming language which consists of short statements that tell the machine what to do. Both TI and H-P were working to reposition their products in this developing market segment.

Hewlett-Packard had dominated the top end of the market from the beginning. With its late 1981 introduction of several new products, H-P put its calculator somewhere in the increasingly gray border between programmable calculators and hand-held computers. For example, the Hewlett-Packard Interface Loop (HP-IL) provided a link that let the HP-41 calculator control and communicate with other machines and computers, including the company's HP-80 personal computer. Complementary products included a battery operated printer, a digital cassette drive, cassettes that significantly expanded the calculator's memory, and a device that other companies could build into their computers to make them compatible with the system. The company aimed the new system at its favorite customers: engineers and scientists. The products would allow H-P to sell accessory products to people who already owned the popular HP-41 series calculators, and to attract new customers who would prefer to pay $325 and add components later, instead of paying $2000 or more for a personal computer.

Analysts expected both Texas Instruments and Tandy Corporation (Radio Shack) would be strong competitors, especially at the high-priced end of the market. However, as *Business Week*[5] and the *Wall Street Journal*[6] were quick to point out, the Japanese producers were not limiting their horizons to the high end of the calculator market. They were clearly working on strategies and products that would expand pocket computers to the mass market. One of Casio's vice presidents eventually expected to have a pocket computer low enough in price to do away with all the scientific calculators in the market. It seemed clear that H-P would have to be both technologically innovative and cost-effective if it intended to be competitive in this market.

Business Segment Performance (1978–1981)

Hewlett-Packard reported data by business segment, with both electronic office systems and hand-held calculators and computers included in electronic data products. The other business segments were electronic test and measurement, medical electronic equipment, and analytical instrumentation. Exhibit 1 provides data on net sales, earnings before taxes, identifiable assets, and capital expenditures for these four business segments. Exhibit 2 compares electronic data products with the other business segments combined together to provide a summary comparison of their comparatively newer, more competitive, and higher risk line of business with their basic and more traditional business activities. The electronic data products appeared to have provided greater growth in profit margins, asset turnover, and return on assets, although the level of returns was higher in the more traditional businesses.

STRATEGIC IMPLEMENTATION

Structural Changes

The January 1982, Hewlett-Packard Corporate Organization Chart (Exhibits 3 and 4) shows that a number of changes have been made since Mr. Young became Chief Executive Officer. Ralph Lee, Executive Vice President-Operations retired in 1980 after 35 years with H-P. Paul Ely, Vice President and General Manager-Computer Systems, and Bill Terry, Vice President and General Manager-Instruments, were subsequently made Executive Vice Presidents-Operations.

Bill Doolittle had been promoted from Vice President-International to Senior Vice President-International. Al Oliverio had been promoted from Vice President-Marketing to Senior Vice President-Marketing. Ed van Bronkhorst had been promoted from Vice President to Se-

EXHIBIT 1
Selected data on business segments (millions)

	1978	*1979*	*1980*	*1981*	*Percent average annual growth 1978–1981*
Net sales					
Electronic data products	$715	$1,060	$1,510	$1,771	36
Electronic test and measurement	731	986	1,200	1,349	23
Medical electronic equipment	163	193	230	273	19
Analytical instrumentation	98	122	159	185	24
Earnings before taxes					
Electronic data products	124	183	285	319	38
Electronic test and measurement	180	242	271	284	17
Medical electronic equipment	26	27	37	50	25
Analytical instrumentation	16	16	24	32	28
Identifiable assets					
Electronic data products	587	767	1,000	1,169	26
Electronic test and measurement	452	594	709	817	22
Medical electronic equipment	120	131	146	175	14
Analytical instrumentation	71	83	94	99	16
Capital expenditures					
Electronic data products	90	115	148	174	25
Electronic test and measurement	49	46	85	89	28
Medical electronic equipment	7	5	11	18	52
Analytical instrumentation	7	6	11	9	17

Source: Hewlett-Packard *Annual Reports.*

nior Vice President, Corporate Treasurer, and Chief Financial Officer. Franco Mariotti had been promoted from Managing Director-Europe to Vice President-Europe. Dick Alberding had been promoted from General Manager-Medical Group to Vice President-Medical Group. Dr. Bernard Oliver retired as an officer and director of the company in May 1981. He had been with H-P for 29 years as head of corporate research and development activities. John Doyle, Vice President of Personnel, replaced Oliver as Vice President, Research and Development. Appointed Director of Personnel, succeeding Doyle, was Bill Craven, General Manager of the McMinnville Division (Medical Group) since 1976. Exhibit 5 provides background information on these executive officers.

Corporate Manufacturing Services had been shifted from being part of corporate staff reporting to administration to having a direct reporting relationship to operations. An Internal Audit department had been set up and reported directly to John Young. The Computer Systems Group had been split into four separate entities —the Technical Computer Group, the Business Computer Group, the Computer Peripherals Group, and the Computer Terminals Group. The products of these four groups continued to be marketed through one organization, the Computer Marketing Group. The Instruments Group had been divided into the Microwave and Communication Instrument Group and the Electronic Measurements Group. The products of these two groups continued to be marketed through one organization, Instrument Marketing. The hand-held calculator and personal computer activities had been elevated to product group status, the Personal Computation Group. As a result, there were ten product groups instead of the six in 1978. There remained however, the same six marketing organizations.

Leadership

According to the *San Jose Mercury*[7] John Young's team of employees was learning to play the electronics game by Young's rules which demanded diligent planning, close attention to cost-effectiveness, and no last-minute surprises. Although many had originally doubted that he could fill the shoes of the two founders, these critics have since admitted they like the way

EXHIBIT 2
Comparison of electronic data products and other business segments combined[a]

	1978	*1979*	*1980*	*1981*	*Percent average annual growth 1978–81*
Net sales (millions)					
Electronic data products	$715	$1,060	$1,510	$1,771	36
Other segments combined	992	1,301	1,589	1,807	22
Earnings before taxes (millions)					
Electronic data products	$124	$ 183	$ 285	$ 319	38
Other segments combined	222	285	332	366	18
Identifiable assets (millions)					
Electronic data products	$587	$ 767	$1,000	$1,169	26
Other segments combined	643	808	949	1,091	19
Capital expenditures (millions)					
Electronic data products	$ 90	$ 115	$ 148	$ 174	25
Other segments combined	63	57	107	106	26
Strategic ratio analysis					
EBT/sales (percent)					
Electronic data products	17.3	17.3	18.9	18.0	2
Other segments combined	22.4	21.9	20.9	20.3	−3
Sales/identifiable assets (times)					
Electronic data products	1.22	1.38	1.51	1.51	8
Other segments combined	1.54	1.61	1.67	1.66	3
EBT/identifiable assets (percent)					
Electronic data products	21.1	23.9	28.5	27.3	9
Other segments combined	34.5	35.3	35.0	33.5	−1

[a]Electronic Test and Measurement, Medical Electronic Equipment, and Analytical Instrumentation.

EXHIBIT 3

Hewlett/Packard Corporate Organization, January 1982

Viewed broadly, Hewlett-Packard Company is a rather complex organization made up of many business units that offer a wide range of advanced electronic products to a variety of markets around the world. Giving it common direction and cohesion are shared philosophies, practices and goals as well as technologies.

Within this broad context, the individual business units—called product divisions—are relatively small and self-sufficient so that decisions can be made at the level of the organization most responsible for putting them into action. Consistent with this approach, it has always been a practice at Hewlett-Packard to give each individual employee considerable freedom to implement methods and ideas that meet specific local organizational goals and broad corporate objectives.

Since its start in 1939, the HP organization has grown to more than 40 product divisions. To provide for effective overall management and coordination, the company has aligned these divisions into product groups characterized by product and/or market focus. Today there are ten such groups or segments. Six sales-and-service forces, organized around broad product categories, represent the product groups in the field.

HP's corporate structure is designed to foster a small-business flexibility within its many individual operating units while supporting them with the strengths of a larger organization. The accompanying chart [Exhibit 4] provides a graphic view of the relationship of the various groups and other organizational elements. The organization has been structured to allow the groups and their divisions to concentrate on their product-development, manufacturing and marketing activities without having to perform all the administrative tasks required of a company doing business worldwide. Normal and functional lines of responsibility and communication are indicated on the chart; however, direct and informal communication across lines and between levels is encouraged.

Here is a closer look at the company's basic organizational units:

PRODUCT DIVISION

An HP product division is a vertically integrated organization that conducts itself very much like an independent business. Its fundamental responsibilities are to develop, manufacture and market products that are profitable and which make contributions in the marketplace by virtue of technological or economic advantage.

Each division has its own distinct family of products, for which it has worldwide marketing responsibility. A division also is responsible for its own accounting, personnel activities, quality assurance, and support of its products in the field. In addition, it has important social and economic responsibilities in its local community.

PRODUCT GROUPS

Product groups, which are composed of divisions having closely related product lines, are responsible for coordinating the activities of their respective divisions. The management of each group has overall responsibility for the operations and financial performance of its members. Further, each group has worldwide responsibility for its manufacturing operations and sales/service forces. Management staffs of the four U.S. sales regions and two international headquarters (European and Intercontinental Operations) assist the groups in coordinating the sales/service functions.

The group management structure provides a primary channel of communication between the divisions and corporate departments.

CORPORATE OPERATIONS

Corporate Operations management has responsibility for the day-to-day operation of the company. The executive vice presidents in charge of Corporate Operations are directly responsible to HP's president for the performance of their assigned product groups; they also provide a primary channel of communication between the groups and the president.

EXHIBIT 3 ***(continued)***

CORPORATE ADMINISTRATION

The principal responsibility of Corporate Administration is to insure that the corporate staff offices provide the specialized policies, expertise and resources to adequately support the divisions and groups on a worldwide basis. The executive vice president in charge of Corporate Administration also reports to the president, providing an important upward channel of communication for the corporate staff activities.

The Marketing and International offices, through the U.S. sales regions and two international headquarters, insure that—on a worldwide basis—all corporate policies and practices are followed and that local legal and fiscal requirements are met.

CORPORATE RESEARCH AND DEVELOPMENT

HP Laboratories is the corporate research and development organization that provides a central source of technical support for the product-development efforts of HP product divisions. In these efforts, the divisions make important use of the advanced technologies, materials, components, and theoretical analyses researched or developed by HP Labs. Through their endeavors in areas of science and technology, the corporate laboratories also help the company evaluate promising new areas of business.

BOARD OF DIRECTORS

The Board of Directors and its chairman have ultimate responsibility for the legal and ethical conduct of the company and its officers. It is the board's duty to protect and advance the interests of the stockholders, to foster a continuing concern for fairness in the company's relations with employees, and to fulfill all requirements of the law with regard to the board's stewardship. The board counsels management on general business matters and also reviews and evaluates the performance of management. To assist in discharging these responsibilities, the board has formed various committees to oversee the company's activities and programs in such areas as employee benefits, compensation, financial auditing, and investment.

PRESIDENT

The president has operating responsibility for the overall performance and direction of the company, subject to the authority of the Board of Directors. Also, the president is directly responsible for corporate development and planning functions, and for HP Labs.

EXECUTIVE COMMITTEE

This committee meets weekly for the purpose of setting and reviewing corporate policies, and making coordinated decisions on a wide range of current operations and activities. Members include the Executive Committee chairman, the chairman of the Board, the president and the executive vice presidents for Operations and Administration. All are members of the Board of Directors.

OPERATIONS COUNCIL

Primary responsibilities of this body are to review operating policies on a broad basis and to turn policy decisions into corporate action. Members include the executive vice presidents, product group general managers, the senior vice presidents of Marketing and International, the vice president—Europe, and the managing director of intercontinental.

Source: Hewlett-Packard Corporate Public Relations.

EXHIBIT 4

Hewlett-Packard corporate organization as of January 1982. (*Source:* public document, Hewlett-Packard Corp.)

Board of Directors — Dave Packard, Chairman of the board; Bill Hewlett, Chairman—Executive committee

Chief Executive Officer — John Young, President

Administration

Bob Boniface, Executive vice-president

Corporate Staff
- Corporate controller: Jerry Carlson, Controller
- Corporate services: Bruce Wholey, Vice-president
- Government relations: Jack Beckett, Director
- International: Bill Doolittle, Senior vice-president
- Patents and licenses: Jean Chognard, Vice-president
- Personnel: Bill Craven, Director
- Public relations: Dave Kirby, Director
- Secretary: Jack Brigham, secretary and general counsel
- Marketing: Al Oliverio, Senior vice-president
- Treasurer: Ed van Bronkhorst, Senior vice-president

Europe
Franco Mariotti, Vice-president
Field Sales Regions: Germany, France, United Kingdom, South/Eastern Europe, Northern Europe
Manufacturing: United Kingdom, Germany, France

Intercontinental
Alan Bickell, Managing director
Field sales regions: Japan, Far East, Australia, South Africa, Latin America
Manufacturing: Singapore, Malaysia, Puerto Rico, Brazil, Japan

U.S./Canada Sales
Field sales regions: Eastern, Mid-West, Southern, Neely (Western), Canada
Corporate parts center

Operations

Paul Ely, Executive vice-president

Computers
- Technical Computer Group — Doug Chance, General manager
  - □ Data systems
  - □ Roseville
  - □ Desktop computer
    - ○ Engineering Systems
  - □ Boblingen Desktop
  - □ Computer I.C.
    - ○ Cupertino I.C.
    - ○ Systems Technology
- Computer Peripherals Group — Dick Hackborn, General manager
  - □ Boise
  - □ Disc Memory
  - □ Greeley
  - □ Vancouver
- Business Computer Group — Ed McCracken, General manager
  - □ Computer Systems
  - □ Information Networks
    - ○ Pinewood
  - □ Boblingen General Systems
  - □ Application Systems
- Computer Terminals Group — Cyril Yansouni, General manager
  - □ Data Terminals
  - □ General systems
  - □ Grenoble
  - □ Puerto Rico
- Computer Marketing Group — Jim Arthur, General manager
  - □ Computer
    - ○ Systems Remarketing
  - □ Computer Support
  - Worldwide Sales
    - ○ Computer Supplies

Bill Terry, Executive vice-president

Instruments
- Microwave and Communication Instrument Group — Hal Edmondson, General manager
  - □ Colorado Telecom
  - □ Queensferry Telecom
  - □ Stanford Park
  - □ Spokane
  - □ Manufacturing
  - □ Signal Analysis
  - □ Network
  - □ Measurement
  - □ Santa Rosa Technology Center
- Electronic Measurements Group — Bill Parzybok, General manager
  - □ Boblingen Instrument
  - □ San Diego
  - □ Colorado Springs
    - ○ Logic Systems
    - ○ Oscilloscope
    - ○ Graphics Displays
  - □ YHP Instrument
  - □ Loveland Instrument
  - □ Lake Stevens Instrument
  - □ New Jersey
  - □ Santa Clara
    - ○ Lasers
- Instrument marketing — Bob Brunner, Group marketing manager
  - □ Instrument Support
  - Worlwide Sales

Dean Morton, Executive vice-president
- Components Group — John Blokker, General manager
  - □ Microwave Semiconductor
  - □ Optoelectronics
  - □ Malaysia
- Components Sales/Service Worldwide
- Medical Group — Dick Alberding, Vice-president
  - □ Andover
  - □ Boblingen Medical
  - □ McMinnville
  - □ Waltham
- Medical Sales/Service Worldwide
- Analytical Group — Lew Platt, General manager
  - □ Avondale
  - □ Scientific Instruments
  - □ Waldbronn
- Analytical Sales/Service Worlwide
- Personal Computation Group — Dick Moore, General Manager
  - □ Corvallis
  - □ Personal Computer
  - □ Brazil
  - □ Singapore
- Personal Computation Marketing Worldwide

Reporting to the President

HP Laboratories
John Doyle, Vice-president, research and development
Research Centers: Computer research, Physical research, Technology research

Corporate Development
Fred Schroder, Director

Internal Audit
George Abbott, Manager

Corporate Manufacturing Services
Ray Demere, Vice-president

□ Division ○ Operation (product line international locations)

EXHIBIT 5
Executive officers of Hewlett-Packard

David Packard; age 69; Chairman, HP. Mr. Packard is a co-founder of the Company and has been a director since 1947.[a] He has served as Chairman of the Board of Directors since 1972 and was the Company's President from 1947 to 1964. Mr. Packard also served as Chairman of the Board and Chief Executive Officer from 1964 to 1968 when he was appointed U.S. Deputy Secretary of Defense. Mr. Packard is a Director of Caterpillar Tractor Company; Standard Oil Company of California; The Boeing Company; and Genentech, Inc.

William R. Hewlett; age 68; Chairman of the Executive Committee, HP. Mr. Hewlett is a co-founder of the Company and has served on its Board of Directors since 1947. Mr. Hewlett served as Executive Vice President of the Company from 1947 to 1964 when he was appointed President. He served as President and Chief Executive Officer from 1969 to 1977 and was Chief Executive Officer and Chairman of the Executive Committee from November 1977 to May 1978 when he retired as Chief Executive Officer. Mr. Hewlett remains the Chairman of the Company's Executive Committee. He also is a Director of Chrysler Corporation and Utah International, Inc., a mining company.

John A. Young; age 49; President and Chief Executive Officer, HP. Mr. Young has served as President and Chief Executive Officer of the Company since May 1978. He was appointed President and Chief Operating Officer of the Company as of November 1, 1977, and has been a member of the Company's Board of Directors since 1974. Prior to his appointment as President and Chief Operating Officer, Mr. Young served as Executive Vice President from 1974. Mr. Young is a Director of Wells Fargo & Company; Wells Fargo Bank, N.A.; Dillingham Corporation; and SRI International. He also serves on the Board of Trustees of Stanford University.

Robert L. Boniface; age 57; Executive Vice President, HP. Mr. Boniface has been a Director of the Company since 1974. He has served as an Executive Vice President of the Company since 1975 and was Vice President, Administration from 1974 to 1975. Mr. Boniface served as Vice President, Marketing from 1970 to 1974.

Paul C. Ely, Jr.; age 49; Executive Vice President, HP. Mr. Ely was named an Executive Vice President of the Company in July 1980 and was elected to the Board of Directors effective September 1980. Mr. Ely is responsible for the Company's Computer Groups. Prior to his appointment as Executive Vice President, Mr. Ely served as Computer Group General Manager from 1974 and as Vice President from 1976.

Dean O. Morton; age 49; Executive Vice President, HP. Mr. Morton was elected a Director of the Company in September 1977. He was appointed a Vice President of the Company in 1973 and was also appointed General Manager of the Company's Medical Products Group in 1974. Mr. Morton served in those dual capacities until he assumed his present position in November 1977. Mr. Morton is also a Director of State Street Investment Corporation and Cobe Laboratories, Inc.

William E. Terry; age 48; Executive Vice President, HP. Mr. Terry was named an Executive Vice President of the Company in July 1980 and was elected to the Board of Directors effective September 1980. Mr. Terry is responsible for the Company's Instrument Groups. Prior to his appointment as Executive Vice President, Mr. Terry served as Vice President and General Manager of the Company's Instrument Group from 1974. Mr. Terry served as General Manager of the Company's Data Products Group from 1971 to 1974. Mr. Terry is a Director of Applied Magnetics Corporation; Altus Corporation, a manufacturer of lithium batteries; and Kevex Corporation, a manufacturer of x-ray spectrometers.

William P. Doolittle; age 63; Senior Vice President, International, HP. Mr. Doolittle has been a Director of the Company since 1971 and served as Vice President, International from 1963 until he assumed his present position in July 1981. Mr. Doolittle is also a director of Machine Intelligence Corp. and Creative Strategies International.

Alfred P. Oliverio; age 54; Senior Vice President, Marketing, HP. Mr. Oliverio served as Vice President, Marketing from 1974 until he assumed his present position in July 1981.

EXHIBIT 5 *(continued)*

Edwin E. van Bronkhorst; age 57; Senior Vice President, Treasurer, HP. Mr. van Bronkhorst served as Vice President and Treasurer of the Company from 1963 until his appointment as Senior Vice President and Treasurer in July 1981. He also serves as the Company's Chief Financial Officer. He was named a Director of the Company in 1962 and currently serves as a Director of ROLM Corporation, a manufacturer of computerized communication systems; Northern California Savings and Loan Association; and TRIAD Systems Corporation, a manufacturer of microcomputer-based data processing systems primarily for the auto parts distribution industry.

Richard C. Alberding; age 50; Vice President, Medical Products Group, HP. Mr. Alberding was appointed to his present position in July, 1981, and has served as general manager of the Company's Medical Products Group since 1977. Mr. Alberding was director of the Company's European operations from 1970 until 1977.

Jean C. Chognard; age 57; Vice President, Patents and Licenses, HP. Mr. Chognard has been Patent Counsel for the Company since 1958 and has been a Vice President of the Company since May 1976.

Raymond M. Demere, Jr.; age 60; Vice President, Manufacturing Services, HP. Mr. Demere has been a Vice President of the Company since 1971 and served as operations manager of the Instrument Group of the Company from 1974 until September 1977 when he was appointed Vice President, Manufacturing Services.

John L. Doyle; age 48; Vice President, Research and Development, HP. Mr. Doyle was appointed Corporate Director of Personnel in June 1976 and thereafter elected Vice President, Personnel in July 1976. In June 1981 Mr. Doyle assumed his present position as Vice President, Research and Development.

Franco Mariotti; age 46; Vice President, Europe, HP. Mr. Mariotti was appointed to his present position in July 1981 and has served as managing director of the Company's European operations since 1977. From 1976 to 1977 Mr. Mariotti served as marketing manager for Europe.

W. Bruce Wholey; age 60; Vice President, Corporate Services, HP. Mr. Wholey has been Vice President, Corporate Services since January 1973.

S. T. Jack Brigham III; age 42; Secretary and General Counsel, HP. Mr. Brigham was elected Assistant Secretary of the Company in May 1974. He served in that capacity as well as General Attorney of the Company until May 1976 when he was elected Secretary and General Counsel of the Company.

Source: Hewlett-Packard 1981 Form 10-K.

[a]Mr. Packard did not serve as a Director during his service as United States Deputy Secretary of Defense from January 1969 to December 1971

Young has changed and redirected the firm. He has placed added emphasis on manufacturing and marketing, dropped technological programs when they weren't cost-effective, and monitored day-to-day details to correct problems before they have snowballed. At the same time he has balanced his approach by stimulating efforts on new products and technologies, such as electronic office systems and hand-held computers with the associated H-P integrated loop. Young has not emphasized formal planning done by corporate planners. Instead, he has pushed a pragmatic system with the operating people doing the planning. Young believed his contribution was having put emphasis on having a lot more time spent in thoughtful consideration of what the company was doing, but not in a formal planning regime.

John Young was reported to be a serious chief executive with a dry sense of humor, a logical thinker who often asked leading questions to get his managers to come around to his way of thinking, and an efficient worker who did not tolerate incompetence. Associates saw him as a "numbers man" with a top priority of profits. Despite his devotion to numbers and planning, Young also followed two basic and more subtle tenets of the H-P way of life: managing by wandering around and showing respect and empathy for employees. Exhibit 6 provides a brief outline of "The HP Way." For all his formal position power, Young has relied

EXHIBIT 6
The HP way

BUSINESS PRACTICES

Pay as we go—No long-term borrowing
- Helps to maintain a stable financial environment during depressed business times.
- Serves as an excellent self-regulating mechanism for HP managers.

Market expansion and leadership based on new product contributions
- Engineering excellence determines market recognition of new HP products.
- Novel new-product ideas and implementations serve as the basis for expansion of existing markets or diversification into new markets.

Customer satisfaction second to none
- Sell only what has been thoroughly designed, tested, and specified.
- Products must have lasting value, having high reliability (quality) and customers discover additional benefits while using them.
- Offer best after-sales service and support in the industry.

Honesty and integrity in all matters
- Dishonest dealings with vendors or customers (such as bribes and kickbacks) not tolerated.
- Open and honest communication with employees and stockholders alike.
- Conservative financial reporting.

PEOPLE PRACTICES

Belief in our people
- Confidence in, and respect for, HP people as opposed to dependence on extensive rules, procedures, etc.
- Trust people to do their job right (individual freedom) without constant directives.
- Opportunity for meaningful participation (job dignity).
- Emphasis on working together and sharing rewards (teamwork and partnership).
- Share responsibilities; help each other; learn from each other; provide chance to make mistakes.
- Recognition based on contribution to results—sense of achievement and self-esteem.
- Profit sharing; stock purchase plan; retirement program, etc., aimed at employees and company sharing in each other's success.
- Company financial management emphasis on protecting employee's job security.

A superior working environment
- Informality—open, honest communications; no artificial distinctions between employees (first-name basis); management by wandering around; and open-door communication policy.
- Develop and promote from within—lifetime training, education, career counseling to give employees maximum opportunities to grow and develop with the company.
- Decentralization—emphasis on keeping work groups as small as possible for maximum employee identification with our businesses and customers.
- Management-by-Objectives (MBO)—provides a sound basis for measuring performance of employees as well as managers; is objective, not political.

MANAGEMENT STYLE

Management by wandering around
- To have a well-managed operation, managers and supervisors must be aware of what happens in their areas—at several levels above and below their immediate level.

EXHIBIT 6 ***(continued)***

Since people are our most important resource, managers have direct responsibility for employee training, performance and general well being. To do this, managers must move around to find out how people feel about their jobs—what they think will make their work more productive and meaningful.

Open door policy

Managers and supervisors are expected to foster a work environment in which employees feel free and comfortable to seek individual counsel or express general concerns.

Therefore, if employees feel such steps are necessary, they have the right to discuss their concerns with higher-level managers. Any effort through intimidation or other means to prevent an employee from going up the line is absolutely contrary to company policy—and will be dealt with accordingly.

Also, use of the Open Door policy must not in any way influence evaluations of employees or produce any other adverse consequences.

Employees also have responsibilities—particularly in keeping their discussions with upper-level managers to the point and focused on concerns of significance.

Source: Measure, September–October 1981, p. 14.

heavily on consensus-style management. He has met often with his executive committee, and few major decisions have been made without the agreement of everyone around the table. Members of the committee were expected to be independent thinkers, but Young has used a subtle approach based on logic to bring people around to his point of view. When Young has not agreed with a colleague's opinion, he has asked questions. These were not confrontational kinds of questions, but they were penetrating. Young would then go along with whatever course the executive eventually recommended. Young saw himself as being good at the non-directive approach and worked hard at being a good coach.

High on Young's list of priorities for the 80's was for H-P to become a low-cost manufacturer. Young admitted this had not been one of H-P's strengths. His concern for cost-effectiveness was almost legendary. When he initially assumed the presidency, he put a lot of effort into convincing his management team that the company could do a better job of managing assets, particularly inventory and accounts receivable. One of the first things he axed was research for research's sake. Yet about 70% of total company product orders in 1981 resulted from products developed after 1977. Under Young, technology has received more of a profit-and-loss kind of consideration and evaluation. In 1981, research and development was increased to 9.7% of sales, an increase of 1.1% over the previous year. Further, John Young has restructured H-P Laboratories entirely. He has also created over the last three years a computer and semi-conductor research facility staffed with 100 professionals. He thought this would become one of the top such facilities in the United States.

In September 1979, an attitude survey was taken in which 7,966 employees were asked to evaluate more than 100 topics at H-P, including pay, benefits, supervision, management, job satisfaction, and many other items. Exhibit 7 provides results on major items and a comparison to national norms. With a 67% favorable response, employees rated H-P management well above the national norm of 46%. The rating covered such questions as the fairness of management decisions and the concern of managers for the well-being of the people they managed. As reported in the March–April issue of *Measure*[8] (HP's magazine), four of the top 22

EXHIBIT 7
H-P attitude survey

	Percent favorable responses	
	H-P employees	*National sample*[a]
Work organization	70	65
Work efficiency	67	63
Management	67	46
Job training and information	61	56
Work associates	81	78
Supervision	70	61
Overall communications	58	41
Performance and advancement	75	58
Pay	52	39
Benefits	70	53
Job satisfaction	76	66
Organizational identification	84	59
Organization change	28	25
Working conditions	59	44
Job stability	56	60
Policies and practices	81	69
Reactions to the survey	77	55

Source: Measure, "Open Line," March–April 1981, p. 12b.
[a]200 Top U.S. Companies.

issues generated by the survey analysis showed concern about top management and the application of management philosophy. The quality of some managers was questioned; management-by-objectives and management-by-wandering-around were criticized for not being used widely enough; and the use of the Open Door Policy was sometimes frustrated by a feeling of threat of retribution. The fundamental responses to these concerns were seen by top management as chiefly matters of local responsibility and action, although corporate support in the form of training, communication, and management evaluation was believed to be important. The startup of more than 300 quality teams at many locations was believed to improve both productivity and the practice of MBO. The Open Door Policy as well as MBWA were topics of messages by Young in various issues of *Measure*. Both of these policies were seen by John Young as important to the creation of a feeling of openness and providing informal opportunities for everyone to hear and be heard. He believed the desired result was to achieve mutual trust and respect for both the people and the process involved. He has tried to make it clear both in his communications and his actions that the H-P manager has no greater responsibility.

PERFORMANCE (1978–1981)

Since 1978, when John Young became CEO, Hewlett-Packard has grown rapidly. The annual growth rate of net sales has averaged 27.4% and that of net earnings has averaged 26.9%. The growth rates for 1980–1981 of 15.5% and 16% respectively, however, were substantially lower than previous years. The 1981 *Annual Report*[9] indicated that the major cause of the reduced growth was the adverse economic conditions in the U.S. and abroad. Net sales were somewhat below projections, and incoming orders were considerably lower than expectations. These shortfalls, coupled with a high level of committed expenses for new product development and product introductions, put heavy pressure on operating profit. Two changes were made in 1981 that somewhat modified earnings. The first was a $14 million reduction in accrued pension expense for the year, which increased net earnings by $7 million. This change resulted from a scheduled five-year review of the initial funding assumptions used for the U.S. Supplemental Pension Plan begun in 1976. The second was an $8 million reduction in income taxes, resulting from the Economic Recovery Tax Act of 1981. Without these two adjustments, the company's net earnings would have been $297 million, up only 10.4% from 1980. Exhibit 8 provides a four-year consolidated summary of various measures of performance. Exhibit 9 provides an analysis of operating results. Exhibit 10 is a consolidated balance sheet. Exhibit 11 is a consolidated statement of changes in financial position, showing how funds were provided and how they were used. Exhibit 12 provides a strategic ratio analysis of H-P's performance during this period. Exhibit 13 includes information on sales, profits, and research and development expenses for selected companies and industries.

EXHIBIT 8

Hewlett-Packard four-year consolidated summary[a] for the years ended October 31[b]

	1978	*1979*	*1980*	*1981*
Net sales	$1,737	$2,361	$3,099	$3,578
Costs and expenses				
Cost of goods sold	808	1,106	1,475	1,703
Research and development	154	204	272	347
Marketing	264	362	459	526
Administration and general	215	291	370	422
	1,441	1,963	2,576	2,998
Earnings before taxes	296	398	523	580
Provision for taxes	143	195	254	268
Net earnings	153	203	269	312
Per share[a]				
Net earnings	1.32	1.72	2.23	2.55
Cash dividends	.12	.17	.20	.22
At year-end				
Total assets	1,462	1,900	2,337	2,758
Long-term debt	10	15	29	26
Common shares outstanding[a]	116	118	120	123
Thousands of employees	42	52	57	64

Source: Hewlett-Packard *Annual Reports*.

[a]Reflects the 2-for-1 stock splits in 1979 and 1981.

[b]Millions except for employee and per share amounts.

EXHIBIT 9

	Percent increase from prior year				*Percent of net sales*			
	1978	*1979*	*1980*	*1981*	*1978*	*1979*	*1980*	*1981*
Net sales	27.0	35.9	31.3	15.5	100.0	100.0	100.0	100.0
Cost of goods sold	29.3	36.9	33.4	15.5	45.7	46.8	47.6	47.6
Research and development	23.2	32.5	33.3	27.6	8.9	8.6	8.8	9.7
Marketing	26.9	37.1	26.8	14.6	15.2	15.3	14.8	14.7
Administrative and general	18.8	35.3	27.1	14.1	12.4	12.3	11.9	11.8
Earnings before taxes	29.3	34.5	31.4	10.9	17.0	16.9	16.9	16.2
Provision for taxes	32.4	36.4	30.3	5.5	8.2	8.3	8.2	7.5
Net earnings	26.4	32.7	32.5	16.0	8.8	8.6	8.7	8.7

EXHIBIT 10
Consolidated balance sheet[a]

	1978	*1979*	*1980*	*1981*
Assets				
Current assets				
Cash and temporary cash investments	$ 189	$ 248	$ 247	$ 290
Accounts and notes receivable	371	491	622	682
Inventories				
Finished goods	99	120	148	186
Purchased parts and fabricated assemblies	257	358	397	456
Other current assets:	36	52	77	91
Total current assets	952	1,269	1,491	1,705
Property, plant, and equipment				
Land	44	53	69	78
Buildings and leasehold improvements	405	491	645	789
Machinery and equipment	272	348	447	581
	721	892	1,161	1,448
Accumulated depreciation	245	301	372	469
	476	591	789	979
Other assets	34	40	57	74
	1,462	1,900	2,337	2,758
Liabilities and shareholders' equity				
Current liabilities				
Notes payable and commercial paper	85	147	143	144
Accounts payable	71	109	104	143
Employee compensation, benefits, and accruals	171	237	297	308
Accrued taxes on income	88	106	147	109
Total current liabilities	415	599	691	704
Long-term debt	10	15	29	26
Deferred taxes on earnings	35	51	70	108

EXHIBIT 10 *(continued)*
Consolidated balance sheet[a]

	1978	1979	1980.	1981
Shareholders' equity				
Common stock	29	59	60	123
Capital in excess of par	247	267	333	358
Retained earnings	727	909	1,154	1,439
Total shareholders' equity	1,002	1,235	1,547	1,920
	$1,462	$1,900	$2,337	$2,758

Source: Hewlett-Packard *Annual Reports.*
[a]In millions; for fiscal years ending October 31.

EXHIBIT 11
Consolidated statement of changes in financial position[a]

	1978	1979	1980	1981
Funds provided				
Net earnings	$153	$203	$269	$312
Items not affecting funds:				
Depreciation and amortization	56	72	93	120
Other, net	11	27	27	53
Total from operations	220	302	389	485
Proceeds from sale of stock	29	37	50	67
Increase in accounts payable and accrued liabilities	59	104	55	50
Total funds provided	308	443	494	602
Funds used				
Investment in property, plant, and equipment	159	191	297	318
Increase in accounts and notes receivable	99	120	131	60
Increase in inventories	77	122	67	97
Increase in other current assets	8	16	25	14
Decrease (increase) in accrued taxes	(26)	(18)	(41)	38
Dividends to shareholders	14	20	24	27
Other, net	(1)	(5)	(12)	6
Total funds used	330	446	491	560
Increase (decrease) in cash and temporary cash investment, net of notes payable and commercial paper	(22)	(3)	3	42
Net cash at beginning of year	126	104	101	104
Net cash at end of year	104	101	104	146

Source: Hewlett-Packard *Annual Reports.*
In millions; for fiscal years ending October 31.

EXHIBIT 12
Strategic ratio analysis

Fiscal year	*Profit margin (earnings/ sales) (percent)*	*Asset turnover (sales/ assets) (times)*	*Return on assets (earnings/ assets) (percent)*	*Financial leverage (assets/ net worth) (times)*	*Return on net worth (earnings/ net worth) (percent)*
1978	8.81	1.19	10.5	1.46	15.3
1979	8.60	1.24	10.7	1.54	16.4
1980	8.68	1.33	11.5	1.51	17.4
1981	8.72	1.30	11.3	1.44	16.3

EXHIBIT 13
Sales, profits, and R & D data on selected companies and industries

	Sales		*Profits*		*R & D Expense*			
	1981 Millions of dollars	*Percent annual change (1977–81)*	*1981 Millions of dollars*	*Percent annual change (1977–81)*	*1981 Millions of dollars*	*Percent of sales*	*Percent of profit*	*Dollars per employee*
Selected companies								
AT&T	58214	12.2	6888	10.6	507.2	0.9	7.4	594
Datapoint	396	40.1	49	53.8	34.7	8.8	71.2	5091
Digital Equipment	3198	31.1	343	33.2	251.2	7.9	73.2	3987
Hewlett-Packard	3578	28.4	312	27.9	347.0	9.7	111.2	5422
Lanier Business Products	303	35.9	26	39.4	4.7	1.5	18.4	1163
IBM	29070	12.3	3308	5.4	1612.0	5.5	48.7	4542
Texas Instruments	4206	21.0	109	2.7	219.4	5.2	202.2	2621
Wang Laboratories	856	60.2	78	73.3	66.9	7.8	85.7	4240
Xerox	8691	14.3	598	8.4	526.3	6.1	88.0	4350
Industry composites								
Instruments	14106	18.6	740	17.4	647.5	4.6	87.5	2571
Information processing								
Computers	60057	15.5	5311	9.4	3845.5	6.4	72.4	4231
Office equipment	14716	17.9	771	13.2	729.2	5.0	94.6	3324
Peripherals & services	5800	29.3	365	35.7	344.1	5.9	94.2	3284

Source: *Business Week*, "R & D Scoreboard," July 5, 1982, pp. 54–72.

A TIME FOR EVALUATION

John Young had just reviewed the changes made in strategy and strategic implementation while he had served as chief executive officer. He wondered whether the strategic changes made had been the right ones and whether any additional changes might be needed. He believed the performance of the various business segments might offer a valuable point of departure for his analysis. He also felt that this seemed like an appropriate time to review the changes made in organization structure, his management and leadership of the company, and the organization's overall corporate performance during these recent years of growth and strategic change. He believed that enough time had passed that a reasonably objective assessment could be made as to whether he had provided the necessary strategies and leadership to the Hewlett-Packard Company during this difficult transition period.

NOTES

1. *Wall Street Journal*, "Digital Equipment and Hewlett-Packard Enter Electronic Office Systems Market, October 30, 1981, p. 48.
2. *Business Week*, Two Giants Bid for Office Sales,"
3. *Electronics*, "H-P: A Drive into Office Automation," November 3, 1981, pp. 106–10.
4. *Business Week*, "When 'Calculator' Is a Dirty Word," June 14, 1982, p. 62.
5. Ibid.
6. *Wall Street Journal*, "Calculator Makers Add Features and Cut Prices to Find a Niche in a Crowded Market," December 21, 1981, p. 23.
7. *San Jose Mercury*, "H-P—Now It's the House That Young Built," August 24, 1981, pp. 1D, 7D.
8. *Measure*, "Open-Line," March–April 1981, pp. 12a–h.
9. *Hewlett-Packard Company*, "1981 Annual Report."

ACKNOWLEDGMENTS

Business Week, "When 'Calculator' Is a Dirty Word," June 14, 1982, p. 62.

Business Week, "Two Giants Bid for Office Sales," November 9, 1981, pp. 86–96.

Electronics, "H-P: A Drive into Office Automation," November 3, 1981, pp. 106–10.

Hewlett-Packard Company, "Annual Reports," 1978, 1979, 1980, 1981.

Hewlett-Packard Company, "Form 10-K," 1978, 1979, 1980, 1981.

Measure, "Open Line," March–April 1981, pp. 12a–h.

Measure, "Why Do HP People Do Things the Way They Do," September–October, 1981, pp. 11–14.

San Jose Mercury, "H-P—Now It's the House That Young Built," August 24, 1981, pp. 1D, 7D.

Wall Street Journal, "Digital Equipment and Hewlett-Packard Enter Electronic Office Systems Market," October 30, 1981, p. 48.

Wall Street Journal, "Calculator Makers Add Features and Cut Prices to Find a Niche in a Crowded Market," December 21, 1981, p. 23.

EXERCISE 15–18

- Describe the product/market strategies you see implicit in this case. Explain.
- From your analysis of industry data (library or other sources) and the case, prepare a Hofer fifteen-cell portfolio diagram on the Hewlett-Packard product divisions.
- In what way is the management style ("The Hewlett-Packard Way") and Mr.

Young's actions helpful or harmful in the implementation of the product or corporate strategies? Explain.

- Describe the factor that serves to link the product line choices of Hewlett-Packard. Is this a strength or a weakness?
- Describe Hewlett-Packard's corporate strategy as you (not Hewlett-Packard) see it. Explain how you came to develop this perspective of the company's chosen strategy.
- You have been asked by one of the Hewlett-Packard's competitors to suggest a strategy for their company to use that might take advantage of a weakness of Hewlett-Packard. What would you recommend? Explain.

16

THE MULTINATIONAL FIRM

In Chapter 15 we examined in detail the development of a superordinate corporate strategy used to guide the configuration of activities in a multibusiness organization. In the highly integrated firm, the principal line of business serves as the focal point for the strategies of each of the business units serving the central line. Strategies concerning supplier units of raw materials involve protecting sources of supply and providing those supplies at low cost. Strategies concerning distribution and marketing units are keyed to protection of markets and providing secure and low-cost targeted distribution. In both cases, the focal point is the main line of business.

Where the production or distribution and marketing capacity exceeds the needs of the central line of business by a significant margin, however, managers of the secondary lines of business must develop identifiable strategies that not only meet the needs of the main line of business, but also provide the opportunity to take advantage of their capacity to generate additional revenues.

As the integrated business achieves a reasonably attainable market share in mature and saturated markets, management may seek opportunities for additional investment: first, in related lines of business, to take advantage of natural marketing opportunities; next, by investing in nonrelated lines of business. Here the interest is that of developing income from cash generated from the principal business. Management's interest has shifted from the energy business or the wood products business or the automobile parts and accessories business to the *money* business, seeking ways of employing excess funds to gain revenue for the corporation's shareholders.

The evolution of the multinational firm can take a similar progressive track. The domestic firm's interest in international transactions can arise originally as a search for low-cost, secure sources of supply. Historically, the trading nations of Europe and elsewhere have long sought sources of timber, hides, chemicals, coal, ores, and other materials to serve their own manufacturing or processing industries. Third World nations have had a long history of serving as the extractive source of materials for more advanced nations. Our own country served as a source of timber, hides, sugar, cotton, flax, and hemp for Britain and other European nations.

A second source of interest in international trade for the domestic firm may be the need for new product markets. As domestic markets saturate, international markets become increasingly attractive, even though the costs of transportation and servicing of these markets is higher than would be the case in one's own country. For more advanced countries, a reciprocal trade arrangement often is found to be attractive. The advanced country buys raw materials and sells manufactured or processed goods to the less advanced. The heavily populated nations of Africa and Asia have for many years had great appeal to industries seeking additional markets for products in saturated domestic markets.

Where the interest in international trade is the result of a need to integrate the activities of the units (both domestic and foreign), the parent organization is likely to view the enterprise as an entity rather than a portfolio of separate units and will permit little autonomy. The tendency for a low level of autonomy is also found when the multinational group is large, the product is fairly standardized, the foreign unit serves a market larger than that in its own country, and the multinational holds a large portion of its equity.[1]

As the general manager contemplates the possibility of a move into an international context, a number of factors should be considered. Obviously, in many countries, the language, mode of dress, stage of economic development, political system, customs and culture are markedly different than in one's home country. Less obvious but of equal or greater significance are the effects of economic activity on internal and external political relationships. Most countries welcome trade with other nations. When the extent of foreign trade begins to dominate the local economy, however, the

[1] G. Garnier, "Context and Decision Making Autonomy in the Foreign Affiliates of U.S. Multi-National Corporations," *Academy of Management Journal* 25(4) (1982) pp. 893–904.

political strength of the foreign-trading partner is enhanced to the point where local interests have, for practical purposes, lost effective control over their own home communities or country. Host countries, therefore, may be cautious as trade activity increases and may use a variety of strategies to avoid foreign-country dominance in domestic matters.

Within the foreign country, increased trade can enhance the political positions of the party in power and may thereby create resistance and resentment in the political opposition. Similarly, the growth in influence brought about by enhanced foreign trade may anger and alienate the political and commercial competitors of the trader. Thus, U.S. trade with countries in the Mideast may not only create anti-American sentiments in the host country among the opposition party, but may also create additional tensions among Soviet-bloc nations with which we compete for trade and political influence throughout the world. In addition, neighboring countries may see the increase in economic strength of the host country as increasing the threat to their own security. A wealthy Libya, for example, may concern Algerians and Egyptians worried about the military security of their borders.

Although the constraints may not be made explicit, these political forces serve to restrict the extent of commerce with a given trading partner. Controls in one's home country may also restrict the extent of imports and exports. Restrictions on the sale of weapons systems, military hardware, high-technology industrial products, and critical raw materials are only some of the kinds of products on which government restrictions might be placed. For many general managers, a careful examination of the controls on the movement of materials and goods should be a starting point in considering international commerce.

The support structure for economic activity is also a critical component in the formulation of a strategy involving international trade. An active and stable banking system, ready sources of reliable power, water and sewage treatment, a supply of trained or trainable labor, an all-weather system of roads, a means of communication, and a stable and secure government are elements in the host country that enable commercial activity to flourish and thrive. Strategists from the United States may neglect to consider the effects of their own normative assumptions about a support structure. As one example, managers may forget that although all of our citizens may travel in our country without restriction, freedom of movement is not available in all countries throughout the world.

The availability and quality of labor is another key component in support for economic health. Although labor may be available in underdeveloped nations, it is often unskilled, illiterate, or semiliterate and may be trainable to only semiskilled occupations. An additional consideration is that in developed nations, labor may have the requisite training or education levels but may be organized by highly politicized labor unions.

The critical nature of each factor in a country's list of economic attributes is dependent, to a large extent, on the nature of the business involved. For a shoe-manufacturing company seeking a factory site for its low-priced line of footwear, the ready availability of low-skilled and inexpensive labor is advantageous rather than a limiting factor because its products can be manufactured by semiskilled labor. A company interested in establishing a technologically advanced assembly plant, on the other hand, might be restricted to those countries in which a sufficiently large pool of better-educated and more-readily trained employees might be available. For the general manager interested in establishing a plant that will process large quantities of materials, the presence of a rail or waterway system would be very helpful. Where these are missing, the company may include the construction of needed transportation in its investment planning or it may seek sites in countries where the transportation system can accommodate or be adapted to serve the organization's needs.

Natural features of the terrain, climate, or environment must also be considered when contemplating commerce in another country. In Southeast Asia, the wet season, with torrential and nearly nonstop rains, brings outdoor construction and agriculture to a stop for its duration. In Canada, Scandinavia, and other northern countries, the severe cold for 6 or more months each year has restricted population growth in the north and has contributed to a highly seasonal pattern of economic activity. In countries near the equator, the excessive midday heat has caused the development of a cultural practice of midday closure of businesses and an extension of the working day to evening hours.

The analysis of the relative attractiveness of various countries can take the form of simple lists of positive and negative attributes. The manager must then somehow compile and weight these elements in order to arrive at a composite judgment. A somewhat more systematic means of evaluating opportunities in different countries can be constructed from information available from boards of trade and from the U.S. Department of Commerce. Boulton reports on the use of a BCG matrix and import and export growth rates to develop a diagram of relative attractiveness of a number of selected industries.[2]

The matrices used in the BCG and GE strategy-formulation approaches offer a means for analysis in the selection of country and industry. For a particular country, the BCG matrix (see Figure 16–1) can serve as the backdrop for a depiction of market size for each of several products (by circles of various sizes) located on a grid measured by market attractiveness and company strength.

For the organization with capital and management, this type of descriptive device may suggest opportunities for exploration and possible investment. A country in which domestic production is rising much more rapidly than domestic sales suggests the need for export markets. For another country's producers, this would suggest the potential entry of an aggressive competitor into its own markets. For another country's marketer, it might mean the availability of those exported products as additions to the company's product line.

Where domestic consumption is rising more rapidly than domestic production, the situation suggests an opportunity for the foreign producer to join the competition for that demand and (potentially) to ship products to that country for import.

[2] William R. Boulton, *Business Policy: The Art of Strategic Management* (New York: Macmillan, 1984), p. 75.

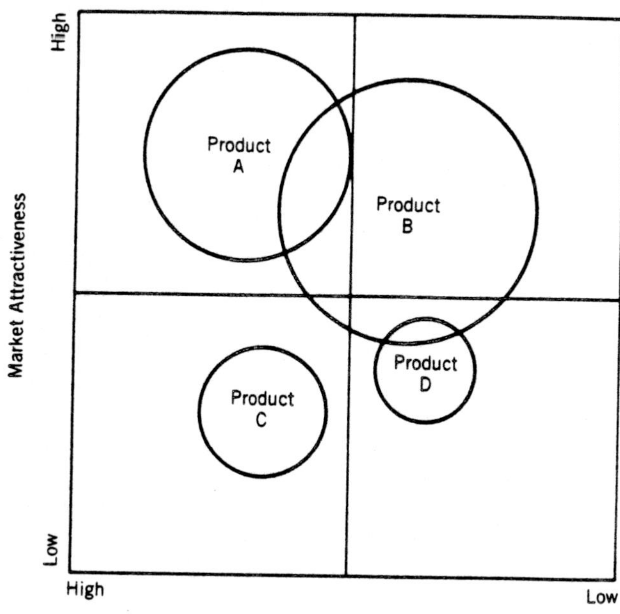

FIGURE 16–1 Product/market selection matrix country of "grovania."

EXERCISE 16–1

The following information is provided about a number of industries in the nation of "Grovania." Examine the data, then respond to the questions. Prepare for demonstration and explanation in class or as a written assignment.

Product	*Last Year*	*This Year*
Cheese		
Domestic Sales	3,400	4,400
Export Sales	500	700
Imports	2,200	3,100
Yogurt		
Domestic Sales	1,350	1,500
Export Sales	680	700
Imports	150	350
Bacon		
Domestic Sales	5,560	5,400
Export Sales	4,900	4,800
Imports	1,680	2,050

Ham		
Domestic Sales	3,060	3,430
Export Sales	2,050	1,700
Imports	2,440	1,540

- Prepare a four-cell matrix from the data above, with the following instructions:
  Calculate the rate of growth for imports for the products listed. Repeat for the exports of these products.
  Average the rate of growth of imports. Your answer is ______________.
  Average the rate of growth of exports. Your answer is ______________.
  Use the average rate of growth as a center line for the two axes on your diagram. Set the average rate of growth to be equal to 1. Rates of growth greater than the average will be represented by values greater than 1. Rates slower than average will be represented by values less than 1. Use export growth as the vertical axis and import growth as the horizontal axis. Label each axis.
  Represent each product's sales activity by a circle. The size of each circle should reflect the relative size of total sales attributed to the country's commercial activity in this product.
  Place each circle on the diagram in its appropriate place.
- Examine the diagram you have just completed. As an advisor to the agricultural-products producing interests in your area of the United States, what products in "Grovania" pose the greater competitive threat? What products offer a potential opportunity? Explain your answers.
- As an advisor to a company that markets foreign products in the United States, identify the areas of greatest opportunity for your company? What products present the greatest threats? Explain your answers.
- What additional information would be helpful to you in examining international trade opportunities? Explain.

EXERCISE 16–2

Prepare a matrix like the one in Exercise 16–1 for Ireland. Make use of library resources to provide domestic sales and import and export information on the following products for the most recent two years for which you can find data:

- Automobiles.
- Alcoholic Beverages.
- Pharmaceuticals.
- Machine Tools.

- Chemical Fertilizers.
- Agricultural Products.

Where technological expertise is needed, and where that talent is not readily available in the host country, the company with that talent (often a single-business enterprise) will be the only type of company with a realistic promise of success. In that case, the company will only be interested in a single product/market, but in different countries.[3]

For the strategist, a variety of combinations of factors can be used in a weighted evaluative scheme. In the example cited by Harrell and Kiefer, market size, market growth, price control, barriers, local-content export requirements, inflation, trade balance, and political factors were arranged in a multiplicative model to arrive at a weighted country-attractiveness measure.

To measure competitive strength, the example used market share, industry position, product fit, profit contribution, profit percentage of dealer cost, and market support. Other combinations could be used, weighted to reflect the importance of each to the company or product involved.

The lists contained in Table 16–1 are representative of some of the factors that should be considered by the general manager in reaching decisions on developing a strategy for international trade for a given country. To some extent, the attributes that make a company strong or weak in a foreign country are similar to those that serve the same function in domestic markets. Extensive experience in the particular country, however, may be an extremely important factor in the company's successful development since previous experience should place the company in an advanced position on the learning curve in its development. Language skills, political contacts, and a knowledge of the culture and customs of the country will also be helpful in both reaching good decisions and in carrying out an international trade strategy in that particular country. You may wish to add items to these partial lists as your understanding of international commerce develops.

The characteristics of the country will range in importance to the prospective trader depending on the product and the type of trade being contemplated. If, for example, our prospective trader is interested in obtaining raw materials and wishes to import them from the country in question, then availability of the material is certainly a key item in considering the attractiveness of a given country. With bulky materials, transportation would also be of great significance as might terrain or climatic conditions. Education level of the population, on the other hand, may have little importance in that particular trading situation. If one were interested in the sale of military hardware, the extent of affiliation with major powers and relationships with the country's neighbors might be of great significance.

[3] G. D. Harrell and R. O. Kiefer, "Multinational Strategic Market Portfolios," *MSU Business Topics* (Winter 1981), pp. 5–15.

TABLE 16–1

Partial list of attributes that make a country attractive or unattractive to a manager interested in developing trade	*Partial list of attributes that make a company strong or weak in that country*
Needed Raw Materials	Capital Resources
Size of Domestic Market	Management Talent
Market Growth	Technological Talent
Tariff	Language Skills
Local Content Export Registration	Market Share
Inflation	Product Reputation
Highway Development	In-country Experience
Rail system	Product Positioning
Seaports	Import/Export Experience
Climatic Conditions	Political Contacts
Terrain	
Banking System	
Political System	
Relationship with Neighbors	
Affiliation to Major Powers	
Cultural Barriers	
Availability of Labor	
Quality of Labor Force	
Education Level	
Labor Union Activity	
Media Availability	
Balance of Payments	
Government Indebtedness	
Standard of Living	
Diversification of Economy	

EXERCISE 16–3

Add any additional items to the list in Table 16–1 you believe should be considered by the general manager in contemplating international trade with another country. Then consider the following situations, and respond to the questions you find with each.

- You are considering acquiring potash (potassium carbonate)—a basic chemical used in glass manufacture and as a fertilizer—from ores mined in a number of foreign sources. Sylvite, the mineral ore used to derive potash, is mined underground and shipped in trainload and shipload quantities to the United States for processing into products to be used by your customers.

Which six factors in the country do you believe to be of greatest significance as you review this decision? List and explain.

Weight each of the six to reflect your assessment of its importance so that the total weight equals 100.

Which four factors in your company's strengths and weaknesses do you believe have the greatest significance as you prepare your analysis? List and explain.

Weight each of the four to reflect your assessment of its importance so that the total weight equals 100.

- Your company is the manufacturer and marketer of a line of baby food products. Your company has had a long and distinguished history of high quality and customer loyalty. The population decline in the United States and the increasing interest in breast feeding of infants has caused your market to saturate and your product/market to enter the decline stage. You have been asked to examine a number of countries to assess the desirability of engaging in an intensive and large-scale marketing effort designed to develop and expand the market for your line of infant and toddler food products. As developed for the U.S. market, your products are packaged under highly sanitary conditions and are ready to be mixed with water or milk. Milk substitutes, packaged ready for use or dried and ready for mixing with water, form a second major product line. The third line is made up of canned meats, fruits and vegetables. These products are precooked, and need only to be warmed to be served.

  Which six factors in the country do you believe to be of greatest significance as you review this decision? List and explain.

  Weight each of the six to reflect your assessment of its importance so that the total weight equals 100.

  Which four factors in your company's strengths and weaknesses do you believe have the greatest significance as you prepare your analysis? List and explain.

- Weight each of the four to reflect your assessment of its importance so that the total weight equals 100.

- Your company manufactures computer keyboards. These assemblies have numerous moving parts and must be hand assembled. Quality control is important because the failure of a keyboard means the failure of a computer. All parts will be manufactured in the host country except the computer chips, which require the use of "clean room" manufacturing facilities. Keys are plastic injection moldings, as are the frames in which the keys are placed. Springs and other components must be placed in appropriate positions in the frames with the keys as the entire keyboard is assembled. Finished keyboards are to be shipped back to your country to be packaged with the monitor, disk drives, and other materials in a single container for shipment to individual retail customers.

Which six factors in the country do you believe to be of greatest significance as you review this decision? List and explain.
Weight each of the six to reflect your assessment of its importance so that the total weight equals 100.
Which four factors in your company's strengths and weaknesses do you believe have the greatest significance as you prepare your analysis? List and explain.

- While on a vacation trip to a foreign country, your souvenir shopping trips led you to a small shop that served as an outlet for native art. To your enthusiastic, but amateur appraisal, the work seemed to be that of astonishingly talented persons. On inquiry, you found that a family of native people had had a long history as artists and that the presence of this work in the dealer's place was, to them, a new venture. Visits to other areas in the country yielded similar situations: families of artists, many working at labor jobs during the day but preparing works of very high-quality art for sale to local patrons. A representative collection sent to a gallery in New York yielded a similar appraisal and an offer to assist in marketing the work of these heretofore unknown artists. You consider the establishment of a small enterprise designed to purchase works of art in the country you had visited and market it in the United States.
  Which six factors in the country do you believe to be of greatest significance as you review this decision? List and explain.
  Weight each of the six to reflect your assessment of its importance so that the total weight equals 100.
  Which four factors in your company strengths and weaknesses do you believe have the greatest significance as you prepare your analysis? List and explain.
  Weight each of the four so that the total weight equals 100.

The Rug Corporation case offers an opportunity to examine a situation in which the diagnostic tools described might be of help to the company's management. As you read through the case, attempt to note possible answers to these questions:

- Consider the product line to be sold by the Rug Corporation. Does this product line suggest an economic standard for assessing possible foreign markets?
- Consider the marketing mix you believe is needed to sell this product. What requirements does this place on the choice of potential market?
- Briefly review the strengths and weaknesses of the company. Then consider the *additional* talents or attributes needed for successful international trade. What constraints might this place on the choice of potential foreign markets?

After reading the case, and noting your answers to these three questions, respond to the questions at the end of the case.

RUG CORPORATION

In September last year, the management of The Rug Corporation (the company) decided against making a manufacturing direct foreign investment in the Commonwealth of Puerto Rico.[1] This decision had followed a brief investigation, lasting five months. The company's management decided that investing abroad at that time would not be in the best interest of the company or its owners. Bill Sikes, the controller and executive responsible for export sales, explained that a lack of experienced managers and a tremendous increase in domestic and export sales were the two most important factors leading to this decision.

The Rug Corporation, a Georgia firm, manufactured scatter rugs, bathroom carpets, and bath sets (covers for toilet tanks and lids). All of the company's products were tufted. The mean average wholesale price was $3.75. The company's products were produced from man-made materials: nylon and polyester face yarn; "typar,"[2] a man-made primary backing; and foam laytex, a secondary backing.

During the fiscal year two years ago, the worldwide petroleum crisis resulted in both increased raw material costs and decreased face yarn supply. Raw material costs, which previously had increased at an annual rate of 3 to 4 percent, rose steadily. By early last year, when raw materials were again in abundant supply, costs had increased an average of 20 to 25 percent.

Because of the decreased supply of face yarn during this period, the company's suppliers placed it on allocation. Only the supply of face yarn was restricted. The company never experienced supply problems for those raw materials used in the production of primary or secondary backing. The allocation program ended approximately six months prior to the company's investigation of investment opportunities in Puerto Rico.

The allocation program and the increase in raw material prices resulted in lower production quantity and decreased sales volume. The company's suppliers allocated raw materials at levels as close as possible to their customer's previous year's purchases. If a customer, for example, had in earlier years purchased 10 percent of a supplier's total production of a certain raw material, the supplier allocated 10 percent of its current year's production to that customer during the period of the shortage.

The effect of this controlled raw material market was that the company began losing certain sales. Increased raw material prices led to a loss of some customers when price increases were added to wholesale prices of finished goods. Further, the overall raw material shortage resulted in the company being unable to increase production levels sufficiently to fill large orders placed by new customers.

Founded fifteen years ago by Mr. John Douglas, the company was one of a group of five separate corporations which were owned

This case was prepared by Dr. Edgar W. Kossack, Assistant Professor of International Business and Marketing, Florida Atlantic University. All names have been disguised.

[1] Although Puerto Rico was, in fact, a self-governing Commonwealth of the United States, protected by the Constitutions of both the United States and Puerto Rico, Mr. Sikes felt that the investment would be similar to investing in a foreign country. He based this opinion on several observations, the most important of which were: (1) Spanish was the mother tongue of Puerto Rico; (2) Puerto Rico was 1,050 miles (2¼ hours by air) from Miami; and (3) Corporate and personal income was not subject to U.S. federal taxation.

[2] "Typar" is a Dupont trade name.

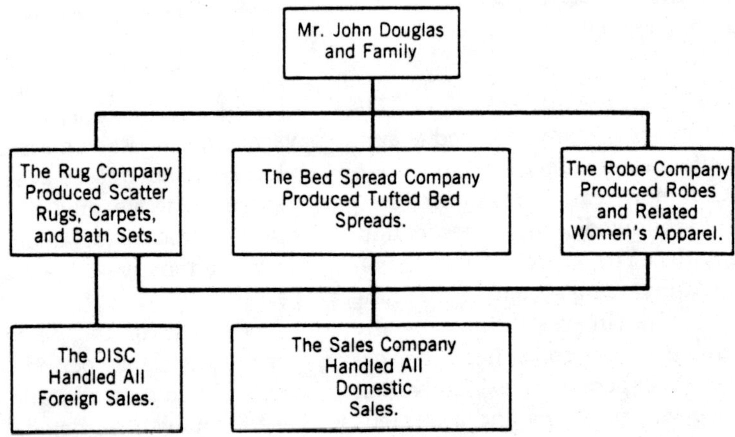

FIGURE 1 Organization chart: The Rug Corporation.

EXHIBIT 1
Sales to major house accounts

Major house accounts	*% of Total house-account sales*
Stamp Companies e.g. S&H Company	15%
Discounters e.g. K-Mart Zayres	30%
Department Stores e.g. Sears Roebuck & Co. J.C. Penney Montgomery Wards	35%
Small Independent Retailers	20%

and managed by Mr. Douglas and his family.[3] Since the founding, management had concentrated its efforts on reaching a satisfactory level of profit as a percentage of sales volume. Management felt that a rate of profit equal to 10 percent of sales before taxes should be reached before concentrating on any other operational goal. By the end of the last fiscal year, management recognized that the profit goal had been reached. The objective then was changed to increasing the company's growth rate.

Growth in sales had reached a 10 percent annual rate earlier. This rate of growth was figured in terms of total sales, and included both volume and price increases. When profit objectives were reached, a decision was made to increase the growth rate objective from 10 percent to 20–25 percent annually. Management felt that further increases in total profits had to be the result of increased sales volume.

The products were sold throughout the United States through two separate sales efforts.[4] Headquarters management negotiated sales to large accounts directly. These house accounts represented approximately 40 percent of the total sales volume. Although the volume of sales to each house account fluctuated from year to year, the percentage of total sales which were negotiated directly by the company had not appreciably changed over recent years. Approximately 20 percent of the products sold to the

[3] The five companies, along with a description of their respective activities, are presented in Case Figure 1.

[4] See Case Figure 2 for a diagram of both domestic and international distribution channels.

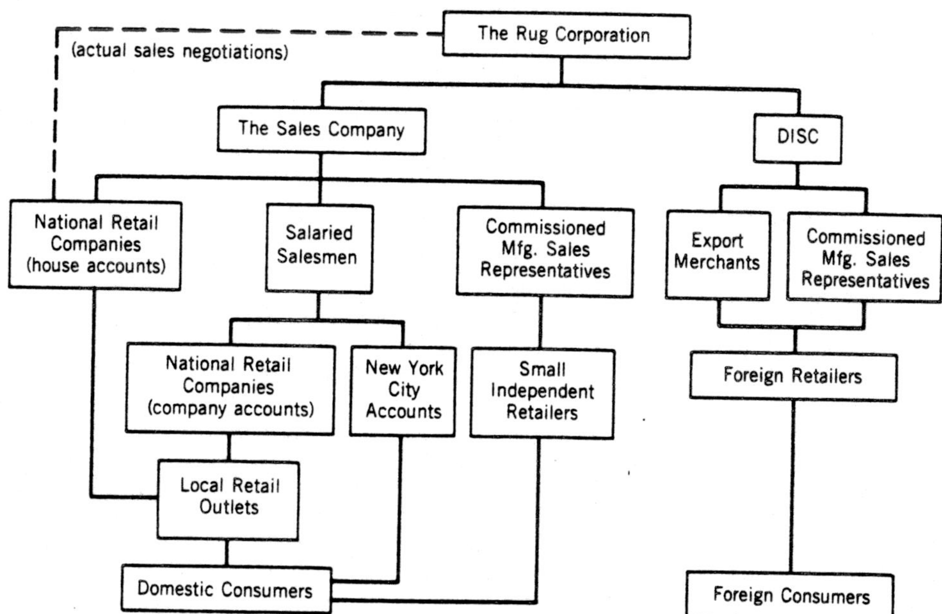

FIGURE 2 Domestic and Foreign Distribution Channels. 'The DISC's sales are funneled through this "paper corporation" at the end of the reporting period.

larger house accounts were resold under the customer's own private brand name.[5]

The Sales Company, a separate sales organization headquartered in New York, handled other accounts. For reporting purposes, all sales were routed through The Sales Company. The New York sales office employed five salaried salesmen and twenty commissioned sales representatives. The commissioned sales representatives also handled noncompetitive products of other manufacturers, and were located at key marketing points throughout the country. Mr. Sikes described the procedure for assigning sales territories as "very fluid." The five salaried salesmen worked out of the New York City sales office. They were assigned to call on "company accounts," or major customers located throughout the domestic market. They also called on any customer maintaining a purchasing office in New York City. Major customers were defined as those retail establishments which, although not large enough to qualify as house accounts, represented sufficient sales volume to require the attention of company salesmen. Further, retail establishments which qualified as company accounts were national companies. The president of The Sales Company doubled as sales manager and also handled certain major company accounts.

The twenty commissioned sales representatives were responsible for covering the remainder of the domestic market and were assigned territories throughout the United States. Mr. Sikes explained that the company made an attempt to be "flexible" in territory assignments. Special agreements were made, at times, to allow a sales representative to call on customers located in neighboring territories. Mr. Sikes explained that a description of territory assignments would be very difficult as a result.

[5] The larger house accounts and their respective sales volume information are listed in exhibit 1.

EXHIBIT 2
Statements of earnings

	Previous years ended June 30					
	5th	*4th*	*3rd*	*2nd*	*Last*	*This year*
Net sales	$9,712,500	$10,545,000	$11,100,000	$12,210,000	$11,160,000	$14,430,000
Cost of products sold	7,187,250	7,803,300	8,325,000	8,913,300	7,923,600	10,245,300
Selling, general, and administrative expenses	2,187,125	2,636,250	2,664,000	3,052,500	2,678,400	3,463,200
Net operating income	$ 97,125	$ 105,450	$ 111,000	$ 244,200	$ 558,000	$ 721,500
Miscellaneous income (net)	19,425	21,090	22,200	24,420	22,320	28,860
Licensing						
Sale of equipment						
Rental income						
Discount						
Net income before taxes	$ 116,500	$ 126,540	$ 133,200	$ 268,620	$ 580,320	$ 750,360
Income taxes	52,425	56,943	59,940	120,879	261,144	337,662
Net earnings	$ 64,075	$ 69,597	$ 73,260	$ 147,741	$ 319,176	$ 412,698

The company had a showroom at the Calhoun, Georgia, plant and The Sales Company maintained a separate showroom at its New York office. Other showrooms were located in Dallas, Texas, and San Francisco, California, and were maintained by the local, commissioned sales representatives. The company advertised only in trade journals and limited its sales and promotional efforts to personal contacts by salesmen.

The domestic carpet and rug industry was a highly competitive industry. There was no accurate count of the exact number of manufacturers of carpets and rugs. On the basis of available information, such as the confidential estimates of the Carpet and Rug Institute,[6] information gathered from sales personnel, major accounts, and personal visits with competitors, Mr. Sikes felt that his company and six close competitors each had about 10 percent of the rug market.[7] Some fifteen to twenty other manufacturers supplied the remaining 30 percent of the market. He described these as companies which "fringe into the market." These were manufacturers of broadloom carpet which also produced a small number of rugs and bath sets, but individually they did not represent a serious threat to the company's market position.

Mr. Sikes characterized this industry as highly competitive. Price, style, design, and the ability to deliver on short notice, were the most important competitive factors. Production tech-

[6] The Carpet and Rug Institute is an association of carpet and rug producers.

[7] See Income Statements, Exhibit 2, and Balance Sheets, Exhibit 3.

nology was standardized so that quality was no longer a competitive distinction. Mr. Sikes felt that, although there were levels of quality, buyers were very knowledgeable and knew that at any given level there was little difference between his company's products and those of the close competitors.

No accurate records were available on total export activities. Although the company owned a small IBM computer, its approximately 18,000 customers were not classified as domestic or foreign. Also, total export sales were hard to identify since some 60 percent of those products exported were sold to large export merchants in New York and Miami. The company's management had no control over the eventual disposition of these products and no knowledge of the identities of ultimate consumers. Further, management believed that some of its domestic customers might export products overseas, but it had no direct knowledge of this.

Although no specific export data were available, Mr. Sikes estimated that, historically, approximately 5 percent of the total sales volume was eventually sold overseas. Of that amount, a portion was sold by the company

EXHIBIT 3
Balance Sheet
June 30, 5th previous year

Current Assets		
Cash		$ 200
Accounts receivable		
Factors	$ 25,637	
Trade	17,862	
Officers and employees	4,308	
Others	691	
Affiliated companies	$647,438	695,936
Current portion of long-term note receivable (secured)		13,700
Inventories, at lower of cost or market		
Finished goods	$135,561	
Work-in-process	183,337	
Raw materials	206,983	
Supplies	15,393	541,274
Prepaid expenses		6,284
Total current assets		$1,257,394
Investments		
Cash value of life insurance	$ 24,981	
Note receivable due after one year	21,774	46,755
Fixed Assets		
Property, plant and equipment	$877,000	
Less accumulated depreciation	356,790	520,210
Total		$1,824,359

Current Liabilities		
Bank overdraft		$ 6,645
Note payable		206,250
Accounts payable		
Trade	$ 251,679	
Affiliated company	136,608	
Officers	11,791	400,078
Payrolls and other compensation		49,193
Taxes withheld from employees		9,214
Accrued taxes including income		66,249
Other liabilities		23,869
Total current liabilities		$ 761,498
Stockholders' Equity		
Common stock		
Issued, 60 shares of $100 par value of which 24 are in treasury	$ 6,000	
Retained earnings	1,116,861	
	$1,122,861	
Less cost of treasury stock	60,000	1,062,861
Total		$1,824,359

EXHIBIT 3 ***(continued)***
Balance Sheet
June 30, 4th previous year

Current Assets		
Cash		$ 200
Accounts receivable		
Factor	$ 15,155	
Trade	16,261	
Officers and employees	5,854	
Others	450	
Affiliated companies	370,531	408,251
Current portion of long-term note receivable (secured)		15,625
Inventories, at lower of cost or market		667,826
Overpayment of income taxes		71,874
Prepaid expenses		5,158
Total current assets		$1,168,934
Cash value of life insurance		29,472
Fixed Assets, at cost less accumulated depreciation of $404,590		554,488
Other Assets		
Note receivable, due after one year (secured)	$ 8,314	
Deposit	20	8,334
Total		$1,761,228

Current Liabilities		
Bank overdraft		$ 81,547
Note payable		227,550
Accounts payable		
Trade	$ 147,168	
Affiliated company	145,681	
Officers	3,614	296,463
Payrolls and other compensation		46,648
Accrued profit sharing expense		22,185
Other liabilities		12,088
Total current liabilities		686,481
Stockholders' Equity		
Common stock		
Issued, 60 shares of $100 par value	$ 6,000	
Retained earnings	1,128,747	
	$1,134,747	
Less cost of treasury stock 24 shares	60,000	$1,074,747
Total		$1,761,228

Balance Sheet
June 30, 3rd previous year

Current Assets		
Cash		$ 13,772
Accounts receivable		
Factors	$ 9,824	
Trade	12,326	
Affiliated companies	701,460	
Officers and employees	7,005	
Other	450	731,065
Current portion of long-term note receivable (secured)		10,613
Inventories, at lower of cost or market		440,265
Prepaid expenses		8,400
Total current assets		$1,204,115

Current Liabilities		
Notes payable		
Bank	$ 180,469	
Officers	5,000	
Other	10,650	$ 196,119
Accounts payable		
Trade	$ 122,880	
Affiliated companies	147,024	
Officers	7,698	277,602
Payrolls and other compensation		39,676
Accrued profit-sharing expense		18,738
Taxes withheld from employees		1,216
Federal and state income taxes		69,631
Other liabilities		9,831
Total current liabilities		$ 612,813

EXHIBIT 3 *(continued)*

Cash value of life insurance		34,058			
Fixed Assets, at cost less accumulated depreciation of $457,974		527,266	Stockholders' Equity Common stock Issued, 60 shares of $100 par value	$ 6,000	
			Retained earnings	1,206,646	
				$1,212,646	
Other Assets Deposits		20	Less cost of treasury stock, 24 shares	60,000	$1,152,646
Total		$1,765,459	Total		$1,765,459

Balance Sheet
June 30, 2nd previous year

Current Assets			Current Liabilities		
Cash		$ 2,356	Notes payable		
Accounts receivable			Bank	$ 155,000	
Trade	$ 14,171		Officers	5,000	$ 160,000
Affiliated companies	768,360		Accounts payable		
Officers and employees	17,855	800,386	Trade	$ 119,675	
Inventories		663,658	Affiliated companies	170,560	
Prepaid expenses		9,025	Officers	1,347	291,582
Total current assets		$1,475,425	Payrolls and other compensation		108,267
			Federal and state income taxes		72,235
Investments			Other liabilities		57,582
			Total current liabilities		$ 689,666
Cash value of life insurance		3,469			
Fixed Assets			Stockholders' Equity		
Land, buildings and improvements	$ 534,137		Common stock Issued, 60 shares of $100 par value	$ 6,000	
Machinery and equipment	471,578		Retained earnings	1,342,541	
	$1,005,715			$1,348,541	
Less accumulated depreciation	506,422	499,293			
Other Assets Deposits		20	Less cost of 24 shares of treasury stock	60,000	$1,288,541
Total		$1,978,207	Total		$1,978,207

Balance Sheet
June 30, Last Year

Current Assets			Current Liabilities		
Cash		$ 17,967	Notes payable—officers		$ 5,000
Accounts receivable			Accounts payable		
Trade	$ 5,742		Trade	$ 196,204	
Affiliated companies	993,260		Affiliated companies	247,585	443,789
Officers and employees	21,902	1,020,904	Payrolls and other compensation		130,081

EXHIBIT 3 *(continued)*
Balance Sheet
June 30, Last Year

Notes receivable		100	Accrued profit-sharing expense		44,608
Inventories		477,727	Taxes withheld from employees		1,707
Prepaid federal income taxes		32,089	State income taxes payable		279
Prepaid expenses		10,409	Other liabilities		8,886
Total current assets		$1,559,196	Total current liabilities		$ 634,350
Investments			Stockholders' Equity		
			Common Stock		
Cash value of life insurance—net of loans of $33,038		10,593	Issued, 60 shares of $100 par value	6,000	
			Retained earnings	$1,464,749	
Fixed Assets				$1,470,749	
Land, buildings and improvements	$ 539,486		Less cost of 24 shares of treasury stock	60,000	1,410,749
Machinery and equipment	487,674				
	$1,027,160		Total		$2,045,099
Less accumulated depreciation	551,870	475,290			
Other Assets		20			
Total		$2,045,099			

either directly to overseas customers or through commissioned sales representatives. The company had a commissioned sales representative in Puerto Rico and Canada. Mr. Sikes guessed that before the shortage of raw materials, direct export shipments broke down as follows:

Market	*% of Total direct-export sales*
Puerto Rico	50%
Japan	10%
Australia	10%
Venezuela	20%
Other European markets	10%

A substantial amount of export sales had been to customers in Puerto Rico. That volume had decreased in recent years because of a lack of aggressive sales effort,[8] increased competition, and, more recently, increases in domestic sales which had focused management's attention away from export problems.

Mr. Sikes described his company's export history as "sporadic." Although individual sales had always been large and profitable, they were never steady. Sometimes, export sales came from an unsolicited contact by an overseas customer. In fact, some sales had been made to customers referred to the company by the U.S. Chamber of Commerce.

Mr. Sikes summarized the export activities of his company and the entire rug industry:

[8] The company's commissioned sales representative in Puerto Rico had recently begun selling other products and was no longer concentrating on the company's products.

Our industry is very weak in exporting. We take whatever falls in our lap. We are not aggressive and don't go looking for export business. We are not willing to take that chance. The attitude of our industry in general has been that we are better businessmen than anybody else in the world. This is not true. Also, the members of our industry feel that foreign customers must be dealt with on a cash-in-advance basis because they are not creditworthy, because they are located overseas. This, I feel, is not true at all.

In an effort to improve the export activities of his company, Mr. Sikes had been instrumental in creating a Domestic International Sales Corporation (DISC).[9] The DISC was incorporated in the fall of last year. During the one reporting period it had been in operation, there had been $275,000 in qualified export sales. All export sales, which could be properly identified, were handled through the DISC. But because of the relatively small volume of export business, the DISC was in reality a "paper corporation." Mr. Sikes admitted that he and his auditors simply "funneled" export sales through the DISC at the end of each fiscal year. He explained that at the end of the last fiscal year he simply went through all sales receipts in an effort to determine those sales which qualified as DISC sales. Qualified export sales for the year were limited to those to the major New York and Miami export merchants and those sales to overseas customers or through foreign sales representatives.

Mr. Sikes had also investigated purchasing export credit insurance through the Foreign Credit Insurance Association (FCIA).[10] A decision on whether to purchase credit insurance offered through the FCIA had not yet been made. To date, export sales had been on a cash-in-advance basis or to customers with an irrevocable and confirmed letter of credit. Domestic sales, in comparison, were made on an open-account basis with a 2 percent discount for payment within ten days and full payment within thirty days.

The company had licensing agreements with manufacturers in Belgium, Brazil, Italy, and Australia. During the tenure of a license agreement, which was usually two years, the company provided the licensee with technical manufacturing know-how. In return, the licensee paid a predetermined annual fee plus a percentage of all sales, above a certain dollar level, of the product produced with the licensed technology. The dollar sales level which was applicable for the percentage-of-sales portion of the fee was set at the licensee's previous level of sales. This percentage-of-sales override fee allowed the company to collect an additional amount for all sales increases which resulted from the licensee using the company's know-how. The license fee was normally between $3,000 and $8,000, with the percentage-of-sales override being between 1 and 2 percent.

Because of the satisfactory experience with exporting activities, Mr. Sikes began early last year looking for ways to increase the company's sales volume through developing overseas sales. He was convinced that the company's new growth objective could be reached through aggressive sales efforts in Puerto Rico and foreign markets. Before the petroleum crisis, some 50 percent of the company's export volume had

[9] A Domestic International Sales Corporation (DISC) is a special corporation through which a domestic firm can channel its exports. The advantage gained by firms exporting through a DISC is an unlimited deferral on a portion of their export related profits for income tax purposes.

[10] The Foreign Credit Insurance Association (FCIA), together with the Export-Import Bank, offers credit insurance on export sales. FCIA policies cover commercial risks, political risks, or both, that result in a foreign customer's failure to pay.

gone to Puerto Rico. This had fallen to about 20 percent. Exports to Japan and Venezuela had fallen from 10 percent and 20 percent respectively to nothing. Further, sales to Canada and the Dominican Republic had begun, and in a very short time had grown impressively. All this convinced Mr. Sikes that there was potential sales volume in the export market.

In April of last year Mr. Sikes received an information package from the Commonwealth of Puerto Rico. The package included descriptions of the general investment environment in Puerto Rico, as well as pertinent economic, geographic, and demographic data. Mr. Sikes met with the company's president, Mr. Douglas, and they decided to contact the Economic Development Administration of the Commonwealth of Puerto Rico, the organization which had sent the package, for further information. Mr. Sikes admitted that his initial thought was that, perhaps by manufacturing in Puerto Rico, his company could regain its previous market share by producing with cheaper labor and saving on the cost of transportation. He also felt that Puerto Rico might be used as a center for exporting goods to South America and, perhaps, some of Africa.

In June of last year two representatives of the Commonwealth of Puerto Rico visited the company's plant in Calhoun, Georgia, and presented a general picture of the Puerto Rican economy to the company's management. During the months that followed, two things led to the company's decision. First, domestic sales increased. Mr. Sikes explained that the general business recession which had contributed to a material decline in the carpet industry was not working to the benefit of the rug industry. Management believed that consumers, who would have replaced damaged or soiled carpets if the economy had not been in the midst of a recession, now began to purchase small rugs to cover the damaged areas. Second, sales in the Canadian market began to grow because of some large sales made by the Canadian sales representative. By September, the growth in sales volume increased to the point where management concluded that the Puerto Rican investment was unnecessary. As Mr. Sikes put it, "We had our hands full trying to handle everything else that we had." Although the executives of the firm discussed the idea for several months, they decided in September of last year not to pursue the investigation further.

Mr. Sikes explained what had happened:

> *So, things happened which helped us decide not to pursue the investment in Puerto Rico. These additional sales just fell into our lap. We were not looking for them. We were looking one place, and the solution came from someplace else . . . we had our solution to our growth problem, and we didn't need to invest in Puerto Rico. But, if our growth rate, in the future, drops back, it is possible that the idea of investing in Puerto Rico or some other country might be brought up again. And, even if our growth rate does not drop back, we may reevaluate our growth goal.*

EXERCISE 16–4

Note: This exercise may be suitable for group research and presentation in class.

- Consider your responses to the study questions outlined at the beginning of the case. Then select no more than three countries (other than Puerto Rico and

Canada) that seem to be appropriate target markets for the Rug Corporation's foreign trade attentions. Explain and justify your choices.

- Prepare a list (as in Table 16–1 and Exercise 16–3) of the six factors of prime importance in selection of a foreign trading partner for the Rug Corporation. Weight the factors to reflect your assessment of the importance of each so that the weights total 100.
- Also prepare a list of the four factors of prime importance in terms of company strengths. Weight the factors to reflect your assessment of the importance of each such that the weights total 100.
- Make use of reference sources (business, international trade, encyclopedias, etc.) to help you in providing scores for each country (including Puerto Rico and Canada) for each of the six factors you have identified in the earlier question. Total the weighted scores to reach a total score for *country attractiveness.*
- From these same reference sources and your understanding of the company's strengths and weaknesses, provide scores for each of the four factors you have identified *for each country* including Puerto Rico and Canada. Total the weighted scores to reach a total score for *company competitive strength* for each country.
- Make use the weighted total scores to position each country in a nine-cell matrix that uses country attractiveness as the vertical axis and competitive strength as the horizontal axis. As in the earlier applications of the 9-cell matrix, arrange the scales so that highest scores in both dimensions would place the country in the upper leftmost cell of the matrix.
- With which country should the Rug Corporation initiate trade? Explain.
- Suppose your scores on all countries are so low that all countries are placed in the area of the matrix that calls for divestiture or liquidation. What should be done then? Explain.

In the Brown & Sharpe Manufacturing Company case, this prominent manufacturer of machine tools is actively involved in international trade with a number of nations, including the Soviet Union. Its domestic sales suffered from the recession in the mid 1970s, a factor that encouraged the company to continue to explore the possibility of expanding its foreign sales effort. Read the case thoroughly, then respond to the questions at its conclusion.

BROWN & SHARPE MANUFACTURING COMPANY

COMPANY BACKGROUND

The second oldest company in the history of the United States, Brown & Sharpe Manufacturing Company, was founded in Providence, Rhode Island, in 1833. At the dawn of the American Industrial Revolution, David Brown and his son Joseph R. Brown formed a partnership to manufacture timepieces. Brown installed clocks in steeples and towers throughout New England as well as in New York. The partners established a reputation for precision, accuracy, and quality, and this reputation has been part of the corporate image ever since those early days.

During the early nineteenth century, major changes took place in the social and economic development of the New England States. Industrialization was slowly replacing an economy mainly based on seafaring and agriculture. The new industry, predominantly textile manufacturing mills, were in need of machinery and as a result machine tool builders were in great demand.

Joseph Brown, who in 1841 took over from his father, had a creative talent for producing innovative mechanical precision tools. His watches and clocks won citations and awards throughout the country. Recognizing the opportunity to expand his business, Brown entered the machine tool industry during the 1840s. He also took on an apprentice named Lucian Sharpe. This partnership changed the character of the firm and laid the foundation for the modern machine tool enterprise that B. & S. was to become. Their joint efforts produced the precision vernier caliper, a unique precision gear-cutting-and-dividing machine, and other innovative machinery. They manufactured drills to make percussion nipple holes in Civil War muskets as well as sewing machines. These developments called for a new legal structure of their enterprise and on January 1, 1868, J. R. Brown and L. Sharpe became incorporated as the Brown and Sharpe Manufacturing Company.

Brown's major contributions to the technology of that time was his construction of a universal milling machine, followed in 1876 by a universal grinding machine. These machines were the first in a line of machinery that continues to be in use throughout the world today. Under the presidency of Henry D. Sharpe, Sr., who followed in Lucian Sharpe's footsteps in 1899, B. & S. gained a worldwide reputation and their machine tool line became the greatest in the industry. Very early on, the company recognized the potential of foreign markets. By the late 1880s, there was an agent in London for the market in Great Britain and her colonies; an agent in Berlin for commercial traffic in Germany, Austria, and Hungary; and an agent in Moscow for Eastern Europe and Russia.[1]

The company kept building on the work of J. R. Brown and its research and development produced a steady stream of new and improved machinery over the years. The company's success resulted in the need to expand the physical plant. It moved several times to new locations; the latest one took place in 1964 when the organization moved to Precision Park, a 160-acre tract of land in North Kingston, Rhode Island.

In 1951, Henry D. Sharpe, Jr., replaced his father as president of B. & S. The new president gradually reorganized the company along divisional lines (Exhibits 1–3). At the moment, the corporate structure encompasses the following divisions.

This case was prepared by William R. Allen of Suffolk University as the basis for classroom discussion.

[1] Howard F. Brown, "*The Saga of Brown and Sharpe*," Thesis, University of Rhode Island, 1971.

1 *The Machine Tool Division*, located at Precision Park, designs and manufactures single-spindle automatic screw machines, surface and universal grinding machines, and numerically controlled machining centers.

2 *The Industrial Products Division*, also headquartered at Precision Park, manufactures a wide line of electronic, optical, and mechanical precision gaging-and-inspection equipment, machinists' tools, including micrometers, vernier calipers, vises, turret tools, accessory equipment and fluid transfer pumps. At a facility located in Centredale, Rhode Island, the Industrial Products Division also manufactures or markets high-speed steel and carbide drills, reamers, milling cutters, end mills, special cutting tools, and other metal-cutting specialties.

3 *The Hydraulics Division*, in Manchester, Michigan, produces a broad line of industrial fluid-power-control valves, hydraulic power units, and Gerator pumps.[2] In addition, the company operates plants in Great Britain, Switzerland, and France.

During the 1950s and 1960s, several new companies were acquired to expand and diversify the existing product lines. At the same time, the breakthrough in electronics had, and still has, a major impact on machine tool design. The generations of numerically controlled machinery have added another dimension to product lines.

The B. & S. success story has not been continuous, however. Several times during its existence, it had to face very hard times, indeed. Employment over the last 50 years has fluctuated between 12,000 to 2,000 workers. The machine tool industry is a cyclical industry and downturns occur with a certain regularity. However, not since the depression in the 1930s has the downturn in business been as steep as in 1975. Brown & Sharpe had a loss of about $3 million during this year.

FLUCTUATIONS IN THE MACHINE TOOL BUSINESS

Demand in the machine tool business is subject to wide fluctuations. A prosperous and expanding economy with increased capital spending spurs machine tool buying. A declining economy usually means immediate cutbacks in capital spending with a resultant decline in demand for machine tools. Because of lead times for most machinery is from 8 to 18 months, downturns and upswings in the industry are slightly out of phase with the general economy.

> *The recurring sequence of changes that constitute a business cycle—expansion, downturn, contraction, and upturn—is not periodic. The phases of business cycles repeat themselves, but their duration varies considerably and so does their intensity and scope.*
>
> *Business cycles have existed in the United States, Great Britain, and France for nearly two hundred years, and they have marked the industry of modern nations practicing free enterprise since the latter part of the 19th century—if not longer. Earlier centuries, while free from business cycles, did not escape the ordeal of economic instability. In recent decades, the Soviet Union and other nations that organize their economic activity through state enterprises and governmental edicts have also escaped business cycles; but they have not escaped fluctuations.*[3]

[2] Promotional pamphlet of the history of Brown & Sharpe.

[3] Arthur F. Burns, *The Business Cycle in a Changing World* (New York: National Bureau of Economic Research, 1969), pp. 7, 8.

Over the years, numerous efforts to discover the pertinent factors that influence the downturn and upswing in the economy and in a particular industry have been successful to varying degrees.

> *Diversity and individuality are no less characteristic of business cycles than the family resemblance among them, and this fact inevitably complicates the task of understanding the nature and causes of business cycles.*[4]

The crucial point, then, is for the industry and the individual to come up with as accurate a forecast of the demand for their product as possible. A company's future may well depend to a large extent on the capabilities of the economic consulting specialist. As Mr. Larry Ford, product manager, remarked, "We are in the forecasting business."

The realization of the interdependence of national economies has made the forecasting exercise increasingly complex. The company doing business abroad can only make a reliable forecast if they consider the economic indicators in all their markets.

> *Already some 100 companies, including Campbell Soup, G. D. Searle, Union Carbide, and Shell Oil, are using the data-gathering and forecasting services of the builders of the few international econometric models.*[5]

Because of their relative newness, these models are not yet perfected. Major problems arise from the fact that the data lag 2 months or more and that there is a lack of uniformity in the basis of the figures. However, a major deterrent in the use of the models is their cost. A basic charge of $10,000 to $20,000 is the norm.

Even with information as accurate as possible, there is no guarantee that management will make the right decisions. The problems in the machine tool industry are compounded by the fact that production requires a considerable lead time.

The machine tool industry saw its largest decline in new orders since the depression in 1975 (55%). Joseph T. Bailey, chairman of Warner & Swasey Co., was quoted in *Business Week* of January 19, 1976, as saying that shipments could be even 25% lower this year than those in 1975. (Exhibit 4) Mr. Bailey didn't see any real growth until the nation's industrial capacity—now hanging around 70%—would get up to around 85% again. The general feeling among the industry's management is that they are at the bottom of the cycle, ready to move upward (Figure 1).

> *Sharpe says, "Recovery for us is a very slow process" and points out that during the last recession, "things really bottomed out in 1970 and it wasn't really until 1973 that the incoming business picked up. And this was translated into significant improvement in shipments in 1974."*[6]

The company has been building up inventory in order to make fast deliveries when conditions improve.

The export of machine tools did not suffer to the same extent from the downturn. Reasons for the steady climb of export figures during the 1970s are the devaluation of the dollar and the increasing worldwide demand for machine tools. In 1971, about 10% of sales of the machine tool division of B. & S. came from the overseas market. In 1974, this figure had climbed to 12%. The British operation in Plymouth had net sales in 1974 of $6,793,256 with

[5] *Business Week*, April 26, 1976, p. 91.

[4] Burns, *The Business Cycle*, pp. 24, 25.

[6] "Brown & Sharpe: A Troubled Cyclical," *Financial World*, June 18, 1975.

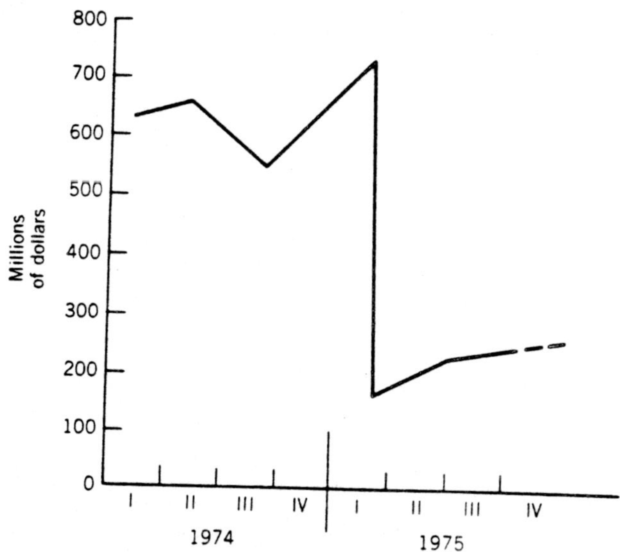

FIGURE 1 The lag that worries machine tool makers. Data: National Machine Tool Builders Assn.

exports generating about 50% of the sales volume.

As Mr. Ford explained, one way to smooth out production is to expand the export market. The company recognizes three different markets for their products.

1 The traditional market consisting of the USA, Western Europe, Japan, Canada, Austroasia, and some parts of Latin America.
2 Developing markets in nonsocialist countries.
3 The markets in countries with centrally planned economies.

The markets 2 and 3 will become traditional markets if demand can be forecasted with a degree of reliability.

B. & S.'s first efforts are channeled into maintaining and servicing their traditional markets. When demand in this market winds down (after peaking of the cycle, see Figure 2), the marketing effort emphasizes the development and maintenance of markets in developing countries such as Spain, the Philippines, and Taiwan. Near or at the lowest point of the cycle, Eastern European countries enter the market.

DOING BUSINESS WITH THE USSR

The USSR is the world's largest country and has around 250 million inhabitants. It has immense natural resources (the USSR ranks first in reserves of petroleum, iron ore, and coal), which are only partially explored and exploited. At this time, the Soviet economy is expanding at a higher rate than the industrialized west.[7]

The State Committee for Planning (Gosplan) directs every phase of the Soviet economy with five-year plans that cover broad economic

[7] "Doing Business with the USSR; a Guide for Western Corporations," *A Business International European Research Report*, Geneva, November 1971.

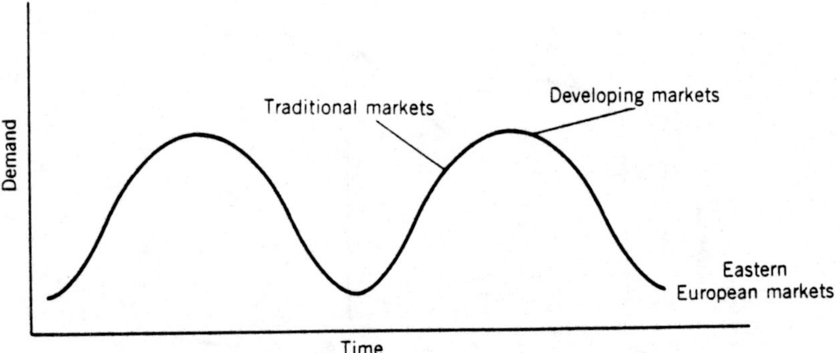

FIGURE 2 Relationship between cyclical demand and different markets.

goals and one-year plans that are concerned with immediate and specific goals. This committee and the Council of Ministers guide the Ministry of Foreign Trade, which, in turn, composes the Foreign Trade Plan. This plan has a considerable amount of details and specifics. The actual purchase of foreign goods is handled by the Foreign Trade Organizations. The Soviet trade missions and delegations and agencies such as Amtorg in New York serve as counselors to the exporter.

Negotiating a contract in the Soviet Union takes considerable time. The successful American negotiator needs patience, persistence, and perseverence. The Russian negotiating team is made up of specialists on the product under consideration. They are tough negotiators, and it is imperative to establish pricing directives beforehand in anticipation of their all-out effort to bargain on each point of the pricing policy. Personal relationships between the Russian and American negotiating teams are of great importance.

SALES OPPORTUNITIES IN THE USSR

> *Most machine tools currently in use throughout the Soviet Union are relatively modern, only about one-third of them being considered obsolete. Most of the forthcoming Soviet purchases will be for installation in new production facilities rather than for replacement of existing machinery.*
>
> *The substantial Soviet market for machine tool accessories, parts, tools, and dies—$960 million in 1974, is expected to rise to approximately $1.3 billion in 1978. The United States has benefited from increased Soviet trade with the West. Imports from the United States should represent 8% of imports in 1978.*[8]

Exports from the United States are restricted by the U.S. government on high-technology machinery. These are precisely the machines (with highly developed numerical control) that the Russians are most interested in. The industry has a lobby in Washington that works to change these barriers to free trade. They point out that Sweden is selling the Russians the high-technology machinery at the moment. As they have access to these products in any case, the industry feels the restrictions are not serving any purpose.

[8] Global Market Survey, Metalworking and Finishing Equipment," U.S. Department of Commerce, January 1975, pp. 170, 172.

> *The Soviet market for machining centers is largely supplied by imports, since domestic production is limited and Soviet technology is assessed by trade sources as lagging 2 to 3 years behind the Western level. Imports are projected to rise to $70 million in 1978.*[9]

German companies have been the leading suppliers to date, followed by British, French, Italian, and American manufacturers. Cincinnati Milacron and Brown & Sharpe are the most prominent suppliers of machining centers from the United States. Soviet manufacturers are interested in increasing purchases from the United States because of the higher speeds in positioning or tool changing as well as the greater accuracy, attained by the U.S.-designed machining centers.

> *The Soviets are striving to catch up with Western countries in technological advances in numerically controlled systems. Although the Soviets are striving toward full development of their own systems, based on the "Minsk" computers, they have not achieved the sophistication of equipment offered by Western Industry and will continue to import this advanced machinery until the technological gap can be closed.*[10]

BROWN AND SHARPE IN THE USSR

B. & S.'s business connections with the USSR go back to the 1880s. However, after the Second World War, the company did not export to Russia till the 1970s. And this time, the plant in Plymouth, England, took the initiative.

There was a recession in Britain in 1971. To move out of the trough in the cycle management decided to actively tap their tertiary market, the USSR. Mr. Ford, (who worked for the Plymouth subsidiary for 6 years) and the general manager of the plant contacted the Trade Delegation of the USSR in London. This initial contact led to a trip to Russia in November 1970. The company's contact in Russia was Stankoimport Department 1, which handles the import of machine tools in bulk. It wasn't until April 1971 that the first contract was signed. In between there were several trips back and forth concerning negotiations that could last up to 3 weeks. During this time, Mr. Ford built up mutual trust and developed important contacts in the different trade organizations and ministries. His openness, noncontroversial stance, and frank enjoyment of such Russian pastimes as an evening with the Bolshoi or a meal in a truly Russian restaurant, brought him lasting friendships. In view of the importance of personal relationships in negotiating with the Russians, this was a favorable development. The more tangible development was the sale of $3 million worth of machine tools, which were shipped between January 1972 and March 1973. Because of their unwieldy bureaucracy, the Russians purchased a great amount of replacement parts and accessories at the same time. This order exceeded the initial expectations of B. & S.'s management team.

Department 1 of Stankoimport purchases in bulk and disperses the machinery to the different industries all over the country. Their objective is to trade off price versus quality. But for B. & S. quantity is not always an advantage. The plant in the United Kingdom has a capacity of 10 machines per month and the Russians asked for 132 machines. For this reason, the time element figures prominently in production and pricing strategies. For example, the company starts to negotiate at a trough in the cycle, negotiations take up months if not years, lead time on delivery is from 1 year to 18 months, and the result is that the industry is by that time in an upturn. At that point B. & S. will want to service its traditional markets, which provide the higher contribution margins. The Russians use the argument that the company should add capacity

[9] "Global Market Survey," p. 173.

[10] "Global Market Survey," p. 174.

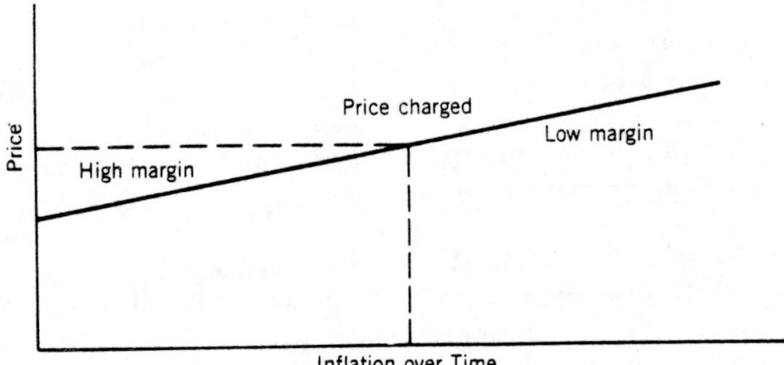

FIGURE 3 Inflation over time.

that would result in economies of scale. However, B. & S. refuses to follow such a strategy because it would result in a dependence on an unpredictable market.

The time element magnifies pricing problems as well, especially in . . . the United Kingdom, which has been ravaged by inflation over the last few years. The trouble is that the Russians do not want to include an escalation clause in their contract. Therefore the initial price has to be sufficiently inflated to take care of this situation (Figure 3). Another reason for padding the price is the fact that the Russians bargain on several pricing features one at a time. They always expect discounts, include a penalty for late delivery of ± 5%, and take off another percentage (up to 20 and 30%) to make up for problems with the goods that might turn up later (retention). It is important to them to gain on all these points because they are evaluated on them by their superiors. B. & S. did deliver the goods on time so that they did not have to subtract a percentage as a penalty discount. They also did not have to subtract anything for retention. The whole contract was executed very smoothly and B. & S. established a good reputation in the USSR.

Because of the time element B. & S. would be better off if it started negotiations before nearing the trough of the cycle. As noted earlier, the key to this problem is to construct an adequate forecasting model so that a strategy could be developed with the objective to fill in the troughs of the recessionary cycles (Figure 4).

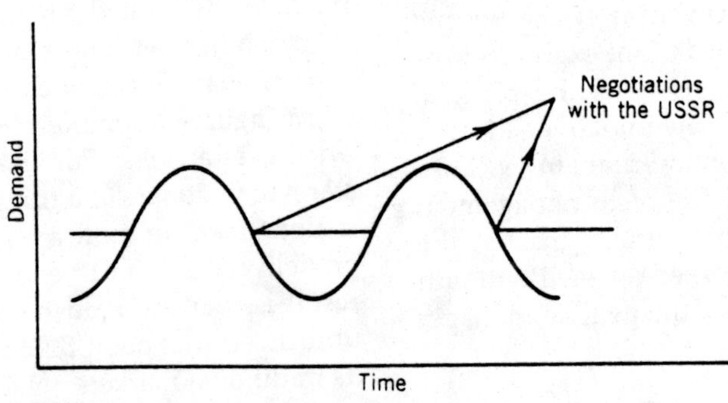

FIGURE 4

However, the Russians prefer to negotiate at the bottom of the cycle because that puts them in a better bargaining position.

Trade shows are the major form of promotion for B. & S., and their stand on the Moscow trade fair has always been a great success. The Russians try to get their hands on practically every machine on exhibition. The question is how to develop this market to its full potential taking into account their government restrictions and the unpredictability and, therefore, instability of the market.

EXHIBIT 1
Organization chart corporate structure

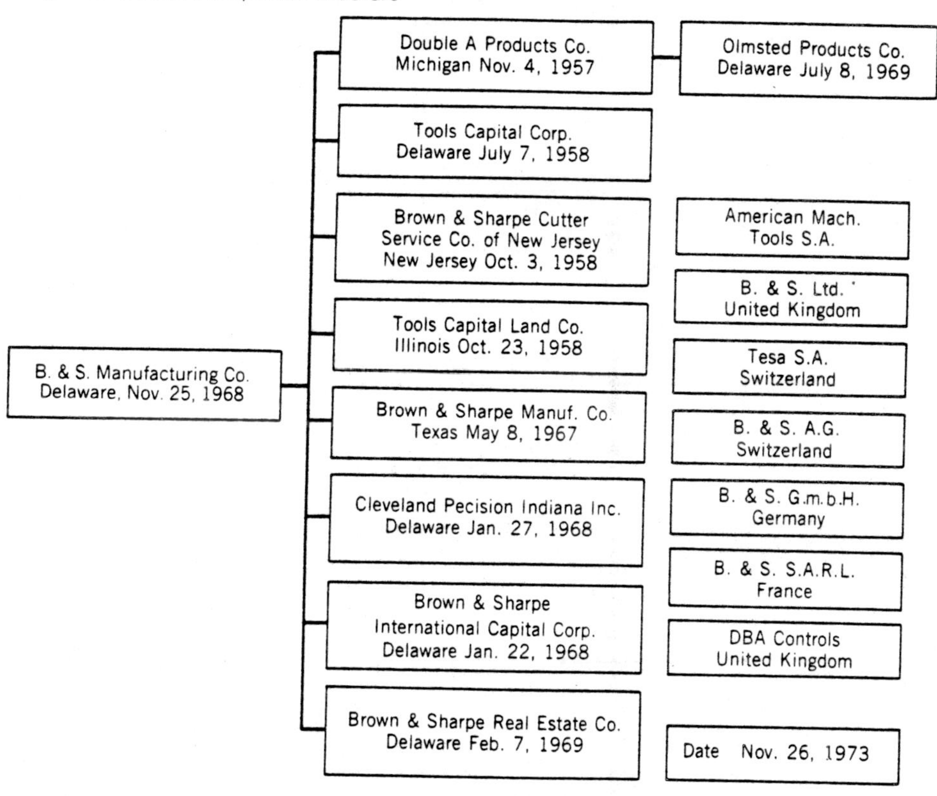

EXHIBIT 2
Organization chart

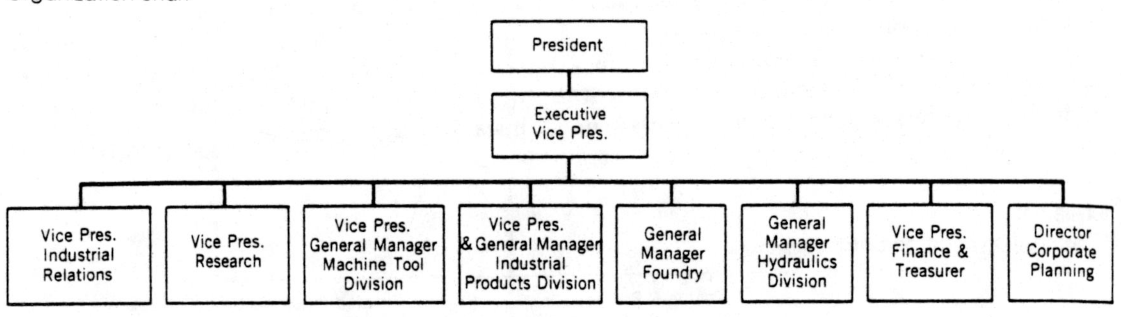

EXHIBIT 3
Organization chart machine tool division

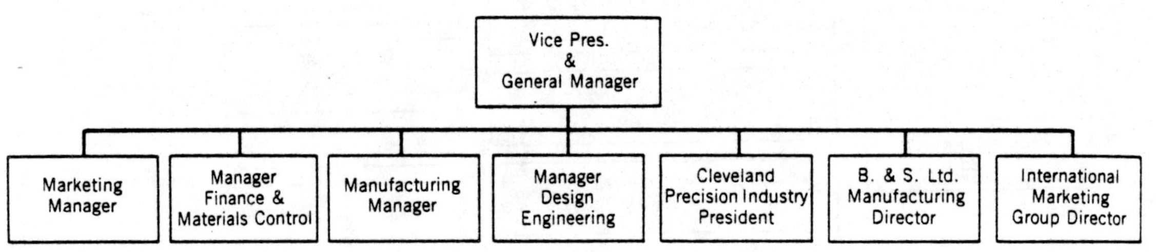

EXHIBIT 4
Metal-working machinery

	Revenues 1975 000	*% change yr ago*	*Net income 1975 000*	*% change profits as yr ago*	*% of sales 1975*	*1974*
Industry Average:		+4.1		−7.8	3.6	4.0
Cincinnati Milacron Inc.	$450,188	−0.6	$9,946	−3.1	2.2	2.3
Warner & Swasey Co.	251,888	−3.7	7,050	−15.6	2.8	3.4
Acme-Cleveland Corp.	234,323	+36.4	6,955	−21.8	3.0	3.3
Kearney & Trecker Corp.	90,449	+31.2	8,369	+76.4*	9.3	6.9
Brown & Sharpe Mfg. Co.	86,871	−12.8	(2,265)	—	—	3.6
Gleason Works	83,530	+1.0	2,050	—	2.5	—

Source: "Industry Week," March 22, 1976.
*An extraordinary credit or charge, represents at least 10% of net income.

EXERCISE 16–5

Prepare an analysis of the B. & S. case in terms of strengths, weaknesses, values, management objectives and all of the factors related to the development of business strategies that we have discussed in earlier chapters.

- What do you believe to be B. & S.'s principal competitive advantage? Explain.
- Explain how this advantage might be of assistance in exploring foreign markets.
- Examine the global strategy depicted by the diagram in Figure 2 of the case. Evaluate the wisdom of this strategy, first in conventional strategy-formulation terms, then in light of the analytic framework developed in this chapter.
- To what extent does trade with controlled economies help or hurt the B. & S. company?
- To what extent does U.S. foreign policy affect the business of B. & S.?
- What might be done by B. & S. to escape or avoid the effects of U.S. foreign policy?
- What might be the political, ethical, or moral issues involved in such a circumvention of official U.S. government policies? Explain.

We have now discussed environmental factors that are of importance to the strategist in the host country. We shall next examine the reasons for an organization's entree into international trade and some of the structures used to assist in the execution of chosen strategies.

ORGANIZATIONAL STRUCTURES AND THE MULTINATIONAL FIRM

Organizational structuring in the multinational firm follows many of the same dynamics discussed in Chapter 13. Organizations respond to the requirements of size, the environment in which they are embedded, and to the goal-attainment needs described by their strategists. As many (if not most) multinational firms grow out of extensions of the interests and needs of domestic companies seeking raw materials or markets, most forays into international trade evolve out of searches for materials through the purchasing or operations function or from explorations for new customers by the marketing function.

A persuasive theoretical framework for the examination and development of organizational structure for the multinational firm incorporates four broad classes of strategy:

1 *Volume expansion* emphasizes an increase in the flow of products to new markets

in other countries. It involves the export of finished goods to markets remote from the production sites in the home country. It may be limited initially to the employment of sales agents or locally owned outlets. Carried out more extensively, this strategy may involve a large-scale sales and distribution effort designed to support an intensive marketing campaign.

2 *Resource acquisition* involves a flow of resources *into* the home country. It is an adaptation of vertical integration and is used to secure low-cost materials. The foreign operation is often characterized by its extractive, labor-intensive nature. Capital investment will be made only to the minimum extent necessary to carry out operations overseas. The operation will be managed in a spare, relatively mechanistic manner by a limited number of expatriate managers.

3 *Reciprocity,* in its simplest form, involves only two countries and an exchange of goods and services between the two. In a reciprocal arrangement, resources again flow into the home country. In this case, however, the local country typically processes raw material (with cheap labor) and thereby adds value to the goods shipped. In a more complex reciprocal arrangement, goods acquired in one country may be shipped to another for processing and then on to a third country for use or for further conversion. In the reciprocity strategy, the production of local administrative and management to operations personnel will be higher than in either of the two strategies described earlier. Communications will tend to be multidirectional. As the reciprocal network becomes more complex, greater decision-making autonomy is needed in the local offices. Organizations tend to become less mechanistic and more flexible in meeting organizational needs as they arise.

4 *Integrated operations,* is a strategy in which local organizations serve as profit centers. Foreign and domestic markets are given equal weight in decision making. Products and services are adapted to meet the needs of local or regional markets. The organization is staffed with a large proportion of local management personnel. A high degree of autonomy exists within broad parameters established by the home office. The local organization structure is fully developed, with the full range of business functions represented.[4]

Table 16–2 briefly summarizes the suggested effects of these four multinational corporate strategies on the structure of local operations.

The Culpepper Tackle, Inc., case is used to help in examining (by means of this framework) the home/local organizational issues involved in entering an international market. Before reading the case, refer to Table 16–2 to refresh your memory about the types of strategy and some of the dimensions of local structural implications. When you have finished reading the case, answer the questions that follow it.

[4] T. T. Herbert, "Strategy and Multinational Organization Structure: An Interorganizational Relationships Perspective" *Academy of Management Review* 9(2) (1984), pp. 259–71.

TABLE 16–2
Home/local structural implications of strategy

Local structural implications	*Strategy*			
	Volume expansion	*Resource acquisition*	*Reciprocity*	*Integrated operations*
Structure type	Functional line	Functional line; wide span of control	Functional/product; line-and-staff	Functional/divisional
Formalization	Bureaucratic	Bureaucratic	Somewhat less bureaucratic	Less bureaucratic
Decision locus	Home	Home	Policy-home; operations-local	Local
Staff locus	Home	Home	Small local staff	Local
Communication	One-way	One-way	Two-way, lateral	Two-way
Control	Tight; loose local operations	Tight	Looser	General
Performance measures	Quantitative, cost	Quantitative, cost center	Profit or cost center; somewhat less rigid or quantitative	Profit center; ROI
Managerial personnel	Few; most locals	Expatriates	Larger administrative component; expatriate/local mix	Locals
Home office relationship	Close control by home office	Close control by home office	Less close control by home office	Loose; autonomous operations within policy
Output	Limited product line	Limited product line	Limited product line	Full line
Investment/profits policy	Bare-bones investment; repatriation of profits	Bare-bones investment; repatriation of profits	Greater investment; local investment of profits	Local investment and capital sources

CULPEPPER TACKLE, INC., AND THE CENTRAL AMERICAN OPERATIONS

Culpepper Tackle, Inc., is a diversified manufacturer of fishing lures and accessories with principal manufacturing facilities and corporate headquarters located in the Southwest. One-hundred percent of the capital stock of Culpepper Tackle, Culpepper Manufacturing, and Draper Tackle is owned by Olin Culpepper, who is the president and chief executive officer of all three companies in addition to being chairman of the board of the three companies. Olin Culpepper, age 50, is an aggressive, hard working individual who compensated for his lack of formal education beyond high school by dedicating himself to provide a quality product to his customers. Olin is an extremely religious individual who is a deacon in his local Baptist church. He is also involved in matters of civic nature and is looked upon in the community with a great deal of admiration and respect.

HISTORY OF THE COMPANY

Culpepper started his company on savings he had accumulated as a fishing guide. His first manufacturing facility was located in the basement of his home, where he poured lead jigs and spinner baits. His operation was truly the "mom and pop" type organization with his wife, Edna, getting much of the credit for the early successes of the company. Olin likes to tell of the early days when he would attend fishing shows and expositions with his "product in his pocket."

Culpepper Tackle continued to grow throughout the 1960's and in 1967, Culpepper moved into its present facility. Due to the increased sales growth of the company, many additions have been made since the initial move.

Olin maintains an excellent rapport with his 100 employees. He abhors the typical businessman's image of a suit and tie, and prefers blue jeans and knit shirts. People are constantly amazed at his informality and ability to get along with his employees. Many department heads have been with the company since its beginning, and there is a sense of undivided loyalty to Olin. No union exists within the Culpepper organization, nor has a union organization effort ever been attempted.

Top management at Culpepper includes Olin's brother-in-law, Fred Jenkins, who has been with Olin since 1960; Olin's wife, Edna; Olin's son, Bobby; a CPA, Jerry Wilson; and Billy Joe Monroe, age 29, who directs the sales force. Jenkins serves as the vice-president and in this function oversees much of the production of Culpepper operations, Bobby Culpepper serves in an advertising and promotion capacity, and Edna Culpepper serves as the head of the office staff. Among top management, only Jerry Wilson, the CPA, has a college degree. Mr. Culpepper considers Jenkins, to be his top man; together they have built Culpepper into a nationally known fishing tackle company. The management team is summarized in Exhibit 1.

Most of the individuals employed with Culpepper Tackle are middle-aged women working to supplement their husbands' income. The manufacturing and assembly of fishing lures is very labor intensive, consequently, cost of labor is the primary expenditure involved in producing fishing tackle. There are ten depart-

The research and written case information were presented at a Case Research Symposium and were evaluated by the Case Research Association's Editorial Board. This case was prepared by Mike Garner, Muthuraman Karuppan, Kelly Jennings, Mary Curtis and Bill Stevens under the supervision of Dr. Robert D. Hay of the University of Arkansas as a basis for class discussion.

EXHIBIT 1
Culpepper Tackle management team

Position	*Experience and duties*
Vice-President	Fred Jenkins, brother-in-law to Olin, employed since 1960, oversees production operations.
Office Manager	Edna Culpepper, Olin's wife oversees general office activities.
Controller	Jerry Wilson, CPA, handles financial matters.
Special Projects	Bobby Culpepper, Olin's son has "grown up" in the business.
Sales Supervisor	Billy Joe Monroe, an old acquaintance of Olin's, has "repped" for many other sporting goods companies.

ment heads; they report directly to the vice president, Fred Jenkins, whom they like and admire. The departments, in manufacturing process sequence are: (1) raw materials, (2) weighting, pinning, and glueing, (3) in-process storage, (4) racking for painting, (5) painting, (6) hooking, (7) packaging, (8) boxing, (9) finished goods storage, (10) shipping. A manufacturing flow chart appears in Exhibit 2 and a simplified plant layout is shown in Exhibit 3.

MANAGEMENT PHILOSOPHY

Olin has always prided himself at being involved in every aspect of his business. He negotiates the yearly working capital loan from the local bank; assists in production; does all the major hiring, but will delegate any dismissal functions; is in constant demand because of his position as a promotion man for the company; and when there is any major decision to be made, Olin is the one who makes it. He looks down at individuals who are negative in approach to the ideas he values and believes are profitable to the firm. The salesmen in the field often ask to speak to Olin when any problem arises, and as a result Billy Joe Monroe is bypassed in his role as supervisor of sales. Mr. Culpepper recognizes a potential problem since Monroe has failed to win the respect of many of the salesmen who represent Culpepper.

PRODUCT RESEARCH AND DEVELOPMENT

In no other area is the company more dependent on Olin than in the area of research and development. Mr. Culpepper has developed and patented 90 percent of the lures currently sold by Culpepper Tackle, Inc.; he rarely markets a new idea that is not his own. He primarily develops his lures by first "whittling the prototype out of wood" and sending it to have a mold and other requirements made. He tests the lures at the lake below the plant for its functioning accuracy, and if satisfied with its performance, he puts it into production. He is also constantly working in new colors for the lures in an attempt to give the fishermen a wide variety of colors and selections. His stated primary goals are to (1) satisfy the fisherman, and (2) make a reasonable profit doing it. He has established the policy of sending two new lures back to the fisherman for every one returned because of defective workmanship. He also prints on his packaging that he welcomes any comments from fishermen on his lures and appreciates any suggestions on how he might improve them. Olin tries to price his product "at the market" because of the competitive nature of the product

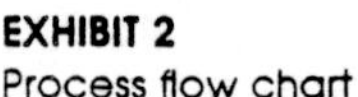

EXHIBIT 2
Process flow chart

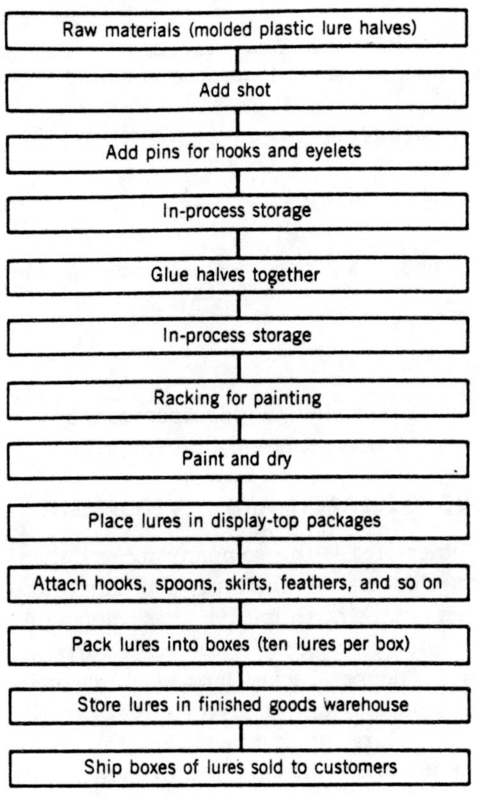

and the unyielding supply of foreign lures which are marketed on the American scene.

PRESENT MARKETING PROCEDURE

Currently, Culpepper has no factory salesmen. Each region of the United States is handled by independent sales organization rep groups. For example, Louisiana, Mississippi, Arkansas, and Oklahoma are currently being serviced by a two-man rep group. Texas, which delivers the largest percentage of Culpepper sales, is serviced by another two-man rep group. Although salesmen are paid ten percent of gross collections, no attempt is made to hold salesmen responsible for bad accounts. Insurance on all accounts is required by the lending institution, thus, cutting down on losses from bad debts. Fifty percent of Culpepper sales are made to major jobbers or wholesalers, who in turn sell to small retailers. Major customers, such as K-Mart, Walmart, Woolworth, and Sears, purchase directly from the factory on special pricing terms worked out by Olin with the buyers from these chains. Sales figures for the most popular products through all channels are listed in Exhibit 4.

Each August when the industry's major trade exposition is held in Chicago, Olin attempts to get his business "booked" at the exposition, which aids in the planning of his production requirements. In exchange, Culpepper gives early advantages, such as extra discounts, to those companies that will make commitments for January shipments. Usually the buyer will receive his shipment in two parts, around the 1st of October and the 1st of January.

DECISIONS AND EVENTS IN THE HISTORY OF THE COMPANY

In early 1970, Olin began looking at ways to expand the sales of his company. Bass fishing, along with other forms of outdoor recreation, was growing by leaps and bounds. National tournaments, in which large cash prizes were offered, had generated interest in the sport of fishing. According to the U.S. Fish and Wildlife Services, in 1976, there were nearly 54 million anglers in the United States. Sixty-nine percent of them were men. Fishing ranked No. 1 as the participant sport for men and No. 2 for women. Forty-nine percent of all anglers were pan fishers, mainly fishermen who fish from the shore or boat, with a worm (or other bait) on the hook, hoping to land the small tasty fish that fit so well into a frying pan. Bass fishermen who cast in warm waters account for about twenty-seven percent. The remainder are anglers who

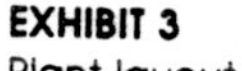

EXHIBIT 3
Plant layout.

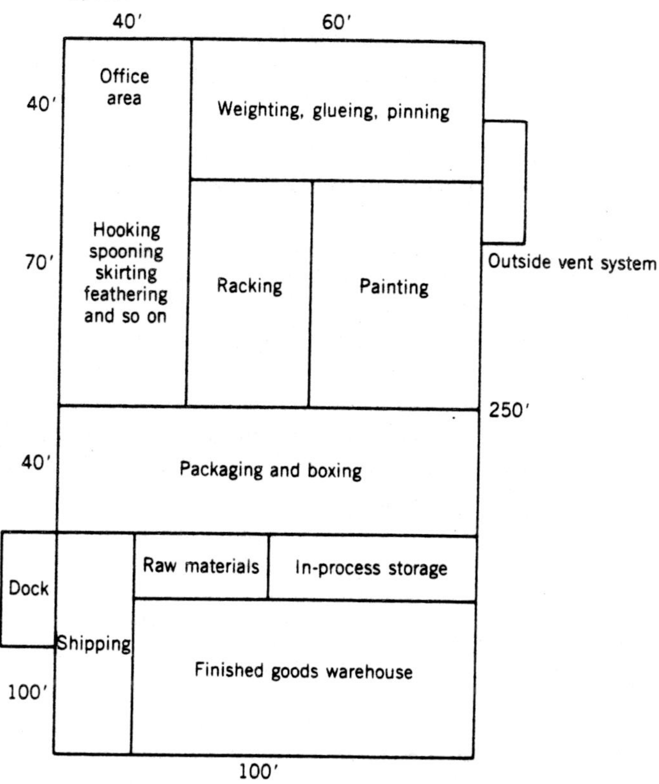

EXHIBIT 4

Year	*Grabber*	*Hotshot*	*Silverein*	*Supper blade*	*By-god*	*Spinner*
1966		648,000	730,000			
1967		840,000	850,000	410,000	81,000	
1968		945,000	830,000	470,000	110,000	
1969		1,030,000	830,000	432,000	132,000	36,850
1970		930,000	810,000	415,000	162,600	38,975
1971		838,000	785,000	403,000	162,600	55,400
1972		769,000	730,000	403,000	172,400	58,675
1973		687,000	735,000	375,000	163,800	51,740
1974	2,100,000	692,000	700,000	300,000	160,080	52,950
1975	1,938,000	525,000	525,000	275,000	161,500	68,460
1976	2,348,000	510,000	473,333	286,000	158,600	69,750
1977	2,432,000	400,000	440,000	290,000	151,750	70,625
1978	2,240,000	480,000	430,000	265,000	149,650	71,790

work cold waters, seeking trout among other fish.

Although the number of fishing licenses sold in the United States has been steadily increasing, the dollar amounts spent by anglers have more than doubled during the same period (1970–1978). Olin firmly believed that these factors coupled with the increase in population and disposable income was a definite plus for the industry (Exhibit 5).

Olin was extremely concerned about foreign competition, especially from the Japanese, but believed there was enough business for everyone. To maintain his market position, Olin believed he should try to diversify his operations and transfer his established name to other fishing related products.

Boats and Trailers

With this in mind, Olin entered the very lucrative, but highly competitive bass boat market. A building, with a designed capacity of ten boats per day, was constructed at the site of the lure manufacturing facility. Molds were ordered, and production officially began in June of 1970. Problems soon developed in the manufacturing processes, and in September 1970, the company was still only producing two boats a day. Olin's policy has always been to hire local labor; consequently the personnel involved in the manufacture of the "Bass Bomber" had little experience in this field, and the turnover of employees became a serious problem. Many believed that the attention which Olin was giving to his boat project would in turn hurt his lure operation. Luckily this was not the case, although Olin wished he had never thought about the boat production. In addition, the dealer network for the distribution of the boats failed to materialize in the manner in which Olin had hoped. The dealers, whom Olin believed were firmly committed, decided to handle other established boat lines. In addition, Olin had many "friends" who were forever wanting a "good deal" on a boat, and it was difficult for him to turn them down. When Olin received a visit from an OSHA official in 1972 telling him that his boat operation did not comply with government standards, this seemed like another stab in the back.

At the same time that Olin had entered the boat market, he also began the manufacture of boat trailers, on which he held a design patent. This manufacturing operation fared somewhat better than the boat production.

Olin has long wondered whether this entire operation should be eliminated completely or improved sufficiently to remove all the related problems. Jerry Wilson estimated that the operation could be sold at a net loss of $150,000.

EXHIBIT 5

	Sales (millions)					
Year	*Industry*	*Culpepper*	*U.S. disposable income (millions)*	*Fishing licenses sold in the U.S. (millions)*	*Cost to anglers (millions)*	*U.S. population (millions)*
1971	617.26	2.33	686,000	31.1	91	207.1
1972	698.87	2.60	801,000	33.0	107	208.8
1973	733.82	3.03	985,000	33.5	118	210.4
1974	770.50	3.10	1,074,000	34.3	128	211.9
1975	809.03	3.86	1,186,000	34.7	142	213.6
1976	849.48	4.11	1,309,000	34.9	155	215.1
1977	891.96	4.30	1,455,000	36.0	167	216.2
1978	936.55	5.08	1,601,000	36.8	179	218.3

Maintaining Plastic Supplies

In 1974, reacting to reports that plastic would soon be in short supply due to a shortage of petroleum, Olin went into the open market where he was forced to buy inferior plastic at astronomical prices. He purchased 1,000,000 pounds of raw plastic at $.50 per pound. Much to his dismay, supplies in 1975 were plentiful, with prices falling to around $.30 a pound.

Draper Tackle Acquired

In 1974, Culpepper Tackle acquired Draper Tackle, a division of Brunswick Corporation. Draper Tackle manufactured jigs and was an established name in the jig market as much as Culpepper was in the hard lure market. Olin had known the original developer of Draper Lures, Sonny Draper, before he sold the company to Brunswick. Brunswick was discouraged with the performance of this subsidiary and contacted Olin about a possible acquisition of the entire inventory, assets, and equipment. Olin and Jenkins travelled to Nashville, Tennessee, where the company was located, and were impressed with all the latest equipment that Brunswick had acquired for the company, although Olin thought it was probably too fancy. Olin hypothesized that the cost of Draper Tackle had probably "eaten them up" and the company had probably gotten lost in the large corporate hierarchy of Brunswick. He also felt that Brunswick lacked the management expertise in this area. Negotiations between Olin, Brunswick, and Olin's banker resulted in a sale of Draper Tackle to Culpepper for $200,000. Olin believed he had practically stolen the company, because he estimated that the value of the equipment alone exceeded the amount paid for the company, not to mention getting a company well established in a market in which Olin wanted to be a leader. To the surprise of many, Draper Tackle operated profitably, but Olin wondered if it would be better to sell the line to independent salesmen (those not selling Culpepper products).

Fishing Rods and Plastic Worms

In 1975, Culpepper Tackle entered two new markets: fishing rods and plastic worms. Both were highly competitive and required a large initial investment. However, Olin believed with the proper promotion and product development he could make inroads into the market of such leaders as Fenwick and Shakespeare, and Childer. Culpepper's rod, "Whip Stick," was produced on a subcontract basis with area women doing the wrappings of the rods in their homes.

Initial acceptance of the "Whip stick" was good, although the $75 sales price was somewhat above the competition. Olin had made the decision to let the present salesmen, who sold his lures, also sell his rods, since they could give the sales presentation for the rods while they were selling lures. The only problem was that Olin paid commissions of seven percent on rods whereas a commission of ten percent was paid on lures. He soon realized that the primary salesmen's emphasis would be on lures, overlooking the sales pitch for his rods. He wondered whether he should (1) let a different set of reps sell his rods, (2) increase the commission to ten percent which would increase the price of his rod beyond competition, or (3) get out of the rod business. Olin had reduced the sales price of rods, but the 1978 sale of rods was less than $200,000 (see Exhibit 6). Jerry Wilson estimated the company probably would lose $10,000 on rods when the final figures were complete.

EXHIBIT 6

Year	*Rods*
1975	37,300
1976	22,250
1977	12,340
1978	5,320

Similar circumstances existed with the worm line. Culpepper began marketing a worm called the "rattletail worm" and the initial response from buyers was positive. For some reason, salesmen were reluctant to sell the worm, despite the ten percent sales commission. This was discouraging to Olin.

The Computer

By 1975, Jerry Wilson was pressuring Olin to lease a system 3 IBM computer for about $2,000 a month. Adams felt that invoices, inventories, payroll, and raw materials could be done more efficiently and effectively with this tool. Although Olin resisted this pressure due to the extra cost and his lack of understanding of what he referred to as an "idiot machine," he grudgingly agreed after the accountant agreed to oversee its operation in order to cut expenses. The possibility of leasing some of the available time to other firms also influenced his decision.

The Move to Metric

In 1977, Culpepper believed the country was moving to "metric." At the time, all hard lures were being sold in dozen packs, and if Olin were to change to metric, he would be the innovator by going to ten-count packs. Olin believed the whole changeover could be done for $10,000, but serious concerns were voiced by Jenkins and the others that it would be one tremendous hassle and costs would be high. The company went to a metric system in late 1977. Buyer acceptance was slow, due to a lack of education in the metric system, but Olin foresaw a growing acceptance. Weights and sizes of lures were listed in both ounces and grams.

THE GRABBER

In early 1974, the biggest thing to hit the fishing market happened. An elderly man in Tennessee had developed a revolutionary lure that set the fishing world buzzing. Called the Grabber, it was hand carved and caught many fish. National publications such as *Sports Afield* and *Outdoor Life* did cover stories on the lure and hailed as the "lure of the 70's." People were paying up to $15 a day just to rent the lure and to lose one would cost $50. The problem for the elderly man was his inability to make the lure fast enough to supply the overwhelming demand. Culpepper, along with several other manufacturers, anxiously sought the manufacturing rights to the lure. Olin managed to secure the exclusive rights to the lure after extensive negotiations with the inventor. Olin agreed to pay the man a per dozen royalty on all sold and on any adaptations which Culpepper might later make to the lure. Everything was set for mass production of the lure, and Olin set out to secure a design patent.

The demand for the Grabber lure outstripped the capacity of the Culpepper manufacturing facilities. Also there was a crucial time lag between the molding of the lure, which was being done in Chicago and the actual receipt of it back in the home plant. It was at this point that Olin began serious consideration of establishing his own molding company. He was acquainted with a German tool maker in Chicago named Olson who was interested in establishing his own operation. Olson had accumulated, since his emigration from Germany before the war, $50,000 that he was willing to invest as part of the initial capital outlay. Olin contributed $50,000 and the Culson Corporation was established with equal ownership between Olin and Olson.

One year later, Olin began noticing that it was taking Olson longer and longer to deliver the molded lures. This was partly the fault of Olin because he had in the interim designed a self-watering plastic flower pot. Sales of this item were beyond expectation and so to keep up with the demand, the production run for Culpepper's lures was decreased. To further compound matters Olson had accepted orders from Timex and AMF for moulded plastic casings.

Financial statements for both Culpepper Tackle and Culson Corporation are shown in Exhibits 7 and 8, respectively.

EXHIBIT 7
Culpepper Manufacturing, Inc., and Consolidated Subsidiaries condensed comparative balance sheet

	For the year ended Dec. 31	
	1978	*1977*
Assets		
Current assets		
Cash	$ 475,214.08	$ 433,667.72
Accounts rec.	190,459.18	146,484.84
Note rec.	-0-	47,689.05
Inventory	2,066,389.95	1,464,554.24
Prepaid expenses	6,377.83	3,932.60
Prepaid income tax	66,141.60	-0-
Deposit on equip. purch.	10,500.00	-0-
Total current assets	$2,815,082.64	$2,096,328.45
Fixed assets		
Buildings, equip. and other	1,537,342.46	$ 822,821.33
Less allow. for depreciation	358,659.15	237,723.63
Total fixed assets	$1,164,683.31	$ 585,097.70
Other assets		
Notes rec. now current	-0-	73,097.70
Investment in stock	4,200.00	4,200.00
Patents and trademarks	11,471.25	2,145.90
Misc. inventories	-0-	2,384.20
Advances to affil. foreign co.	-0-	55,675.41
Advances to stockholder	15,029.35	-0-
Utility deposits	350.00	830.90
Total assets	$4,010,816.55	$2,819,760.26
Liabilities and capital		
Current liabilities		
Accounts payable	$ 279,384.90	$ 351,960.00
Notes payable	881,039.39	899,973.20
Accrued expenses	381,191.90	214,537.15
Federal and state income payable	-0-	214,213.37
Total current liabilities	$1,541,616.19	$1,680,683.92
Long-term liabilities		
Long-term debt excluding current installments	1,043,550.69	361,607.40
Other liabilities		
Advances from stockholder	-0-	4,570.69
Total liabilities	$2,585,165.88	$2,046,862.01

(continued)

EXHIBIT 7 *(continued)*
Culpepper Manufacturing, Inc., and Consolidated Subsidiaries condensed comparative balance sheet

	For the year ended Dec. 31	
	1978	*1977*
Capital		
Common stock, no par value		
1,000 shares authorized		
200 shares issued	28,000.00	28,000.00
Retained earnings	1,397,649.67	744,898.25
Total capital	$1,425,649.67	$ 772,898.25
Total liabilities and capital	$4,010,816.55	$2,819,760.26
Gross operating income		
Sales of merchandise	$5,075,236.10	$4,301,235,69
Other income	28,163.56	9,508.76
Total	$5,103,399.66	$4,310,744.45
Cost of sales		
Cost of manuf. goods sold	2,818,445.15	2,839,100.14
Excise taxes	341,638.92	403,082.33
Manufacturing royalties	45,013.42	77,751.30
Total	3,205,097.49	3,319,933.77
Gross operating profit	1,898,302.17	990,810.68
Operating expenses	394,927.16	164,010.64
Net operating income	1,503,375.01	826,800.04
Other deductions (net)	200,670.57	88,635.20
Net income before income taxes	1,302,704.44	738,164.84
Income taxes	791,351.40[a]	370,042.67
Net income to retained earnings	$ 511,353.04	$ 368,122.17

[a]Includes additional assessment from years 1974–1976.

CENTRAL AMERICAN OPERATIONS

In a little over six months, one million of the Grabber lures were sold to distributors. Combined with the needed capacity of the other lure operations and assembly, Culpepper realized he must find other manufacturing facilities. He had heard from a mutual friend that a Central American country was extremely interested in acquiring U.S. industries. Olin made an initial visit to the country with Fred Jenkins and was very impressed with the possibility of establishing a plant there. Labor rates were very low, $5 per person per 12 hour day, and considering the labor intensive product Culpepper Tackle produced, this option seemed very advantageous.

In order to minimize the capital investment of the company, Olin believed, initially it would probably be wise to lease manufacturing facilities rather than purchase the land and build. He also hoped to transfer his rod operation facility after the lure operation was well established.

In late 1976, a building was leased and Fred Jenkins was sent to set up the plant and train the locals. Raw materials were shipped via a plane from New Orleans. (See Appendix A for additional details from Fred Jenkins.) Communication problems and a coordination of raw material shipments slowed shipments of finished products back to the United States.

The political situation was very bad and the U.S. Embassy would often call Jenkins to warn him not to leave his home during the night for fear of terrorist action.

Olin was pleased with the quality of the product he was receiving from the Central American country, and expressed his desire that operations there be expanded to include a wider range of Culpepper lures. The plant there employed 140 people. A breakdown on the manu-

EXHIBIT 8
Culson Corporation condensed balance sheet

	For the year ended Dec. 31	
	1978	*1977*
Assets		
Current assets		
Cash	$ 572,138.00	$ 356,237.00
Inventories	312,842.60	214,106.20
Other	15,358.00	8,932.00
Total current assets	$ 900,338.60	$ 579,275.20
Fixed assets		
Property, plant and equipment	1,761,569.60	1,601,969.60
Accumulated depreciation	618,011.80	351,227.80
Total fixed assets	$1,143,557.80	$1,250,741.80
Other assets	21,611.80	17,883.60
Deferred charges	81,415.60	91,539.00
Total assets	2,146,923.80	1,939,439.60
Liabilities and capital		
Current liabilities		
Accounts payable and accrued expenses	247,067.80	158,041.80
Notes payable	122,733.80	209,791.40
Total current liabilities	369,801.60	367,833.20
Long-term debt	1,144,691.80	1,149,825.60
Total liabilities	1,514,493.40	1,417,658.80
Capital		
Capital stock	140,000.00	140,000.00
Retained earnings	492,430.40	281,780.80
Total capital	632,430.40	421,780.80
Total liabilities and capital	$2,146,923.80	$1,939,439.60

EXHIBIT 8 *(continued)*
Condensed income statement

	For the year ended Dec. 31	
	1978	*1977*
Gross operating income		
Plastic molding	$2,795,660.00	$1,716,400.00
Tooling sales and services	585,410.00	432,460.00
Less: discounts	(13,979.00)	(8,582.00)
Total	3,367,091.00	2,140,278.00
Cost of sales	2,642,743.60	1,751,302.00
Gross operating profit	724,347.40	388,976.00
Operating expenses	229,196.80	183,999.20
Net operating income	495,150.60	204,976.80
Other deductions		
Interest expenses	105,177.80	34,553.40
Amortization	9,934.40	-0-
Total	115,112.20	34,553.40
Net income before taxes	380,038.40	170,423.40
Provision for income taxes	169,388.80	33,619.60
Net income to retained earnings	$ 210,649.60	$ 136,803.80

facturing cost for Grabber between the domestic and the Central American plant is given in Exhibit 9.

There were several problems regarding the Central American operations. The cost of transportation was increasing, communication problems between the two locations were difficult, political unrest there continued, and, most importantly, the operations were occupying too much of Jenkins' time. Olin returned the much needed Jenkins to the United States when he trained an SMU graduate, a native, to take over the operations there. Also a telex system was established to allow closer contact.

As sales continued to grow in 1978, Olin wondered whether he should try to expand operations in South America or in light of the political situation and rising costs, pull out completely. Several U.S. businessmen had been kidnapped and killed and terrorist activity was rampant.

Olin was also concerned about maintaining his overall market share, which traditionally had fluctuated around 3 percent. Another major area of concern facing Olin was the subject of alternative ways of financing future growth, if any.

EXHIBIT 9
Breakdown on cost — Grabber

	Domestic	*Central American*[a]
Raw materials	.21	.21
Glueing	.08	.03
Painting	.15	.06
Hooking	.07	.03
Packaging	.05	.03
Subtotal	.56	.36
Transportation		.03
Duty		.02
Total	.56 cents	.41 cents

[a]The Central American plant produces ¾ of the Grabbers sold in the U.S., and the Grabber retails locally at 90 cents.

APPENDIX A

ADDITIONAL INFORMATION CONCERNING CULPEPPER TACKLE, INC., AND CONSOLIDATED SUBSIDIARIES (REPORTED BY VICE-PRESIDENT)

Our plant in Central America was approved for a ten-year period. During this period, we have the right to ship merchandise and materials there without any duty whatsoever. However, there are a few things we have to comply with as follows:

1 A strict account procedure must be maintained for their government so that we can prove to them at anytime that the raw materials we ship there come back to the United States, or they are in inventory there. In the case of machinery and equipment, we must be able to show them where it is or what disposition has been made of it.

2 We are not allowed to sell any of our products or equipment in the Central American market.

At the end of the ten-year duty free period, this agreement may be renewed upon application and at the discretion of their government (and their government is a lot more cooperative than ours; the only drawback is that most of their accounting and legal procedures are the same as when Columbus visited them).

TRANSPORTATION

Our Central American country is bounded by 3 other nations and the Pacific Ocean. Most boat shipments are made from Houston and New Orleans on cargo transports. These are usually container shipments and have to go through a port in Guatemala — overland by truck to our country. This is to limit the expense of using the Panama Canal and reduce the amount of time in transit. This is the least expensive way of transporting raw materials and merchandise, and it has a cost of .05 cents per pound in a minimum shipment of 2,000 pounds. This, on the surface, seems cheap, but we have to get this material to New Orleans either by commercial carrier or our truck and this adds another .05 cents. When the cargo arrives in Guatemala, it is placed on a cargo transport and goes overland. When this truck reaches the border, it is also met by a customs guard and he rides with this shipment until it is delivered to our plant door. The seal is broken and the material unloaded.

Commercial trucks are also available to Dallas but we were always afraid to try this because of the long journey through Mexico.

The cargo rates are fantastic by air, $.18 per lb. from the U.S. and $.12 per lb. on their return. Where fast service is essential and our shipments are needed in a hurry, we ship by air. In fact, 90 percent of our shipments are air freight. Sometimes though, to ship by air is not necessarily faster than boat, because of the complicated customs procedures. It takes one full-time employee to handle shipments with customs. It can take three days to a week to clear customs with a shipment and the time it takes is controlled more or less by the temperament of the customs officials. We have never had to pay a bribe that is so common in Mexico, but the paperwork involved is unbelievable.

LABOR

Our plant is located in a country of 4½ million people. Unemployment is possibly the highest in the world, and the density of population is second only to Japan.

When we set up the company, we had four stockholders, Olin, myself, Alfredo and Ricardo Garcia. We had included two nationals from that country as it is best to have them in case of political takeovers, etc. They will usually not bother a company that has some control by their own people. In the near future, we will see if this helps or not.

Everyday we have from 40 to 100 people outside the plant seeking employment. This in itself keeps your employees on the ball as they all know there is someone outside to replace them. The natives are a very hard working, trainable people, and are the best workers I have been around.

When a person is hired it is as follows:

1 At a rate of $4.80 per day upon completion of a 90–120 day training period. Their government gives us a break in that we pay a reduced rate on labor of approximately $3.00 per day, until such time as the employee becomes productive.

2 When an employee reaches a permanent status we,
   a. Sign this employee to a contract of one year.
   b. Must pay those employees every day they come to the plant.
   c. Are obligated, if an employee is present six days a week to recognize that this entitles [him or her] to receive pay for the seventh day even though [he or she does] not work (we have very few absences from work because of this).
   d. Must give each employee a bonus of one month's pay for every year worked. This is the reason that we sign contracts for one year only.
   e. Give two weeks vacation for every full year.
   f. Agree that permanent status entitles the employee to social security benefits which includes hospitalization and the right to apply for government housing. This cost is paid by our company.

FINANCIAL

It takes from $8,000 to $10,000 a week to keep the plant in operation and to take care of the overhead. Bear in mind that this is labor cost only as we furnish all the raw materials. We have set up prices that we pay the plant on the basis of what is done—whether it is complete, etc. We try to operate the plant there on a break-even basis with a small reserve.

We pay Alfredo $.15 per line when he glues it, paints it, hooks and packages it. We pay him $.03 for a complete jig packaged. We pay him from $.03 to $.08 for glueing bodies and $.01 for pouring lead heads.

The labor cost involved with our plant on the same item is about 70 percent less than our U.S. labor cost. So if we are receiving merchandise that has a labor cost of 30 percent of what we can do here, we have a lot of room left for transportation and other overhead costs.

The best I have been able to figure as to the values is that when the products are shipped to us, we can expect to sell these at approximately 60 percent more than the labor cost of Alfredo's invoices.

We employ 140 workers at the plant.

EXERCISE 16–6

Identify the type of strategy being used by Mr. Olin. Use the categories of strategic types found in Table 16–2. Explain.

- Describe in a three- to four-page typewritten paper the local structural implications of this strategy on Culpepper's Central American unit. Be explicit and describe how you will assure that these structural components will be accomplished.
- Draw the organization chart for Culpepper suggested by Table 16–2 for this type of strategy.

The International Division is an umbrella designation for an organizational unit that can be used to serve three of the four strategies described in Table 16–2. This form is well suited to resource acquisition, volume expansion, and reciprocal strategies. Where the fully integrated strategy is involved, however, a geographic regional or broad product-group organization form is preferred.

Several general guidelines for organization from *within* the international division have been suggested:

1. Where product lines are relatively similar, an international division organized into geographic regions often provides needed coordination in regions where languages and cultures have similarities.
2. Where product lines are quite different or where they require highly specialized support services, a product-line organization within the international division is preferred.
3. A functional organization form for the international division is used where the superiority of the company lies in a particular function. If, for example, a critical

competitive advantage is the manufacturing capability of the company, retaining functional control over manufacturing would assure that the management of that function would be expert in production, and highly knowledgeable about the details of manufacturing that provide the competitive edge.[5]

EXERCISE 16-7

Your company, Kirschner's Kandies, manufactures an extensive line of candy for sale to supermarkets in the United States. Although your entire product line requires sugar as a principal ingredient, about 40% of the product line is chocolate coated or contains chocolate as an ingredient. Although a significant competitor, your company is much smaller than companies such as Brach or Hershey. Your market share has grown slowly but steadily, an indication of good product acceptance in U.S. markets.

Your production facilities are now in use for two shifts of operations 5 days per week and, therefore, have capacity for additional production. You are concerned about your sources of raw materials. Major users of sugar and cocoa have been engaged in backward vertical integration and extensive use of long-term contracts with their raw materials suppliers.

Your vice president of operations has been unusually astute in his assessments of market conditions for sugar and cocoa, and has been able to handle nearly all purchases through the spot market. He will retire next year and you have no natural replacement for his special skills.

- Suggest a strategy involving international trade which might help you in alleviating this situation. Explain in some detail how you plan to execute this strategy.
- Describe and sketch the organizational structure you would use to help in carrying out your selected strategy.

EXERCISE 16-8

Following several years of operation under the structure described in Exercise 16-7, your marketing vice president has approached you with some thoughts about opening new markets overseas. Domestic markets for sweets have not grown extensively due to dietary and other concerns, and the company's sales have flattened. The marketing vice president visited an international trade show in Europe with a shipment of sample candies and came away impressed by the likelihood of product acceptance in European markets. His samples were quickly used up, and he had

[5] Herbert, "Strategy and Multinational Organization Structure," p. 263.

several inquiries from European distributors about the possibility of handling the Kirschner's Kandies line.

- What kind of international strategy does this situation suggest? Explain.
- How would you organize to carry out the strategy suggested? Sketch the organization chart for this organization.
- If your European sales resulted in a doubling of your present production, what other strategy might you consider? Explain. Describe and sketch a chart for the organization you would recommend to help you to carry out this strategy.

A field study of the organization of 93 U.S. multinational organizations has added another important variable, the extent of dependence of the company on the foreign operation, and has supported the theoretical organizational arrangements suggested by Herbert.[6] It appears that, in practice, multinational firms will make use of a functional organization where product diversity is low regardless of the extent to which the company is dependent on foreign operations. Where the importance of the foreign operation is high and where product diversity increases, the organization will begin to make use of the geographic organizational form, *to a point*. At very high levels of product diversity, the organization will shift to either the international division form or to a product division configuration.

Conglomerates tend to retain the product organization form and do not make use of the area or international organizational form, in part to avoid disturbing the autonomy of their divisions.[7] Figure 16–2 is a graphic representation of the results of this study.

[6] Herbert, "Strategy and Multinational Organization Structure," pp. 259–71.

[7] J. D. Daniels, R. A. Pitts, and M. J. Tretter, "Strategy and Structure of U.S. Multinationals: An Exploratory Study," *Academy of Management Journal* 27(2) (1984), pp. 292–307.

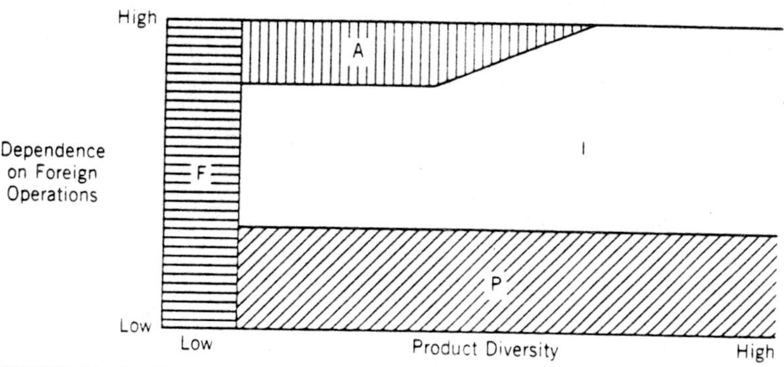

FIGURE 16–2 Structural evolution of nonconglomerate U.S. multinational firms. F = Functional; P = Product; I = International Division; A = Area.

EXERCISE 16-9

Compare the theoretical suggestions of Herbert and the results of the exploratory field study of Daniels, Pitts, and Tretter.

- Where does field research support theory and where does it differ? Explain.
- Build, if you can, a composite set of guidelines for organization design in the multinational organization. (Note: You may wish to incorporate the results of the research of Garnier [referred to earlier] on organizational structure.) Prepare to present your work in class or to hand it in as a written assignment.

WEIRICH SPORTING EQUIPMENT COMPANY*

The Weirich Company, based in the United States, has long been associated with sporting equipment in Europe and Scandinavia, markets that account for approximately 42% of corporate sales, and 50% of profits. As a manufacturer of team sports equipment for baseball, football (American), field hockey, hurling, soccer, and rugby, the product line has been varied by sport, but relatively limited within each sport. Marketing and sales have been accomplished through direct sales contact with team owners and managers by Weirich sales representatives. The Weirich line has maintained a good reputation over the years and contacts established by the Weirich representatives have been longlasting. The company's organization chart is seen in Figure 1.

The company's products now occupy nearly 70% of team markets in the company's international service area. Efforts to expand the share further have been unsuccessful. Although your representatives have been unable to prove it, they feel reasonably sure that your competitors have secured their position by means of kickbacks or other gratuities to purchasing agents or team managers. As a consequence of the flattening of sales in your present markets, you have considered a number of alternatives.

The most attractive, at least initially, is a proposal to broaden your line of products. The marketing department in your Scandinavian area has proposed the expansion of this department's sales by adding new product lines. The products suggested (shoes, specialized clothing, leather products) would make use of Weirich's production facilities and contractors, but it would be marketed to the general public in the case of shoes, to industrial purchasers of clothing to be used for safety protection of employees in hazardous occupations, and to the farm-equipment industry for a variety of leather products used in handling animals.

* This case was prepared by this author

EXERCISE 16-10

- If the recommendations for change are accepted for the Scandinavian department, what organizational changes might be needed? Explain. Sketch the organization chart that would reflect these changes.

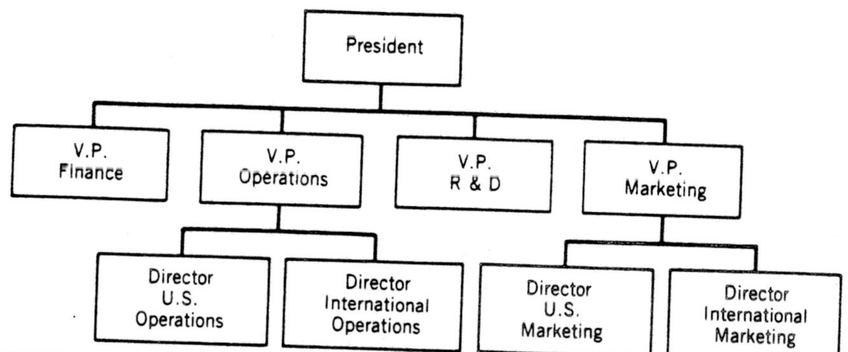

FIGURE 1 Partial organization chart, Weirich Sporting Equipment Co.

- If the recommendations for change are adopted for all parts of the company, what organizational changes might be needed? Explain. Sketch the organization chart that would reflect these changes.

After several years of operation under the newly expanded product line, corporate sales have grown substantially. European and Scandinavian markets now account for 63% of sales and 80% of profit. Sales in the United States have grown, but market share has diminished somewhat, as more aggressive domestic competitors have opened retail outlets for team-sport equipment and have been more aggressively pricing their lines.

Your sales representatives in Europe and Scandinavia have found that several team owners have reached the age where they would like to reduce the scope of their interests. Several have had profitable businesses that they now plan to sell in order that they can spend their later years enjoying the contact with professional sports. Two prospects seem to be particularly appealing:

1 Jules Bisset, owner and sponsor of a team of cyclists in Lyon, is also the owner of a highly successful milling business. His mills serve the needs of bakeries in a large region in that portion of France. He has delegated the management of the firm to Jacques LeClerc, an experienced milling manager and long-term employee who has agreed to remain under contract to manage the firm for a minimum of 5 years in return for a modest equity interest.

2 Pedersen Canneries is a Danish fisheries company owned by Arno Christensen, a sporting enthusiast and part owner of a world-class Danish soccer team. His company is also quite successful, and he has a sizable fleet of fishing craft, two canneries, and an established worldwide reputation and distribution network. Arno has agreed to remain in management during a transition period in which he would complete the development of his replacement who is to be drawn from the higher-level management team of the company.

Each of these possibilities represents a large investment to the company. Weirich has been conservatively run, however, and has acquired large balances in cash and investment accounts. The purchase of either firm, therefore, would not jeopardize the corporation's financial position. If either company were purchased, domestic sales would drop from 37% of corporate totals to approximately 25%.

EXERCISE 16-11

As an organizational consultant to Weirich, what recommendations would you make regarding organization design, given the purchase of either the fisheries or the milling company? Explain your reasoning and describe possible alternate organizations (and draw the charts) for the forms from which you have made your choice.

As this chapter concludes, we should reflect on the additional complexities introduced by business involvement in different nations. As we have seen, the interest in foreign trade can arise through the search for resources or markets. The search for appropriate trading partners, however, is complicated by a range of economic, social, political, cultural, and lingual dimensions. In part because of the risks involved in foreign trade, the risks related to the extent of capital investment are affected by political concerns as well as by market factors. Organizational governance patterns are affected by social, political, and long-range business strategic concerns. Structures are also complicated but are similar to those used in other multibusiness situations. It is easy to see that the multinational firm represents the highest level of abstraction and complexity to the strategist. Strategy formulation for these organizations clearly calls for the greatest attention to information gathering and methodical analysis to assure that alternatives and choices have been carefully prepared.

The concluding case for this chapter is the internationally famous Levi Strauss & Company. Your analysis should encompass each of its major product/markets and should be a comprehensive treatment of strategies for operating divisions and for the corporation. You should make a complete analysis of major divisions in the manner suggested in the chapters dealing with single businesses and then conclude by analyzing the multibusiness nature of Levi Strauss with a lengthy commentary on its multinational strategy.

This exercise can be considered for a group project, but it would be more meaningful as a relatively lengthy (6 to 20 typewritten pages) written case analysis.

LEVI STRAUSS & CO.

Levi Strauss, a Bavarian immigrant who was lured to the West during the gold rush in search of prosperity, did not strike it rich in gold, but he found his fortune in jeans. His first pair of jeans was sold in 1853 to a San Francisco gold digger who wanted a sturdy pair of pants which would hold up in the mines. In time, his jeans became so popular that young Strauss set up a shop in San Francisco. Today, the headquarters of Levi Strauss and Company (L.S. & CO.) stands near the same location as young Strauss's shop.

 The case was prepared by Neil H. Snyder, Debie Alford, Karen Davis, Allison Gillum, Jim Tucker and Jeff Walker of the McIntire School of Commerce, University of Virginia. This case is designed to be used as a basis for discussion rather than to illustrate either effective or ineffective handling of an administrative situation.

It was not until the 1930s that Levi's jeans reached the eastern market. Although attempts were made to promote jeans for resort wear, the basic clientele continued to be limited. World War II, however, created a sharp increase in demand, and they were sold only to individuals engaged in defense work. It also marked a turning point for Levi Strauss. L.S. & CO. had been largely a wholesale operation prior to WW II, but after the war, they began concentrating on manufacturing and direct sales. Before the war, L.S. & CO.'s annual sales were around $8 million, but by 1961 sales reached $51 million, mainly because of aggressive product diversification.

In 1981, L.S. & CO. was the largest manufacturer of jeans in the world, controlling about one-third of the jeans market. Additionally, they were the largest firm in the apparel industry with products in virtually every product line, and sales and profits by far the greatest in the apparel industry. According to L.S. & CO. Chairman of the Board, Peter E. Haas, "We'd like to outfit people from the cradle to the grave."

Levi's success has resulted in part from their skill in sensing an emerging new market and responding quickly and in part from their strong management and exceptional brand name acceptance. In addition, a focus on identifying market opportunities through segmentation in recent years has aided a diversification strategy. As a result, the company's growth and success has been strong despite the extreme competitiveness and cyclical nature of the apparel industry.

Top managers at L.S. & CO. are optimistic about the 1980s. Emphasis in the future will be on expanding womenswear and activewear and increasing the international market. A 1978 assessment by the *Wall Street Transcript* is valid today. It states, "There are few firms in any industry comparable to Levi Strauss from the standpoint of dynamic growth, above average return of equity, competitive strength and strong international consumer franchise" (*Wall Street Transcript*, January 23, 1978).

KEY EXECUTIVES*

Walter A. Haas, Jr., joined the Company in 1939 and served as its President from 1958 to 1970 and as its Chief Executive Officer from 1970 to 1976. He was named Chairman of the Board in December 1970, and Chairman of the Executive Committee in April 1976. He served in both of these positions until his retirement in 1981. He also served as a director since 1943. Mr. Haas controls 10.4% of the Company's stock. This figure includes shares owned by his wife, children, and estates and trusts for which he votes. He is the great grandnephew of Levi Strauss. He was 64 years old in November 1981.

Peter E. Haas joined the Company in 1945 and became Executive Vice President in 1958. He became President of the Company in December 1970, and Chief Executive Officer in April 1976. In November 1981, he became Chairman of the Board. Mr. Haas controls 12% of the Company's stock. This figure includes stock owned by his family and stock owned by trusts and estates for which he has the voting power. He graduated from the University of California in 1940 and from Harvard University's Graduate School of Business in 1943. He is the great grandnephew of Levi Strauss and was 61 years of age in 1981.

Robert T. Grohman joined the Company in April 1975, as President of Levi Strauss International and was elected a Vice President of the Company in May 1974. In 1975 he was appointed International Group President and Senior Vice President. He has been Executive Vice President since April 1976 and was President of

* The information included in this section was obtained from "Notice of Annual Meeting of Stockholders and Proxy Statement," Levi Strauss and Company, April 2, 1980, p. 1; Standard and Poor's Register of Corporations, Directors, and Executives, 1980, Vol. 2; and Standard and Poor's Industry Surveys, Vol. 1, Section 3, July 31, 1980, p. A95.

the Operating Groups for fiscal years 1977–1980. He was named chief member of the office of the President in June 1978. In November 1981 he became President and Chief Executive Officer. He has served as a director since 1974. He was 56 in 1981.

Francis J. Brann joined the Company in 1965 and was elected Vice President in November 1972. He assumed the position of Levi Strauss International Division Area Manager Central Europe in June 1974 and the position of President of the Canada and Latin America Divisions in January 1976. In July 1976, he was elected Senior Vice President and assumed the position of Senior Vice President, Corporate Planning and Policy in December 1976. He was named Executive Vice President of the U.S. Sportswear Group in June 1978 and was promoted to President of Levi Strauss U.S.A. in January 1980. He joined the Board of Directors in July 1979. Mr. Brann graduated from the University of San Francisco in 1961 and from City College of New York, Graduate Business School in 1965. In 1981 he was 43.

Thomas W. Tusher joined the Company in 1969. He was named President of Levi Strauss International in January 1980, having served as Executive Vice President of the International Group since December 1976. During most of 1976, he held the position of President of the European Division. Prior to 1976, he functioned as general manager for various International divisions and areas. He was elected Vice President of the Company in April 1976, and Senior Vice President in December 1977. He joined the Board of Directors in July 1979. Mr. Tusher graduated from the University of California in 1963 and from Stanford University, Graduate Business School in 1965. In 1981 he was 39 years old.

Robert D. Haas joined the Company in January 1973 as Project Analyst in Inventory Management and became Jeanswear Product Manager in August 1973. He then joined the Levi Strauss International group as Marketing Services Manager in October 1975. He became Director of Marketing in May 1976, and Assistant General Manager-Far East Division in December 1976. In November 1977, he was elected Vice President of the Company and was appointed Director of Corporate Marketing Development. He was elected Senior Vice President-Corporate Planning and Policy in June 1978, and was appointed President of the New Business Group in January 1980, when he joined the Board of Directors. On December 1980, he became President of the Operating Groups. In 1981 he was 38.

Exhibit 1 contains the names, positions and ages of the key executives of Levi Strauss.

THE APPAREL INDUSTRY

If one were forced to select one word which describes the nature of competition in the apparel industry, it would have to be fierce. In the United States alone, there are more than 15,000 manufacturers in the apparel industry. However, the industry is experiencing a trend toward consolidation (large firms diversifying by buying smaller firms). This fact is evidenced by a 16 percent reduction in the number of domestic producers over the past 5 years. For the larger firms in the industry, consolidation via acquisition has led to rapid diversification of product lines and to an increased ability to cope with fluctuations in market demand. At the same time, it has resulted in market concentration. Currently, 5 percent of the firms in the apparel industry generate over 70 percent of industry sales.

Blue Bell, Inc. (manufacturer of Wrangler jeans), V.F. Corporation (producer of Lee Jeans), and L.S. & CO. are the major competitors in the apparel industry in terms of sales. In 1979, Blue Bell had sales of \$1.029 billion and V.F. Corporation had sales of \$544 million. Sales growth in these two companies has been steady, but slow. From 1974 to 1979, Blue Bell and V.F. experienced a 17.7% and 8.8% average annual sales

EXHIBIT 1
Key executives

Name	*Position and office*	*Age*
J. P. Berghold	Vice President and Treasurer	42
Thomas C. Borrelli	Vice President and President of the Jeanswear Division	60
Francis J. Brann	Senior Vice President and President of Levi Strauss USA, Director	42
James W. Cameron	Vice President-Human Resources	49
Harry H. Cohn	Vice President and Executive Vice President of Group III—Levi Strauss USA, Director	50
Robert T. Grohman	President, Chief Executive Officer, Director	56
Peter E. Haas	Chairman of the Board, Director	61
Robert D. Haas	Senior Vice President and President of the Operating Groups, Director	38
Walter A. Haas, Jr.	Retired November 1981, Director	64
Thomas E. Harris	Vice President-Community Affairs	
Roy C. Johns, Jr.	Vice President-Corporate Communications	51
Peter T. Jones	Senior Vice President and General Counsel, Director	50
David A. Kaled	Vice President-Corporate Planning and Policy	37
Robert B. Kern	Vice President, Corporate Secretary, Director	60
James A. McDermott	Vice President and Executive Vice President of Group II—Levi Strauss USA	44
Robert F. McRae	Vice President and President of the Canada Division	48
Richard D. Murphy	Vice President-Controller	37
Gerald E. O'Shea	Vice President and Assistant to the Chief Operating Officer	58
Alfred V. Sanguinetti	Senior Vice President and President of Group I—Levi Strauss USA, Director	52
Karl F. Slacik	Senior Vice President-Finance and Chief Financial Officer	51
Peter T. Thigpen	Vice President and Executive Vice President of Group I—Levi Strauss International	41
Thomas W. Tusher	Senior Vice President and President of Levi Strauss International, Director	39
William K. Warnock	Vice President, Executive Vice President of Diversified Apparel Enterprises and President of Koret of North America.	59

Sources: 10-K Report for the fiscal year ended November 25, 1980, Standard and Poor's Register of Corporation Directors and Executives 1980, Vol. 2, published by Standard and Poor's Corporation, New York.

growth, respectively. In comparison, L.S. & CO. had sales of $2.1 billion in 1979, and their sales have more than doubled since 1975.

Market Saturation

According to Standard and Poor's, the United States apparel market has been saturated by both foreign and domestic producers. While imports of apparel have been growing gradually since the 1950s, in recent years imports have captured a considerable portion of the domestic market. Imports have continued to increase, albeit at a decreasing rate. Import volume doubled in the 1975 to 1978 period. Thus, domestic producers have found that it is becoming increasingly difficult to pass along to their customers the increased costs of raw materials, labor, energy, etc. In response to this trend, domestic manufacturers are turning toward mechanization, adoption of a global view of the business, diversification toward products that are more import-resistant, and a reliance on brand-name marketing and product exclusivity to counteract pressure on price.

Automation, particularly in design and cutting, is being used to increase productivity and thereby reduce average unit costs. In general, significant automation initiatives have been limited almost exclusively to larger firms who can afford the increased investment in plant and equipment. Thus, automation has resulted in a weakening of the competitive position of smaller firms. One consolation for smaller producers, however, is that the largest production cost component in the apparel industry is the cost of fabric. Except for better fabric utilization, automation affects directly only a small portion of total production costs, and service centers which offer automated pattern marking and cutting on a pay-as-you-go basis to smaller firms have been established. Furthermore, many smaller firms have focused on market niches to avoid severe price competition.

Designer Jeans

For a short time, designer jeans such as Gloria Vanderbilt, Calvin Klein, and Jordache were perceived as threats to the major producers of jeans. However, by 1981 the designer jean fad seemed to have peaked, and consumers began returning to the basic styles. Furthermore, designer jeans never accounted for more than an estimated 3 percent of the jean market.

Counterfeiting of Jeans

Jean counterfeiting is an emerging threat to the manufacturers of popular name brand jeans. Counterfeiting is a profitable undertaking since counterfeiters need not invest heavily to establish demand for their products (jean manufacturers have already done this), and they have no regard for product quality (jean manufacturers will bear the cost of dissatisfied customers).

For the most part, consumers who buy counterfeit jeans are unaware that they are not the real thing. These jeans are sold for a lower price than the "true brand," and they are often of inferior and/or inconsistent quality. Counterfeiters use lighter weight fabric; the seams in counterfeit jeans often come apart after one washing; and the zippers and rivets in counterfeit jeans are of low quality. Additionally, many counterfeiters purchase phony labels from label-makers in New York and attach the labels to jean seconds and irregulars purchased from other jeans manufacturers. Counterfeiting is a major concern of apparel manufacturers. They perceive counterfeits as a threat to their franchise and to overall sales.

In 1980 alone, L.S. & CO. uncovered a U.S. counterfeiting operation that produced approximately 50,000 fake pairs of Levi jeans per month. Moreover, L.S. & CO. recently won a $500,000 settlement in London from the operators of an international counterfeiting operation selling fake Levi jeans in Europe. This underscores the tremendous value of Levi's trademark.

Outlook for the Domestic Apparel Market

The future of the domestic apparel industry looks extremely good for various product lines such as activewear, sportswear, womenswear, jeans, and western styles. As the baby boom population moves into a higher age bracket, emphasis on leisure remains high; the proportion of women in the work force is increasing; and the population is shifting to the Sunbelt. Thus, these segments should continue to grow.

Many firms who are surviving the effects of increased competition are doing so primarily because of diversification into various segments of the apparel market. By broadening their scope and focusing on different markets, firms find it easier to avoid the potentially serious negative effects resulting from rapid style changes which characterize the industry.

Activewear is becoming an important factor in the apparel industry, and it is expected to remain popular through the 1980s. The success of activewear is due largely to the popularity of sports and physical fitness in the United States. Additionally, activewear has both functional and fashionable qualities which make it versatile enough for use as everyday wear. Since "casual is the wave of the future" (*U.S. Industrial Outlook*, 1980; p. 367) and the refreshed, relaxed and youthful appearance is also in vogue, the outlook for activewear is very good. Furthermore, the popularity of activewear is inducing strong growth in related sportswear apparel. L.S. & CO. is the only major apparel producer offering a full line of activewear.

Industry experts believe that womenswear has an exceptionally promising future, since more women are entering the labor market. There is evidence of a strong trend toward dressier fashions, sportswear, activewear, and separates for women. This trend looks promising to the executives at L.S. & CO. since their recent acquisition of Koracorp Industries made them a leader in the production of women's sportswear.

The future of western styles looks bright also. Their popularity is expected to continue because of the trend in the United States and foreign countries toward wearing rugged American styles. From the perspective of the apparel producer, western styles are appealing for a number of reasons. First, most western style clothes are made from cotton materials which are readily available and easy to work with. Second, they are durable, versatile, and comfortable. Thus, demand for these products is expected to remain strong for many years. Finally, corduroy products, which add color and variety to western styles, are experiencing increased demand. L.S. & CO. is encouraged by this trend since they are the leading producer of western styles in the world.

The Outlook for the International Market

As the United States apparel market has become more saturated, growth-oriented apparel producers in the U.S. have directed their attention toward the market potential overseas. Between 1974 and 1979, the value of U.S. apparel exports increased from $332.7 million to $819 million. Furthermore, industry analysts believe that by 1985, 4 percent of total U.S. apparel production will be exported. Large U.S. apparel firms have relied on their financial, marketing, and research and development capabilities to compete successfully with foreign producers. Additionally, the popularity of American styles overseas has resulted in increased demand for name brand U.S. products.

Countries in Western Europe, such as Italy, Belgium, Austria, Switzerland, and West Germany offer the most promising possibilities for future export growth. According to *U.S. Industrial Outlook* (1980 p. 367), growth prospects in these countries look good for several reasons. First, they have high standards of living. Second, they are experiencing declining domestic production. Finally, apparel imports in these countries are increasing rapidly.

THE STRUCTURE AND PRODUCTS OF LEVI STRAUSS & CO.

Levi Strauss designs, manufactures, and markets casual wear for just about every taste. Their product line includes everything from jeans, skirts, and suits to shoes. The majority of their products are manufactured and sold under the Levis® trademark. In 1980, Levi Strauss and Company consolidated its three operating divisions into two units, Levi Strauss U.S.A. and Levi Strauss International. It also has miscellaneous other divisions and a corporate staff. Each unit contains several divisions which facilitate production and marketing in various segments of the casual wear market.

EXHIBIT 2
Operating structure of L.S. & CO.

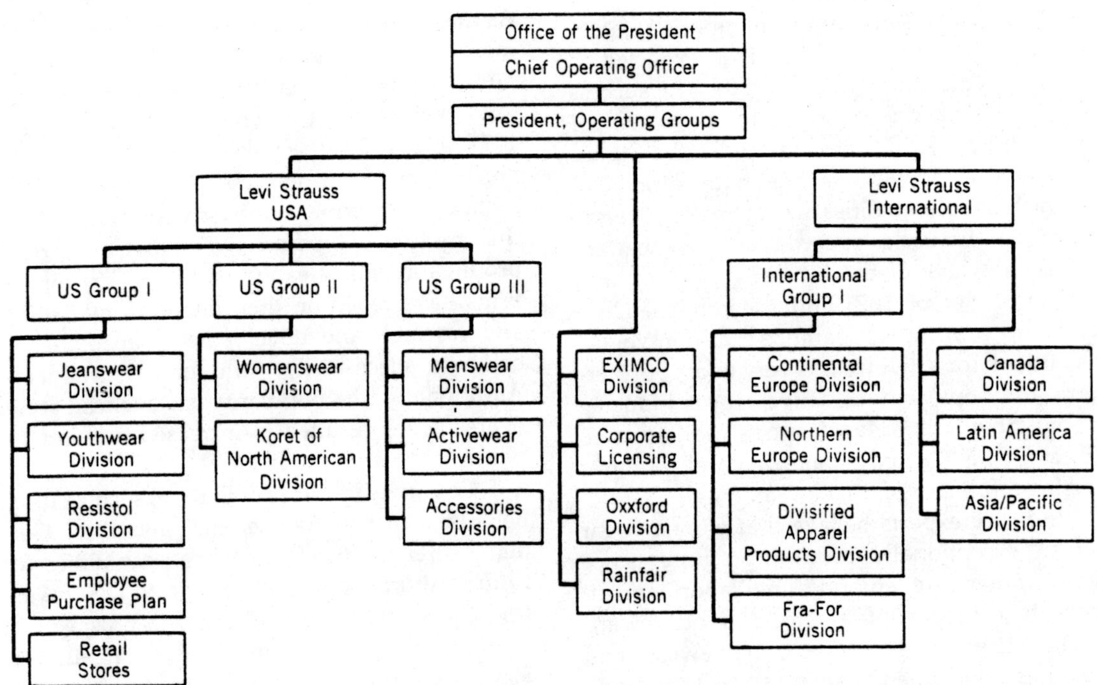

Source: 1980 Annual Report.

Levi Strauss U.S.A.

Levi Strauss U.S.A. consists of 3 groups which are divided into operating divisions: Jeanswear, Youthwear, Resistol Hats, Womenswear, Koret of North America, Menswear, Activewear, Accessories, Employee Purchase Plan, and Retail Stores. L.S. & CO.'s Jeanswear division is the largest jeans manufacturer in the United States, and the largest division in the company. Additionally, it is responsible for producing all styles of jeans (i.e., straightleg, bell bottom, prewashed). However, this group also produces various styles of shirts, jackets, vests, shorts, and western wear for men.

The Youthwear division is the second major product division in the U.S.A. Unit. It produces apparel for children from toddlers to teens, but it focuses primarily on the 7-to-14-year-old market. Like the Jeanswear division, its products range from jeans, jackets, shirts, and overalls to T-shirts. Sportswear for youngsters is a new product recently added to the Youthwear division.

Resistol Hats is the world's largest producer of brand-name western and dress hats. This divison was formally part of Koracorp Industries which was a large and successful manufacturer in its own right.

Womenswear is another important product division in the U.S.A. Unit. Products included in this division are pants, shirts, sweaters, and shorts. A recent introduction to the Womenswear line, "Bend-Over"® pants, which are made from a stretch material, is the hottest selling product in the group.

In Levi Strauss's 1979 Annual Report, the following statement was made concerning the Womenswear group:

> *Womenswear, the company's most rapidly growing division, nearly doubled its sales last year. . . . This sharp growth indicates the division's potential in the vast womenswear market, which exceeds the menswear in size.*

Koret of North America Division was formerly Koret of California®. They produce high brand-loyalty apparel products.

The Menswear Division manufactures stretch pants called Levi's Action Slacks which are becoming popular. Among the other products in the Menswear Division are men's shirts, vests, sweaters, and jackets.

Activewear is the newest product division in the U.S.A. Unit. This division manufactures such products as warm-up suits, shorts, skiwear, and other sports apparel for both men and women. According to L.S. & CO.'s 1979 Annual Report, "The division's entry into the marketplace followed a three-year comprehensive study of the activewear market. . . . The activewear market was found to be large and highly fragmented, with no major American brands offering a full range of products." L.S. & CO.'s top managers indicate they will place substantial emphasis on activewear in the future as they attempt to carve out a niche for themselves in the market.

The Accessories Division produces a wide range of products such as belts, hats, and wallets. The Accessories Division produces the smallest sales volume of any product line in Levi Strauss & Co.

Exhibit 3 shows sales figures for Levi Strauss U.S.A. from 1976 to 1980.

EXHIBIT 3
Division's percentage of total sales (dollar amounts in millions)

	1979 Sales	*% Sales*	*1978 Sales*	*% Sales*	*1977 Sales*	*% Sales*	*1976 Sales*	*% Sales*
Levi Strauss USA								
Division Jeanswear	743.1	57	658.7	61	695.5	65	569.1	66
Youthwear	217.8	17	184.2	17	171.6	16	126.8	15
Sportswear and Activewear	120.7	09	120.6	11	108.8	10	94.1	11
Menswear	197.4	15	99.2	09	62.8	06	47.4	05
Accessories	15.6	01	14.3	01	33.6	03	26.5	03
Total	1294.6		1077.0		1072.3		863.9	
Levi Strauss International								
Europe	389.7	53	305.7	52	237.4	49	146.1	41
Canada	139.6	19	114.8	20	122.7	25	111.4	31
Latin America	134.7	18	103.5	18	79.3	16	51.7	15
Asia/Pacific	74.1	10	61.0	10	47.6	10	46.7	13
Total	738.1		585		487		355	

Source: 1979–1976 Annual Reports for Levi Strauss & Co.

Levi Strauss International

Levi Strauss International is the second component in the company's structure. The international unit is divided into 4 groups (International Group I and Canada, Latin America, and Asia/Pacific Divisions) of which the International Group I is the largest. The International Group I is further divided into operating divisions. L.S. & CO.'s primary export product is jeans, but sportswear, youthwear, and womenswear have proven to be successful export items as well.

Exhibit 3 shows sales figures for the International Division from 1976 to 1980.

Other Operating Units

Four operating divisions have been separated from the two main operating units (Levi Strauss USA and Levi Strauss International) due to their unique nature.

The EXIMCO Division was set up to develop special markets for L.S. & CO. and to manage sales in Eastern Europe, China, Switzerland, and Hong Kong. It provides Levi Strauss with the ability to take advantage of new opportunities in international markets.

The Oxxford Division produces top quality men's suits in the U.S., and the Rainfair Division produces industrial clothing and coated compounded products for industry. Both of these divisions produce products formerly produced by Koracorp Industries.

PRODUCTION FACILITIES

Levi Strauss & Company has numerous plants and distribution centers located in North America and throughout Asia, Latin America, and Europe. Exhibit 4 presents a list of facilities L.S. & CO. owns or leases. According to *Fortune* magazine (November 19, 1979; p. 86), "During the next 5 years, the company plans to spend some $400 million to build no fewer than 40 new factories and enlarge several existing ones; more than $250 million will go into production facilities for sweaters, blazers, and a variety of other garments that were not in the company's product line a few years ago."

MARKETING

The marketing orientation of Levi Strauss has undergone significant change since the company's inception in the 1850s. Originally, Levi's jeans were worn almost exclusively by gold miners who considered them to be essential equipment because they were both rugged and durable. However, in the 1950s jeans became a teenage fad, and later they became a trend. Thus, L.S. & CO. adjusted their marketing orientation to take advantage of this trend. Currently, Levi's products are oriented toward the more fashion conscious 20-to-39-year-old age group. There are 71.1 million people in this age group in the United States today, and there will be 77.6 million people in this age group by 1985.

Brand Awareness

L.S. & CO. is the leading producer in the apparel industry. Much of their success can be attributed to the marketing strength they developed over many years of producing and selling jeans. The most important competitive advantage L.S. & CO. has, and their most important marketing strength as well, is wide consumer acceptance of the Levi's brand. L.S. & CO. sells high quality products at reasonable prices, and this fact is recognized throughout the world.

Distribution

L.S. & CO. sells most of their products through department stores and specialty outlets. In addition, they promote many accessories (i.e., belts, hats, and totebags) inside retail establishments by using attractive point-of-sale racks

EXHIBIT 4
Facilities owned

Location	*Number of facilities*	*Square feet*	*Purpose*
Arkansas	1	295,000	Distribution Center
	3	156,000	Manufacturing
California	3	282,000	Manufacturing
	2	323,400	Distribution Center
Georgia	2	197,900	Manufacturing
Illinois	1	111,000	Manufacturing
Kentucky	1	324,200	Distribution Center
Nevada	1	315,800	Distribution Center
New Jersey	1	50,000	Manufacturing
New Mexico	2	189,700	Manufacturing
North Carolina	2	262,400	Manufacturing
Pennsylvania	1	126,700	Manufacturing
South Carolina	1	54,600	Manufacturing
Tennessee	9	898,900	Manufacturing
Texas	16	1,559,900	Manufacturing
	1	123,000	Curing
	2	1,399,000	Distribution Center
Virginia	2	99,700	Manufacturing
Wisconsin	2	283,000	Manufacturing
Argentina	1	72,700	Manufacturing
Australia	1	103,600	Manufacturing
	1	37,000	Distribution Center
Belgium	4	213,500	Manufacturing
Brazil	1	38,300	Manufacturing
	1	250,000	Manufacturing and Distribution Center
Canada	4	236,200	Manufacturing
	1	96,000	Manufacturing and Warehousing
	1	183,000	Distribution Center
France	6	317,400	Manufacturing
	1	77,200	Manufacturing and Warehousing
	1	116,600	Manufacturing and Distribution Center
Mexico	1	253,800	Manufacturing and Distribution Center
	1	104,000	Manufacturing
Puerto Rico	1	54,000	Manufacturing
	1	20,000	Distribution Center
Sweden	1	18,800	Distribution Center
United Kingdom	3	178,000	Manufacturing
	1	96,000	Distribution Center
Total	85	9,518,300	

EXHIBIT 4 *(continued)*
Facilities leased

Location	*Number of facilities*	*Square feet*	*Purpose*	*Term expires (3)*
Arkansas	5	238,400	Manufacturing	1981–1989
	2	45,000	Warehousing	1982–1989
California	1	18,000	Manufacturing	1985
	1	155,000	Distribution Center	2013
	2	85,000	Warehousing	1986–2001
Georgia	2	145,900	Manufacturing	1984–1996
New Mexico	2	116,000	Manufacturing	1992–1994
	1	50,300	Manufacturing and Warehousing	1989
North Carolina	1	25,000	Warehousing	1984
Ohio	1	105,000	Manufacturing	2006
South Carolina	1	92,000	Manufacturing	1991
Tennessee	3	142,900	Manufacturing	1983–1998
	3	75,500	Warehousing	1982–1986
Texas	9	377,700	Manufacturing	1981–1997
	1	200,000	Manufacturing and Warehousing	2009
	1	15,900	Warehousing	1983
	1	310,000	Distribution Center	1998
Utah	1	29,000	Manufacturing	1993
Argentina	1	51,000	Distribution Center	1982
Australia	1	83,600	Manufacturing and Warehousing	1983
Belgium	1	88,300	Distribution Center	1986
	1	65,000	Warehousing	1981
Canada	1	105,900	Distribution Center	2002
	8	429,300	Manufacturing	1981–2002
	2	31,200	Warehousing	1981–1986
France	1	32,300	Manufacturing and Warehousing	1981
	1	37,000	Distribution Center	1986
Germany	1	171,800	Distribution Center	1987
Hong Kong	1	93,200	Manufacturing	1982
	1	50,700	Warehousing and Distribution Center	1981
Italy	1	43,100	Distribution Center	1983
Japan	2	26,800	Distribution Center	1985
Netherlands	1	17,900	Distribution Center	1985
Norway	1	11,300	Distribution Center	1981
Philippines	1	38,800	Manufacturing	1984
	1	32,500	Distribution Center	1984
Switzerland	1	16,800	Distribution Center	1981
United Kingdom	2	116,000	Manufacturing	1999–2000
	1	144,000	Distribution Center and Warehousing	2000
	1	20,000	Distribution Center	1981
Total	70	3,933,100		

Source: 10-K Report for financial year end November 25, 1980.

which complement the products on display. Pants specialty stores began to play a more dominant role in L.S. & CO.'s distribution system in the early 1970s. These stores and the more broadly oriented "Levi's Only" stores represent welcomed alternatives to distributing almost exclusively through department stores where sales have been sluggish recently. Approximately 90% of the products sold in "Levis's Only" stores are manufactured by Levi.

Advertising

L.S. & CO. employs both national and local advertising, and they utilize all advertising media (i.e., T.V., radio, magazines, and newspapers). L.S. & CO.'s promotions emphasize quality and style as the two most important attributes of their products. The slogan "quality never goes out of style" appears whenever the Levi's brand name is advertised.

L.S. & CO. maintains flexibility in their advertising programs so they can shift their emphasis to high volume markets quickly. They focus on anticipating consumer demand and gearing their advertising accordingly, rather than attempting to dictate consumer preferences. Furthermore, they employ advertising programs which parallel and compliment their special selling support.

Other Marketing Strengths

Diversification. Levi's extensive diversification is a major strength. They offer a wide variety of products to consumers throughout the United States and the world. This diversity makes L.S. & CO. less vulnerable to dramatic shifts in consumer preferences for any particular product or in any particular place.

Dependable delivery. L.S. & CO. employs an advanced computer system to define fashion trends and anticipate changes in consumer demand for apparel. This system enables L.S. & CO. to manufacture and inventory products which are selling well or are expected to sell well. Thus L.S. & CO. has achieved a reputation for dependable delivery.

Market research. When Levi Strauss develops a new product, they utilize test marketing to determine the most effective approach for advertising it. They concentrate on understanding the nature of demand for the product by identifying trends which might affect that demand and determining if that demand can be served. First, they segment the markets they serve according to consumers' preferences and the types of retail outlets which serve them. Then, they identify locations where the Levi's brand has achieved acceptance. Thus, L.S. & CO. adjusts its advertising to meet the needs of specific products in specific markets.

Marketing Weaknesses

Despite their numerous marketing strengths and their number one position in the apparel industry, L.S. & CO. has marketing weaknesses as well. First, their pricing policy is subject to Federal Trade Commission (FTC) regulations. Specifically, the FTC does not permit forced price maintenance by manufacturers at the retail level. In recent years, this has cost L.S. & CO. millions of dollars for out-of-court settlements of cases in which they were accused of price maintenance. As a result, L.S. & CO. is susceptible to price wars. Retailers will drastically cut the price of Levi products to attract customers to their stores from their competitors. This may pose a possible threat to the quality image of a branded product.

PERSONNEL

The apparel industry employs approximately 1,134,000 production workers, and employment in the industry has been stable for 5 years. Heavy concentrations of jobs in the apparel industry are found in New York, Pennsylvania, California, North Carolina, and Texas, but most production is done in the South due to the low cost of labor.

Apparel production is highly labor intensive, and apparel industry wages are among the lowest of all manufacturing industries. This is because the production process used by apparel firms is suited to employing unskilled and semiskilled workers. Two major unions represent apparel workers (International Ladies Garment Union and Amalgamated Clothing and Textile Workers Union), and 81 percent of workers in the apparel industry are women.

L.S. & CO. employed over 44,700 individuals in 1979. Seventy-five percent (75%) of them were production workers, and over 60 percent of L.S. & CO. production workers were union members. Relations between L.S. & CO. and the production workers are satisfactory. As evidence of this fact, there has never been a major interruption in production due to labor disputes.

At L.S. & CO., in 1979, 11 percent of officials and managers were minority persons; 15 percent of officials and managers and 4 percent of sales personnel were women; and the Board of Directors includes both minority persons and women. Further, L.S. & CO. supports minority economic development, and management's community concern is evidenced by its objective of allocating at least 3 percent of aftertax profits to social responsibility efforts. All L.S. & CO. plants have strong community relations programs, and L.S. & CO. encourages all employees to be socially concerned and socially active.

RESEARCH AND DEVELOPMENT

Research is considered one of L.S. & CO.'s most important competitive advantages. Their Product Research and Development Department is responsible for the company's progress in new fabrics and garments, and their goal is to improve functional performance. Additionally, an Equipment Research and Development Center is maintained by L.S. & CO. so that it can remain a leader in automated and semi-automated production equipment. Further, Corporate Marketing Research has an online computerized data bank to monitor major fashion directions, general apparel pricing, retail point-of-sale trends, the company's image, and consumer attitudes toward products currently offered. Research also pretests the effectiveness of proposed advertisements and receptivity of the market place to new products.

FINANCIAL MATTERS AT LEVI STRAUSS

Exhibits 5, 6, 7, and 8 present L.S. & CO.'s ten-year financial summary, consolidated income statement, consolidated balance sheets, and consolidated statement of changes in financial position, respectively.

FUTURE

At L.S. & CO. the word future means diversification. In November of 1977 L.S. & CO. began a coordinated corporate strategy of diversification which it intends to continue into the future "at full speed." Four facts suggest this course of action:

1 "In all probability the jeans business in the U.S. is slowly maturing" (*Business Week,* May 19, 1979).
2 L.S. & CO. is generating more cash than it needs to finance its 20 percent annual growth in jeans.
3 Market research shows better returns could be made by putting the Levis® Trademark on other products.

4 In all likelihood antitrust laws would block an attempt by L.S. & CO. to acquire another jeans-maker.

Peter Haas, Chairman of the Board, states "diversification has become the most prudent course we can follow."

Fortune magazine (November 19, 1978) foresees two dangers in L.S. & CO.'s diversification plans. "One danger inherent in these ambitious plans is that keeping track of all the ever-changing fashions and maintaining the huge assortment of sizes and styles in all the new fields could tax the company's managerial capabilities beyond their limits." Also L.S. & CO. is "vulnerable to the same profit-eroding markdowns the minute inventories get out of hand."

Robert T. Grohman, President and Chief Executive Officer, says, "In order to maintain something close to the rate of growth we have experienced in the last five years, we are looking at much more rapid expansion in other segments." He adds, "We are not a fringe house and we are not high-fashion innovators, but we are looking at product lines that have a long-term appeal to the mainstream consumer." Furthermore, Grohman says, "Our size and diversification give us tremendous flexibility."

Brenda Gall of Merrill Lynch, Pierce, Fenner & Smith says of L.S. & CO., "They have instant name recognition, strong ties with retailers and the marketing talent to identify and go after basic, profitable product lines. They have many opportunities ahead of them, and their growth rate over the last five years is not unsustainable."

EXHIBIT 5
Ten-year financial summary Levi Strauss & Co. and subsidiaries (in millions except per share amount)

	1980	1979	1978	1977
Net Sales	$ 2,840.8	$ 2,103.1	$ 1,682.0	$ 1,559.3
Gross Profit	$ 1,040.2	$ 793.8	$ 623.6	$ 562.6
Interest Expense	25.0	12.4	11.2	20.0
Income Before Taxes	401.9	345.6	280.4	270.0
Provision for Taxes on Income	178.2	154.1	135.4	140.2
Net Income	$ 223.7	$ 191.5	$ 145.0	$ 129.8
Earnings Retained in the Business	$ 170.2	$ 151.1	$ 110.0	$ 108.0
Cash Flow Retained in the Business	213.3	176.9	125.5	128.7
Income Before Taxes as % of Sales	14.1	16.4	16.7	17.3
Net Income as % of Sales	7.9	9.1	8.6	8.3
Net Income as % of Beginning Stockholders' Equity	32.8	33.3	31.3	35.8
Current Assets	$ 1,122.5	$ 1,047.1	$ 824.2	$ 694.2
Current Liabilities	452.4	489.7	302.4	263.5
Working Capital	670.1	557.4	521.8	430.7
Ratio of Current Assets to Current Liabilities	2.5/1	2.1/1	2.7/1	2.6/1
Total Assets	1,455.5	1,291.1	973.9	824.2
Long-Term Debt—Less Current Maturities	$ 138.8	$ 99.1	$ 83.3	$ 80.6
Stockholders' Equity	831.6	681.2	575.3	463.9
Capital Expenditures	$ 119.8	$ 51.3	$ 42.9	$ 31.4
Depreciation	25.4	18.2	16.1	13.7
Property, Plant & Equipment—Net	280.8	188.5	141.3	119.3
Number of Employees	48,000	44,700	35,100	37,200
Per Share Data:				
Net Income	$ 5.36	$ 4.58	$ 3.28	$ 2.93
Cash Dividends Declared	1.30	1.00	.80	0.50
Book Value (on shares outstanding at year end)	20.34	16.50	13.14	10.66
Market Price Range	44–30	34½/17	19⅜–13⅝	15⅞–12⅛
Average Common and Common Equivalent Shares Outstanding	41,763,108	41,784,058	44,229,872	44,257,346

Source: 1980 Annual Report for Levi Strauss & Company.

1976	*1975*	*1974*	*1973*	*1972*	*1971*
$ 1,219.7	$ 1,015.2	$ 897.7	$ 653.0	$ 504.4	$ 432.0
$ 439.9	$ 347.4	$ 275.5	$ 184.4	$ 160.3	$ 129.6
12.2	13.1	13.7	10.1	4.3	4.4
206.8	136.7	72.7	33.8	48.1	35.7
102.1	71.9	37.9	22.0	23.0	16.0
$ 104.7	$ 64.7	$ 34.9	$ 11.9	$ 25.0	$ 19.7
$ 94.8	$ 58.6	$ 29.6	$ 6.6	$ 20.9	$ 16.3
110.6	71.7	45.7	17.7	28.0	22.5
17.0	13.5	8.1	5.2	9.5	8.3
8.6	6.4	3.9	1.8	5.0	4.6
39.5	31.4	19.8	7.0	16.8	23.2
$ 570.1	$ 407.6	$ 383.5	$ 305.5	$ 252.4	$ 202.8
226.6	155.4	188.1	155.7	98.2	67.9
343.5	252.2	195.3	149.8	154.2	134.9
2.5/1	2.6/1	2.0/1	2.0/1	2.6/1	3.0/1
678.0	496.3	470.4	382.7	307.1	247.9
$ 79.2	$ 68.7	$ 72.8	$ 48.1	$ 37.6	$ 28.4
362.4	265.2	206.0	176.4	169.7	148.8
$ 19.5	$ 10.4	$ 24.3	$ 28.8	$ 17.6	$ 15.6
11.6	9.3	9.7	8.3	6.4	5.1
102.4	82.1	82.3	68.0	48.0	39.6
32,500	29,700	30,100	29,100	25,100	21,400
$ 2.35	$ 1.47	$ 0.80	$ 0.27	$ 0.57	$ 0.47
0.23	0.14	0.12	0.12	0.10	0.08
8.25	6.08	4.73	4.05	3.90	3.42
$13\frac{3}{8}$–9	$10\frac{3}{4}$–$3\frac{1}{8}$	$5\frac{5}{8}$–$3\frac{1}{8}$	$12\frac{1}{2}$–$4\frac{1}{2}$	15–$10\frac{1}{8}$	$16\frac{1}{8}$–$8\frac{3}{8}$
44,476,748	43,899,028	43,520,320	43,520,320	43,520,320	42,344,000

EXHIBIT 6
Consolidated statement of income Levi Strauss & Co. and subsidiaries

(Dollars in thousands except per share amounts)	*Year ended* November 30, 1980 (53 weeks)	November 25, 1979 (52 weeks)	November 26, 1978 (52 weeks)
Net sales	$2,840,844	$2,103,109	$1,682,019
Cost of goods sold	1,800,665	1,309,263	1,058,439
Gross profit	1,040,179	793,846	623,580
Marketing, general and administrative expenses	635,870	464,086	344,536
Operating income	404,309	329,760	279,044
Interest expense	25,018	12,449	11,178
Interest and other income, net	(22,606)	(28,238)	(12,503)
Income before taxes	401,897	345,549	280,369
Provision for taxes on income	178,208	154,095	135,400
Net income	$ 223,689	$ 191,454	$ 144,969
Net income per share	$ 5.36	$ 4.58	$ 3.28
Average common and common equivalent shares outstanding	41,763,108	41,784,058	44,229,872

Source: 1980 Annual Report for Levi Strauss & Co.

EXHIBIT 7
Consolidated balance sheets Levi Strauss & Co. and subsidiaries

(Dollars in thousands)	*November 30, 1980*	*November 25, 1979*
Assets		
Current Assets:		
Cash	$ 36,192	$ 27,454
Temporary investments of cash	51,693	195,297
Trade receivables (less allowance for doubtful accounts: 1980—$9,368; 1979—$8,340)	446,461	340,131
Inventories:		
Raw materials and work-in-process	252,538	216,820
Finished goods	275,017	225,001
Other current assets	60,606	42,411
Total current assets	1,122,507	1,047,114
Property, Plant and Equipment (less accumulated depreciation: 1980—$113,301; 1979—$101,989)	280,783	188,495
Other Assets	52,070	55,510
	$1,455,360	$1,291,119

EXHIBIT 7 *(continued)*
Consolidated balance sheets Levi Strauss & Co. and subsidiaries

(Dollars in thousands)	*November 30, 1980*	*November 25, 1979*
Liabilities and Stockholders' Equity		
Current Liabilities:		
Current maturities of long-term debt	$ 14,963	$ 15,832
Short-term borrowings	48,642	53,535
Accounts payable	135,006	154,929
Accrued liabilities	93,875	83,802
Compensation and payroll taxes	55,313	57,636
Pension and profit sharing	20,982	27,545
Taxes based on income	68,309	85,069
Dividend payable	15,335	11,357
Total current liabilities	452,425	489,705
Long-Term Debt—Less current maturities	138,754	99,126
Deferred Liabilities	32,552	21,098
Stockholders' Equity:		
Common stock—$1.00 par value: authorized 100,000.000 shares: shares issued—1980—43,998,808, 1979—21,999,404	43,999	21,999
Additional paid-in capital	59,837	82,424
Retained earnings	806,257	636,010
	910,093	740,433
Less treasury stock, at cost: 1980—3,105,482 shares: 1979—1,354,949 shares	78,464	59,243
Total stockholders' equity	831,629	681,190
	$1,455,360	$1,291,119

EXHIBIT 8
Consolidated statement of changes in financial position Levi Strauss & Co. and subsidiaries

	Year ended		
(In thousands)	*November 30, 1980 (53 weeks)*	*November 25, 1979 (52 weeks)*	*November 26, 1978 (52 weeks)*
Working Capital Provided By:			
Operations:			
Net income	$ 223,689	$191,454	$144,969
Add items not currently involving working capital:			
Depreciation and amortization	30,004	20,430	17,606
Other, net	13,066	5,380	(2,140)
Working capital provided by operations	266,759	217,264	160,435

EXHIBIT 8 ***(continued)***
Consolidated statement of changes in financial position Levi Strauss & Co. and subsidiaries

	Year ended		
(In thousands)	*November 30, 1980 (53 weeks)*	*November 25, 1979 (52 weeks)*	*November 26, 1978 (52 weeks)*
Common stock issued in acquisition of Koracorp Industries Inc.	—	37,261	—
Proceeds from long-term debt	54,586	8,400	14,411
Common stock issued to employees	6,322	4,999	5,077
Working capital provided	327,667	267,924	179,923
Working Capital Used For:			
Additions to property, plant and equipment	119,824	51,254	42,863
Cash dividends declared	53,442	40,391	34,972
Acquisition of Koracorp Industries Inc. (less working capital of $34,961):			
Property, plant and equipment	—	17,702	—
Other assets	—	4,885	—
Goodwill	—	39,341	—
Long-term liabilities assumed	—	(26,054)	—
Purchases of treasury stock	26,130	87,451	3,611
Reductions in long-term debt	14,958	15,505	11,766
Other, net	640	1,862	(4,379)
Working capital used	214,994	232,337	88,833
Increase in working capital	$ 112,673	$ 35,587	$ 91,090
Increase (Decrease) in Working Capital, Represented by Change in:			
Cash and temporary investments of cash	$(134,866)	$(32,070)	$ 93,880
Trade receivables, net	106,330	99,006	37,886
Inventories	85,734	143,327	4,391
Other current assets	18,195	12,624	(6,188)
Current maturities of long-term debt and short-term borrowings	5,762	(48,003)	20,290
Accounts payable and accrued liabilities	9,850	(83,667)	(51,983)
Other current liabilities	21,668	(55,630)	(7,186)
Increase in working capital	$112,673	$ 35,587	$ 91,090

Source: 1980 Annual Report for Levi Strauss & Co.

17

DEVELOPING AND EMERGING ISSUES

In this text, we have been concerned with the development of competence in strategic management from the perspective of the general manager. The early chapters were devoted to an examination of areas of functional concern in an integrated way. We were concerned with a comprehensive and coherent set of managerial decisions and actions, a set that supported a managerial choice of direction, mission, or strategic goal.

In Chapters 7, 8, and 9, we made use of three types of tools used to help the general manager to knit the major functional areas together and thereby to aid in the process of reaching decisions affecting the business as an entity. These three models introduce time as a significant dimension in general-management decision processes. Knowledge of the dynamics of cost structures gained in two of these models enables the general manager to fine-tune the organization's efforts to find the points of profit maximization. In the third model, a knowledge of the state of maturity of a product can aid in planning for organizational, financial, and human needs and in harvesting the fruits of the organization's efforts.

In all of this early material we have emphasized the role of the general manager as an effective *implementer* of a chosen strategy. We began with unifunctional subjects and concluded with multifunction, time-related, and integration-oriented decision processes. The progression from simple and structured topics to much more complex and much less structured material is consistent with the way in which we learn and the way in which we gain experience in business organizations. In business careers, we are assigned simple tasks at first, and we learn to deal with complexities as we gain competence. With experience, we find ourselves increasingly dealing with complexity in progressively less-certain environments. The daily production schedule has now become a 5-year forecast of operations. The weekly marketing department assignment sheet has become a marketing plan for a new product introduction. This text material in its structure, has attempted to follow the same educational development pattern.

EXERCISE 17–1

Reflect on your work in this course to date. Does the summary outlined in the preceding paragraph accurately describe the development of your knowledge in the first third of the course? Please comment, and be prepared to discuss your observations in class.

In the major portion of the text, which included Chapters 10 through 14, we developed an understanding of the concept of strategy formulation. A model of the strategy formulation process was presented and chapter material was devoted to a careful development of skills used in the analysis of the factors needed to array and choose a strategy. Text materials that addressed the development of organizational structure and policies for use in strategy implementation were provided, as was a discussion of the evaluation of strategies. Although this material is relatively structured in its use of a model of the strategy-formulation process, it is much more complex than the extrapolative processes used in break-even analysis or operational forecasting. In addition, these discussions introduce political and competitive forces, consumer whim, managerial values, choices and egos, and a myriad of forces that may affect the destiny of the business. It is, however, a model of managerial *choice* rather than a deterministic planning framework. Success in closing the gap between where the organization is and where its management would like it to be is determined not only by its ability to carry out a given strategy, but also by the cognitive skills needed by strategists to conceive plausible alternative solutions and to be effective in their selection.

EXERCISE 17–2

Sketch, from your own memory, the strategy formulation model. Then, refer to the model to check your recollection. Was this model helpful? Describe at least two other applications for which the model might be useful.

The last portion of the book, which we have just concluded, extends this complexity to multiple-product situations in which strategies need to be established for each product/market and in which the collective efforts of all product divisions must be harnessed to achieve the objectives of a corporate strategy. Multinational enterprises add other dimensions of ambiguity, complexity, and risk. Once again, we have moved from the specific to the more general, from structured to less-structured situations, from the known to the less well known.

In this chapter we hope to extend our thinking into the next several years, to consider some of the environmental factors likely to have a significant impact on strategy formulation for all organizations, and to discuss some of the issues of special interest to the strategist.

LOOKING AHEAD

As we contemplate the conditions we see as most likely during the last few years of the 1980s and into the first half of the 1990s, it seems clear that our world industrial economy will be much more evenly competitive than it has been in our industrial history. We face genuinely difficult competition from our foreign trading partners in a wide range of industries. The productivity gains that were the principal competitive advantage of the United States in the first half of the twentieth century no longer dominate international trade. The power of the rebuilt industries of Japan and Germany and the emerging technological strength of Korea are examples of dramatic changes that have taken place in the 40 years since World War II. Our country can no longer expect to dominate its chosen markets by means of its productive capability. In market after market, our foreign trading partners have offered superior products at better prices than have been available from domestic suppliers.

Postwar industrial redevelopment, of course, has been a major factor in providing a more modern technology for Japan and Germany than that used in other countries. Government support and low labor costs have also been of help to these countries in building their export trading activity. These factors, however, only explain a portion of the advantage earned by our foreign competitors. In fact, very careful control of quality at very high levels, close attention and quick response to customer needs and wishes, and meticulous attention to production control have built these competitors into dominant forces in their chosen markets.

The competitive edge the United States seems to have sustained is that of generating ideas, of creating solutions to complex problems, innovating in the application of new materials and technologies, and serving as the cultural, style, and social trend setter for more affluent countries. In mature markets, our natural resources give us special advantages in agribusiness and in coal-based energy and chemical production. In developing technologies and product/markets, we seem to be able to establish an advantage. As style setters, we maintain a competitive advantage in consumer products, appliances, and numerous other cultural amenities. We have found, however, that the strength of our foreign competitors and the rapidity of their response to new technologies offers a very brief period of advantage. Innovations in the adaptation of management techniques has been a strength of Asian competitors. European competitors have also adapted management techniques but offer competition in the development of new products as well.

The complementary nature of comparative advantages will be a distinctive feature of international trade in the years ahead. Competition will be intense and will involve the deliberate use of materials, labor, capital and ideas drawn from sources throughout the world. We will continue to see an extension of worldwide trade, internationally marketed products, and the recognition of international competition as the principal fact of business life.

EXERCISE 17–3

From your knowledge of world economics and geopolitics and/or your reading of library and popular literature, what other factors may seriously affect domestic business interests? List two or three, and prepare a rationale in support of your choices in written form.

Several issues related to organizational governance are likely to materially affect strategic thinking by general managers in the next 10 years. First, there is growing evidence of a lack of satisfaction with the internal direction and control in many organizations.

- Class action suits have been instituted by stockholders unhappy because of a management or a board of directors the plaintiffs felt were unresponsive.
- In the auto industry, the United Auto Workers succeeded in placing a union official on the board of directors of one of the major auto makers.
- A perceived lack of concern for the interests of the public at large by government authorities has led to the placement of citizens charged with representing the public on boards of directors.
- Takeover raids by entrepreneurial financiers have in many cases disclosed to thousands of stockholders the extent to which their company's financial performance has lagged behind competing firms.
- The leveraged buyout of a publicly held company by a group of managers has

made use of the value of the company itself in support of the offer of the buyer group.

Corporate gadflies have been a nuisance to boards of directors since the inception of the corporation. In the past, they have been annoying but not threatening, and could be dismissed with impunity. In our litigious society, however, the gadfly has found support in the courts and has forced the attention of the corporation on problems its management had heretofore been able to ignore.

In the other situations, listed above, corporate governance systems were apparently unresponsive to external interests, and consequently had not adequately adapted to the needs of a broader constituency. The lack of sensitivity to the needs of the public at large might be justified if one were to hold the views of Milton Friedman. Public interests, he would argue, should be represented by government, not by adjustments in the economic judgments made in the management of the company. Government, it seems, is unwilling to leave the best interests of citizens to the tender mercies of an impersonal market economy. Instead, we see a directed public presence in governance and a direct line of information from the boardroom to the public.

Although criticized by many, the Chrysler Corporation's action in agreeing to place a UAW official on the corporation's board may have been a step toward a new dimension in major corporation responsiveness through the existing governance structure. We have yet to see the corporation's customer represented in governance but for some time have had client (student) representation on boards of trustees and advisory boards in universities and colleges.

In the cases involving raids or buyouts, the proponents of the purchasers argue that the management has not adequately represented the interests of the owners of the company. If they had, they explain, then stock prices would not have fallen to the levels that make the raid attractive to the company's shareholders. Where the takeover is hostile, the company's management is often charged with rejecting the suitor corporation, not in the best interests of the owners, but instead in defense of their own interests as highly paid managers.

The class action suit, the corporate raid, or the buyout offer are serious attempts at challenging the legitimacy of management and thereby changing corporate direction or ownership. To the general manager and strategist, response to these threats to governance may seriously interrupt the corporate strategy, and will divert managerial attention and time from the pursuit of that strategy and toward the defense of management's flanks. To paraphrase the old adage, the swamp draining strategy is difficult to accomplish while fending off the raiding (or litigating) alligators.

We have been concerned with strategies directed at success in a product/market or technological context. Environmental factors have been regarded as offering opportunities, boundaries, or constraints to managerial action. Ansoff extends our thinking by suggesting that we need to consider strategies in several contexts:[1]

[1] H. L. Ansoff, "The Changing Shape of the Strategic Problem," in Dan E. Schendel and Charles W. Hofer, *Strategic Management: A New View of Business Policy and Planning* (Boston: Little, Brown, 1979), pp. 30–47.

- Product/market/technology strategy—the traditional strategy for dealing with the marketplace.
- Capability strategy—the strategy needed to achieve the capability required to carry out a new strategy.
- Societal strategy—the strategy needed to exist in an environment viewed increasingly as uncertain and constraining rather than more optimistically offering unlimited opportunity.
- Legitimacy strategy—The strategy needed for dealing with the public's increasing dissatisfaction with unlimited growth as a mode of business operation and with the primacy of ownership in governance.

In describing a more complex view of strategy formulation in the 1980s, Ansoff has said that "the historical preoccupation with product/market/technology strategies must be broadened to include the other types of strategies shown"[2] (see Figure 17-1).

Although Ansoff is concerned with changes in the environment, other authors have identified a number of problems caused by managerial attitudes and practices. In summarizing administrative issues for the 1980s, Paine and Anderson note several practices that tend to focus attention on short-term objectives rather than on long-run strategic goals. Short-term profit orientation, the use of traditional financial measures such as ROI, and the short tenure of top managers have resulted in high ROI and cash flows but in a failure to meet capital needs and competition in the long run. The authors comment that many corporate positions are held by financial executives who have had little if any background in the principal elements of the business. A lack of mastery of the art of international competition and a failure to make use of the creativity of the organization's work force are also issues noted.[3]

In reflecting on many of the tools we have used in this book, the authors' comments hit close to the mark. We do make use of financial tools, which are largely short-run in nature. Also, the old habits and practices we learned painfully over the years are difficult to change. We have learned to deal openly with disagreement in our organizations (open disagreement with the boss was unheard of years ago), but we have not learned how to deal with problems of differences in ideology or with attacks on the legitimacy of the enterprise or our own positions of influence within the organization.

We have come to understand that our resources are finite and our environment fragile. We are only now beginning to understand that our organizations may be curtailed, closed, or controlled as society sees fit. Economic activity and politics have never been separated in practice, despite an artificial separation in their study. As we discussed Chapter 16 on multinational businesses, the political ramifications of eco-

[2] Ansoff, "Changing Shape of the Strategic Problem," p. 43.

[3] Frank T. Paine, and C. R. Anderson, *Strategic Management* (Chicago: Dryden Press, 1983), p. 379.

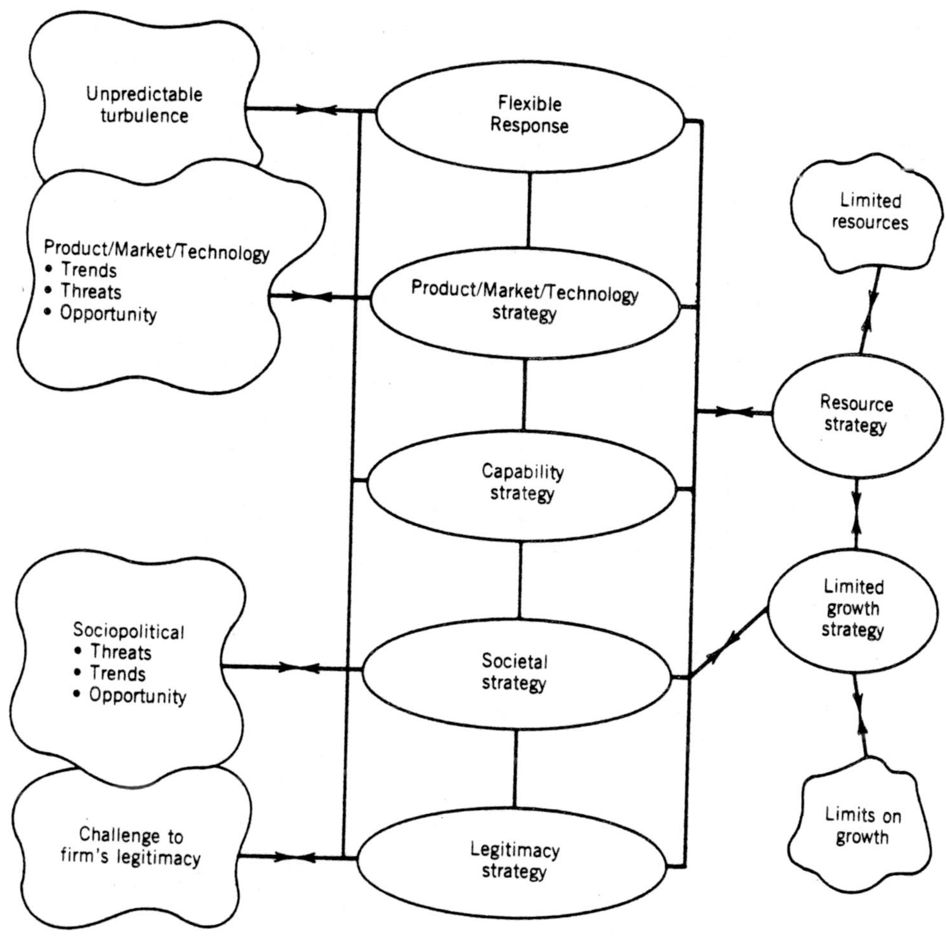

FIGURE 17–1 The "ultimate" strategic problem. *Source:* Ansoff, H. I. *The Changing Shape of the Strategic Problem* p. 42.

nomic activities have an impact within a host country and in the network of political relationships in which the host country is embedded.

The identical pattern of political, social, and economic effects is found as companies seek domestic sites for their business operations. State and local politicians scramble to claim credit for the successful location of employers in their political districts because economic trophies are important ingredients in political careers at all levels of government. Losers remember their losses and promise to even the score at the polls. Economic growth often causes population shifts. A decline in the tax base in one region can seriously affect the government and education infrastructure in the region losing workers. In the region gaining employment, growth can cause serious problems in housing, school systems, and law enforcement as population growth absorbs the existing resources of the region.

Social, political, and cultural attributes of communities are also ingredients in the competition for talented employees. In an increasingly national and international marketplace for employment, talented technicians, engineers, physicians, and scholars are attracted by the quality of life in the community as much as the quality of their work in considering employment opportunities. Industry in the United States has been able to attract a range of highly talented people from Europe and Asia in large part because of the high standard of living in this country.

We have found, to our dismay, that the pursuit of quality of life as an employment objective has in many communities brought about a decline in the quality that brought in employment at the outset. Talented computer scientists and engineers have expressed concern about living in a silicon valley (the Palo Alto area) or its equivalent elsewhere. Many would prefer a more heterogeneous community with a broader range of interests and populated by persons with a variety of backgrounds. Our communities, like our physical environment, are fragile and easily damaged by imbalances in their component elements.

ISSUES FOR STRATEGISTS

Managerial Values and Organizational Futures

Contemporary thinking on strategy formulation suggests that although environmental factors have a strong influence on the range of strategic choice (consistent with a contingency view), the personal values and choices of strategy formulators are increasingly important in the choice of strategy actually employed.

Although the environment provides a feasible space within which a profit or growth-maximizing strategic solution is possible, managerial values provide an additional set of constraints that limit business gain in order to achieve strategists' personal objectives or to enable the strategists to live within a set of personal-value guidelines. For the most part, these choices are made as expressions of personal standards without adequate consideration of the long-term effects on the organization. These constraints may offer satisfaction to one or two executives, but they may also curtail growth, inhibit the employment of talented employees, or focus organizational attention on products with less than attractive commercial futures. With these potential consequences of strict adherence to a particular set of managerial values, it seems clear that the long-term survival and health of the organization will not only require a careful review of future organizational needs, but also the long-term consequences of the effect of managerially imposed constraints.[4]

[4] Raymond E. Miles and Charles C. Snow, *Organizational Strategy, Structure, and Process* (New York: McGraw-Hill, 1978), p. 273.

Rapidity of Change

The dramatic effect of technological, social, political or competitor forces has shortened or made more problematic the life of ongoing strategies. A managerially sound response to such a shift in environmental conditions may involve the establishment of an entirely new strategy, a process that we have found can be an extensive and time-consuming process. In military and geopolitical life, dramatic shifts in the critical environmental factors are expected. Sound strategic responses are even more crucial and organizational issues significantly more complex.

A system for dealing with this type of situation is that of developing an array of planned responses built on a number of scenarios of situations that might develop in the future. In effect, government and military officials have developed an array of alternative strategies. Each has been subjected to careful analysis and discussion and is designed to achieve strategic objectives within the framework of the environmental changes posited by the scenario. Scenarios will not perfectly predict environmental changes or their complexity. They provide, however, a framework for *approximating* environmental change and permit the development of a strategic response that reflects considered judgment rather than the impulse borne of the pressure of the moment.

Strike, flood, or tornado plans are examples of contingency strategies used by business organizations. Given the frequency of dramatic change in many businesses, strategists should give serious consideration to the use of scenario analysis to more effectively deal with rapid changes in competitive conditions, loss (or gain) of a major customer, or other potential problems. Although we cannot possibly anticipate all dramatic or radical changes, those that seem most plausible can be outlined and alternate strategies developed. In terms of management processes, the preparation of scenarios and strategies should be an invaluable opportunity for management development and should offer an opportunity for the strategy formulation and execution team to improve its communication and decision-making processes.

Political Skills

As we look at the years ahead, it seems clear that our business strategists must learn to develop strategies that are sensible *politically*. Public agencies learned long ago that their wars at the bargaining table could be won as much, or more, through the collective impact of public sentiment than by their skills in negotiation. Our major corporations have begun to realize that their executives must learn to reach the public, to express their goals in public forums, and to appeal to a wide range of public interests if they are to thrive.

We have had very few business leaders who were effective as politicians. Despite the fact that consummate skills in corporate politics were needed to master the intricate power relationships of business life and to gain high positions in the corporation, they have had little value in the political arenas outside the boardroom or the executive suite. Perhaps the problem is linked to ideologies. In the corporation, and perhaps even across the bargaining table, the corporation executive deals with people who share a common ideology or a common ethic and whose motives follow patterns similar to his or her own. In addition, the selection processes used in employment and development further screen the players, thereby reducing the variance in political response.

Public politics, on the contrary, has no screening, varied ideologies, a range of motive agendas, and (at least in the United States) a cultural predisposition to challenge authority. For the typical competitive business executive, the compromise mandated by political forces offers something less than satisfaction. Further, the challenges to legitimacy, so common in political life, engender in many executives an instant hostility that makes even compromise unlikely.

In the decade ahead, we must be prepared to face the challenges to our legitimacy and to recognize that a strategy that appears to maximize gains in a product/market context may be unacceptable socially or politically. The key to organizational survival in the long term will be the business executive who can recognize the need to develop strategies to cope with the social and political realities, and who is prepared to build and execute those strategies in a political rather than hierarchical power structure.[5]

As we conclude this study of the processes of strategy formulation and general management, it should be apparent that the use of the systematic processes outlined in these pages will be materially helpful in assuring that judgment is based on sound analysis and careful preparation. The complexities, opportunities, uncertainties, and challenges of the next decade further emphasize the need for continuing to build competence: to learn and use well-developed strategic skills and to display the courage to make timely decisions. To those of you who have now begun to exercise that competence, one can offer the wishes for the future extended to airmen in recent wars . . . "good luck, and good hunting."

[5] See also J. L. Bower, "Business Policy in the 1980's," *Academy of Management Review* 7(4) (1982), pp. 630–38.